THE MANAGEMENT OF ORGANIZATIONS

Edited by

Michael L. Tushman

Charles O'Reilly

David A. Nadler

Ballinger Series on

THE MANAGEMENT OF ORGANIZATIONS

Michael L. Tushman

Charles O'Reilly

and

David A. Nadler

Series Editors

THE MANAGEMENT OF ORGANIZATIONS:
Strategies, Tactics, Analyses

Edited by

Michael L. Tushman

Graduate School of Business
Columbia University

Charles O'Reilly

Graduate School of Business
University of California, Berkeley

David A. Nadler

Delta Consulting Group

1817

Harper & Row, Publishers, New York
BALLINGER PUBLISHING COMPANY

Grand Rapids, Philadelphia, St. Louis, San Francisco
London, Singapore, Sydney, Tokyo

International Standard Book Number: 0–88730–380–3 (cloth)   0-88730-381-1 (paper)

Library of Congress Catalog Card Number: 89–14954

Printed in the United States of America

Library of Congress Cataloging-in-Publication Data

The management of organizations / edited by Michael L.
   Tushman, Charles O'Reilly, David A. Nadler.
      p. cm.
    ISBN 0–88730–380–3 (cloth)   ISBN 0-88730-381-1 (paper)
    1. Organizational behavior.   2. Organizational effectiveness.
  3. Management.   I. Tushman, Michael L.   II. O'Reilly, Charles.
  III. Nadler, David A.
  HD58.7.H354   1989   89–14954
  658.4—dc20   CIP

              92 93 94 95 HC 9 8 7 6 5 4

Table of Contents

Preface

This book has evolved from our efforts to better understand how organizations work and how managers deal with organizational and competitive challenges. In our work with a variety of managers in different firms, industries, and countries, we have been struck by the ever-increasing challenge of the manager's job as organizations and work requirements become more complex. One challenge generic to managers is the necessity to be effective in two time frames simultaneously: managers must work on solving today's problems while organizing to deal with tomorrow's challenges. Ironically, work on current issues often sows the seeds for tomorrow's problems. Throughout this book, managers are asked to weigh the trade-offs between short-run efficiency and long-term adaptability. This managerial duality, and the concomitant need to engage in different kinds of problem-solving efforts simultaneously, pervades the readings.

Our objective is to help managers take advantage of the growing literature on organizations. Our task has been to synthesize and organize this extensive literature in a way that is useful to practicing managers. We present a set of concepts, models, and tools that will help managers (1) diagnose and solve short-term performance problems and (2) build organizations with the capacity to be adaptive and innovative as competitive conditions change. We ask the reader to take advantage of his or her experience and the management literature to build organizations that are effective in the short term and adaptive over time.

The readings in the book are framed around a core organizing model—the congruence model. This diagnostic model provides the book's backbone; it is used as an organizing scheme for the book's content and as an analytic tool in managerial problem solving. While the congruence model is the organizing framework for the book, we present other concepts as submodels to aid in more detailed problem solving on motivation, organization design, management of culture, executive leadership, and change. In every case, we have tested and used these tools with managers from CEOs to first-level supervisors.

This book is organized into six sections. As we focus on managerial problem solving, we begin by addressing the manager's role and the issue of strategy and objective formulation, offering a specific tool for organization diagnosis and problem solving. We then move through sections on formal organization arrangements, culture and the informal organization, individual motivation and decision making, organization change, and executive leadership. Although we move from macro-organization issues (e.g., organization design) to micro-issues (e.g., individual motivation), after Section I there is no inherent sequence to the sections.

Each section consists of a series of readings that provide concepts, models, and tools that facilitate understanding of the section's topic. Several criteria guided our selection of readings. Each article must reflect research-based knowledge that can be directly tied to managerial practice. We avoided readings with no research base, as well as those research-based readings with no managerial utility. We do not cover all perspectives on each topic. Rather, we provide readers with a point of view for each section that has both a research anchor and managerial relevance.

Several themes run through our book:

1. We take a *strategy-based perspective*. Managers—at any level, in any industry, in any country—cannot engage in effective problem solving without clear strategy and/or objectives. Given the importance of performance targets, Section I begins with a discussion on the generic role of the manager and the critical issue of setting objectives based on an evaluation of opportunities and threats. We consider strategy/objective formulation as both a top-down and a bottom-up phenomenon, with importance to the first-level supervisor as well as the CEO.

2. Our book focuses on *managerial problem solving*. We use the congruence model as a specific tool to help managers identify performance problems, engage in systematic data gathering and diagnosis, and evaluate alternative interventions. This approach to organization problem solving asks managers to evaluate the relations between social and technical factors and pushes them to manage down, across (with peers), up with the boss, and perhaps outside the organization (with suppliers, vendors, or customers).

3. *Managing for short-run efficiency and long-term adaptability* requires dealing with congruence as a double-edged sword. Managing for internal consistency is associated with short-run efficiency but also long-term inertia. This managerial paradox highlights the importance of vigilant problem solving and of creating formal and informal conditions within the organization to enhance organization learning.

4. Because organizations exist in changing environments, *managing organization change* is a vital topic. Throughout the book we present tools to help managers implement incremental as well as strategic organization change. While Section V is dedicated to managing change, each section's readings highlight the importance of effective implementation skills.

5. The key to both short- and long-term organization effectiveness is the manager and his or her team. Our fifth theme is *building and maintaining an executive team* that retains its ability to attend to and deal with both organizational and competitive challenges. While Section VI focuses on executive leadership, each section highlights the importance of the man-

ager's setting a vision and objectives for the organization and creating the formal and informal conditions to enhance vigilant organization problem solving.

6. We do not provide cookbook solutions to managerial problems. We do provide a set of *general problem solving concepts and tools*. The research and our consulting and executive education experience suggest that these tools apply to managers in any organization, in any country. While the specifics of a particular problem will differ, the problem-solving approaches, tools, and concepts we present seem to be generically applicable.

This book is a synthesis of our various attempts to organize the research in organization behavior and theory in a way that might be useful to practitioners. We have tested and refined the concepts and tools with our MBA students, in our executive education work, and in our consulting projects over the past ten years. We are convinced of the utility of an overall point of view, or model, as a way to facilitate managerial problem solving and to integrate new knowledge on organizations.

This book continues in the tradition of our earlier work by providing an integrative model and a set of focused readings that are, in turn, linked via the congruence model. Many colleagues have been helpful in the development of this book. In particular, Elaine Romanelli was instrumental in getting the three of us together. Debora Ancona has contributed in idea development and in work with clients. Colleagues in several organizations have helped us enormously, including Jon Lane at Data General, John Murphy and Alan Mather at GTE, Bill James and Peter Keane at Procter and Gamble, Richie Herrink at IBM, Jerry Pike at Syntex, Stan Winvick at AMD, and Jerry Abarbanel at Dunn and Bradstreet. Carol Franco, India Koopman, and Marjorie Richman at Ballinger have all put in extra effort to make this book finally see the light of day. Perhaps of greatest importance, our colleagues at the graduate schools of business at Columbia and Berkeley and at the Delta Consulting Group helped us continue to experiment with our own ideas and to learn from a remarkable set of professionals.

In summary, we remain committed to the belief that, in the spirit of Kurt Lewin, the best theories are practical and useful. We believe the fundamental role of the management field is to develop and disseminate tools to aid in the creation, development, and enhancement of effective and adaptive organizations. This book is a piece of that larger effort.

Michael L. Tushman
Charles O'Reilly
David A. Nadler

SECTION
I

Managers, Strategies, and Organizations

INTRODUCTION AND OVERVIEW

The job of the manager continues to become more challenging. Changes in technology, regulation, international competition, and economic conditions make it more difficult to sustain competitive advantage. Further, as organizations themselves grow more complex, managers need to develop skills in managing not only *downward* but also *across* with peers from other functions, perhaps in other countries, *up* with more senior colleagues, and *outside* with critical suppliers, vendors, or customers. Managers are challenged to create successful and adaptive units by external competitors and customers as well as by internal colleagues.

We take a problem solving approach to the manager's job. Managers need to be effective problem solvers and decision makers in their ever more complex organizations. Decisions must often be made with limited information, perhaps limited expertise, within tight time constraints. Managers rarely have sufficient expertise and influence to deal with increasingly complicated decisions. In most settings, they are inherently dependent on subordinates, peers, and systems to help make and implement decisions. As managers are promoted, this dependence on other individuals, groups, and systems increases.

The most effective managers come to grips with this complexity and dependence. One source of insight in understanding organizations is the research base in organization behavior, theory, and strategy built over the past thirty years. This research base provides important insights into how and why organizations operate. Our challenge is to build on this research base and develop useful, pragmatic *tools* for managers. Tools to help managers systematically diagnose the causes of performance problems prior to taking action.

1

Organizing frameworks, or models, are the most basic tools to simplify the complexity of organizations. Organizing models are road maps that help managers understand the determinants of behavior and predict future outcomes. These models provide a framework for gathering and interpreting data and linking these diagnostic data to managerial action. These models do not crank out solutions to managerial problems. Rather, they are systematic diagnostic tools that help managers solve problems based on a blend of research-based insight and experience-based intuition.

Managers already have implicit models of how and why their organizations operate. Our observation is that the more explicit and amenable to adaptation based on experience and research-based insight these models are, the more effective managers can be. Further, if a problem-solving framework is shared by the manager and his or her colleagues, it provides a common ground and language for joint problem solving.

This book provides an integrated set of problem-solving models. These models are, in turn, organized according to a more general model of organization problem solving—the congruence model. While the congruence model is not the only general problem-solving model available (indeed, the readings present several alternative approaches), we use it as our basic organizing framework. Managers in a host of organizations around the world have found this problem-solving approach helpful.

The congruence model is the general road map through which we will find our way through organizations. Each section of the book corresponds to a component of the congruence model. These sections provide submodels that delve into specific aspects of the congruence model in greater detail. For example, Section II uses information-processing ideas as a framework to better understand the issues in designing formal organization arrangements. This book attempts, through the congruence model, to organize different concepts and models of organization behavior into a simple, integrated, and thus useful format.

THE CONGRUENCE MODEL

In Chapter 3, the reading "A Model of Diagnosing Organizational Behavior" discusses the congruence model in detail. It is useful to give here a brief overview of the model so we can begin to use it immediately as an integrating device and organizing framework for the book.

There are many different ways of thinking about organizations and the patterns of behavior that occur within them. During the past three decades organizations have come to be seen as complex, open social systems. Organizations are seen as mechanisms that take input from the larger environment and transform that input into output.

While the systems perspective is useful, systems theory by itself may be too abstract to be a useful managerial tool. For this reason, there have been attempts to develop more specific models based on the general systems paradigm. Building on the input, transformation process, and output perspective, we can describe the system of organizational behavior and effectiveness (Figure 1). The major inputs to organizations are the environment, which provides constraints, demands, and opportunities; the resources available to the organization; and the organization's history. A fourth input, and perhaps the most crucial, is the organization's strategy. Strategy is the set of key decisions about how to configure the organization's resources in light of the demands, constraints, and opportunities of the environment and the historical context.

Input	Environment	Resources	History	Strategy
Definition	All factors, including institutions, groups, individuals, events, and so on, that are outside the organization being analyzed, but that have a potential impact on that organization.	Various assets to which the organization has access, including human resources, technology, capital, information, and so on, as well as less tangible resources (recognition in the market, and so forth).	The patterns of past behavior, activity, and effectiveness of the organization that may affect current organizational functioning.	The stream of decisions about how organizational resources will be configured to meet the demands, constraints, and opportunities within the context of the organization's history.
Critical Features for Analysis	1. What demands does the environment make on the organization? 2. How does the environment put constraints on organizational action?	1. What is the relative quality of the different resources to which the organization has access? 2. To what extent are resources fixed rather than flexible in their configuration(s)?	1. What have been the major stages or phases of the organization's development? 2. What is the current impact of such historical factors as strategic decisions, acts of key leaders, crises, and core values and norms?	1. How has the organization defined its core mission, including the markets it serves and the products/ services it provides to these markets? 2. On what basis does it compete? 3. What supporting strategies has the organization employed to achieve the core mission? 4. What specific objectives have been set for organizational output?

FIGURE 1.   Key Organizational Inputs

The organization's output includes organization performance as well as group and individual performance. Organization outputs reflect actual performance, while strategy/objectives reflect desired performance.

The organization, then, is the mechanism that takes input and transforms it into output. Organization performance is driven by the interrelations between four major organization components. The first component comprises the tasks of the organization—or the work to be done—and their critical characteristics. The tasks to be done reflect the strategic decisions of managers about the nature of the organization's core mission and how it will be achieved. A second component is the individuals—the organization's human resource

Component	Task	Individual	Formal Organizational Arrangements	Informal Organization
Definition	The basic and inherent work to be done by the organization and its parts.	The characteristics of individuals in the organization.	The various structures, processes, methods, and so on that are formally created to get individuals to perform tasks.	The emerging arrangements, including structures, processes, relationships, and so forth.
Critical Features for Analysis	1. The types of skill and knowledge demands the work poses. 2. The types of rewards the work can provide. 3. The degree of uncertainty associated with the work, including such factors as interdependence, routineness, and so on. 4. The constraints on performance demands inherent in the work (given a strategy).	1. Knowledge and skills individuals have. 2. Individual needs and preferences. 3. Perceptions and expectancies. 4. Background factors.	1. Organization design, including grouping of functions, structure of subunits, and coordination and control mechanisms. 2. Job design. 3. Work environment. 4. Human resource management systems.	1. Leader behavior. 2. Intragroup relations. 3. Intergroup relations. 4. Informal working arrangements. 5. Communication and influence patterns.

FIGURE 2.   Key Organizational Components

profile. Given tasks and individuals to perform them, the organization needs a third component—formal organizational arrangements. These include all the various formal structures, processes, systems, relationships, and jobs that motivate individuals and facilitate their performance of organizational tasks. Finally, there are the informal organizational arrangements. These emerge over time; they are neither written nor formalized, but influence much behavior. These arrangements include patterns of communication, power, and influence; values and norms; and so forth.

How do these four components relate to one another? Each component can be thought of as having a relationship with each other component (Figure 2). Each part, then, can be thought of as having a relative degree of congruence and consistency, or fit. There are six possible relationships in the model; its basic hypothesis is that *organizations will be most effective when their major components are congruent with each other.* Problems of organizational effectiveness stem from either lack of congruence, or fit, among the organizational components or from inappropriate strategies/objectives.

This model represents a contingency approach to thinking about organizational effectiveness. There is no one best organization design, style of management, or method of working. The question is whether the organizational design, for example, fits with the nature of the work being done, the individuals, and the informal arrangements. Different patterns of organization and management will be more appropriate in some situations than others.

ORGANIZATION OF THIS BOOK

This book is organized into six sections, each of which corresponds to a specific component of the congruence model. Section I focuses on the managerial role and the issue of strategy/objective formulation and introduces the notion of managerial problem solving via the congruence model. Section II focuses on formal organization arrangements—choosing formal structures, systems, and procedures to get today's work done as well as tomorrow's. Section III presents several readings on the informal organization, including group processes, leadership within groups, power, conflict, and management of culture. Section IV deals with individual motivation, decision making, and commitment processes in the short run as well as with managing individuals over a career. Section V discusses the roots of organizational inertia and presents several approaches to managing organization change and adaptation. Readings discuss managing both incremental and strategic change. Section VI returns to the role of the executive and the executive team in setting vision and strategy and in building organizations to be efficient and adaptive.

READINGS IN SECTION I

Section I has three chapters. Chapter 1 concentrates on the role of the manager. Peters sets the stage by challenging managers to be both more competitive and more compassionate. Leavitt's provocative article argues that the most effective managers must not only be concerned with problem solving but also pathfinding and implementation. Chapter 2 introduces the basic concepts of strategy and objective formulation. The Porter and MacMillan articles present several ideas on business and competitive analysis and on strategic anticipation. Pascale argues that traditional top-down approaches to strategy formulation completely miss potential learning, which comes from a bottom-up approach to strategy. Pascale also introduces a perspective on organization problem solving that complements the congruence model. In Chapter 3, Nadler and Tushman develop the congruence model in detail. Miles and Snow present a complementary organization model and introduce the issue of organizational adaptation. Greiner presents an evolutionary perspective on organizations upon which Section V builds.

THE MANAGERIAL ROLE

Facing Up to the Need for a Management Revolution

Tom Peters

Can America make it? A huge trade imbalance, a sliding currency, falling real wages and a dismal productivity record. A decade ago, these were the hallmarks of a struggling British economy. Today they characterize an American economy which is struggling . . . against fierce competition from the Far East.

Financial Times (of London)
May 9, 1987[1]

Excellence Isn't—There are no excellent companies. The old saw "If it ain't broke, don't fix it" needs revision. I propose: "If it ain't broke, you just haven't looked hard enough." Fix it anyway.

No company is safe. IBM is declared dead in 1979, the best of the best in 1982, and dead again in 1986. People Express is the model "new look" firm, then flops twenty-four months later.

In 1987, and for the foreseeable future, there is no such thing as a "solid," or even substantial, lead over one's competitors. Too much is changing for anyone to be complacent. Moreover, the "champ to chump" cycles are growing ever shorter—a "commanding" advantage, such as Digital Equipment's current edge in networks that allow vast numbers of computers to interact with one another, is probably good for about eighteen months, at best.

There are two ways to respond to the end of the era of sustainable excellence. One is frenzy: buy and sell businesses in the brave hope of staying out in front of the growth industry curve. This is the General Electric idea: in the last six years, it has acquired over 325 businesses at a cost of over $12 billion, and dumped more than 225, getting $8 billion in return.[2]

The second strategy is paradoxical—meeting uncertainty by emphasizing a set of new basics: world-class quality and service, enhanced responsiveness through greatly increased flexibility, and continuous, short-cycle innovation and improvement aimed at creating new markets for both new and apparently mature products and services.

The latter is Ford's approach to transformation. Quality really has become Job One at Ford. The once all-powerful finance function has assumed a less dominant role, and manufacturing, the prime source of quality, is no longer low in the organizational pecking order. And product development techniques have been set on their ear with the unconventional, but wildly successful, Team Taurus approach; it combined supplier, worker, dealer, and customer input from the start.

If the word "excellence" is to be applicable in the future, it requires wholesale redefinition. Perhaps: "Excellent firms don't believe in excellence—only in constant improvement and constant change." That is, excellent firms of tomorrow will cherish impermanence—and thrive on chaos.

THE ACCELERATING AMERICAN DECLINE

You need not look far to find cause for alarm:

1. Our average business productivity grew at 3 percent a year from 1950 to 1965. From 1965 to 1973, the rate was 2 percent; and since 1973, it's barely crept along at 1 percent. Manufacturing productivity looks worse. It grew at 2.5 percent a year from 1950 to 1985; that contrasts with Japan at 8.4 percent, Germany and Italy at 5.5 percent, France at 5.3 percent, Canada at 3.5 percent—and much-aligned Britain at 3.1 percent.

2. U.S. per capita GNP, called by some the truest measure of a nation's international economic standing, slipped below Japan's in 1986; it also trails the per capita GNP of such European nations as West Germany, Switzerland, Sweden, and Denmark.

3. The average wage for a 25–34-year-old white male declined 26 percent from 1973 to 1983 in constant dollars; the comparable figure for 35–44-year-olds was little better, a decline of 14 percent. This figure is more useful to look at than others. Given the increase in work force participation by women, overall family income has slowly risen. But the economic fate of the individual white male remains the bellwether indicator of progress (or lack of it).

4. The national savings rate, long the lowest in the industrial world, continues to decline. Despite supply-side economic stimulants such as the 1981 tax cut, savings as a share of disposable personal income plummeted from 7.5 percent to 3.9 percent from 1981 to 1986. At year's end 1986, it stood at 2.8 percent. Only our dramatic shift as a nation from premier net lender to premier net borrower has kept investment afloat.

5. In 1986, 138 banks failed, the largest number in one year since the Great Depression; the pace in 1987 is ahead of 1986's. By contrast, 10 banks toppled in 1981.

6. Economists estimate that as many as 30 million people have been dislocated by the "restructuring" in manufacturing during the last decade. Since 1980, the *Fortune 500* have shed a staggering 2.8 million jobs.

7. The plain truth is that every major manufacturing or service firm—from the Bank of America and Citicorp, to Du Pont and Gen-

8

eral Motors, to IBM and Intel and the Hospital Corporation of America—is undergoing trauma.

Alarming as these indicators are—and a host of similar ones—it is the chaos in trade that is most revealing of our poor performance. It alone provides the harsh, industry-by-industry evidence of our decline.

The fact that the trade deficit is currently (April 1987) running at $152 billion, despite the dollar's plunge against the yen and mark since September 1985, is a powerful indication that, while the problem may have been exacerbated by the dollar's strength of a few years back, we are getting clobbered primarily because of the generally poor quality of what we produce and a failure, as a result of questionable service and slow responsiveness, to make use of our onshore, close-to-the-world's-biggest-market advantage.

Textile-makers all but gave up decades ago, and begged for protective relief; while foreign wages were and are often still low, the industry's repeated failure to modernize and adapt to new market needs was the root cause. Then, one by one, steel, autos, and machine tools also begged for—and got—access to the protectionist trough. Finally, 1986 brought the spectacle of Silicon Valley's once proud barons spending more time in Washington than at the factory; their pleas for protection against Japan's alleged "dumping" (selling below cost to gain market share) culminated in the imposition of tariffs of 100 percent on certain Japanese electronics products. But though Japanese hands are not entirely clean, it was long-term disinterest in the factory (the nuts and bolts of producing top-quality products) and arrogance toward even large customers that most severely damaged our semiconductor industry—not Japanese "dumping" or protectionist barriers within Japan.

In 1986, despite continuing bright spots such as computers and aircraft, even the trade balance in high-technology goods went into the red. That was also a first-time losing year for construction equipment and agriculture. In the latter case, despite billions in subsidies, we have simply not awakened to the fact that most of the rest of the world, including India and China, is now self-sufficient in grain. Commodity prices in general remain in a trough, and any upticks are likely to be temporary. That is, the United States can no longer depend on its natural resources to be a source of enduring trade surplus.

A Decline in Service Too

The various service industries are faring little better than manufacturing and agriculture. A formidable $41 billion positive trade balance in services in 1981 has all but disappeared.[3] In a recent *Harvard Business Review* article, "Will Service Follow Manufacturing into Decline?," James Brian Quinn and Christopher Gagnon were glum:

> It will take hard and dedicated work not to dissipate our broad-based lead in services, as we did in manufacturing. Many of the same causes of lost position are beginning to appear. Daily we encounter the same inattention to quality, [over]emphasis on scale economies rather than customers' concerns and short-term financial orientation that earlier injured manufacturing. Too many service companies have . . . concentrated on cost-cutting efficiencies they can quantify, rather than on adding to their product's value by listening carefully and . . . providing the services their customers genuinely want. Haven't we heard this once before? The cost of losing this battle is unacceptably high. . . . If [services] are disdained or mismanaged, the same forces that led to the decline of U.S. manufacturing stand ready to cut them to pieces.[4]

That's bad news indeed, since the service sector now employs 75 percent of us.

Some Rays of Light, but on Net, Trouble

To be sure, the picture isn't entirely grim. And many of these indicators have their flip sides. For instance, although Japanese productivity growth has been several times ours in recent years, we still hold an absolute productivity advantage over the Japanese. In absolute terms they are far ahead of us in targeted industries (steel, autos, semiconductors), but far behind in others (agriculture, the service sector as a whole).

And while the *Fortune 500* continue their job-shedding binge, our vital capital markets, among other things, have spurred a small-business-led surge in job creation, in high-tech as well as hamburgers.

Yet, while the bag is mixed, almost all leading indicators—e.g., productivity growth, competitive assessments of leading industries such as financial services and semiconductors, the trade balances with almost any other industrialized nation—clearly show that our postwar economic hegemony is at an end. Though we still harbor fond memories of days when the rules of the game governed everyone but us, we are now, at best, "one of the big players"; decisions of the Japanese and German ministries of finance are at least as important as those of the U.S. Federal Reserve Board or Department of the Treasury.

All of this is, of course, exacerbated by our failure to come to grips with our awesome budget deficit. One simply can't (1) run a constant deficit of $100 to $200 billion a year, (2) blithely devalue the dollar by over 50 percent vis-à-vis Japan, and (3) shift from chief creditor to chief debtor nation overnight—while expecting the economic waters to remain calm. The U.S. standard of living has declined, by definition, as the dollar has plummeted. More inflation surely looms if the dollar is not stabilized. And a recession may well lie ahead.

Thus, it is essential to address the macroeconomic folly of continued deficits, among other matters. But it is equally important not to be lulled by the glib talk of macroeconomic wizards. Sound macroeconomic policy will help, but the underlying source of our problematic economic performance is a cataclysmic change in competitive conditions, which has in surprisingly short order turned almost every traditional U.S. strength, at the level of the individual firm, into weakness.

AN ERA OF UNPRECEDENTED UNCERTAINTY

Merging and Demerging: Shuffle for Shuffle's Sake

Madness *is* afoot. On the same day in early March 1987, Chrysler buys AMC and USAir swallows Piedmont.

The Chrysler move comes amidst predictions of overcapacity in U.S. auto production—and not long after a decision at General Motors to shut down eleven plants. In the airline industry, prior to late 1986, only USAir, Piedmont, Delta, and American had eschewed major mergers; they also happened to be the four most profitable airlines, with number one American making twenty-four times as much as United, which was the largest airline in 1986 and fraught with problems after trying to swallow much of Pan Am. In 1987, Texas Air will be biggest, after swallowing Continental, Eastern, and People Express. Its digestion problems are all too well documented. So why have the four best so quickly succumbed to major mergers?

Don't look to GE for an answer. On the one hand, its former top strategic planner (now a line executive vice-president) is quoted by *Business Week* in early 1987 as saying that nine out of ten acquisitions "are a waste of time and a destruction of shareholders' value."[5] Then the same article goes on to report that GE is thinking of acquiring United Technologies—a conglomerate with revenues of $16 billion.

Certainly most studies suggest that, in general, mergers don't pan out.[6] For instance, business strategist Michael Porter, of the Harvard Business School, recently concluded a study of merger behavior among thirty-three big U.S. firms from 1950 through 1980. As a group, they subsequently unloaded 53 percent of all their acquisitions during this period and sold off a whopping 74 percent of their acquisitions in unrelated new fields (those purchases that were to have made them safe by positioning them in "guaranteed" growth sectors, according to the press releases). Likewise, when consultants McKinsey & Co. made an extensive study in 1986 of mergers between 1972 and 1983 that involved the two hundred largest public corporations, they determined that a mere 23 percent were successful (as measured by an increase in value to shareholders). The highest success rate (33 percent) was found with small acquisitions made in related fields, the lowest (8 percent) resulted from the merger of large firms in unrelated areas.

Structural economist Frederic Scherer has observed, after years of meticulous study: "On average, mergers decrease efficiency." An economist at the Securities and Exchange Commission was more blunt: Asked to comment on a proposal to further relax antitrust restrictions, he replied, "Most industries in which we have competitive difficulties are not exactly filled with pigmy companies. . . . You don't put two turkeys together and make an eagle."

The mergers do grab headlines. But Ray Miles, dean of the business school of the University of California at Berkeley, is not alone when he points out, "Current 'merger mania' notwithstanding, it seems likely that the 1980s and 1990s will be known as decades of large-scale disaggregation."[7] New terms such as "breakup value" and "de-integration" are heard daily in the halls of the *Fortune 500*. A 1987 *Forbes* analysis of Litton Industries, caustically titled "But the Grass Looked Greener Over There," speaks eloquently to the overall issue of frenzied buying and selling:

> Restructuring. The magic word of the mid-1980s. Just say the syllables: re-struc-tur-ing. They cure all ills, excuse all past mistakes and justify huge writedowns in assets. But does restructuring always accomplish what it originally sets out to accomplish? The trouble with much of what goes on in the name of restructuring is that it is a policy for tomorrow based on today's known circumstances. Take the case of Litton Industries, Inc. That $4.5 billion (revenues) conglomerate has been repeatedly restructured in its 33-year history. The latest restructuring, completed in 1985, refocused the company into three main lines of business, each of which looked extremely promising when the restructuring began four years earlier. Alas. Soon after the reorganization was essentially complete, each of the three chosen businesses ran into problems. . . . The Litton of the future is essentially in place, says [its chief executive officer]. "Now our job for the next several years is to make what we have perform." But one wonders: Will Litton have to restructure again in a few years? Or will management finally settle down to making what it has work?[8]

Mergers and de-mergers are just one part of the madness. Strategies change daily, and the names of firms, a clear indicator of strategic intent, change with them. In rapid succession, U.S. Steel became USX, American Can became Primerica, and United Airlines became Allegis for a while. General Electric has been a bit more coy than the rest; it has not made the official change to GE, but "encourages" the use of the initials rather than the words. The new names share a common trait—they're all more vague than their predecessors.

So U.S. Steel is almost out of steel, as the change in its name suggests. And why not? The year of the change, 1986, brought LTV, the second-largest U.S. steelmaker after swallowing Republic Steel in 1984, to bankruptcy. The company, with $8.2 billion in revenues, became the biggest industrial firm every to go belly up. (Texaco, at $32 billion, eclipsed the record in early 1987. Most record-breaking feats these days seem to be bad-news stories.)

Internationalism: Yes and No

Despite protectionist movements in the United States and other nations, transactions that cross international borders are sharply on the rise. Seldom does a week pass without major joint ventures among partners from more than one country. Nomura buys into Salomon Brothers. Boeing and the Japanese make a deal. McDonnell-Douglas then attempts to join up with Airbus Industries in an effort to match Boeing's newest partnership.

Global financing is also changing the landscape. On the one hand, financial markets are opening up rapidly, and everyone is increasingly connected to everyone else. High-speed computers and communications technology make possible the arrangement of the most exotic financing in a dozen currencies in a matter of days—which facilitates such developments in manufacturing as "global sourcing," wherein firms shop freely among several nations, usually for the lowest-cost source of numerous components. This in turn brings increasing de-integration or "hollowing" of firms; tasks routinely done inside most firms, from watering the plants in the lobby to manufacturing subcomponents, are now subcontracted to outsiders small and large, domestic and foreign.

But strong as the trend toward transcending national boundaries is, the countertrend is also strong. Protection is one element. Debt is another. The United States has lent a trillion dollars to developing countries, and about two-thirds of that debt is held by private banks. Huge debt restructurings are common, and more major defaults, such as Brazil's in early 1987, are anticipated. The quandary is inescapable. The only way the debt-strapped nations can pay back their loans is by exporting what they produce, whether manufactured goods or commodities. This drives them to aggressive selling tactics, which trigger a further protectionist response. Talk about Catch-22.

Predictability Is a Thing of the Past

Nothing is predictable. Currency-exchange transactions now total $80 trillion a year, only $4 trillion of which is required to finance trade in goods and services. The rest is essentially currency speculation, one reason that the overall financial situation has been labeled the "Casino Society." The prices of the major currencies, once stable within 1 percent over decades, now swing 5 percent a week, and 50 percent a year. The prices of energy, agricultural products, and metals are also volatile.

So we don't know from day to day the price of energy or money. We don't know whether protection and default will close borders, making a mess of global sourcing and trade alike, or whether global financing will open things up further.

We don't know whether merging or demerging makes more sense, and we have no idea who will be partners with whom tomorrow or next week, let alone next month.

We don't know who our competitors will be, or where they will come from. New foreign competition appears each day—not only in new services and end products (1986 was the year of the Hyundai and the Yugo, and 1987 brings Daihatsu, the ninth Japanese auto company to export to the United States), but also in the form of the invisible subcomponents of purportedly American products (at one point most of the innards of the IBM personal computer were made abroad).

New competitors financed by venture capital and a sustained market for Initial Public Offerings (IPOs) spring up like mushrooms in banking and health care and pizza delivery and temporary business services, and in semiconductors, supercomputers, and biotechnology, too. Other "new" competitors are units spun off from big firms (often following a hostile takeover or a leveraged buyout, two of a vast number of new financing schemes speeding the pace of corporate overhaul) or downsized, newly autonomous units within big firms.

Technology's Unsettling Impact—On Everything

Technology is yet another wild card affecting every aspect of doing business. As mentioned, it has revolutionized financing. It has also forever changed:

1. Manufacturing: The technology of miniaturization is (a) reducing optimal factory size dramatically and (b) allowing factories of all sizes to turn out a huge variety of products, with greatly reduced setup times.
2. Design: Such innovations as computer-aided engineering are slashing the length of design-to-manufacture cycles.
3. Distribution: Electronics, computer, and telecommunications technologies are making it possible to (a) shorten substantially the time required between order and delivery, (b) poll customers instantly, (c) engage in almost numberless permutations and combinations of globe-spanning partnerships. They are also (d) breathing new life into the independent user, such as the corner grocer, whose optical scanner and computer give him newfound power in dealing with big producers. Likewise, (e) distribution companies, such as Ingram in books and McKesson in drugs, make it possible for smaller user firms to achieve almost all the purchase-price economies that big buyers can achieve.
4. Product definition: There is a blurring of service/product distinctions, given the enhancement of almost every product, from tractors to bank cards, by "software" services and the "intelligence-added" features provided courtesy of the microprocessor.

Consumers Are on the Move Too

On the consuming end of things, more uncertainty is added. Tastes are changing: (1) Thanks to the Japanese, Germans, and others, there is a vastly increased awareness of quality. (2) The rapid rise in the number of women in the work force and of two-wage-earner families leads to new needs (e.g., convenience goods and services). (3) Changes in the kinds of jobs available and, hence, in the distribution of incomes may create something like a two-class society—with an increased number of "haves" demanding greater variety and quality, and an increased number of "have-nots" demanding more durable basic goods, in the face of increasingly poor prospects. And (4) with a TV or two in every home, and a car or two in most driveways, the demand for these products is shifting from a desire for the product per se, almost regardless of quality, to a demand for customized alternatives with special features tailored for ever narrower market segments.

The Interaction of Forces: All Bets Are Off

Of course, more important than any one of these sets of uncertainties—financial, international, technological, or markets/tastes—is the interaction among them. For instance, the drive for more product variety is abetted by the technology which can meet such needs, the explosion of international competitors (producers of both end products and subcomponents) with a piece of the action, and the similar, finance-driven explosion of start-up domestic firms vying for a piece of the more specialized action too.

Sum up all these forces and trends, or, more accurately, multiply them, then add in the fact that most are in their infancy, and you end up with a forecaster's nightmare. But the point is much larger, of course, than forecasting. The fact is that *no firm can take anything in its market for granted.*

Suppose you are considering next year's strategy for a maturing product. Here's what you might well find:

- a new Korean competitor
- an old Japanese competitor continuing to reduce costs and improve quality
- a dozen domestic start-ups, each headed by talented people claiming a technology breakthrough
- one old-line domestic competitor that has slashed overhead costs by 60 percent and is de-integrating via global sourcing as fast as it can
- another old-line domestic competitor that has just fended off a hostile takeover; in doing so, it may have (odds 50 percent) sold off the division that competes with you to another strong competitor with a great distribution system
- a competitor that has just introduced an electronics-based distribution system that wires it to each of its 2,500 principal distributors, slashing the time required to fill orders by 75 percent
- yet another competitor that is tailor-making its products to suit the requirements or tastes of tiny groups of customers, thanks to a new, flexible Computer Integrated Manufacturing (CIM) system
- consumers demanding consistently high quality in every component of the product, from inner workings to fits and finishes
- a wildly gyrating currency market that confounds your own global sourcing decisions
- the probable interruption of supply from two offshore manufacturing plants where governments have defaulted on loan interest and principle payments

It is because this scenario is now *average*—for every banker, health care administra-

tor, public utility executive, and soup maker, let alone computer maker—that our organizations *all* require major surgery. Violent and accelerating change, now commonplace, will become the grist of the opportunistic winner's mill. The losers will view such confusion as a "problem" to be "dealt" with.

Old Assumptions Askew

Today, only a small motivated firm with . . . highly qualified labor and good vertical mobility instead of oppressive hierarchy can hold up in a world whose principal characteristic is instability.

> Andrea Saga
> *Submerged Industry,*
> on the dominant role of
> the gray economy in spearheading
> Italy's economic revival

Henry Ford made great contributions, but his Model T was not a quality car.

> W. Edwards Deming
> father of statistical
> process control and the
> Japanese quality revolution[9]

U.S. industry, run as it was by our forefathers in the tradition of our ancestors, grew big and powerful and restless. We built the biggest steel mills, the biggest oil refineries, the biggest chemical plants, the largest automobile assembly lines, the largest smelters in the world. Boy, could we make product! We didn't always make the best, but we made the most at the lowest price and U.S. industry became a model for the rest of the world. We were the model for size, productivity, for efficiency—but not necessarily for quality. You've heard the expressions, "It ran like a Swiss watch," or "It had the precision of a German machine." We in the U.S. really didn't care. We left the specialized, high quality niche in the marketplace to others, while we concentrated on huge scale, high volume, mass production economics. . . . But then in the '60s and '70s we began to get some hint . . . that some of our assumptions were askew. For one thing, we started to experience some competition from foreign producers—not just because they could make their products cheaper and faster, but because they were, for God's sake, better. The car didn't fall apart at 30,000 miles, and when you bought their television set, it didn't mean taking the repairman into the family.

> Dr. Irving G. Snyder, Jr.
> Vice President and Director
> of Research & Development
> Dow Chemical USA
> from a speech: "The Quality Revolution—
> It Just Ain't in Our Genes"

Two assumptions at the very core of our economic system are now causing untold harm: (1) bigger is better, and biggest is best; (2) labor (human beings at work) is to be ever more narrowly specialized, or eliminated if possible.

THE AMERICAN PENCHANT FOR GIANTISM

Big, not best, has always been the American calling card. In fact, I bet you can't drive more than seventy-five miles in any direction, from anywhere in the United States, without running into a "biggest in the world" of some sort. Wide-open spaces and an apparently limitless frontier set it all in motion. U.S. farmers, starting with the Pilgrims, would cultivate land, wear it out, and blithely move west five miles. Today almost every farm you see is a history lesson told by hulks of rusted cars and agricultural equipment, and homes and yards are filled with broken Christmas toys and power lawn mowers.

Have you ever seen a rusted auto or tractor body in Germany, Switzerland, or Japan? The Europeans and the Japanese have lived within limits for centuries, and have had to be more careful with resources—that is, quality-conscious.

When we began to manufacture, we adopted agriculture's early habits—mass, not quality. Big railroads spurred us on by making vast markets for cheap goods accessible to industry. Railroad tycoons then used naked power to create and control huge business combinations; independents who wouldn't go along faced outrageous rail rates and were often forced out of business. The rise of big combines coincided with the War Department's perfection of mass-production techniques starting in the Civil War and culminating little more than a half-century later, during World War I. Britain may have invented most tools of mass production, but Americans copied and perfected them, and applied them to commercial use. (It's ironic that we are now the premier inventors, and Japan the "copycat" perfecters.)

This all-American system—long production runs, mass operations—paid off with victory in World Wars I and II, and cemented subsequent U.S. economic dominance. But we won World War II with *more* tanks and planes, not, in general, *better* ones. And then overseas economies revived and started looking to our enticing markets. Their only entryways were through niche markets and by offering superb quality to overcome our skepticism, such as that engendered by the inferior image of Japanese products in 1955.

The emphasis on quality fit nicely with European and Japanese skills, in particular their bent for craft (non-specialized) labor and their use of the worker as the primary means of adding value to a product. As well, their historic lack of excessive vertical integration (as in the Ford Motor Company, which once owned the iron mines from which came the iron for the steel forged in the River Rouge mills that in turn went into the cars) provided unique flexibility and was the basis for the short production runs needed to conquer small niche markets. We stuck to our penchant for big, becoming enamored of large-scale automation after World War II. The Japanese took our unused designs for smaller, more flexible machine tools, cornered that market, and also raised rapid product changeover to a high art.

And so today, we are in trouble. Quality and flexibility will be the hallmarks of the successful economy for the foreseeable future. A recent poll of Korean businessmen, *Fortune* reports, revealed that "they preferred Japanese suppliers to American by a margin of two to one. The Koreans complained about mediocre product quality, slow delivery times, and poor service, and added that U.S. companies were reluctant to accept small orders."[10] (This is all the more dramatic, given the longstanding enmity between the Japanese and the Koreans.)

The Koreans are right, but it is gut-wrenching to turn our backs on bigness. GE chairman Jack Welch tells security analysts he wants his company to be number one in "market value"—to be worth the most on the stock market.[11] Does he want to be remembered for superb products? for creating jobs? Who knows? He seldom talks about products; and as for jobs, GE has slashed over 100,000 jobs from its payroll, not counting acquisitions, since he came aboard. And as one *Forbes* writer puts it, GE's Fairfield headquarters "has the look and feel of a colossal investment banking house on the prowl for takeover targets"—with nary a product in sight.

Size drives even entrepreneurs, who all too quickly drift from a desire to be special to a desire to be big, and, they anticipate, safe. People Express founder Don Burr's ill-fated acquisition of Frontier Airlines is all too typical.

Listen to the chatter when the *Fortune 500* comes out. Few chiefs comment on their profit or return on assets. The question is: "What's your rank?" "Making the *Fortune 500*"—an attribute based on size alone—is the Holy Grail for most nonmembers; moving up is the Holy Grail for most members.

The Japanese Passion Whose Time Has Come

There are two principal schools of thought about the Japanese miracle. Economists would have us believe their success is due to consist-

ent, conservative macroeconomic policy—the confluence of interest between companies and their bankers, and between the bankers and the government. For instance, the conservative alliance represented by the all-powerful Ministry of Finance and the more visible Ministry of International Trade and Industry (MITI) directs low-cost loans to targeted industries and protects youthful (or recovering) industries. The sociologists and management theorists sing a different tune, explaining the same phenomenon in terms of group cohesion, lifetime employment, and other management and family (e.g., child-rearing) practices.

The plain fact is, of course, that both have a point. Both factors have contributed to Japan's success.

But there are other, more novel explanations that make sense too. One such focuses on the unique, age-old Japanese passion for smallness, in a world where the advantages of smallness seem to be fast eclipsing the once generally perceived value of giantism. For instance, in *Smaller Is Better: Japan's Mastery of the Miniature*, Korean writer O-Young Lee suggests that "Japan, with its tradition of smaller is better . . . its sensitivity to information, is perfectly positioned to take the lead in the coming age of reductionism."[12]

Lee does a thorough job of tracing the roots of Japan's attachment to smallness. Japanese fairy tales, for example, feature "little giants" who turn needles into swords, bowls into boats, in contrast to such characters of Western folk legend as Paul Bunyan. But the language may provide the most important clue. For instance, the Japanese word for "craftsmanship" is literally "delicate workmanship," and that for feminine beauty is "detailed woman." On the other hand, "large" is literally "not delicately crafted" and "worthless" is "not packed in." There are many more prefixes, more frequently used, that mean "small" than "big." And so on.

The folding fan, miniature gardening, the tea ceremony, and other ritual staples of

Japanese life all stem, according to Lee, from a passion for reductionism.[13] For meditation, the Japanese naturally gravitate to small spaces—small inner courts, say, within already small houses—while Americans (and Koreans and Chinese, for that matter) head for the wide-open spaces when they need to reflect. In fact, the Japanese are contemptuous of almost everything large, says Lee, adding that "Nothing comes harder to the Japanese than living with objects of no use. They cannot bear the unnecessary, the excess."[14]

This deep-seated Japanese trait has major economic consequences in these, the early days of the electronic (miniaturization) age. Sony, for instance, has pioneered in miniaturization—of tape recorders and radios (the Walkman), of VCRs, and of the disk audio, and now video, player.

Though it was a U.S. firm that invented the transistor, and initially supplied transistors to Sony, it was Sony which first mastered the consumer application of the technology.[15] Many other examples, of course, could be added, such as the development of the first electronic calculator by Sharp in 1963. Lee concludes: "That reduction is a hallmark of Japanese electronics should come with little surprise if we recall our discussion of the [Japanese] rock garden. . . . [T]he essence of rock gardening aesthetic was summed up in the words of the garden designer Tessen Soki: 'A thousand miles is shrunk down to one foot.' "[16] (Japan's total dominance of the market in miniaturized consumer goods is illustrated by its astonishing $9 billion positive trade balance in consumer electronics alone,[17] which is nearly half the size of its more ballyhooed automotive surplus.)

In summary, says Lee, "It has been a thousand years since Sei Shonagon wrote, 'All things small, no matter what they are, all things small are beautiful.' How ironic that we should now be hearing the same refrain from the other side of the Pacific!"[18]

One need look no further than a 1987 Mazda ad in a Lufthansa in-flight magazine for evidence supporting Lee's thesis. The ad simply could not have been conceived in America. Its beautiful artwork features a photograph of eleven ancient, delicately crafted Japanese wooden combs. The ad's lead was "Combing Through the Details." The copy proceeds:

A comb looks like a very simple item. But it is deceptively simple. We tend to forget that in the past combs were all hand made. That every tooth, and the space between each tooth, was filed to the same width. This uniformity is all the more astonishing when we remember it was achieved by eye. One mistake and the comb would be ruined. This made combs valuable possessions. And the fact that they were personal items engendered the belief in ancient Japan that one's comb was the repository of one's soul. No wonder the making of it was approached with an almost religious devotion. The comb, an example of how devotion to the basics can lead to simply stunning results. Mazda. Where a devotion to the basics of automotive engineering leads to simply stunning results.

The ad, then, (1) uses the small and delicate as exemplar (a comb in this instance), (2) underscores the tie to ancient Japan and craftsmanship, and (3) "sells" the emphasis on details as Mazda's principal competitive strength.

Now GM has tried a similar tack, using the lead line "No one sweats the details like GM." The similarity is superficial, to say the least. "Sweat" and the image of delicate and ancient combs are, figuratively and literally, worlds apart!

Re-interpreting History I: Has Big Ever Been More Efficient?

The new market realities demand flexibility and speed. The new technologies permit their achievement—but only if we turn our backs decisively on our love affair with size and its handmaidens, stability and predictability. And a useful step in weaning ourselves from the obsession with size might be to recognize that it has never yielded the promised results.

"Bigness has not delivered the goods, and this fact is no longer a secret." With these words, economists Walter Adams (a former president of Michigan State University) and James Brock launch their 1986 book *The Bigness Complex*.[19] After a review of hundreds of studies, they conclude: "Scientific evidence has not been kind to the apostles of bigness and to their mythology."[20]

Adams and Brock don't even require us to deal with the many forces—the instability, the technology of miniaturization, the explosion in products, services, and competitors, and the changing markets just described—that are all currently pushing toward the predominance of small enterprises or business units. They argue, and my own observations coincide with theirs, that the highly touted economies of scale have never been all they were cracked up to be.

In fact, astute observers of the industrial landscape have been questioning the efficiency of bigness for decades. A report on U.S. Steel done by a management consultant in the 1930s concluded even then that the firm was "a big, sprawling, inert giant, whose production operations were improperly coordinated; with an inadequate knowledge of the costs or the relative profitability of the many thousands of items it sold; with production and cost standards generally below those considered everyday practice in other industries; with inadequate knowledge of its domestic markets and no clear appreciation of its opportunity in foreign markets; with less efficient production facilities than its rivals had."[21]

Also in the 1930s, the legendary General Motors chairman Alfred Sloan turned self-critical, observing that "in practically all our activities we seem to suffer from the inertia resulting from our great size. . . . There are so many people involved and it requires such a tremendous effort to put something new into effect that a new idea is likely to be considered insig-

nificant in comparison with the effort that it takes to put it across. . . . Sometimes I am forced to the conclusion that General Motors is so large and its inertia so great that it is impossible for us to be leaders."[22]

In a classic 1956 study, economist Joe Bain examined the cost advantages flowing to multi-plant, as opposed to single-plant, firms in twenty industries.[23] In no case was owning more than one plant a major advantage! More recently, Frederic Scherer studied the fate of fifteen former subsidiaries of conglomerates that had been sold to their former managers. All but one showed substantial improvements in profit—despite the heavy burden of debt incurred in the buyouts. Among the reasons for the dramatic improvement, Scherer notes these: "Cost-cutting opportunities that had previously gone unexploited were seized. Austere offices were substituted for lavish ones. Staffs were cut back sharply. . . . Inexpensive computer services were found to substitute for expensive in-house operations. Make vs. buy decisions were reevaluated and lower-cost alternatives were embraced. Efforts were made to improve labor-management relations by removing bureaucratic constraints that had been imposed by the previous conglomerate's headquarters. Tight inventory controls were implemented, cutting holding costs by as much as one-half."[24]

The movement toward efficiency through smallness is accelerating in virtually every industry today. Language itself provides the first clue:

- In steel, there is an unsung U.S. success story—the one-third of the market now held by profitable, fast-growing firms such as Nucor Corporation and Chaparral Steel. These two have excelled in "mini-mills." Now, the *mini-mill* is about to be eclipsed by the *micro-mill:* further miniaturization, thanks to new technologies, will make it economical to dot little mills every 25 miles or so along the road, in support of local markets.

- A recent *Industry Week* analysis of Allen-Bradley observes that "the Milwaukee-based firm found that its motor starters were losing market share to imports. . . . The design was obsolescent. . . . [T]he company designed and built a . . . *minifactory* [my emphasis] to make them in Milwaukee. Allen-Bradley has cashed in on the flexibility of its *'factory within a factory'* [my emphasis]. It has boosted the variety of starters from 125 originally to 600—without adding floorspace or hardware. . . . Its flexibility gives the company a quick-response capability that translates into a marketplace edge. . . . Now it exports motor starters again and is recouping its domestic share as well."[25]
- In photo-finishing, the *mini-lab* is allowing corner shops with a $250,000 line of credit to do what only Kodak could do ten years ago. The same is true in optometry, where the same word is in vogue.
- The evidence even cascades from the shelves of the corner grocery store, where, for example, the products of a host of *microbrewers* are pushing the venerable Budweiser to the rear.

More sweeping evidence comes from *U.S. News & World Report*'s year-end analysis for 1986. It attributes much of the productivity vitality of the Los Angeles basin—population about 13 million—to the astonishing fact that "some 90 percent of those employed in the . . . area work in small firms with fewer than 50 people that can change course fast to stay competitive."[26]

Once upon a not-so-ancient time, as noted above, Ford owned the mines that provided the iron that went into the steel from which its cars were made. Today, too much of such vertical integration is hurting many of the old industrial giants. For instance, most of

Chrysler's $500-per-car cost advantage over GM accrues from the fact that it purchases 70 percent of its components outside the firm; the comparable GM proportion is 30 percent. Not surprisingly, de-integration is now a strategic priority at GM. As Gordon Forward, founder of Chaparral, puts it, "The big is coming out of manufacturing in this country." The *Economist* confirms the trend:

> Disbursement of production towards ever-smaller manufacturing units is progressing remorselessly. . . . Industrial boutiques [those new terms again], run by small, independent operators with all the latest computer-aided . . . techniques are emerging as contractors to mainstream corporations, many of which might eventually be forced to offload their own manufacturing units and buy in tailor-made products. . . . [That is], Henry Ford's soul-destroying, wealth-creating assembly lines are out of date. Most of the things factories make now—be they cars, cameras or candlesticks—come in small batches designed to gratify fleeting market whims. The successful manufacturing countries in the 21st century will be those whose factories change their products fastest.

Reinterpreting History II: Has Big Ever Been More Innovative?

After efficiency, the second advantage of bigness touted by its advocates has been innovativeness. On this point, the authors of *The Bigness Complex* begin by presenting the advocates' conventional wisdom—

> Ostensibly, giant firms might be presumed for a variety of reasons to be superior inventors and innovators: They can afford to hire armies of the best brains and to outfit them in elaborate, extensive and sophisticated laboratories. Their massive size should permit them to bear the potential losses of risky research into fundamentally new products and production processes. They can further reduce risks by operating a large portfolio of individual projects, so that the

success of any one project can compensate for the failures and losses of other projects. They have established channels of distribution and that should enable them to quickly bring new products to market.[27]

—and then proceed to slash away:

Reality and the available evidence show that despite all these theoretical advantages, small firms . . . are far more efficient innovators than industrial giants . . . small firms are more prolific inventors than giant companies; small firms exert significantly greater research and development effort than large ones; small firms devise and develop inventions at substantially lower costs than large firms; and the giant organizations seem to suffer a number of debilitating and apparently endemic disadvantages as regards invention and innovation.[28]

Adams and Brock review numerous studies, such as one by the National Science Board (part of the National Science Foundation) which reveals that only 34 percent of major technical innovations come from giant firms (over 10,000 employees)—far less than those firms' share of industrial output. Moreover, "the smallest firms produced about four times as many innovations per R&D dollar as the middle-size firms and 24 times as many as the largest firms."

They continue with this *coup de grâce:* "Now do giant firms display any appetite for undertaking more fundamental and risky research projects. That is, contrary to the image that bigness is conducive to risk-taking, there is no statistically significant tendency for corporate behemoths to conduct a disproportionately large share of the relatively risky R&D or of the R&D aimed at entirely new products and processes. On the contrary, they generally seem to carry out a disproportionately small share of the R&D aimed at entirely new products and processes."[29] Yet another study reveals that small firms spend three to ten times

more than large ones to develop similar new products.[30] Even firms venerated for research, such as Du Pont, are challenged by these authors: "A study . . . found the bulk of the firm's commercially important products to have been invented *outside* the firm."[31]

Brock and Adams do a much-needed job in conveying the macroeconomists' view of the shortcomings of size. Eli Ginzberg of Columbia University and George Vojta, formerly Citicorp's top strategic planner, examine the phenomenon from the managerial perspective in *Beyond Human Scale: The Large Corporation at Risk:*

The large corporation at risk moves along a familiar path. Growth in earnings and return on capital tend to moderate. Often the deceleration of the rate of profits conceals an accumulation of potential corporate deficits, which are permitted to remain hidden, at least for a time, by accounting conventions and/or regulatory procedures. . . . [A] slow secular decline in a major arena is often misread as a cyclical phenomenon that time will cure. This misreading allows top management to procrastinate before taking corrective action. . . .

Burdened by the high costs of internal coordination and ineffective utilization of its human resources, the large enterprise is increasingly vulnerable to the entry of small and medium firms into its markets. Its vulnerability is usually in the specialized segments of these markets, where the small firm can be more attentive and responsive to selected customer groups. These new competitors, unburdened by massive prior investments and free of the heavy costs of internal coordination, are frequently able to offer superior products and thereby capture the small end of the market. The large-scale competitor must therefore focus increasingly on the upper end, where transaction size and gross profitability are still large enough to cover its costs. Over time, many large corporations must yield large segments of what had earlier been highly profitable markets to the new competition. . . . At this stage the firm is on the brink of major trauma. It confronts large write-offs, is vulnerable to takeover bids, and many even have to file for bankruptcy.[32]

While these two studies contain damning evidence, neither emphasizes the degree to which current trends are underscoring the inadequacies of bigness. The best contemporary analysis has been done by Michael Piore and Charles Sabel of MIT in *The Second Industrial Divide*. They catalogue "the break-up of mass markets," "the decomposition of large markets," "the disintegration of mass markets," "particularized demand," and, the ultimate, "fragmented markets becoming pulverized." Surprisingly, they are not talking about new arenas such as biotechnology and semiconductors, but about chemicals, steel, textiles, autos, and computers. And they propose a survivor's strategy, "flexible specialization," by which they mean smaller economic units or firms providing a wider variety of products for narrower markets. I will discuss such a strategy below. The point here is simply this: What has been the most venerated tradition in American economics, or, indeed, the American psyche—that big is good; bigger is better; biggest is best—isn't so. It wasn't so. And it surely won't be so in the future.

THE OTHER AMERICAN TRADITION: MINIMIZATION OF LABOR'S ROLE

If bigness is now problematic (and never really was very good), what about that other sacred cow of the American economic belief system, the minimization of the role of labor? It began with a unique American device—the specializing of jobs into narrow skills. The Japanese and Europeans have a centuries-old craft-guild tradition (based on broad-based skills). Extreme specialization never took root in either setting. But neither the craft tradition nor the crafts-

men came to America with the great waves of immigrants; instead, there were masses of illiterate peasants to labor in our giant factories. And when labor finally did organize, the result was to lock in place the narrow job jurisdictions that the moguls of mass production had so painstakingly invented.

The central idea behind narrow job classifications is the conception of labor as a mechanical tool; cost minimization (low wages) and the widespread application of labor-replacing automation are natural concomitants. So is the fact that old American firms and, more frighteningly, new ones thoughtlessly ship work offshore to find cheaper labor. No one speaks more eloquently of the stark choices we face than Robert Reich in *Tales of a New America:*

> . . . high wage economies can no longer depend on standardized mass production. Big Ideas . . . can be shipped in blueprints or electronic symbols anywhere on the globe. Workers in South Korea, Taiwan, or Mexico can churn out turbo-charged automatic vacuums just as well as American workers can, and for far lower wages. Indeed, today [an inventor] is as likely to license a South Korean or Taiwanese company to manufacture the [Big Idea] as he is to sell out to Westinghouse. If Westinghouse docs get hold of [the] Big Idea, it is apt to build its own factory overseas.
>
> In a world where routine production is footloose and billions of potential workers are ready to underbid American labor, competitive advantage lies not in one-time breakthroughs but in continual improvements. Stable technologies get away. Keeping a technology requires elaborating upon it continuously, developing variations and small improvements in it that better meet particular needs. . . .
>
> Where innovation is continuous, and products are ever more tailored to customers' particular needs, the distinction between goods and services begins to blur. Thus when robots and computerized machine tools are linked through software that allows them to perform unique tasks, customer service becomes a part

of production. When a new alloy is molded to be a specified weight and tolerance, service accounts for a significant part of the value added. . . . Reports that American workers can no longer compete in manufacturing and must shift to services are only half-right. More precisely, they can keep high wages only by producing goods with a large component of specialized services, or to state the same thing differently, providing services integral to the production and use of specific goods.

The point is this: In the new global economy, nearly everyone has access to Big Ideas and the machines and money to turn them into standardized products, at about the same time, and on roughly the same terms. *The older industrial economies have two options: They can try to match the wages for which workers elsewhere are willing to labor. Or they can compete on the basis of how quickly and well they can transform ideas into incrementally better products* [my emphasis].

The first path—toward stable mass production—relies on cutting labor costs and leaping into wholly new product lines as old ones are played out. For managers this path has meant undertaking (or threatening) massive layoffs, moving (or threatening to move) to lower-wage states and countries, parceling out work to lower-cost suppliers, automating to cut total employment, and diversifying into radically different goods and services. For workers this path has meant defending existing jobs and pay scales, grudgingly conceding lower wages and benefits, shifting burdens by accepting lower pay scales for newly-hired workers, seeking protection from foreign competition, and occasionally striking.

The second path . . . involves increasing labor value. For managers this path means continuously retraining employees for more complex tasks, automating in ways that cut routine tasks and enhance worker flexibility and creativity, diffusing responsibility for innovation, taking seriously labor's concern for job security and giving workers a stake in improved productivity via profit-linked bonuses and stock plans. For workers this second path means accepting flexible job classifications and work rules, agreeing to wage rates linked to profits and productiv-

ity improvements, and generally taking greater responsibility for the soundness and efficiency of the enterprise. The second path also involves a closer and more permanent relationship with other parties that have a stake in the firm—suppliers, dealers, creditors, even the towns and cities in which the firm resides.

On this second path, all those associated with the firm become partners in its future. . . . Each member of the enterprise participates in its evolution. All have a commitment to the firm's continued success. Both paths can boost profits and improve competitiveness in the short run. But only the second can maintain and improve America's standard of living over time.[33]

A Grim Prognosis

Today's and tomorrow's winning hand is becoming increasingly clear—quality and flexibility. Essential to them both are (1) smaller units and (2) highly skilled workers serving as the chief source of incremental improvements in products and services.

It is a simple case of what "goes around, comes around"? Long-standing Japanese and European traditions—less dependence on big scale, more dependence on broadly skilled labor—are now conducive to economic success. Our denigration of these two factors may prove disastrous.

Worse yet, we have no tradition to fall back on as we seek new models. This is not, as some have labeled it, a "back to basics" movement. Quality and flexibility through skilled labor have never been an American custom.

THE SHAPE OF THE NEW AMERICAN COMPETITOR

Uniformity has given way to broader choices . . . Mass markets have splintered. Size has lost its significance as it becomes increasingly clear that a company's rank in the *Fortune 500* is of limited importance.

Martin Davis
Chairman, Gulf + Western
Fortune, December 1985[34]

In the face of the uncertainties catalogued above, there are those who *are* thriving, in every economic sector. Interestingly, the winners increasingly share common traits. Most pronounced is the emergence of the specialist producer of high value-added goods or services,[35] or niche creator, which is either a stand-alone firm or a downsized, more entrepreneurial unit of a big firm.

Specialists in Steel, Autos, and Chemicals . . .

A quick *tour d'horizon* admits no exception to this trend. Begin with the toughest of industries, steel. While USX, LTV, Bethlehem, and the rest of the integrated firms totter, mini-mill /micro-mill leaders such as Nucor Corporation and Chaparral, and specialists like Worthington Industries, thrive. Productivity in each of these large firms is several times the industry average. Worker involvement is uniformly high, and quality and responsiveness to customers are phenomenal. In many markets, business is being won back from overseas.

The auto market is flying apart. Hyundais dot the highway. Chrysler's president says we will soon have "the Big Thirty, not the Big Three," and industry analyst Maryann Keller comments that "The U.S. Market [has become] a collection of niche markets." Chrysler was following a niche strategy when it acquired AMC primarily for its Jeep Division. And Ford has won by adding value to its product through design distinction and high quality. GM, on the other hand has been losing out: aiming for the "mass market" that no longer exists, it produced look-alike models, and did not deign to enter small niches, such as that for four-wheel

drive and turbos, until very late in the game. The huge firm, says Keller, was "nibbled to death rather than chewed" by smaller, more highly focused competitors.

In chemicals, big firms are writing off billions of dollars in assets in basic commodity chemicals aimed at undifferentiated markets; they are racing, instead, into what the industry calls "downstream" (closer to the river's mouth, or customers) products—numerous specialty, high value-added chemicals to address the narrow needs of smaller markets. Monsanto had a rosy profit picture in 1986; in just five years it has reduced its dependence on bulk chemicals from 26 percent to 3 percent of assets. Du Pont is creating numerous swift-moving business units, closer to the market.

. . . and Computers and Semiconductors

In September 1986, *Financial World* reviewed the computer industry, observing: "Despite analysts' predictions of an industry shakeout, that only a handful of huge companies would survive, the computer industry is actually *more* fragmented than ever."[36] The *Economist,* in January 1987, concurred: "The way in which market forces have humbled IBM is a lesson to trustbusters everywhere. Only a few years ago the American Justice Department and the EEC Commission threatened to break it up or maim it, so as to end its near-monopoly of the computer market. Today it is struggling to remain a blue-chip. In 1986 it suffered a 27 percent fall in net profits . . . while increasing its sales by a tiny 2.5 percent to $51 billion. Can IBM now mount as successful a counter-attack against its competitors as it did against too-hasty trustbusters?"[37]

In fact, IBM is under attack from the world of the future (Hypres is succeeding, where a quarter-billion-dollar IBM development project failed, in introducing the first products using exotic Josephson Junction technology)—and in supercomputers (Cray et al.), superminicomputers (Convex et al.), engineering work stations (Apollo et al.), minicomputers and networks (Digital Equipment et al.), and personal computers (Apple et al.). A February 1987 issue of *High Technology* assesses the state of the vital "parallel/multiprocessor computers" market.[38] It lists nineteen products, from Elxisi's 6400 to Sequent's Balance 2100 to BBN's Butterfly to NCube. Elxisi? BBN? Who?

In semiconductors, the commodity, or so-called merchant chip, market once dominated by Fairchild, National Semiconductor, et al., has all but been lost to Japan. We were victimized even in this new arena by our century-old addiction to mass production and our aversion to labor. With a few exceptions such as IBM, which produces chips only for internal consumption, the big U.S. producers emphasized invention over polishing manufacturing skills. Mass production facilities were built willy-nilly as product demand soared. The best engineers did not go into production. Silicon Valley's labor practices, except for engineers, often make Detroit's look humanistic. Since demand exceeded supply in the days in which these firms' philosophies were taking shape, rudeness, not responsiveness, was the approach to customer affairs.

Now the worm has turned, as it did on Detroit. Computer companies and other purchasers not only found the Japanese chip to be of higher quality, they found the Japanese firm to be more responsive to their needs—from 6,000 miles away—than their next-door neighbors.

The way out of the box, if there is one, appears to be customer-centered specialization. Thus Intel is betting much of its future on an entrepreneurial Application Specific Integrated Circuit (ASIC) unit—a group whose operations are entirely separated from those of the rest of the firm. The greater good-news story in U.S. semiconductors, however, may be the 113 specialist start-ups between 1977 and 1986 that constitute the so-called Third Wave;

only six have failed, and the new bunch will do over $2 billion in sales in 1987.[39] Some, such as LSI Logic, which was just founded in 1981 but is projecting sales of $300 million in 1987, have become powerhouses. They give us a wide lead in what may well turn out to be the most important part of the industry.

Forget Bigness in Packaged Goods Too

The story is repeated in packaged goods and foods. Take Kitchen Privileges of Alexandria, Virginia, a specialist firm that serves specialists.[40] It is a commercial kitchen (seventeen ovens, walk-in freezer, etc.) specifically designed to be rented. And it is, by giants such as Campbell Soup, to help test-market new products, and by start-ups like Ultimate Brownies. Consumers, especially in the burgeoning two-worker-family sector, are demanding more and more fresh specialized products. Big producers such as Campbell and entrepreneurs by the thousand are satisfying them by deluging a market increasingly fragmented into niches with goods designed to fit.

Campbell has in fact had two sweeping reorganizations in the last five years. The first created over fifty fleet-of-foot business units, the second decentralized marketing into regional offices in an effort to get closer to the distribution channel. Flexible manufacturing systems the firm is introducing add yet another dimension of responsiveness.

Procter & Gamble is following a similar path, attempting to streamline its very hierarchical, functionally centered organization. The firm's past successes cannot be denied, but its old approach is far too cumbersome for today's fast-changing markets.

Ditto the Service Sector

The situation in the service sector is no different. The business section of the January 3, 1987, issue of the Kansas City *Times* proclaims:

24

"Niche stores again outdo retail giants in holiday sales." The new household names and profit stars in retailing are firms such as The Limited, The Gap, and Nordstrom. Even the specialists are specializing—The Limited's Victoria's Secret, Limited Express, and Henri Bendel; The Gap's Banana Republic. Meanwhile, the giants, from Safeway to Carter Hawley-Hale, sputter, fight takeover threats, and attempt to transform their cavernous retail spaces into collections of Limited-like boutiques. (Countertrends can be found, to be sure, such as warehouse stores in retailing. However, these stores will likely end up with a very limited share of the market. In fact, sales per store in warehouse operations have been declining since 1983.)

In financial services, the "financial supermarket," with its one-stop shopping for all financial services, died stillborn: for example, Merrill Lynch, formulator of the idea, sold off its commercial real estate unit in 1986. And the giant banks, with rare exceptions, look much less "solid" than only a few years ago; the Bank of America is the premier acute-care case—while superregionals such as Banc One of Columbus, Ohio, are surging ahead and smaller specialists such as the University National Bank & Trust of Palo Alto, California are growing fast and yielding eye-popping returns to assets. Indeed, a look at *Business Week*'s 1986 list of the top 200 banks reveals that the further down the list you go, the better the returns get. Only one of the twenty-three biggest banks (The Morgan) returned more than 1 percent on assets, while fully twenty of the smallest fifty topped that magic mark.

In health care, too, the mega-firms like American Medical International and Hospital Corporation of America were seen as a wave of the future just a few years ago. They roamed the countryside gobbling up small hospitals, and some experts were predicting that most health care in the United States would be delivered by a half-dozen firms by the mid-nineties. Now the giants are struggling. On May 31, 1987, for instance, HCA announced that it was selling off 104 hospitals, for $1.8 billion; it is left with 75, some 50 psychiatric centers, and a number of management contracts. On the other hand, regional hospitals that have specialized are doing well. So are ambulatory-care centers and superspecialists such as Service Master, a Chicago-area firm whose principal business is contracting to clean hospitals. It's over a billion dollars in size, with a five-year return to equity that was tops among the *Business Week 1000* in 1986. (Incidentally, ServiceMaster is going great guns with its mundane but specialized service in Japan, too.)

More evidence of the specialist advance in services is the burgeoning of temporary services and franchising. Only a few years ago the word "temp" brought to mind stenographers and receptionists. The industry which grew at a compound annual rate of almost 20 percent from 1970 to 1984, now provides Kelly today for that secretary substitute, and they'll ask you if you want a WordStar or a MacWrite person.

Typical of the specialist winner in franchising is Minit-Lube, or "McOil Change," as *Forbes* dubbed the several-hundred-unit chain:

Stand in the spotless driveway of Minit-Lube, a fast-growing auto lubrication franchise, where cars are streaming into Minit-Lube's bays, three abreast. Why is this chain so successful? Perhaps it is because, aside from the drive-through car bays, Minit-Lube looks nothing like a greasy automotive business. It's clean, painted white and surrounded by neatly trimmed lush landscaping. . . . The place should have been named McOil Change. The customer pulls up, is greeted by a smiling employee trained to make eye contact. The customer then places the standard order—a check or fill of brake and power-steering fluids, motor oil, battery water and filters for air and oil. Thereafter, a uniformed service team springs into action. One pops the hood to check and fill fluids. Another vacuums the interior and cleans windows. A third, from a pit below, works his way along the drive shaft, grease gun and wrench in hand, lubricating joints, draining the oil and replacing the filter. Within ten minutes the driver is on his way. The bill: $20. Sears charges the same just for an oil change and lubrication, and it can take up to an hour.[41]

The Winning Look Is Clear

This tour is hardly complete, but it does give the flavor of the sorts of firms that are turning up winners. And even were most of the recent mergers to reverse history's trend and work, the movement toward specialization and more moderately sized business units would in no way be blocked. A GE swallows an RCA, but its first move is to put each acquired business unit, such as NBC, through a starvation diet, similar to the one GE's homegrown corporate and business unit staffs have been subjected to. The truly close-to-the-market units within GE and its acquisitions, and within Du Pont, IBM, and P&G, are being reshaped to look and act more like The Limited, Minit-Lube, or Worthington Industries.

Take all the evidence together, and a clear picture of the successful firm in the 1990s and beyond emerges. It will be:

- flatter (have fewer layers of organization structure)
- populated by more autonomous units (have fewer central-staff second-guessers, more local authority to introduce and price products)
- oriented toward differentiation, producing high value-added goods and services, creating niche markets
- quality-conscious
- service-conscious
- more responsive
- much faster at innovation
- a user of highly trained, flexible people as the principal means of adding value

Figure 1 summarizes the case I've made so far. A series of forces, arrayed on the left side of the chart, are interacting with one another to create a completely new context for doing business, labeled "outcome." The outcome can only be dealt with, I believe, by firms which share a common set of traits, labeled "shape of a winner."

THE GOOD NEWS: THERE IS GOOD NEWS

You want evidence of transformation not led by major mergers? How about Ford at $60 billion, Chrysler at $23 billion, Dana at $4 billion, Brunswick at $3 billion, Milliken at $2 billion, Campbell Soup at $4 billion, McKesson at $6 billion? You want examples of those squarely in the middle of it? Try Du Pont or Procter & Gamble. How about winners who have hiccuped but so far not made a major misstep in tumultuous markets? Consider Cray, Apple, Digital Equipment, Nucor, Worthington, Chaparral, ServiceMaster, American Airlines, Banc One, Federal Express, The Limited, Nordstrom.

But is there anyone big who seems to have known the formula all along? I began this discussion by declaring that there were no excellent companies. Were I to admit an exception, it would be 3M. If ever there was a perpetual-motion machine, it is this $9 billion firm. Its trick has been to understand value-added differentiation and perpetual market creation long before such tactics became necessary. Every unit of the corporation, whether it serves "mature" markets or exotic new ones, is charged with continual reinvention. And the firm's minimum acceptable profit margins per unit are astronomical—only attainable with truly superior products and service.

So in every industry there are places to visit, people to learn from. Johnsonville Sau-

Shape of a Winner

- Niche-oriented market creators (short production runs)
- Flat (fewer layers)
- Fast (responsive, adaptive)
- Quality-conscious
- Internationalist (even if small)
- Smaller (stand-alone, small within big)
- Gain sharing, participation, adding value through people

Outcome

- Uncertainty
- End of isolation
- Demise of mass (markets and production)
- More choices
- Market fragmentation
- Product and service explosion
- Demand for quality and fast response
- More complexity
- Midsize firms
- Cleaned-up portfolios and more competitive big firms' business units

Generic Uncertainty

- Oil @ $5 or $35 a barrel
- 1 trillion Eurodollars
- $80 trillion in annual currency = trading/gyrating exchange rates
- Casino society (junk bonds, availability of venture capital, strong market for initial public offerings, leveraged buyouts)
- $1 trillion in developing-country debt
- Mergers, divestitures, de-integration, joint ventures
- Record business and bank failures (and record start-ups)

Technology Revolution

- Design (fast collection of customer data, reduced design-to-manufacture time)
- Manufacturing (smaller, more flexible factories)
- Distribution (electronic linkages, power to customers)

New Competitors

Foreign
- Developed (e.g., Japan, Germany)
- Newly industrialized (e.g., Korea)
- Rapidly industrializing (e.g., Brazil)

Domestic
- Smaller firms resulting from the entrepreneurial explosion
- Downsized and de-integrated units within big firms, spun-off elements from big firms

Changing Tastes

- More options
- Two-wage-earner families
- More affluence (top third)
- Less affluence (bottom third)
- Saturation of markets for the "commodities" of yesteryear
- Demand for superior quality

FIGURE 1. Forces at Work and Their Apparent Resolution

27

sage of Sheboygan Falls, Wisconsin, installed a remarkable organization structure, with little hierarchy, lots of employee involvement, and substantial profit-sharing; its market share in the Milwaukee area soared from 7 to 50 percent in ten years. I wrote about the firm in *U.S. New & World Report*—and was delighted to learn that the column spurred visits by plant managers from 3M and General Mills. Another column, about the stellar customer service and economic performance of Sewell Village Cadillac of Dallas, led to a visit by a team from a Procter & Gamble plant.

So the role models are there—in steel, textiles, and autos, as well as computers, retailing, health care, and banking.

THE BAD NEWS: PACE

General Motors was and remains a pioneer in workplace experiments. From its joint venture with Toyota called the New United Motor Manufacturing, Inc. (NUMMI), to its assembly plant in Lakewood, Georgia, a lot has been going on.

But not enough. The firm's relative cost position has deteriorated. Its management ranks, despite radical (by past standards) surgery, remain hopelessly bloated. Its committee-driven designs still lag and its product development cycles are still two to three times longer than those of its best competitors. And it still can't figure out how to take on small markets. Top that off with a bad case of merger indigestion from Hughes and EDS alike. Moreover, technology, rather than people, is still its theme. (All of this was, almost certainly, what led to GM's precipitous 20 percent loss of market share in just one year, as of May 1987. Never mind whether or not GM will recover, as it may well do—the simple fact that the world's largest industrial firm could tumble that fast, despite extraordinary incentives to car buyers aimed at stemming the tide, is stunning evidence of the changing times.)

No one is complacent. Ford, though topping GM in profits in 1986 for the first time in sixty-two years, knows it has barely scratched the surface in its attempt to achieve superior quality and shorter product development cycles. It looks to Toyota as the premier firm in its industry. IBM is scurrying, too; one long-time observer of the firm estimates that its payroll has 50,000 more people than it needs to accomplish its current mission.

But is even Ford moving fast enough? It's not at all clear. Radical changes in organizational structure and procedures are called for. Layers of management must be reduced in most big firms by 75 percent. Product development time and order lead time must be slashed by 90 percent. Electronic/telecommunications linkups to customers and suppliers must be developed posthaste. Just listening to customers and dealers needs to become the norm—and as yet it's not.

All this adds up to a requirement, not for structural or procedural tinkering, but for a revolution in organization: more autonomous units—guided by a coherent vision rather than by memorandums and managers-as-cops, and manned by involved workers with a big stake in the action and hell-bent upon constant improvement. And this in turn means that new attitudes are also required—especially commitment on the part of managers to the idea that suppliers, workers, unions, distributors, and customers are all partners in the common endeavor.

But the wholesale changes in attitude have not yet occurred, and without them we are doing immeasurably dumb things. We are, for example, letting work drift offshore in pursuit of the lowest-cost production. But, as I'll argue below, to lose control of the plant is to lose control of the future—of quality, responsiveness, and the source of most innovation, which in manufacturing industries occurs in the palpable, on-premises interaction among plant team, designer, marketer, and customer.

We are misusing automation. Americans still see it as a tool to reduce the need for labor, not as a tool to aid labor in adding value to the product. In consequence, efforts to staff our plants with robots are not working.

We are still churning businesses, via merger and divestiture, in hopes of obtaining some ideal portfolio, fit for the future. There is none. No industry is safe. There is no such thing as a safe, fast-growth haven. The new attitudes toward people and adding value are required as much in financial services and entertainment as in autos and steel. Look at the revolution wrought by The Limited or Federal Express, linking people power and computer network power; most service firms are light-years behind.

Take Roger Milliken of Milliken & Co. His genius in 1980 was to see that the answer to competition in the "mature" textile market was unparalleled quality attained largely through people. He revolutionized the company then. But he's almost unique because he saw in 1984 that the first revolution was wholly inadequate to meet the worldwide competitive challenge. So he made another revolution, re-ordering every relationship in the firm in pursuit of unparalleled customer responsiveness. Two revolutions in six years.

It is Roger Milliken's brand of urgency—and taste for radical reform—that must become the norm. For Milliken's two revolutions (and the firm was a star to begin with) are still only barely meeting the competitive challenge.

IMPLICATIONS FOR PUBLIC POLICY

Management, I believe, holds the key to a competitive resurgence in the United States. Nonetheless, certain policy prods could help

immeasurably in speeding the necessary transformation.

As a conclusion to this introductory analysis, I will offer only the barest of outlines—suggestions for several steps that policymakers can take:

1. *Promote more, not less, competition.* That is, turn up the heat. *First, pass no protectionist legislation.* Protect an industry, ancient and recent history alike suggest, and it gets sloppier, or at least fails to improve at an acceptable rate. Playing fields are not, and never have been, level. We should utilize existing trade management legislation, which is fully adequate, and not add more. The objective is to get better and different, not to try to hide from a newly energized world economy. (In this regard, the trade bill which will likely pass in 1987—the most restrictive since Smoot-Hawley in 1930—is a giant step backwards.)

   Second, don't tie the corporate raiders' hands. Raiders are no altruists, and their acts cause much unnecessary pain. And, to be sure, some of the moves corporations make to forestall raiders are dysfunctional—for example, making inappropriate mergers so as to create a balance sheet that scares a raider off, or shuttling jobs offshore in a crash, but ultimately misguided, effort to slash costs. But on balance, the raiders are, along with the Japanese, the most effective force now terrorizing inert corporate managements into making at least some of the moves, such as downsizing, that should have been made years ago.

   Third, get rid of the entire capital-gains tax after a certain holding period passes. The start-up firms are the breath of fresh air in the economy—we encouraged them with the 1981 capital-gains tax break, and have now discouraged them with the omnibus tax act of 1986. In general, support financial incentives that favor start-ups and spin-offs/divestitures such as leveraged buy-outs.

2. *Retool and involve the work force.* The work force must become the prime source of value added. We need to give employers the incentive to hire people and constantly upgrade skills. *First, provide a special tax incentive for all funds, including employee wage costs, spent on training and pay-for-knowledge programs. Provide a further tax incentive for wage increases that result directly from skill upgrading. Provide general tax deductibility for employee off-the-job skill upgrading, whether or not it's related to the current job. I also support, to aid displaced workers, some form of Individual Training Account,* as proponents have labeled it. Sizable tax-deductible contributions by employees, similar to IRAs, might be made over an extended period. The money would revert to the employee at retirement or some such time, but upon displacement would be issued, in voucher form, for use in certified training programs.

A second, sweeping plank is aimed at giving employers an even higher incentive to hire and involve employees. Inspired, in particular, by the ideas discussed by Martin Weitzman in *The Share Economy,* I propose, for employers, that *a major, old-fashioned investment tax credit plan be allowed on wages distributed as bonuses via profit-distributing bonus plans and quality- and productivity-based gain-sharing plans. For employees, I suggest a big tax exemption, possibly with limits, for all income from profit-distribution and productivity-based gain-sharing plans.* (Such a bold incentive would be required to compensate for greater uncertainty—the real possibility of lower pay in bad times.)

Third, greater employee assurance is required as foreign competition heats up even further, and smaller firms become increasingly dominant. *Extended and increased trade adjustment assistance is desirable* to combat the former (though it should be highly skewed to force rapid enrollment in retraining programs, for instance). Portable pensions and other dislocation-ameliorating housing and health-care programs will be required as well.

3. *Stop the mindless offshore job drift.* The loss of jobs per se may be less significant than the loss of control of our destiny, as certain manufacturing activities migrate offshore. *I propose a new form of domestic content legislation.* The term is usually applied to the percentage of domestic content in imports. My alternative is to provide some tax credit for domestic products, based upon the percentage of domestic content, up to, say, 50 percent. A particularly thorny subset of this issue is start-ups—for instance, high-tech firms—that never do establish their own manufacturing operations. The capital-gains tax formula for start-ups could be a sliding one, depending on the percent of value added by onshore manufacture.

4. *Push internationalism.* We need to shed our lingering isolationism. Concepts I support include (a) *a value-added tax (VAT) to pay for the programs I have proposed here, but excluding goods sold for export,* (b) *tax benefits favorable to Americans working abroad,* (c) *provision of more readily available financing sources for smaller or mid-sized firms seeking export markets,* and (d) *educational incentives to induce much more foreign-language education.*

5. *Support expanded research and development.* The R&D tax credit and the basic-research credit which supports business and university linkages will both be phased out by the end of 1988, thanks to the 1986 tax act. At the least, they should be restored. Support for high levels of basic research, especially in non-defense areas, is a must. Additionally, we might provide special tax breaks to firms that bring university researchers on board, or that support cooperative education programs, especially in engineering and science.

This brief sketch is not meant to be exhaustive. It does not include any mention of major policy levers that influence the overall business climate (areas where others are more expert than I), and it includes only some of the types of policies that would hasten the transformation of our firms.[42]

I find myself turning more frequently to public policy considerations because of my growing frustration. The changes are being made—by management. The changes can be made—by management. But they are not being made fast enough by management. The issue is not the unions. Nor is it "unfair" Japanese practices, unless learning our language or paying attention to details that commercial and individual consumers care about is unfair.

We must look at what's working, and move fast to adapt and emulate the best. The speed of the transition is the most pressing issue.

REFERENCES

1. "Rebuilding the U.S. Model," *Financial Times,* May 9, 1987, p. 26.
2. Edwin A. Finn, Jr., "General Eclectic," *Forbes,* March 23, 1987, p. 75.
3. James Brian Quinn and Christopher Gagnon, "Will Service Follow Manufacturing into Decline," *Harvard Business Review* (November/December 1986), p. 95.
4. Ibid., p. 103.
5. James R. Norman, "General Electric Is Stalking Big Game Again," *Business Week,* March 16, 1987, p. 113.
6. Michael Porter, "The State of Strategic Thinking," *The Economist,* May 23, 1987, pp. 18, 22.
7. Raymond E. Miles and Charles C. Snow, "Network Organizations: New Concepts for New Forms," *California Management Review* (Spring 1986), p. 62.
8. John Heins, "But the Grass Looked Greener over There," *Forbes,* April 27, 1987, p. 54.
9. "Business Guru Finds a Following," *San Jose Mercury News,* April 17, 1987, p. 13D.
10. Sylvia Nasar, "Competitiveness: Getting It Back," *Fortune,* April 27, 1987, p. 223.
11. Finn, op. cit., p. 75.
12. O-Young Lee, *Smaller Is Better: Japan's Mastery of the Miniature* (New York, NY: Kodansha International, 1984), p. 19.
13. Ibid., p. 35.
14. Ibid., p. 87.
15. Ibid., pp. 154–156.
16. Ibid., p. 156.
17. The overall annual U.S. electronic trade deficit with Japan runs over $20 billion.
18. Lee, op. cit., p. 169.
19. Walter Adams and James W. Brock, *The Bigness Complex: Industry, Labor and Government in the American Economy* (New York, NY: Pantheon Books, 1986), p. xi.
20. Ibid., p. 46.
21. Ibid., p. 35.
22. Ibid., pp. 39–40.
23. Ibid., pp. 45–46.
24. Ibid., pp. 44–45.
25. Jack Thornton, "New Marketing Muscle," *Industry Week,* May 4, 1987, p. 38.
26. "California Doing Its Own Thing," *U.S. News & World Report,* December 22, 1986, p. 25.
27. Adams and Brock, op. cit., p. 50.
28. Ibid., p. 52.
29. Ibid., p. 54.
30. Ibid., p. 55.
31. Ibid., p. 52.
32. Eli Ginzberg and George Vojta, *Beyond Human Scale: The Large Corporation at Risk* (New York, NY: Basic Books Inc., 1985), pp. 218–219.
33. Robert B. Reich, *Tales of a New America* (New York, NY: Times Books, 1987), pp. 118, 119, 120, 121, 147, 148.
34. Martin Davis, "Two Plus Two Doesn't Equal Five," *Fortune,* December 9, 1985, p. 175.
35. By the term "high value-added" I simply mean products or services which emphasize innovative design tailored for narrow markets and resulting from more intense listening to customers; superior quality; exceptional service and responsiveness to customers. This is in contrast to the Model T strategy—"any color as

long as it's black"—followed by so many firms to this day.

36. "Chipping Away," *Financial World*, September 30, 1986, p. 4.

37. "IBM Humbled," *The Economist*, January 31, 1987, p. 17.

38. Dwight B. Davis, "Parallel Computers Diverge," *High Technology* (February 1987), p. 20.

39. Michael S. Malone, "America's New-Wave Chip Firms," *Wall Street Journal*, May 27, 1987, p. 28.

40. Caroline E. Mayer, "Cooking Up a Hot Idea," *Washington Post*, January 26, 1987, p. 1 (Business).

41. John Merwin, "McOil Change," *Forbes*, August 11, 1986, p. 91.

42. It also flies in the face of the basic intention of tax reform—less use of the tax code to manipulate firms' outcome. While I acknowledge the adverse consequences of thousands of special interest loopholes, I think this is precisely the wrong time to turn our back on the most effective weapon to aid rapid industrial transformation—tax policy.

Management and Management Education in the West: What's Right and What's Wrong?

Harold Leavitt

This article describes three distinct elements in the management process: path-finding (#1); problem-solving (#2) and implementing (#3). Business schools have tended to emphasise #2 approaches with less attention to #3 and often total ignorance of #1; whilst in recent years #3 has become recognised as much more important. We also need to re-establish the importance of the #1 approach: management needs its visionaries, dreamers and aesthetes.

In the last 5 years American management has undergone some heavy pummeling. Before that American managers had been a proud, indeed arrogant lot; confident of the superiority of their managerial skills relative to Europe and the rest of the world. But the emergence of the new industrial Japan rather quickly changed all that. The Japanese have taken huge bites out of our domestic automobile market, bites that could easily prove fatal. They have also taken much of our steel market (and yours), and they are threatening my home territory in the Silicon Valley of California; and they are doing it all not simply by price-cutting but by turning out high quality and technologically advanced products.

It is not surprising, then, that American managers are a little humbler this year; indeed

they are full of doubt and uncertainty. And so are management educators. For there is a chain of reasoning pervading the American scene that runs something like this: First, the Japanese are good, very good. Second, by contrast, American Companies look bad, very bad; they seem bumbling and inefficient. The American press and public are making the most of the American decline, as, of course, are European managers tired of being treated like naive novices.

But carry the logic further. The decline of American management is closely correlated with the rise of the American business school. For the last quarter century American business schools have been turning out MBA's in very large numbers at very high salaries. These graduates have been around long enough to achieve positions of power and leadership throughout American industry. And as you here at the London Business School know well,

American management educators were certainly as arrogant as American businessmen when LBS got started, back in the sixties. The last step in that chain of logic is now surely obvious: If the Japanese are good, and the American managers aren't as good as they looked and if those managers are also MBA's then the ultimate blame looks reasonably clear. The real source of our malaise must be the educators, the professors, in those blasted business schools. And just to add a little salt to the wound, the Japanese have done what they've done without business schools!

Since this set of lectures is intended to look at the state of the art in management education, it behooves us to do more than attack the professors. We can also ask, in a more analytic way "What's gone wrong? And what needs to be done to set it right"? In the rest of this talk I want to consider those issues, but to do so I need to break the larger problem down into some smaller pieces. One way to reduce it is to eliminate macro questions like the broad structure of U.S. and Japanese industry. Let's *not* look, for example at issues like Japan Inc. versus the U.S. and its anti-trust laws. Let's discuss instead the internal issues of management to which much of the Japanese incline and the American decline have been ascribed. The Japanese are good, we are told, because they develop cadres of loyal people committed to their work, to the quality of their products and to their companies. And we in the West don't. So let's think *relatively* small—about internal company management, and let's further decompose internal management processes into some even smaller categories.

A MODEL OF THE MANAGING PROCESS

Herewith, then, a simple-minded model of what the internal managing process is about.

You may disagree and disapprove. I do not tout the model as correct or complete, but only as a useful way to start toward breaking down the questions of what's gone wrong and what needs to be set right.

I propose a three-part model. It says the managing process is about, in more or less reverse order *implementing, problem-solving* and *path-finding,* implementing is about action, about getting things done, making things happen. Implementing is getting the bricks laid, the service performed, the product delivered. But managing is also about *problem-solving.* That is, managing is not just about doing; it is also about thinking. It involves reducing complex problems to simpler forms, setting up choices, and deciding among alternative courses of action. But behind both of those segments there is a third, a much fuzzier element, more difficult to define and communicate, but incontrovertibly real and critical. I shall call that third component the *path-finding* part of the managing process. Path-finding is about getting the right questions rather than the right answers. It is about selecting the problem, not solving it. It is *not* about figuring out how to get there from here, nor even about making sure that we do get there; rather about pointing to where it is that we ought to try to go. #1 Path-finding then, is about mission, innovation, vision. #2 Problem-solving is about analysis, thought, reason; and #3 Implementing is about acting, changing, doing.

The model then looks something like Figure 1. I have purposely drawn wavy vertical lines between segments to indicate that the boundaries between them are often unclear, and also to suggest that movement from one to another (from path-finding to problem-solving or problem-solving to implementing, and all other combinations) is often difficult and critical in the managing process. It is not enough, that is, for the manager to be competent in each of these three. The manager had also better be

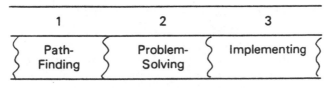

FIGURE 1. A Model of The Managing Process

skillful at moving the ball across the boundaries between them.

#3. IMPLEMENTING

Let me take a few of your minutes to add a little meat to these bones. May I ask you to think with me about #3, the implementing part of managing. This aspect of the managing process has one critical attribute that distinguishes it from much non-managerial implementing. *It must always be done through other people.* In other areas of life we can often implement our own decision. But in managing human organizations we must invariably get other people to mow our lawns. Implementing in organizations, therefore, almost always requires some persuading or commanding or manipulating or forcing other people to do what you want done. The implementing part of the managing process, because it involves changing human behaviour, thus becomes a largely *emotional* process. It deals not so much with the rational parts of people as with their passions, their fears and their loyalties. It is not through reason that we persuade our employees to improve product quality; it is through fear, greed, love, loyalty, affection, commitment or some other emotional mechanism.

Another aspect of the implementing of the managing process: Some professions and occupations provide training and practice at persuading, commanding, leading other people, and some do not. And some individuals are better at it than others. If one were to pick from the American scene a recent public fig-ure who has been particularly notable as an implementer, my first choice would be President Lyndon Johnson. Johnson, while he was president, was not viewed by most observers as a great intellectual leader, nor as a great problem-solver or decision-maker. Nor was he seen as a great path-finder. You may recall that he did try to establish the vision of a "new society," but that notion somehow never took hold, and I think most of us in the States never really believed that he believed it. But what is remembered about Mr. Johnson is his ability to walk through the halls of Congress twisting arms and stroking egos, establishing friendships and making compromises, so that he got things done. He studies the people he dealt with very carefully and individually. He got things done through relationships. The folklore he left behind reflects those characteristics. His favourite sayings were pragmatic, indeed earthy. One of his favourites: "Don't spit in the soup, we all have to eat." Another: When one of his aides came to him to ask, "Mr. President, why are you now establishing an alliance with John Smith who has always been your enemy and who for years has been trying to destroy you?" Johnson is said to have replied, "I'd rather have him inside the tent pissing out than outside pissing in." This is not the rhetoric of your great British statesman. But it does nicely reflect Johnson's concern for doing what one has to do to get the doggone job done.

Let's take that whole issue one step further. Imagine a young person coming to you to ask: "How do I learn to become a great implementer? What shall I study? What occupation shall I enter?" It does not seem difficult to iden-

35

tify some professions in which implementing skills are critical to effective performance and hence emphasized in the training process. How about salesmen? How about litigating lawyers—your barristers that is, as distinct from your more analytic solicitors. Litigators, at least the ones I have encountered in American law firms, are doers, movers and shakers, indeed killers. They worry about whether to put Italian women on the jury; or whether they would be better off with Irish men. They worry about the idiosyncracies and characteristics of the opposing lawyers, and those of the judge. They work on people's emotions and impulses as a good salesman might.

But we need to add some other categories of occupations here which in combination may look like a strange set of bedfellows indeed. For it is not only the salesmen and litigators and politicians who are implementers. So are company commanders (and all field commanders) in the military; and first line supervisors on the shop floor. All those are people who must get other people to do it.

Still another category of people belong to this implementing set: the psychiatrists, psychologists and others in the "helping professions." For they too, whether they admit to it or not, are (a) trying to change people's behaviour, (b) trying to do it via emotional means, and (c) dealing either one-on-one or one-on-a-small-group of unique individuals.

At least two generalizations emerge from such a picture of the implementing process and the kinds of people who try to do it well. First, in all the varied kinds of implementing, human emotionality and human irrationality are the stuff of which change is made. Emotion is not "noise" in the system as it might be in more analytic aspects of the world. And second, most of those implementing people still think small; that is, they tend to think about people singly or in small numbers. People, for most true blue implementers, have names, faces, personalities and idiosyncracies.

#2. PROBLEM-SOLVING AND DECISION-MAKING

We can similarly consider the #2 portion of the managing process: problem-solving and decision-making. If the key word in implementing is *emotion,* then the key word in the problem-solving portion of our model is *analysis.* Problem-solving is seen by us in the West (and particularly educators) as a rational, analytical process. It is a process that can be taught, that can be to an ever greater extent quantified. The problem-solving, decision-making manager is not so much a doer as a thinker. The image is one of the steel-trap intellect poring over the data and coming up with the right decision.

The recent public figure who at least by stereotype best fits that image is Robert McNamara, especially when he was directing the U.S. Department of Defense. McNamara was held in awe by many of his contemporaries because of his brilliantly orderly, systematic and rational mind. And the folklore and stories about him reflects just that. Here's one: Mr. McNamara is listening to a presentation in which the presenter shows slide after slide after slide covered with graphs and numbers. At the 154th slide Mr. McNamara says "Stop! Slide No. 154 contradicts slide No. 3." And everyone in the group is awed by this capacity to process all that information so effectively. You may recall, however, that Mr. McNamara was not nearly as successful in implementing his decisions as he was in making them. There were a lot of generals out in the field who viewed him as an intruder into their territories, and who resisted (often effectively) those carefully laid out procedures and controls imposed from the Pentagon. Nor do we remember Mr. McNamara as a great visionary. His most memorable skill was as an analyst, a decomposer of complex problems, who could then re-order them to come up with sensible solutions.

If we ask, as we did about implementing, which occupations or professions might serve as training grounds for greatness in problem-solving, a reasonable answer is fairly easy. One place to look is to the American Business School after about 1960. I would estimate that about 80% of the MBA curriculum in top rated American business schools even now is concerned with just this issue of analytic problem-solving. Starting about 1960 there was a great influx into business schools of new kinds of faculty: mathematicians, statisticians, computer scientists, systems analysts, and econometricians. New labels began to appear on courses and groups and departments: decision science, management science, operations research, data analysis, and Old courses become more quantitative: accounting, marketing, finance shared not only a strong quantitative orientation but a commitment to programming the hitherto unprogrammable; coupled with a faith that last year's judgements could be this year's specified operationalized programs.

It is important to add, however, that what we now call *organizational behaviour* also got its start at about the same time—though on a much smaller scale. And it is also important to point out that this heavy push towards numbers in business schools was extremely sensible at the time. Some very wise people perceived correctly that rapid growth in technology and the emerging computer offered a rich and promising vein to be mined to improve management practice. So the movement that pushed American business schools toward quantification was a visionary movement, a progressive movement away from the existing view of business education as a simulation of then current business practice. In any case there are lots of occupations for a young person to go into if he or she wants to try to become a great problem-solver/decision-maker. If one does not opt for an MBA, one can go into engineering or accountancy or financial analysis or consultancy or one can become a tax lawyer.

So beginning about 1960, American management education made its big push toward analytic problem-solving; using methods which contrasted sharply with the simulaneously evolving implementing side. While the implementing types—mostly social scientists—thought small and emotional, the problem-solvers—mostly economists, accountants, and operations researchers—thought large (either about non-human systems or very large, human organizations) and thought rational. And the two did not live well together. For the stereotypical true-blue analyst not only was reason good but emotion was bad. Emotion represented noise in the human system. If people were really what God had intended them to be they would not be emotional; they would be reasonable. While for the true-blue implementers emotion was the important stuff of which change was made. It was through emotion that one generated passionate commitment, loyalty and love. So a continuing conflict emerged, one that is alive and well even today. Indeed it has proved itself a highly productive conflict. But more of that later.

#1. PATH-FINDING

Let's turn briefly now to part #1 of our model of managing, the path-finding part; and let us ask some of the same questions again. If *implementing* carries large emotional components, and if *problem-solving* carries large rational/analytical components, how shall we characterize path-finding? The issue is not one of influence or persuasion, nor is it one of reasoning or systemic analysis. The issue here is purpose, mission, direction. The Path-finding part is the home territory of the visionary, the dreamer, the innovator, the entrepreneur. The issue here is deciding what we want to be when we grow up, what we want our organizations to become. This is a highly personal and subjective area, with answers, where there are any, emerging from within the self more than from what's out there. This is the ephemeral land of values, beliefs and aesthetics.

Do we need such soft subjective "female" thinking to manage our organizations? The answer is affirmative, whether we derive it from social or political or organizational observations. The path-finding role has always been critical to the rises and falls of institutions. Among recent Americans, Martin Luther King serves for me as an ideal model of a path-finder. His most remembered phrase was "I have a dream," and indeed he did; a vision of what might be. From among recent American presidents, John Kennedy comes to my mind. And in your country, from the American perspective at least, Winston Churchill seemed to fill the bill as a war-time leader. It's worth noting that those whom we cite as memorable path-finders must perforce be those who were also skilful as #3 implementers. For those dreamers and visionaries who do *not* attract working followers are not remembered. Or if they are remembered, it is as ineffectual and impractical dreamers; "visionaries" as distinct from "men and women of vision."

It is obvious that path-finders need not be nice people. People with strong commitments and deep beliefs are often intransigent, single-minded, unforgiving or wicked. Some great path-finders were more than unpleasant; they were very bad guys. Adolph Hitler qualifies, and Jim Jones of Jonestown in Guyana. And probably so too do many of the robber barons of British and American industrial history.

In business the path-finders are most likely to be found among entrepreneurs and founders of companies. The Watsons of IBM, or Hewlett and Packard or perhaps Freddie Laker. Not always loveable, these path-finders, not necessarily even successful, but stubborn, committed believers.

To which occupations and professions, then, shall we send our sons and daughters if they too wish to become great path-finders? That question about #1 is much more difficult

that for parts #2 or #3. We might want to send them to places that appear distant from the contemporary management scene. We could send them to live among artists and architects, or among philosophers and religionists, or among theoretical physicists; but whatever we do, we should *not* send them to business schools.

WHERE HAVE WE GONE WRONG?

So now we have a model, one model, of what the manageing process is about. And we have, I hope, outlined the three major chunks of that model. We have said that the skillful manager needs not only to be skilled to some degree in each of those, but that he or she also needs to be able to move fluidly among them; to move from conception to decision to action. And we have asserted further that over the last quarter of a century American management education, and British management education, too, have concentrated most heavily on the #2 problem-solving part of the model, paying some but much less attention to the #3 implementing part, while completely neglecting #1, path-finding. Indeed we have done more than neglect path-finding, we have downright fought it. Both the problem solvers and the implementers, who usually fight like the devil with one another, have shared a common interest in keeping the path finders out. The problem solvers don't want soft-headed subjective dreamers around. Path-finders can seldom offer hard evidence for their choices, and hard evidence is the sine qua non of modern problem-solving. And the #3 implementers (at least the participative, humanistic group) disapprove of the deviant, strongly individualistic quality of most path-finders. Path-finding associates with powerful and dominant individual leaders. It smacks of a cult of personality. Besides, we don't know how to teach #1 anyway—or do we?

Where, then, have things gone wrong with American managing? I asserted back at the start of this talk that by breaking the management process down into smaller units, we might locate the problem areas and perhaps offer ways to go about correcting them. It's time we got on with those issues.

Two key areas leap forward almost immediately. The first and more familiar one centers on the nature of the #2—#3 relationship. How does an organization move smoothly from #2 decision to #3 action? Often modern organizations seem to move from decision to inaction. That question has plagued us for a long time, and clearly that's one area where the Japanese seem to do things a lot more effectively than we do. They seem to be able to get their people at all levels to buy into company decisions and to carry them out loyally, carefully and effectively. Neither you in the UK nor we in the States have nearly as good a record on that score, although some of us think that we may still be a little better at that game than you are.

The other problem is, of course, the path finding problem. I propose to you that we in the States and you in the UK have both neglected our common heritage on this one. In both our countries we used to extol our path finders, we encouraged and nurtured them, taught our children to emulate them, and helped them to grow everywhere in our lands. But the emergence of large bureaucratic organizations; the development of orderly and specialized, systematic, top-down organizational designs; the rejection of leadership as an attribute of individuals in favour of blander concepts of power equalization, all these have contributed to decline in vital, innovative, fire-starting path finding behaviour in our two nations.

So let me take the last few minutes of this talk to try to elaborate on those two problems; and to offer some suggestions for dealing with them.

THE #2—#3 RELATIONSHIP

The #2—#3 problem is astonishingly simple, relative to its importance. It boils down to something like this: Should #2 precede #3? Or should they be interactive? To sharpen the issue, imagine a hypothetical and extreme rational analyst's position. We shall call that the #2 view of the #2—#3 relationship. That view holds (in caricature, at least) that the proper relationship between problem-solving and implementing is serial. That #2 precedes #3. Diagrammatically it would look like this, #2 → #3. It is an incontrovertibly, logical, common sense "truth." We decide first; *then* we act. Planning *precedes* action. Doing follows thought. Certainly we do not go somewhere first, and then decide where we wanted to go. We do not fire and *then* aim.

This #2 view, based so deeply in common sense rationality, has led us in organizations to *specialize* these two broad set of activities, developing specialized #2 planning and decision-making people on the one hand, and acting, implementing and working #3 people on the other. And the specialization and separation of those two sets of human activities has gotten us into lots of trouble.

There is of course, another approach to the same set of issues. We can call it the view from #3. Again, in caricature this #3 view argues that the proper relationship between #2 (problem solving) and #3 (implementing) is an interactive one. The diagramatic arrow should be double-headed like this: #2 ⇄ #3. It is not logic, but *psychologic,* that drives the argument for that apparently absurd view. The #3 arguments runs something like this: "Although it makes logical sense to solve problems first and then to implement the solutions, it does

39

not make psychological sense to do so in organizations. The reason is that in organizations many human beings are always involved in the process. If the human bodies doing the problem solving and the decision making are a different set from the bodies assigned to carrying out the decisions, trouble will follow."

That point of hand off, where #2's have to pass the ball to #3's, is where the trouble usually starts. The reason is simple (and probably nevertheless a fundamental): people don't like other people's babies nearly as much as they like their own. #3's will find all sorts of reasons for disapproving of #2's plans that have been passed on to them. On the other hand #3's love their own decisions, and will fight hard to make them work.

The counter argument (from the #2's) is also clear and sensible: "Those soft-headed #3 types want to mess everything up. They want everybody in on all decisions, with the consequences that all that 'democratic' decision-making slows everything down and generates ugly, mediocre decisions that only a committee could love." The good clear decisions made by #2 people who know how to make them, (and now have the responsibility for making them) give way to trade-offs and compromises that convert handsome horses into misshapen camels.

The two positions are of course both right and both wrong. But given that debate, where are we now and where should we go? In America at least, from about 1910 to about 1960 the #2's were winning all the points. The great push in American industry was towards the orderly, the systematic and the specialized. From time study to the assembly line to industrial engineering to more recent forms of systems analysis, the trend was toward planning and systemizing, with ever increasingly specialized staff groups to collect the data and do the analyses that would in effect dictate the "proper" decisions.

In the early fifties things began to

change. By that time the small voices of a few #3's were beginning to be heard. In the States, they were voices like Fritz Roethlisberger's and Douglas McGregor's and Rensis Likert's. A weak #3 counter-wave developed during the sixties and seventies then gained strength rapidly in the late seventies and early eighties as the Japanese success helped the #3 cause, generating fear, fury and self-doubt among hard headed American managers. In the last few years #3 has waxed, and #2 has been waning just a little. But it is not only the groupy, apparently bottoms-up Japanese success that has generated all this new interest in the #3 posture. The growth of the service and high technology sectors of our economy have both stimulated a positive reconsideration of the #3 view. The #2 position, to work successfully, requires high degrees of specialization of jobs and tight controls. We did that pretty well when our employees used their arms and legs more than their heads. But our technology for specifying, measuring and controlling the head work of service workers, engineers and software technicians is rather primitive. So the old #2 game simply doesn't work very well. Stop watches and time clocks do more harm than good when used on our R & D teams. So we have trotted out and sought to modernize our unexploited #3 methods.

This continuing and sometimes bitter conflict between the #2 and #3 view has not been entirely destructive. The #2 view drives always toward tighter controls, more specialization, more orderly methods, more evaluation of individual performance, more emphasis on rewards tied to productivity. The #3 view wants participation, more meetings, more motivation, evaluation of unit (not individual) productivity. An extreme #2 army would be made up of well trained, well organized, obedient but reluctant troops. A #3 army would be peopled by an eager, enthusiastic, undisciplined mob.

Between those two there is room for innovations, and if we look at some of the major managerial inventions of the last thirty years, those that have prospered seemed to me to be those which have walked the narrow line between these two views. Just one example here: the concept of decentralization. Alfred P. Sloan proposed it, and everybody in America loves it. #2's and #3's both believe almost fervently in decentralization. Astonishingly, until one looks inside, #2's love for decentralization is based on very different reasons from #3's. #2's love it because it provides mechanisms of control. Decentralization pinpoints responsibility in a few key profit centres, and by controlling at those points one can control the whole huge organization. But if you are a #3 type, that isn't the reason you believe in decentralization. You like it because small is beautiful. And the more you can break larger into smaller units, the more possible it is for members of those units to deal directly with one another. Moreover, decentralization adds diversity to the system, as each sub-unit can do more of its own thing in its own way. And, even further, the short communication lines within decentralized units makes for greater freedom and autonomy for each individual. For #3's, then, decentralization messes up the organization, making it *less* orderly, and more human. And that is what's good. For #2's, the same decentralization provides order in an otherwise dangerously chaotic world.

I will leave it to the reader to consider other management "tools", like Peter Drucker's *Management by Objective,* or a more recent entry—*Matrix Organization.* I believe those that have prospered or will prosper in the near future must be able to offer attractive bait to both #2's and #3's.

While this whole struggle between #2 and #3 has been in some sense productive, it has not been productive enough. We have never resolved the conflict, we have mostly compromised it. We have yet to resolve, in Western style, a relationship between #2 and #3 that is consistent with our cultures and with

our needs to cut costs, increase productivity and improve quality.

THE PATH-FINDING ISSUE

We return finally to #1, path-finding, the orphan of western management and management education. What, if any, is the function of path-finding in the larger managing process? Do we need path-finders and path-finding? I propose the role of the path-finder is a construction process. It is quite possible to build solid buildings without architects. A good engineer can make sure that our structure will be physically sound; and that it will include a heating system appropriate to the climate and the building's volume. And if we couple that engineer with a good building contractor, that team will make sure that the right beams are placed properly, that the brick-layers lay the right bricks in the right places, and that the stairs go both up and down.

We don't *need* an architect. What the architect adds is not something necessary, but something beautiful. What we get is design, aesthetics. We get more than quonset huts. We get the opera house in Sydney, or our particular vine-covered cottage in the country.

Note the nature of this architectural problem: Assume a specified budget of x pounds; assume a paid-for piece of land suitable as a site for a small house in an area my family likes. We now call upon an architect to "design" a house for us. How many houses can be designed to meet all those constraints? And by what criterion function do we select the "right" house? The word "right", here, seems to have very little meaning, relative say, to, the "right" answer to a math problem. A reasonable architect can produce in a few days ten to twenty sketches of "right" houses that would all meet the budgetary and physical specifications. Under such circumstances how does one make choices? How does one decide which house to build? The answer is love. It's when the family finds the sketch that turns them on; when the children and Momma and Poppa jump up and down and shout "We love it!" Then we have found the right answer. The criteria are internal and subjective. They involve notions of aesthetics much finer, like that "design" part of the architect's role, is a generator and selector of designs, of possibilities. Path-finding is first divergent, not convergent.

But we must note, too, that architect's designs often turn out to be infeasible. The design for the opera house in Sydney began at a projected cost of about 8 million dollars, if I recall correctly; but ended up costing something over 100 million dollars. One reason was that the engineers could not find materials and methods that could handle the stresses that such a shape would generate. Path-finders, that is to say, often dream impossible dreams. As the managing process flows from #1 to #2 and #3, dreams must be compromised, modified or killed. And yet, from what my Australian friends tell me the people of Sydney just love their opera house. Was it "worth" that extra 90+ millions of dollars? If you're a #1, love is quite enough. That opera house is another small step for mankind.

The #1 view, whether in construction or in management, is a pro-active view. Unlike the re-active #2 view, the #1 types don't try to forecast the future, they try to create it. They do not ask "How shall our organization adapt to the world of the future?" They ask "What organization do we believe to be right and beautiful? Then let us worry about how we can get the world out there and our own people to help us build it."

In the U.S. and in the U.K. that pro-active, let's-build-a-better-mousetrap view is a strong part of our culture, our history, our faith. We need it now as much as we ever did. Let's not let the growth of larger bureaucracies and higher technologies "modernize" us into extinction.

2

BUSINESS STRATEGY

Corporate Strategy

Michael Porter

Strategic planning was born amid a flurry of optimism and industrial growth in the 1960s and early 1970s. It quickly became a fad. No self-respecting chief executive could do without a strategic-planning staff, no business school without a planning curriculum. Today, strategic planning has fallen out of fashion. Other concerns—corporate culture, quality, implementation—are seen as the new tickets to success. After all, Japanese companies supposedly don't prepare strategic plans.

The criticism of strategic planning was well deserved. Strategic planning in most companies has not contributed to strategic thinking. The answer, however, is not to abandon planning. The need for strategic thinking has never been greater. Instead, strategic planning needs to be rethought and recast. While some companies have taken the first steps in doing so, few have transformed strategic planning into the vital management discipline it needs to be.

From *The Economist*, May 23, 1987, copyright 1987 by *The Economist*. Reprinted by permission.

THE GENESIS

To understand how strategic planning needs to change, one must understand the history of planning's development and the forces that have driven it. Strategic planning, scarcely 30 years old, grew out of two streams of thinking about management practice. The first was the developments in programme planning and budgeting that came out of the second world war. Many companies installed formal budgeting as a tool to improve the control of their operations. Annual budgets were soon stretched into five-year plans because of the growing recognition that the financial consequences of decisions were often long term.

A second stream of thought, pioneered in the 1950s at the Harvard Business School, highlighted the importance of having an overall corporate strategy. Management theory had concentrated on the functions of business—eg, production, finance, marketing, logistics, control. Each was pursued as a separate subject, with its own concepts and methodologies. Yet there was no theory on how to integrate these functions. Companies had always had overall strategies, but these remained implicit and largely intuitive. As firms grew and became more complex, however, they needed a systematic approach to setting strategy. Strategic planning emerged as the answer.

Many companies established formal long-range planning systems. Top managers issued planning guidelines, specifying the goals to be met and the information expected. In return they were given thick planning books, replete with five year financial projections. Every year, senior staff spent hours poring over the plans.

Strategic thinking rarely occurs spontaneously. Without formal planning systems, day-to-day concerns tend to prevail. The future is forgotten. Formal planning provided the discipline to pause occasionally to think about strategic issues. It also offered a mechanism for communicating strategy to those who had to carry it out, something that seldom happened when the formulation of strategy remained the private province of the chief executive.

Corporate planners were the high priests of this process. They drafted guidelines, set schedules, cajoled line managers and coached top executives in carrying out the planning process. Planners were also gradually installed in business units to encourage planning at lower levels.

The need for professional strategic planners and for detailed guidelines reflected the unfamiliarity of most executives with this new management discipline. Without guidelines, few managers knew what constituted strategic thinking. The strategic planner offered the same type of specialised skills as other functional experts did.

While the early emphasis was on installing a formal planning process, managers and academics soon realised that the process raised difficult and subtle questions which they had to tackle. The original notions in strategic planning had been driven not by the needs of those managing a particular factory or business but by the top managements of diversified firms. Corporate boards faced knotty questions of what businesses to compete in and how to allocate resources among them. The problem had become particularly acute in the 1960s and early 1970s, after many large companies had diversified widely. They had an abundance of investment opportunities but, relatively speaking, a dearth of capital to exploit them.

The history of General Electric, a pioneer in strategic planning, vividly illustrates the issues that concerned many companies. General Electric was competing in a wide range of businesses including jet engines, computers, electronics and nuclear power. Each had a prodigious appetite for capital; GE simply could not satisfy them all. It needed some way of deciding which ones to sustain and which ones to abandon.

Top managers of diversified firms also faced a more subtle and even more widespread problem. They had the formal power to choose which businesses to spend money on, but lacked detailed knowledge of them. Too often, choices were not made at all. Skilful company executives, with facile answers to every head office question, obtained finance because the conglomerate's managers had little ammunition with which to deny their requests.

These dilemmas brought forth a flurry of "solutions", many proffered by the growing number of strategic consulting firms. In one way or another, their proposals were all tools for "portfolio planning", based on the notion that a diversified corporation could be likened to a portfolio of stocks. Portfolio-planning tools allowed a diversified corporation to plot all its businesses on a simple chart with axes that measured each one's competitive position (see the chart for a well-known example). Depending on where a business fell, there was a well-defined strategic prescription—invest, harvest, or divest. These tools allowed head-office staff to visualise the enterprise as a whole,

44

and provided a basis for evaluating the optimistic assertions of the line managers.

Each variation of portfolio planning was built on a somewhat different concept of what determined the success of an individual company. The most popular was the variant shown in the chart, which was conceived by the Boston Consulting Group. It highlighted the importance of relative market share—based on the so-called experience curve, which posited that the company with the largest cumulative volume would have the lowest cost. Other versions emphasised the stage of the business in the product life-cycle and various other proxies for industry attractiveness or competitive position. These tools became the basis for the five-year plans required of each business. Line managers were expected to fill out forms which allowed head office to place its business on such charts.

By the late 1970s, strategic planning was well into its second decade. There was a general feeling that a new, important management discipline had been created. Chief executives could say they practised strategic planning, corporate planners were in demand, and strategic consultants thrived. Some consultants and government officials even began to apply the new

techniques to countries to formulate industrial policy. Self-satisfaction prevailed.

At the same time, however, seeds of doubt were being sown. By the mid-1980s, they had blossomed into widespread criticism and even outright hostility. It became fashionable to dismiss strategic planning as unimportant—and worse, as the cause of corporate problems, not their solution.

The attack on planning took several forms. The first was a growing recognition that the processes for strategic planning were not promoting strategic thinking. Instead of clarifying and communicating strategy, the outcome of laborious strategic-planning exercises was thick binders which had little, if any, impact on action. Form dominated substance. Meaningless long-term projections obscured strategic insight. Strategic planners had captured the process, filling out plans which were reviewed by yet other planners. Line managers tolerated planning, but increasingly dismissed it as an irrelevant ritual.

The techniques of planning also came under fire. Early techniques, such as the experience curve, product-cycle theory and portfolio planning, promised easy answers based on simple concepts of competition. These techniques each posited a single variable in competition—the experience effect, the product life cycle, changing the game—and only one corresponding route to success. Building the largest market share, selling the laggards or creating a "new game" were seen with deceptive precision as reliable guides for strategic action.

Unfortunately, there was too little substance behind these prescriptions. How, for example, was a new game to be discovered, or market-share leadership achieved? Worse, companies began finding that the premises behind these prescriptions did not always hold. Having the largest share was frequently not the most profitable position, as Bank of America has learned. Becoming a low-cost producer by investing to move rapidly down the experience

Discarded distinctions

Stars

Question Marks

Annual market growth, % less than <10%> greater than

Cash Cows

Dogs

Relative market share* less than <1·0> greater than

*Share of company analysed divided by share of largest or competitor company.

curve is not always the way to win, as Texas Instruments found out in small computers and watches. Portfolio planning is not a panacea for managing a conglomerate, as countless companies have had to admit as they have sold their failed acquisitions (see table).

Finally, strategic planning was attacked for leaving out important determinants of corporate success. The ascendance of Japanese companies was seen as evidence that American management techniques, notably strategic planning, were a failure. Japanese companies concentrated on quality, productivity and teamwork, not, it seemed, on fancy planning techniques and the next quarter's earnings per share. Japanese methods were therefore touted as the new keys to success.

Corporate culture also emerged as a new theme, popularised in part by the runaway success of "In Search of Excellence". Companies lavished attention on the "soft" side of management. Next came the love affair with entrepreneurship (or intrapreneurship). Entrepreneurs clearly did not need to fill out strategic plans—one more reason to dismiss planning.

It had suddenly become embarrassing to talk about strategic planning. Some companies went so far as to dismantle their planning processes altogether, sometimes with a relish that belied years of frustration.

THINKING IS STRATEGY

The need for strategic thinking has never been greater. Few companies, whether they are in oil, computers, banking or retailing, have escaped the growing competition that has characterised the past decade. Slower growth, deregulation, globalisation and rapid and radical technological change have shaken up industry after industry.

The questions that good planning

seeks to answer—the future direction of competition, the needs of the customer, the likely behaviour of competitors, how to gain a competitive advantage—will never lose their relevance. What has been under attack is not these questions, but the techniques and organisational processes which companies used to answer them. The solution is to improve strategic planning, not to abolish it. The need to plan formally has not changed—otherwise strategic thinking will be crowded out by day-to-day pressures.

Some companies have misinterpreted their earlier difficulties with strategic planning, and reduced it to an annual discussion of important issues facing each business. This is a serious mistake as well. One cannot identify and frame issues clearly without articulating what a firm's environment and strategy are supposed to be.

There are no substitutes for strategic thinking. Improving quality is meaningless without knowing what kind of quality is relevant in competitive terms. Nurturing corporate culture is useless unless the culture is aligned with a company's approach to competing. Entrepreneurship unguided by a strategic perspective is much more likely to fail than succeed. And, contrary to popular opinion, even Japanese companies plan. The successful ones are

Hopes dashed

Diversification and divestment by 33 large American companies, 1950–80

	Proportion divested
	%
All acquisitions	53
Acquisitions in entirely new fields	61
Acquisitions in unrelated new fields	74
Start-ups	44
Joint ventures	50

Source: Harvard Business Review. May–June 1987.

strong believers in planning, and avid students of their industries and competitors.

If strategic planning is to be reborn as an indispensable management tool, it must change its ways. Many companies have recognised the shortcomings in their planning process and tried to correct them. Yet few have done so effectively.

To be effective, strategic planning must use a proper process, because strategy cannot be separated from implementation. Strategic thinking cannot occur only once a year, according to a rigid routine. It should inform a company's daily actions. Moreover, the information necessary for good strategic thinking is equally vital to running a business—designing marketing material, setting prices and delivery schedules, etc.

Strategic planning must therefore become the job of line managers, not of head-office staff. The best systems will employ multifunctional planning teams in which line managers from sales, marketing, manufacturing, logistics and other areas, under the leadership of the general manager, debate and resolve the trade-offs among functions essential for good strategy.

While the size of strategic planning staffs should be pared down in most companies, planners have not become less important. Instead, their role should shift from doers to facilitators and integrators. In my experience, the most effective strategic planners are line executives on rotation rather than planning specialists. Today, every executive needs to understand how to think strategically. A stint in planning also gives line managers a broad perspective that becomes invaluable in general management positions. At the same time, strategic planners with line experience bring to their job an expertise and a credibility that no professional planner can match.

Good strategic thinking also requires fewer planning guidelines. They should specify the kinds of information required, and leave it

to line managers to decide how to present this information. Each year the guidelines should highlight new areas for special attention— whether they be cost, information technology, or the like. A good strategic plan should conclude with the detailed actions which are to be agreed upon and carried out. This, coupled with the involvement of line managers, ensures that strategic plans do not merely gather dust.

How plans are reviewed is perhaps the most vital way of ensuring that a planning process stays healthy. In most companies, a review consists of elaborate presentations by managers, followed by perfunctory questioning. Planning under these circumstances is soon viewed as a waste of time. The most effective systems are those in which a written plan is submitted in advance of a meeting between line managers and head-office staff, and presentations are limited to a short summary of what actions are proposed. The meeting should encourage hard questioning, so as to define expectations and flag problems.

THE ROLE OF PLANNING IN MANAGEMENT

There is a dangerous tendency today to practise single-issue management. The latest fad, corporate culture, is embraced as the answer to improving a company's performance. The truth, of course, is that there is no easy answer. Quality, manufacturing, corporate culture, entrepreneurship and strategic thinking are all important. Concern for one does not imply lack of concern for another. The most effective companies manage to integrate and make consistent all these aspects of management.

The converse is also true. The embarrassing decline of many of the so-called "Excellent Companies" is a reflection that their corporate values and behaviour fell out of sync with the imperatives of their competitive environment. One cannot ignore strategic thinking in favour of maintaining a supportive culture, just as one cannot ignore quality no matter how elegant is the strategic plan.

My own view is that strategic thinking is the glue that holds together the many systems and initiatives within a company. Without it, the consistency of actions in the many parts of an organisation is not assured. Other academics and managers put more emphasis on organisation and culture as the central concerns of management. This is fine, as long as neither strategy nor implementation is given short shrift.

THE INGREDIENTS

Every company, whether diversified or not, should have a strategic plan for each of its businesses. I favour a set of analytical techniques for developing strategy that have grown out of my research over the past 15 years. Whatever techniques one uses, however, a good plan should contain the following elements:

· An analysis of the industry in which the firm competes. The attractiveness of the whole industry is as important to success as is the company's own position, a fact which strategic planning initially overlooked. A sound plan should assess how the industry might change in the future, taking account of such factors as technological changes, substitute products and government policy.

· Sources of competitive advantage. A sound plan must contain an explicit awareness of the sources of competitive advantage in the industry. Competitive advantage comes in two basic types: lower cost, or differentiation, relative to competitors. To understand competitive advantage, a good plan must reflect the factors that determine a business's cost position. It must also con-

tain a clear articulation of who the buyers are and what they value.

· An analysis of existing and potential competitors who might affect the company. All competitive advantage is relative, a point left out of earlier introspective approaches to planning. Analysis of the competition must move beyond keeping press clippings on competitors and analysing their financial statements, to understanding the logic of each competitor's strategy, how it thinks, and its likely future moves.

· An assessment of the company's competitive position. In analysing its own position, a company must move from the vague notion of strengths and weaknesses to a central (and precise) concern with its competitive advantages and disadvantages. A sound plan must contain a best estimate of the company's relative cost position as well as an objective assessment of where it stands in all areas of importance to buyers.

· Selection or ratification of strategy. The chosen strategy should be built on competitive advantage and how it can be sustained. Sustaining advantage requires continuous improvement and change, not a static solution in which strategy can be set and forgotten. There is no formula for achieving competitive advantage, only approaches that are tailored to individual companies. Goals such as becoming number one or number two in the industry are often inappropriate. In developing a strategic vision the emphasis should be on competitive advantage and, in turn, on a company's performance.

· Actions. The chosen strategy must be translated into concrete actions, including needs for capital spending and for staff training and development.

A sound corporate plan for a diversified company must be more than merely the sum of the plans of its individual parts. Such corporate plans are rare, however: the practice of developing a corporate strategy lags far behind the ability to think strategically in individual businesses.

The ultimate truth about corporate strategy has two elements. One is the way the corporation adds value above and beyond what could be achieved if business units were independent. In order to add value, the diversified corporation must materially enhance the competitive advantage of its individual businesses. If it does not, shareholders would be better off if the diversified firm were broken up, and the bits sold, something which corporate raiders are proving every day.

Second, the most effective way in which the corporation can add value is by developing links between its business units that lead to synergy. While synergy is viewed by many as another passé concept, in reality it has never been more important. Early efforts at synergy did not work because the concept was ill-defined and proved hard to implement. Recent thinking is starting to shed light on what synergy is as well as how to achieve it organisationally. The most successful diversified companies—Marriott, Johnson & Johnson, Canon—are proving that it can be done.

ERRORS TO AVOID

Even with an ideal planning process, strategic thinking still requires the creative acts of synthesis and choice. In assessing the quality of the chosen strategies that are the outcome of strategic planning, five crucial errors are made time and again:

· *Restructuring as strategy.* The 1980s has been a decade of restructuring. Companies have cut costs, closed factories, trimmed employment, terminated unprofitable product lines, and put pressure on their suppliers. The results have been heartening and sometimes dramatic. Profitability has increased: firms are leaner and meaner.

But restructuring is not a strategy. It is a means of dealing with the failure of past strategies. The strategic agenda for many companies is still unfinished. Now that the easy cutting phase is over, the real challenge is to build. This will involve the creation of new and lasting competitive advantages, and the development of new products and services.

I see too few companies that have made the transition from restructuring to building. Unless they do, it is only a matter of time before they will be restructuring again.

· *Buying competitors instead of beating them.* Managers, particularly in America and Europe, have rediscovered an easy way to gain market share—buying competitors. This frequently results in immediate improvements in performance, the result of eliminating redundancies and spreading fixed costs. At the same time, industry prices often recover rapidly as the number of rivals shrinks.

With some exceptions, this sort of strategic thinking is, in the long run, bad for companies—and for countries. It is another example of the absence of strategic vision; the desire for the quick fix rather than the creation of some new economic value for the buyer. It is hard to think of many truly great companies that have succeeded by buying their competitors. The Toyotas, DuPonts, Marks & Spencers and Procter & Gambles have beaten their competitors through innovation and dynamism. Buying competitors is a drug which makes managers feel good in the short term but ultimately saps the energy and creativity of an organisation.

· *Alliances.* Under competitive pressure, many companies are turning to coalitions— what are sometimes termed strategic alliances. The idea is that teaming up—though not merging—with another company, often a foreign competitor, will offset weaknesses in each and produce a winning combination.

Alliances do have a role in strategic thinking, but a more limited one than is suggested by the recent spate of them. Alliances are never the solution to a company's strategic dilemmas. They carry formidable costs in terms of organisational coordination and run the grave risk of dissipating competitive strengths. The best alliances are narrow, covering well-defined areas of mutual benefit. Attempting to solve a company's strategic problems through alliances is, ultimately, a non-strategy.

- *Imitation instead of innovation.* Most strategic thinking is still imitative. Managers emulate their competitors when they select strategies. They lack the conviction to set themselves apart. Most banks, for example, have pursued the same strategy in response to deregulation. They have embraced "relationship banking", entered the same product lines, made the same type of acquisitions in new geographic areas, and even reorganised into the same business units. The same is true of most motor companies, electric utilities and entertainment firms.

The essence of strategic thinking is creating a sustainable competitive advantage. This is simply not possible if a company imitates its competitors. Sustainable competitive advantage arises from altering the bases of competition—new product attributes, new types of services, new production methods, new delivery systems. This is what Morgan Guaranty has done in banking, American Airlines and Singapore Airlines in air transport, Benetton in clothing, and SSIH, with its Swatch, in watches. Strategic plans that do not meet the test of innovation are simply not good enough.

Managers, with the help of those who evaluate and reward them, must overcome the fear of being different. The way they are judged should not encourage them to prefer failing with the same strategy as everyone else, but to dare to succeed with a unique strategy.

- *Diversification for growth's sake.* The allure of diversification is as strong as ever in most companies. Many are making the same strategic mistakes that have been prevalent for decades: making acquisitions in new fields where they cannot add any value, simply to grow.

Such ill-conceived diversification was once largely an American phenomenon. Despite massive divestitures, American companies have become only slightly wiser. Restructuring to raise profits and then growing via questionable acquisitions: that is the extent of strategic thinking in far too many American companies, and the great tragedy of the American economy. The practice seems to be spreading. Britain is in the midst of a diversification boom. Japanese firms are starting to make acquisitions in seemingly random areas. The Korean *chaebol* are diversifying helter skelter and are showing the strains in terms of erratic decisions. Even West German companies are weakening—Daimler-Benz's acquisition of AEG Telefunken, for example, is one where the true synergies are hard to discern.

Diversification is bad strategic thinking in the long run unless the various businesses in the corporate portfolio gain competitive advantage from being there. The kind of diversification so common today, based on vague similarities among businesses, is another example of non-strategy. The resulting corporate growth makes it look as though something is happening. In fact, nothing of economic value is being created.

50

Business Strategy

Ian MacMillan

This chapter provides a highly condensed overview of business strategy formulation and outlines and discusses the key steps involved. For the purpose of this chapter, the focus is on business, as opposed to corporate, strategy formulation. By *corporate strategy* is meant the strategy for securing and maintaining a successful portfolio of businesses. It involves the major decisions made regarding the deployment of resources among different businesses in the corporate portfolio. By *business strategy* is meant the strategy for securing and maintaining a position of competitive success in a product/market area. Major decisions must be made regarding the deployment of resources in a specific product/market area to secure the area from competitive attack; these decisions take place within the confines of a broader corporate strategy.

There are many ways of viewing strategy formulation, starting with the evolutionary process described by Mintzberg et al. (1976) and Wrapp (1967), who argue that strategic decisions usually evolve as organization experience evolves. In fact, Mintzberg (1976) makes a clear distinction between *intended* strategies, which are conscious managerial decisions but may never be realized, and *emergent* strategies, which emerge as a result of competitive forces in the marketplace but were not necessarily intended.

Hofer (1975) and Miller (1975), among others, suggest a contingency theory approach. They argue that specific characteristics of the

organization and its environment give rise to strategies that succeed only if they are tailored to the key competitive conditions the organization faces. Empirical work by Hambrick et al. (1982) and particularly Hambrick and Lei (1985) demonstrates convincingly that this is the case—a number of key environmental contingency variables must to be taken into account in formulating strategy.

Between these viewpoints are a broad body of authors who argue that strategy formulation must be formalized and who lay out general approaches to strategy formulation (Ansoff, 1965; Newman and Logan, 1971; Andrews, 1971; Katz, 1970; Hofer and Schendel, 1978.) There is still some debate as to the effectiveness of strategy formulation. Among others, Ansoff et al. (1971), Thune and House (1970), and Herold (1972), support the hypothesis that strategy "pays." Grinyer and Norburn (1975), and Kudla (1979) reject it, while Rue and Fulmer (1973) achieved mixed results. More recent evidence suggests that whether or not comprehensive strategic planning pays off is a function of both the environment and the types of planning processes used (Frederickson, 1985; Ramanujam and Venkatraman, 1987).

In this chapter, it is assumed that the concept of formal strategic planning has survived the market test. Studies by Steiner (1972) and Kudla (1979) have indicated a willingness on the part of most U.S. Fortune 500 companies to invest significant time, funds and effort in the process.

The focus will be on strategy *formulation,*

as opposed to such implementation problems as organization design and planning and control systems to support the strategy. The chapter briefly reviews the following steps of the strategy formulation process, recommended by various authors:

- *Environmental analysis* identifyies the key threats and opportunities in the future of the business and the critical factors for success in the industry.
- *Business analysis* identifies key strengths and weaknesses.
- *Strategy formulation* determines the desired relationship between the organization and its future environment and develops strategies to achieve this relationship.
- *Strategic anticipation* prepares for opponents' responses.

ENVIRONMENTAL ANALYSIS

Environmental analysis consists of two major parts: structural analysis and trend analysis. *Structural analysis* determines the key relations of the firm to its environment. It is accomplished through *environmental mapping,* which identifies the key organizations that have a vested interest in the strategy of the business; *industry chain analysis,* which analyzes the entire chain of industries that link the business from its raw material suppliers through to the final customer; and *industry attractiveness assessment,* which assesses the attractive and unattractive features of the industry in which the firm participates. *Trend analysis* determines the key trends that may affect the business. It consists of *macroeconomic trend analysis,* which considers what takes place in the society as a whole, and *industry chain trends analysis,* which assesses the impact of macroeconomic trends on the critical links in the industry chain together with trends taking place within the industry chain itself.

Structural Analysis

Environmental Mapping   A number of organizations surrounding the business have a vested interest in its decisions. Typical of such interest groups are competitors, suppliers, financial organizations, stockholders, government regulatory bodies, political interest groups, unions, and local community groups, depending on the organization. The recent experience of even the largest corporations with such interest groups suggests their ability to influence corporate direction is such that strategic decisions cannot be made unilaterally; realistic strategies may have to take the vested interests of surrounding organizations into account. Consequently, an essential ingredient of structural analysis is environmental mapping—a specific analysis of the interest groups that currently take an active interest in the business strategy or may do so in the future.

In carrying out such an analysis, it may prove wise to take the following steps (MacMillan and Jones, 1986; Kennedy, 1965). First, identify the key interest groups that have a vested interest in the decisions made by the business. Then, identify the key issues they will raise with the business and the positions they will take on the issues. Next, estimate the power of each interest group and the basis of that power. Finally, identify any issues over which different groups will be in conflict (such as dividend payments versus wage rates or profits versus regulatory compliance). Of particular importance are issues likely to elicit conflicting demands from powerful groups. Environmental mapping should provide an estimate of the future points of conflict between the organization and its key interest groups, the scope of such conflict, and the basis of such conflict; an indication of what major constraints could be placed on the strategic decisions to be made; and an explanation of where support and opposition can be expected from these interest groups.

Given this background, the next structural analysis that may be worth pursuing is industry chain analysis.

Industry Chain Analysis Few businesses are not part of an industry chain. Figure 1 depicts a "typical" chain. Analysis of the chain is important not only in identifying the competitive conditions in the particular business's industry but also in the rest of the chain. It is concerned with identifying the critical links in the chain and the way in which the business depends on them.

Factors to look for in a chain analysis include recent shifts in demand at any link; the degree of concentration of competitors, since the greater the concentration in a particular link, the greater the impact of any disruption in that link; major social and regulatory pressures on that link; recent price level shifts at that link, since any decrease in real prices at a link in the chain may be transmitted to industries behind it, and any price increase at a link may be transmitted to industries ahead of it; and, finally, critical resource dependencies (raw materials, labor, equipment, etc.) at any link, which increase the probability that disruption might occur at that link and might progress up or down the chain. Chain analysis should be confined to the most important links and may provide warning signals of major cost, price, and supply and demand pressures that could affect the business in the strategic planning period.

Recent work by Porter (1985) has strongly reinforced the need to analyze the industry chain in detail. Porter suggests the key to long-run successful strategies lies in being able to identify the place in the chain where the real value added takes place. The profits in a particular industry chain accrue to those firms that can find and sustain positions at those links in the chain where, given certain inputs, the firm's processing of these inputs adds significant value to those purchasing the firm's outputs. For instance, a firm like IBM "takes in" a stream of mechanical and electric components and, in the eyes of customers, adds a huge amount of value in terms not only of assembly but also distribution, delivery, service, and system support for the mainframe computers it markets. Porter suggests that the fundamental key to successful strategy lies in being able to find defensible and therefore sustainable value added opportunities in the chain and that firms that cannot do this are doomed to inferior profitability.

The preceding analyses provide a contextual background for the next stage of the analysis: assessment of industry attractiveness.

Assessment of Industry Attractiveness The results of environmental mapping and industry chain analysis provide the basis for deciding the attractiveness of the industry in which the business is operating. The factors to consider in assessing the attractiveness of the industry are listed in Table 1. At least as important as identifying the factors that currently lead to success in the industry is the assessment of the forces driving competitive behavior in the industry. Here, Porter (1980) has made a major contribution. Applying principles of industrial organiza-

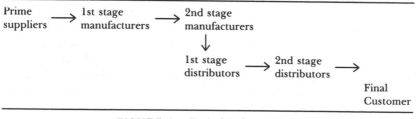

FIGURE 1. *Typical Industry Chain*

TABLE 1.   Factors Which Could Enhance Industry Attractiveness

Market Factors	Industry Factors	Cost Factors	Investment Factors	Interest Group Factors
Large market size	High degree of pricing control	Low capital intensity	Short payback on investment	High social acceptability
High market growth rate	Weaker dispersed competition	Low labor intensity	Low potential for excess capacity	Low degree of unionization
High market segmentability	High industry profitability	Low marketing cost/sales	High ease of entry and exit	Low regulatory vulnerability
High customer profitability	Low cyclical vulnerability	Low manufacturing cost/sales	Low degree of vertical integration	
Low concentration of customers	Low inflation vulnerability	Low inventory/sales		
	Low energy dependence	Low R&D/sales		
	High technological stability			
	Low supply vulnerability			
	Low environmental impact vulnerability			

Source: Strategic Planning Institute, Cambridge, Mass.

tion, he suggests five major forces that shape the nature of competition in an industry and that should be analyzed to assess whether the industry's current attractiveness will increase or decrease.

1. *Entry of new competitors.* By systematically studying the barriers facing firms that desire to enter the industry, we can predict whether the industry is likely to get more crowded. (Factors to analyze are listed in Table 2).
2. *Bargaining power of buyers.* An analysis of the extent to which downstream customers are increasing their bargaining power in relation to the firm reveals whether the firm will be able to hold onto future profits. (Factors to look for are in Table 2).
3. *Bargaining power of suppliers.* As in bargaining power of buyers, but for the firm's suppliers.
4. *Threat of substitution.* Future profitability could be seriously damaged by the emergence of firms with alternative ways of satisfying the customers' needs (plastic replacing metal or wood, word processors replacing typewriters).
5. *Rivalry among competitors.* Finally, factors such as very high levels of investment or very high dependence on a few, key sought-after customers influence the vigor of competition. (Table 2 lists some of the factors that precipitate highly rivalrous conditions).

The systematic analysis of these factors provides guidelines for determining the critical factors for success in the industry. To be successful, a company operating in a small, high-growth market with many small competitors, high industry profits, high inflation rates, cyclical vulnerability, and rapid technological change must behave differently from a company in a large, slow-growing market with low

TABLE 2. *Forces Driving Competitive Behavior*

Bargains to Entry	Buyer Power	Supplier Power	Rivalry
High economies of scale	Large purchases	Few suppliers	Slow industry growth
High product differentiation	Standard product purchased	No substitutes for us	High fixed costs
High capital required	Low switching costs	Our purchases not important	Low differentiation of products
High switching costs	Buyer makes low profits	Our industry not important	Low switching costs
Exclusive distribution access	Purchases not important	Hard for us to switch	Capacity expansions in large chunks
Proprietary technology	Many substitutes available	Suppliers can integrate forward	High exit barriers
Exclusive supply access	Very knowledgeable buyers		Product important to all competitors
Cost advantages			Many balanced competitors
Government support			

Source: Derived from M. E. Porter, *Competitive Strategy* (New York: The Free Press, 1980).

industry profits and a few larger competitors, all of which are highly unionized and highly energy dependent.

Success factors for the first company could include the ability to lead in product technology, to maintain or gain share in the expanding market via a strong marketing force, to negotiate prices that allow the company to keep up with inflation, and to identify ways of smoothing disruptive effects of cyclical sales without increasing costs (such as long-term contracts). Success factors for the second company could include the ability to reduce manufacturing and energy costs; to negotiate satisfactory contracts with unions with minimum disruption of production; to achieve control or near control of the major distribution systems; and to efficiently identify, design, develop, and manufacture custom products.

This concludes the structural component of environmental analysis. The problem is that the environment changes, so attention must be given to trend analysis.

Trend Analysis

Macroeconomic Trends. The origins of change in the industry chain usually stem from trends in the society as a whole. Thus, the first level of trend analysis is concerned with trends in the society and economy in which the firm is embedded.

At the national level, there are several types of trends the firm should identify. First are broad demographic trends: shifts in the age distribution of the population, the geographical distribution, the distribution of ethnic groups, the proportions of ethnic groups, the size of families, the income of families, education, and occupation would be identified and projected into the future. Second are broad economic trends: projections would be made of the trends in gross domestic product, consumer spending power, government expenditures, government fiscal and monetary policy, national productivity, and general business activity. Third are broad sociopolitical trends: trends in cultural values and attitudes would be identified; the policies of the important political parties, particularly those of the incumbent party, analyzed; and the effects of the implementation of these policies projected. Fourth are ecological trends: trends in the physical environment and their effects on the nation would be projected.

A detailed analysis of every aspect of these trends is not necessary. What the firm requires is some idea of the direction in which the nation is moving. Many of these analyses are conducted by government departments or private consultants specializing in this type of work.

The basic purpose of macroeconomic trend analysis is to identify the impacts these trends may have on the business, either directly or along links in the industry chain. For instance, shifts in social demographics may lead to restructuring in the retail industry, which could lead to the reevaluation of a manufacturer's plant locations and distribution channels. (The impact on retailing of the growth and regional concentration trends in the senior citizen population could eventually work back down the chain and affect packaging, branding, pricing and delivery systems.)

Out of the macroeconomic and sociopolitical analyses should emerge some assessments of the major *impacts* on the industry in which the business operates. Some of these trends may have a negative influence, in which case they are regarded as *threats;* some may have a positive influence, in which case they are regarded as *opportunities.*

Industry Chain Trends   Clearly, major trends in the industry chain have the potential to affect the business. In analyzing these trends, it is important to focus on the critical links identified in the structural analysis of the chain. For each critical link in the industry chain, it may be necessary to conduct the following types of analyses.

First, on the basis of the national analysis, consumer spending patterns and market growth should be projected to get an idea of the expected trends in competitive activity at that link. The likelihood of new competitors entering the field and of existing competitors increasing their activity should be identified and the effects on the market estimated. Second would be an analysis of labor. Trends in union activity and attitudes toward unionization, in wage levels, in labor supply, and in labor efficiency should be identified and their effects projected. Third would be an analysis of raw material supplies. A fourth analysis could concern technology. Current technological development and its effects would be projected. A fifth analysis could concern trends in the money market. Subsequent analyses could focus on trends at regional (state and local) levels.

The object is to determine whether any of the factors identified in the industry attractiveness assessment are changing in a way that will cause the attractiveness to substantially change. As is the case with macroeconomic trend analysis, major trends that reduce industry attractiveness, or the ability of the firm to compete, are identified as threats. Major trends that increase industry attractiveness, or the firm's ability to compete, are identified as opportunities. In the light of these trends, the critical success factors must also be reviewed to assess what factors will determine success in the future as opposed to the present.

The analysis of industry chain trends completes the environmental analysis. The strategist should have the following results:

1. Key future interest groups and the major issues on which conflict/support can be expected.
2. Critical factors for future success in the industry.
3. Threats and opportunities facing the industry.

The next step for the strategist is to focus on the business itself, which leads to business analysis.

BUSINESS ANALYSIS

The purpose of business analysis is to identify the strengths and weaknesses of the business in relation to its competitors. Business analysis comprises three major steps. First is *analysis of key strategic variables,* such as product policy; market policy (to determine where the firm is performing well and poorly); distribution policy; and support functions, such as manufacturing and R&D, (to determine if the firm is focusing its efforts consistently within the areas of good performance). Second is *competitive analysis,* in which the firm's position compared with competitors assessed for areas of strength and weakness. Explanation of the differences determines the firms actual strengths and weaknesses. Finally is a comparison with future environmental trends, which identifies the strengths and weaknesses likely to persist in the future.

Analysis of Key Strategic Variables

Katz (1970) discusses the importance of clearly identifying what he calls the key strategic variables of the firm. These strategic variables represent the policy commitments the firm has made to reflect its desired relationship with its environment.

Product Policy. Analysis of sales volume and contribution to profits by product category often reveals that a large proportion of sales volume and contribution to profits is generated by a relatively small proportion of the products. It is where these concentrations of sales and profits take place that provides the clues to what are the business's real strengths.

For instance, in Figure 2, product A is a strong contributor to total sales as well as to total profits. This product is one of the major products of the business. Product C may be even more important, since it generates high profits from moderate sales. However, it is probably a prime target for competitive attack. Product B could be receiving more attention than it deserves by virtue of the fact that it is a high sales volume generator but contributes only moderately to profits. Product D must be seriously considered: unless there is a very real strategic reason for the low profits, (such as share gain) price should be increased. This will reduce sales but improve profits. Product E is a prime candidate for deletion unless there are compelling reasons to keep it.

Thus, the key product policy question is: In what product categories are sales and profits concentrated? This often requires creative determination of the key "dimensions" for categorizing products, since products can be categorized in many ways—by price range, size, color, quality, configuration, and materials. While many of these dimensions may be irrelevant, for each business some are critical. One of the creative challenges of business analysis is determining the dimensions that are critical.

Market Policy. A similar analysis of sales and profits by market or customer type will provide clues to where the real market strengths of the firm lie. As is the case with product policy, markets can be categorized by many dimensions: by customer type (there are a host of sociodemographic and socioeconomic dimensions), by geographic region, by end-usage patterns, and by reason for purchase (new, replacement), to name but a few. The strategic challenge is to identify the important dimensions that will answer the key question: In what market categories are sales and profits concentrated?

Distribution Policy. Analysis of sales and profits by distribution channel provide the clues for discovering the firm's distribution strengths. As above, the key dimensions need to be identified to determine which channels provide the bulk of sales and profits.

| | | Contribution to Total Profits | | |
		High	Medium	Low
Contribution to total sales	High	A	B	D
	Medium	C		
	Low			E

FIGURE 2.   *Sales and Profit Contribution Analysis*

Other Key Policy Variables.   The above three analyses identify products, markets, and distribution channels that are strong performers and those that are weak performers. The next question is whether the firm is deploying its resources appropriately to the strong performers. Along this line, the firm needs to consider other key policy variables. The search here is for consistency between the firm's posture in the product/market/distribution arena and its other major policy decisions. Katz (1970) and Rothschild (1976, 1979) indicate what some of these policy variables may be.

- *Promotion policy.* What fundamental efforts are employed to attract the attention of final consumer and intermediate purchasers? Are these appropriate in the light of actual sales and profit concentrations? Desired sales and profit concentrations?
- *Price policy.* Is the pricing of the products in various markets and channels appropriate? For instance, in Figure 2 some concern was expressed about the low margins of products B and D. Unless there is some compelling strategic reason not to raise their prices, they should be moved up.
- *Innovation policy.* How are R&D funds allocated? Is this appropriate in the light of product and market concentrations? What research funds go to product innovation? To process innovation?
- *Manufacturing policy.* Are manufacturing, scheduling, inventory, delivery, and quality consistent with the key products/markets/ channels served?
- *Key personnel policy.* Where are the best people deployed? How are they promoted and rewarded? Is this consistent with the firm's product/market/channel posture?
- *Investment and discretionary spending policy.* Are organization funds deployed appropriately? To what product/market/channels are the last few dollars in the various divisional budgets allocated? An analysis of

these discretionary expenditures can reveal differences between the attention focused on various product/market/channel activities and the degree of success in each area.

Finally, a review of the firm's position in regard to its key interest groups may indicate the need for other key policy commitments such as the following:

- *Regulation policy.* What will be the policy regarding regulation? Compliance, reluctant compliance, or outright resistance to regulation?
- *Labor policy.* What are the policies toward labor unions? Toward other forms of organized labor? What approach will the firm take? Fight? Avoid? Compromise?

It is important to recognize that the major analytical challenge is to identify, for the specific industry, what its specific strategic variables are. Each industry and firm has a unique set of policy variables that are major determinants of future success. For instance, the mining industry requires key commitments to exploration policy and options policy (options to mine certain explored areas). In the publishing industry, editorial and options policies are important. Hence, the above list is merely a specification of common strategic variables. The challenge to the strategist is to identify those key to the specific business under analysis.

The business analysis highlights inconsistencies between the firm's current posture in the market and its major policy commitments to these markets. Such inconsistencies must be explained or corrected. They could also highlight inconsistencies between the firm's current policy commitments and the critical factors for success in the future. Finally, the identified areas of product/market/channel concentrations also highlight where the firm is doing well and poorly. The question now is *why* this is happening. To answer this question, comparisons with competitors must be made.

Competitive Analysis

To the extent that information is available, the firm must conduct policy analyses for its competitors similar to those carried out for itself. The object is to identify where the firm is outperforming competitors; the explanation of these differences then leads to identification of key strengths. Thus, it is important to determine why the firm is outperforming competitors rather than merely where this occurs. This is what explains the strengths of the firm. (For instance, outselling competitors in Texas is not a strength, but the *reason* for it is a strength.)

It is also important to determine why the firm is doing worse than competitors. Since this may be the result of a strategic choice not to compete heavily in a certain product, market, or channel, it is important to know whether this relatively poor performance is the result of choice or a fundamental weakness. A review of the critical factors for success from the environmental analysis may help explain such weaknesses.

In sum, competitive analysis should yield *key strengths of the business*—where the firm outperforms competitors and why; *key weaknesses of the business*—where the firm underperforms and why; and the *key policy variables*—which determine the posture of the firm in relation to its environment.

Comparison with Future Environment

A review of the trend analyses leads to questions as to whether the current strengths of the firm are appropriate to the future. In this process, the product/market/channel strengths of both the firm and its major competitors are reviewed in light of expected trends in the environment, and an estimate is made of which cur-

rent strengths will persist or become obsolete and which current weaknesses will persist or disappear. This completes the business analysis. The stage is now set for strategy formulation.

STRATEGY FORMULATION

The strategy formulation process consists of *mission development,* in which the basic purpose of the business is specified; *specification of objectives and constraints,* by which objectives are set and the major constraints imposed by corporate strategy or external interest groups are identified; the actual *strategy formulation,* in which offensive and defensive strategies are formulated and along with the key policy commitments to support them; and, finally, *strategic anticipation,* in which competitive counterresponses are anticipated.

Although the following discussion of strategy formulation appears to be a straightforward, step-by-step process, this may well not be the case. Several iterations may be required, as the strategist revises mission, objectives, and strategy with regard to expected competitive and interest group responses.

Statement of Mission

The determination of the firm's current and future strengths and weaknesses and of the industry's major threats, opportunities, and critical success factors finally places the strategist in the position of being able to ask what the mission of the business should be. The mission statement answers the question, What business are we in? It addresses the fundamental raison d'etre of the business in its environment. In other words, a mission statement specifies the functional role the business plays in the larger economy. Hofer and Schendel (1978) argue that effective management of a business stems from a clear understanding of this mission on the part of senior management.

In formulating mission, the strategist must make the tradeoff between a broad mission that spreads management and resources thin and a narrow mission that focuses resources but limits flexibility. Thus, a casualty insurance company may have a mission statement as broad as "We are in the business of insurance against risk worldwide" or as narrow as "We are in the business of providing line and theft coverage to retailers in the Northeastern United States." The first statement could take the company as far afield as Australia, with a vast array of insurance services. The second is very specific and focused, but leaves little room for flexibility.

Scope of mission can be decided only in light of major environmental threats and opportunities, which may indicate the need for a broadening or narrowing of the current mission. The result should be a statement that specifies what part of society the business will participate in and what the functional role of the business role will be.

The next step is to specify the objectives that will be sought and the constraints that will be imposed on the business in pursuing the mission.

Specification of Objectives and Constraints

Hofer and Schendel (1978) and Katz (1970) list a variety of objectives that the business strategist may consider. These include growth, profits, resource utilization, efficiency, contributions to various stakeholders (such as suppliers, customers, employees, stockholders, and society at large), risk/reward tradeoffs, and survival. However, objectives are not unilaterally decided. The key interest group analysis will indicate what objectives will be demanded by interest groups surrounding the firm. To the extent that such demands will be irrefutable,

the strategist should include them as part of the objective set.

At minimum, three major sets of objectives should be included, although conscious tradeoffs among them will have to be made. These are growth, profitability, and competitive performance (such as market share). In other words, the strategist needs to decide how fast the business should grow, how profitably this growth will take place, and how well the business should do in relation to competitors.

Work by Miles and Snow (1980) suggests that the business should make clear decisions on the fundamental nature of the strategies it wishes to pursue. Their study identifies four classes of strategies that companies pursue: *prospecting strategies*, in which the firm proactively and aggressively pursues growth through continual innovation in new products and markets; *defending strategies*, in which the firm basically concentrates on establishing a highly profitable and strong position in a selected industry and defends it aggressively in response to change; *analyzing strategies*, in which the firm selectively fosters growth and innovation in dynamic markets segments and defends its mature segment; and *reacting strategies*, in which the firm merely reacts to competitive initiatives.

The important finding of this work is that even though defenders and analyzers tended to do well in mature industries while prospectors and analyzers tended to do well in dynamic industries, reactors generally did not do well and successful defenders and prospectors were found in *all* types of industries. The key point is that regardless of whether the firms chose to be defenders, prospectors, or analyzers, having selected that basic strategy the successful firm developed a fine-tuned, balanced, and above all *consistent* set of policies, procedures, objectives, goals, and programs to pursue the fundamental strategic approach selected.

The extent to which the strategist will be

allowed to trade off among growth, profits, and relative market share is a function of the constraints that will be imposed. Constraints are imposed from two sources. First, the firm may be subject to corporate constraints emanating from the objectives and key policy decisions of the corporate strategy; second, the key interest group analysis will indicate the constraints that may be imposed by powerful suppliers, customers, labor representatives, banks, regulatory bodies, and so on. To the extent that these constraints are nonnegotiable, they must be accepted as valid constraints on strategic direction.

Having identified the major constraints on strategy and decided on appropriate or acceptable objectives, the next need is to formulate a strategy to achieve these objectives. It is important to divide strategy into two components (MacMillan and Jones, 1986): an *offensive strategy,* which seeks to use strengths to capitalize on opportunities, and a *defensive strategy,* which seeks to bolster weaknesses that may be reinforced by threats. Before addressing each type of strategy, the nature of the current competitive environment bears some discussion.

Competitive Dynamics and Strategic Initiative.

In several industries, the advent of global competitors and high rates of change in markets and technology in recent years has precipitated the need to carefully consider the dynamics of competition. In the wake of the serious shake-outs that continue to take place, three conditions appear to have emerged that will increasingly drive firms to look for dynamic strategies to pursue. These are discussed next, together with the implications.

1. *Today's competitors are "survivors."* After the turbulent competition of the past decade, the surviving competitors are highly competent and aggressive and have significant resources. The implication is that any competitive advantage the firm may currently hold will eventually be eroded away by the actions of these competent, resourceful opponents. It is not a question of whether the competitive advantage *will* be eroded but of *when.* As a result, the task for today's strategist is to constantly plan and pursue the next move; even as the firm is benefiting from the current competitive advantage, it should be laying the groundwork for the next competitive advantage.

2. *Today it costs more to stay in the game.* There are few industries in which the stakes have not increased dramatically in the last decade, and this trend will continue. Thus, the challenge is to find ways in which major competitive moves can be made that consume the minimum necessary resources. Creative ways must be sought to reduce the amount of investment required to stay in the game and still make the investments needed to remain competitive.

   Another uncomfortable reality is that cost reduction is no longer a strategic option; it has become an imperative. Management must be vigilant in driving down costs, yet at the same time maintain quality. Firms unable to maintain quality while they effect continuous cost reduction simply will not survive.

3. *Today the game is more uncertain.* The irony is that even as it becomes more costly to stay in the game, the aggressiveness and competence of today's competitors threaten the success of any major move the firm makes. However costly a move may be, it will not necessarily be successful. Businesses thus face the dilemma of simultaneously having to invest more and seeing the probability of success decrease. This creates the challenge to make every competitive move in such a way that its chances of success are as high as possible—by knowing the competition; by knowing the

competitive forces shaping the industry (Porter, 1980); and by thoroughly understanding the customers, the distribution channels, and the providers of service for the product. Resources cannot be squandered in vainglorious efforts; the stakes are too high.

Clearly, a firm's offensive strategy must formally recognize these dynamics: The firm makes a strategic move that, if successful, seizes the competitive initiative and obliges others in the industry to respond to it. Once a firm takes the initiative, there is a period when it has effective strategic control of the industry as the competitors marshal their resources for the counterattack. If in the meantime the firm does not prepare and execute the next move, it will lose the initiative and end up being one of those controlled rather than being the controller of its strategic destiny. From the time the initiative has been taken to the time competitors have effectively responded is all the time available to put this next initiative in place.

Research in the area of competitive responses indicates that when competitors delay, it is either because they can't respond or because they won't respond. The cases where a competitor can't counterattack have been well documented in the work of Porter (1980, 1985) and Yip (1982) in their discussinos of entry barriers. (Typical examples are listed in Table 2.) Today, delays usually mean the competitor won't respond. This is because of competitive inertia—the natural inertia that comes with large organizations. Competitive anticipation therefore requires a thorough knowledge of each competitor. In modern strategy there is no longer "competition"—only specific competitors, each of which responds according to its own inertial patterns.

Thus, as far as the offensive strategy is concerned, there is a need to constantly search for new initiatives, using the options listed in Table 3, to sequentially take the initiative and then anticipate when the competitors will react, taking into account their response barriers and their inertia.

The essence of dynamic strategy is depicted in Figure 3. By making some initiative-seizing move, the firm captures strategic control, which plays out over time as the wave in the figure. At first, it takes the firm a certain amount of time to launch and establish its competitive edge. Once it is established, there follows a period of exploitation during which the firm has strategic control and can generate supernormal profits. This is followed by a period of counterattack by the various competitors, which eventually erode the advantageous position. From the end of the launch period to the period of rapid erosion is the strategic window—the only time the firm has to establish its next initiative.

Each industry will have its own typical wave form, while different types of initiatives will elicit different response profiles; the response to a new product introduction will differ from the response to a segmentation move or the introduction of a new distribution method or a service enhancement. Clearly, therefore, real strategic insight is needed to manage the strategic wave, and a great deal depends on the ability to anticipate competitive reaction. This is discussed after a brief discussion of offensive and defensive strategy.

Offensive Strategy

In developing an offensive strategy, the options available to the firm and its competitors should be reviewed. Rothschild (1979), Hofer and Schendel (1978), and Porter (1985) identify a number of major offensive strategic options. These are identified in Table 3. Depending on

TABLE 3. *Strategic Options: Offensive Strategies*

Market segmentation	Whereby the competitor identifies and focusses on specific segments of the market
Product innovation	Whereby the competitor introduces new products as the major thrust of competitive direction
Service competition	Whereby the competitor enhances service as a major competitive weapon
Distribution competition	Whereby the securing of major distribution channels and superior delivery is sought
Promotion competition	Whereby the major emphasis is on promoting of product
Process innovation	Whereby the competitor reduces costs by introduction of the latest process technology
Logistics innovation	Reduction of costs of manufacturing, distribution, inventory
Price competition	Whereby pricing is used as the major competitive weapon
Market diversification	New Markets are sought, either geographically or market segments which were not previously served
Related and unrelated product diversification	New Products are sought for existing markets
Credit competition	Terms of payment, and assistance in funding of purchases by the customer, are used as a means of securing sales
Supply control competition	Securing control of critical supplies or controlling costs of supplies
Forward integration	Moving into activities down the chain
Back integration	Moving into activities up the chain
Conglomerate diversification	New products are brought to new managers

the specific opportunities in the industry (identified in the environmental analysis), and the status of the competition (identified in the competitive analysis), several of the options in Table 3 may be viable for one or more competitors in the industry.

The success of a strategy often depends largely on what options are chosen by competitors. If several competitors select the same op-

tion as the basis on which they will compete in the future, the result is a war of attrition in which all competitors expend their resources on keeping up with one another. In trying to assess the likelihood of competitors' moves, it is important to recognize that few can select all options; after all they are subject to their own resource limitations. The problem is to determine whether they will select the same option

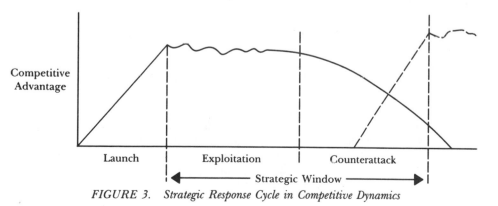

FIGURE 3. *Strategic Response Cycle in Competitive Dynamics*

as the firm and precipitate a war of attrition. The concept of strategic anticipation discussed below can be of help in trying to determine whether the competitor will commit substantial resources in pursuit of the option.

Defensive Strategy

Unfortunately, it may not be possible for all resources and effort to go toward the offensive strategy; defensive measures may be called for as well. In formulating a defensive strategy, threats that have been identified are reviewed with the object of assessing whether they are reinforced by a weakness of the firm. Where the threats and weaknesses of the firm coincide, the firm is most vulnerable, and resources may have to be deployed to reduce this vulnerability. In particular, if the firm expects competitors to attack the business at these points of high vulnerability, resources may have to be used to contain such attacks and bolster these weaknesses.

Katz (1970) argues that resources deployed for defensive purposes should be kept to a minimum, since the strategist must trade off the limited resources of the business between offensive and defensive strategies. In making the tradeoffs between the perhaps substantial resources required to implement offensive and defensive strategies, it should be recognized that to the extent that the firm invests in defensive strategies, it is largely reacting to competitors' moves. To the extent that it can afford to invest in offensive strategies that avoid direct confrontation, it is gaining more control over its own destiny, at least until the period of counterattack. To the extent that it

cannot find any offensive strategic directions, particularly if the industry is highly unattractive, it may have to resort to purely defensive options. Hofer and Schendel (1978) suggest several such options (see Table 4).

Once the appropriate offensive and defensive strategies have been decided, the reformulation of strategic variables becomes necessary. These variables should be reviewed in light of the strategy selected to ensure consistency, in much the same way as for the original business analysis. In other words, a consistent set of policies should be established to guide decisions on product, market, channel, price, promotion, and so forth to reinforce the direction to be taken in the future. Finally, the entire strategy should be reviewed in light of the statement of mission, the impact on objectives, and anticipated competitive response. If objectives cannot be met, reformulation of mission, objectives, and strategy may be necessary.

As far as competition is concerned, the strategic anticipation process may reveal responses that could also cause the business to reformulate strategy. We turn now to the problem of anticipating competitive responses.

Strategic Anticipation

The guidelines for strategic anticipation draw heavily on the work of two authors, Allison (1971) and Thompson (1967), who in turn have used many other authors' contributions in the development of their arguments. The topic is discussed more extensively in MacMillan and Jones (1986) and in MacMillan, McCaffery, and van Wyck (1985).

Allison (1985) discusses the ways in

TABLE 4.   Strategic Options: Defensive Strategies

Scope reduction	Divestiture of assets and reduction of costs to a level where small select segments can be served from an appropriately small asset and cost base
Merger	With some other competitor to pool market share and thus achieve economies of scale
Sale	To a company outside the industry wanting access to the market
Liquidation	Liquidating of the business altogether

which complex strategic decisions are made from the perspective of three distinct but not mutually exclusive perspectives: rational actor, organization process, and bureaucratic politics.

Competitor as a Rational Actor   One way of anticipating strategic responses is to consider the competitor as a rational actor—to imagine the way Competitor A would respond if it were a single, purposive person with specific goals in mind. The essence of using the rational actor perspective is to put ourselves in the position of the competitor facing our strategic move and to try to determine what the most rational counterresponse would be. This requires as clear an idea as possible of the following: What are the competitor's objectives? What goals is it emphasizing? What are the major policy commitments it has made regarding products, markets, distribution channels, promotion methods, and pricing? Where is discretionary income being directed? How are key personnel rewarded?

With some knowledge of the competitor's objectives, strategy, and resource deployments, it is possible to put ourselves in its shoes and to decide what responses the competitor could make when faced with a strategic move on our part. The next two approaches help to determine the factors that would influence its decisions.

Competitor as an Organization   The problems of coordinating a complex organization are substantial. This coordination problem results in the development of a large number of bureaucratic rules, procedures, and policies under which the various managers must act. The opponent must also control the activities of its managers to ensure that they carry out their assigned tasks. To cope with this problem, the competitor develops control systems that monitor and then reward managers according to how well the tasks have been performed. The organizational process model recognizes that the possible response of a competitor is in-

fluenced by these bureaucratic processes in many ways.

If the strategic move a firm makes has never been encountered by a competitor, the competitor may not have a set of rules, policies, or procedures to counter it. In many cases, it may respond by continuing as it always has or by countering the move in a way that most closely "fits the rules." Because policies that act as the guidelines for decision-making in the organization may be difficult to change, there is a tendency for organizations to keep them.

In planning the activities of its divisions, the competitor must commit its resources. It is therefore disruptive if a particular manager makes sudden demands for new resources. The specific perspective of one division may make it rather unsympathetic to problems encountered in another division, and this can give rise to parochial conflicts and conflicts of jurisdiction as each division tries to solve the problem in terms of its perspective. It is therefore important to analyze the following: What types of major rules, policies and programs are used by the competitor? These may influence the visibility of the firm's move, increase the time it takes to recognize the move, and limit the responses the competitor can generate. What major control systems does the competitor employ? How are departments evaluated? How often are they measured? At what level in the organization are decisions relevant to the move made? How is the competitor organized? What are its major departments? Will the strategic move directly affect more than one department? Will it affect them in different ways? Are there likely to be conflicts among departments? The better the firm's knowledge of these factors, the better it can assess the competitor's likely responses to them.

Competitor as a Political Entity   The last model views the competitor as a political system in which powerful and influential interest groups, surrounding the organization or within it, place demands on the organization to achieve their own purposes. Key interest groups perceive any response to the firm's strategy in terms of their interests. This influences the way the organization may react. Certain responses that seem rational may not be tolerated by a group believing they may harm its interests. This applies at the level of specific decision-makers as well. People within the competitor's organization will assess their responses to the initiating firm's move in terms of how they will be rewarded for the outcome and the risks associated with it.

With this as background, it is suggested that the competitor be analyzed in a political context, much in the same way that the environmental mapping of the strategist's own organization takes place. Questions to be asked are: What major interest groups have a vested interest in the competitor's response? What issues are they raising? What positions are they taking? How powerful are these interest groups? This analysis should indicate what constraints are imposed on the organization and what responses will be prescribed unless the organization can convince the relevant interest groups to relax the constraints. A knowledge of these factors provides a sense of the likelihood that some responses will not be considered because the proposal may be too risky for the opposing organization in general or the opposing decision-maker in particular.

The results of a political model perspective indicate which responses are likely to be acceptable to the competitor and its interest groups. This puts the firm in a position to anticipate the competitor's likely counter-strategies.

The insight provided by applying these three models allows us to develop some estimates of the expected counterresponses. These estimates are taken into account in refining the firm's offensive and defensive strategies.

SUMMARY

At this stage the strategist should have an *offensive strategy* geared to applying strengths to take advantage of opportunities; a *defensive strategy* to bolster weaknesses that are reinforced by threats; a *set of policy commitments* for the key strategic variables of the business, which are consistent with the strategy and with trends in the environment; an estimate of the *competitive counterresponses;* an assessment of the *key interest groups* that will have a vested interest in the results of the strategy and of the issues that will arise and the groups' positions on these issues. From here on, the strategy needs to be converted into an implementation plan indicating what major steps should be taken to execute the strategy and what resources must be deployed.

BIBLIOGRAPHY

Allison, G. T. *Essence of Decision.* Boston: Little Brown, 1971.

Andrews, K. *The Concept of Corporate Strategy.* Homewood, Ill.: Dow-Jones, 1971.

Ansoff, H. I. *Corporate Strategy, An Analytic Approach to Business Policy Expansion.* New York: McGraw-Hill, 1965.

Ansoff, H. I., R. C. Brandenburg, F. E. Portner, and R. Radosevich. *Acquisition Behavior of U.S. Manufacturing Firms: 1946–65.* Nashville: Vanderbilt University Press, 1971.

Grinyer, P. H., and D. Norburn. "Planning for Existing Markets: Perception of Executives and Financial Performance." *Journal of the Royal Statistical Society Series A* 138, part 1 (1975): 70–97.

Hambrick, D. C., and D. Lei. "Toward Empirical Prioritization of Contingency Variables for Business Strategy." *Academy of Management Journal* 28, no. 4 (1985): 763–788.

Hambrick, D. C., I. C. MacMillan, and D. L. Day. "Strategic Attributes on Performance in the BCG Matrix." *Academy of Management Journal* 25, no. 3 (September 1982): 510–531.

Herold, D. M. "Long-Range Planning and Organizational Performance." *Academy of Management Journal* 15 (March 1972): 91–102.

Hofer, C. W. "Towards a Contingency Theory of Business Strategy." *Academy of Management Journal* (December 1975): 356–379.

Hofer, C. W., and D. E. Schendel. *Strategy Formulation: Analytical Concepts.* St. Paul, Minn.: West Publishing, 1978.

Katz, R. L. *Management of the Total Enterprise.* Englewood Cliffs, N.J.: Prentice Hall, 1970.

Kennedy, J. S. "Practice and Theory in Negotiations." In Webster, R. D., "New Directions in Marketing," *Proceeding of the 48th National Conference: American Marketing Association.* Chicago: American Marketing Association, 1965.

Kudla, R. J. "The Effects of Strategic Planning on Common Stock Returns." *Academy of Management Journal* 12, no. 1 (March 1980).

MacMillan, I. C., and P. E. Jones. *Business Strategy: Power and Politics.* St. Paul: West Publishing, 1985.

MacMillan, I. C., M. L. McCaffery, and G. van Wijk. "Competitive Responses to Easily Imitated New Products." *Strategic Management Journal* 6 (1985): 75–86.

Miller, D. "Towards a Contingency Theory of Business Strategy Formulation." *Proceedings of the National Meeting of the Academy of Management.* New Orleans: Academy of Management (August 1975).

Mintzberg, H., D. Raisinghani, and A. Theoret. "The Structure of Unstructured Decision Processes." *Administrative Science Quarterly* 21, no. 2 (June 1976).

Newman, W. H., and J. P. Logan. *Strategy, Policy, and Central Management.* Cincinnati: South Western Publishing, 1971.

Porter, M. E. *Competitive Strategy.* New York: The Free Press, 1980.

Porter, M. E. *Competitive Advantage.* New York: The Free Press, 1985.

Ramanujam, V., and N. Venkatraman. "Planning System Characteristics and Planning Effectiveness." *Strategic Management Journal* 8, no. 5 (1987): 453–468.

Rothschild, W. E. *Putting It All Together.* New York: AMACOM, 1976.

Rothschild, W. E. *Strategic Alternatives.* New York: AMACOM, 1979.

Rue, L. W., and R. M. Fulmer. "Is Long Range Planning Profitable?" *Proceedings of the Business Policy and Planning Division of the Academy of Management,* paper no. 8. Boston: Academy of Management (August 1973).

Salter, M. E. and W. A. Weinhold. *Diversification Through Acquisition.* New York: The Free Press, 1979.

Steiner, G. A. *Pitfalls in Comprehensive Long Range Planning.* Oxford, Ohio: The Planning Executive Institute, 1972.

Thompson, J. D. *Organizations in Action.* New York: McGraw-Hill, 1967.

Thune, S. S., and R. J. House. "Where Long Range Planning Pays Off." *Business Horizons* 13 (August 1970): 81–87.

Wrapp, H. E. "Good Managers Don't Make Policy Decisions." *Harvard Business Review* 45, no. 5 (Sept.–Oct. 1967): 72–84.

Yip, G. *Barriers to Entry: A Corporate Strategy Perspective.* Lexington, Mass.: Lexington Books, 1982.

Perspectives on Strategy:
The Real Story
Behind Honda's Success

Richard Pascale

PERSPECTIVE ONE: THE HONDA EFFECT

At face value, "strategy" is an innocent noun. Webster defines it as the large-scale planning and direction of operations. In the business context, it pertains to a process by which a firm searches and analyzes its environment and resources in order to 1) select opportunities defined in terms of markets to be served and products to serve them, and 2) makes discrete decisions to invest resources in order to achieve identified objectives.[1]

But for a vast and influential population of executives, planners, academics, and consultants, strategy is more than a conventional English noun. It embodies an implicit model of how organizations should be guided and consequently, preconfigures our way of thinking. Strategy formulation 1) is generally assumed to be driven by senior management whom we expect to set strategic direction; 2) has been extensively influenced by empirical models and concepts; and 3) is often associated with a laborious strategic planning process that, in some

© [1975] by the Regents of the University of California. Reprinted from the *California Management Review*, vol. 26, No. 3, (Spring 1984). By permission of The Regents.

companies, has produced more paper than insight.

A $500-million-a-year "strategy" industry has emerged in the United States and Europe comprised of management consultants, strategic planning staffs, and business school academics. It caters to the unique emphasis that American and European companies place upon this particular aspect of managing and directing corporations.

Words often derive meaning from their cultural context. *Strategy* is one such word and nowhere is the contrast of meanings more pronounced than between Japan and the United States. The Japanese view the emphasis we place on "strategy" as we might regard their enthusiasm for Kabuki or sumo wrestling. They note our interest not with an intent of acquiring similar ones but for insight into our peculiarities. The Japanese are somewhat distrustful of a single "strategy," for in their view any idea that focuses attention does so at the expense of peripheral vision. They strongly believe that *peripheral vision* is essential to discerning changes in the customer, the technology or competition, and is the key to corporate survival over the long haul. They regard any propensity to be driven by a single-minded strategy as a weakness.

The Japanese have particular discomfort

with strategic concepts. While they do not reject ideas such as the experience curve or portfolio theory outright they regard them as a stimulus to perception. They have often ferreted out the "formula" of their concept-driven American competitors and exploited their inflexibility. In musical instruments, for example, (a mature industry facing stagnation as birthrates in the U.S. and Japan declined), Yamaha might have classified its products as "cash cows" and gone on to better things (as its chief U.S. competitor, Baldwin United, had done). Instead, beginning with a negligible share of the U.S. market, Yamaha plowed ahead and destroyed Baldwin's seemingly unchallengeable dominance. YKK's success in zippers against Talon (a Textron division) and Honda's outflanking of Harley-Davidson (a former AMF subsidiary) in the motorcycle field provide parallel illustrations. All three cases involved American conglomerates, wedded to the portfolio concept, that had classified pianos, zippers, and motorcycles as mature businesses to be harvested rather than nourished and defended. Of course, those who developed portfolio theory and other strategic concepts protest that they were never intended to be mindlessly applied in setting strategic direction. But most would also agree that there is a widespread tendency in American corporations to misapply concepts and to otherwise become strategically myopic—ignoring the marketplace, the customer, and the problems of execution. This tendency toward misapplication, being both pervasive and persistent over several decades, is a phenomenon that the literature has largely ignored.[2] There is a need to explicitly identify the factors that influence how we conceptualize strategy—and which foster its misuse.

Honda: The Strategy Model

In 1975, Boston Consulting Group presented the British government its final report: *Strategy Alternatives for the British Motorcycle Industry.* This 120-page document identified two key factors leading to the British demise in the world's motorcycle industry:

· market share loss and profitability declines, and
· scale economy disadvantages in technology, distribution, and manufacturing.

During the period 1959 to 1973, the British share of the U.S. motorcycle industry had dropped from 49 percent to 9 percent. Introducing BCG's recommended strategy (of targeting market segments where sufficient production volumes could be attained to be price competitive) the report states:

> The success of the Japanese manufacturers originated with the growth of their domestic market during the 1950s. As recently as 1960, only 4 percent of Japanese motorcycle production was exported. By this time, however, the Japanese had developed huge production volumes in small motorcycles in their domestic market, and volume-related cost reductions had followed. This resulted in a highly competitive cost position which the Japanese used as a springboard for penetration of world markets with small motorcycles in the early 1960s.[3]

The BCG study was made public by the British government and rapidly disseminated in the United States. It exemplifies the necessary (and I argue, insufficient) strategist's perspective of

· examining competition primarily from an intercompany perspective,
· at a high level of abstraction,
· with heavy reliance on micro-economic concepts (such as the experience curve).

Case writers at Harvard Business School, UCLA, and the University of Virginia quickly condensed the BCG report for classroom use in case discussions. It currently enjoys extensive use in first-term courses in Business Policy.

Of particular note in the BCG study, and in the subsequent Harvard Business School rendition, is the historical treatment of Honda.

The mix of competitors in the U.S. motorcycle market underwent a major shift in the 1960s. Motorcycle registrations increased from 575,000 in 1960 to 1,382,000 in 1965. Prior to 1960 the U.S. market was served mainly by Harley-Davidson of U.S.A., BSA, Triumph and Norton of U.K. and Moto-Guzzi of Italy. Harley was the market leader with total 1959 sales of $16.6 million. After the second world war, motorcycles in the U.S.A. attracted a very limited group of people other than police and army personnel who used motorcycles on the job. While most motorcyclists were no doubt decent people, groups of rowdies who went around on motorcycles and called themselves by such names as "Hell's Angels," "Satan's Slaves" gave motorcycling a bad image. Even leather jackets which were worn by motorcyclists as a protective device acquired an unsavory image. A 1953 movie called "The Wild Ones" starring a 650cc Triumph, a black leather jacket and Marlon Brando gave the rowdy motorcyclists wide media coverage. The stereotype of the motorcyclist was a leather-jacketed, teenage trouble-maker. Honda established an American subsidiary in 1959—American Honda Motor Company. This was in sharp contrast to other foreign producers who relied on distributors. Honda's marketing strategy was described in the 1963 annual report as "With its policy of selling, not primarily to confirmed motorcyclists but rather to members of the general public who had never before given a second thought to a motorcycle. . . ." Honda started its push in the U.S. market with the smallest, lightweight motorcycles. It was superior to the lightweight being sold by Sears, Roebuck in America at that time. It had a three-speed transmission, an automatic clutch, five horsepower (the American cycle only had two and a half), an electric starter and step through frame for female riders. And it was easier to handle. The Honda machines sold for under $250 in retail compared with $1,000–$1,500 for the bigger American or British machines. Even at that early date Honda was probably superior to other competitors in productivity.

By June 1960 Honda's Research and Development effort was staffed with 700 designers/engineers. This might be contrasted with 100 engineers/draftsmen employed by . . . (European and American competitors). In 1962 production per man-year was running at 159 units, (a figure not reached by Harley-Davidson until 1974). Honda's net fixed asset investment was $8170 per employee . . . (more than twice its European and American competitors). With 1959 sales of $55 million Honda was already the largest motorcycle producer in the world.

Honda followed a policy of developing the market region by region. They started on the West Coast and moved eastward over a period of four-five years. Honda sold 2,500 machines in the U.S. in 1960. In 1961 they lined up 125 distributors and spent $150,000 on regional advertising. Their advertising was directed to the young families, their advertising theme was "You Meet the Nicest People on a Honda." This was a deliberate attempt to dissociate motorcycles from rowdy, Hell's Angels type people.

Honda's success in creating demand for lightweight motorcycles was phenomenal. American Honda's sales went from $500,000 in 1960 to $77 million in 1965. By 1966 the market share data showed the ascendancy of Japanese producers and their success in selling lightweight motorcycles.

U.S. Market Share (%)	
Honda	63
Yamaha	11
Suzuki	11
Harley-Davidson	4
BSA/Triumph and Others	11

Starting from virtually nothing in 1960, the lightweight motorcycles had clearly established their lead.[4]

Quoting from the BCG report:

> The Japanese motorcycle industry, and in particular Honda, the market leader, present a [consistent] picture. The basic philosophy of the Japanese manufacturers is that high volumes per model provide the potential for high productivity as a result of using capital intensive and highly automated techniques. Their marketing strategies are therefore directed towards developing these high model volumes, hence the careful attention that we have observed them giving to growth and market share [see figure below].
>
> The overall result of this philosophy over time has been that the Japanese have now developed an entrenched and leading position in terms of technology and production methods. . . . The major factors which appear to account for the Japanese superiority in both these areas are . . . specialized production systems, balancing engineering and market requirements, and the cost efficiency and reliability of suppliers.[5]

As evidence of Honda's strategy of taking a position as low cost producer and exploiting economies of scale, other sources cite Honda's construction in 1959 of a plant to manufacture 30,000 motorcycles per month well ahead of existing demand at the time. (Up until then Honda's most popular models sold 2,000–3,000 units per month.)[6]

The overall picture depicted by the quotes above exemplifies the "strategy model." Honda is portrayed as a firm dedicated to being the low price producer, utilizing its dominant market position in Japan to force entry into the U.S. market, expanding that market by redefining a leisure class ("Nicest People") segment, and exploiting its comparative advantage via aggressive pricing and advertising. Richard Rumelt, writing the teaching note for the UCLA adaptation of the case states: "The fundamental contribution of BCG is not the experience curve per se but the ever-present assumption that differences in cost (or efficiency) are the fundamental components of strategy."[7]

The Organizational Process Perspective

On September 10, 1982, the six Japanese executives responsible for Honda's entry into the U.S. motorcycle market in 1959 assembled in Honda's Tokyo headquarters. They had gathered at my request to describe in fine grain detail the sequence of events that had led to Honda's ultimate position of dominance in the U.S. market.[8] All were in their sixties; three were retired. The story that unfolded, greatly abbreviated below, highlights miscalculation, serendipity, and organizational learning—counterpoints to the streamlined "strategy" version related earlier.

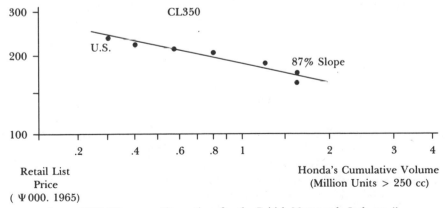

Source: BCG "Strategy Alternatives for the British Motorcycle Industry."

Any account of Honda's successes must grasp at the outset the unusual character of its founder, Sochiro Honda and his partner, Takeo Fujisawa. Honda was an inventive genius with a large ego and mercurial temperament, given to bouts of "philandering" (to use his expression).[9] In the formative stages of his company, Honda is variously reported to have tossed a geisha out a second-story window,[10] climbed inside a septic tank to retrieve a visiting supplier's false teeth (and subsequently placed the teeth in his mouth),[11] appeared inebriated and in costume before a formal presentation to Honda's bankers requesting financing vital to the firm's survival (the loan was denied),[12] hit a worker on the head with a wrench,[13] and stripped naked before his engineers to assemble a motorcycle engine.[14]

Post-war Japan was in desperate need of transportation. Motorcycle manufacturers proliferated, producing clip-on engines that converted bicycles into makeshift "mopeds." Honda was among these but it was not until he teamed up with Fujisawa in 1949 that the elements of a successful enterprise began to take shape. Fujisawa provided money as well as financial and marketing strengths. In 1950 their first D type motorcycle was introduced. They were, at that juncture, participating in a fragmented industry along with 247 other manufacturers. Other than its sturdy frame, this introductory product was unnoteworthy and did not enjoy great commercial success.[15]

Honda embodied a rare combination of inventive ability and ultimate self-confidence. His motivation was not primarily commercial. Rather, the company served as a vehicle to give expression to his inventive abilities. A successful company would provide a resource base to pursue, in Fujisawa's words, his "grandiose dream." Fujisawa continues, "There was no end to his pursuit of technology."[16]

Fujisawa, in an effort to save the faltering company, pressed Honda to abandon their noisy two-stroke engine and pursue a four-stroke design. The quieter four-stroke engines were appearing on competitive motorcycles, therefore threatening Honda with extinction. Mr. Honda balked. But a year later, Honda stunned Fujisawa with a breakthrough design that doubled the horsepower of competitive four-stroke engines. With this innovation, the firm was off and running, and by 1951 demand was brisk.[17] There was no organization, however, and the plant was chaotic.[18] Strong demand, however, required early investment in a simplified mass production process. As a result, *primarily* due to design advantages, and secondarily to production methods, Honda became one of the four or five industry leaders by 1954 with 15 percent market share.[19]

For Fujisawa, the engine innovation meant increased sales and easier access to financing. For Mr. Honda, the higher horsepower engine opened the possibility of pursuing one of his central ambitions in life—to race his motorcycle and win. Winning provided the ultimate confirmation of his design abilities. Racing success in Japan came quickly. As a result, in 1959 Honda raised his sights to the international arena and committed the firm to winning at Great Britain's Isle of Man—the "Olympics" of motorcycle racing. Again, Honda's inventive genius was called into play. Shifting most of the firm's resources into this racing effort, Honda embarked on studies of combustion that resulted in a new configuration of the combustion chamber that doubled horsepower and halved weight. Honda leapfrogged past European and American competitors—winning in one class, then another, winning the Isle of Man manufacturer's prize in 1959 and sweeping the first five positions by 1961.[20]

Fujisawa, throughout the fifties, sought to turn Honda's attention from his enthusiasm with racing to the more mundane requirements of running an enterprise. By 1956, as the innovations gained from racing had begun to pay off in vastly more efficient engines, Fujisawa pressed Honda to adapt this technology for a commercial motorcycle.[21] Fujisawa had a particular segment in mind. Most motorcyclists in Japan were male and the machines were used primarily as an alternative form of transportation to trains and buses. There were, however, a vast number of small commercial establishments in Japan that still delivered goods and ran errands on bicycles. Trains and buses were inconvenient for these activities. The pursestrings of these small enterprises were controlled by the Japanese wife—who resisted buying conventional motorcycles because they were expensive, dangerous, and hard to handle. Fujisawa challenged Honda: Can you use what you've learned from racing to come up with an inexpensive, safe-looking motorcycle that can be driven with one hand (to facilitate carrying packages).[22]

In 1958, the Honda 50cc Supercub was introduced—with an automatic clutch, three-speed transmission, automatic starter, and the safe, friendly look of a bicycle (without the stigma of the outmoded mopeds). Owing almost entirely to its high horsepower but *lightweight 50cc engine* (not to production efficiencies), it was affordable. Overnight, the firm was overwhelmed with orders. Engulfed by demand, they sought financing to build a new plant with a 30,000 unit per month capacity. "It wasn't a speculative investment," recalls one executive. "We had the proprietary technology, we had the market, and the demand was enormous."[23] (The plant was completed in mid-1960.) Prior to its opening, demand was met through makeshift, high cost, company-owned assembly and farmed-out assembly through subcontractors.[24] By the end of 1959, Honda had skyrocketed into first place among Japanese motorcycle manufacturers. Of its total sales that year of 285,000 units, 168,000 were Supercubs.[25]

Fujisawa utilized the Supercub to restructure Honda's channels of distribution. For many years, Honda had rankled under the two-tier distribution system that prevailed in the industry. These problems had been exacerbated by the fact that Honda was a late entry and had been carried as secondary line by distributors whose loyalties lay with their older manufacturers. Further weakening Honda's leverage, all manufacturer sales were on a consignment basis.

Deftly, Fujisawa had characterized the Supercub to Honda's distributors as "something much more like a bicycle than a motorcycle." The traditional channels, to their later regret, agreed. Under aimicable terms Fujisawa began selling the Supercub directly to retailers—and primarily through bicycle shops. Since these shops were small and numerous (approximately 12,000 in Japan), sales on consignment were unthinkable. A cash-on-delivery system was installed, giving Honda significantly more leverage over its dealerships than the other motorcycle manufacturers enjoyed.[26]

The stage was now set for exploration of the U.S. market. Mr. Honda's racing conquests in the late fifties had given substance to his convictions about his abilities. While still heavily occupied by the Isle of Man, success fueled his quest for new and different challenges.

To the onlooker from Japan, the American market was vast, untapped, and affluent. In addition, Honda had experimented with local Southeast Asian markets in 1957–58 with little success. With little disposable income and poor roads, total Asian exports had reached a meager 1,000 units in 1958.[27] The European market, while larger, was heavily dominated by its own name brand manufacturers, and the popular mopeds dominated the low price, low horsepower end. Spurred in part by ambition and in part by a process of deduction, Fujisawa and Honda focused attention on the United States.

Two Honda executives—the soon-to-be named president of American Honda, Kihachiro Kawashima and his assistant—arrived in the U.S. in late 1958.* Their itinerary: San Francisco, Los Angeles, Dallas, New York, and Columbus. Mr. Kawashima recounts his impressions:

My first reaction after travelling across the United States was: How could we have been so stupid as to start a war with such a vast and wealthy country! My second reaction was discomfort. I spoke poor English. We dropped in on motorcycle dealers who treated us discourteously and in addition, gave the general impression of being motorcycle enthusiasts who, secondarily, were in business. There were only 3,000 motorcycle dealers in the United States at the time and only 1,000 of them were open five days a week. The remainder were open on nights and weekends. Inventory was poor, manufacturers sold motorcycles to dealers on consignment, the retailers provided consumer financing; after-sales service was poor. It was discouraging.

My other impression was that everyone in the United States drove an automobile—making it doubtful that motorcycles could ever do very well in the market. However, with 450,000 motorcycle registrations in the U.S. and 60,000 motorcycles imported from Europe each year it didn't seem unreasonable to shoot for 10 percent of the import market. I returned to Japan with that report.

In truth, we had no strategy other than the idea of seeing if we could sell something in the United States. It was a new frontier, a new challenge, and it fit the "success against all odds" culture that Mr. Honda had cultivated. I reported my impressions to Fujisawa—including the seat-of-the-pants target of trying, over several years, to attain a 10 percent share of U.S. imports. He didn't probe that target quantitatively. We did not discuss profits or deadlines for breakeven. Fujisawa told me if anyone could succeed, I could and authorized $1 million for the venture.

The next hurdle was to obtain a currency

---

*Mr. Kihachiro Kawashima subsequently became Executive Vice President of Honda Motor Co., Ltd. Japan.

allocation from the Ministry of Finance. They were extraordinarily skeptical. Toyota had launched the Toyopet in the U.S. in 1958 and had failed miserably. "How could Honda succeed?" they asked. Months went by. We put the project on hold. Suddenly, five months after our application, we were given the go-ahead—but at only a fraction of our expected level of commitment. "You can invest $250,000 in the U.S. market," they said, "but only $110,000 in cash." The remainder of our assets had to be in parts and motorcycle inventory.

We moved into frantic activity as the government, hoping we would give up on the idea, continued to hold us to the July 1959 start-up timetable. Our focus, as mentioned earlier, was to compete with the European exports. We knew our products at the time were good but not far superior. Mr. Honda was especially confident of the 250cc and 305cc machines. The shape of the handlebar on these larger machines looked like the eyebrow of Buddha, which he felt was a strong selling point. Thus, after some discussion and with no compelling criteria for selection, we configured our start-up inventory with 25 percent of each of our four products— the 50cc Supercub and the 125cc, 250cc, and 305cc machines. In dollar value terms, of course, the inventory was heavily weighted toward the larger bikes.

The stringent monetary controls of the Japanese government together with the unfriendly reception we had received during our 1958 visit caused us to start small. We chose Los Angeles where there was a large second and third generation Japanese community, a climate suitable for motorcycle use, and a growing population. We were so strapped for cash that the three of us shared a furnished apartment that rented for $80 per month. Two of us slept on the floor. We obtained a warehouse in a run-down section of the city and waited for the ship to arrive. Not daring to spare our funds for equipment, the three of us stacked the motorcycle crates three high—by hand, swept the floors, and built and maintained the parts bin.

We were entirely in the dark the first year. We were not aware the motorcycle business in the United States occurs during a seasonable

April-to-August window—and our timing coincided with the closing of the 1959 season. Our hard-learned experiences with distributorships in Japan convinced us to try to go to the retailers direct. We ran ads in the motorcycle trade magazine for dealers. A few responded. By spring of 1960, we had forty dealers and some of our inventory in their stores—mostly larger bikes. A few of the 250cc and 305cc bikes began to sell. Then disaster struck.

By the first week of April 1960, reports were coming in that our machines were leaking oil and encountering clutch failure. This was our lowest moment. Honda's fragile reputation was being destroyed before it could be established. As it turned out, motorcycles in the United States are driven much farther and much faster than in Japan. We dug deeply into our precious cash reserves to air freight our motorcycles to the Honda testing lab in Japan. Throughout the dark month of April, Pan Am was the only enterprise in the U.S. that was nice to us. Our testing lab worked twenty-four-hour days bench testing the bikes to try to replicate the failure. Within a month, a redesigned head gasket and clutch spring solved the problem. But in the meantime, events had taken a surprising turn.

Throughout our first eight months, following Mr. Honda's and our own instincts, we had not attempted to move the 50cc Supercubs. While they were a smash success in Japan (and manufacturing couldn't keep up with demand there), they seemed wholly unsuitable for the U.S. market where everything was bigger and more luxurious. As a clincher, we had our sights on the import market—and the Europeans, like the American manufacturers, emphasized the larger machines.

We used the Honda 50s ourselves to ride around Los Angeles on errands. They attracted a lot of attention. One day we had a call from a Sears buyer. While persisting in our refusal to sell through an intermediary, we took note of Sears's interest. But we still hesitated to push the 50cc bikes out of fear they might harm our image in a heavily macho market. But when the larger bikes started breaking, we had no choice. We let the 50cc bikes move. And surprisingly, the retailers who wanted to sell them weren't motorcycle dealers, they were sporting goods stores.

The excitement created by the Honda Supercub began to gain momentum. Under restrictions from the Japanese government, we were still on a cash basis. Working with our initial cash and inventory, we sold machines, reinvested in inventory, and sunk the profits into additional inventory and advertising. Our advertising tried to straddle the market. While retailers continued to inform us that our Supercub customers were normal everyday Americans, we hesitated to target toward this segment out of fear of alienating the high margin end of our business—sold through the traditional motorcycle dealers to a more traditional "black leather jacket" customer.[28]

Honda's phenomenal sales and share gains over the ensuing years have been previously reported. History has it that Honda *"redefined"* the U.S. motorcycle industry. In the view of American Honda's start-up team, this was an innovation they backed into—and reluctantly. It was certainly not the strategy they embarked on in 1959. As late as 1963, Honda was still working with its original Los Angeles advertising agency, its ad campaigns straddling all customers so as not to antagonize one market in pursuit of another.

In the spring of 1963, an undergraduate advertising major at UCLA submitted, in fulfillment of a routine course assignment, an ad campaign for Honda. Its theme: You Meet the Nicest People on a Honda. Encouraged by his instructor, the student passed his work on to a friend at Grey Advertising. Grey had been soliciting the Honda account—which with a $5 million a year budget was becoming an attractive potential client. Grey purchased the student's idea—on a tightly kept nondisclosure basis. Grey attempted to sell the idea to Honda.[29]

Interestingly, the Honda management team, which by 1963 had grown to five Japanese executives, was badly split on this advertising decision. The President and Treasurer favored another proposal from another agency. The Director of Sales, however, felt strongly that the Nicest People campaign was the right one—and his commitment eventually held sway. Thus, in 1963, through an inadvertent sequence of events, Honda came to adopt a strategy that directly identified and targeted that large untapped segment of the marketplace that has since become inseparable from the Honda legend.[30]

The Nicest People campaign drove Honda's sales at an even greater rate. By 1964, nearly one out of every two motorcycles sold was a Honda. As a result of the influx of medium income leisure class consumers, banks and other consumer credit companies began to finance motorcycles—shifting away from dealer credit, which had been the traditional purchasing mechanism available. Honda, seizing the opportunity of soaring demand for its products, took a courageous and seemingly risky position. Late in 1964, they announced that thereafter, they would cease to ship on a consignment basis but would require cash on delivery. Honda braced itself for revolt. While nearly every dealer questioned, appealed, or complained, none relinquished his franchise. In one fell swoop, Honda shifted the power relationship from the dealer to the manufacturer. Within three years, this would become the pattern for the industry.[31]

The "Honda Effect"

The preceding account of Honda's inroads in the U.S. motorcycle industry provides more than a second perspective on reality. It focuses our attention on different issues and raises different questions. What factors permitted two men as unlike one another as Honda and Fujisawa to function effectively as a team? What incentives and understandings permitted the Japanese executives at American Honda to respond to the market as it emerged rather than

doggedly pursue the 250cc and 305cc strategy that Mr. Honda favored? What decision process permitted the relatively junior sales director to overturn the bosses' preferences and choose the Nicest People campaign? What values or commitment drove Honda to take the enormous risk of alienating its dealers in 1964 in shifting from a consignment to cash? In hindsight, these pivotal events all seem ho-hum common sense. But each day, as organizations live out their lives without the benefit of hindsight, few choose so well and so consistently.

The juxtaposed perspectives reveal what I shall call the "Honda Effect." Western consultants, academics, and executives express a preference for oversimplifications of reality and cognitively linear explanations of events. To be sure, they have always acknowledged that the "human factor" must be taken into account. But extensive reading of strategy cases at business schools, consultants' reports, strategic planning documents as well as the coverage of the popular press, reveals a widespread tendency to overlook the process through which organizations experiment, adapt, and learn. We tend to impute coherence and purposive rationality to events when the opposite may be closer to the truth. How an organization deals with miscalculation, mistakes, and serendipitous events *outside its field of vision is often crucial to success over time.* It is this realm that requires better understanding and further research if we are to enhance our ability to guide an organization's destiny.

PERSPECTIVE TWO: SHIFTS IN THE NATURE OF COMPETITION

The "microeconomic" and "miscalculation" models focus on different factors and attribute success to different causal events. Both perspectives are valuable; which one is more valuable depends, in part, on the environment in which an organization finds itself. Which view of reality is most appropriate in the environmental context of the eighties?

Two decades ago, American companies were, with rare exception, the flagships of the world's industrial armada. Across a diverse range of products and services, one found dominant American companies, each a world leader in its industry, each having carved out a seemingly impregnable strategic enclave. In twenty years, this picture has changed.

Let us consider the extent and nature of this change. Beginning with the Department of Commerce's list of twenty major industries, eliminating those industries heavily regulated (e.g., transportation [railroads and airlines], utilities, banking); those industries selling primarily to government (e.g., defense and aerospace); and those industries where competition is primarily of a regional rather than a national nature (e.g., construction, food chains). We are left with thirteen industries within which firms compete on a national and often international basis and whose success is primarily self-determined (i.e., not heavily dependent upon geographical advantages or governmental regulation). Identifying the leading firm in each of these industries based on *Fortune* 500 rankings, we can trace their movements over the past twenty years—1962 through 1982—in terms of market share positions and gains or losses in comparative advantage. These provide the coordinates for Figure 1.

Individual companies focus on changes *within* their industrial environment. When we aggregate across industries, we observe trends impacting upon all participants. Figure 1 reveals that nine of the leading firms declined both in share and competitive advantage. Two additional companies lost competitive advantage while retaining parity in share. Only Boeing and IBM gained along the market share and competitive advantage dimensions. What factors account for this deterioration in competitive position over the past twenty years?

The early sixties was, above all, a period of industrial expansion. The Index of Industrial Production registered a 15.6 percent *increase* from 1960 to 1963, compared with a *decrease* of 9.1 from 1979 to 1982.[32] In nearly all sectors, there were increases in primary demand enabling participants to grow without doing so at one another's expense. Interest rates were low (prime rates averaging 4.5 percent in 1961, as compared with an average 18.87 percent in 1981), and investors embraced risks in their determination to capitalize on the optimism of the times. Technological change fuelled continual product and process innovation with the result that productivity increases followed almost effortlessly. Table 1 summarizes these and other factors.

Another ingredient important in securing a firm's competitive position was technological advantage. Bell Laboratories's patents for the first transistors guaranteed a seven-year strategic haven during which time it exploited high margins and recouped its investments. Xerox copiers and IBM's 360 enjoyed much the same competitive respite as did, in one form or another, nearly every other industrial leader. However, patents and proprietary process technology preserve advantage as long as the players of an industrial family honor the rules. This was to change as competition shifted from the domestic to the international arena.

The international pecking order of the sixties (that is, one nation's standing in relation to others), was determined by factors largely separate from the industrial sphere. National status was dependent on military strength, technological leadership (measured by Nobel prizes and megafeats such as space shots), Olympic gold medals, and a country's centrality in the world geopolitical dialogue. NATO, not GNP, was the dominant acronym at the time.

The environment fostered set piece competition. To oversimplify, oligopolistic competitors focused primarily on domestic markets, participants shared implicit rules.

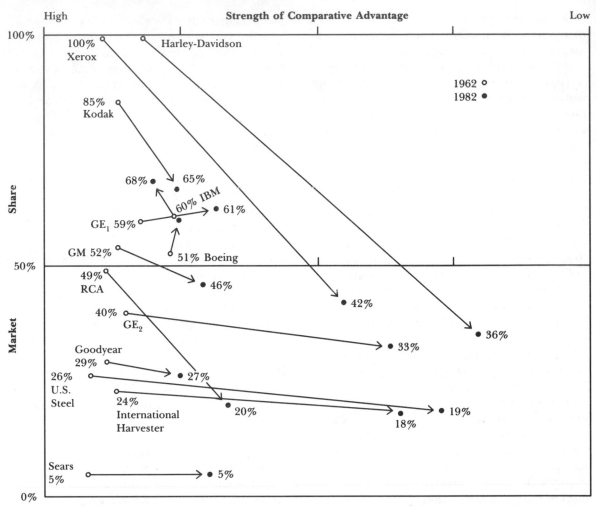

FIGURE 1.   Market Share and Comparative Advantage Trends in Thirteen Key Industries, 1962–1982

Market defined as follows: Xerox: plain copiers; Harley-Davidson: motorcycles; Kodak: photographic film; IBM: mainframe computers; GE (General Electric): generators. GE₂: electrical appliances (refrigerators); GM: passenger cars. Boeing: commercial widebody jet aircraft; RCA: color TVs; Goodyear: OEM tires; U.S. Steel: finished steel; International Harvester: farm tractors; Sears: mass-market retailing.

These factors fostered competitive stability—abundantly the case in automotive manufacturing and consumer electronics. That is not to say that some industries, such as steel, had not begun to encounter competitive pressures. But relatively speaking, from the post-war period through the mid-sixties, a strategic enclave, once established was defended with comparative ease.

The arts of war have been forever at the mercy of changing armaments; technology changes faster than beliefs. Each leap—from arrow to rifle to infrared seeking missile—renders an era of military knowledge obsolete and imposes a painful reexamination and transition. Military science is the kin of managerial science. The stable industrial world culminating in the sixties was accompanied by a body of

TABLE 1. *Dramatic Changes Over Two Decades Undermine Secure Market Position*

	Environmental Shifts	
	From (1960s)	To (1980s)
Growth rates	• Rapid growth in most industries with room for most serious competitors	• Slowed growth or stagnation squeezing incremental growth out of competition
Nature of competition	• Oligopolistic competitors in most industries	• Encroachment of international rivals
	• Primary focus on domestic markets and competitors	• Focus on international competition
		• Domestic scale economies finance penetration pricing in overseas markets
	• Implicit "rules" shared by domestic competitors foster stability	• New competitors each playing by different rules (e.g., niche vs. scale strategies) force continued innovation, price cutting, quality improvements all resulting in competitive instability
Expressions of nationalism	• National status dependent on military, technological leadership and level of involvement in international diplomatic dialogue	• The "new mercantilism"
		• International status and domestic prosperity linked to trade expansionism
	• Internal domestic focus	• Focus on international trade and economic linkages among trading partners
Economic environment	• Expansionistic, low interest rates	• Stable or contracting economic climate
	• Risk seeking investor climate	• High interest rates
	• Inflation	• Risk adverse investor climate in most industries
Technology	• Rapid technological changes with numerous products early in life cycle	• Slowed technological change in many industries
	• Patents serve to protect technological advantage with secure domestic	• Maturing products
		• Fierce international competitive surveillance and "reverse engineering" dilute patent protection and rapidly equalize technological advance
IMPLICATIONS	• Few secure enclaves	• Relative stability, security
	• Changing rules	
	• Intense competition from international rivals	

managerial beliefs which in the hindsight of the eighties, endowed us with the tactics of Gallipoli in a theater more akin to Vietnam.

The perceived nature of competition in the sixties made strategy the king of management functions. Conceptual rather than operational thinking prevailed, giving impetus to management consulting firms armed with matrices, experience curves, and other microeconomic paraphernalia. Business schools proliferated as did courses emphasizing the quantitative sciences in an era when success was secured via bold-stroke actions rather than nuance. Qualitative refinements in organizational process and operations management were frosting on the managerial cake. The danger, as our military analogue implies, is that such beliefs, once internalized, tend to persist beyond their time—even when environmental circumstances render them inappropriate.

In the late sixties, research at Harvard Business School exposed an industrial anomaly that has proven a precursor of our times.[33] The major home appliance industry (refrigerators, stoves, dishwashers, washers, and dryers) was revealed to defy the conventional wisdom of market behavior. Dominated by large oligopolistic competitors (Sears, General Electric, Westinghouse) the industry's most profitable participants were its smaller firms (such as Maytag). Whereas other oligopolistic markets fostered stability and protection for their dominant members, in this topsy-turvy industry, the large manufacturers (e.g., G.E.) were squeezed on one hand by continual price pressures from retailers (e.g., Sears) and on the other by the continuing technological innovation of smaller manufacturers (e.g., Tappan and Maytag). The consumer was the prime beneficiary: quality increased, technological innovation blossomed, and prices in real dollars remained steady or declined.

The explanation for this harsh competitive behavior lay in the asymmetry of the participants. Sears, a mass retailer, competed via price leadership; G.E., the manufacturer, competed on quality leadership, innovation parity, and required market share to support its production economies; smaller survivors lived by their technological wits and innovated in order to keep G.E. and Sears at bay. (By achieving sufficient product differentiation, they were able to justify higher margins.)

Enter the 1980s

We have read, ad nauseam, about the industrial climate of this decade, of the iron law of economic stagnation by which one firm's gain is via another's loss. We have read, too, of higher interest rates and more conservative investors. These are no doubt contributing factors. But in addition, slower technological change in many industries has been accompanied by intense competitive surveillance and rapid technological transfer. Particularly across international boundaries, patent protection is mitigated by reverse engineering and outright infringement. As a result, technology is rapidly equalized.

Another powerful, but often underemphasized, factor in these environmental shifts, is the increasing centrality of the "new mercantilism." National status and, indeed, a nation's domestic prosperity are linked directly to trade. Balance of payments, exchange rates, GNP growth, and unemployment are all inextricably intertwined. Heightened national self-interest has placed the spotlight on the success of each country's contestants in key industries. One firm's competitive response is thus linked to a coordinated national response—involving diplomatic exchanges, threats of trade sanctions, central bank behavior, and protective domestic pricing.

In aggregate, the forces depicted have drastically reshaped competitive activity. Most importantly, they have transformed a great many stable and secure domestic markets into battle zones that more closely resemble the major home appliance example cited earlier.

International competitors seem more prone to play by different rules. Some invest to achieve scale economies, some for quality leadership, others for price leadership, still others pursue a niche strategy stressing innovation. Under these circumstances, there is no impregnable strategic stance. As in the home appliance example, every participant, in order to survive, behaves in a way that destabilizes his counterparts. Innovators achieve a breakthrough, draw off customers, and start a share swing. To avoid losing share, the most cost efficient producer must follow, rendering his existing product and process technology obsolete. The low price strategy of still another player, content to follow in technology, creates a cost/price squeeze on the rest . . . forcing further innovation and the cycle repeats itself.

Survival for all but the most favored players requires a new competitive response and new organizational capabilities. For those remaining in the upper left-hand corner of Figure 1, defense of the status quo is sufficient. (IBM and Boeing, for example, seem to need to do no more than what they have always done.) For those with high share and weakening competitive advantage, the microeconomic concepts of scale efficiencies are highly applicable. (Insofar as price is *the* key success factor, being larger and reinvesting to sustain low price position assures continued success.) As long as a firm's position remains secure, much of what the old strategy model prescribes still obtains.

But for the vast majority of the firms charted in Figure 1, the shift is down scale, with weakening share position and weakening competitive advantage. For these firms, future success is more dependent on flexibility. In particular, three organizational factors become important:

· operational efficiency
· incremental product improvements, and
· the capacity to sense opportunity and execute an effective response.

For most of the firms in Figure 1, these are the key success factors for the eighties. Older, generalized ways of thinking about strategy must expand to adequately grapple with this new challenge.

PERSPECTIVE THREE: THE CASE FOR MULTIPLE PERSPECTIVES

The argument developed thus far is as follows: first, traditional biases favor analytical and microeconomic tools shaping corporate strategy. Secondly, strategy alone, even if more broadly defined, is not adequate to achieve the levels of innovation and responsiveness that competition in the eighties demands. This is not to assert that management thinking has been solely limited to formulations of strategy alone. In fact, if we pick up *Business Week, Forbes,* or *Fortune* the odds are high stories about efforts to change or turnaround will focus on not one but three "essentials": a new *strategy,* a *reorganization* to fit the strategy, and a new or rejuvenated *system* to track the factors meriting central attention.

We need a still broader framework. A 1972 study comparing a dozen Japanese subsidiaries in the United States with a dozen American counterparts produced a surprising finding: the Japanese firms had no monopoly on high productivity. In fact, a near-equal mix of Japanese and American firms shared these honors.[34] When the high performing firms (regardless of national ownership) were aggregated, they were found to share much in common. Most notably, they explicitly focused on more than strategy, structure, and systems:

· they paid conscious and concrete attention to management style and had devised ways of transforming style from the intangible realm of personality into a pragmatic instrument of executive direction;

- they did not relegate the hiring and socialization of new employees to a haphazard process governed by personnel departments: instead these firms shared amazing commonality in the step-by-step process through which they welded employees into a productive and committed workforce; and
- they paid attention to the firm's overarching value system, linking its relationship to employees, customer, and society as a whole.

In sum, in addition to 1) strategy, 2) structure, and 3) systems, the high performing firms paid equal attention to 4) style, 5) staff (i.e., their human resources), and 6) shared values. Their use of all *six* of these levers, and their ability to get them all to mesh together, contributed centrally to squeezing more out of their organizations in terms of innovations, responsiveness, and operational efficiency. Let us examine each dimension in sequence.

Perspective #1: Strategy

An earlier section has addressed the shortcomings of the narrowly defined microeconomic strategy model. The Japanese avoid this pitfall by adopting a broader notion of "strategy." In our recent awe of things Japanese, most Americans forget that the original products of the Japanese automotive manufacturers badly missed the mark. Toyota's Toyopet was square, sexless, and mechanically defective. It failed miserably, as did Datsun's first several entries into the U.S. market. More recently, Mazda miscalculated badly with its first rotary engine and nearly went bankrupt. Contrary to myth, the Japanese did not from the onset embark on a strategy to seize the high-quality small car market. They manufactured what they were accustomed to building in Japan and tried to sell it abroad. Their success, as any Japanese automotive executive will readily agree, did not re-

sult from a bold insight by a few big brains at the top. On the contrary, success was achieved by senior managers humble enough not to take their initial strategic positions too seriously. What saved Japan's near-failures was the cumulative impact of "little brains" in the form of salesmen and dealers and production workers, all contributing incrementally to the quality and market position these companies enjoy today. Middle and upper management saw their primary task as guiding and orchestrating this input from below rather than steering the organization from above along a predetermined strategic course.

The Japanese don't use the term "strategy" to describe a crisp business definition or competitive master plan. They think more in terms of "strategic accomodation," or "adaptive persistence," underscoring their belief that corporate direction evolves from an incremental adjustment to unfolding events. Rarely, in their view, does one leader (or a strategic planning group) produce a bold strategy that guides a firm unerringly. Far more frequently, the input is from below. It is this ability of an organization to move information and ideas from the bottom to the top and back again in continuous dialogue that the Japanese value above all things. As this dialogue is pursued, what in hindsight may be "strategy" evolves. In sum, "strategy" is defined as "all the things necessary for the successful functioning of organization as an adaptive mechanism." Skillful use of the other levers help make adaptation possible.

Perspective #2: Organizational Structure

For many American managers, reorganizing is the ultimate quick fix. Rearrange the boxes; never mind whether you change behavior inside the boxes.

There is no contention here that how one clusters various activities in an organization is unimportant to getting work done. The problem is, as with *any* of the other six factors taken in isolation, organizational structure is necessary but insufficient. The Coca-Cola Company spent the decades of the 1960s and 1970s in a continuous state of reorganization. The field force was decentralized, matrixed, recentralized. Pepsi-Cola steadily gained ground. Not until the eighties, under steadier guidance and with meticulous attention given to support *systems,* field management *style,* recruitment and training of *staff,* and *shared values,* did Coca-Cola begin to recapture its leadership against its major competitor.

Organizational fads, especially in rapid succession of one another, are a strong indicator of naiveté. No survey of American enterprise over the past two decades could fail to notice the succession of structural fads that have come and gone, each promoting itself as the optimum solution. There was functional organization, then the decentralization of the fifties and sixties, followed by the matrix format of the late sixties and seventies—organizational equivalents of a face-lift—and often just as cosmetic. These solutions almost always failed to live up to expectations. The boxes changed but most everything else stayed the same.

One's ability to get things done in corporations seldom depends upon one's job description and formal authority alone. A great part of one's efficacy stems from knowledge, proven track record, reputation and the trust and confidence of others. These factors are especially important at the *interfaces* between one's job and someone else's. No matter how well conceived an organization is structured, these interfaces between functions exist and successful managers build bridges across them with informal relationships. When a reorganization occurs it destroys these relationships. Not surprisingly, organizations then require six to eighteen months for its members to reestablish new interfaces. Frequent reorganizations are very traumatic as they continually disrupt

these essential networks before they become fully rooted.

Reorganization is like open heart surgery—sometimes it is necessary. But if a patient can contain a heart ailment through adequate rest, regular exercise, and by not smoking, it is preferable to the risks of the operating table. Organizations would do well to use other mechanisms to get their existing structure to work whenever possible—rather than resorting too quickly to a structural remedy.

The structural "lever" encounters a fatal flaw in that it imposes a two-dimensional way of thinking upon a phenomenon that cannot be captured in two dimensions. The givens of organizations are ambiguity, uncertainty, imperfection, and paradox. Structural remedies, by their unambiguous two-dimensional nature, impose a falsehood—organizational charts:

· suggest a clarity in reporting relationships that, in fact, retain significant elements of interpersonal *ambiguity;*
· announce finite changes that are, in fact, the outcome of an *uncertain* stream of events;
· suggest mechanistic linkages that deny systemic and interpersonal *imperfections;* and
· by the very act of representing *one* organizational solution (rather than another) deny an inherent *paradox*—that paradox being that today's solution to how one organizes, however appropriate, sows the seeds for the next generation of problems.

Structural solutions are simply not fine enough instruments in and of themselves to assure these delicate tradeoffs. To succeed, structure requires reinforcement from the other managerial factors.

Perspective #3: Systems
Systems pertain to such things as forms and computer printouts, to how information flows

up, down, and across the hierarchy of an organization. Systems to a large extent prescribe how communication occurs—and as a result, tend to configure how appropriately and quickly an organization can respond. Senior management can revise a strategy by a simple decree. Likewise, a structural reorganization is readily conceived and announced. But systems often remain unchanged. Stop to consider the forms we fill in, the reports we receive and promulgate, the incentive systems that reward us, and the procedures that guide us and regulate our lives. Systems condition us like mice in a maze; they gobble up an enormous portion of our discretionary energies. They are not chic, they are not pretty, they're not fast in how they work or how they change. (In fact, their maintenance in organizations is regarded as a low-status activity.) But systems insidiously and powerfully influence how people spend their lives at work each day.

"Hard copy" systems focus on things written in ink on paper—procedures that are written down, computer printouts, tables of numbers, forms, and so forth. In addition, all organizations have informal systems, that is, unwritten understandings that employees internalize about "how business gets done around here." Every organization has unwritten habits and routines. Two important ones are systems for conflict resolution and meeting formats. All organizations evolve rules about how one deals with conflict. In some organizations, it is dealt with openly and directly; in others it is handled in a roundabout way. Likewise, most organizations develop acceptable patterns for meetings. Informal rules provide guidelines as to who talks, who listens, whether presentations are formal monologues or informal dialogues, whether presenters use models and data with lots of analysis, whether they focus on the competition, market assumptions, or the bottom line. Informal systems also determine who gets mentored and the legitimate avenues for favoritism. Informal criteria are

usually the first to signal fast-track candidates. These largely unseen and unwritten rules account for a great deal.

The Japanese culture pays attention to informal systems. A great many of the most important rules are implicit. There are rituals for bowing and for who has to bow most deeply, for gift giving, and for eating. Japanese life, to a much greater extent than is true in the Western world, is regulated by these unwritten rituals. As a result, survival in Japanese society requires a certain degree of astuteness at perceiving these unwritten rules. This contributes to the ability of Japanese managers to read the unwritten rules of their organization as clearly as most Westerners can read a balance sheet. Not surprisingly, they expect the informal rules to mesh with the formal ones. In most American organizations, we are far less conscious of whether this meshing occurs and, as a result, many of our formal systems are undermined by the informal ones. In summary, fuller and more meticulous attention to both formal and informal systems is a precondition to improved organizational functioning.

Perspective #4: Style

A manager's style breathes life into strategy and systems. Regrettably, most readers equate style with certain personality traits. Once so defined, "style" is relegated to the idiosyncratic and intangible domain of psychology.

A most useful way of thinking about style is to equate it to how a manager allocates time and attention. Henry Mintzberg once researched the managerial span of attention.[36] The average length of time spent on any one thing is nine minutes. Management time is chaotic, fragmented, and filled with interruptions. This is the nature of managerial work. Nonetheless, from that chaos subordinates perceive a pattern, whether intended or not. Subordinates observe how bosses allocate their time, what issues really capture their attention, and from this they interpolate what the boss really cares about.

The three most powerful mechanisms for conveying time and attention messages are within an arm's length of where one sits each day. One of them is the in-basket, another is the telephone, and the third is one's calendar. What goes into the pending tray and yellows with age and what items get turned around immediately? What things get circled, and what comments are written in the margins? Is the "metamessage" of style—cost? quality? budget overruns? new product innovation? The people down the line read these messages with uncanny accuracy.

Consider the telephone. Who gets calls? Who doesn't? What question does the boss ask? What behavior is complimented? What draws criticisms, and what doesn't draw comments at all? What is the cumulative pattern that derives from the way the boss uses the phone?

Lastly the calendar. Who gets in, and who's screened out? When the boss is outside the office, where is he—with the controllers, customers, on the production line?

In aggregate, the calendar, the in-basket, and the telephone tells us a lot about one's style. "Style" defined as symbolic behavior provides every manager with a potent lever of influence and we need not transform our personalities to use it. The effective employment of this managerial lever results from nothing less or more than the self-discipline to allocate our time and attention to *do* what we *say* our priorities are.

Perspective #5: Staff

There is a set of consistent steps that organizations go through to develop a cadre of committed and productive employees. IBM and Procter & Gamble, each in very different ways, do this well. First of all, they target malleable applicants just beginning or very early in their careers. They invest in careful selection. They avoid overselling the candidate and hiding blemishes. They allow the applicant to see rather clearly what the firm is like, permitting applicants to deselect themselves. In addition, of course, the firm plays its part in screening out those who don't fit the mold.

Socialization process begins in the trenches. No employee skips this step. One needs to learn the territory via immersion in the basics of the industry. It's like the infantry: one has to learn to shoot a gun, dig a foxhole, and hit a target.

Next comes coherent, frequently spaced, and predictable rewards. IBM sets quotas that 80 percent of its sales force can reach, then provides detailed and frequent performance reviews to stretch each candidate beyond to reach his own potential. At IBM, almost everyone on the marketing side has to be able to sell computers and keep the customer happy; one doesn't get promoted otherwise, no matter how good one is at other things. Procter & Gamble establishes a six-rung performance ladder that every successful professional candidate is expected to climb within the first two years. The reward systems are unambiguous and generally unbeatable. This clarity and impartiality, it should be noted, derives from *systems* measures and incentives that are honed for simplicity. At P&G it's: What have you done for market share? What are you doing for profits? At IBM it's: What have you sold? Is the customer satisfied?

Nothing enforces reward systems as powerfully as social leverage. Every high performing firm in the sample had periodic get-togethers in which results were reviewed across one's peer group: The boss would start with one person, ask for his report or result and go around the circle. It creates a powerful incentive. The participant finding himself at the bottom one week is powerfully motivated to avoid that embarrassment the next.

We have noted that socialization is

sparked by a shared boot camp experience among a cadre of carefully selected young employees. It is strengthened by the social level of peer comparisons and group norms and reinforced by reward systems that establish unequivocal standards of performance. Yet a fourth support derives from reinforcing folklore. Every organization has a folklore about watershed events or actions. Odds are high, if we listen carefully, that employees can summarize in one or two pithy sentences the essence of what they interpret the folklore to be. When the moral of the stories are inconsistent with what management is striving to achieve, folklore breeds cynicism and a wait-and-see attitude. Folklore acts as a guiding theory of how the firm really works. As such, it powerfully influences how employees respond to management's initiatives.

Last among the determinants of a coherent and committed staff is the availability of consistent role models. There is no more powerful way for instructing younger members of an organization than role models who present a consistent picture of what a person needs to be like to be a winner. Amazingly, many organizations leave role models to chance. The result is a mixed and confusing picture: one promotion seems related to people skills; another seems to underscore office politics; still another honors a reclusive financial wizard. There is no clear pattern. No training program in existence can instruct more powerfully than consistent role models.

Effective socialization requires consistency and meticulous attention to all the ingredients we have discussed. When managed carefully, it promotes behavioral congruence and cohesiveness. For some, this smacks of an Orwellian nightmare. For others it is ho-hum common sense. Nonetheless, most organizations do it very badly, and our outstanding organizations tend to do it well.

The socialization process described is found in most self-sustaining Japanese, American, and European companies. Its primary dividend is the coherence it provides about "how we do business around here." As such, it greatly enhances the strategic process by facilitating the dialogue up and down the hierarchy. Senior managers who shared the same socialization process and common career experiences as those in the field, can communicate with the field in a kind of shorthand. Remember: organizational responsiveness relies on effective communication with minimum politics and the minimal friction loss resulting from conflicting agendas. A meticulous socialization process directly serves this objective.

Perspective #6: Shared Values[37]

Shared values refer to the overarching value system that ties the purposes of the corporation to the customer, society, and higher order human values. They do not pertain to economic goals such as profit, sales, R.O.I., or market share. For example, IBM's Thomas Watson once stated: "We must be prepared to change all the things we are in order to remain competitive in the environment, but we must never change our three basic beliefs: 1) Respect for the dignity of the individual, 2) Offering the best customer service in the world, and 3) Excellence." In a similar vein, AT&T's value system has for ninety years emphasized 1) "Universal" service, 2) Fairness in handling personnel matters, 3) A belief that work should be held in balance with commitments to one's family and community, and 4) Relationships (i.e., from one manager to another). These four factors are deemed essential in getting things done in a large highly structured company. What makes IBM's or AT&T's value systems so important is that they are not empty slogans. They are deeply internalized. It is hard to talk to an employee of one of these organizations at any length before they surface in one way or another.

What does a strong set of shared values

accomplish? It provides a kind of "magnetic north" for an organization which keeps it true to its commitments to employees, the customer, and society. The problem with secular economic values is that their ends often justify inappropriate means: in order to achieve sales or R.O.I. objectives an executive may cut corners on customer service or treat employees in a capricious manner. Having a "magnetic north" helps define the permissible range of behavior in such circumstances. It acts as a kind of a "tie breaker," assisting an employee in making a close call, tilting him or her in the direction that the boss would want taken even though the boss isn't there to personally guide the decision.

Employment involves a social contract as well as a contract prescribing the exchange of labor for capital. In many Western organizations, that contract, while never explicit, often assumes little trust by either party in the other. If the only basis for the relation of company and employee is an instrumental one, it should not be surprising that many people in our organizations do what they must do to get their paycheck but little more. Shared values that concern themselves with the development and well-being of employees establish the moral context for this social contract. If such shared values are consistently honored, then employees tend to identify more fully with the company. They see the firm's interest and their own as more congruent and tend to invest themselves more fully in the organization.

Most consultants will confirm that they have been called in to solve a client's problem only to discover in the course of conducting interviews that someone in the client organization already had the solution. But because communication channels were blocked, or, more often, because the individual with the good idea was "turned off" and convinced that the organization wouldn't listen, no initiative was taken. The potential initiator hesitated to invest himself, in the last analysis, because trying is linked

to caring, and history had taught him that the firm was not worth caring that much about. We begin to see here the direct connection between shared values and an organization's ability to tap into the "little brains."

Without a doubt, the most significant outcome of the way Japanese organizations manage themselves is that they are better at getting employees to be alert, to look for opportunities to do things better, and to strive by virtue of each small contribution to make the company succeed. It is like building a pyramid or watching a colony of ants: thousands of "little people" doing "little" things, *all with the same basic purpose,* can move mountains.

A recent study of product innovation in the scientific instruments and tool machinery industries indicates that 80 percent of all product innovations are initiated by the customer.[38] The majority of ideas doesn't flow from R&D labs down but from the customer up. To be sure, customers don't do the actual inventing, but their inquiries and complaints plant the seeds for improvements. Given these statistics, it matters a lot whether a company's sales force and others operating out at the tentacles of its field system are vigilant. They need to be open to new ideas *and* willing to initiate within their organization. Here is a key to success of many Japanese companies. We saw this occurring at American Honda. Staying alert and taking entrepreneurial initiative were major tenets of the Honda value system. The Japanese executives at American Honda could count on the fact that if they "erred" in these directions, they were acting as top management would want them to.

To be sure, the case for shared values can be overstated. Self-sustaining firms tend to have a *style* of management that is open to new ideas, ways of handling *staff* that encourage innovation, *systems* that are customer focused and that reward innovation, *skills* at translating ideas into action and so forth. But the ideas don't flow unless the employee *believes* in the corporation and identifies enough with its purposes to "give up" his good ideas. Further, any of us who work in organizations knows how hard they are to move. One has to *really* believe an organization *cares* in order to invest the energy and effort needed to help it change. Such commitment derives from shared values. And if we look at outstanding American firms that have a sustained track record of keeping up with or ahead of competition, we see this to be the case. Hewlett-Packard, Procter & Gamble, 3M, Boeing, Caterpillar are examples. Each has a highly developed value system that causes its employees to identify strongly with the firm. Perhaps the intense loyalty that these firms inspire is just an interesting idiosyncrasy. I believe, on the contrary, that this bond of shared values is fundamental to all of the rest. It is probably the most underpublicized "secret weapon" of great self-sustaining companies.

CONCLUSION

The intent of the "strategy model" has always been to assess the relationship of a firm with its environment, and identify the key elements of the managerial mix that are relevant to an effective organizational response. Given this charter to view the firm and its environment as an organic whole, our challenge is to develop a more adequate model. The central contention of this paper is that six dimensions are better than one or two or even three. Strategy, structure, and systems are not enough.

A multiple perspective disciplines us against the cognitive and perceptual biases that produce the "Honda Effect." It keeps us honest by drawing us into the interior of organization, forcing us to focus on the fine grain details that drive an effective strategic process. So doing, we learn how each of the S dimensions goes back in history—how the *strategies* that have been attempted, the firm's history of *reorganizations*, the *systems* that have been layered one upon another, the different *styles* of former leaders, and so forth—how each contributes to the legacy of what the firm is today and what stands in the way of moving it forward. Finally, attention to multiple dimensions causes us to grapple with the interdependence of each— that neither strategy nor structure nor any of the factors stands alone. Change efforts that shift only one or two of the factors and leave the remainder alone almost always fail. Only when we move on the multiple fronts across all six factors do we achieve lasting change. This has powerful implications for diagnosis and for practice.

REFERENCES

1. Joseph L. Bower, *Managing the Resource Allocation Process,* Division of Research, Graduate School of Business Administration, Harvard University, Cambridge, Massachusetts, 1970, pp. 7–8.
2. A recent set of articles have begun to address this problem. See R. H. Hayes and W. J. Abernathy, "Managing Our Way to Economic Decline," *Harvard Business Review* (July/August 1980), p. 67; see also R. H. Hayes, and J. G. Garvin, "Managing As If Tomorrow Mattered," *Harvard Business Review* (May/June 1982), p. 71.
3. Boston Consulting Group, *Strategy Alternatives for the British Motorcycle Industry,* Her Majesty's Stationary Office, London, 30 July 1975, p. XIV.
4. D. Purkayastha, "Note on the Motorcycle Industry—1975," 9-578-210, Harvard Business School, Cambridge, Massachusetts, Rev. 1/81, p. 5, 10, 11, 12.
5. Boston Consulting Group, *Strategy Alternatives,* p. 59; also p. 40.
6. Tetsuo Sakiya, *Honda Motor: The Men, The Management, The Machines* (Tokyo, Japan: Kadonsha International, 1982), p. 119.
7. Richard P. Rumelt, "A Teaching Plan for *Strategy Alternatives for the British Motorcycle Industry,"*

Japanese Business: Business Policy. The Japan Society, New York, NY (1980), p. 2.

8. Anon. *Honda: A Statistical View,* Overseas Public Relations Department of Honda Motor Co., Ltd., Tokyo, Japan (1982), p. 11.

9. Tetsuo Sakiya, "The Story of Honda's Founders," *Asahi Evening News,* June 1–August 29, 1979, Series #19, Series #12; also Series #10, Series #2 and 3.

10. Interviews with Honda executives, Tokyo, Japan, July 1980.

11. Sakiya, *Honda Motor,* p. 69; also Sakiya, "Honda's Founders," Series #4.

12. Sakiya, "Honda's Founders," Series #7 and 8.

13. Sakiya, *Honda Motor,* p. 72.

14. Sakiya, "Honda's Founders," Series #2.

15. Sakiya, *Honda Motor,* pp. 65–69; Sakiya, "Honda's Founders," Series #6.

16. Sakiya, *Honda Motor,* p. 73.

17. Ibid, pp. 71–72.

18. Ibid, p. 71.

19. Data provided by Honda Motor Company, Tokyo, Japan, September 10–12, 1982.

20. Sakiya, "Honda's Founders," Series #11.

21. Ibid, Series #13; also Sakiya, *Honda Motor,* p. 117.

22. Sakiya, "Honda's Founders," Series #11.

23. Richard T. Pascale, Interviews with Honda executives, Tokyo, Japan, September 10, 1982.

24. Ibid.

25. Data provided by Honda Motor Company.

26. Pascale interviews.

27. Ibid.

28. Ibid.

29. Ibid.

30. Ibid.

31. Ibid.

32. The U.S. Federal Reserve Board's "Index of Industrial Production," based on 235 different data series, registered a 15.6% increase (from 66.2 to 76.5) from 1960 to 1963 compared with a 9.1% decrease (from 152.5 to 138.6) from 1979 to 1982.

33. Michael Hunt, "Strategy in the Electric Appliance Industry" (Unpublished Ph.D. dissertation, Harvard Graduate School of Business Administration, Cambridge, Massachusetts, 1971). Also see Michael Hunt, "Teaching Note on the Home Appliance Series," Harvard Graduate School of Business Administration, Cambridge, Massachusetts, 1971.

34. Richard T. Pascale, and A. G. Athos, *The Art of Japanese Management* (New York, NY: Simon & Schuster, 1981).

35. Development of the managerial implications of structure, systems, style, and staff draw heavily on the ideas of Thomas J. Peters. Also see R. H. Waterman, T. J. Peters, and J. R. Phillips, "Structure Is Not Organization," *Business Horizons,* No. 80302 (June 1980).

36. Henry Mintzberg, *The Nature of Managerial Work* (New York, NY: Harper & Row, 1973).

37. Much of this material on shared values is built upon the ideas of Anthony G. Athos. See Pascale and Athos, *The Art of Japanese Management.*

38. Eric von Hippel, "Users as Innovators, *Technology Review* (January 1978) pp. 31–39.

3

ORGANIZATION, CONGRUENCE, AND EFFECTIVENESS

A Model for Diagnosing Organizational Behavior: Applying a Congruence Perspective

David A. Nadler

Michael L. Tushman

Managers must continually identify and find solutions to problems caused by mismatched components within the organization. A unique approach that will help managers perform this vital function is offered.

Management's primary job is to make organizations operate effectively. Society's work gets done through organizations and management's function is to get organizations to perform that work. Getting organizations to operate effectively is difficult, however. Understanding one individual's behavior is challenging in and of itself; understanding a group that's made up of different individuals and comprehending the many relationships among those individuals is even more complex. Imagine, then, the mind-boggling complexity of a large organization made up of thousands of individuals and hundreds of groups with myriad relationships among these individuals and groups.

But organizational behavior must be managed in spite of this overwhelming complexity; ultimately the organization's work gets done through people, individually or collectively, on their own or in collaboration with technology. Therefore, the management of organizational behavior is central to the management task—a task that involves the capacity to *understand* the behavior patterns of individuals, groups, and organizations, to *predict* what behavioral responses will be elicited by various managerial actions, and finally to use this un-

Reprinted, by permission of the publisher, from *Organizational Dynamics* (Autumn 1980). © 1980 American Management Association, New York. All rights reserved.

derstanding and these predictions to achieve *control.*

How can one achieve understanding and learn how to predict and control organizational behavior? Given its inherent complexity and enigmatic nature, one needs tools to unravel the mysteries, paradoxes, and apparent contradictions that present themselves in the everyday life of organizations. One tool is the conceptual framework or model. A model is a theory that indicates which factors (in an organization, for example) are most critical or important. It also shows how these factors are related—that is, which factors or combination of factors cause other factors to change. In a sense then, a model is a roadmap that can be used to make sense of the terrain of organizational behavior.

The models we use are critical because they guide our analysis and action. In any organizational situation, problem solving involves the collection of information about the problem, the interpretation of that information to determine specific problem types and causes, and the development of action plans accordingly. The models that individuals use influence the kind of data they collect and the kind they ignore; models guide people's approach to analyzing or interpreting the data they have; finally, models help people choose their course of action.

Indeed, anyone who has been exposed to an organization already has some sort of implicit model. People develop these roadmaps over time, building on their own experiences. These implicit models (they usually are not explicitly written down or stated) guide behavior; they vary in quality, validity, and sophistication depending on the nature and extent of the experiences of the model builder, his or her perceptiveness, his or her ability to conceptualize and generalize from experiences, and so on.

We are not solely dependent, however, on the implicit and experience-based models that individuals develop. Since there has been extensive research and theory development on the subject of organizational behavior over the last four decades, it is possible to use scientifically developed explicit models for analyzing organizational behavior and solving organizational problems.

We plan to discuss one particular model, a general model of organizations. Instead of describing a specific phenomenon or aspect of organizational life (such as a model of motivation or a model of organizational design), the general model of organization attempts to provide a framework for thinking about the organization as a total system. The model's major premise is that for organizations to be effective, their subparts or components must be consistently structured and managed—they must approach a state of congruence.

In the first section of this article, we will discuss the basic view of organizations that underlies the model—that is, systems theory. In the second section, we will present and discuss the model itself. In the third section, we will present an approach to using the model for organizational problem analysis. Finally, we will discuss some of the model's implications for thinking about organizations.

A BASIC VIEW OF ORGANIZATIONS

There are many different ways of thinking about organizations. When a manager is asked to "draw a picture of an organization," he or she typically draws some version of a pyramidal organizational chart. This is a model that views the stable, formal relationships among the jobs and formal work units as the most critical factors of the organization. Although this clearly is one way to think about organizations, it is a very limited view. It excludes such factors as leadership behavior, the impact of the environment, informal relations, power distribution, and so on. Such a model can capture only a small part of what goes on in organizations. Its perspective is narrow and static.

The past two decades have seen a growing consensus that a viable alternative to the static classic models of organizations is to envision the organization as a social system. This approach stems from the observation that social phenomena display many of the characteristics of natural or mechanical systems. In particular, as Daniel Katz and Robert L. Kahn have argued, organizations can be better understood if they are considered as dynamic and open social systems.

What is a system? Most simply, a system is a set of interrelated elements—that is, a change in one element affects other elements. An *open system* is one that interacts with its environment; it is more than just a set of interrelated elements. Rather, these elements make up a mechanism that takes input from the environment, subjects it to some form of transformation process, and produces output. At the most general level, it should be easy to visualize organizations as systems. Let's consider a manufacturing plant, for example. It is made up of different related components (a number of departments, jobs, technologies, and so on). It receives inputs from the environment—that is, labor, raw material, production orders, and so on—and transforms these inputs into products.

As systems, organizations display a number of basic systems' characteristics. Some of the most critical are these:

- *Internal interdependence.* Changes in one component or subpart of an organization frequently have repercussions for other parts; the pieces are interconnected. Again, as in the manufacturing plant example, changes made in one element (for example, the skill levels of those hired to do jobs) will affect other elements (the productiveness of equipment used, the speed or quality of production activities, the nature of supervision needed, and so on).

- *Capacity for feedback*—that is, information about the output that can be used to control the system. Organizations can correct errors and even change themselves because of this characteristic. If in our plant example plant management receives information that the quality of its product is declining, it can use this information to identify factors in the system itself that contribute to this problem. However, it is important to note that, unlike mechanized systems, feedback information does not always lead to correction. Organizations have the potential to use feedback to become self-correcting systems, but they do not always realize this potential.

- *Equilibrium*—that is, a state of balance. When an event puts the system out of balance the system reacts and moves to bring itself back into balance. If one work group in our plant example were suddenly to increase its performance dramatically, it would throw the system out of balance. This group would be making increasing demands on the groups that supply it with the information or materials it needs; groups that work with the high-performing group's output would feel the pressure of work-in-process inventory piling up in front of them. If some type of incentive is in effect, other groups might perceive inequity as this one group begins to earn more. We would predict that some actions would be taken to put the system back into balance. Either the rest of the plant would be changed to increase production and thus be back in balance with the single group, or (more likely) there would be pressure to get this group to modify its behavior in line with the performance levels of the rest of the system (by removing workers, limiting supplies, and so on). The point is that somehow the system would develop energy to move back toward a state of equilibrium or balance.

· *Equifinality.* This characteristic of open systems means that different system configurations can lead to the same end or to the same type of input-output conversion. Thus there's no universal or "one best way" to organize.

· *Adaptation.* For a system to survive, it must maintain a favorable balance of input or output transactions with the environment or it will run down. If our plant produces a product for which there are fewer applications, it must adapt to new demands and develop new products; otherwise, the plant will ultimately have to close its doors. Any system, therefore, must adapt by changing as environmental conditions change. The consequences of not adapting are evident when once-prosperous organizations decay (for example, the eastern railroads) because they fail to respond to environmental changes.

Thus systems theory provides a way of thinking about the organization in more complex and dynamic terms. But although the theory provides a valuable basic perspective on organizations, it is limited as a problem-solving tool. This is because a model systems theory is too abstract for use in day-to-day analysis of organizational behavior problems. Because of the level of abstraction of systems theory, we need to develop a more specific and pragmatic model based on the concepts of the open systems paradigm.

A CONGRUENCE MODEL OF ORGANIZATIONAL BEHAVIOR

Given the level of abstraction of open theory, our job is to develop a model that reflects the basic systems concepts and characteristics, but that is more specific and thus more usable as an analytic tool. We will describe a model that specifies the critical inputs, the major outputs, and the transformation processes that characterize organizational functioning.

The model puts its greatest emphasis on the transformation process and specifically reflects the critical system property of interdependence. It views organizations as made up of components or parts that interact with each other. These components exist in states of relative balance, consistency, or "fit" with each other. The different parts of an organization can fit well together and function effectively, or fit poorly and lead to problems, dysfunctions, or performance below potential. Our *congruence model of organizational behavior* is based on how well components fit together—that is, the congruence among the components; the effectiveness of this model is based on the quality of these "fits" or congruence.

The concept of congruence is not a new one. George Homans in his pioneering work on social processes in organizations emphasized the interaction and consistency among key elements of organizational behavior. Harold Leavitt, for example, identified four major components of organization as being people, tasks, technology, and structure. The model we will present here builds on these views and also draws from fit models developed and used by James Seiler, Paul Lawrence and Jay Lorsch, and Jay Lorsch and Alan Sheldon.

It is important to remember that we are concerned about creating a model for *behavioral* systems of the organization—the system of elements that ultimately produce behavior patterns and, in turn, organizational performance. Put simply, we need to deal with questions of the inputs the system has to work with, the outputs it must produce, the major components of the transformation process, and the ways in which these components interact.

Inputs

Inputs are factors that, at any one point in time, make up the "givens" facing the organization. They're the material that the organization has to work with. There are several different types of inputs, each of which presents a different set of "givens" to the organization (see Figure 1 for an overview of inputs).

The first input is the *environment,* or all factors outside the organization being examined. Every organization exists within the context of a larger environment that includes individuals, groups, other organizations, and even larger social forces—all of which have a potentially powerful impact on how the organization performs. Specifically, the environment includes markets (clients or customers), suppliers, governmental and regulatory bodies, labor unions, competitors, financial institutions, special interest groups, and so on. As research by Jeffrey Pfeffer and Gerald Salancik has suggested, the environment is critical to organizational functioning.

The environment has three critical features that affect organizational analysis. First, the environment makes demands on the organization. For example, it may require certain products or services at certain levels of quality or quantity. Market pressures are particularly important here. Second, the environment may place constraints on organizational action. It may limit the activities in which an organization may engage. These constraints range from limitations imposed by scarce capital to prohibitions set by government regulations. Third, the environment provides opportunities that the organization can explore. When we analyze an organization, we need to consider the factors in the organization's environment and determine how those factors, singly or collectively, create demands, constraints, or opportunities.

The second input is the organization's *resources.* Any organization has a range of different assets to which it has access. These include employees, technology, capital, information, and so on. Resources can also include less tangible assets, such as the perception of the organization in the marketplace or a positive organizational climate. A set of resources can be shaped, deployed, or configured in different ways by an organization. For analysis purposes, two features are of primary interest. One concerns the relative quality of those resources or their value in light of the environment. The second concerns the extent to which resources can be reshaped or how fixed or flexible different resources are.

The third input is the organization's *history.* There's growing evidence that the way organizations function today is greatly influenced by past events. It is particularly important to understand the major stages or phases of an organization's development over a period of time, as well as the current impact of past events—for example, key strategic decisions, the acts or behavior of key leaders, the nature of past crises and the organization's responses to them, and the evolution of core values and norms of the organization.

The final input is somewhat different from the others because in some ways it reflects some of the factors in the organization's environment, resources, and history. The fourth input is *strategy.* We use this term in its broadest context to describe the whole set of decisions that are made about how the organization will configure its resources against the demands, constraints, and opportunities of the environment within the context of its history. Strategy refers to the issue of matching the organization's resources to its environment, or making the fundamental decision of "What business are we in?" For analysis purposes, several aspects of strategy are important to identify. First, what is the core mission of the organization, or how has the organization defined its basic purpose or function within the larger system or

Input	Environment	Resources	History	Strategy
Definition	All factors, including institutions, groups, individuals, events, and so on, that are outside the organization being analyzed, but that have a potential impact on that organization.	Various assets to which the organization has access, including human resources, technology, capital, information, and so on, as well as less tangible resources (recognition in the market, and so forth).	The patterns of past behavior, activity, and effectiveness of the organization that may affect current organizational functioning.	The stream of decisions about how organizational resources will be configured to meet the demands, constraints, and opportunities within the context of the organization's history.
Critical Features for Analysis	1. What demands does the environment make on the organization? 2. How does the environment put constraints on organizational action?	1. What is the relative quality of the different resources to which the organization has access? 2. To what extent are resources fixed rather than flexible in their configuration(s)?	1. What have been the major stages or phases of the organization's development? 2. What is the current impact of such historical factors as strategic decisions, acts of key leaders, crises, and core values and norms?	1. How has the organization defined its core mission, including the markets it serves and the products/services it provides to these markets? 2. On what basis does it compete? 3. What supporting strategies has the organization employed to achieve the core mission? 4. What specific objectives have been set for organizational output?

FIGURE 1.   Key Organizational Inputs

environment? The core mission includes decisions about what markets the organization will serve, what products or services it will provide to those markets, and how it will compete in those markets. Second, strategy includes the specific supporting strategies (or tactics) the organization will employ or is employing to achieve its core mission. Third, it includes the specific performance or output objectives that have been established.

Strategy may be the most important single input for the organization. On one hand, strategic decisions implicitly determine the nature of the work the organization should be doing or the tasks it should perform. On the other hand, strategic decisions, and particularly decisions about objectives determine the system's desired outputs.

In summary, there are three basic inputs—environment, resources, and history—and a fourth derivative input, strategy, which determines how the organization responds to or deals with the basic inputs. Strategy is critical because it determines the work to be performed by the organization and it defines desired organizational outputs.

Outputs

Outputs are what the organization produces, how it performs, and how effective it is. There has been a lot of discussion about the components of an effective organization. For our purposes, however, it is possible to identify several key indicators of organizational output. First, we need to think about system output at different levels. In addition to the system's basic output—that is, the product—we need to think about other outputs that contribute to organizational performance, such as the functioning of groups or units within the organization or the functioning of individual organization members.

At the organizational level, three factors must be kept in mind when evaluating organizational performance: (1) goal attainment, or how well the organization meets its objectives (usually determined by strategy), (2) resource utilization, or how well the organization makes use of available resources (not just whether the organization meets its goals, but whether it realizes all of its potential performance and whether it achieves its goals by building resources or by "burning them up"), and (3) adaptability, or whether the organization continues to position itself in a favorable position vis-à-vis its environment—that is, whether it is capable of changing and adapting to environmental changes.

Obviously, the functioning of groups or units (departments, divisions, or other subunits within the organization) contribute to these organizational-level outputs. Organizational output is also influenced by individual behavior, and certain individual-level outputs (affective reactions such as satisfaction, stress, or experienced quality of working life) may be desired outputs in and of themselves.

The Organization as a Transformation Process

So far, we've defined the nature of inputs and outputs of the organizational system. This leads us to the transformation process. Given an environment, a set of resources, and history, "How do I take a strategy and implement it to produce effective performance in the organization, in the group/unit, and among individual employees?"

In our framework, the organization and its major component parts are the fundamental means for transforming energy and information from inputs into outputs. On this basis, we must determine the key components of the organization and the critical dynamic that shows how those components interact to perform the transformation function.

Organizational Components

There are many different ways of thinking about what makes up an organization. At this point in the development of a science of organizations, we probably do not know the one right or best way to describe the different components of an organization. The task is to find useful approaches for describing organizations, for simplifying complex phenomena, and for identifying patterns in what may at first blush seem to be random sets of activity. Our particular approach views organizations as composed of four major components: (1) the task, (2) the individuals, (3) the formal organizational arrangements, and (4) the informal organization. We will discuss each of these individually (see Figure 2 for overviews of these components).

The first component is the organization's *task*—that is, the basic or inherent work to be done by the organization and its subunits or the activity the organization is engaged in, particularly in light of its strategy. The emphasis is on the specific work activities or functions that need to be done and their inherent characteristics (as opposed to characteristics of the work created by how the work is organized or

Component	Task	Individual	Formal Organizational Arrangements	Informal Organization
Definition	The basic and inherent work to be done by the organization and its parts.	The characteristics of individuals in the organization.	The various structures, processes, methods, and so on that are formally created to get individuals to perform tasks.	The emerging arrangements, including structures, processes, relationships, and so forth.
Critical Features for Analysis	1. The types of skill and knowledge demands the work poses. 2. The types of rewards the work can provide. 3. The degree of uncertainty associated with the work, including such factors as interdependence, routineness, and so on. 4. The constraints on performance demands inherent in the work (given a strategy).	1. Knowledge and skills individuals have. 2. Individual needs and preferences. 3. Perceptions and expectancies. 4. Background factors.	1. Organization design, including grouping of functions, structure of subunits, and coordination and control mechanisms. 2. Job design. 3. Work environment. 4. Human resource management systems.	1. Leader behavior. 2. Intragroup relations. 3. Intergroup relations. 4. Informal working arrangements. 5. Communication and influence patterns.

FIGURE 2.   *Key Organizational Components*

structured in this particular organization at this particular time). Analysis of the task would include a description of the basic work flows and functions with attention to the characteristics of those work flows—for example, the knowledge or skills demanded by the work, the kinds of rewards provided by the work, the degree of uncertainty associated with the work, and the specific constraints inherent in the work (such as critical time demands, cost constraints, and so on). Since it's assumed that a primary (although not the only) reason for the organization's existence is to perform the task consistent with strategy, the task is the starting point for the analysis. As we will see, the assessment of the adequacy of other components depends to a large degree on an understanding of the nature of the tasks to be performed.

A second component of organizations involves the *individuals* who perform organizational tasks. The issue here is identifying the nature and characteristics of the organization's employees (or members). The most critical aspects to consider include the nature of individual knowledge and skills, the different needs or preferences that individuals have, the perceptions or expectancies that they develop, and other background factors (such as demographics) that may potentially influence individual behavior.

The third component is the *formal organizational arrangements*. These include the range of structures, processes, methods, procedures, and so forth that are explicitly and formally developed to get individuals to perform tasks consistent with organizational strategy. The broad term, organizational arrangements, encompasses a number of different factors. One factor is organization design—that is, the way jobs are grouped together into units, the internal structure of those units, and the coordination and control mechanisms used to link those units together. A second factor is the way jobs are designed within the context of organizational designs. A third factor is the work envi-

ronment, which includes a number of factors that characterize the immediate environment in which work is done, such as the physical working environment, the available work resources, and so on. A final factor includes the organization's formal systems for attracting, placing, developing, and evaluating human resources.

Together, these factors create the set of formal organizational arrangements—that is, they are explicitly designed and specified, usually in writing.

The final component is the *informal organization*. Despite the set of formal organizational arrangements that exists in any organization, another set of arrangements tends to develop or emerge over a period of time. These arrangements are usually implicit and unwritten, but they influence a good deal of behavior. For lack of a better term, such arrangements are frequently referred to as the informal organization and they include the different structures, processes, and arrangements that emerge while the organization is operating. These arrangements sometimes complement formal organizational arrangements by providing structures to aid work where none exist. In other situations they may arise in reaction to the formal structure, to protect individuals from it. They may therefore either aid or hinder the organization's performance.

Because a number of aspects of the informal organization have a particularly critical effect on behavior, they need to be considered. The behavior of leaders (as opposed to the formal creation of leader positions) is an important feature of the informal organization, as are the patterns of relationships that develop both within and between groups. In addition, different types of informal working arrangements (including rules, procedures, methods, and so on) develop. Finally, there are the various communication and influence patterns that combine to create the informal organization design.

Organizations can therefore be thought of as a set of components—the task, the individuals, the organizational arrangements, and the informal organization. In any system, however, the critical question is not what the components are, but what the nature of their interaction is. This model raises the question: What are the dynamics of the relationships among the components? To deal with this issue, we must return to the concept of congruence or fit.

The Concept of Congruence

A relative degree of congruence, consistency, or "fit" exists between each pair of organizational inputs. The congruence between two components is defined as "the degree to which the needs, demands, goals, objectives, and/or structures of one component are consistent with the needs, demands, goals, objectives, and/or structures of another component."

Congruence, therefore, is a measure of how well pairs of components fit together. Consider, for example, two components—the task

and the individual. At the simplest level, the task presents some demands on individuals who would perform it (that is, skill/knowledge demands). At the same time, the set of individuals available to do the tasks have certain characteristics (their levels of skill and knowledge). Obviously, if the individual's knowledge and skill match the knowledge and skill demanded by the task, performance will be more effective.

Obviously, too, the individual-task congruence relationship encompasses more factors than just knowledge and skill. Similarly, each congruence relationship in the model has its own specific characteristics. Research and theory can guide the assessment of fit in each relationship. For an overview of the critical elements of each congruence relationship, see Figure 3.

The Congruence Hypothesis

The aggregate model, or whole organization, displays a relatively high or low degree of sys-

Fit	Issues
Individual/Organization	How are individual needs met by the organizational arrangements? Do individuals hold clear or distorted perceptions of organizational structures? Is there a convergence of individual and organizational goals?
Individual/Task	How are individual needs met by the tasks? Do individuals have skills and abilities to meet task demands?
Individual/Informal organization	How are individual needs met by the informal organization? How does the informal organization make use of individual resources consistent with informal goals?
Task/Organization	Are organizational arrangements adequate to meet the demands of the task? Do organizational arrangements motivate behavior that's consistent with task demands?
Task/Informal organization	Does the informal organization structure facilitate task performance or not? Does it hinder or help meet the demands of the task?
Organization/Informal organization	Are the goals, rewards, and structures of the informal organization consistent with those of the formal organization?

FIGURE 3.   *Definitions of Fits*

tem congruence in the same way that each pair of components has a high or low degree of congruence. The basic hypothesis of the model, which builds on this total state of congruence, is as follows: "Other things being equal, the greater the total degree of congruence or fit between the various components, the more effective will be the organization—effectiveness being defined as the degree to which actual organization outputs at individual, group, and organizational levels are similar to expected outputs, as specified by strategy."

The basic dynamic of congruence sees the organization as most effective when its pieces fit together. If we also consider strategy, this view expands to include the fit between the organization and its larger environment—that is, an organization is most effective when its strategy is consistent with its environment (in light of organizational resources and history) and when the organizational components are congruent with the tasks necessary to implement that strategy.

One important implication of the congruence hypothesis is that organizational problem analysis (or diagnosis) involves description of the system, identification of problems, and analysis of fits to determine the causes of problems. The model also implies that different configurations of the key components can be used to gain outputs (consistent with the systems characteristic of equifinality). Therefore the question is not how to find the "one best way" of managing, but how to find effective combinations of components that will lead to congruent fits among them.

The process of diagnosing fits and identifying combinations of components to produce congruence is not necessarily intuitive. A number of situations that lead to congruence have been defined in the research literature. Thus in many cases fit is something that can be defined, measured, and even quantified; there is, in other words, an empirical and theoretical basis

for assessing fit. The theory provides considerable guidance about what leads to congruent relationships (although in some areas the research is more definitive and helpful than others). The implication is that the manager who wants to diagnose behavior must become familiar with critical aspects of relevant organizational behavior models or theories so that he or she can evaluate the nature of fits in a particular system.

The congruence model provides a general organizing framework. The organizational analyst will need other, more specific "submodels" to define high and low congruence. Examples of such submodels that might be used in the context of this general diagnostic model include the following: (1) the job characteristics model to assess and explain the fit between individuals and tasks as well as the fit between individuals and organizational arrangements (job design), (2) expectancy theory models of motivation to explain the fit between individuals and the other three components, (3) the information processing model of organizational design to explain the task-formal organization and task-informal organization fits, or (4) an organizational climate model to explain the fit between the informal organization and the other components. These models and theories are listed as illustrations of how more specific models can be used in the context of the general model. Obviously, those mentioned above are just a sampling of possible tools that could be used.

In summary, then, we have described a general model for the analysis of organizations (see Figure 4). The organization is seen as a system or transformation process that takes inputs and transforms them into outputs—a process that is composed of four basic components. The critical dynamic is the fit or congruence among the components. We now turn our attention to the pragmatic question of how to use this model for analyzing organizational problems.

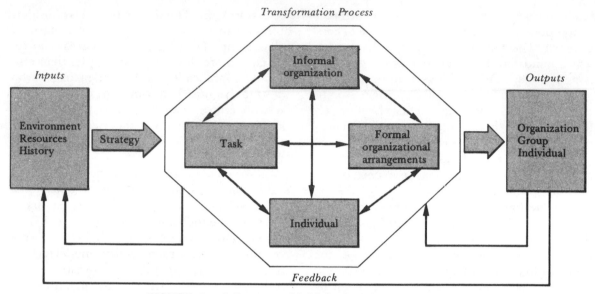

FIGURE 4.   A Congruence Model for Organization Analysis

A PROCESS FOR ORGANIZATIONAL PROBLEM ANALYSIS

The conditions that face organizations frequently change; consequently, managers are required to continually engage in problem-identification and problem-solving activities. Therefore, managers must gather data on organizational performance, compare the data with desired performance levels, identify the causes of problems, develop and choose action plans and, finally, implement and evaluate these action plans. These phases can be viewed as a generic problem-solving process. For long-term organizational viability, some type of problem-solving process must operate—and operate continuously.

Experience with using the congruence model for organizations for problem analysis in actual organizational settings has led to the development of an approach to using the model that's based on these generic problem-solving processes (see Figure 5). In this section, we will "walk through" this process, describing each step in the process and discussing how the model can be used at each stage. Here are the steps in the problem-analysis process:

1. *Identify symptoms:* In any situation initial information (symptomatic data) may indicate that there are problems, but not what the problems are or what the causes are. Symptomatic data are important because the symptoms of problems may indicate where to look for more complete data.

2. *Specify inputs:* Once the symptoms are identified, the starting point for analysis is to identify the system and the environment in which it functions. This means collecting data about the nature of environment, the type of resources the organization has, and the critical aspects of its history. Input analysis also involves identifying the overall strategy of the organization—that is, its core mission, supporting strategies, and objectives.

3. *Identify outputs:* The third step is an analysis

Step	Explanation
1. Identify symptoms.	List data indicating possible existence of problems.
2. Specify inputs.	Identify the system. Determine nature of environment, resources, and history. Identify critical aspects of strategy.
3. Identify outputs.	Identify data that define the nature of outputs at various levels (individual, group/unit, organizational). This should include desired outputs (from strategy), and actual outputs being obtained.
4. Identify problems.	Identify areas where there are significant and meaningful differences between desired and actual outputs. To the extent possible, identify penalties; that is, specific costs (actual and opportunity costs) associated with each problem.
5. Describe components of the organization.	Describe basic nature of each of the four components with emphasis on their critical features.
6. Assess congruence (fits).	Conduct analysis to determine relative congruence among components (draw on submodels as needed).
7. Generate and identify causes.	Analyze to associate fit with specific problems.
8. Identify action steps.	Indicate the possible actions to deal with problem causes.

FIGURE 5. *Basic Problem Analysis Steps Using the Congruence Model*

of the organization's outputs at the individual, group, and organizational levels. Output analysis actually involves two elements: (1) defining the desired or planned output through an analysis of strategy that explicitly or implicitly defines what the organization wants to achieve in terms of output or performance indicators, and (2) collecting data that indicate the type of output the organization is actually achieving.

4. *Identify problems:* Symptoms may indicate problems—in this case, significant difference between desired or planned output and actual output. Such problems might be discrepancies (actual vs. expected) in organizational performance, group functioning, individual behavior, or affective reactions. These data tell us what problems exist, but they still don't tell us the causes. (Note: Where data are available, it's frequently also useful to identify the costs associated with the problems or the *penalties* the organization incurs by not fixing the problem. Penalties might be actual costs—increased expenses, and so on—or opportunity costs, such as revenue lost because of the problem.)

5. *Describe organizational components:* At this step the analysis to determine the causes of problems begins. Data are collected about the nature of each of the four major organizational components, including information about the component and its critical features in this organization.

6. *Assess congruence (fits):* Using the data collected in step 5 as well as applicable submodels or theories, an assessment is made of the positive or negative fit between each pair of components.

7. *Generate hypotheses about problem causes:*

Once the components are described and their congruence assessed, the next step is to link together the congruence analysis with the problem identification (step 4). After analyzing to determine which are the poor fits that seem to be associated with, or account for, the output problems that have been identified, the patterns of congruence and incongruence that appear to cause the patterns of problems are determined.

8. *Identify action steps:* The final step in problem analysis is to identify possible action steps. These steps might range from specific changes to deal with relatively obvious problem causes to a more extensive data collection designed to test hypotheses about relatively more complex problems and causes.

In addition to these eight steps, some further steps need to be kept in mind. After possible actions are identified, problem solving involves predicting the consequence of various actions, choosing the course of action, and implementing and evaluating the impact of the chosen course of action. It is, of course, important to have a general diagnostic framework to monitor the effects of various courses of action.

The congruence model and this problem-analysis process outline are tools for structuring and dealing with the complex reality of organizations. Given the indeterminate nature of social systems, there is no one best way of handling a particular situation. The model and the process could, however, help the manager in making a number of decisions and in evaluating the consequences of those decisions. If these tools have merit, it is up to the manager to use them along with his or her intuitive sense (based on experience) to make the appropriate set of diagnostic, evaluative, and action decisions.

FUTURE DIRECTIONS

The model we've presented here reflects a particular way of thinking about organizations. If that perspective is significant, the model might be used as a tool for handling more complex problems or for structuring more complex situations. Some directions for further thought, research, and theory development could include these:

1. *Organizational change.* The issue of organizational change has received a good deal of attention from both managers and academics. The question is how to effectively implement organizational change. The problem seems to center on the lack of a general model of organizational change. It is hard to think about a general model of organizational change without a general model of organizations. The congruence perspective outlined here may provide some guidance and direction toward the development of a more integrated perspective on the processes of organizational change. Initial work in applying the congruence model to the change issue is encouraging.

2. *Organizational development over time.* There has been a growing realization that organizations grow and develop over time, and that they face different types of crises, evolve through different stages, and develop along some predictable lines. A model of organizations such as the one presented here might be a tool for developing typology of growth patterns by indicating the different configurations of tasks, individuals, organizational arrangements, and informal organizations that might be most appropriate for organizations in different environments and at different stages of development.

3. *Organizational pathology.* Organizational problem solving ultimately requires some

sense of the types of problems that may be encountered and the kinds of patterns of causes one might expect. It is reasonable to assume that most problems encountered by organizations are not wholly unique, but are predictable. The often expressed view that "our problems are unique" reflects in part the lack of a framework of organizational pathology. The question is: Are there basic "illnesses" that organizations suffer? Can a framework of organizational pathology, similar to the physician's framework of medical pathology, be developed? The lack of a pathology framework, in turn, reflects the lack of a basic functional model of organizations. Again, development of a congruence perspective might provide a common language to use for the identification of general pathological patterns of organizational functioning.

4. *Organizational solution types.* Closely linked to the problem of pathology is the problem of treatment, intervention, or solutions to organizational problems. Again, there's a lack of a general framework in which to consider the nature of organizational interventions. In this case, too, the congruence model might be a means for conceptualizing and ultimately describing the different intervention options available in response to problems.

SUMMARY

This article has presented a general approach for thinking about organizational functioning and a process for using a model to analyze organizational problems. This particular model is only one way of thinking about organizations; it's clearly not the only model, nor can we claim it's definitively the best model. It is one tool, however, that may be useful for structuring the complexity of organizational life and helping managers create, maintain, and develop effective organizations.

SELECTED BIBLIOGRAPHY

For a comprehensive review and synthesis of research in organizational behavior, see Marvin Dunnette's *Handbook of Industrial and Organizational Psychology* (Rand-McNally, 1976). Daniel Katz and Robert Kahn's seminal work on organizations as systems, *The Social Psychology of Organizations* (John Wiley & Sons, 1966), has been revised, updated, and extended in their 1978 edition. See their new book for an extensive discussion of organizations as open systems and for a unique synthesis of the literature in terms of systems ideas.

For a broad analysis of organizational behavior, see David Nadler, J. Richard Hackman, and Edward E. Lawler's *Managing Organizational Behavior* (Little, Brown, 1979) and see Charles Hofer and Daniel Schendel's *Strategy Formulation: Analytical Concepts* (West, 1978) for a discussion of strategy.

For an extensive discussion of output and effectiveness, see Paul Goodman and Johannes Pennings's *New Perspectives on Organizational Effectiveness* (Jossey-Bass, 1977) and Andrew Van de Ven and Diane Ferry's *Organizational Assessment* (Wiley Interscience, 1980).

For more detail on organizational arrangements, see Jay R. Galbraith's *Designing Complex Organizations* (Addison-Wesley, 1973); on job design and motivation, see J. Richard Hackman and Greg Oldham's *Work Redesign* (Addison-Wesley, 1979); and on informal organizations, see Michael Tushman's "A Political Approach to Organizations: A Review and Rationale" (*Academy of Management Review*, April 1977) and Jeffrey Pfeffer's new book, *Power and Politics in Organizations* (Pitman Publishing, Inc., 1980).

Submodels corresponding to the various components of our congruence model would include: J. Richard Hackman and Greg Oldham's job design model; Victor Vroom and Edward Lawler's work on expectancy theory of motivation and decision making—see Vroom's *Work and Motivation*

(Wiley, 1964) and Lawler's *Motivation in Work Organizations* (Wadsworth Publishing Co., 1973); Jay R. Galbraith, Michael Tushman, and David Nadler's work on information processing models of organizational design; and George Litwin and Robert Stringer's work on organization climate—see Litwin and Stringer's *Motivation and Organizational Climate* (Harvard University Graduate School of Business Administration, 1968).

David Nadler's "An Integrative Theory of Organizational Change," to appear in the *Journal of Applied Behavioral Science* in 1981, uses the congruence model to think about the general problems of organizational change and dynamics. Several distinct levers for change are developed and discussed. Other pertinent books of interest include: Jay R. Galbraith's *Organization Design* (Addison-Wesley, 1979), Jay R. Galbraith and Daniel A. Nathanson's *Strategy Implementation: The Role of Structure and Process* (West, 1978), George C. Homans's *The Human Group* (Harcourt Brace Jovanovich, Inc., 1950), Paul R. Lawrence and Jay W. Lorsch's *Developing Organizations: Diagnosis and Action* (Addison-Wesley, 1969), Harold J. Leavitt's "Applied Organization Change in Industry" in J. G. March's (ed.) *Handbook of Organizations* (Rand-McNally, 1965), Harry Levinson's *Organizational Diagnosis* (Harvard University Press, 1972), Harry Levinson's *Psychological Man* (Levinson Institute, 1976), Jay W. Lorsch and Alan Sheldon's "The Individual in the Organization: A Systems View" in J. W. Lorsch and P. R. Lawrence's (eds.) *Managing Group and Intergroup Relations* (Irwin-Dorsey, 1972), David A. Nadler and Noel M. Tichy's "The Limitations of Traditional Intervention Technology in Health Care Organizations" in N. Margulies and J. A. Adams's (eds.) *Organization Development in Health Care Organizations* (Addison-Wesley, 1980), Edgar H. Schein's *Organizational Psychology* (Prentice-Hall, 1970), and James A. Seiler's *Systems Analysis in Organizational Behavior* (Irwin-Dorsey, 1967).

Fit, Failure, and the Hall of Fame

Raymond E. Miles

Charles C. Snow

There is currently a convergence of attention and concern among managers and management scholars across basic issues of organizational success and failure. Whether attention is focused on the very survival of organizations in aging industries, the pursuit of excellence in mature industries, or the preparation of organizations for the rapidly approaching challenges of the 21st century, the concern is real and highly motivated. U.S. managers and organizations have been indicted for low productivity, and management scholars have recognized the fragmentation of their literature and called for a new synthesis.

Clearly, neither organizational success or failure has an easy explanation. Nevertheless, it is becoming increasingly evident that a simple though profound core concept is at the heart of many organization and management research findings as well as many of the proposed remedies for industrial and organizational renewal. The concept is that of *fit* among an organization's strategy, structure, and management processes.

Successful organizations achieve strategic fit with their market environment and support their strategies with appropriately designed structures and management processes. Less successful organizations typically exhibit poor fit externally and/or internally. A conceptual framework can be built upon the process of fit that will prove valuable to both managers and management scholars as they sift through current theories, perspectives, and prescriptions in search of an operational consensus. The main features of such a framework are structured around four main points:

- *Minimal* fit among strategy, structure, and process is essential to all organizations operating in competitive environments. If a misfit occurs for a prolonged period, the result usually is failure.
- *Tight* fit, both internally and externally, is associated with excellence. Tight fit is the underlying causal dynamic producing sustained, excellent performance and a strong corporate culture.
- *Early* fit, the discovery and articulation of a new pattern of strategy, structure, and process, frequently results in performance records which in sporting circles would merit Hall of Fame status. The invention or early application of a new organization form may

provide a more powerful competitive advantage than a market or technological breakthrough.

- *Fragile* fit involves vulnerability to both shifting external conditions and to inadvertent internal unraveling. Even Hall of Fame organizations may become victims of deteriorating fit.

MINIMAL FIT, MISFIT, AND FAILURE

The concept of fit plays an undeniably important role in managerial behavior and organizational analysis. Fit is a process as well as a state—a dynamic search that seeks to *align* the organization with its environment and to *arrange* resources internally in support of that alignment. In practical terms, the basic alignment mechanism is *strategy,* and the internal arrangements are *organization structure and management processes.* Because in a changing environment it is very difficult to keep these major organizational components tightly integrated, perfect fit is most often a condition to be strived for rather than accomplished.

Although fit is seldom referred to explicitly, it has appeared as the hallmark of successful organizations in a variety of settings and circumstances. For example, in our own studies of organizational behavior in many widely different industries, we have regularly found that organizations of different types can be successful provided that their particular configuration of strategy, structure, and process is internally and externally consistent.[1] In his landmark historical analysis, Alfred Chandler found that the companies now recognized as the pioneers of the divisional organization structure were among the first to identify emerging markets, develop diversification strategies to meet these market needs, and to revamp their organization structures to fit the new strategies.[2] In their

study of the management of innovation in electronics firms, Tom Burns and G. M. Stalker found that organizations pursuing innovation strategies had to use flexible, organic structures and management processes; rigid, mechanistic approaches did not fit with such strategies.[3] Finally, in another highly acclaimed study, Paul Lawrence and Jay Lorsch found that successful organizations in three quite different industries were those that were sufficiently differentiated to deal with the complexities of their industrial environments while simultaneously being tightly integrated internally.[4]

These and other studies conducted by organization theorists have essentially if not directly reaffirmed the importance of fit. In addition, recent research in sociology and economics has supported the idea that achieving at least minimal fit is closely associated with organizational success. Industrial economists have identified a set of generic strategies that generally fit most industries, as well as some of the organizational and managerial characteristics associated with these strategies.[5] Sociologists, borrowing concepts and theories from biology, have examined, within different populations of organizations, certain features that fit (or do not fit) particular environments.[6] In sum, the concept of fit may at first glance appear to be obvious, but many studies from several disciplines indicate that while fit is fundamental to organizational success, it is enormously difficult to achieve and/or maintain.

Fit and Survival

It is appropriate to distinguish between degree of fit as well as the nature of fit, specifically that *minimal fit is required for organizational survival.* Under some circumstances, organizations that are "misfits" in their industries may survive, but sooner or later they must adjust their behavior or fail. For example, in one of our studies, the objective was to determine if certain strategies were both feasible and effective in different industries.[7] The industries selected for study were air transportation, autos, plastics, and semiconductors. We found that in general some strategies were effective and others were not. Organizations that we called "Defenders," "Prospectors," and "Analyzers" were all effective; i.e., they met the test of minimal fit in each industry. On the other hand, organizations identified as "Reactors" were generally ineffective, except in the air transportation industry which was highly regulated at the time (1975). Reactors are organizations that have either a poorly articulated strategy, a strategy inappropriate for the industrial environment, or an organization structure and management system that does not fit the strategy. The findings from this study suggest that in competitive industries, there is a set of feasible strategies (e.g., Defender, Prospector, Analyzer) each of which can be effective. Moreover, misfits—organizations whose behavior lies outside of the feasible set—tend to perform poorly unless they are in a "protected" environment such as that provided by government regulation.

Fit and Misfit

The line of demarcation between minimal fit and misfit, however, is not obvious. No whistles blow warning an organization that its internal or external fit is coming undone. The process is more likely to be marked by a general deterioration whose speed is affected by competitive circumstances. For example, an in-depth study of the major firms in the tobacco industry during the years 1950–1975 illustrates the point.[8] Few American industries have experienced the degree of negative pressure that was exerted on the tobacco industry during these years, and the experiences of four companies (Philip Morris, R. J. Reynolds, American Brands, Liggett & Meyers) pointedly show how organizations struggle to maintain an alignment with their shifting environments over time.

Each of the companies responded differently to severe, uncontrollable jolts such as the Sloan-Kettering Report linking smoking to cancer (1953), the Surgeon General's Report reaffirming this conclusion (1964), and events leading to and concluding with a ban on broadcast advertising of cigarettes (1970). Philip Morris, relying on a Prospector strategy, engaged in a series of product and market innovations that propelled the company from last among the major firms in 1950 market share to first today. R. J. Reynolds largely pursued an Analyzer strategy—rarely the first-mover in product-market innovations but always an early adopter of the successful innovations of its competitors—and today it ranks a close second to Philip Morris. Both of these companies currently exhibit a minimal if not strong fit with environmental conditions in the tobacco industry.

American Brands followed a Defender strategy in which it tried to maintain its traditional approach in the face of these environmental changes. This strategy essentially amounted to continued reliance on nonfiltered cigarettes even though the filtered cigarette market segment was growing steadily. American Brands, probably not wanting to cannibalize its sales of nonfiltered cigarettes, was at least ten years behind Philip Morris and R. J. Reynolds in entering the filtered cigarette market, and, during this period, the company fell from first to fourth place in overall market share. The company's internal fit among strategy, structure, and process was a good one throughout the mid-1950s to mid-1960s, but its strategic fit with the market underwent a gradual decline. Certainly, in retrospect, one could argue that American Brands was a misfit during this time, and the firm paid for it in declining performance.

Lastly, Liggett & Meyers behaved almost as a classic Reactor throughout this quarter-century period. It demonstrated substantially less internal consistency than its competitors, fared poorly in its product-market strategy, and doggedly hung on to its approach despite unfavorable performance. Described by one source as "always too late with too little," Liggett & Meyers in the late 1970s was searching for someone to purchase its tobacco business. Here was a misfit bordering on failure.

In the case of the tobacco industry, major environmental changes resulted in declining fit and performance for one company and near-failure for another. Organizational misfit does not, however, have to come from external changes; it can result from internal shifts generated by the organization itself. To illustrate internally generated misfit, consider the well-known case of organizational disintegration and resurrection, the Chrysler Corporation.[9]

From a strong position as the country's second largest automobile manufacturer in the 1930s, Chrysler arguably began to decline in the post-World War II period when it changed its strategy without significantly altering its organization structure or management processes. Prior to the 1950s, Chrysler kept its capital base as small as possible, subcontracted out a substantial part of its production, and rode its suppliers hard to keep costs down. But then Chrysler decided to emulate both General Motors and Ford, even to the point of matching their product lines model for model. From the early 1960s until its Federal bailout in the 1970s, Chrysler seemed determined to be a full-line, worldwide, direct competitor of Ford and GM.

To support this product-market strategy, however, Chrysler was late in forming a subsidiary to monitor its distributors, late in making the necessary foreign acquisitions, and often late in designing its greatly broadened product line which was done mostly by a single, centralized engineering group. In fact, Chrysler largely remained a functionally departmentalized and centralized organization long after it adopted a strategy of diversifica-

tion. Managerial problems in the areas of cost control, inventory, and production merely added to the misfit between Chrysler's strategy and its structure and management system. Despite its recent public attention and economic rebound, the company has not yet achieved stable performance.

In sum, the consequence of misfit is declining performance if not complete failure. Organizational misfits can be protected by a benign environment, sometimes for lengthy periods of time, but minimal fit is required for survival in competitive environments. However, minimal fit, as the term implies, does not guarantee excellent performance.

TIGHT FIT: THE FOUNDATION FOR EXCELLENCE

Corporate excellence requires more than minimal fit. Truly outstanding performance, achieved by many companies, is associated with tight fit—both externally with the environment and internally among strategy, structure, and management process. In fact, *tight fit is the causal force* at work when organizational excellence is said to be caused by various managerial and organizational characteristics.

In the late 1940s and early 1950s, Peter Drucker studied a number of top U.S. corporations, including General Motors, General Electric, IBM, and Sears, Roebuck.[10] Based on his observations, Drucker associated the widely acclaimed achievements of these organizations with such managerial characteristics as delegation and joint goal setting (MBO) and with organizational characteristics emphasizing the decentralization of operating decisions. He saw overstaffing as a threat to corporate responsiveness and argued that the best performance comes when jobs are enriched rather than narrowed. Finally, he felt that the overall key to the success of these companies was that they knew what business they were in, what their competencies were, and how to keep their efforts focused on their goals.

Some thirty years later, Thomas Peters and Robert Waterman studied 62 U.S. companies and produced their own checklist of characteristics associated with corporate excellence.[11] As had Drucker before them, they noted that organizations with records of sustained high performance tended to have a clear business focus, a bias for action, and lean structures and staffs that facilitated the pursuit of strategy.

Drucker clearly acknowledged the importance of organization structure and was convinced at the time that the federally decentralized (i.e., multidivisional) organization structure was the design of the future. He did not, however, probe the relationship between alternative strategies and their appropriate structures and management processes. Similarly, while Peters and Waterman stressed structural leanness and responsiveness as universally valuable characteristics, they also noted the requirement of achieving a close fit among the seven "S's" of strategy, structure, skills, systems, style, shared values, and staff (people). Again, however, Peters and Waterman did not discuss the possible alternative organization forms appropriate for different strategies. In our view, the observations of Drucker, Peters, and Waterman are accurate and extremely valuable. The discovery thirty years apart of the association of similar characteristics with organizational excellence is a powerful argument for the validity of that association—but it is not an explanation of why that association exists nor of the causal force that may be involved.

Both the managerial and organizational characteristics described by these observers, and the outstanding performance achieved by the organizations that they have examined, are the result of the achievement—by discovery or by design—of tight fit. That is, such characteristics as convergence on a set of core business values—doing what one does best, a lean action-oriented structure that provides opportunities for the full use of people's capabilities at all levels, etc.—essentially flow from the achievement of tight fit with the environment and among strategy, structure, and process. In short, the causal dynamic of tight fit tends to operate in four stages:

· First, the discovery of the basic structure and management processes necessary to support a chosen strategy create a *gestalt* that becomes so obvious and compelling that complex organizational and managerial demands appear to be simple.
· Second, *simplicity* leads to widespread understanding which reinforces and sustains fit. Organization structure and key management processes such as reward and control systems "teach" managers and employees the appropriate attitudes and behaviors for maintaining focus on strategic requirements.
· Third, simplicity *reduces the need for elaborate coordinating mechanisms,* thereby creating slack resources that can be reallocated elsewhere in the system.
· Fourth, as outstanding performance is achieved and sustained, its *association* with the process by which it is attained is reinforced, and this serves to further simplify the basic fit among strategy, structure, and process.

It should be emphasized that we do not specify "finding the right strategy" as an important element of this causal linkage. In fact, finding strategy-structure-process fit is usually far more important and problematic. It may be that there is less to strategy than meets the eye. At any moment, in any given industry, it is likely that several organizations are considering the same strategic moves: to diversify, retrench, acquire other firms, etc. For example, in the

1920s, the top executives of Sears, Roebuck did not have a secret crystal ball that forecast the effects of the automobile on retail trade. Indeed most organizations—including Sears' major competitor, Montgomery Ward—saw similar trends. It was the case, however, that well ahead of competitors Sears developed a structure that would allow it to operate as a high-quality, low-cost nationwide retailing organization.

It is valuable, of course, that the chosen strategy be articulated—for example, Sears pursued the image of "a hometown store with nationwide purchasing power." Nevertheless, it is when the blueprint of how to achieve such strategic goals is drawn that real understanding begins to emerge throughout the system. As clarity involving means emerges, that which was enormously complex and apparently beyond accomplishment, now seems straightforward and easy to achieve.

The process of searching for, discovering, and achieving tight fit is pervasive. At the individual level, for instance, learning to drive a car, fly an airplane, or serve a tennis ball are all activities that at first appear complex and difficult to learn but once mastered seem to be relatively simple. Mastery occurs, however, only when the gestalt is apprehended, felt, and understood. The same learning process occurs within organizations. The Baltimore Orioles, for example, believe they know how and why they won the recent World Series and have enjoyed success over the years. Strategy, structure, and process fit and are well understood by members at all levels of the organization. From the front office to the manager, coaches, and players (including those in the farm system), it seems clear how one goes about building a world-champion team. Much of the same could be said for Procter & Gamble, Johnson & Johnson, Minnesota Mining & Manufacturing, McDonald's, Schlumberger, and other excellent companies.

In sum, what we are suggesting is that focus, leanness, action, involvement, identification, etc., are likely *products* of tight fit. Fit simplifies complex organizational and managerial arrangements, and simple systems facilitate leanness, action, and many other observed manifestations of excellence. As one understands the system, one feels more a part of it, and as one's role becomes clear to self and others, participation is facilitated, almost demanded. Closeness and understanding provide a common culture, and stories and myths emerge that perpetuate key aspects of culture.

EARLY FIT: A KEY TO THE HALL OF FAME?

To this point we have argued that minimal fit is necessary for an organization's survival and that tight fit is associated with excellent performance. We now suggest that *early fit—the discovery and articulation of a new organization form—can lead to sustained excellence* over considerable periods of time and thus a place in some mythical Hall of Fame.

Picking a Hall of Fame company is difficult. In sports, Hall of Fame performers are individuals who have been selected only after their careers are over, and sometimes selection is preceded by an interval of several years so that the decision is relatively objective, based on complete information, and final. Organizations, on the other hand, are ongoing systems; therefore, any given Hall of Fame nominee might immediately have one or more "off" years. Nevertheless, some organizations would be likely to appear on every pundit's Hall of Fame list, and we believe that most of these organizations would share the characteristic of an early organizational breakthrough that was not quickly or easily matched by their competitors at the time.

There are, of course, many ways that companies can achieve a competitive advantage. For example, obtaining a patent on a particular product or technology gives a firm an edge on its competitors. Cornering the supply of a key raw material through location or judicious buying may permit a company to dominate a particular business. An innovative product design or the development of a new distribution channel can provide an organization with a competitive lead that is difficult to overcome. Yet all of these competitive advantages are more or less temporary—sooner or later competitors will imitate and improve upon the innovation and the advantage will disappear. Such abilities, therefore, do not guarantee induction into the Hall of Fame.

Sustained corporate excellence seems to have at least one necessary condition: the invention or early application of—and rapid tight fit around—a new organization form. Achieving early fit succeeds over the proprietary advantages mentioned above because a new organization form cannot be completely copied in the short or even intermediate run. In this century, certain firms would appear to merit Hall of Fame nomination based on broad criteria such as product excellence, management performance, market share and responsiveness, and the like. We will discuss five of our own nominees all of which meet these criteria but also share the characteristic of early fit through invention or application of a new organization form: Carnegie Steel, General Motors, Sears, Roebuck, Hewlett-Packard, and IBM.

Carnegie Steel

Carnegie Steel was one of the first companies to employ the fully-integrated functional organization form complete with centralized management and technical specialization.[12] In his early thirties, Andrew Carnegie left a position with the railroad to concentrate on manufacturing steel rails. Convinced that the management methods he and others had pioneered on the railroad could also be applied to the manufacturing sector, Carnegie essentially started the

modern steel business in the U.S. and he played a major role in forging the world's first billion-dollar corporation, U.S. Steel.

At the heart of Carnegie Steel's success was its reliance on centralized management (particularly cost accounting and control) and full vertical integration. Carnegie recognized early the benefits of vertical integration in the fragmented, geographically dispersed steel industry in the latter half of the 19th century, and his company integrated backward into the purchase of ore deposits and the production of coke as well as forward into manufacture of finished steel products. Vertical integration permitted a new external alignment in the steel industry: substantially larger market areas could now be served much more quickly, efficiently, and profitably. Carnegie Steel supplemented its functional organization structure with careful plant design and transportation logistics, continuous technological improvements, successful (though limited) product diversification, and innovative human resources management practices and labor relations. Thus, internally, there was rapid development of a tight fit between management processes and the company's pioneering strategy and structure.

Carnegie Steel, of course, did not invent the vertically integrated, functional organization form; elements of this model were already available. However, the company's early and complete use of this form dramatically altered the steel business in a way that was not matched by competitors for decades. (See Table 1 for the evolution of major organization forms and our prediction of the next new form.)

General Motors

General Motors has the strongest claim as the inventor of the "federally decentralized" or divisional organization structure. Among the early automobile makers, William C. Durant was one of the strongest believers in the enor-

TABLE 1.   Evolution of Organization Forms

	Product-Market Strategy	Organization Structure	Inventor or Early User	Core Activating and Control Mechanisms
1800	Single product or service. Local/regional markets	Agency	Numerous small owner-managed firms	Personal direction and control
1850	Limited, standardized product or service line. Regional/national markets	Functional	Carnegie Steel	Central plan and budgets
1900	Diversified, changing product or service line. National/international markets	Divisional	General Motors Sears Roebuck Hewlett-Packard	Corporate policies and division profit centers
1950	Standard and innovative products or services. Stable and changing markets	Matrix	Several aerospace and electronics firms (e.g., NASA, TRW, IBM, Texas Instruments)	Temporary teams and lateral resource allocation devices such as internal markets, joint planning systems, etc.
2000	Product or service design. Global changing markets	Dynamic network	International construction firms; Global consumer goods companies: Selected electronics and computer firms (e.g., IBM)	Broker-assembled temporary structures with shared information systems as basis for trust and coordination.

mous potential market for the moderate-priced car.[13] Acting on his beliefs, Durant put together a group of companies engaged in the making and selling of automobiles, parts, and accessories. In 1919, the total combined assets of Durant's General Motors made it the fifth largest company in the U.S. But although Durant had spotted a potentially large opportunity, and had moved rapidly to create an industrial empire to take advantage of it, he had little interest in developing an organization structure and management system for the enterprise he had created.

Indeed, in combining individual firms into General Motors, Durant relied on the same organizational approach of volume production and vertical integration that he had used in his previous managerial positions and that was popular at the time. However, this approach led to little more than an expanding agglomeration of different companies making automobiles, parts, accessories, trucks, tractors, and even refrigerators. An unforeseen collapse in the demand for automobiles in 1920 precipitated a financial crisis at General Motors, which was quickly followed by Durant's retirement as President. Pierre du Pont, who had been in semi-retirement from the chemical company, agreed to take the presidency of GM. One of du Pont's first actions was to approve a plan devised by Alfred P. Sloan, a high-level GM executive whose family firm had been purchased by Durant, that defined an organization structure for General Motors.

Sloan's plan, which went into effect in early 1921, called for a general office to coordinate, appraise, and set broad goals and policies for the numerous, loosely controlled operating divisions of GM. The general officers individually were to supervise and coordinate different groups of divisions and collectively were to help make policy for the corporation as a whole. Staff specialists were to advise and serve both the division managers and the general officers and to provide business and financial information necessary for appraising the performance of the individual units and for formulating overall policy. Although most of Sloan's proposals had been carried out by the end of 1921, it was not until 1925 that the original plan resulted in a smooth-running organization. The multidivisional decentralized structure allowed GM to diversify a standard product, the automobile, to meet a variety of consumer needs and tastes while maintaining overall corporate financial synergy.

From 1924–1927, General Motors' market share rose from 19 to 43 percent. Unlike its major competitor, Ford, which was devastated by the Depression, GM's profits grew steadily throughout the Depression and World War II. It has been the leading automobile manufacturer in the world since its implementation of the divisional structure and for years was the corporate model for similar structural changes in other large American industrial enterprises.

Sears, Roebuck

Just as General Motors can make a strong claim to the invention of the divisional structure for product diversification, Sears, Roebuck can claim to have been one of the earliest users of this structure outside of manufacturing. Sears has long enjoyed its reputation as the world's most successful retailer.[14] Since its inception in 1895, Sears has undergone two periods where it achieved an "early fit" among its competitors. The first phase of the Sears story began in 1895 when Julius Rosenwald, a consummate administrator, joined Richard Sears, a brilliant merchandiser, and together they built a company catering to the American farmer. Sears, Roebuck's Chicago mail-order plant was a major innovation in the retailing business. Designed by Otto Doering in 1903, this modern mass-production plant preceded by five years Henry Ford's acclaimed automobile assembly line, and it ushered in the "distribution revolution" that was so vital a factor in early 20th century America's economic growth.

The second phase of the Sears story began in 1924 when Robert E. Wood left Montgomery Ward to join the company. Since farmers could now travel to cities in their automobiles and the urban population was more affluent, retail selling through local stores appeared to be more promising than mail-order sales. Promoted to President in 1928, Wood, with his new hand-picked management team, moved ahead rapidly to create a nationwide retail organization. Montgomery Ward and other retail chains of the period (e.g., J. C. Penney, Eaton's, Woolworth's, Grant's, Kresge's) have not been able to this day to match Sears' performance.

The organization form developed at Sears bore many similarities to GM's multidivisional structure, but it was geared toward retailing rather than manufacturing. Whereas GM diversified by product, Sears diversified by geographic territory. Each of the territorial units became full-fledged autonomous divisions with their managers responsible for overall operating results, and the Chicago headquarters remained a central office with staff specialists and general executives. Sears' ultimate tight internal and external fit was not accomplished nearly as rapidly as those of Carnegie Steel or General Motors, but it was achieved first among Sears' competitors and gave the company a competitive advantage that has not, until recently, been seriously threatened.

Hewlett-Packard

The decentralized, divisional structure developed by General Motors and Sears (along with a few other outstanding companies such as Du

Pont and Standard Oil of New Jersey) flourished in the 1950s under the spotlight of publicity from management consulting firms and from academics like Peter Drucker. For most companies, however, the divisional structure did not serve as a proprietary advantage but merely as a necessary means of maintaining alignment with a market demanding diversity. Nevertheless, one outstanding company, a Hall of Fame nominee on many early ballots, has taken this organization structure to new heights in its pursuit of leading-edge technological developments in an emerging industry. The company is Hewlett-Packard and the industry, of course, is electronics. Founded in 1939 by William Hewlett and David Packard, this company is the world's largest manufacturer of test and measurement instruments as well as a major producer of small computers. The company is noted for its strong corporate culture and nearly continuous high performance in a very demanding industrial environment.

From the beginning, Hewlett-Packard has pursued a strategy that brings the products of scientific research into industrial application while maintaining the collegial atmosphere of a university laboratory. This means that the firm concentrates on advanced technology and offers mostly state-of-the-art products to a variety of industrial and consumer markets. A given product line and market are actively pursued as long as the company has a distinctive technological or design advantage. When products reach the stage where successful competition depends primarily on low costs and prices, Hewlett-Packard often moves out of the arena and turns its attention to a new design or an entirely new product. As a company that achieved early fit, its technological diversification rivals General Motors' product diversification and Sears' territorial diversification.

Hewlett-Packard's strategy of technological innovation is supported by an organization structure and management system that may be unparalleled in flexibility. The fundamental business unit is the product division, an integrated, self-sustaining organization with a great deal of independence. New divisions arise when a particular product line becomes large enough to support its continued growth out of the profit it generates. Also, new divisions tend to emerge when a single division gets so large that the people involved start to lose their identification with the product line. Most human resources management practices—especially those concerning hiring, placement, and rewards—are appropriately matched with the company's structural and strategic decentralization.

International Business Machines

Any Hall of Fame list must include IBM.[15] One of the largest producers of calculating, computing, and office machinery, IBM is arguably the best managed company in the United States, perhaps the world. Paradoxically, IBM's nomination to the Hall of Fame cannot be based on the invention of a particular organization form—nor, for that matter, a management innovation or technological break-through. The company is simply good at everything it does; it is a polydextrous organization that is consistently quick to adopt and refine any approach that it can use to its advantage.

The company was born when Thomas Watson, Sr. joined the Computing-Recording Corporation in 1914 and renamed it International Business Machines in 1924. However, the modern IBM dates to the stewardship of Thomas Watson, Jr., who was chief executive officer from 1956 to 1971. Today IBM is the most profitable U.S. industrial company, and its form of organization is a combination of time-honored and advanced approaches.

IBM takes advantage of two key characteristics of the functional organization, vertical integration and production efficiency. For example, IBM is the world's largest manufacturer of memory chips and installs its entire output in its own machines. And beginning in the late 1970s, a series of huge capital improvements has made IBM one of the most automated and lowest-cost producers in the industry.

IBM has also relied to a limited extent on acquisitions, a characteristic most often associated with the divisional organization. Unlike many large conglomerates, the company is very selective about its acquisitions, the most recent of which is intended to help IBM create the futuristic electronic office.

Finally, IBM uses a variety of the most advanced approaches to organization and management. First, the company has created at least 15 internal new ventures groups in the last few years to explore new business opportunities. The new units are independently run, but they can draw on IBM resources. Second, the company has increased its use of subcontracting. In its most recent product venture, the personal computer, IBM relied largely on parts obtained from outside suppliers and is selling the machine through retail outlets like Sears and ComputerLand as well as its own sales network. Software for the machine was developed by inviting numerous software firms to supply ideas and materials. Third, besides being a vigorous competitor, IBM has formed many successful cooperative agreements with other companies, especially in Japan and Europe. It is generally acknowledged that substantially more cooperative arrangements involving business firms, as well as governments and universities, will be needed in coming years to supplement traditional competitive practices. And, lastly, IBM is international in scope. It is the leading computer firm in virtually every one of the approximately 130 countries where it does business.

In sum, a close, current look at the Hall of Fame companies just described would probably not uncover the maintenance of perfect fit. As suggested earlier, even these organizations are vulnerable to external and internal slippage, perhaps even distortion. Therefore, it is important to explore the processes by which tight fit may be eroded.

THE FRAGILITY OF FIT

As noted earlier, fit is a process as well as a state. Environmental factors outside an organization's control are constantly changing and may require incremental or major strategic adjustment. Strategic change, in turn, is likely to require changes in organization structure and/or management processes. When environmental jolts are extreme, some organizations may be unwilling or unable to adjust—recall the earlier examples from the tobacco industry and witness the recent plight of several airline companies under deregulation.

However, environmental change is not the only cause of alignment deterioration. For example, misfit may occur when organizations voluntarily change their strategies but fail to follow through with appropriate structural and managerial adjustments, as illustrated by the case of Chrysler. An even more intriguing alignment-threatening process is also demonstrable, one which may well account for more deterioration of fit than either environmental jolts or unsupported strategic changes. This process involves voluntary internal structure and process changes that are made without concern for their longer-run consequences for strategy and market responsiveness. Although usually subtle and long-term in its development, this process of internal unraveling underscores the point that an organization's fit at any given time may be quite fragile.

Recall the earlier description of how the discovery of tight fit results in system simplicity: When strategy, structure, and process are completely aligned, both goals and means are visible, and task requirements are obvious and compelling. Resources previously required for coordination or troubleshooting can be redeployed in the primary system, and even tighter fit may result. However, as the spotlight of tight fit illuminates the overall system for everyone to see and understand, its bright glare may also begin to highlight the organization's inherent deficiencies. That is, each pattern of fit has its own distinct contribution to make. For example, the functional organization form is ideal for efficient production of standard goods or services and the divisional form is most appropriate for diversification. Each form not only has its own strengths but also its own built-in limitations. The form best suited for efficiency is vulnerable to market change, and the form suited to diversification is sometimes clearly redundant.

As the pattern of fit becomes increasingly clear to managers and employees of excellent (tight fit) companies, they can easily describe why the organization prospers. But at least some members of these same companies can also point to the system's shortcomings. For example, in a vertically integrated, centralized, functional organization, perceptive managers will advocate the creation of task forces, project groups, or even separate divisions to facilitate quick development of new products or services. Conversely, one can anticipate in a decentralized, divisional structure that cost-conscious managers will suggest standardizing certain components or services across divisions in order to reduce redundancy and achieve scale economies. Most organizations regularly make minor adjustments in their structures and processes to accommodate demands for which their systems were not designed. In some organizations, however, what begins as a limited adjustment may over time grow into a crippling, step-by-step unraveling of the entire system. Moreover, this may occur without conscious long-term planning or even awareness. Two brief examples, both associated with companies on our Hall of Fame list, serve as illustrations.

At General Motors, once Sloan's federally decentralized structure was fully in place,

managers began to recommend standardization of various product components and production processes. Some aspects of engineering and production had been coordinated across divisions from the beginning, but the advocates of full-scale standardization finally began to override the divisional structure in the 1950s. Many readers may recall the "scandal" that occurred when buyers discovered that the General Motors' engine in their cars had not been made by that division and, in some cases, even by a division of lower status. In fact, those engines had been manufactured according to policies that reflected increasing interdivisional coordination and centralization of decision making. During the 1950s and 1960s when General Motors appeared invulnerable to competition—foreign or domestic—the cost of increased centralization and coordination was probably not visible. It almost appeared that the company could have its diversity and its cost savings, too. One wonders how much more rapidly General Motors might have responded to the challenge of foreign competition if it had been able to do so by simply aiming the operations of one autonomous division toward Japan and another toward Europe. In general, the more attention that is devoted to the known shortcomings of a particular organization form, the more likely is the possibility of unraveling a successful fit.

Could a similar process occur at Hewlett-Packard in the 1980s? In recent months, the company has been beset with problems caused by its decentralized management system and entrepreneurial culture, including overlapping products, lagging development of new technology, and a piecemeal approach to key markets.[16] The response to these problems was the launching of several programs to improve planning, coordinate marketing, and strengthen the firm's computer-related research and development efforts.

Hewlett-Packard's current CEO, John Young, recognizes that these organizational changes involve trade-offs; the benefits obtained from cross-divisional coordination have to be weighed against the threats to the entrepreneurial spirit of the various divisions. That is, the use of program managers and strategic coordinators to align product designs, to force the divisions to share components, and to coordinate pricing and marketing strategies has generated a number of successful cross-divisional development projects. However, these successes have been offset by a wave of manager and engineer defections to other companies. Thus, only time will tell if this reorganization improves the company's internal fit or begins to unravel the core threads among strategy, structure, and process that have produced Hewlett-Packard's success.

The moral of these examples is not that managers of excellent companies should not try to improve performance. Rather, it is that rearranging organization structure and management systems may in some cases preclude an organization from pursuing its desired strategy. Managers of truly outstanding companies recognize the strengths and limitations of alternate organization forms, and they will not undo a crucial link among strategy, structure, or process in order to "solve" predictable problems.

FUTURE FIT: A NEW ORGANIZATION FORM

Our argument concerning the effects of minimal, tight, and early fit on organizational performance is based on the belief that the search for fit has been visible in organizations for at least the past 100 years. But will this search continue in the future? We believe it will. In fact, many managers are now considering a new organization form and are experimenting with its major components and processes in their organizations. The reality of this new form,

therefore, simply awaits articulation and understanding.

In this century, there have been three major breakthroughs in the way organizations have been designed and managed (see again Table 1). The first breakthrough occurred at the turn of the century in the form of the functional organization. Prior to that time, small firms had relied on an informal structure in which the owner-manager's immediate subordinates acted as all-purpose "agents" of the chief executive, solving whatever problems arose. There was very little of the technical specialization found in today's organizations. The functional form allowed those companies that adopted it to become very large and to specialize in a limited set of products and markets. Next came the divisional form, which facilitated even more organizational growth, but, more importantly, it facilitated diversification in both products and markets. The third breakthrough was the matrix structure in which elements of the functional and divisional forms were combined into a single system able to accommodate both standard and innovative products or projects.

Now a promising new organization form is emerging, one that appears to fit the fast-approaching conditions of the 21st century. As was true of previous forms, elements of this new form are sprouting in several companies and industries simultaneously.

- *Large construction firms.* The construction industry has long been known for its use of subcontracting to accomplish large, complex tasks. Today, the size and complexity of a construction project can be immense, as evidenced by the multinational consortium of companies now building an entire city in Saudi Arabia. Under such circumstances, companies must be able to form a network of reliable subcontractors, many of them large firms which have not worked together before. Some companies, therefore, have found it advantageous to focus only on the overall design and management of a project, leaving the actual construction to their affiliates.

· *Global consumer goods companies.* Standardized products such as clothes, cameras, and watches can be designed, manufactured, and marketed throughout the world. Companies engaged in this type of business are prime examples of the "world enterprise": buying raw materials wherever they are cheapest, manufacturing wherever costs are lowest, and selling wherever the products will bring the highest price. To do so, however, requires many different brokers—individuals and groups who bring together complementary resources. All of the participants in the process—designers, suppliers, manufacturers, distributors, etc.—must be coupled into a smooth-running operation even though they are continents apart.

· *Electronics and computer firms.* Certain firms in these industries already are dealing with conditions that in the future will be widespread: rapid change, demassification, high technology, information abundance, and so on.[17] In these companies, product life cycles are often short and all firms live under the constant threat of technological innovations that can change the structure of the industry. Individual firms must constantly redesign their processes around new products. Across the industry, spinoff firms are continually emerging. Thus, a common development model includes venture capitalists working with high-technology entrepreneurs in the development, manufacture, and distribution of innovative products or services.

Across these three examples, some key characteristics of the new organization form are clearly visible. Organizations of the future are likely to be *vertically disaggregated:* functions typi-cally encompassed within a single organization will instead be performed in independent organizations. That is, the functions of product design and development, manufacturing, and distribution, ordinarily integrated by a plan and controlled directly by managers, will instead be brought together by *brokers* and held in temporary alignment by a variety of *market mechanisms.*

For example, one form of a vertically disaggregated organization held together by a market mechanism is the franchise system, symbolized by McDonald's or H&R Block. In a franchise system, both the product or service and its basic recipe are provided by the parent corporation to a local management group. Such a model, however, seems appropriate only for a limited set of standard goods or services. In our view, a more flexible and comprehensive approach—and hence a better analog of the organization of the future—is the "designer" system associated with companies such as Yves St. Laurent or Gucci. In these companies, design skills can be applied in a variety of arenas, from electronics to household goods to personal products or services. Similarly, production expertise can be contracted for and applied to a wide array of products or services, as can skills in marketing and distribution. Thus, we expect the 21st century firm to be a temporary organization, brought together by an entrepreneur with the aid of brokers and maintained by a network of contractual ties. In some instances, a single entrepreneur will play a lead role and subcontract for various services. This same individual may also serve as a consultant to others attempting to form their own organizational networks. In other cases, linkages among equals may be created by request through various brokers specializing in a particular service.

Given these characteristics, we have found it useful to refer to this emerging form as the *dynamic network* organization. However, the full realization of this new type of organization awaits the development of a core activating and control mechanism comparable to those that energized the previous organization forms (e.g., the profit center in the divisional form). Our prediction is that this mechanism essentially will be a broad-access computerized information system. Note that most of today's temporary organizations (e.g., a general contractor) have been put together on the basis of lengthy experience among the key participants. Under future conditions of high complexity and rapid change, however, participants in the network organization will first have to be identified, trust between the parties will be a major issue, and fixed-fee contracts specified in advance will usually not be feasible. Therefore, as a substitute for lengthy trust-building processes, participants will have to agree on a general structure of payment for value added and then hook themselves together in a full-disclosure information system so that contributions can be mutually and instantaneously verified. Properly constructed, the dynamic network organization will display the technical expertise of the functional form, the market focus of the divisional form, and the efficient use of resources characteristic of the matrix. And, especially important, it will be able to quickly reshape itself whenever necessary.

CONCLUSION

The United States is in a period of economic challenge and organizational upheaval. There are myriad prescriptions for industrial and organizational renewal, and many of the factors linked to organizational success are being rediscovered today after a thirty-year hiatus. Our own analysis, however, indicates that these characteristics, while important, are merely manifestations of a more fundamental, dynamic process called fit—the search for an organization form that is both internally and externally consistent. We have argued that minimal fit is

necessary for survival, tight fit is associated with corporate excellence, and early fit provides a competitive advantage that can lead to the organization Hall of Fame. Tomorrow's Hall of Fame companies are working on new organization forms today.

REFERENCES

1. Raymond E. Miles and Charles C. Snow, *Organizational Strategy, Structure, and Process* (New York: McGraw-Hill, 1978).
2. Alfred D. Chandler, Jr., *Strategy and Structure* (New York: Doubleday, 1962).
3. Tom Burns and G. M. Stalker, *The Management of Innovation* (London: Tavistock, 1961).
4. Paul R. Lawrence and Jay W. Lorsch, *Organization and Environment* (Boston: Harvard Graduate School of Business Administration, 1967).
5. Michael E. Porter, *Competitive Strategy* (New York: Free Press, 1980).
6. Michael T. Hannan and John H. Freeman, "The Population Ecology of Organizations," *American Journal of Sociology,* vol. 82 (March 1977): 929–964; and Howard E. Aldrich, *Organizations and Environments* (Englewood Cliffs, NJ: Prentice-Hall, 1979).
7. Charles C. Snow and Lawrence G. Hrebiniak, "Strategy, Distinctive Competence, and Organizational Performance," *Administrative Science Quarterly,* vol. 25 (June 1980): 317–336.
8. Robert H. Miles, *Coffin Nails and Corporate Strategies* (Englewood Cliffs, NJ: Prentice-Hall, 1980)
9. The description of Chrysler Corporation was adapted from James Brian Quinn, *Chrysler Corporation,* copyrighted case, The Amos Tuck School of Business Administration, Dartmouth College, 1977.
10. Peter F. Drucker, *The Practice of Management* (New York: Harper & Row, 1954).
11. Thomas J. Peters and Robert H. Waterman, *In Search of Excellence: Lessons from America's Best Run Companies* (New York: Free Press, 1983), Chapter 3.
12. The description of Carnegie Steel was adapted from Paul R. Lawrence and Davis Dyer, *Renew-*

ing American Industry (New York: Free Press, 1983), Chapter 3.

13. The description of General Motors was adapted from Chandler, op. cit., Chapter 3.

14. The description of Sears, Roebuck was adapted from Chandler, op. cit., Chapter 5; and from Drucker, op. cit. Chapter 4.

15. The description of IBM was adapted from "The Colossus That Works," *Time*, July 11, 1983, pp. 44–54.

16. "Can John Young Redesign Hewlett-Packard?" *Business Week*, December 6, 1982, pp. 72–78.

17. For a complete discussion of these conditions, see Alvin Toffler, *The Third Wave* (New York: Bantam Books, 1981); and John Naisbitt, *Megatrends* (New York: Warner Books, 1982).

Evolution and Revolution as Organizations Grow

Larry E. Greiner

A small research company chooses too complicated and formalized an organization structure for its young age and limited size. It flounders in rigidity and bureaucracy for several years and is finally acquired by a larger company.

Key executives of a retail store chain hold on to an organization structure long after it has served its purpose, because their power is derived from this structure. The company eventually goes into bankruptcy.

A large bank disciplines a "rebellious" manager who is blamed for current control problems, when the underlying cause is centralized procedures that are holding back expansion into new markets. Many younger managers subsequently leave the bank, competition moves in, and profits are still declining.

The problems of these companies, like those of many others, are rooted more in past decisions than in present events or outside market dynamics. Historical forces do indeed shape the future growth of organizations. Yet management, in its haste to grow, often overlooks such critical developmental questions as: Where has our organization been? Where is it now? And what do the answers to these questions mean for where we are going? Instead, its gaze is fixed outward toward the environment and the future—as if more precise market projections will provide a new organizational identity.

Companies fail to see that many clues to their future success lie within their own organizations and their evolving states of development. Moreover, the inability of management to understand its organization development problems can result in a company becoming "frozen" in its present stage of evolution or, ultimately, in failure, regardless of market opportunities.

My position in this article is that the future of an organization may be less determined by outside forces than it is by the organization's history. In stressing the force of history on an organization, I have drawn from the legacies of European psychologists (their thesis being that individual behavior is determined primarily by previous events and experiences, not by what lies ahead). Extending this analogy of individual development to the problems of organization development, I shall discuss a series of developmental phases through which growing companies tend to pass. But, first, let me provide two definitions:

1. The term *evolution* is used to describe prolonged periods of growth where no major upheaval occurs in organizational practices.

2. The term *revolution* is used to describe those periods of substantial turmoil in organization life.

As a company progresses through developmental phases, each evolutionary period creates its own revolution. For instance, centralized practices eventually lead to demands for decentralization. Moreover, the nature of management's solution to each revolutionary period determines whether a company will move forward into its next stage of evolutionary growth. As I shall show later, there are at least five phases of organization development, each characterized by both an evolution and a revolution.

KEY FORCES IN DEVELOPMENT

During the past few years a small amount of research knowledge about the phases of organization development has been building. Some of this research is very quantitative, such as time-series analyses that reveal patterns of economic performance over time.[1] The majority of studies, however, are case-oriented and use company records and interviews to reconstruct a rich picture of corporate development.[2] Yet both types of research tend to be heavily empirical without attempting more generalized statements about the overall process of development.

A notable exception is the historical work of Alfred D. Chandler, Jr., in his book *Strategy and Structure.*[3] This study depicts four very broad and general phases in the lives of four large U.S. companies. It proposes that outside market opportunities determine a company's strategy, which in turn determines the company's organization structure. This thesis has a valid ring for the four companies examined by Chandler, largely because they developed in a time of explosive markets and technological advances. But more recent evidence suggests that organization structure may be less malleable than Chandler assumed; in fact, structure can play a critical role in influencing corporate strategy. It is this reverse emphasis on how organization structure affects future growth which is highlighted in the model presented in this article.

From an analysis of recent studies,[4] five key dimensions emerge as essential for building a model of organization development:

1. Age of the organization.
2. Size of the organization.
3. Stages of evolution.
4. Stages of revolution.
5. Growth rate of the industry.

I shall describe each of these elements separately, but first note their combined effect as illustrated in Figure 1. Note especially how each dimension influences the other over time; when all five elements begin to interact, a more complete and dynamic picture of organizational growth emerges.

After describing these dimensions and their interconnections, I shall discuss each evolutionary/revolutionary phase of development and show (a) how each stage of evolution breeds its own revolution, and (b) how management solutions to each revolution determine the next stage of evolution.

Age of the Organization
The most obvious and essential dimension for any model of development is the life span of an organization (represented as the horizontal axis in Figure 1). All historical studies gather data from various points in time and then make comparisons. From these observations, it is evi-

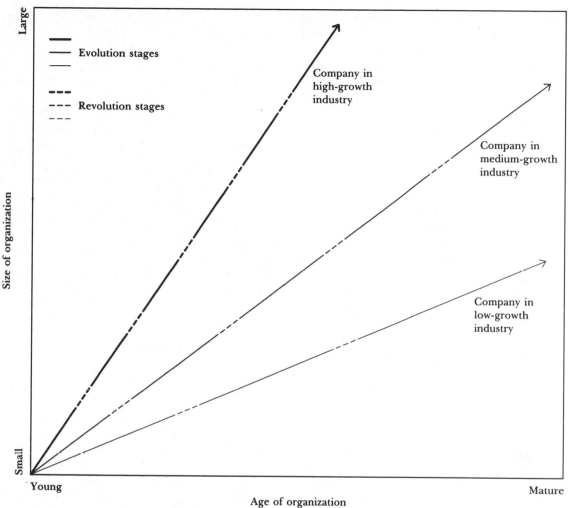

FIGURE 1   *Model of Organization Development*

dent that the same organization practices are not maintained throughout a long time span. This makes a most basic point: management problems and principles are rooted in time. The concept of decentralization, for example, can have meaning for describing corporate practices at one time period but loses its descriptive power at another.

The passage of time also contributes to the institutionalization of managerial attitudes. As a result, employee behavior becomes not only more predictable but also more difficult to change when attitudes are outdated.

Size of the Organization

This dimension is depicted as the vertical axis in Figure 1. A company's problems and solutions tend to change markedly as the number of employees and sales volume increase. Thus, time is not the only determinant of structure; in fact, organizations that do not grow in size can retain many of the same management issues and practices over lengthy periods. In addition to increased size, however, problems of coordination and communication magnify, new functions emerge, levels in the management hierarchy multiply, and jobs become more interrelated.

Stages of Evolution

As both age and size increase, another phenomenon becomes evident: the prolonged growth that I have termed the evolutionary period. Most growing organizations do not expand for two years and then retreat for one year; rather, those that survive a crisis usually enjoy four to eight years of continuous growth without a major economic setback or severe internal disruption. The term evolution seems appropriate for describing these quieter periods because only modest adjustments appear necessary for maintaining growth under the same overall pattern of management.

Stages of Revolution

Smooth evolution is not inevitable; it cannot be assumed that organization growth is linear. *Fortune*'s "500" list, for example, has had significant turnover during the last 50 years. Thus we find evidence from numerous case histories which reveals periods of substantial turbulence spaced between smoother periods of evolution.

I have termed these turbulent times the periods of revolution because they typically exhibit a serious upheaval of management practices. Traditional management practices, which were appropriate for a smaller size and earlier time, are brought under scrutiny by frustrated top managers and disillusioned lower-level managers. During such periods of crisis, a number of companies fail—those unable to abandon past practices and effect major organization changes are likely either to fold or to level off in their growth rates.

The critical task for management in each revolutionary period is to find a new set of organization practices that will become the basis for managing the next period of evolutionary growth. Interestingly enough, these new practices eventually sow their own seeds of decay and lead to another period of revolution. Companies therefore experience the irony of seeing a major solution in one time period become a major problem at a latter date.

Growth Rate of the Industry

The speed at which an organization experiences phases of evolution and revolution is closely related to the market environment of its industry. For example, a company in a rapidly expanding market will have to add employees rapidly; hence, the need for new organization structures to accommodate large staff increases is accelerated. While evolutionary periods tend to be relatively short in fast-growing industries, much longer evolutionary periods occur in mature or slowly growing industries.

Evolution can also be prolonged, and revolutions delayed, when profits come easily. For instance, companies that make grievous errors in a rewarding industry can still look good on their profit and loss statements; thus they can avoid a change in management practices for a longer period. The aerospace industry in its infancy is an example. Yet revolutionary periods still occur, as one did in aerospace when profit opportunities began to dry up. Revolutions seem to be much more severe and difficult to resolve when the market environment is poor.

PHASES OF GROWTH

With the foregoing framework in mind, let us now examine in depth the five specific phases of evolution and revolution. As shown in Figure 2,

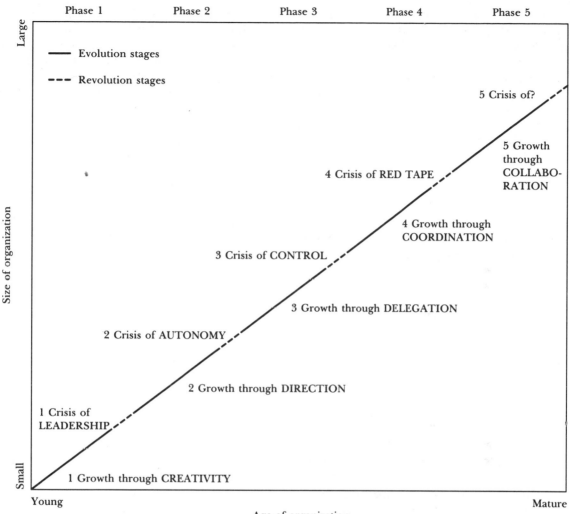

FIGURE 2. *The Five Phases of Growth*

each evolutionary period is characterized by the dominant *management style* used to achieve growth, while each revolutionary period is characterized by the dominant *management problem* that must be solved before growth can continue. The patterns presented in Figure 2 seem to be typical for companies in industries with moderate growth over a long time period; companies in faster growing industries tend to experience all five phases more rapidly, while those in slower growing industries encounter only two or three phases over many years.

It is important to note that *each phase is both an effect of the previous phase and a cause for the next phase.* For example, the evolutionary management style in Phase 3 of the exhibit is "delegation," which grows out of, and becomes the solution to, demands for greater "autonomy" in the preceding Phase 2 revolution. The style of delegation used in Phase 3, however, eventu-

127

ally provokes a major revolutionary crisis that is characterized by attempts to regain control over the diversity created through increased delegation.

The principal implication of each phase is that management actions are narrowly prescribed if growth is to occur. For example, a company experiencing an autonomy crisis in Phase 2 cannot return to directive management for a solution—it must adopt a new style of delegation in order to move ahead.

Phase 1: Creativity . . .

In the birth stage of an organization, the emphasis is on creating both a product and a market. Here are the characteristics of the period of creative evolution:

- The company's founders are usually technically or entrepreneurially oriented, and they disdain management activities; their physical and mental energies are absorbed entirely in making and selling a new product.
- Communication among employees is frequent and informal.
- Long hours of work are rewarded by modest salaries and the promise of ownership benefits.
- Control of activities comes from immediate marketplace feedback; the management acts as the customers react.

. . . & the leadership crisis. All of the foregoing individualistic and creative activities are essential for the company to get off the ground. But therein lies the problem. As the company grows, larger production runs require knowledge about the efficiencies of manufacturing. Increased numbers of employees cannot be managed exclusively through informal communication; new employees are not motivated by an intense dedication to the product or organization. Additional capital must be secured, and

new accounting procedures are needed for financial control.

Thus the founders find themselves burdened with unwanted management responsibilities. So they long for the "good old days," still trying to act as they did in the past. And conflicts between the harried leaders grow more intense.

At this point a crisis of leadership occurs, which is the onset of the first revolution. Who is to lead the company out of confusion and solve the managerial problems confronting it? Quite obviously, a strong manager is needed who has the necessary knowledge and skill to introduce new business techniques. But this is easier said than done. The founders often hate to step aside even though they are probably temperamentally unsuited to be managers. So here is the first critical developmental choice—to locate and install a strong business manager who is acceptable to the founders and who can pull the organization together.

Phase 2: Direction . . .

Those companies that survive the first phase by installing a capable business manager usually embark on a period of sustained growth under able and directive leadership. Here are the characteristics of this evolutionary period:

- A functional organization structure is introduced to separate manufacturing from marketing activities, and job assignments become more specialized.
- Accounting systems for inventory and purchasing are introduced.
- Incentives, budgets, and work standards are adopted.
- Communication becomes more formal and impersonal as a hierarchy of titles and positions builds.
- The new manager and his key supervisors take most of the responsibility for instituting direction, while lower-level supervisors

are treated more as functional specialists than as autonomous decision-making managers.

. . . & *the autonomy crisis.* Although the new directive techniques channel employee energy more efficiently into growth, they eventually become inappropriate for controlling a larger, more diverse and complex organization. Lower-level employees find themselves restricted by a cumbersome and centralized hierarchy. They have come to possess more direct knowledge about markets and machinery than do the leaders at the top; consequently, they feel torn between following procedures and taking initiative on their own.

Thus the second revolution is imminent as a crisis develops from demands for greater autonomy on the part of lower-level managers. The solution adopted by most companies is to move toward greater delegation. Yet it is difficult for top managers who were previously successful at being directive to give up responsibility. Moreover, lower-level managers are not accustomed to making decisions for themselves. As a result, numerous companies flounder during this revolutionary period, adhering to centralized methods while lower-level employees grow more disenchanted and leave the organization.

Phase 3: Delegation . . .

The next era of growth evolves from the successful application of a decentralized organization structure. It exhibits these characteristics:

- Much greater responsibility is given to the managers of plants and market territories.
- Profit centers and bonuses are used to stimulate motivation.
- The top executives at headquarters restrain themselves to managing by exception, based on periodic reports from the field.
- Management often concentrates on making

new acquisitions which can be lined up beside other decentralized units.
- Communication from the top is infrequent, usually by correspondence, telephone, or brief visits to field locations.

The delegation stage proves useful for gaining expansion through heightened motivation at lower levels. Decentralized managers with greater authority and incentive are able to penetrate larger markets, respond faster to customers, and develop new products.

. . . & *the control crisis.* A serious problem eventually evolves, however, as top executives sense that they are losing control over a highly diversified field operation. Autonomous field managers prefer to run their own shows without coordinating plans, money, technology, and manpower with the rest of the organization. Freedom breeds a parochial attitude.

Hence, the Phase 3 revolution is under way when top management seeks to regain control over the total company. Some top managements attempt a return to centralized management, which usually fails because of the vast scope of operations. Those companies that move ahead find a new solution in the use of special coordination techniques.

Phase 4: Coordination . . .

During this phase, the evolutionary period is characterized by the use of formal systems for achieving greater coordination and by top executives taking responsibility for the initiation and administration of these new systems. For example:

- Decentralized units are merged into product groups.
- Formal planning procedures are established and intensively reviewed.
- Numerous staff personnel are hired and located at headquarters to initiate companywide programs of control and review for line managers.

- Capital expenditures are carefully weighed and parceled out across the organization.
- Each product group is treated as an investment center where return on invested capital is an important criterion used in allocating funds.
- Certain technical functions, such as data processing, are centralized at headquarters, while daily operating decisions remain decentralized.
- Stock options and companywide profit sharing are used to encourage identity with the firm as a whole.

All of these new coordination systems prove useful for achieving growth through more efficient allocation of a company's limited resources. They prompt field managers to look beyond the needs of their local units. While these managers still have much decision-making responsibility, they learn to justify their actions more carefully to a "watchdog" audience at headquarters.

. . . & *the red-tape crisis.* But a lack of confidence gradually builds between line and staff, and between headquarters and the field. The proliferation of systems and programs begins to exceed its utility; a red-tape crisis is created. Line managers, for example, increasingly resent heavy staff direction from those who are not familiar with local conditions. Staff people, on the other hand, complain about uncooperative and uninformed line managers. Together both groups criticize the bureaucratic paper system that has evolved. Procedures take precedence over problem solving, and innovation is dampened. In short, the organization has become too large and complex to be managed through formal programs and rigid systems. The Phase 4 revolution is under way.

Phase 5: Collaboration . . .

The last observable phase in previous studies emphasizes strong interpersonal collaboration in an attempt to overcome the red-tape crisis. Where Phase 4 was managed more through formal systems and procedures, Phase 5 emphasizes greater spontaneity in management action through teams and the skillful confrontation of interpersonal differences. Social control and self-discipline take over from formal control. This transition is especially difficult for those experts who created the old systems as well as for those line managers who relied on formal methods for answers.

The Phase 5 evolution, then, builds around a more flexible and behavioral approach to management. Here are its characteristics:

- The focus is on solving problems quickly through team action.
- Teams are combined across functions for task-group activity.
- Headquarters staff experts are reduced in number, reassigned, and combined in interdisciplinary teams to consult with, not to direct, field units.
- A matrix-type structure is frequently used to assemble the right teams for the appropriate problems.
- Previous formal systems are simplified and combined into single multipurpose systems.
- Conferences of key managers are held frequently to focus on major problem issues.
- Educational programs are utilized to train managers in behavioral skills for achieving better teamwork and conflict resolution.
- Real-time information systems are integrated into daily decision making.
- Economic rewards are geared more to team performance than to individual achievement.
- Experiments in new practices are encouraged throughout the organization.

. . . & *the ? crisis.* What will be the revolution in response to this stage of evolution?

Many large U.S. companies are now in the Phase 5 evolutionary stage, so the answers are critical. While there is little clear evidence, I imagine the revolution will center around the "psychological saturation" of employees who grow emotionally and physically exhausted by the intensity of teamwork and the heavy pressure for innovative solutions.

My hunch is that the Phase 5 revolution will be solved through new structures and programs that allow employees to periodically rest, reflect, and revitalize themselves. We may even see companies with dual organization structures: a "habit" structure for getting the daily work done, and a "reflective" structure for stimulating perspective and personal enrichment. Employees could then move back and forth between the two structures as their energies are dissipated and refueled.

One European organization has implemented just such a structure. Five reflective groups have been established outside the regular structure for the purpose of continuously evaluating five task activities basic to the organization. They report directly to the managing director, although their reports are made public throughout the organization. Membership in each group includes all levels and functions, and employees are rotated through these groups on a six-month basis.

Other concrete examples now in practice include providing sabbaticals for employees, moving managers in and out of "hot spot" jobs, establishing a four-day workweek, assuring job security, building physical facilities for relaxation *during* the working day, making jobs more interchangeable, creating an extra team on the assembly line so that one team is always off for reeducation, and switching to longer vacations and more flexible working hours.

The Chinese practice of requiring executives to spend time periodically on lower-level jobs may also be worth a nonideological evaluation. For too long U.S. management has

assumed that career progress should be equated with an upward path toward title, salary, and power. Could it be that some vice presidents of marketing might just long for, and even benefit from, temporary duty in the field sales organization?

IMPLICATIONS OF HISTORY

Let me now summarize some important implications for practicing managers. First, the main features of this discussion are depicted in Table 1, which shows the specific management actions that characterize each growth phase. These actions are also the solutions which ended each preceding revolutionary period.

In one sense, I hope that many readers will react to my model by calling it obvious and natural for depicting the growth of an organization. To me this type of reaction is a useful test of the model's validity.

But at a more reflective level I imagine some of these reactions are more hindsight than foresight. Those experienced managers who have been through a developmental sequence can empathize with it now, but how did they react when in the middle of a stage of evolution or revolution? They can probably recall the limits of their own developmental understanding at that time. Perhaps they resisted desirable changes or were even swept emotionally into a revolution without being able to propose constructive solutions. So let me offer some explicit guidelines for managers of growing organizations to keep in mind.

Know Where You Are in the Developmental Sequence
Every organization and its component parts are at different stages of development. The task of top management is to be aware of these stages; otherwise, it may not recognize when the time

TABLE 1.   *Organization Practices During Evolution in the Five Phases of Growth*

Category	Phase 1	Phase 2	Phase 3	Phase 4	Phase 5
Management focus	Make & sell	Efficiency of operations	Expansion of market	Consolidation of organization	Problem solving & innovation
Organization structure	Informal	Centralized & functional	Decentralized & geographical	Line-staff & product groups	Matrix of teams
Top management style	Individualistic & entrepreneurial	Directive	Delegative	Watchdog	Participative
Control system	Market results	Standards & cost centers	Reports & profit centers	Plans & investment centers	Mutual goal setting
Management reward emphasis	Ownership	Salary & merit increases	Individual bonus	Profit sharing & stock options	Team bonus

for change has come, or it may act to impose the wrong solution.

Top leaders should be ready to work with the flow of the tide rather than against it; yet they should be cautious, since it is tempting to skip phases out of impatience. Each phase results in certain strengths and learning experiences in the organization that will be essential for success in subsequent phases. A child prodigy, for example, may be able to read like a teenager, but he cannot behave like one until he ages through a sequence of experiences.

I also doubt that managers can or should act to avoid revolutions. Rather, these periods of tension provide the pressure, ideas, and awareness that afford a platform for change and the introduction of new practices.

Recognize the Limited Range of Solutions
In each revolutionary stage it becomes evident that this stage can be ended only by certain specific solutions; moreover, these solutions are different from those which were applied to the problems of the preceding revolution. Too often it is tempting to choose solutions that

were tried before, which makes it impossible for a new phase of growth to evolve.

Management must be prepared to dismantle current structures before the revolutionary stage becomes too turbulent. Top managers, realizing that their own managerial styles are no longer appropriate, may even have to take themselves out of leadership positions. A good Phase 2 manager facing Phase 3 might be wise to find another Phase 2 organization that better fits his talents, either outside the company or with one of its newer subsidiaries.

Finally, evolution is not an automatic affair; it is a contest for survival. To move ahead, companies must consciously introduce planned structures that not only are solutions to a current crisis but also are fitted to the *next* phase of growth. This requires considerable self-awareness on the part of top management, as well as great interpersonal skill in persuading other managers that change is needed.

Realize That Solutions Breed New Problems
Managers often fail to realize that organizational solutions create problems for the future

132

(i.e., a decision to delegate eventually causes a problem of control). Historical actions are very much determinants of what happens to the company at a much later date.

An awareness of this effect should help managers to evaluate company problems with greater historical understanding instead of "pinning the blame" on a current development. Better yet, managers should be in a position to *predict* future problems, and thereby to prepare solutions and coping strategies before a revolution gets out of hand.

A management that is aware of the problems ahead could well decide *not* to grow. Top managers may, for instance, prefer to retain the informal practices of a small company, knowing that this way of life is inherent in the organization's limited size, not in their congenial personalities. If they choose to grow, they may do themselves out of a job and a way of life they enjoy.

And what about the managements of very large organizations? Can they find new solutions for continued phases of evolution? Or are they reaching a stage where the government will act to break them up because they are too large.

CONCLUDING NOTE

Clearly, there is still much to learn about processes of development in organizations. The phases outlined here are only five in number and are still only approximations. Researchers are just beginning to study the specific developmental problems of structure, control, rewards,

and management style in different industries and in a variety of cultures.

One should not, however, wait for conclusive evidence before educating managers to think and act from a developmental perspective. The critical dimension of time has been missing for too long from our management theories and practices. The intriguing paradox is that by learning more about history we may do a better job in the future.

NOTES

1. See, for example, William H. Starbuck, "Organizational Metamorphosis," in *Promising Research Directions,* edited by R. W. Millman and M. P. Hottenstein (Tempe, Arizona, Academy of Management, 1968), p. 113.
2. See, for example, the *Grangesberg* case series, prepared by C. Roland Christensen and Bruce R. Scott, Case Clearing House, Harvard Business School.
3. *Strategy and Structure: Chapters in the History of the American Industrial Enterprise* (Cambridge, Massachusetts, The M.I.T. Press, 1962).
4. I have drawn on many sources for evidence: (a) numerous cases collected at the Harvard Business School; (b) *Organization Growth and Development,* edited by William H. Starbuck (Middlesex, England, Penguin Books, Ltd., 1971), where several studies are cited; and (c) articles published in journals, such as Lawrence E. Fouraker and John M. Stopford, "Organization Structure and the Multinational Strategy," *Administrative Science Quarterly,* Vol. 13, No. 1, 1968, p. 47; and Malcolm S. Salter, "Management Appraisal and Reward Systems," *Journal of Business Policy,* Vol. 1, No. 4, 1971.

Formal Organization Arrangements: Structure and Systems

INTRODUCTION AND OVERVIEW

Formal organization arrangements set the context within which individuals and groups operate. Organization arrangements include formal structure, rules, systems, and procedures that provide opportunities and constraints for managerial action. Organization arrangements are a powerful determinant of behavior, since they affect decision-making premises, locus and flows of information and influence, and human resource flows. Organization arrangements are an important managerial lever in that they are powerful determinants of behavior and are easily shaped by managerial action.

Organization arrangements include a range of organization characteristics. *Strategic grouping* is the most basic aspect of organization arrangements. Any manager must allocate scarce resources; these resources can be allocated by function, product, market, geography, or some combination (e.g., matrix forms). The choice of strategic grouping needs to be driven by strategy/objectives. Given a choice of fundamental form, managers need to decide the *number and structure of subunits* (e.g., research, development, engineering units). The choice and structure of subunits are driven by strategy and task considerations.

Grouping and subunit design split the organization into pieces. *Formal linking mechanisms* are required to achieve linkage between interdependent units. *Management systems,* including reward, planning and control systems, and linking roles, are all formal mechanisms to achieve coordination across interdependent groups. The more complex or intense the linkage requirements, the more complex the required formal linking mechanisms. Finally, formal *human resource management systems,* including career, appraisal, and socialization practices, are formal mechanisms that ensure the effective recruitment, socialization, and development of human resources. These human resource mechanisms need to be linked to business strategy.

One important aspect of the manager's job is to choose and/or adapt organization arrangements to get work done. Formal design must follow function. While the degree of leverage over organization arrangements will vary by level in the firm, all managers have some degree of influence over the design and/or use of grouping, linking, and reward mechanisms. Section II introduces a set of ideas, based on information-processing logic, on managing formal organization arrangements. The readings suggest there is no one best organization form. Rather, organization arrangements must fit strategic/task demands subject to individual, cultural, and historical constraints. Finally, formal organization arrangements need to facilitate task accomplishment in both the short and long term. We begin our discussion of internal entrepreneurship and organization learning in this section, leaving a more thorough discussion of adaptation until Section V.

READINGS IN SECTION II

Using information-processing concepts as a framework to think about organization arrangement choices, Nadler and Tushman discuss strategic grouping and linking decisions and their linkage to strategic and work requirements. While the previous readings focused on organization arrangements for today's strategy and task demands, Burgelman's suggests that different designs must be considered to enhance internal entrepreneurship and innovation.

The next set of articles in the section concerns formal management systems. Stata and Maidique focus on designing bonus systems to enhance short- and long-term performance, while Kerr's essay reemphasizes the importance of designing reward systems to enhance work accomplishment. Posner's article discusses the importance of combining financial awards with nonfinancial rewards.

The last two articles in this section discuss the importance of management systems. Pfeffer observes that organization demography affects innovation, conflict patterns, politics, and adaptation. He suggests that human resource systems can be designed to shape demographic patterns via selection, hiring, promotion, and developmental practices. Schuler relates human resources practices and organization design to innovation and entrepreneurship.

4

FORMAL ORGANIZATION ARRANGEMENTS: STRUCTURE AND SYSTEMS

Strategic Linking: Designing Formal Coordination Mechanisms

David A. Nadler

Michael L. Tushman

Cases:

Jean Shaeffer, President of Federal Engineering, is grappling with an important decision for her engineering products firm (see Figure 1). Currently the industry leader in scientific instruments and process control products, her firm has not gotten any of the burgeoning systems business. This new market requires the production of integrated systems tailored to different user-needs. While Federal Engineering, with its divisional structure, has been able to provide first quality instruments, it has not been able to produce competitive systems. Some-

how, Federal's systems have been late and of low quality and have generated substantial customer dissatisfaction. Shaeffer's hunch is that while her firm has excellent technical talent, the distinct groups just do not work well together. There are priority difficulties, a lack of information sharing, and a lack of working together for the good of the systems business. Shaeffer's dilemma is that she must not jeopardize the instrument business while attacking the firm's problems in the systems area.

Roger Laffer, Senior Strategy Officer for Office Products Corporation, has been asked by the firm's CEO to help come up with an institutional framework for corporate technology transfer (see Figure 2). While this firm has been

From *Strategic Organization Design* by David Nadler and Michael L. Tushman. Copyright © 1988 by Scott, Foresman and Company. Reprinted by permission.

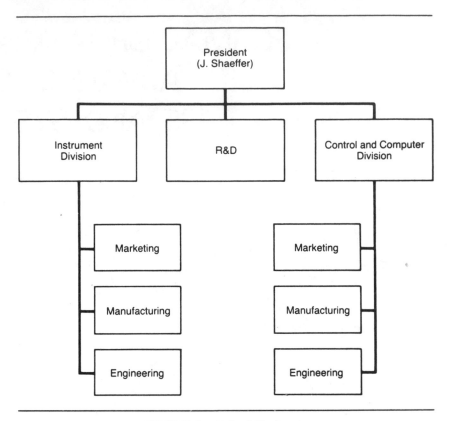

FIGURE 1.   *Federal Engineering*

widely known for its technological and market excellence in computers, printers, and office products, the firm has a dismal record in capitalizing on technologies across existing business units. Laffer feels that the corporation's focus on distinct products/market niches hinders its ability to deal with opportunities that did not neatly fit into corporate categories. Laffer wonders whether a revised structure, along with top management support, could provide an institutional infrastructure to support technology transfer.

Both Shaeffer and Laffer are dealing with problems of strategic linking. Both must develop a set of formal linking mechanisms that will work to enhance, encourage, and facilitate coordination between distinct groups in their firms. Strategic linking issues follow directly from strategic grouping choices. Strategic grouping focuses resources by product, market, discipline, or geography. This grouping of resources puts some resources together *and* splits other resources. For example, a disciplinary-organized pharmaceutical laboratory focuses attention on disciplines but scatters individuals who are interested in therapeutic areas. In a product organization, functional expertise is split among product areas. Strategic linking involves choosing formal structures that link units that have been split during strategic grouping. Once strategic grouping decisions have been made, the next step is to coordi-

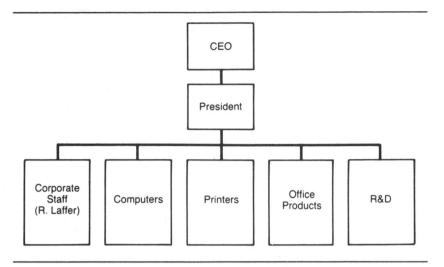

FIGURE 2.   *Office Products Company*

nate, or link, the units so that the firm can operate as an integrated whole.

Where grouping decisions are driven by strategy considerations, strategic linking is driven by the degree of **task interdependence** between areas. Different degrees of task interdependence require different types of formal linking mechanisms. The objective is to build linking mechanisms that allow adequate information processing between groups. Linking mechanisms that are not adequate to handle necessary information will result in poorly coordinated work. Those linking mechanisms that are more extensive than necessary will hinder information flow and result in unnecessary cost. This chapter discusses different types of work interdependence, presents a range of formal linking mechanisms, and concludes with a methodology for making linking decisions (see Figure 3).

VARIETIES OF TASK INTERDEPENDENCE

Strategic grouping results in a set of groups that are dedicated to product, markets, func-

tion, and/or discipline. Strategic grouping provides the basic architecture of the firm at each level of analysis. Strategic linking involves choosing those sets of formal linking mechanisms to coordinate the different groups so the organization functions as a whole. For example, at Federal Engineering, Jean Shaeffer must choose a set of formal linking mechanisms to link the two divisions together in service of the systems business.

Linking follows directly from grouping and, as with strategic grouping, must be accomplished at multiple levels of analysis. Our design problem involves choosing the right set of linking mechanisms to deal with: (1) work flows between distinct units, (2) the need for disciplinary- or staff-based professionals to have contact across the firm, and (3) work flows associated with emergencies, crises, or other nonroutine events.

The conceptual thread across work flow, disciplinary linkages, and work flows under crisis conditions is work-related interdependence. Managers choose linking mechanisms to deal with this source of uncertainty. The greater the task interdependence, the greater the need for coordination and joint problem solving. The more complex the degree of work/task interde-

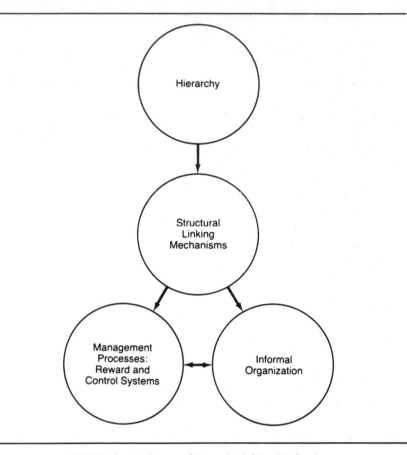

FIGURE 3.   *A Range of Formal Linking Mechanisms*

pendence, the more complex the formal linkage devices must be to handle work-related uncertainty. On the other hand, groups that are only weakly interdependent have relatively little need for coordination and joint problem solving and therefore need simple formal linking devices.

Consider branch banks located throughout a city. Each branch bank runs essentially independently of each other except for the common sharing of advertising and marketing resources. Similarly, business units within a diversified firm with completely different product/market niches are also essentially independent of each other except for those corporate resources that are shared between divisions (e.g., technology, staff). Both of these examples illustrate **pooled interdependence**. Units that operate independently but are part of the same organization and therefore share scarce resources must deal with the pooled nature of their interdependence. Units with pooled interdependence have a minimal amount of coordination and linking requirements (see Figure 4).

At Olympic Oil, the Petroleum Products Division extracts petroleum from the ground and provides the raw material for the Polymer Chemistry Division (see Figure 5). This division makes a variety of products that various end-use divisions use in the production of consumer

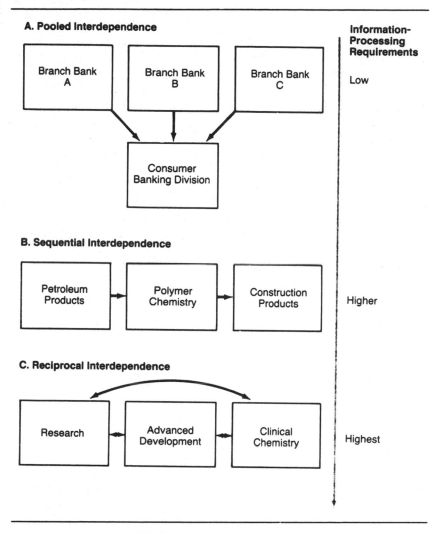

FIGURE 4.   Forms of Interdependence

and construction products. Similarly, in the back office of a bank, checks move through a series of groups before they exit the bank. These examples illustrate **sequential interdependence** (review Figure 4). Sequentially interdependent units must deal with a greater degree and variety of problem-solving and coordination requirements than units that have pooled interdependence. Groups that have sequential interdependence must attend to close

coordination and timing so that work flows remain smooth and uninterrupted; each unit in the work flow is dependent on prior units.

At Federal Engineering, Marketing must work with R&D and with Production in the development of new products. Each functional area must be in close contact with the others to ensure the synthesis of market, technological, and production considerations. Similarly, in an advertising agency, the media, creative, and ac-

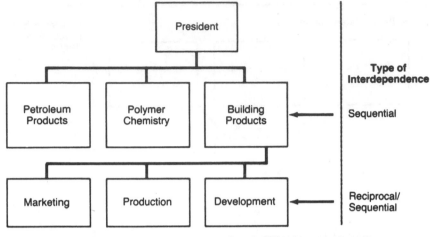

FIGURE 5.   Olympic Oil

count services areas must work closely with each other in the development of ad campaigns for their clients. These examples illustrate **reciprocal interdependence**, that is, interdependence in which each group must work with each other unit in the production of a common product (review Figure 4). Reciprocal interdependence imposes substantial coordination and problem-solving requirements between units; no one unit can accomplish its task without the active contribution of each other unit.

Pooled, sequential, and reciprocal interdependence represent different degrees of work-related interdependence. Reciprocal interdependence imposes greater coordination costs and complexity than sequential, which, in turn, requires greater coordination than pooled interdependence. Beyond work flows, accentuated task interdependence can also arise in emergency, temporary, or crisis situations, in which units that normally only pool their activities must suddenly work together. For example, in our branch bank example, if one part of town suffers a black out, then the other branch banks must work together more closely to deal with the emergency. Similarly, independent product divisions that share a common technology must work together for those unique corporate ventures that attempt to combine the strengths of the two divisions.

Finally, quite apart from work flow considerations, knowledge-based staff and/or professionals must retain contact across organization boundaries or they will become overly specialized and/or lose touch with the state-of-the-art in their respective fields. The greater the rate of change in the discipline or staff areas, the greater the professionally anchored interdependence. At Warner-Lambert, for example, biologists in various areas of the corporation held monthly seminars to inform each other of current biological developments. This need for continual updating was much less critical in the more routine toxicological areas.

Whether driven by work flows, crises, or professionally anchored need for collaboration, these differing degrees of work-related interdependence impose different information processing requirements. Those units that have pooled interdependence (or in which the rate of change of the underlying knowledge base is low) have fewer coordination demands and information processing requirements than units that have reciprocal interdependence (or in which the rate of change of the underlying knowledge base is rapid). The designer's challenge is to choose the appropriate set of linking mechanisms to deal with the information-processing requirements that arise from work-related interdependence.

Finally, just as strategic grouping is relevant at multiple levels of analysis, so too is the assessment of work-related interdependence. For example, at Olympic Oil (review Figure 5), the divisions are sequentially interdependent. However, within each division, the respective functional areas must attend to reciprocal interdependence as they attempt to develop new and innovative products in their respective markets. Similarly, at Federal Engineering, not only was there reciprocal interdependence between the functional areas, but within R&D, each discipline was reciprocally interdependent in new product development efforts. Thus, the degree of task/work interdependence is not constant across organizations. The degree of work-related interdependence must be assessed at each level of analysis.

STRATEGIC LINKING: A RANGE OF LINKING MECHANISMS

Various types of formal mechanisms can be used to link, or coordinate, the efforts of organizational groups. Our objective is to choose those structural linking mechanisms that provide adequate information flows, procedures, and structures to deal with the information requirements imposed by work-related interdependence. Formal linking mechanisms that are not sufficient to handle linking requirements will result in poorly coordinated work. Those linking mechanisms that are more extensive than need be will result in unnecessary costs and overcomplexity. Structural linking mechanisms can be analyzed in terms of their ability to handle information flows and complex problem-solving requirements.[1]

Hierarchy

The most simple form of structural linking is the **hierarchy**: the formal distribution of power and authority. The hierarchy of authority follows directly from grouping decisions. For example, in a divisional structure, the divisional general managers report to the president of the firm, while functional managers report to their respective divisional general managers (review Figure 1). Coordination and linking between managers at the same level can be accomplished via their common boss. The common boss serves as an information channel, can exercise control over how much and what types of information move between groups, and can adjudicate problems that arise in his or her area.

The formal hierarchy is the simplest and one of the most pervasive formal linking mechanisms. Focused, sustained, and consistent behavior by the manager can both direct and set the stage for the effective coordination between organizational groups. The hierarchy is, however, a limited linking mechanism. Because of inherent cognitive/information-processing capacity, even modest amounts of task interdependence, exceptions, crises, or environmental uncertainty can overload the individual manager. When linking requirements begin to overload the first common supervisor (e.g., see earlier Shaeffer, Laffer examples), other formal mechanisms must be used to complement the manager as a linking mechanism.

Structural Linking

Liaison Roles. At Federal Engineering, the development of process control systems requires the close coordination between the Instrument and Control Divisions. While some linking occurs via the hierarchy (i.e., through Shaeffer), much more intense problem solving occurs between two **liaison individuals**. John O'Connor and Phil Dinsky, respected members of the two divisions, are the point-men on the systems business. These two individuals serve as sources of information and expertise for problems and as contacts and advisors on systems work that affects their two divisions.

O'Connor and Dinsky represent formal liaison roles—formal roles that serve as information conduits and initiators of problem-solving endeavors deep in the organization. These liaison roles are responsible for enhanced information flows and coordination between units, although they rarely have authority to back up their positions. The liaison role is not usually a full-time responsibility but rather is done in conjunction with other activities (see Figure 6).

Cross-Unit Groups. At Federal Engineering, the Air Force is a particularly important cus-

tomer; Federal Engineering supplies the Air Force with a range of products and services. There are numerous Air Force complaints, however, of sloppy coordination and incomplete and/or inconsistent information among Federal Engineering professionals. To provide focused Air Force coordination between the different divisions, Shaeffer convened an Air Force integrating committee. This committee brought all key Federal Engineering actors together—a cross-unit group—to ensure a common posture toward the Air Force (see Figure 7).

The Air Force coordinating committee is one example of a range of possible group-based formal coordinating mechanisms. Groups made up of task-relevant representatives meet to focus on particular clients, prod-

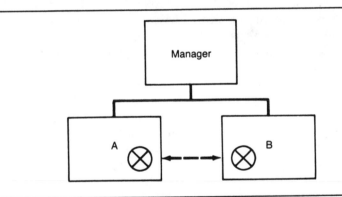

FIGURE 6.   *Liaison Roles*

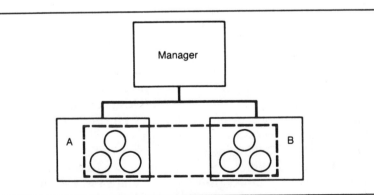

FIGURE 7.   *Cross-Unit Groups*

ucts, markets, and/or problems. These groups can be permanent, temporary, or ad hoc. Their objective is to assure that relevant expertise comes together to deal with their joint task/problem.

In contrast with liaison roles, cross-unit groups provide a more extensive forum for information exchange, for coordination, and for the resolution of conflict between work units. Although these task forces, teams, or groups may form as need be, it may also be appropriate to design cross-unit groups into the structure if there are ongoing cross-unit projects. In a medical center, for example, a representative group of individuals from the key divisions might be responsible for establishing and adjusting guidelines and processes that affect work flows across divisions.

Integrator Role or Department. If problem-solving requirements increase and more decisions affecting multiple groups must be made at lower levels of the organization, teams and/or liaison individuals might not be sufficient. Cross-unit groups may result in no one person feeling accountable for the total performance of the group. Conflicts sometimes arise within cross-unit groups or between liaison individuals, yet the first common boss might not have the expertise and/or time to adjudicate these differences. A solution to the need for real-time problem solving and for bringing general management's point of view to lower levels in the organization is to appoint an individual as **integrator**. This integrator role is responsible for taking a general management point of view in helping multiple-work groups accomplish a joint task, such as a specific product or project (see Figure 8).

Product, brand, geographic, and account managers are examples of formal roles created to bring a general management perspective to specialized managers who bring focused expertise, yet relatively narrow concerns to team meetings. Integrators have the formal responsibility of achieving coordination across the organization. While integrators report to senior management, they usually do not have formal authority to direct their functional and/or disciplinary colleagues. Because of this dotted-line relationship to members of their team, integrators must rely on expertise, interpersonal competence, and team and conflict-resolution skills to shape the efforts of frequently recalcitrant team members.

Integrator roles must acquire functional

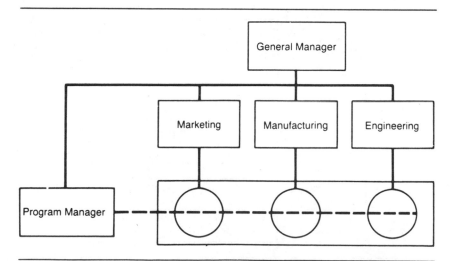

FIGURE 8.   Integrators (Project, Brand, Program, Account Managers)

or disciplinary resources to accomplish their work. When there are several projects, accounts, or products, each of these must compete with one another for resources. For example, in a functional organization, if there are five new product efforts, each of these must acquire scarce resources and attention from functional managers. To increase the power of the product/project organization and to help coordinate resources among products, a product development department is sometimes created (see Figure 9).

In product/project organizations, the product side of the organization has its own senior manager who reports along the same line as the functional managers. This senior manager formally represents the product side of the organization at senior levels and assists in resource allocation across projects. However, the functional organization still reports to its functional supervisors and has a dotted-line relationship with the project/product manager. While our example has centered on project/product integrator roles, the role is quite general. It is a role to counter the consequences of strategic grouping, to achieve coordination and real-time problem solving at lower levels of complex organizations.

Matrix Structures. Some strategies require equal attention to several strategic contingencies, for example, products and markets or

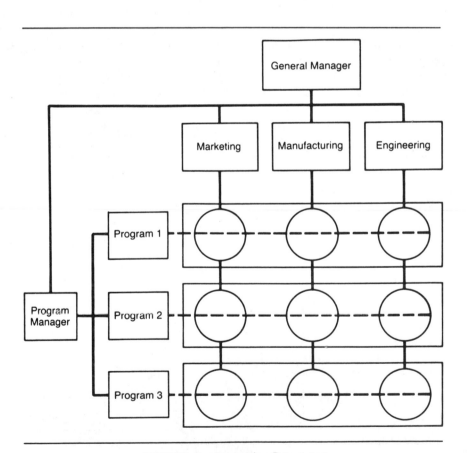

FIGURE 9. *Integrating Department*

product and geography. Similarly, in highly uncertain environments with highly interdependent tasks, great pressures for coordination may come from both the functional and product sides of the organization. Whenever strategy requires the simultaneous maximization of several dimensions (e.g., product, market, geographic, time) and/or when information-processing requirements demand simultaneous consideration of several dimensions, integrating roles are not sufficient to handle the enormous information-processing requirements. When it is important to give equal attention to several critical contingencies and when information-processing demands are substantial, **matrix structures** are appropriate.

A matrix organization structurally improves coordination between multiple perspectives by balancing the power between dimensions of the organization and by installing

systems and roles to achieve multiple objectives at once. For example, an R&D facility that wants to maximize disciplinary competence *and* product focus might invest in a matrix structure. Directors of the different laboratories would then report to both their disciplinary and product managers. The dotted-line relationship (seen in the integrator role) becomes solid; key members of the laboratory have two bosses.

Figure 10 presents a matrix organization structure. It has two chains of command. On the right side, the functional departments continue to exist. The organization still benefits from the information exchange and control provided by the grouping of people by function. On the left is another chain of command, with a product manager for each major new product coordinating the activities of individuals across functional groups. Thus, those managers within each function who head product

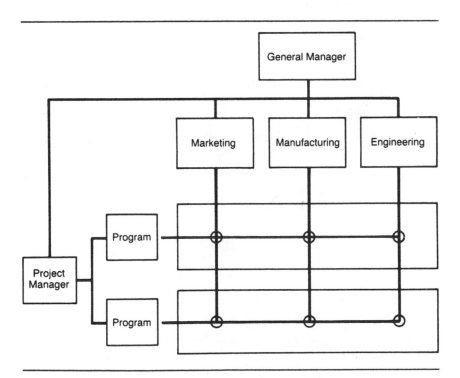

FIGURE 10. Matrix Organization

activities report to two bosses at once, a functional boss and a product boss. In this way, information is processed both within and across functional groups and coordination of different product-oriented activities is achieved.

Matrix structures are very complex. They require dual systems, roles, controls, and rewards. Systems, structures, and processes must be developed to handle both dimensions of the matrix. Further, matrix managers must deal with the difficulties of sharing a common subordinate, while the common subordinate must face off against two bosses. As seen in Figure 11, the general manager is the single boss, where each of the sides of the matrix come together. This individual must assure equal power and influence to each side of the matrix. Otherwise the organization will revert back to a single-focus organization. Below the matrix manager there is also a clear hierarchy. His or her subordinates report to one boss. The matrix is most directly felt by the matrix manager and the two matrix supervisors. It is this relatively narrow slice of the organization that really sees matrix systems, roles, procedures, and processes. This set of four roles must constantly balance the pressures and conflicts in a structure that attempts to work several strategic directions at once.

While the matrix structure is the most complex and conflictual linking mechanism, it is also the only structure that attempts to maximize several strategically important considerations at once. Given its complexity and inherent instability, a matrix structure should be reserved for situations in which no other linking alternative is workable.[2]

Making Structural Linking Decisions

Costs and Benefits of Linking Options. Structural linking mechanisms vary by cost and resources utilized, their dependence on the informal organization, and their inherent information-processing capacities. The essence of making linking decisions is to choose those formal linking mechanisms that most effectively handle work-related interdependence. Using overly complex linking mechanisms will be too costly and inefficient, while using too simple linking mechanisms will not get the work done. The hierarchy of structural linking mechanisms

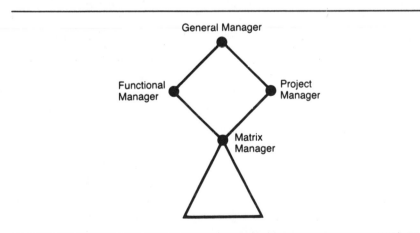

FIGURE 11. *Matrix Organization: Another Perspective*

can be evaluated along the following set of dimensions:

1. The cost and/or amount of resources devoted to each mechanism differs greatly. The formal hierarchy or liaison roles require sustained attention to coordination by a few key individuals. Matrix structures, on the other hand, require dual structures, systems, and procedures. Matrix structures also require time, energy, and effort devoted to committees and teams that attend to both axes of the matrix. The more extensive the linking mechanism in terms of individuals involved, systems, and procedures, the more resources must be devoted and the more costly the linking mechanism.

2. Formal linking mechanisms also differ in their dependence on the informal organization. Where the hierarchy and some liaison roles rest firmly on the formal organization, cross-group units, integrator roles, and matrix structures depend more and more on a healthy informal organization. Those more complex linking mechanisms actually build on organization conflict. These linking mechanisms require an informal organization that can handle the ambiguity and conflict associated with substantial work-related interdependence. Indeed, without an informal organization that deals openly with conflict, that has collaborative norms and values, and that can deal with the complexities of dual-boss relations, matrix organizations will not work. Thus, the more complex the formal linking mechanism, the greater the dependence on the informal system.

3. Finally, information-processing capacities of the various linking mechanisms are different. The hierarchy and liaisons are limited by individual cognitive limitations. These simple linking mechanisms deal well with simple interdependence but cannot deal with substantial uncertainty or complex work interdependence. Integrator roles, task forces, and matrix structures push decision making deep into the system and take advantage of many more resources and perspectives. These linking mechanisms allow for multiple points of view and real-time problem solving and error correction, and they are not dependent on individuals.

More complex linking mechanisms can handle more information and deal more effectively with uncertainty than can simpler linking mechanisms. Liaison roles can only relay limited amounts of information and, while they can identify issues needing coordination, their ability to resolve conflicts is limited. Cross-unit groups can identify issues needing coordination and can involve the requisite number of individuals in inter-unit problem solving. Figure 12 compares information-processing capacity with cost and dependence on the informal organization for the set of structural linking devices.

Making Strategic Linking Decisions. Jean Shaeffer at Federal Engineering required a structure that would continue to produce top-quality scientific instruments *and* would compete more effectively for the systems business. Shaeffer decided to keep her product organization but to add a systems-business manager. Reflecting the importance of the systems business, this systems manager reported directly to Shaeffer and was fully responsible for the systems business. The systems manager was evaluated on systems business and acquired resources from relevant divisions within Federal Engineering. Divisional employees working on systems business were evaluated by their divisional managers as well as the systems manager.

Roger Laffer did some diagnostic work on his firm's technology transfer problem and

	Cost	Dependence on Informal Organization	Information-Processing Capacity
	Low	Low	Low
Hierarchy	↑	↑	↑
Liaison			
Cross-Unit Groups			
Integrator Roles/Departments			
Matrix Organization	↓	↓	↓
	High	High	High

FIGURE 12.   Consequences of Structural Linking Mechanisms

discovered that there was no corporate vehicle to capitalize on technology transfer opportunities. While the divisions had plenty of ideas, there was no corporate instrument to evaluate and/or take action on those ideas. Laffer recommended the creation of a technology transfer board. This committee would be made up of senior technologists and divisional general managers and would be a corporate focal point for technology transfer. The committee was charged with evaluating, pushing, and funding technology transfer opportunities throughout the corporation. This technology transfer board was headed by a senior manager with both technological and market competence and was actively supported by the president and CEO.

Shaeffer and Laffer both faced problems in strategic linking. Shaeffer's organization had to deal with substantial work-related interdependence and considerable time pressure. Shaeffer's choice of a project organization with a powerful project manager reflects the demands of the reciprocal interdependence between divisions. Laffer's task force/committee solution to his firm's technology transfer problem reflects the pooled nature of the work interdependence and the weak-to-moderate perceived time pressure. Consistent with work requirements, Shaeffer chose a complex set of linking mechanisms, whereas Laffer chose a simpler, committee-based linking mechanism.

More generally, the problem in strategic linking is to choose those *sets* of formal linking mechanisms that effectively deal with work-related interdependence. The linking mechanisms discussed here are not mutually exclusive. Rather, managers must choose those sets of linking devices that are able to deal with the work-related uncertainty. For example, at Federal Engineering, Shaeffer must utilize the hierarchy, liaison individuals, cross-group teams, and project organization, all in service of the systems effort. Shaeffer added the project organization only because simpler linking mechanisms were not sufficient for the systems business. Thus, more complex formal linking mechanisms are utilized to deal with work interdependence with which more simple mechanisms are unable to cope.

Structural linking involves choosing the set of formal linking mechanisms that deals with work-related interdependence. Managers must balance the cost of more complex linking mechanisms with their increased information-processing capacity. Structural linking mechanisms must be extensive enough to handle information-processing requirements. Overly complex linking mechanisms will be costly to the organization in terms of time, money, energy, and effort. For example, a matrix organization to handle Laffer's problem would only create confusion and chaos in his technology transfer efforts. On the other hand, linking mechanisms that are not adequate to meet work, professional, or problem demands will result in poorly coordinated work. For example, if Shaeffer used a committee or task force to deal with the systems business, it is highly unlikely that the systems business would be taken seriously throughout Federal Engineering.

The choice of structural linking mechanisms should, then, be based on work-related interdependence. Those more complex linking requirements require more complex formal linking devices. Managers must choose those sets of linking mechanisms that match the information-processing demands of their unit's work interdependence. A mismatch between information-processing requirements and the choice of linking devices will be associated with relatively poor coordination and lower organization performance (see Figure 13).

STRATEGIC LINKING IN ACTION

Formal linking mechanisms address the communication and information-processing needs that arise from grouping decisions. When grouping decisions both group together and split apart resources, linking mechanisms work to achieve coordination between interdependent units. As grouping decisions are made at several levels of analysis, so too are linking decisions. At Olympic Oil (review Figure 5), management must make linking decisions at the

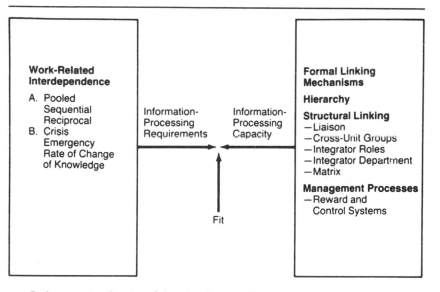

—Performance is a function of choosing that set of formal linking mechanisms to deal with work-related interdependence.

—As interdependence changes, so too should linking mechanisms change.

—Structural linking is required at multiple levels of analysis.

FIGURE 13. *Strategic Linking: Formal Coordinating Mechanisms*

corporate, divisional, and functional levels. As each level deals with different degrees of work interdependence, the choices of structural linking mechanisms will differ. For example, the sequential interdependence at the corporate level can be handled via a senior team or committee; more complex linking mechanisms are required to deal with reciprocal interdependence within the division. Linking decisions, like grouping decisions, are important at each level of an organization.

Structural linking is an important managerial tool. Whereas strategic grouping decisions are single decisions made at each level of analysis, there may be a host of structural linking mechanisms within a particular unit. For example, in an R&D facility, structural linking might be accomplished via a matrix organization throughout the laboratory. Further, special task forces might be utilized to deal with the impact of new technologies on the organization, a top team might be convened to deal with a new competitive threat, and informal committees might be established to share expertise across disciplines within the laboratory. Linking, then, can be a powerful and flexible tool to deal with the different coordination requirements that exist within all organizations. Again, the choice of linking mechanism must be contingent on work-related interdependence.

Finally, as work interdependence shifts over time, so too should the choice of linking mechanisms. For example, if Laffer's technology transfer board (a simple linking mechanism) comes up with a viable candidate for internal development, the increased task interdependence between divisions will require some form of project organization to provide direction and real-time coordination efforts. Again, the choice of linking mechanisms must deal with the requisite task interdependence. As task interdependencies are not fixed, neither can our choices of structural linking mechanisms be fixed (review Figure 13).

MANAGEMENT PROCESSES: REWARD AND CONTROL SYSTEMS

Closely related to formal linking mechanisms is the design of formal reward and evaluation systems. Individuals are motivated by those factors that affect their formal as well as informal rewards. Individuals pay attention to those dimensions on which they are evaluated. As such, any formal linking mechanism must also be tied to complementary formal reward and control systems. If there is an inconsistency between structural linking mechanisms and reward patterns, coordination will suffer. For example, if a sales department is rewarded for sales volume and manufacturing is rewarded for gross margin, then these two groups are working at cross-purposes. No set of structural linking mechanisms can deal with these reward inconsistencies.

As with the choice of linking mechanisms, the choice of reward and control systems must be contingent on work requirements. More complex tasks require complex and subtle reward systems, while simple tasks require elementary reward systems. For example, at Federal Engineering, members of the systems team must be evaluated both for quality instruments as well as for their contribution to the systems business. These more complex reward systems must assess hard and soft criteria, both of which are critical for successful systems products.

Whatever the nature of the reward and/or control systems, they should (1) have clearly specified and operational objectives, (2) reward the total task as well as component tasks, (3) eliminate zero-sum situations, and (4) clearly link performance to valued outcomes. Bonus and incentive systems should be clearly linked to subunit performance and organizational performance. At both Federal Engineering and Laffer's office products company, the choices of structural linking mechanisms must be bolstered with formal reward and incentive systems that clearly evaluate and reward individuals for their contributions to the systems business and technology transfer.[3]

NOTES

1. Our linking ideas build on much earlier work, including J. Galbraith, *Designing Complex Organizations,* (Reading, MA: Addison-Wesley, 1973); L. Sayles and M. Chandler, *Managing Large Systems,* (New York: Harper & Row, 1971); L. Sayles, "Matrix Management: The Structure with a Future," *Organizational Dynamics* (Autumn 1976); R. Katz and T. Allen, "Project Performance and the Locus of Influence in the R&D Matrix," *Academy of Management Journal* 28 (1985) 67–87; A. Van de Ven, A. Delbecq, and R. Koenig, "Determinants of Coordination Modes Within Organizations," *American Sociological Review* 41 (1976) 322–37.

2. See S. Davis, and P. Lawrence, *Matrix,* (Reading, MA: Addison-Wesley, 1977) for an in-depth discussion of matrix organizations.

3. For much more detail on reward and control systems and their linkage to organization design, see E. Lawler, *Pay and Organization Development,* (Reading, MA: Addison-Wesley, 1981); R. Dunbar, "Designs for Organizational Control," in P. Nystrom and W. Starbuck, eds., *Handbook of Organization Design,* (New York: Oxford University Press, 1981); E. Lawler and J. Rhode, *Information and Control in Organizations,* (Santa Monica, CA: Goodyear, 1976).

Designs for Corporate Entrepreneurship in Established Firms

Robert Burgelman

As firms grow large, their capacity to maintain a certain growth rate, based on pursuing opportunities in their mainstream areas of business, eventually diminishes. Sooner or later, firms—Apples and IBMs alike—have to find and exploit opportunities in marginally related, even unrelated, areas through internal corporate venturing and/or acquisition.

Systematic research shows that such diversification is both difficult and risky. Not surprisingly, various authors have argued that firms should maintain the "common thread"[1] and "stick to the knitting."[2] This may be good advice for firms which have not sufficiently exploited their incremental opportunities. It does, however, assume away the fundamental problem and offers little in terms of how firms could improve their capacity to engage in *corporate entrepreneurship:* extending the firm's domain of competence and corresponding opportunity set through internally generated new resource combinations.[3]

In the light of received theory of strategy and organization, the term "corporate entre-

preneurship" seems oxymoronic. This article presents a new model of strategic behavior in large, established firms which identifies entrepreneurial activity as a natural and integral part of the strategic process. The model sheds more light on why the strategic management of entrepreneurial activities constitutes a real challenge for corporate management. This article also proposes a conceptual framework which corporate management may find useful for improving its capacity to deal effectively with entrepreneurial initiatives. This, in turn, provides the basis for discussing conditions under which various organization designs for corporate entrepreneurship may be appropriate and raises some issues and problems associated with implementing such designs.

A NEW MODEL OF THE STRATEGIC PROCESS

Based on a field study of the internal corporate venturing process in one large, established firm and on the re-analysis of landmark studies in the field of strategic management, I have proposed a new model of the strategic process (see Figure 1).[4] Figure 1 shows two fundamentally

© [1984] by the Regents of the University of California. Reprinted from the *California Management Review,* vol. 26, No. 3. By permission of The Regents.

Support from the Strategic Management Program of Stanford University's Graduate School of Business is gratefully acknowledged.

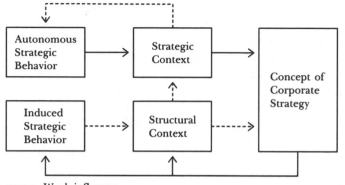

FIGURE 1. A Model of the Interaction of Strategic Behavior, Corporate Context, and the Concept of Strategy

different strategic processes going on simultaneously in large, complex firms.

Induced Strategic Behavior Loop

The bottom loop of the model corresponds to the traditional view of top driven strategic management. The current *concept of strategy* represents the more or less explicit articulation of the firm's theory about the basis for its past and current successes and failures. It provides a more or less shared frame of reference for the strategic actors in the organization, and provides the basis for corporate objective-setting in terms of its business portfolio and resource allocation.

The concept of strategy induces strategic activity in the firm. *Induced* strategic behavior fits in the existing categories used in the firm's strategic planning, and takes place in relation to its familiar external environments. Examples of such strategic behavior emerge around, among others, new product development projects for existing businesses, market development projects for existing products, and strategic capital investment projects for existing businesses.

The current concept of strategy corresponds to a *structural context* aimed at keeping strategic behavior at operational levels in line with the current concept of strategy. Structural context refers to the various administrative mechanisms which top management can manipulate to influence the perceived interests of the strategic actors at the operational and middle levels in the organization. It intervenes in the relationship between induced strategic behavior and the concept of strategy, and operates as a selection mechanism on the induced strategic behavior.

The so-called "excellent companies"[5] all seem to have found *their* way of making the induced strategic behavior loop work exceedingly well. Operational and middle level managers in these firms understand what strategic actions are required in view of the corporate development needs, even though there may be very little explicit attention given to formal "strategy." Managers in such companies identify with the corporate ways and means, yet maintain an element of creative independence. Marks and Spencer, 3M, and Hewlett-Packard are examples of excellent implicit management of the induced strategic behavior loop. General Electric with its SBU system and, until recently, Texas Instruments with its OST system are examples of excellent explicit management of the induced strategic behavior loop.

Autonomous Strategic Behavior Loop

During any given period of time, the bulk of strategic activity in large, complex firms is likely to be of the induced variety. The present model, however, proposes that large, resource-rich firms are likely to possess a reservoir of entrepreneurial potential at operational levels that will express itself in autonomous strategic initiatives. *Autonomous* strategic behavior introduces new categories for the definition of opportunities. Entrepreneurial participants, at the product/market level, conceive new business opportunities, engage in project championing efforts to mobilize corporate resources for these new opportunities, and perform strategic forcing efforts to create momentum for their further development. Middle level managers attempt to formulate broader strategies for areas of new business activity and try to convince top management to support them. This is the type of strategic behavior encountered in the study of internal corporate venturing.[6] Such autonomous strategic initiatives attempt to escape the selective effects of the current structural context, and they make the current concept of corporate strategy problematical. They lead to a redefinition of the corporation's relevant environment and broaden the scope of its business portfolio.

Autonomous strategic behavior takes shape outside of the current concept of strategy. Yet, to be successful, it needs eventually to be accepted by the organization and to be integrated into its concept of strategy. The process through which this can be achieved has been identified as the process of *strategic context* determination. Strategic context determination intervenes in the relationship between autonomous strategic behavior and the concept of strategy. It encompasses the activities through which middle level managers question the current concept of strategy and provide top management with the opportunity to rationalize, retroactively, successful autonomous strategic behavior. This, in turn,

changes the basis for the further inducement of strategic behavior.

The model thus suggests that corporate entrepreneurship is typically constituted by the interlocking strategic activities of managers at multiple levels in the firm's organization. It subsumes two important findings from the literature on innovation in organizations:

- Different processes are involved in generating and implementing innovations.[7]
- There may be a conflict between being excellent at incremental innovation and the capacity for more radical innovation.[8]

It also provides a theoretical explanation for the seemingly contradictory findings of Peters and Waterman that excellent companies seem to have *both* an extraordinarily strong CEO whose influence pervades the entire organization *and* independent mavericks who engage in activities outside the regular channels of hierarchical decision-making.[9] Finally, it provides a preliminary conceptualization of the experimentation-and-selection process through which diversity becomes transformed into a new order in large, complex organizations.

The Managerial Challenge Posed by Autonomous Strategic Behavior

Consider the following vignettes:

> In 1966, calculators were largely mechanized. A young man working for one of the calculator companies brought a model for an electronic calculator to Hewlett-Packard. His own firm was not interested in it because they didn't have the electronic capability. In spite of unfavorable market research forecasts, William Hewlett personally championed the project.[10]

> Back in 1980, Sam H. Eletr, a manager in Hewlett-Packard's labs, tried to persuade the company's new product people to get into biotech-

nology. "I was laughed out of the room," he said. But venture capitalists didn't laugh. They persuaded Mr. Eletr to quit Hewlett-Packard and staked him to $5.2 million to start a new company. Its product: gene machines, which make DNA, the basic material of the genetic code—and the essential raw material in the burgeoning business of genetic engineering. Now, three years later, Hewlett-Packard has formed a joint venture with Genentech Inc. to develop tools for biotechnology. One product it is considering: gene machines.[11]

How should corporate management deal with such autonomous strategic behavior? Clearly, not every new idea or proposal can or should be adopted and developed. Yet, it is not a gratuitous exercise in Monday morning quarterbacking to ask whether the managements of the firms involved in the vignettes had made a *strategic* analysis of the proposals and whether they did indeed make a *strategic* decision not to pursue the proposals of their internal entrepreneurs.

From a strategic management perspective, it does not seem adequate to reject the electronic calculator because "we don't have an electronics capability" or to reject the gene-making machine because "we are not in biotechnology." It seems likely that there must have been some important relevant capabilities in place which allowed the internal entrepreneurs to come up with the proposal and perhaps even develop a prototype in the first place! Even if there is no apparent significant relationship with current capabilities and skills, it is still important to consider the strategic opportunities and/or threats potentially implied by the entrepreneurial proposal. It is precisely these efforts—to extend the firm's domain of competence, to elaborate and recombine the current capabilities, and to define new, unanticipated opportunities—which make internal entrepreneurial activity a vital part of the strategic process in large, established firms.

From a strategic management perspec-

tive, the problem is *how* could corporate management improve its capacity to deal with autonomous strategic behavior, given that, by definition, it does not fit with the current corporate strategy. What is now needed is an analytical framework which can be used by corporate management to assess entrepreneurial proposals and which also leads to tentative conclusions about the use of various organization design alternatives to structure the relationships between entrepreneurial initiatives and the corporation.

A FRAMEWORK FOR ASSESSING INTERNAL ENTREPRENEURIAL PROPOSALS

The conceptual framework focuses on two key dimensions of strategic decision-making concerning internal entrepreneurial proposals. One is the expected *strategic importance* for corporate development. The other is the degree to which proposals are related to the core capabilities of the corporation, i.e., their *operational relatedness*.

Assessing Strategic Importance

How can management assess, as accurately as possible, the strategic importance of an entrepreneurial initiative? Even though this is one of the most important top management responsibilities, it is also one for which top management is often not well equipped. Corporate level managers in large, diversified firms tend to rise through the ranks, having earned their reputation as head of one or more of the operating divisions. By the time they reach the top management level, they have developed a highly reliable frame of reference to evaluate business strategies and resource allocation proposals pertaining to the main lines of business of the corporation. By the same token, their substantive knowledge of new technologies and markets is limited.[12]

There is a tendency for top management to rely on corporate staffs, consultants, and informal interactions with "peers" from other companies to make assessments of new business fields. Such information sources have merit, but they are no substitute for efforts to understand the deeper substantive issues involved in a specific proposal. The latter efforts should be based on requiring middle level managers to "educate" corporate management and to encourage middle level managers to "champion" new proposals based on their own substantive assessments. Such *substantive* interaction between different levels of management is likely to improve top management's capacity to make strategically sound assessments, making them rely less on purely quantitative projection.[13]

It would be useful for top management to have a checklist of critical issues and questions in these substantive interactions. Examples of these are:

- How does this initiative maintain our capacity to move in areas where major current or potential competitors might move?
- How does this help us to find out where *not* to go?
- How does it help us create new defensible niches?
- How does it help mobilize the organization?
- To what extent could it put the firm at risk?
- When should we get out of it if it does not seem to work?
- What is missing in our analysis?

Strategic assessment will sometimes result in a classification of a proposal as "very" or "not at all" important. In other cases, the situation will be more ambiguous and lead to assessments like "important for the time being" or "maybe important in the future." Key to the usefulness

of the analysis is that such assessments are based on specific, substantive factors.

Assessing Operational Relatedness

The second key dimension of strategic decision-making concerns the *degree* to which the entrepreneurial proposal requires capabilities and skills that are different from the core capabilities and skills of the corporation. This is relevant for a number of reasons. First, new business proposals may either be driven by newly developed capabilities and skills or they may drive the development of new capabilities and skills, both of which have very different implications.[14] Second, entrepreneurial proposals typically are based on new combinations of corporate capabilities, and this may reveal potential opportunities for positive synergies (or threat of negative synergies). Often, internal entrepreneurs will weave together pieces of technology and knowledge which exist in separate parts of the organization and which would otherwise remain unused.

In order to be able to make the required assessments of the dimension of operational relatedness, corporate management should rely on substantive interactions with middle level managers who champion entrepreneurial projects. To guide these interactions, corporate management again needs a checklist of critical issues and questions in these substantive interactions. Some examples are:

- What are the key capabilities required to make this project successful?
- Where, how, and when are we going to get them if we don't have them yet, and at what cost?
- Who else might be able to do this, perhaps better?
- How will these new capabilities affect the capacities currently employed in our mainstream business?
- What other areas may possibly require suc-

cessful innovative efforts if we move forward with this project?
· What is missing in our analysis?

A useful tool to help corporate management with this assessment is to develop an accurate inventory of current capabilities and skills in various functional areas and to spell out in detail how each area of business activity uses these capabilities and skills. Such a capabilities/businesses *matrix* should be regularly updated and should provide a reference frame for each new entrepreneurial proposal. In light of this, new proposals will sometimes be classified as "very" or "not at all" related. In other cases, the situation will again be somewhat unclear and lead to a "partly related" assessment. In the context of the matrix, these assessments should be made in specific, substantive terms for each proposal.

The assessment framework can now be used to discuss the use of various organization design alternatives for the different types of entrepreneurial proposals.

DESIGN ALTERNATIVES FOR CORPORATE ENTREPRENEURSHIP

Having assessed an entrepreneurial proposal in terms of its strategic importance and operational relatedness, corporate management must choose an organization design for structuring the relationship between the new business and the corporation which is commensurate with its position in the assessment framework. This involves various combinations of *administrative* and *operational* linkages.

Determining Administrative Linkages
The assessment of strategic importance has implications for the degree of *control* corporate

management needs to maintain over the new business development. This, in turn, has implications for the administrative linkages to be established.

If strategic importance is high, strong administrative linkages will be in order. This means, basically, that the new business must be folded into the existing structural context of the firm. Corporate management will want a say in the strategic management of the new business through direct reporting relationships, substantive involvement in planning/budgeting processes, and involvement in trade-offs between the strategic concerns of the new and existing businesses. Measurement and reward systems must reflect clearly articulated strategic objectives for the new business development. Low strategic importance, on the other hand, should lead corporate management to examine how the new business can best be spun off.

In more ambiguous situations, where strategic importance is judged to be somewhat unclear as yet, corporate management should relax the structural context, and allow the new business some leeway in its strategic management. In such situations, the strategic context of the new business remains to be determined. This requires mechanisms facilitating substantive interaction between middle and corporate levels of management, and measurement and reward systems capable of dealing with as yet unclear performance dimensions and strategic objectives.

Determining Operational Linkages
The degree of operational relatedness has implications for the *efficiency* with which both the new and the existing businesses can be managed. This, in turn, has implications for the required operational linkages.

If operational relatedness is judged to be high, strong coupling of the operations of the new and existing businesses is probably in order. Corporate management should ensure that both new and existing capabilities and skills are used well through integration of work flows, adequate mutual adjustment between resource users through lateral relations at the operational level, and free flows of information and know-how through regular contacts between professionals in the new and existing businesses. Low operational relatedness, on the other hand, may require complete decoupling of the operations of new and existing businesses to avoid interferences and concomitant wasteful (because unnecessary) communications and negotiations.

In situations where operational relatedness is partial and not completely clear, loose coupling seems most adequate. In such situations, the work flows of new and existing businesses should remain basically separate, and mutual adjustment should be achieved through individual integrator roles or through task force type mechanisms, rather than directly through the operational level managers. Information and know-how flows, however, should remain as uninhibited as is practical.

Choosing Design Alternatives

Various combinations of administrative and operational linkages produce different design alternatives. These correspond to choices which corporate management has to make regarding the different situations identified in the assessment framework. Figure 2 shows nine such design alternatives.

The design alternatives discussed here are not exhaustive, and the scales for the different dimensions used in the assessment framework remain rudimentary. Much room is left for refinement through further research. By the same token, the framework represented in Figure 2 allows for a preliminary conceptual underpinning for a number of practices encountered in today's business environment.

1. *Direct integration.* High strategic importance and operational relatedness require strong administrative and operational linkages. This means that there is a need to integrate the new business directly into the mainstream of the corporation. Such integration must anticipate internal resistance for reasons well documented in the organizational change literature. The role of "champions"—those who know the workings of the current system very well—are likely to be important in such situations. The need for direct integration is perhaps most likely to occur in highly integrated firms, where radical changes in product concept and/or in process technologies could threaten the overall strategic position of the firm.[15]

2. *New product/business department.* High strate-

		Very Important	Uncertain	Not Important
Operational Relatedness	Unrelated	3. Special Business Units	6. Independent Business Units	9. Complete Spin Off
	Partly Related	2. New Product Business Department	5. New Venture Division	8. Contracting
	Strongly Related	1. Direct Integration	4. Micro New Ventures Department	7. Nurturing and Contracting
		Very Important	Uncertain	Not Important

Strategic Importance

FIGURE 2.   *Organization Designs for Corporate Entrepreneurship*

gic importance and partial operational relatedness require a combination of strong administrative and medium-strong operational linkages. This may be achieved by creating a separate department around an entrepreneurial project in that part (division or group) of the operating system where potential for sharing capabilities and skills is significant. Corporate management should monitor the strategic development of the project in substantive terms and not allow it to be folded (and "buried") into the overall strategic planning of that division or group.[16]

3. *Special business units.* High strategic importance and low operational relatedness may require the creation of specially dedicated new business units. Strong administrative linkages are necessary to ensure the attainment of explicit strategic objectives within specified time horizons throughout the development process. It will often be necessary to later on combine and integrate some of these business units into a new operating division in the corporate structure.[17]

4. *Micro new ventures department.* Uncertain strategic importance and high operational relatedness seem typical for the "peripheral" projects which are likely to emerge in the operating divisions on a rather continuous basis. For such projects, administrative linkages should be loose. The venture manager should be allowed to develop a strategy within budget and time constraints but should otherwise not be limited by current divisional or even corporate level strategies. Operational linkages should be strong, to take advantage of the existing capabilities and skills and to facilitate transferring back newly developed ones. Norman Fast has discussed a "micro" new ventures division design,[18] which would seem to fit the conditions specified here.

5. *New venture division (NVD).* This design is proposed for situations of maximum ambiguity in the assessment framework.[19] The NVD may serve best as a "nucleation" function. It provides a fluid internal environment for projects with the potential to create major new business thrusts for the corporation, but of which the strategic importance remains to be determined as the development process unfolds. Administrative linkages should be fairly loose. Middle level managers supervising a few ventures are expected to develop "middle range" strategies for new fields of business: bringing together projects which may exist in various parts of the corporation, and/or can be acquired externally, and integrating these with some of the venture projects they supervise, to build sizable new businesses. Operational linkages should also be fairly loose, yet be sufficiently developed to facilitate transferring back and forth relevant know-how and information concerning capabilities and skills. Long time horizons—eight to twelve years—are necessary, but ventures should not be allowed to languish. High quality middle level managers are crucial to make this design work.

6. *Independent business units.* Uncertain strategic importance and negligible operational relatedness may make external venture arrangements attractive. Controlling ownership with correspondingly strong board representation may provide corporate management with an acceptable level of strategic control without administrative linkages.[20]

7. *Nurturing plus contracting.* In some cases, an entrepreneurial proposal may be considered unimportant for the firm's corporate development strategy, yet be strongly related to its operational capabilities and skills. Such ventures will typically address "interstices" in the market which may be too small for the company to serve profit-

ably but which offer opportunities for a small business.[21] Top management may want to help such entrepreneurs spin off from the corporation and may, in fact, help the entrepreneur set up his or her business. This provides a known and, in all likelihood, friendly competitor in those interstices, keeping out other ones. Instead of administrative or ownership linkages, there may be a basis for long-term contracting relationships in which the corporation can profitably supply the entrepreneur with some of its excess capabilities and skills. Strong operational linkages related to these contracts may facilitate transfer of new or improved skills developed by the entrepreneur.

8. *Contracting.* The possibilities for nurturing would seem to diminish as the required capabilities and skills of the new business are less related. Yet there may still be opportunities for profitable contracting arrangements and for learning about new or improved capabilities and skills through some form of operational linkages.

9. *Complete spin off.* If strategic importance and operational relatedness are both low, complete spin off will be most appropriate. A decision based on a careful assessment of both dimensions is likely to lead to a well founded decision from the perception of both the corporation and the internal entrepreneur.

Implementing Design Alternatives

In order to implement designs for corporate entrepreneurship effectively, three major issues and potential problems need to be considered. First, corporate management and the internal entrepreneur should view the assessment framework as a tool to clarify—at a particular moment in time—their community of interests and interdependencies and to structure a non-zero sum game. Second, corporate manage-

ment must establish measurement and reward systems which are capable of accomodating the different incentive requirements of different designs. Third, as the development process unfolds, new information may modify the perceived strategic importance and operational relatedness, which may require a renegotiation of the organization design.

To deal effectively with the implementation issues and potential problems, corporate management must recognize internal entrepreneurs as "strategists" and perhaps even *encourage* them to think and act as such. This is necessary because the stability of the relationship will be dependent on both parties feeling that they have achieved their individual interests to the greatest extent, given the structure of the situation. On the part of corporate management, this implies attempts to appropriate benefits from the entrepreneurial endeavor, but only to the extent that they can provide the entrepreneur with the opportunity to be more successful than if he or she were to go it alone. This, in turn, requires simultaneously generous policies to help internal entrepreneurs based on a sound assessment of their proposals and unequivocal determination to protect proprietary corporate capabilities and skills vigorously.[22]

CONCLUSION

Until recently, the Schumpeterian distinction between entrepreneurial and administrated ("bureaucratic") economic activity could be considered adequate. However, in the light of the turbulence of recent industrial developments, this distinction loses much of its relevance. Large, established corporations and new, maturing firms alike are confronted with the problem of maintaining their growth, if not their existence, by exploiting to the fullest the unique resource combinations they have assembled.

Increasingly, there is an awareness that internal entrepreneurs are necessary for firms to achieve growth. The internal entrepreneur, like the external entrepreneur, enacts new opportunities and drives the development of new resource combinations or recombinations. As a result, new forms of economic organization—a broader array of arrangements—are necessary.

In turn, new theories of the firm and a more nuanced view of the role of hierarchies, contracts, and markets are required. The conceptual foundations of these theories are currently being laid in such fields as the economics of internal organization, agency theory, the theory of legal contracts, and theories of organization design and change. Usually, practitioners are already ahead, experimenting with new organizational forms and arrangements. In the process, they generate new data and raise the basis for new research questions.

A better understanding of the process of corporate entrepreneurship will facilitate the collaboration between firms and their internal entrepreneurs.

REFERENCES

1. H. Igor Ansoff, *Corporate Strategy* (New York, NY: McGraw-Hill, 1965).
2. T. J. Peters and R. H. Waterman, *In Search of Excellence* (New York, NY: Harper and Row, 1983).
3. For a discussion of the theoretical foundations of corporate entrepreneurship, see R. A. Burgelman, "Corporate Entrepreneurship and Strategic Management: Insights from a Process Study," *Management Science,* 29 (1983): 1649–1664.
4. R. A. Burgelman, "A Model of the Interaction of Strategic Behavior, Corporate Context, and the Concept of Strategy," *Academy of Management Review,* 8 (1983): 61–70.
5. Peters and Waterman, op. cit.
6. R. A. Burgelman, "A Process Model of Internal Corporate Venturing in the Diversified Major Firm," *Administrative Science Quarterly,* 28 (1983): 223–244.
7. J. Q. Wilson, "Innovation in Organization: Notes Toward a Theory," in J. D. Thompson, ed. *Approaches to Organizational Design* (Pittsburgh, PA: University of Pittsburgh Press, 1966), pp. 195–218.
8. W. Abernathy, *The Productivity Dilemma* (Baltimore, MD: The Johns Hopkins University Press, 1978).
9. Peters and Waterman, op. cit.
10. R. M. Atherton and D. M. Crites, "Hewlett-Packard: A 1975–1978 Review" (Boston, MA: Harvard Case Services, 1980).
11. This quote was taken from "After Slow Start, Gene Machines Approach a Period of Fast Growth and Steady Profits." *The Wall Street Journal,* December 13, 1983.
12. Henry Kissinger has made the interesting observation that top policy-makers are, basically, strategies-in-action whose fundamental strategic premises are a *given* by the time they reach their positions. See H. A. Kissinger, *White House Years* (Boston, MA: Little Brown, 1979).
13. See also R. A. Burgelman, "Managing the Internal Corporate Venturing Process," *Sloan Management Review* (Winter 1984), pp. 33–48.
14. A. R. Fusfeld, "How to Put Technology into Corporate Planning," in Technology Review, *Innovation* (1976), pp. 53–57.
15. An example of the need for direct integration is documented by Twiss's account of the development of "float glass" at Pilkington Glass, Ltd. See B. Twiss, *Managing Technological Innovation* (London: Longman, 1980); see also A. C. Cooper and D. Schendel, "Strategic Responses to Technological Threats." *Business Horizons* (1976), pp. 61–69, for a discussion of the difficulties firms face when confronted with radical changes in their mainstream operations.
16. An example where the proposed approach might have been useful is provided by one of the major, diversified automotive supplier's handling of electronic fuel injection development. In spite of having the required technology, there was strong resistance from the firm's carburetor division, and the automotive group

management level did not support the development either. Only after a new group level manager took charge of the strategic management of the project and brought in additional operational capabilities and skills did the project take off.

17. IBM's use of the Special Business Unit design to enter the personal computer business is an example. See "Meet the New Lean, Mean IBM," *Fortune,* June 13, 1983, p. 78.

18. N. D. Fast, *The Rise and Fall of Corporate New Venture Divisions* (Ann Arbor, MI: V.M.I. Research Press, 1979).

19. For a discussion of major problems associated with the NVD, see R. A. Burgelman, "Managing the New Venture Division: Research Findings and Implications for Strategic Management," *Strategic Management Journal,* (forthcoming). See also N. D. Fast, op. cit.

20. IBM's use of Independent Business Units is one example where the corporation keeps complete ownership. See Fortune, June 13, 1983. An example of joint ownership is provided by how Bank of America has organized its Venture-Capital Business. See "Despite Greater Risks, More Banks Turn to Venture-Capital Business," *The Wall Street Journal,* November 28, 1983.

21. For a discussion of the concept of "interstice," see E. T. Penrose, *The Theory of the Growth of the Firm* (Oxford: Blackwell, 1968).

22. For an account of some examples, see "Spin Offs Mount in Silicon Valley," *The New York Times,* January 3, 1984.

On the Folly of Rewarding A, While Hoping for B

Steven Kerr

Whether dealing with monkeys, rats, or human beings, it is hardly controversial to state that most organisms seek information concerning what activities are rewarded and then seek to do (or at least pretend to do) those things, often to the virtual exclusion of activities not rewarded. The extent to which this occurs of course will depend on the perceived attractiveness of the rewards offered, but neither operant nor expectancy theorists would quarrel with the essence of this notion.

Nevertheless, numerous examples exist of reward systems that are fouled up in that behaviors which are rewarded are those which the rewarder is trying to discourage, while the behavior he desires is not being rewarded at all.

In an effort to understand and explain this phenomenon, this paper presents examples from society, from organizations in general, and from profit-making firms in particular. Data from a manufacturing company and information from an insurance firm are examined to demonstrate the consequences of such reward systems for the organizations involved, and possible reasons why such reward systems continue to exist are considered.

SOCIETAL EXAMPLES

Politics

Official goals are "purposely vague and general and do not indicate . . . the host of decisions that must be made among alternative ways of achieving official goals and the priority of multiple goals . . ." (8, p. 66). They usually may be relied on to offend absolutely no one, and in this sense can be considered high acceptance, low quality goals. An example might be "build better schools." Operative goals are higher in quality but lower in acceptance, since they specify where the money will come from, what alternative goals will be ignored, etc.

The American citizenry supposedly wants its candidates for public office to set forth operative goals, making their proposed programs "perfectly clear," specifying sources and uses of funds, etc. However, since operative goals are lower in acceptance, and since aspirants to public office need acceptance (from at least 50.1 percent of the people), most politicians prefer to speak only of official goals, at least until after the election. They of course would agree to speak at the operative level if "punished" for not doing so. The electorate

From *Academy of Management Journal,* 1975, 18, Number 4. Reprinted by permission.

could do this by refusing to support candidates who do not speak at the operative level.

Instead, however, the American voter typically punishes (withholds support from) candidates who frankly discuss where the money will come from, rewards politicians who speak only of official goals, but hopes that candidates (despite the reward system) will discuss the issues operatively. It is academic whether it was moral for Nixon, for example, to refuse to discuss his 1968 "secret plan" to end the Vietnam war, his 1972 operative goals concerning the lifting of price controls, the reshuffling of his cabinet, etc. The point is that the reward system made such refusal rational.

It seems worth mentioning that no manuscript can adequately define what is "moral" and what is not. However, examination of costs and benefits, combined with knowledge of what motivates a particular individual, often will suffice to determine what for him is "rational."[1] If the reward system is so designed that it is irrational to be moral, this does not necessarily mean that immorality will result. But is this not asking for trouble?

War

If some oversimplification may be permitted, let it be assumed that the primary goal of the organization (Pentagon, Luftwaffe, or whatever) is to win. Let it be assumed further that the primary goal of most individuals on the front lines is to get home alive. Then there appears to be an important conflict in goals—personally rational behavior by those at the bottom will endanger goal attainment by those at the top.

But not necessarily! It depends on how the reward system is set up. The Vietnam war was indeed a study of disobedience and rebel-

---

[1]In Simon's (10, pp. 76–77) terms, a decision is "subjectively rational" if it maximizes an individual's valued outcomes so far as his knowledge permits. A decision is "personally rational" if it is oriented toward the individual's goals.

lion, with terms such as "fragging" (killing one's own commanding officer) and "search and evade" becoming part of the military vocabulary. The difference in subordinates' acceptance of authority between World War II and Vietnam is reported to be considerable, and veterans of the Second World War often have been quoted as being outraged at the mutinous actions of many American soldiers in Vietnam.

Consider, however, some critical differences in the reward system in use during the two conflicts. What did the GI in World War II want? To go home. And when did he get to go home? When the war was won! If he disobeyed the orders to clean out the trenches and take the hills, the war would not be won and he would not go home. Furthermore, what were his chances of attaining his goal (getting home alive) if he obeyed the orders compared to his chances if he did not? What is being suggested is that the rational soldier in World War II, *whether patriotic or not,* probably found it expedient to obey.

Consider the reward system in use in Vietnam. What did the man at the bottom want? To go home. And when did he get to go home? When his tour of duty was over! This was the case *whether or not* the war was won. Furthermore, concerning the relative chance of getting home alive by obeying orders compared to the chance if they were disobeyed, it is worth noting that a mutineer in Vietnam was far more likely to be assigned rest and rehabilitation (on the assumption that fatigue was the cause) than he was to suffer any negative consequence.

In his description of the "zone of indifference," Barnard stated that "a person can and will accept a communication as authoritative only when . . . at the time of his decision, he believes it to be compatible with his personal interests as a whole" (1, p. 165). In light of the reward system used in Vietnam, would it not have been personally irrational for some orders to have been obeyed? Was not the military implementing a system which *rewarded* disobedience, while *hoping* that soldiers (despite the reward system) would obey orders?

Medicine

Theoretically, a physician can make either of two types of error, and intuitively one seems as bad as the other. A doctor can pronounce a patient sick when he is actually well, thus causing him needless anxiety and expense, curtailment of enjoyable foods and activities, and even physical danger by subjecting him to needless medication and surgery. Alternately, a doctor can label a sick person well and thus avoid treating what may be a serious, even fatal ailment. It might be natural to conclude that physicians seek to minimize both types of error.

Such a conclusion would be wrong.[2] It is estimated that numerous Americans are presently afflicted with iatrogenic (physician *caused*) illnesses (9). This occurs when the doctor is approached by someone complaining of a few stray symptoms. The doctor classifies and organizes these symptoms, gives them a name, and obligingly tells the patient what further symptoms may be expected. This information often acts as a self-fulfilling prophecy, with the result that from that day on the patient for all practical purposes is sick.

Why does this happen? Why are physicians so reluctant to sustain a type 2 error (pronouncing a sick person well) that they will tolerate many type 1 errors? Again, a look at the reward system is needed. The punishments for a type 2 error are real: guilt, embarrassment, and the threat of lawsuit and scandal. On the other hand, a type 1 error (labeling a well person sick) "is sometimes seen as sound clinical practice, indicating a healthy conservative approach to medicine" (9, p. 69). Type 1 errors also are likely to generate increased income and

a stream of steady customers who, being well in a limited physiological sense, will not embarrass the doctor by dying abruptly.

Fellow physicians and the general public therefore are really *rewarding* type 1 errors and at the same time *hoping* fervently that doctors will try not to make them.

GENERAL ORGANIZATIONAL EXAMPLES

Rehabilitation Centers and Orphanages

In terms of the prime beneficiary classification (2, p. 42) organizations such as these are supposed to exist for the "public-in-contact," that is, clients. The orphanage therefore theoretically is interested in placing as many children as possible in good homes. However, often orphanages surround themselves with so many rules concerning adoption that it is nearly impossible to pry a child out of the place. Orphanages may deny adoption unless the applicants are a married couple, both of the same religion as the child, without history of emotional or vocational instability, with a specified minimum income and a private room for the child, etc.

If the primary goal is to place children in good homes, then the rules ought to constitute means toward that goal. Goal displacement results when these "means become ends-in-themselves that displace the original goals" (2, p. 229).

To some extent these rules are required by law. But the influence of the reward system on the orphanage's management should not be ignored. Consider, for example, that the:

1. Number of children enrolled often is the most important determinant of the size of the allocated budget.
2. Number of children under the director's care also will affect the size of his staff.

---

[2]In one study (4) of 14,867 films for signs of tuberculosis, 1,216 positive readings turned out to be clinically negative; only 24 negative readings proved clinically active, a ratio of 50 to 1.

3. Total organizational size will determine largely the director's prestige at the annual conventions, in the community, etc.

Therefore, to the extent that staff size, total budget, and personal prestige are valued by the orphanage's executive personnel, it becomes rational for them to make it difficult for children to be adopted. After all, who wants to be the director of the smallest orphanage in the state?

If the reward system errs in the opposite direction, paying off only for placements, extensive goal displacement again is likely to result. A common example of vocational rehabilitation in many states, for example, consists of placing someone in a job for which he has little interest and few qualifications, for two months or so, and then "rehabilitating" him again in another position. Such behavior is quite consistent with the prevailing reward system, which pays off for the number of individuals placed in any position for 60 days or more. Rehabilitation counselors also confess to competing with one another to place relatively skilled clients, sometimes ignoring persons with few skills who would be harder to place. Extensively disabled clients find that counselors often prefer to work with those whose disabilities are less severe.[3]

Universities

Society *hopes* that teachers will not neglect their teaching responsibilities but *rewards* them almost entirely for research and publications. This is most true at the large and prestigious universities. Clichés such as "good research and good teaching go together" notwithstanding, professors often find that they must choose between teaching and research oriented activities when allocating their time. Rewards for good teaching usually are limited to outstanding teacher awards, which are given to only a small percentage of good teachers and which

usually bestow little money and fleeting prestige. Punishments for poor teaching also are rare.

Rewards for research and publications, on the other hand, and punishments for failure to accomplish these, are commonly administered by universities at which teachers are employed. Furthermore, publication oriented resumés usually will be well received at other universities, whereas teaching credentials, harder to document and quantify, are much less transferable. Consequently, it is rational for university teachers to concentrate on research, even if to the detriment of teaching and at the expense of their students.

By the same token, it is rational for students to act based upon the goal displacement which has occurred within universities concerning what they are rewarded for. If it is assumed that a primary goal of a university is to transfer knowledge from teacher to student, then grades become identifiable as a means toward that goal, serving as motivational, control, and feedback devices to expedite the knowledge transfer. Instead, however, the grades themselves have become much more important for entrance to graduate school, successful employment, tuition refunds, parental respect, etc., than the knowledge or lack of knowledge they are supposed to signify.

It therefore should come as no surprise that information has surfaced in recent years concerning fraternity files for examinations, term paper writing services, organized cheating at the service academies, and the like. Such activities constitute a personally rational response to a reward system which pays off for grades rather than knowledge.

BUSINESS RELATED EXAMPLES

Ecology

Assume that the president of XYZ Corporation is confronted with the following alternatives:

---

[3]Personal interviews conducted during 1972–1973.

1. Spend $11 million for antipollution equipment to keep from poisoning fish in the river adjacent to the plant; or
2. Do nothing, in violation of the law, and assume a one-in-ten chance of being caught, with a resultant $1 million fine plus the necessity of buying the equipment.

Under this not unrealistic set of choices it requires no linear program to determine that XYZ Corporation can maximize its probabilities by flouting the law. Add the fact that XYZ's president is probably being rewarded (by creditors, stockholders, and other salient parts of his task environment) according to criteria totally unrelated to the number of fish poisoned, and his probable course of action becomes clear.

Evaluation of Training

It is axiomatic that those who care about a firm's well-being should insist that the organization get fair value for its expenditures. Yet it is commonly known that firms seldom bother to evaluate a new GRID, MBO, job enrichment program, or whatever, to see if the company is getting its money's worth. Why? Certainly it is not because people have not pointed out that this situation exists; numerous practitioner oriented articles are written each year to just this point.

The individuals (whether in personnel, manpower planning, or wherever) who normally would be responsible for conducting such evaluations are the same ones often charged with introducing the change effort in the first place. Having convinced top management to spend the money, they usually are quite animated afterwards in collecting arigorous vignettes and anecdotes about how successful the program was. The last thing many desire is a formal, systematic, and revealing evaluation. Although members of top management may actually *hope* for such systematic evaluation, their reward systems continue to *reward* ignorance in this area. And if the personnel department ab-

dicates its responsibility, who is to step into the breach? The change agent himself? Hardly! He is likely to be too busy collecting anecdotal "evidence" of his own, for use with his next client.

Miscellaneous

Many additional examples could be cited of systems which in fact are rewarding behaviors other than those supposedly desired by the rewarder. A few of these are described briefly below.

Most coaches disdain to discuss individual accomplishments, preferring to speak of teamwork, proper attitude, and a one-for-all spirit. Usually, however, rewards are distributed according to individual performance. The college basketball player who feeds his teammates instead of shooting will not compile impressive scoring statistics and is less likely to be drafted by the pros. The ballplayer who hits to right field to advance the runners will win neither the batting nor home run titles and will be offered smaller raises. It therefore is rational for players to think of themselves first and the team second.

In business organizations where rewards are dispensed for unit performance or for individual goals achieved without regard for overall effectiveness, similar attitudes often are observed. Under most Management by Objectives (MBO) systems, goals in areas where quantification is difficult often go unspecified. The organization therefore often is in a position where it *hopes* for employee effort in the areas of team building, interpersonal relations, creativity, etc., but it formally *rewards* none of these. In cases where promotions and raises are formally tied to MBO, the system itself contains a paradox in that it "asks employees to set challenging, risky goals, only to face smaller paychecks and possibly damaged careers if these goals are not accomplished" (5, p. 40).

It is *hoped* that administrators will pay attention to long-run costs and opportunities and will institute programs which will bear fruit later on. However, many organizational reward systems pay off for short-run sales and earnings only. Under such circumstances it is personally rational for officials to sacrifice long-term growth and profit (by selling off equipment and property, or by stifling research and development) for short-term advantages. This probably is most pertinent in the public sector, with the result that many public officials are unwilling to implement programs which will not show benefits by election time.

As a final, clear-cut example of a fouled-up reward system, consider the cost-plus contract or its next of kin, the allocation of next year's budget as a direct function of this year's expenditures. It probably is conceivable that those who award such budgets and contracts really hope for economy and prudence in spending. It is obvious, however, that adopting the proverb "to him who spends shall more be given," rewards not economy, but spending itself.

TWO COMPANIES' EXPERIENCES

A Manufacturing Organization

A midwest manufacturer of industrial goods had been troubled for some time by aspects of its organizational climate it believed dysfunctional. For research purposes, interviews were conducted with many employees, and a questionnaire was administered on a companywide basis, including plants and offices in several American and Canadian locations. The company strongly encouraged employee participation in the survey and made available time and space during the workday for completion of the instrument. All employees in attendance during the day of the survey completed the questionnaire. All instruments were collected directly by the researcher, who personally administered each session. Since no one employed by the firm handled the questionnaires,

and since respondent names were not asked for, it seems likely that the pledge of anonymity given was believed.

A modified version of the Expect Approval scale (7) was included as part of the questionnaire. The instrument asked respondents to indicate the degree of approval or disapproval they could expect if they performed each of the described actions. A seven point Likert scale was used, with one indicating that the action would probably bring strong disapproval and seven signifying likely strong approval.

Although normative data for this scale from studies of other organizations are unavailable, it is possible to examine fruitfully the data obtained from this survey in several ways. First, it may be worth noting that the questionnaire data corresponded closely to information gathered through interviews. Furthermore, as can be seen from the results summarized in Table 1, sizable differences between various work units, and between employees at different job levels within the same work unit, were obtained. This suggests that response bias effects (social desirability in particular loomed as a potential concern) are not likely to be severe.

Most importantly, comparisons between scores obtained on the Expect Approval scale and a statement of problems which were the reason for the survey revealed that the same behaviors which managers in each division thought dysfunctional were those which lower-level employees claimed were rewarded. As compared to job levels 1 to 8 in Division B (see Table 1), those in Division A claimed a much higher acceptance by management of "conforming" activities. Between 31 and 37 percent of Division A employees at levels 1–8 stated that going along with the majority, agreeing with the boss, and staying on everyone's good side brought approval; only once (level 5–8 responses to one of the three items) did a majority suggest that such actions would generate disapproval.

TABLE 1. *Summary of Two Divisions' Data Relevant to Conforming and Risk-Avoidance Behaviors (extent to which subjects expect approval)*

Dimension	Item	Division and Sample	Total Responses	Percentage of Workers Responding		
				1, 2, or 3 Disapproval	4	5, 6, or 7 Approval
Risk avoidance	Making a risky decision based on the best information available at the time, but which turns out wrong	A, levels 1–4 (lowest)	127	61	25	14
		A, levels 5–8	172	46	31	23
		A, levels 9 and above	17	41	30	30
		B, levels 1–4 (lowest)	31	58	26	16
		B, levels 5–8	19	42	42	16
		B, levels 9 and above	10	50	20	30
	Setting extremely high and challenging standards and goals and then narrowly failing to make them	A, levels 1–4	122	47	28	25
		A, levels 5–8	168	33	26	41
		A, levels 9+	17	24	6	70
		B, levels 1–4	31	48	23	29
		B, levels 5–8	18	17	33	50
		B, levels 9+	10	30	0	70
	Setting goals which are extremely easy to make and then making them	A, levels 1–4	124	35	30	35
		A, levels 5–8	171	47	27	26
		A, levels 9+	17	70	24	6
		B, levels 1–4	31	58	26	16
		B, levels 5–8	19	63	16	21
		B, levels 9+	10	80	0	20
Conformity	Being a "yes man" and always agreeing with the boss	A, levels 1–4	126	46	17	37
		A, levels 5–8	180	54	14	31
		A, levels 9+	17	88	12	0
		B, levels 1–4	32	53	28	19
		B, levels 5–8	19	68	21	11
		B, levels 9+	10	80	10	10
	Always going along with the majority	A, levels 1–4	125	40	25	35
		A, levels 5–8	173	47	21	32
		A, levels 9+	17	70	12	18
		B, levels 1–4	31	61	23	16
		B, levels 5–8	19	68	11	21
		B, levels 9+	10	80	10	10
	Being careful to stay on the good side of everyone, so that everyone agrees that you are a great guy	A, levels 1–4	124	45	18	37
		A, levels 5–8	173	45	22	33
		A, levels 9+	17	64	6	30
		B, levels 1–4	31	54	23	23
		B, levels 5–8	19	73	11	16
		B, levels 9+	10	80	10	10

Furthermore, responses from Division A workers at levels 1–4 indicate that behaviors geared toward risk avoidance were as likely to be rewarded as to be punished. Only at job levels 9 and above was it apparent that the reward system was positively reinforcing behaviors desired by top management. Overall, the same "tendencies toward conservatism and apple-polishing at the lower levels" which divisional management had complained about during the interviews were those claimed by subordinates to be the most rational course of action in light of the existing reward system. Management apparently was not getting the behaviors it was *hoping* for, but it certainly was getting the behaviors it was perceived by subordinates to be *rewarding*.

An Insurance Firm

The Group Health Claims Division of a large eastern insurance company provides another rich illustration of a reward system which reinforces behaviors not desired by top management.

Attempting to measure and reward accuracy in paying surgical claims, the firm systematically keeps track of the number of returned checks and letters of complaint received from policyholders. However, underpayments are likely to provoke cries of outrage from the insured, while overpayments often are accepted in courteous silence. Since it often is impossible to tell from the physician's statement which of two surgical procedures, with different allowable benefits, was performed, and since writing for clarifications will interfere with other standards used by the firm concerning "percentage of claims paid within two days of receipt," the new hire in more than one claims section is soon acquainted with the informal norm: "When in doubt, pay it out!"

The situation would be even worse were it not for the fact that other features of the firm's reward system tend to neutralize those

described. For example, annual "merit" increases are given to all employees, in one of the following three amounts:

1. If the worker is "outstanding" (a select category, into which no more than two employees per section may be placed): 5 percent.
2. If the worker is "above average" (normally all workers not "outstanding" are so rated): 4 percent.
3. If the worker commits gross acts of negligence and irresponsibility for which he might be discharged in many other companies: 3 percent.

Now, since (a) the difference between the 5 percent theoretically attainable through hard work and the 4 percent attainable merely by living until the review date is small and (b) since insurance firms seldom dispense much of a salary increase in cash (rather, the worker's insurance benefits increase, causing him to be further overinsured), many employees are rather indifferent to the possibility of obtaining the extra one percent reward and therefore tend to ignore the norm concerning indiscriminant payments.

However, most employees are not indifferent to the rule which states that, should absences or latenesses total three or more in any six-month period, the entire 4 or 5 percent due at the next "merit" review must be forfeited. In this sense the firm may be described as *hoping* for performance, while *rewarding* attendance. What it gets, of course, is attendance. (If the absence-lateness rule appears to the reader to be stringent, it really is not. The company counts "times" rather than "days" absent, and a ten-day absence therefore counts the same as one lasting two days. A worker in danger of accumulating a third absence within six months merely has to remain ill (away from work) during his second absence until his first absence is more than six months old. The limiting factor is that at some point his salary ceases, and his sickness benefits take over. This usually is sufficient to get the younger workers to return, but for those with 20 or more years' service, the company provides sickness benefits of 90 percent of normal salary, tax-free! Therefore . . .)

CAUSES

Extremely diverse instances of systems which reward behavior A although the rewarder apparently hopes for behavior B have been given. These are useful to illustrate the breadth and magnitude of the phenomenon, but the diversity increases the difficulty of determining commonalities and establishing causes. However, four general factors may be pertinent to an explanation of why fouled up reward systems seem to be so prevalent.

Fascination with an "Objective" Criterion

It has been mentioned elsewhere that:

> Most "objective" measures of productivity are objective only in that their subjective elements are (a) determined in advance, rather than coming into play at the time of the formal evaluation, and (b) well concealed on the rating instrument itself. Thus industrial firms seeking to devise objective rating systems first decide, in an arbitrary manner, what dimensions are to be rated, . . . usually including some items having little to do with organizational effectiveness while excluding others that do. Only then does Personnel Division churn out official-looking documents on which all dimensions chosen to be rated are assigned point values, categories, or whatever (6, p. 92).

Nonetheless, many individuals seek to establish simple, quantifiable standards against which to measure and reward performance. Such efforts may be successful in highly predictable areas within an organization but are likely to cause goal displacement when applied anywhere else.

Overconcern with attendance and lateness in the insurance firm and with the number of people placed in the vocational rehabilitation division may have been largely responsible for the problems described in those organizations.

Overemphasis on Highly Visible Behaviors

Difficulties often stem from the fact that some parts of the task are highly visible while other parts are not. For example, publications are easier to demonstrate than teaching, and scoring baskets and hitting home runs are more readily observable than feeding teammates and advancing base runners. Similarly, the adverse consequences of pronouncing a sick person well are more visible than those sustained by labeling a well person sick. Team-building and creativity are other examples of behaviors which may not be rewarded simply because they are hard to observe.

Hypocrisy

In some of the instances described the rewarder may have been getting the desired behavior, notwithstanding claims that the behavior was not desired. This may be true, for example, of management's attitude toward apple-polishing in the manufacturing firm (a behavior which subordinates felt was rewarded, despite management's avowed dislike of the practice). This also may explain politicians' unwillingness to revise the penalties for disobedience of ecology laws, and the failure of top management to devise reward systems which would cause systematic evaluation of training and development programs.

Emphasis on Morality or Equity Rather than Efficiency

Sometimes consideration of other factors prevents the establishment of a system which rewards behaviors desired by the rewarder. The felt obligation of many Americans to vote for one candidate or another, for example, may impair their ability to withhold support from politicians who refuse to discuss the issues. Similarly, the concern for spreading the risks and costs of wartime military service may outweigh the advantage to be obtained by committing personnel to combat until the war is over.

It should be noted that only with respect to the first two causes are reward systems really paying off for other than desired behaviors. In the case of the third and fourth causes the system *is* rewarding behaviors desired by the rewarder, and the systems are fouled up only from the standpoints of those who believe the rewarder's public statements (cause 3), or those who seek to maximize efficiency rather than other outcomes (cause 4).

CONCLUSIONS

Modern organization theory requires a recognition that the members of organizations and society possess divergent goals and motives. It therefore is unlikely that managers and their subordinates will seek the same outcomes. Three possible remedies for this potential problem are suggested.

Selection
It is theoretically possible for organizations to employ only those individuals whose goals and motives are wholly consonant with those of management. In such cases the same behaviors judged by subordinates to be rational would be perceived by management as desirable. State-of-the-art reviews of selection techniques, however, provide scant grounds for hope that such an approach would be successful (for example, see 12).

Training
Another theoretical alternative is for the organization to admit those employees whose goals are not consonant with those of management and then, through training, socialization, or whatever, alter employee goals to make them consonant. However, research on the effectiveness of such training programs, though limited, provides further grounds for pessimism (for example, see 3).

Altering the Reward System
What would have been the result if:

1. Nixon had been assured by his advisors that he could not win reelection except by discussing the issues in detail?
2. Physicians' conduct was subjected to regular examination by review boards for type 1 errors (calling healthy people ill) and to penalties (fines, censure, etc.) for errors of either type?
3. The President of XYZ Corporation had to choose between (*a*) spending $11 million dollars for antipollution equipment, and (*b*) incurring a 50–50 chance of going to jail for five years?

Managers who complain that their workers are not motivated might do well to consider the possibility that they have installed reward systems which are paying off for behaviors other than those they are seeking. This, in part, is what happened in Vietnam, and this is what regularly frustrates societal efforts to bring about honest politicians, civic-minded managers, etc. This certainly is what happened in both the manufacturing and the insurance companies.

A first step for such managers might be to find out what behaviors currently are being rewarded. Perhaps an instrument similar to that used in the manufacturing firm could be useful for this purpose. Chances are excellent that these managers will be surprised by what they find—that their firms are not rewarding what they assume they are. In fact, such undesirable behavior by organizational members as they have observed may be explained largely by the reward systems in use.

This is not to say that all organizational behavior is determined by formal rewards and punishments. Certainly it is true that in the absence of formal reinforcement some soldiers will be patriotic, some presidents will be ecology minded, and some orphanage directors will care about children. The point, however, is that in such cases the rewarder is not *causing* the behaviors desired but is only a fortunate bystander. For an organization to *act* upon its members, the formal reward system should positively reinforce desired behaviors, not constitute an obstacle to be overcome.

It might be wise to underscore the obvious fact that there is nothing really new in what has been said. In both theory and practice these matters have been mentioned before. Thus in many states Good Samaritan laws have been installed to protect doctors who stop to assist a stricken motorist. In states without such laws it is commonplace for doctors to refuse to stop, for fear of involvement in a subsequent lawsuit. In college basketball additional penalties have been instituted against players who foul their opponents deliberately. It has long been argued by Milton Friedman and others that penalties should be altered so as to make it irrational to disobey the ecology laws, and so on.

By altering the reward system the organization escapes the necessity of selecting only desirable people or of trying to alter undesirable ones. In Skinnerian terms (as described in 11, p. 704), "As for responsibility and goodness—as commonly defined—no one . . . would want or need them. They refer to a man's behaving well despite the absence of positive reinforcement that is obviously sufficient to explain it. Where such reinforcement exists, 'no one needs goodness.' "

REFERENCE NOTES

1. Barnard, Chester I. *The functions of the executive.* Cambridge, Mass.: Harvard University Press, 1964.
2. Blau, Peter M., and Scott, W. Richard. *Formal organizations.* San Francisco: Chandler, 1962.
3. Fiedler, Fred E. Predicting the effects of leadership training and experience from the contingency model, *Journal of Applied Psychology,* 1972, 56:114–19.
4. Garland, L. H. Studies of the accuracy of diagnostic procedures, *American Journal Roentgenological, Radium Therapy Nuclear Medicine,* 1959, 82:25–38.
5. Kerr, Steven. Some modifications in MBO as an OD strategy, *Academy of Management Proceedings,* 1973:39–42.
6. Kerr, Steven. What price objectivity? *American Sociologist,* 1973, 8:92–93.
7. Litwin, G. H., and Stringer, R. A., Jr. *Motivation and organizational climate.* Boston: Harvard University Press, 1968.
8. Perrow, Charles. The analysis of goals in complex organizations, in A. Etzioni (ed.), *Readings on modern organizations.* Englewood Cliffs, N.J.: Prentice-Hall, 1969.
9. Scheff, Thomas J. Decision rules, types of error, and their consequences in medical diagnosis, in F. Massarik and P. Ratoosh (eds.), *Mathematical explorations in behavioral science.* Homewood, Ill.: Richard D. Irwin, Inc., 1965.
10. Simon, Herbert A. *Administrative behavior.* New York: Free Press, 1957.
11. Swanson, G. E. Review symposium: Beyond freedom and dignity, *American Journal of Sociology,* 1972, 78:702–705.
12. Webster, E. *Decision making in the employment interview.* Montreal: Industrial Relations Center, McGill University, 1964.

May the Force
Be With You

Bruce Posner

How Au Bon Pain discovered a way to turn lackluster clock-punchers into a team of gung ho professionals.

Nobody expected much from Gary Aronson, and he didn't surprise anyone. After dropping out of college before the second semester of his freshman year, he knocked around a while, eventually winding up as manager of a Kentucky Fried Chicken franchise. In 1983, he switched jobs again, this time moving to Au Bon Pain Co., a Boston-based fast-food chain specializing in fancy coffees, croissants, and spotty customer service. That fact notwithstanding, Aronson viewed it as a different kind of company, or so he told himself, perhaps as a way of justifying his cut in pay from $410 to $280 a week. Different Au Bon Pain may have been, but three years later, Aronson was still making a meager $26,000 a year, with which he supported his wife and two children.

At 30, Aronson was frustrated, bored, and wondering why he persisted in the food-service business. Fast-food companies don't want managers, he thought; they want trained dogs who will go through their routines and keep their mouths shut. Aronson himself had a

hard time keeping his shut. He was known in the company for being "difficult" and "opinionated"—a whiner and a complainer. He didn't care. "My heart wasn't in it anymore," he recalls. "I had the feeling of being in a dead-end job. I thought if I was lucky, I might earn $3,000 more in five years." This was assuming, of course, that he didn't get fired, a distinct possibility. So he put in his 45 hours a week and tried to figure out what he was going to do next.

Today, Gary Aronson is still in the food-service business, and still with Au Bon Pain, but he no longer works 45 hours a week. Three mornings a week, you can find him in his store at 3:15, and on other days he's there from 6:00 A.M. until the store closes at 7:00 P.M. He works weekends, too, putting in a total of 65 to 80 hours each week, making sure that the food is fresh, the place is clean, and the customers are satisfied. His face looks weary these days, but he is not complaining. He's too busy thinking up ways to bring in more customers, sell more food, and make the whole operation run more smoothly. "This is the first time in my life I've been treated like a professional," he says.

It's also the first time he's been *paid* like a professional. If he continues at his present

Reprinted with permission, *Inc.* magazine, July 1987. Copyright © 1987 by Goldhirsh Group, Inc., 38 Commercial Wharf, Boston, MA 02110.

rate, he will make at least $80,000 this year. Suddenly he and his wife, Donna, also an employee, are the talk of the company. The betting is that they will be the first pair of Au Bon Pain shopkeepers to arrive at a managers' meeting in a chauffeur-driven limousine.

Companies have traditionally viewed compensation in a fairly narrow context—as just one of the many levers available to influence the direction of a business. Of all the factors that affect a company's performance, compensation is seldom listed among the most important. If the company fails (or succeeds), the owners will usually blame (or credit) the product or the strategy, the financing or the timing. Seldom will they say that the crucial difference between success and failure is the way they structure the system for paying their employees.

And, in some cases, that may be true. After all, many companies succeed with a compensation system that's little different from their competitors', while those that fail usually have a multitude of other problems. And yet it is a fact that a company with an extraordinary record of performance almost always has an extraordinary compensation plan as well. In most cases, it has been installed by the founder, who had a vision of the kind of company he or she wanted, and an acute understanding of the kind of reward system that would inspire employees to create it. Then there are the handful of companies such as Au Bon Pain, which grope their way through a maze of obstacles before finally hitting on a compensation structure that makes most of the other problems go away.

The truth is that Ron Shaich (pronounced *shake*) had not given much thought to the issue before he became president of Au Bon Pain in 1982. He was only 28 years old at the time, with limited experience in business. As a student at Clark University, in Worcester, Mass., he had founded and managed a nonprofit campus convenience store in competition with a local Store 24. He had been so success-

ful, and had had so much fun, that he decided to get his M.B.A., graduating from Harvard Business School in 1978. Thereafter, he worked briefly for a national chain of cookie stores, did some grass-roots political organizing, and dabbled in the world of campaign consulting. But his idealism soon led him back to business. "In politics, you build organizations and then tear them down," he says. Hoping to build something more permanent, he moved to Boston in 1981 and opened a cookie store on a busy downtown street.

The cookie store brought him into contact with Louis Kane, a 50-year-old Boston businessman who had acquired Au Bon Pain in 1978 from a French oven manufacturer. Shaich was interested in buying croissants to sell in his store, but Kane had other things on his mind. His company was in serious trouble, and he did not know how to save it. His expertise lay in real estate, not food service. Impressed with Shaich, Kane suggested a deal: the two would merge their companies, with Shaich becoming a partner, president, and chief of internal operations. Kane would focus on external issues, selecting expansion sites and arranging financing. Shaich agreed.

At the time, Au Bon Pain consisted of three bakery-cafés located on prime Boston real estate and staffed by its own French bakers. It was an expensive operation, and it was losing money at a rapid clip. Beyond that, the company lacked any sense of purpose or direction. Customers were treated carelessly, as if they were intruders, and employee turnover was high, even for a fast-food operation. The situation called for dramatic action. In short order, the new management team got rid of the in-store bakers, eliminated the wholesale side of the business, and brought in Shaich's father, a New Jersey accountant, to design some financial controls. Then they turned to the stores themselves, replacing the old managers with new ones, whom they paid the going rate—about $18,000 per year.

But Shaich was not interested in building just another fast-food business. "I wanted to create a truly better food-service company," he says. Good food—"food you wanted to eat"—was a given, as was making money. He dreamed of a company built around a general, and passionate, concern for its customers. That, he realized, demanded a certain type of employee, "people who did things not because the boss was looking but because they really cared." In order to attract those people, he knew he had to create a different type of environment. "We didn't want to accept the low standards of the rest of the food industry," he says. "We wanted to show the big guys—Pepsi and McDonald's and Sara Lee—that the conventional ways of treating people were not the only ways. We felt we could do better. . . . I wanted an organization where *I'd* want to work."

With that goal in mind, Shaich began to tinker with the compensation system, setting up a program in which managers could earn monthly bonuses for generating sales above a budgeted level, provided the store stayed within bounds on its food and labor costs. It was an idea he borrowed from the famous business-school case study of Lincoln Electric Co., and it seemed like a surefire method of pointing managers in the right direction, thereby reducing the pressures on himself and the rest of the management system as the company grew.

And grow the company did between 1982 and 1984. As stores increased their volume, Au Bon Pain began adding units. Most weeks, Shaich worked 90 hours, spending the bulk of it in the stores, devising systems to handle the growth. Everywhere he went, he carried a message to employees—that growth, if properly managed, would create opportunities for those who took care of customers. "I did everything I could to make people feel that they wanted to be here," he says.

But growth also put strains on the company, strains that promised to get worse with time. For one thing, the Massachusetts labor market was getting tighter and tighter, making it more difficult to find new managers and crew. That situation created opportunities for employees, but dangers for the company. "We were promoting people left and right," says Shaich, "sometimes before they were ready."

By the beginning of 1984, the company had 14 stores, generating annual revenues of more than $6 million, but the company's management resources were stretched perilously thin. The game plan, moreover, called for opening 10 to 15 new units in the next year and, at the same time, moving into the lunch market with a new line of soups and sandwiches. Shaich himself found that he no longer had time to give store managers the support they expected. So in April he brought in a regional manager from McDonald's Corp. as the vice-president of operations. "We wanted to give the stores the best leadership we could find," Shaich says.

It soon became apparent, however, that the addition of another top manager was not going to solve all the problems, many of which seemed to be related to the compensation plan Shaich had installed so optimistically in 1982. It wasn't working. In the atmosphere of constant change and growth, the company could not come up with meaningful budget targets for managers. Beyond that, the systems for recording operating results were overloaded, and people were constantly being moved before their actual numbers came in. As a result, the compensation plan had lost its integrity. Managers realized that their bonuses really depended not on their performance, but on Shaich's perception of it. Not that he was stingy. In the absence of clear guidelines, he tended to give something to everybody, but on such a discretionary basis that the system became known as "pennies from heaven."

To make matters worse, the new vice-president was busily destroying whatever lingering credibility the compensation system had. To fill the slots in the new stores, he hired new managers, many of them from McDonald's, at salaries $6,000 or $7,000 above those of the old managers. The latter were understandably furious, and they told Shaich so; a few even left. But he didn't intervene. "I felt I needed to give the guy the freedom to do his job." Unfortunately, it soon became clear that the guy wasn't doing his job very well, at least when it came to providing support for store managers, whose morale continued to plummet. "He managed downward," says Shaich. "He expected their loyalty but didn't feel he had to earn it. And he showed no interest in taking care of them as people."

By the end of 1984, Shaich began to have the feeling that the company was coming apart at the seams. Customer complaints were increasing, and the turnover problem was growing. Hard as it was to recruit new employees, the average stay had dwindled from one year to a mere seven months. The company also lacked adequate operating standards—governing, say, where to keep the lettuce for sandwiches. Per-unit operating profits, meanwhile, were deteriorating badly, even as sales continued to rise, and some of the worst performers were the new managers brought in by the vice-president of operations.

"Everywhere I looked," Shaich says, "there was another mess to clean up." He was frustrated, but no more so than his managers. They told him bluntly that they didn't trust the company anymore. Finally, in June 1985, Shaich did what he had to do, firing the VP of operations, putting the brake on expansion, and calling his father back to help rebuild the company. Once again, he took charge of operations—and tried to figure out where he had gone wrong.

Things were worse than they had ever been," Shaich says, and he had a point, although on paper the company looked just fine. With 31 units from New Hampshire to Texas, it had annual revenues of $15 million and was still highly profitable. There was plenty of cash available, thanks to the recent sale of a franchise and Kane's success in raising $11.7 million from private sources. Perhaps most important, Au Bon Pain had established a clear identity for itself in the market. With a sandwich menu featuring tarragon chicken and ham with Brie, it could never be mistaken for another burger chain.

But all that was in jeopardy, Shaich realized, thanks to rising turnover, sinking morale, and operational chaos. He moved quickly to reverse the trend. Hoping to boost the managers' spirits, he raised the salaries of the capable ones and returned to the old policy of promoting from within. To aid the recruitment of crew members, he hiked starting wages 50¢ above those of competitors and began giving free televisions to employees who brought in new recruits. Those new people who stayed got college-scholarship assistance. And in case any managers failed to get the message, Shaich sent them all a memo telling them to holler whenever they had to work more than 55 hours a week. More than once, they did, and he dropped everything to go lend a hand.

But important as these measures were, they did not address the company's underlying problems, as Shaich was well aware. Somehow he had to regain the confidence of the people who judged the business every day: its customers. Again, he turned his attention to developing a compensation system that would keep managers focused on the all-important goal of satisfying the customer, but he found that he scarcely knew where to begin. The bonus system had been a dismal failure. What else was there? Looking for ideas, Shaich called a professor he knew at Harvard Business School, who put him in touch with a young colleague by the name of Len Schlesinger.

Schlesinger was a budding expert in the field of organizational behavior. He and Shaich met once, and again, and Schlesinger spent a few days at the company, talking with employees. Shaich liked him. "Len was somebody I could talk to about the business," he says, "and he really seemed to care." So Schlesinger was invited to join the company as a partner and executive vice-president.

For Schlesinger, accepting the offer meant giving up the likelihood of tenure at Harvard, not to mention a lucrative consulting business, but Shaich was persuasive. It was an opportunity, he said, "to build a company—to create a system you *care* about." Schlesinger says that, in the end, his decision came down to one question: "Was I willing to believe my own bullshit?" The answer was yes.

His first job was to help the company come up with a new compensation system. After the "pennies from heaven" fiasco, Shaich wanted a program that would be simple to explain, easy to sell, attractive vis-à-vis competitors, and equitable within the company. It also had to encourage managers to focus on customer satisfaction.

Schlesinger began by assembling a compensation committee from among the company's managers. Together they explored the options. "People were tired of inside deals," he recalls. "So we wanted something that was very mechanistic, something we could defend." In the end, they came up with a simple system under which managers would be paid according to their level of responsibility and the sales activity of their stores.

Under the plan, every store's general manager would earn a base salary of $375 a week. Salaries would then rise as weekly volumes increased, up to $633.75 a week at the highest-volume store. "We were willing to pay more for the high-volume store," says Shaich, "because it was worth more to the company."

Managers responded enthusiastically to the new system, but—unfortunately—it did not accomplish what it was intended to do. Very quickly, managers figured out the fastest way to make more money was to be assigned to a higher-volume store. "The guy we wanted to be focused and caring was spending a lot of his time lobbying for a transfer," says Shaich. "What's more, we *needed* to move them through the system, so they usually got their way." As a result, the new system had minimal impact on the actual performance of the stores.

The situation was further aggravated by continued turnover among crew members, which was running 40% to 45% in the summer and fall of 1985, despite the fact that the company paid hourly workers a premium wage. Nothing they did succeeded in stemming the tide. "We'd run big help-wanted ads," says Shaich, "and we'd get maybe two or three replies for an opening." Often the entire corporate staff—some 50 strong—had to help make sandwiches and serve customers at lunchtime. And there was no end in sight.

"The pressure was really on," Shaich recalls. "I remember thinking, 'Why aren't we located in the Southwest? Why is all this happening to us?'"

In October 1985, Shaich and Schlesinger took a break from the crisis to fly down to Orlando for the annual meeting of the Multi Unit Food Service Operators. Both of them felt battered and weary. They could take some solace in spending a few days with people who were struggling with similar problems, but that didn't help them forget their own. During one of the afternoon sessions, Shaich began doodling on a piece of paper, listing all the company's failings. Soon the page was filled with loops and arrows. The analysis went something like this:

It was hard for managers to find quality recruits, and when they did, there was no time to train them. The result was substandard work. Managers operated on the assumption that recruits wouldn't stay long, and they usually were right. When employees left, managers filled in at the counters, thereby ceasing to be managers. Eventually, they burned out. But though the system kept most managers from succeeding, they were promoted to other stores anyway—where the cycle repeated itself.

And that's exactly what it was, Shaich and Schlesinger agreed: a cycle of failure. Suddenly, 1,000 miles from home, the nature of their troubles seemed crystal clear.

It was a revelation, albeit a rather depressing one. That evening, however, they had a revelation of a different sort. They were having dinner with Ed Eynon, then vice-president for human resources for a company called Golden Corral Corp., headquartered in Raleigh, N.C. A chain of 435 steak houses, Golden Corral had a reputation as an unusual food-service operation. Listening to Eynon, Shaich and Schlesinger quickly found out why.

Several years back, Eynon said, the company had come up with its own solution to the challenge of running a restaurant chain: it had given unit managers a piece of the action. In addition to a modest base salary of $16,000, a typical manager owned 20% to 30% of his restaurant. Some wound up earning $100,000 a year or more; none required much supervision; and turnover among hourly workers had been cut in half. Shaich and Schlesinger could hardly believe their ears. Says Eynon, "I felt like I was bringing water to thirsty men in the desert."

Quenched though they were, they doubted such a system could work in Boston. Nevertheless, the conversation did offer hope that there might be a solution to their problems, and they returned home determined to break the cycle of failure once and for all.

During the next few months, the two inundated the company with resolutions, exhortations, and memos. Schlesinger advocated a coordinated program to attract high-quality people, with clear incentives, better training, and more timely performance reviews. Shaich followed with proposals for a $1 increase in hourly pay; time off to participate in comprehensive training; and additional bonuses to crew members who stayed on board.

As time went along, however, they began to develop nagging doubts that more bells and whistles would do the trick. Burger King, they

heard, had tried similar ploys, to no avail. The cycle seemed to have a life of its own, impervious to adjustments and modifications. Au Bon Pain's own director of planning had to confess at one point that he would have difficulty recommending the place to his brother. On reflection, Shaich himself realized that he could not conceive of working as a store manager at Au Bon Pain—not under the current system.

But the gravity of the situation did not really come home to him until January 1986. One day, he was visiting a Boston-area store, and—before he had a chance to identify himself—a customer came in and ordered a turkey-and-Brie sandwich on a croissant. The employee behind the counter rang up the order, then realized that the store was out of croissants. Fine, the customer said, make it with another kind of bread. That wasn't possible, the employee said; the other bread could only be sold in whole loaves. The manager appeared and asked what the problem was. The employee explained. Well, said the manager to the customer, we can give you your money back. A disappointed customer left the store empty-handed.

There you had it in a nutshell, Shaich thought. The company had gotten so far away from its purpose that customers were being turned away to avoid slicing up a loaf of bread. All Shaich's efforts to develop operating standards had succeeded only in rendering store managers unable to think for themselves. They followed policies and procedures instead of common sense.

New policies and procedures were not the answer. (Who cared if the lettuce was on the left side of the counter instead of the right?) Nor were more stringent appraisal systems or better policing, piecemeal incentives or bigger bonuses. He could provide his staff with all those things, and the customer would *still* leave the store disappointed, without his turkey-and-Brie sandwich.

At last he saw the problem clearly. It was

a waste of time to try to tinker with the system. A year from now, he and his district managers would still be baby-sitting store managers, solving the problems that they seemed incapable of solving themselves. Somehow, the system had to be turned around 180 degrees. Store managers had to want to solve their own problems. They had to be able to decide for themselves that a satisfied customer was worth a couple of slices of bread.

"We had to turn assembly-line foremen into shopkeepers," says Shaich.

Says Schlesinger, "We had to bust the system wide open."

The revolution began in early 1986. Schlesinger and Shaich read everything they could find about the innovative management techniques of successful food-service companies—Chick-fil-A Inc., in Atlanta, for example, and Luby's Cafeterias Inc., in San Antonio. They also hired a Lincoln, Nebr., consulting firm, Selection Research Inc., to help in their search. Then, in April, they flew to California to visit a company called Harman Management Corp., based in Los Altos, that had the distinction of being the first Kentucky Fried Chicken franchisee in the United States.

Executives of both Golden Corral and Selection Research had mentioned Harman as a model of effective management, but Shaich and Schlesinger were skeptical as they pulled into the company's parking lot. They already had doubts about applying to Au Bon Pain the techniques developed by a company operating in such places as Utah and Colorado. When they saw Harman's cinder-block office, their hearts sank. It looked more like a chiropractor's office than the headquarters of their industry's most innovative leader. Inside, their skepticism mounted. There, in the lobby, was a copy of the company's yearbook. "It was incredibly hokey," recalls Schlesinger—filled with pictures of smiling Harmon's employees and their families at company outings.

Then they sat down with Jackie Trujillo, Harman's vice-president of operations, and their skepticism began turning to wonder.

She told them that the company's 200-odd stores did, on average, 20% more volume than company-owned Kentucky Fried Chicken units. Turnover, she said, was not a problem, nor was supervision. Store managers were responsible for watching their own costs, recruiting their own crews, and making their units successful. How was this possible? Well, the managers—like those at Golden Corral—were owners, getting a salary of $18,000 to $20,000, with opportunities to earn a share of profits on top of that. What's more, they had the option to buy 30% to 40% of the stock in their stores. The company's role was to cheer them on with banquets, rankings, and awards.

Schlesinger was furiously taking notes. He and Shaich could not help but contrast the situation to their own. Harman's stock-purchase agreements with managers were 3 or 4 pages long; Au Bon Pain's directives to managers often ran to 20 pages. Au Bon Pain was spending $250,000 a year on help-wanted ads; Harman spent almost nothing. But perhaps the greatest contrast was between themselves and founder Leon W. "Pete" Harman, whom they met later that day. A homespun fellow in his sixties, he seemed to have all the time in the world. They spent an hour chatting leisurely, without a crisis or an interruption. He said lots of people came to see him, searching for solutions to the same kinds of problems. They listened, but they seldom followed his advice, which he found a little baffling. "You know, at a private company, you don't have to be greedy," he said. "You can share it with your good people, and it all comes back to you."

Schlesinger, the former Harvard professor, was impressed. "Here was a guy with maybe a high-school education, and he seemed to have it all figured out. It was the most humbling experience of my life."

That evening, they visited two of Harman's Kentucky Fried Chicken stores and several other fast-food outlets in the same neighborhoods. Again, they were struck by the contrast. At Harman's, if not elsewhere, the bathrooms sparkled, and the crew members were well dressed and upbeat. Indeed, one of the assistant managers tried to recruit them, saying how great it was to work there, and pointing out that the manager was making $100,000 a year. "You could feel it," Shaich says. "Everything we had been talking about was real."

Two weeks later, Shaich and Schlesinger were back on the road, this time heading to Raleigh, N.C., to visit Golden Corral. It was the same story all over again. There, managers worked as hard as their counterparts at Harman's, and the best of them had incomes to match. "The big difference between them and us," says Shaich, "was that they had adjusted the reward level to the point where it was worth all the pain."

By the time the pair returned from North Carolina, they had seen all the proof they needed. There were but two remaining questions: Would it work in Boston? And if so, how? Schlesinger spent two full weeks tinkering with profit-and-loss statements from individual stores. He tried to apply the profit-sharing formulas from Harman's but found that many of Au Bon Pain's stores had too wide a range of volume to produce meaningful incentives. Then it hit him: why not tie the store manager's incentive to "controllable" profits (that is, profit less rent and depreciation), instead of store profits? A manager, after all, could do nothing about his rent. But he *could* adjust his use of labor, shrinkage, and controllable expenses depending on the level of business he did. If the manager took care of his crew, used them when he needed them, and watched his other costs, the stores could become more efficient and profitable than ever. "Our basic premise," says Schlesinger, "was that it was a lot more important to control outputs than to control inputs." It all made sense, and—unlike Harman's system—it seemed equally applicable to low- and high-volume stores.

So they decided to put their plan to the test. The six-month trial period began on July 15, 1986, at two Au Bon Pain stores, selected because their managers were, at best, average performers. One store, managed by Brian McEvoy, was located in a Hartford office building. The other, in a shopping mall in Burlington, Mass., was managed by Gary Aronson.

Schlesinger, who supervised the test, explained the rules to each of the managers. The company was, in effect, leasing the stores to them. It gave them goals for labor and food costs, but agreed to split the controllable profits on a 50-50 basis. They understood and went to work.

Almost at once, the stores began to change. Aronson got rid of one assistant manager to save on overhead, and hired his wife as a crew member. He and his remaining assistant began working longer hours, as many as 80 hours a week, and looking for ways to control costs and boost volume. They reorganized the store to increase its seating capacity; they developed wholesale and catering accounts; and they raised employees' wages. McEvoy took a different approach, holding his own hours to 55 hours a week, but increasing staffing during peak periods to assure prompt service. He also introduced a telephone express ordering service.

Schlesinger was amazed at the speed of the change. Overnight, managers began solving the problems they had previously dumped on the company. "We finally had a system that didn't accept excuses," Schlesinger says. "My role was helping them to build sales." Shaich was equally impressed when he paid a surprise visit to the Hartford store. The place was spotless. "I know when a store is running well," he says. "I could feel the difference. It was everything I had hoped it would be."

The numbers were just as exciting. Crew turnover at Aronson's store, for example, fell to almost nothing. Meanwhile, both stores were beating their targets by substantial margins. By the end of the six months, McEvoy had exceeded his sales goal by $74,000, and his controllable-profit goal by about $27,000. At that rate, he could expect to earn at least $55,000 a year. Aronson did even better: he was ahead by $54,000 on sales and around $45,000 on controllable profit—meaning he was earning close to $75,000 a year. "We were convinced," says Shaich.

The next step was easy. In January 1987, they began rolling the plan out to the rest of the company.

It is a Friday afternoon in April 1987, and Ron Shaich is sitting with Len Schlesinger in an office at the company's headquarters. A store manager named Jim Morgan walks in. Morgan, an effervescent fellow of 26, has been with the company for four years, and right now he is in a hurry. The Boston Marathon is being run the next Monday. He just wants Shaich and Schlesinger to know that he'll be there at the finish line, selling croissants and beverages from his Au Bon Pain pushcart. Does he have the necessary vending permits? Oh, yeah, he took care of that himself. Will he need any help? No, no, he's convinced some friends to give him a hand. The bosses can relax. The situation is wired.

Perhaps nothing better illustrates how profoundly Au Bon Pain has changed in the past year. Time was when Shaich would have had to plead on bended knee to get a manager to take a pushcart to the Boston Marathon. Indeed, he had often pleaded with managers to take pushcarts to the Bayside Exposition Center south of Boston, but his entreaties went unheeded. These days, he doesn't give it a thought. Gary Aronson, who now manages a

store in downtown Boston, has decided to cover Bayside. He expects to be there 60 to 80 days a year.

The new compensation system is working. It is already installed at 10 of the 40 company-owned stores, and those operated by manager/partners are outperforming the others by a wide margin. During the first three months under the new system, partner stores as a group ran 40% ahead of their profit goals, while the nonpartner stores were pretty much on target. So the company is going full speed ahead with plans to convert the remaining stores by year end. Meanwhile, experienced managers from other food-service companies have begun applying for jobs, and Schlesinger and Shaich are extending the concept to district managers and others.

To be sure, the system entails certain risks, especially for store managers. Each of them gets a base salary of $25,000 and a chance to win or lose. Even if the manager wins, and earns the monthly bonus, half of it (up to $7,500) goes into a reserve fund that is not paid out until his or her contract expires, thereby locking successful managers into their stores for the duration. "They're in the same position as company owners," says Shaich. "They can't just walk away." And like company owners, they have to solve their own problems, hire and fire their own people, set their own wage scale, cut their own deals. What they can't do is to compromise on food quality and customer service, which the company regularly monitors through in-store audits and visits by unidentified "mystery" shoppers. Aside from that, they're on their own.

Some managers will no doubt fail and have to be replaced. After all, the system is not for everyone. But for Au Bon Pain it is working so well that even Shaich finds the results hard to believe. The company projects sales of $35 million for 1987, and the stores have never run better, or with less support from headquarters.

"We're out of the picture," he says. "It's a closed loop." The loop is so closed that he and his partners feel confident about letting the company grow at the rate of 12 new stores per year for the next few years.

Not that Shaich feels they have solved all the problems. The journey has been too long, with too many valleys and swamps, for him to believe it is finally over. But now, at last, Au Bon Pain meets his own test for a business. "This," he says, "is the kind of company I'd like to work for."

Bonus System for Balanced Strategy

Ray Stata

Modesto A. Maidique

With both ROA and sales growth as measures of performance, this bonus plan encourages executives to balance long- and short-term results.

Executive bonus plans that are based on results are not particularly new. Many companies reward executives according to how they contribute to individual goals. But what if the goals are twofold and require trade-offs? Few companies that these authors know of have devised a way to compensate executives for achieving a balance between long- and short-term results. In this article, the authors show how Analog Devices—a growing high-technology company—devised an incentive plan that would reward executives for achieving growth in sales while maintaining a high return on assets. Analog's management solved the problem with a bonus matrix where the payout factor is calibrated to the industry's performance. The authors describe the plan, explain how it was designed, and then show, in follow-up interviews with key executives at Analog, how it worked.

In any industry, a company's performance is relative to the competition. Outside an industry

context, particular return on investment and sales growth percentages have limited significance. In an industry where sales growth is averaging 25%, a business with sales growing at a 15% compound annual rate is *losing* market share. Similarly, a business that is returning a respectable 14% on assets in an industry that is returning 18% to 20% is fast becoming a poor cousin of its competitors.

Regardless of its size or industry, a company's relative competitive position depends on its choice of business strategies for its product-market groups and, equally important, on its effective implementation of those strategies. Over the past 20 years, managers have generally come to understand and accept different frameworks for developing corporate strategy.[1] Many have not, however, devised ways of satisfactorily implementing them. As the president of a major high-technology company recently said, "We now know what we have to do—but look around and you'll find we're not getting it done."

A wide range of tools—such as organizational structures, planning and control systems, personnel policies, and information gathering—is available to implement strategy effectively. But we feel that a system linking company goals to the personal goals of executives is fundamental to effective implementation; and the way in which management compensates its executives is the crucial factor in that system.

Further, if not properly designed, the compensation system can actually work against strategy implementation. Some compensation systems, like those where a base salary is gradually increased each year, fail to distinguish the standard of living increase from the "merit raise" (the portion attributable to an executive's contribution toward company goals). In years of high inflation, that distinction becomes increasingly difficult to see. An incentive program based on measurable results, however, will make clear the link between compensation and an individual's contribution to corporate results.

During the past 20 years, 80% of the top *Fortune* "500" industrials have adopted incentive plans aimed at improving the relationship between corporate strategy and executives' actions.[2] But the results have been mixed. Frequent pitfalls are the administration and communication of the plans, the selection of the participants, and problems in measuring performance.[3] More often than not, however, the two major problems with these plans lie in their design:

1. The plans are decoupled from the industry's performance. Thus executives may receive a high reward for achieving a 15% growth rate while the industry grows at a rate of 25%.
2. The plans are one-dimensional. For example, if compensation is based solely on return on assets, managers may be tempted to eliminate assets or investments critical to long-term growth.

Most plans, particularly the one-dimensional type, do not have the flexibility to be consonant with the business strategy and reflect the business's performance relative to its competition. Designers of the plan usually give something up, often simply to make the plan easy to explain.

For example, for several years management at Analog Devices ($130 million in sales in 1980 and 2,000 employees) experimented with a variety of one-dimensional plans, finally concluding that none of them could be made congruent with its goal of balanced financial objectives. Yet Analog's management also wished to develop an incentive plan that would reinforce the alignment of personal interests with company goals and that would attract, motivate, and retain the people and spirit needed to meet those goals.

For these reasons, four years ago Analog's management developed and implemented a new approach to incentive compensation. While the plan is not a panacea, it goes a long way toward resolving the major problems and, to the best of our knowledge, is a unique solution to balancing bonus compensation. In addition, the plan is subject to continuous review and improvement and to use of different measures. We describe here its design, Analog's experience implementing it, and a follow-up survey of participants that we conducted four years after its implementation.

DESIGNING THE COMPENSATION PLAN

Because—like many companies—Analog Devices is diversified and decentralized into divisions, management realized at the outset that it would need two compensation plans, one for corporate objectives and one for division objectives. As the corporate plan is the master, we'll look first at how it was designed (the division plan is a refined version of it).

The Corporate Plan

At the outset, Analog's management decided the plan must be multidimensional to reinforce corporate objectives, which included a balance between short- and long-term results. Thinking that three dimensions made the plan too complicated and difficult to visualize, management settled on two: return on assets (ROA) and sales growth, the two variables that bring into balance the conflict in objectives. (ROA was chosen instead of return on capital or equity to make the payment independent of the financial structure of the company. Operational pretax profits are used to compute ROA to eliminate effects, like tax and interest rates, over which line management has no control.) Most important, management pegged both measures to the relative performance in its industry.

Management believed these were the right choices for a fragmented, rapidly growing industry such as Analog Devices'—that is, data-acquisition products for measurement and control applications. Managers in other industries or in companies with different corporate objectives might, however, choose different criteria.

The two dimensions Analog picked gave management the flexibility it desired; the price it paid was a more complex payout formula. For ease of communication, the designers of the plan converted the formula to a simple matrix with 49 squares (see the *Exhibit*). Each position on the matrix defines a payout factor that is determined by the two coordinates: ROA and sales growth.

The second step in the design of the plan was to calibrate Analog's performance matrix to performance achieved by the leading companies in its industry and to assign payoff factors for each combination of ROA and growth results.

The third step was to decide who would

participate in the plan and what percentage of total executive compensation at various levels in the company would be derived from bonus when the goal performance was achieved.

Now let's look at each of these steps in turn.

Establishing performance measures   In Analog's industry, a significant delay occurs between investments in new product, market development, and the realization of results. For this reason, performance measures of strategic decisions intended to generate long-term corporate growth need to be isolated from measures of decisions affecting short-term business problems or changes in business conditions. And management should be motivated to hold the long-term rate of strategic investment relatively steady rather than merely to achieve short-term profit objectives.

This line of reasoning suggests that a bonus pay-off related to sales growth should be averaged over a long period. Since the delay between initiation of new product development and significant contribution to sales from the investment is about three years, in its bonus plan Analog uses a 12-quarter (three-year) moving average sales growth. The time period between cause and effect will vary in most companies. If the development period is longer than three to five years, sales growth loses its usefulness as an incentive for management performance; the perspective of executives on a single assignment usually does not extend past five years.

On the other hand—due to changes in the business cycle, in competitive developments, or in customer buying habits—business conditions can and do change, sometimes very rapidly. Because of this, managers need to be motivated for short-term management performance and decisions, for which operating pretax ROA is a better measure. Management's job is to adjust operational expense and assets to ensure satisfactory profits and ROA under changing conditions. The business cycle, for instance, is often reflected in changing sales volume, in which case operational expenses and inventories are the appropriate controls.

Analog's management averages profitability over three quarters; it believes that in its industry there should be about one quarter to detect a meaningful change in order rate, another to effect corrective action, and a third quarter to see any meaningful change in results. For Analog, operating return on assets has been the best profitability measure because it covers expense plus asset management. ROA also helps management to focus on inventory and receivables, both critical factors in short-term changes in business conditions.

Return on capital and return on equity are not good measures for these purposes. Decisions affecting debt-to-equity ratio, interest expense, and tax rates are not appropriate short-term controls; often they are not even feasible. Furthermore, in a decentralized organization it is more meaningful to measure and control assets than liabilities.

Calibrating measures with businesses in the industry To establish appropriate performance standards for Analog Devices (that is, to calibrate the matrix), management analyzed the three-year average performance of 15 leading electronics companies whose markets and products are the most closely related to Analog's. These companies were further segmented into three subcategories (semiconductors, instruments, and computers) to better understand how the mix of Analog's business—between semi-conductor components and equipment-level computer-related instruments—would influence its standards for growth and ROA.

Analog's management found that only a handful of companies sustain an outstanding long-term growth above 40% per year. Most of the high-performance companies cluster around 25% per year. Likewise, ROA is rarely above 30%, the norm being closer to 23% for the better companies.

Another consideration that affected Analog's choice of performance standards was its policy to fund a significant portion of its growth from internally generated profits. As it experienced faster growth rates, it needed to provide a strong incentive for management to earn higher ROA to fund this faster growth. In its analysis, management found that leading companies in its industry were also following similar policies. For them, higher growth has usually been accompanied by higher ROA.

Based on these considerations Analog's management set up its bonus matrix (see the *Exhibit*). The matrix is normalized so that the bonus payout factor, K, is 1.00 when the company is achieving its goals of 25% average growth rate and 23% ROA measured before taxes and nonoperating expenses. (The formula shown in the footnote to the exhibit computes the exact bonus payout factor; the matrix provides a rough visual representation of the tradeoffs between growth and profits.)

A 2% increase in pretax ROA performance is equivalent in payoff to about a 5% increase in sales growth rate. The assignment of payoff factors for other combinations of growth and profits can be made to favor growth or profits as may be appropriate for any company's business strategy.

Selecting participants and deciding how to compensate them The plan is flexible about who participates; it is responsive to changing company needs. The system does not require any particular salary level or job grade and can include executives who have been with Analog for less than a year. As a practical matter, however, virtually all of the participants in the plan have been with Analog several years and are at least two grades above that of an entry-level professional. Division general managers initiate recommendations for participation in the plan, but final approval rests with the vice presi-

189

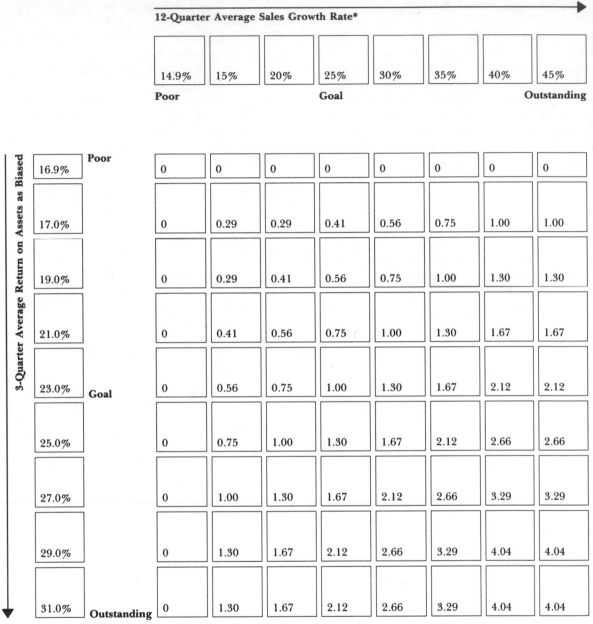

12-Quarter Average Sales Growth Rate*

3-Quarter Average Return on Assets as Biased

ROA \ Sales Growth	14.9% (Poor)	15%	20%	25% (Goal)	30%	35%	40%	45% (Outstanding)
16.9% (Poor)	0	0	0	0	0	0	0	0
17.0%	0	0.29	0.29	0.41	0.56	0.75	1.00	1.00
19.0%	0	0.29	0.41	0.56	0.75	1.00	1.30	1.30
21.0%	0	0.41	0.56	0.75	1.00	1.30	1.67	1.67
23.0% (Goal)	0	0.56	0.75	1.00	1.30	1.67	2.12	2.12
25.0%	0	0.75	1.00	1.30	1.67	2.12	2.66	2.66
27.0%	0	1.00	1.30	1.67	2.12	2.66	3.29	3.29
29.0%	0	1.30	1.67	2.12	2.66	3.29	4.04	4.04
31.0% (Outstanding)	0	1.30	1.67	2.12	2.66	3.29	4.04	4.04

EXHIBIT   Bonus Payoff Function for 1979

Note: The payout is deliberately nonlinear, generating higher incremental payoffs at higher levels of performance. Note the "cutoff" and "saturation" levels. The bias factor allows management to adjust the expected payout from year to year to compensate for unusual circumstances, for example, a year in which deliberate, heavy strategic expenditures are committed that will depress operating ROA. The bias factor is set at the beginning of the year—coincident with the annual plan—and then held constant through the planning period.

*The bonus payoff factor can be calculated from the following formula: Bonus payout factor =

$$K = \left(\frac{\text{ROA\% + bias} - .4 \text{ sales growth}}{33} \right)^{4.5}$$

dent of human resources. As of early 1980, more than 80 executives, including all of the corporate officers and senior individual contributors, were participating in the plan.

Once management had decided who would participate and what performance standards would be used, the next step was to decide what the payoff factors were and how to divide the compensation dollar between fixed and variable compensation. At Analog Devices, executives at various levels in the organization receive a preassigned bonus percentage, which varies from 10% to 25% of their base salary, if they achieve their goal (25% growth and 23% ROA—which defines the position on the bonus matrix where the payoff factor, K, is 1.00).

Top executives with a 25% basic bonus can earn up to 100% of their base salary when they perform outstandingly in terms of both growth and ROA (40% growth and 29% ROA—which defines the position on the bonus matrix where the payoff factor, K, reaches its maximum value of 4.04).

At the lowest level of participation, generally two or three levels below a division general manager, the bonus performance is 10% of base salary for goal performance, with a cutoff when K is 2, or 20% growth.

There are two reasons for the sliding bonus scale. First, high rewards in total compensation for top executives should carry high risks and should only be realized when outstanding results—by competitive standards within the industry—are achieved. Second, lower-level managers should not risk as large a percentage of their total compensation with bonuses since higher-level management decisions can affect results negatively.

A final important issue is how frequently performance should be measured and rewarded. At Analog, management believes a quarterly measure of performance is important since the corporation reports quarterly to the stockholders and to the financial community. Investors these days are interested in consistent

and monotonic results. Accordingly, Analog computes and pays out an executive's bonus each quarter, based on a quarterly moving average of sales growth (12 quarters) and ROA (3 quarters). This aligns management's interests and time frame with those of the stockholders.

Quarterly payouts are also more compatible with the needs of the employee and become in effect another component of compensation. The close coupling of quarterly results to quarterly payout also focuses employee attention on achieving goals.

The Division Plan

In developing the corporate bonus plan, Analog's management also wanted to tailor a similar bonus plan at the division level, which would also be based on each division's potential for growth and profit as well as on opportunities for strategic investments. For instance, a business unit in the test-instrument market may face considerably different market conditions and competition than a business unit in the microprocessor market would.

Management recognized that—in accordance with portfolio analysis—while some divisions might have little growth potential, they might have the ability to deliver high ROA; and other divisions would be able to generate very high growth and return on sales but deliver lower ROA, especially during the start-up phase. That is, some divisions would be "cash cows" and others "stars." In a balanced portfolio, the high ROA, low-growth divisions are as valuable as those at the opposite pole.

The division payoff matrices use the same trade-off between growth and ROA as the corporate matrix—namely, 2 percentage points of ROA and 5 percentage points of average annual growth (see the formula in the exhibit). The same exponent (4.5) also induces nonlinear valuation above or below standard performance for various combinations of ROA and growth. The bias factor allows management to set division ROA standards higher than corporate standards to account for corporate expenses not allocated to the division. It may also set ROA standards lower to compensate for heavy investments during the start-up phase of a new business or product line.

Executives with total group responsibilities or corporatewide staff responsibilities participate on the corporate matrix only, and those whose responsibilities are entirely limited to a division or group participate only on the group or division matrix. Executives who have responsibilities that are primarily division oriented or group oriented but that have significant impact on corporate results participate in both plans equally.

HOW DID IT WORK?

After a major decision, top management's view of its real impact is often obscured by flag waving from managerial cheering sections. At Analog, management decided to conduct a survey to find out what participants in the plan really thought. Over an 18-month period, during which the payout factor moved from 0.58 to 2.0, 10 randomly selected participants who had been assured of anonymity were asked four basic questions:

1. Do you understand the bonus plan?
2. Has it contributed to your understanding of corporate goals and strategy?
3. Has the existence of the plan had an impact on your decisions over the past two years?
4. What is your overall assessment of the plan?

The Spirit of the Plan Is Understood

With the exception of one senior executive who had been instrumental in developing the plan, none of the executives interviewed appeared to have a thorough understanding of the details of the bonus matrix. As one senior marketing manager who had participated in the previous one-dimensional bonus plan explains, "To understand this one you really have to get into it." Yet it was evident that all of the managers interviewed understood the "foundations" (as one person put it) and basic concepts behind the plan. But understanding did not come easily. Several people said it took six months to a year to comprehend the plan.

One engineering manager sums up his first year on the plan this way: "Initially, I had great curiosity about the plan. It was important for me to understand, so I talked to several people in personnel and in other departments about it. I wound up with somewhat conflicting definitions of the bonus matrix; but something else happened. As a consequence of these discussions, I developed a better understanding of the impact of capital equipment decisions on return on assets, depreciation, and marginal contribution. As a consequence, I stopped concerning myself with the details of the plan—for I felt I had understood its spirit."

This spirit seemed to spread to other layers of management as well. "It's simple," one general manager explains. "The plan gives you a chance to reinforce asset management concepts because the topic comes up regularly." But another executive moderates this optimism, recalling that it had taken him at least a year to obtain a solid grasp of the plan. He does not expect the people reporting to him to "make it their own" any faster than he did.

Financial Aspects Linked to Matrix

Executives clearly perceived the link between the *financial* aspects of corporate strategy and the bonus matrix. On the other hand, most of the executives interviewed saw few links between the bonus matrix and overall product-market strategy. Other corporate mechanisms, however, such as the annual strategic plan, had already prompted such connections.

Decision Making Is Affected

Every manager interviewed recalled at least one instance when the plan shaped a major decision. Generally, these decisions were related to capital equipment purchases; but some persons mentioned production goals, others even career choices. The response of one production executive is typical:

"When the new computerized test equipment came, we went wild. Every one of the new products—and some of the old ones—were designed or redesigned to take 'advantage' of the new systems. After the plan was instituted, I did a lot of thinking. What if using the old manual method produced a higher return on assets, despite its labor intensity? After all, if at any time the new equipment was idle, it cost us money. I had some analysis done and it turned out that for *some* products it was better to use the manual method. Now nothing goes into the computerized system until we've checked it thoroughly. I look at things like this now. I'm much less arbitrary."

The careful analysis that is usually lavished by top management on major investments began to permeate lower levels of management. As one general manager explains, "Before, $20,000 and $25,000 investments were made without much notice. Now a $5,000 rise in inventory or even purchase of a $3,000 oscilloscope is carefully scrutinized before it gets to me."

Shortly before he was interviewed, another senior executive had just made a major career decision. He had turned down a position that offered more responsibility, independence, and a better title. This is the way he explains his decision:

"The bonus plan comes into my thinking a lot. It has helped to clarify the corporate objectives and thus facilitated my own decisions.

"Basically, I have cast my lot with Analog. I am here for the long pull. Thus when I heard of this opening, in addition to the usual personal-development questions, I asked myself, 'Where can I have greater impact on sales growth and return on assets?' When analyzed from this perspective, it became clear that if I took the job at this time, I would likely have had a negative impact on both of these areas for the company—and ultimately on my own compensation as well. Thus I decided not to move but to wait for an opportunity in which I could advance my personal development while simultaneously strengthening the corporate entity."

But a few managers are also concerned about possible negative effects on decision making. Running tight on capacity can result in reduced service levels and ultimately reduced sales. Theoretically, the plan takes this into account—one of its axes is sales growth. However, there is a difference in timing. While reductions in inventory may reflect themselves immediately in ROA, the effect of reduced service levels will be subtler and take longer to perceive.

Overall Assessment

The participants interviewed were unanimous in their high regard for the two-dimensional bonus matrix. This approval did not, however, stop them from offering criticisms, all but one of which dealt with bonus size, mix (between corporate and division plans), sensitivity to business performance, and ultimately fairness.

Half of the managers interviewed raised questions about the amount of bonus payout. Some also wondered about whether the distribution factors for lower levels were high enough. Explained one executive, "The annual payout needs to be large enough to buy at least a car with it." Participants on the lowest range of the plan, for instance, would receive about $5,000 pretax maximum using the present scaling—that is, about "half a car." Another executive said, "If cash is going to be the motivational factor, let's make it a significant amount of cash."

Several divisional executives also objected to being compensated on the basis of corporate performance. "The corporate matrix is too distant," one explained. "I really find it difficult to trace our impact on it." Another one observed that although the divisions were the basis of the corporate payout, sometimes "corporate pays out more than our division's plan."

But it was the plan's alleged inequity that drew the strongest criticism. One executive summed up the feeling of several others when he said:

"Setting the division bogie [bias] is an arbitrary process. Each division is at a different stage of development; each general manager has a different relationship with corporate. There's bound to be inequities. How do I know the calibration is fair when the bogies for the other divisions are secret?"

It would be unrealistic to establish causal relationships; however, since the plan was instituted four years ago corporate sales have increased at an annual rate of about 40%, while corporate profit is up from $1.3 million in 1975 to $7.1 million in fiscal 1979. ROA (calculated on the basis of operating profits before tax) has increased from 16% in 1975 to 21% in 1979.

Bonus plans are generally viewed as a means to motivate performance. But one of the main impacts of Analog's bonus plan has been to educate (although it is clear management needs to clarify better how business and personal goals are interrelated). The carrot should not hang on a simple string. Rather than concentrating on profit alone, executives need to recognize the trade-offs between short-term and long-term results and to understand the interplay among growth, strategic investments, operational expenses, and asset management. As the bonus matrix plan points out, corporate performance standards for growth and ROA are not arbitrary. Rather, they are derived from the conditions of the particular industry in which a company competes.

We believe that the two-dimensional plan described here is vastly superior to one-dimensional plans. For a high-growth, high-technology company to flourish, management must mediate the traditional conflict between short-term ROA and long-term growth. The bonus matrix can be the key to striking that balance.

Balancing Contradictions

Obviously, one of the greatest difficulties in the establishment of the conditions for the realization of democracy lies in the contradiction between a planned economy and the active co-operation of each individual. A planned economy of the scope of any big industrial system requires a great deal of centralization and, as a consequence, a bureaucracy to administer this centralized machine. On the other hand, the active control and co-operation by each individual and by the smallest units of the whole system requires a great amount of decentralization. Unless planning from the top is blended with active participation from below, unless the stream of social life continuously flows from below upwards, a planned economy will lead to renewed manipulation of the people.

From Erich Fromm, *Escape from Freedom* (New York: Holt, Rinehart & Winston, copyright © 1969 by Erich Fromm), p. 301. Reprinted with permission.

NOTES

1. See, for instance, Kenneth R. Andrews, *The Concept of Corporate Strategy* (Homewood, Ill.: Dow Jones-Irwin, 1971); see also C. Roland Christensen, Kenneth R. Andrews, and Joseph L. Bower, *Business Policy Text and Cases* (Homewood, Ill.: Dow Jones-Irwin, 1973).

2. Malcolm S. Salter, "Tailor Incentive Compensation to Strategy," HBR March-April 1973, p. 94.

3. John Dearden, "How to Make Incentive Plans Work," HBR July-August 1972, p. 117.

Organizational Demography: Implications for Management

Jeffrey Pfeffer

"IEEE to Ask Gov't to Investigate Lockheed 'Selective Hiring' Policy" was the headline in the September 10, 1984 issue of *Electronic Engineering Times.* Apparently, the news organization had obtained a copy of the July edition of an internal company newsletter in which hiring of engineers between 30 and 45 in the spacecraft engineering area was advocated "to flatten the current bimodal distribution of 40–60-year-olds and 25–30-year-olds, with a gap in the middle." The newsletter cited the need for a more even distribution of workforce experience and education. Beyond the legalities of whether or not hiring on the basis of age is permissible, the situation described in the article is one that is all too familiar in business and other organizations. In the present instance, Lockheed, which has a high proportion of people who spend most of their career with the company, had undergone a period of downturn in the late 1960s and early 1970s, doing little new hiring and losing some engineers to better opportunities elsewhere. Now, in the late 1970s and early 1980s, with renewed expansion, a younger cohort of engineers was being rapidly added. What the company now faced was an older senior management that would begin to retire and a younger, inexperienced group not quite ready to take their place. Thus, there was the need to hire engineers of moderate age and experience to smooth the distribution and provide an orderly transition of management. Of course, this policy would threaten the younger engineers who had been recruited with the promise of rapid promotion and even the older engineers who could foresee pressures for early retirement to make room for the middle group. The article quoted a Lockheed spokesman trying to address both of these issues: "There are going to be more opportunities for younger engineers, but that doesn't mean that there are going to be less opportunities for older employees."

The type of problems represented in the Lockheed situation arise because organizations, until confronted with some kind of crisis, are often fairly insensitive to managing the demography of their workforce (by which I mean simply its composition in terms of age and length of service, as well as its educational and other compositional characteristics). Only when there are crises of succession—conflict between cohorts that differ vastly in age or time in the organization, or other visible manifestations of problems that are caused by demographic issues—is attention paid to this important factor, and then, often only briefly.

Why is there such myopia about this fundamental aspect of organizations? Organizations are full of people. It often seems only natural and appropriate to analyze and manage organizations using individuals as the units of analysis.[1] Moreover, the emphasis on the individual fits prevailing social values and customs; thus, organization theorists have tried to comprehend organizations in terms of the needs, values, attitudes, cognitions, expectancies, and characteristics of individuals.[2] Managers have often followed this lead and have implemented programs of work redesign, leadership training, and other programs focused primarily on changing the psychology of the individuals in place. This emphasis in both theory and practice on individual-level intrapsychic processes has had at least two deleterious effects. First, it has encouraged organization theorists and managers alike to go into the lay psychology business. However, changing attitudes, beliefs, or perceptions as a way of changing behavior is both difficult and occasionally ineffective. Predicating management practice on what goes on inside people's heads means that one must be able to measure intrapsychic processes—not an easy task.

Moreover, management research and practice, in its almost exclusive emphasis on the individual, has lost sight of that fact that organizations are fundamentally relational entities. People in organizations interact with one another, both in formal and informal structures. There are several ways of thinking about organizations which explicitly encompass their relational properties, including measuring and paying attention to networks of interaction directly. Another such perspective involves analyzing the demography of the organizations.

WHAT IS ORGANIZATIONAL DEMOGRAPHY?

Most, if not all, surveys include questions on the backgrounds of the respondents, such as their age and time in the organization. Simi-larly, most organizational personnel information systems contain basic demographic information such as date of hire (and, by inference, time in the organization), age, and sex. The demography of an organization is nothing more than describing it in terms of the distribution on these various dimensions. Organizational demography is based on the data gathered on individuals, but is, in fact, a collective or unit-level property.

Demographic factors are important in understanding and managing organizations because similarity is one of the most important bases of interpersonal attraction;[3] and demographic features such as age, race, and sex both help to determine similarity and also signal that those who share these features are more likely to be similar. People who share experiences and attitudes are more likely to like each other because they will understand each other better, and because liking someone who is similar is self-reinforcing as it ratifies one's own qualities. People in an organization who have gone through a financial crisis or business downturn together will feel closer to each other for having shared the experience, just as employees at People Express who were present during the hectic start-up days have developed a common bond and attraction for each other through that shared experience. Also, attitudinal similarity promotes interpersonal attraction, as we tend to like those who think like we do and have similar beliefs.

Figure 1 presents a model of how demographic similarity, particularly along the dimension of time of entry, promotes the development of cohorts and integration and cohesion within such cohorts. When people enter an organization, they begin immediately to develop networks of relations both in order to solve problems of task interdependence and to provide social support and friendship. People who have been in the organization longer will have already developed extensive communication networks and will therefore have less time or

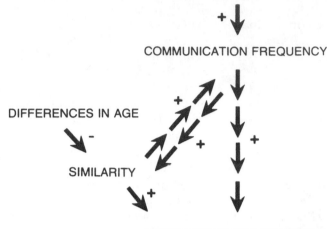

FIGURE 1.

capacity to interact with the new entrants. Thus, other things being equal, the new entrants are likely to interact more with other newer employees who are also just getting to know the place and who have more opportunity to develop relationships with them. Similarity in time of entry and in other dimensions such as age and education will lead to increased communication frequency. Communication frequency both tends to increase similarity in values and perspective and is enhanced further by similarity in attitudes and beliefs. All these factors produce greater integration and cohesion among the group that has entered at the same time. In this way, cohorts based on date of entry into the organization tend to develop. One can observe this effect most strongly in time-of-entry-graded organizations such as law firms, accounting firms, consulting firms, and university faculties, where status and rank are very much based on time of entry and persons tend to enter at one time during the year.

Because similarity is such an important property defining social relations, the most useful measures of organizational demography are those that assess the extent to which a group of persons is heterogeneous or homogeneous.

There are a number of measures that have been developed to measure inequality or diversity in social groups, including the Gini index,[4] measures based on the concept of entropy,[5] and other measures of heterogeneity.[6] A review of these measures by Allison suggested that one of the simplest, the coefficient of variation, is one of the best measures of inequality (or its converse, homogeneity) in a group.[7] The coefficient of variation is simply the standard deviation, divided by the mean value of the variable in question. A second useful measure is the proportion of people in an organization or organizational unit of a certain type.

THE EFFECTS OF DEMOGRAPHY

Demography is measurable; it captures relations among individuals but is a property of the social aggregate and is important in affecting similarity and social relations. It is this latter point, its effect on social relations and behavior, that makes demography important for understanding many things which occur in organizations. Following is a brief review of some of the major research findings on the effects of demography on social systems.

The Effects of Proportions

There is growing recognition that interaction patterns among individuals are determined, at least in part, by the structural features of the interaction, among the most prominent of which is the relative proportion of persons of different types. On a societal level, Marcia Guttentag and Paul Secord have examined, both historically and across countries, the relative numbers of men and women of marriageable ages.[8] They argue that whether there are relatively more men than women (so that women have more dyadic power) or women than men (so that men have dyadic power) helps to account both over time and across cultures for variations in practices such as the bride providing a dowry or the man paying the father of the bride for the privilege of marrying her, the treatment of women in literature and music, practices of monogamy, and labor force participation and fertility of women.

Perhaps better known to organizational analysts is Rosabeth Kanter's arguments on the effects of occupying a token status.[9] Kanter argued that people occupying token status, such as women in managerial ranks in many organizations, received more attention because of their distinctiveness and that this visibility heightened performance pressures. Also, because of their difference from the majority, tokens caused an increased awareness of boundaries and faced pressures to conform to social expectations or stereotypes about women. Women in token status, in situations in which there were few or no other women, confronted problems in interacting with their co-workers and in receiving credit and attention as individuals rather than as representatives of some group. Kanter's study reported that women in token status experienced more turnover and failure.

Two subsequent studies have attempted to further explore the effect of proportions, both examining the proportion of women in particular settings. In one study,[10] two law schools were compared, one in which women constituted about a third of the student body, and the other in which they constituted about one fifth. The women law students tended to pick more traditionally "female" law specialties, participated less in class, and performed more poorly in the school in which they were a small minority. In a study of government agencies with different proportions of women, Charles Bonjean and his colleagues found less direct support for Kanter's predictions.[11] They noted that to the extent minority group members began to become more numerous, their threat to those in power, the majority, grew. The effect of larger numbers as a threat might thus overcome some of the advantages of diminished uniqueness and visibility for any single individual.

The Effects of Cohort Size

In addition to their composition, the size of cohorts also can affect the organization as well as members of the cohort. A cohort is simply a group of people who have entered a social system at a given time. Cohorts are defined in terms of age in societies and in terms of date of entry in most organizational settings. Some organizations even speak of entering groups in terms of classes of cohorts—e.g., in law firms there are first-year associates, second-years, and so forth. Similarly, in other professional organizations in which advancement to partnership or other senior status is the result of a review conducted at a specified time after entry—as in promotion in universities and partnership decisions in accounting and managerial consulting firms—there are clear date-of-entry cohorts and gradings.

Again, the effect of cohort size was investigated first at the societal level. In a provocative work on the effect of cohort size on career prospects and other outcomes, Richard Easterlin argued that in the presence of relatively stable economic growth in the U.S., the variation in cohort size caused by radical changes in fertility behavior during the Great Depression and particularly World War II had consequences for the economic prospects of children born during the baby boom or baby bust years.[12] Children born into large cohorts, Easterlin argued, would have more competition for jobs and positions throughout their lives and would therefore achieve relatively less economic success. He further argued that this reduced economic success would manifest itself in diminished fertility in that cohort as well as greater marital instability.

Paul Maxim has investigated the effect of cohort size on juvenile delinquency.[13] Since criminal behavior is age-related, it is fairly well established that the larger the relative size of a youthful cohort, the higher will be the overall crime rate. However, there is also an argument that larger cohorts will tend to exhibit a higher crime rate than small cohorts of the same youthful age. This is because society has a relatively more difficult time in assimilating a larger cohort, since there are comparatively fewer resources and people to accomplish the socialization compared to the number of persons to be socialized. In particular, a large juvenile cohort strains society's attempts to socialize these youths and also facilitates the development of a unique youth subculture. Using data form Ontario, Canada, Maxim found support for the argument that larger youth cohorts would have higher crime rates than smaller ones.

Shelby Stewman has investigated the effects of cohort sizes on promotion chances in formal organizations, finding a similar pattern of results in terms of economic advancement.[14] Stewman observed that if one was a member of a comparatively small cohort, not only were one's own promotion chances better, but every promotion out of the cohort left even fewer

subsequent competitors to be selected. It therefore seems clear that cohort sizes and the patterns of recruitment that produce either larger or smaller cohorts are important factors affecting mobility prospects and consequences of mobility, such as motivation and career-plateauing issues.

Demography and Turnover

The study of the effects of demography on either societies or organizations is really still in its infancy, but the most studied topic to date has been the effect of demography on organizational turnover. The fundamental set of ideas underlying most of this research includes the following:

- turnover is produced, at least in part, by conflict and disagreement within the organization, as well as by a lack of social integration into the social structure;
- similarity and cohesion are both facilitated by demographic similarity, and particularly, by date-of-entry similarity;
- therefore, to the extent that organizations or units or groups are demographically heterogeneous, particularly in terms of the date of entry, there will be more turnover.

The effect of demography on turnover was investigated first in a sample of academic departments on two University of California campuses.[15] The argument was that turnover should be greater to the extent there were cleavages or gaps between the dates of entry of persons into the organization and to the extent that the organizational length-of-service distribution was lumpy rather than smooth. Turnover would be less, the argument went, if there were persons of more continuous time of entry into the organization, so that distinct cleavages among cohorts would not be present.

In this study, other factors that might affect the amount of turnover (such as department size, the level of resources available to the unit, and the extent to which the department operated in a field with a well-developed scientific paradigm so that there was consensus and uniformity on academic issues) were controlled. Both the size of the older cohort and the number of gaps of five to eight years among adjacent members in the department produced significant effects on turnover (which was classified into six types: assistant, associate, and full professor resignations, full professor early retirements, assistant professor non-renewal of contracts, and a summary measure of turnover including the five preceding types).

A subsequent study examined turnover in top management groups in a sample of 31 U.S. corporations.[16] It measured demography in a more refined way, using distance from other members of the group by either age or date of entry. Controlling for the firm's financial performance and other factors, evidence was again found indicating that demography could predict both the amount of turnover at the corporation level of analysis and who turned over at the individual level of analysis. At the top-management group level, it was the more heterogeneous groups (with larger coefficients of variation of distance) that experienced more turnover; at the individual level, it was the most distant or least similar individuals who tended to leave the group.

Another study examined turnover among nurses in U.S. hospitals.[17] Using the Gini index and the index of diversity as measures of demography, this study found that the more heterogeneous the nurse population in terms of date of entry, the greater the turnover—even after controlling for other factors such as wage levels, the local unemployment rate, and collective bargaining status. These three studies taken together seem to offer fairly strong support for the idea that demographic factors are important in accounting for variation in turnover rates across organizational units.

Demographic Effects on Innovation and Performance

Not only do these turnover effects suggest that demography can be used to help forecast manpower accession requirements and to predict and control turnover, but they may also have some positive consequences for performance, particularly in research and development settings, that can be managed and planned for. Barry Staw was among the first to recognize that turnover, though often associated with costs and ineffectiveness (as in the phrase, "the turnover problem"), was also potentially associated with some positive outcomes as well.[18] In particular, Staw suggested that there were two effects of a long time in the job—one involved increasing skill and familiarity in doing the job, which should positively affect performance; and the second involved diminished interest and motivation because of the loss of novelty and stimulation over time, which should negatively affect performance. The combination of these two effects, Staw reasoned, should produce an inverted U-shaped relationship in which performance should rise for a while (as length of service increased) and then decline (as the diminished motivation and creativity associated from long exposure to the same task overcame the effects of increased proficiency).

This inverted U-shaped effect has been observed when research and development group performance has been plotted against group age, by which is meant the average length of time that members in the group have been on the particular project. Ralph Katz observed that groups with either very young or very old average amount of time on the project performed less well than groups of intermediate age.[19] Katz further went on to show that this was because both intra- and inter-project communication decreased in groups that had been together longer. Groups that were very new had to work out communication and interaction patterns and learn the task, making them somewhat less effective. Groups that had been together on the project a long time routinized behavior to such an extent that communication, and presumably learning and exposure to new ideas, diminished. It was groups intermediate in age that performed most effectively.

SOME IMPLICATIONS FOR MANAGERIAL PRACTICE

The most fundamental implication of the research on the effects of demography on organizations is that we need to pay attention to this variable as both a cause of behavior and as something to be attended to in thinking about growth patterns, accessions, and other aspects of manpower planning. Human resource planning is important to both anticipate demographic issues before they arise and to manage the demography of the firm and its consequences. A sensitivity to demographic effects can help provide a context to understand organizational behavior. More fundamentally, examining the demographic structure of organizations can assist in the human resource planning function.

There are other, more specific implications. Following are a few representative examples to illustrate how a sensitivity to demographic concerns can help managers in their day-to-day work.

Choosing Assistants

Most managers occasionally find themselves in the position of choosing people to assist them. Deans choose associate deans, chief executive officers may have occasion to choose the top executive officers who report to them, the managing partner in a professional firm may choose or otherwise influence the selection of a managing committee which assists in the governance task, and presidents choose their cabinet officers and assistants. In each instance, the natural tendency will be to pick people from one's cohort. For example, to fill six key administrative positions, the new Dean of the Harvard Business School chose people who, for the most part, he knew well. Four of them had entered the business school within three years of the time he did. It is not surprising that he would pick from his own cohort. After all, if our arguments about interaction are correct, these are the people he has interacted with most and thus knows best, has the most confidence in, and with whom he is likely to agree and think alike. One would always want to have, as assistants, people on the same wavelength, whom one can trust, whom one understands implicitly, and whom one is socially integrated with. Such a tendency is observed in many other situations. Indeed, ties formed during school or during the first years on the job are well known for producing contacts that lead to subsequent positions and promotions.

Weighed against the advantages of choosing from within one's cohort may be the possible disadvantages of isolating the administrative structure from other important elements in the organization. Indeed, when I have observed deans or other administrators having some difficulty because of a lack of confidence in the rest of the organization, it is often the case that they have assembled an administrative cadre that leaves them well integrated into one cohort in the organization but isolated from others. If there are distinct cleavages and cohort groups within an organization, particularly one that is professional and tends to be administered on a more collegial and participative basis, it becomes important to choose assistants who represent the various cohorts present in the organization. In this way, these cohorts both feel and are represented in policy-making circles. They become more integrated into the governance structure and are less likely to cause trouble as a united and isolated opposition.

Bringing People In

Since communication is dependent on time of entry and whom one enters with, it is more difficult to bring in people one at a time. To bring in people as a group gives each the opportunity of building links with the others for purposes of both task accomplishment and social support. Bringing in people one at a time makes it more likely that they will not effectively get into the social structure, will suffer decreased performance, and will be more likely to leave.

As an example of a company which acts on this insight, consider the Harris Corporation. Harris hires a large number of new engineers and faces the task of getting these new hires rapidly integrated into the firm and up to speed. They use college affiliations as a way of helping this social integration process. For instance, if you are a graduate from Georgia Tech, the company helps you meet and socialize with other Georgia Tech graduates. By helping people find others who share common backgrounds, the corporation seeks to smooth and hasten their integration into the firm.

Many academic departments implicitly recognize the importance of cohorts in the decisions to admit graduate students and to hire faculty. Particularly in the case of student admissions to doctoral programs, concern is often expressed that persons be brought in as part of a small group rather than as lone individuals. The prediction would be that students admitted as part of a group would have a more successful experience in the program than those who have to make their way alone through the often stressful graduate education experience. Also, some departments often try to hire assistant professors in pairs or groups, to make integration into the school easier and to provide ready access to collegial support of all kinds.

Anecdotal evidence suggests that senior executives brought in from outside the organization by themselves are likely to leave and to perform less effectively. The problems of bringing in executive talent from the outside have often been attributed to lack of knowledge of the particular business. Kotter's research on effective general managers indicates that one of their defining characteristics is an extensive network of personal ties and contacts.[20] Executives brought in from outside not only lack that network but, if they are brought by themselves into pre-existing groups, are unlikely to easily break in to the existing social structure.

If people cannot be added in groups, then sensitivity to the demographic issues involved can lead the organization to take actions to ease the transition and to provide other mechanisms that will facilitate the interaction and social structural development. In the case of chief executive officers, the problem is most often solved by the individuals bringing in others from their previous organization to help them run their new business.[21] However, there are other mechanisms for facilitating integration into the new social structure which can possibly substitute for wholesale replacement of people.

Movement, Rotation, and Development of Personnel

The analysis of interaction and communication behavior as a function of time together has implications for both the development of individuals and the enhancement of organizational performance. In the latter instance, Katz[22] and others strongly suggest that the composition of research and development and other groups from whom innovation is expected should be managed to keep average group age in an intermediate range. Programs of systematic job rotation can possibly help to ensure that both individual and group performance remains more in the high point of the inverted U-shaped curve rather than at either end. Indeed, several companies are trying programs along this line to try to ensure that employees develop requisite experience but do not become stale by being kept in the same place too long. What the work on demography suggests is that focusing such programs on the individual is not sufficient. It is the composition of groups and relationships among individuals that are critical variables to keep in mind.

Many corporations have experimented with so called "fast-track" programs. Such programs are often started in recognition of the need to try to attract and, particularly, retain very promising high-potential managers or other employees. Such programs typically involve an extra measure of exposure to different aspects or divisions of the business on a faster time schedule and more rapid promotion up the organizational ladder. Not all of these programs have met with unqualified success, and the concept of demography can help us understand some of the issues involved. On the one hand, the special attention and enhanced mobility experience and future prospects are clearly motivating, particularly to those in the program obtaining these rewards. However, even the "chosen few" may face some problems as a result of this experience. By being moved frequently, communication networks and personal relationships that might normally form are disrupted. As persons move up the organizational hierarchy rapidly, they are more and more in contact with and dependent upon people from different cohorts and with different experiences. Thus, the fast-track employee becomes a token, or a person in a minority status in some respects, with all the pressures this entails. Moreover, because the individual has moved more rapidly than many of his or her peers, the natural linkages to those who entered at around the same time are severed and the individual can find himself in a position of comparative isolation in the social structure in which he or she must operate.

One foreign country's military service experienced just such a result from its fast-track program. Persons promoted rapidly seemed highly satisfied; but once at the rank of major,

many of them left, and those who remained often expressed dissatisfaction and had various kinds of performance problems. One explanation is that by moving these few individuals up rapidly, they were separated from their peers with whom they had entered the service. At the rank of major, the interdependence required by the duties of the job increased significantly, requiring more lateral communication and getting things done through relationships. Yet, the individuals who were rapidly promoted were now working with people from a different cohort in terms of both time of entry and age. They were in a token status and, moreover, had few social or communication ties to these people. The job environment was difficult, which may help explain what happened to them in terms of turnover and job performance.

This is not to imply that everyone should necessarily be advanced at the same rate or that promotion or mobility should not be used as reward. Rather, the implication is that by paying attention to the potentially disruptive and costly aspects of such programs, some of the costs might be avoided. For instance, instead of focusing only on the individual and individual movement, it might be possible to move and place people in pairs or small groups—which, while still based on ability, are consistent with their time of entry into the organization, age, or other relevant demographic factors. Cohorts remind us of the essentially relational or group aspects of organizations. Many personnel development and rotation policies are keyed to the individual, neglecting ideas of relationships and thereby causing unnecessary problems for both the individuals and the organizations.

As a simple example, when the so-called whiz kids left the military after the Second World War, they went *as a group* to the Ford Motor Corporation. Consider what might have happened to that group, including McNamara and Arjay Miller, had they gone off to a number of different organizations. They would not have been able to take advantage of their experience in working together; and isolated in separate companies, they might have occupied more of a token or minority status, with all the costs that entails. Their success at Ford was probably a function not only of their singular talents but also of the fact that they entered and moved in the organization as a group.

Change

Concepts such as demography and cohorts help us to understand that change in organizations is often, if not predominantly, generational.[23] In other words, change occurs through changes in who is in the organization. Of course, this idea is inconsistent with the belief of many who write in the organizational change literature and who seem to believe that individuals are relatively malleable, at least if the correct change technology is employed. However, studies of both organizations and societies seem to suggest that change through generational replacement, or the replacement of one cohort by another, is at least as important and fundamental as change accomplished by the transformation of those already in place.[24]

Such change may not be inevitable or accomplished without friction. Joseph Gusfield has written an interesting analysis of the Women's Christian Temperance Union.[25] The WCTU was originally populated with persons who saw alcohol as a moral issue and who adopted tactics such as legislation aimed at prohibition and other programs founded on morality and religion. Subsequently, younger and newer persons saw alcohol more as a social or medical problem and advocated a set of activities more consistent with that view. The older persons, who were in control of the WCTU, were able to resist the newer viewpoint and maintain their control over the organization and its view of alcohol. Unfortunately for the WCTU, this failure of generational change led to a decline in the organization's membership and influence.

In general, it seems clear that when or-

ganizations change directions or strategy, they do so most often through a change in personnel. Indeed, matching the demographics and human resources to organizational strategy and operational requirements is a growing topic in the human resource management literature.[26] Academic disciplines change as new ideas get absorbed in graduate schools and then brought into the field by young faculty. Consulting, legal, and accounting practices change, in part, as new techniques and knowledge are developed and transmitted to the newer practitioners of the field. This generational change in disciplines is most evident in engineering, where technical obsolescence is a recognized problem and has led to a premium being placed on the hiring of the newest graduates with the newest and most current knowledge.

If change is generational, accomplished in important respects through the replacement of one cohort by another, then there are several implications. First, change takes time; unless outside forces intervene, a process of generational change is likely to be lengthy. Second, when cohorts do turn over, as in the political leadership in the People's Republic of China and the Soviet Union, it is important to consider which of the succeeding cohorts to bring in. It is possible, as in the case of the WCTU, to find people in the newer cohorts who carry the identical ideas of those being replaced. At the time of turnover among governing cohorts, such a choice as to who and what point of view or orientation will be brought into power becomes critical, for it imprints the organization and its future operations. This analysis suggests that change is carried in cohorts, not in single individuals.

CONCLUSION

Ideas of organizational demography can be useful in sensitizing both managers of organizations as well as organizational researchers and analysts to some fundamental ways of thinking about social structures and in some more specific implications for analysis, prediction, and action. In particular, demographic concepts help orient us to the essentially relational nature of organizations. As Harold Leavitt pointed out a while ago, because of the individualistic values of the society, we tend to think of things in individualistic terms.[27] Thus, we manage careers of individuals; concern ourselves with individual attitudes, needs, and demographic characteristics; and concern ourselves with finding the best individuals and rewarding them individually. The difficulty with this approach is its neglect of the interdependence and relationships that are the essential, indeed defining, characteristic of organizations. For instance, to predict performance or turnover on the basis of an individual's sex is not likely to be productive, though knowing what the sex composition is of the organization or work unit does enable one to make some predictions about performance pressure and social integration. Similarly, tenure in the organization helps to explain turnover, but not as much as when the composition of the whole organization in terms of tenure is considered. The time a person has worked on a research and development team tells us less about the performance of the team than does the average time team members have worked on the particular project together. This shift in focus away from individual to compositional and relational elements is an important feature of demographic analyses.

A second, equally important feature is the shift in orientation toward measurable properties of social units rather than the attention most often paid to intrapsychic processes and psychological constructs. Particularly from the perspective of prediction and management, there is much to be gained from focusing on observable and more manipulable elements of social structure. Thus, one can manage research and development teams to control group age, concern oneself with the demographic composition of top management teams or academic departments to mitigate conflict and facilitate integration, and plan accessions and choose staff to link governance structures across cohorts and other demographic groups. While sensitive to underlying psychological processes of integration, cohesion, and communication, the demographic ideas do not require measurement or management of these variables directly.

Finally, by focusing on cohorts and other salient demographic entities, this perspective helps us bring into focus the importance of generations, generational change, and the relative permanence of social structural arrangements. This is not to suggest that change within persons is impossible, but only that generational or cohort change is another important mechanism by which transformations of organizations occur. Indeed, the literature on organizational change has probably been overly optimistic about the possibility of individual malleability. The concepts of demography suggest how and why permanence becomes institutionalized as well as how change comes about.

Organizational demography is certainly not the only, or perhaps even the most, important concept necessary to analyze and manage organizations. Yet, because of some of the subtle but important shifts in focus it facilitates, it does offer some new insights and some new tools for analyzing formal organizations.

REFERENCES

1. Charles Perrow, *Organizational Analysis: A Sociological View* (Belmont, CA: Wadsworth, 1970), pp. 3–5.
2. See, for example, Gerald R. Salancik and Jeffrey Pfeffer, "An Examination of Need-Satisfaction Models of Job Attitudes," *Administrative Sci-*

ence Quarterly, 22 (September, 1977): 427–456 for a review of much of this literature.

3. Ellen Berscheid and Elaine Walster, *Interpersonal Attraction* (Reading, MA: Addison-Wesley, 1969).

4. Joseph L. Gastwirth, "The Estimation of the Lorenz curve and the Gini Index," *Review of Economics and Statistics,* 54 (1972): 306–316.

5. Henry Theil, *Economics and Information Theory* (Chicago, IL: Rand McNally, 1967).

6. Peter M. Blau, *Inequality and Heterogeneity* (New York, NY: Free Press, 1977).

7. Paul D. Allison, "Measures of Inequality," *American Sociological Review,* 43 (December 1978): 865–880.

8. Marcia Guttentag and Paul F. Secord, *Too Many Women? The Sex Ratio Question* (Beverly Hills, CA: Sage Publications, 1983).

9. Rosabeth Moss Kanter, *Men and Women of the Corporation* (New York, NY: Basic Books, 1977), Ch. 8.

10. Eva Spangler, Marsha A. Gordon, and Ronald M. Pipkin, "Token Women: An Empirical Test of Kanter's Hypothesis," *American Journal of Sociology,* 85 (1978): 160–170.

11. Scott J. South, Charles M. Bonjean, William T. Markham, and Judy Corder, "Social Structure and Intergroup Interaction: Men and Women of the Federal Bureaucracy," *American Sociological Review,* 47 (October 1982): 587–599.

12. Richard A. Easterlin, *Birth and Fortune: The Impact of Numbers on Personal Welfare* (New York, NY: Basic Books, 1980).

13. Paul S. Maxim, "Cohort Size and Juvenile Delinquency: A Test of the Easterlin Hypothesis," *Social Forces,* 63 (March 1985): 661–681.

14. Shelby Stewman and Suresh L. Konda, "Careers and Organizational Labor Markets: Demographic Models of Organizational Behavior," *American Journal of Sociology,* 88 (January 1983): 637–685.

15. Bruce McCain, Charles A. O'Reilly, and Jeffrey Pfeffer, "The Effects of Departmental Demography on Turnover: The Case of a University," *Academy of Management Journal,* 26 (1983): 626–641.

16. W. Gary Wagner, Jeffrey Pfeffer, and Charles A. O'Reilly, "Organizational Demography and Turnover in Top-Management Groups," *Administrative Science Quarterly,* 29 (March 1984): 74–92.

17. Jeffrey Pfeffer and Charles O'Reilly, "Hospital Demography and Turnover Among Nurses," unpublished ms., Palo Alto, CA: Graduate School of Business, Stanford University.

18. Barry M. Staw, "The Consequences of Turnover," *Journal of Occupational Behavior,* 1 (1980): 253–273.

19. Ralph Katz, "Project Communication and Performance: An Investigation Into the Effects of Group Longevity," *Administrative Science Quarterly,* 27 (1982): 81–104.

20. John P. Kotter, *The General Managers* (New York, NY: Free Press, 1982).

21. This is illustrated in Lee Iacocca's description of what he did when he took over the Chrysler corporation, in Lee Iacocca, *Iacocca: An Autobiography* (New York, NY: Bantam Books, 1984).

22. Ralph Katz, op. cit.

23. Theodore L. Reed, "Organizational Change in the American Foreign Service, 1925–1965: The Utility of Cohort Analysis," *American Sociological Review,* 43 (1978): 404–421.

24. Norman B. Ryder, "The Cohort as a Concept in the Study of Social Change," *American Sociological Review,* 30 (1966): 843–861.

25. Joseph R. Gusfield, "The Problem of Generations in an Organizational Structure," *Social Forces,* 35 (1957): 322–330.

26. Andrew D. Szilagyi, Jr., and David M. Schweiger, "Matching Managers to Strategies: A Review and Suggested Framework," *Academy of Management Review,* 9 (1984): 626–637.

27. Harold J. Leavitt, "Suppose We Took Groups Seriously . . . ," in Euguene L. Cass and Frederick G. Zimmer, eds., *Man and Work in Society* (New York, NY: Van Nostrand Reinhold Company, 1975).

Fostering and Facilitating Entrepreneurship in Organizations: Implications for Organization Structure and Human Resource Management Practices

Randall Schuler

Two particularly important factors involved in successful corporate entrepreneurship are organization structure and human resource management practices. By selecting and implementing the appropriate structure and practices, human resource professionals can systematically foster and facilitate innovation and entrepreneurship within their organizations. The more that new and different entrepreneurial activities are needed, the more that complete structural arrangements as well as policy and procedure flexibility are needed. In this article, structural practices appropriate for different degrees of entrepreneurial activity are described. But because appropriate structural practices alone are not sufficient for effectiveness, necessary human resource management practices are also described in detail. Throughout, implications for structural and human resource management practices in advancing entrepreneurship are considered.

What distinguishes entrepreneurial from nonentrepreneurial firms is the rate of new product introduction (innovation). This is not to say that firms are *either* entrepreneurial or nonentrepreneurial, but that the greater the *rate* of new product innovation, the more entrepreneurial the firm (Kanter, 1985; Drucker, 1985). Other things being equal, the greater the rate of product innovation, the greater the level of effectiveness, particularly higher profitability and growth as well as enhanced ability to survive and be competitive. Consequently,

Support for this paper was provided by the NYU Center for Entrepreneurial Studies and the Human Resource Planning Society. The author wishes to thank Ian MacMillan and Susan Jackson for helpful comments and Joe Martocchio in the preparation of an earlier draft of the manuscript.

organizations today consider entrepreneurship, or being more entrepreneurial, a desired state of affairs. The question then looms, "how to become more entrepreneurial?"This article breaks the answer into two major components: organization structure and human resource management practices. While both are under the purview of human resource management professionals in a growing number of organizations (Fombrun et al., 1984), because there has been less discussion regarding the nature of HR practices that foster and facilitate entrepreneurship, *they* are the primary focus of this article and their complementary association with organization structural practices is highlighted. To provide a basis for understanding this association and the organization structure and HRM practices suggestions, it is appropriate to first review what is known about entrepreneurship and entrepreneurism.

ENTREPRENEURISM

Block (1985), defines entrepreneurism as:

> . . . the study of the processes or stages, activities and characteristics involved in the creation or innovation of new products or services that identify and fulfill opportunities within existing businesses or that create and build products or services forming new businesses.

While entrepreneurism is "the study of," entrepreneurship is

> . . . the practice of creating or innovating new products or services within existing businesses or within newly forming businesses or as Kanter suggests it means the creation of new combinations (1985).

So entrepreneurship is the practice or activity of creating, of innovating (Drucker,

1985). Not creating or innovating is nonentrepreneurship or administrativeship. The process of innovation is central to entrepreneurship, or as Drucker (1985) states: "Innovation is the tool of the entrepreneur." The innovation process is distinguished by:

> *Uncertainty*—". . . progress on a new innovation comes in spurts among unforeseen delays and setbacks . . . in the essential chaos of development" (Quinn, 1979). Consequently, ROIs are unpredictable and success is problematic.
>
> *Knowledge-Intensity*—". . . the innovation process is knowledge-intensive, relying on individual human intelligence and creativity. New experiences are accumulated at a rapid pace, the learning curve is steep" (Kanter, 1985). Under these conditions, processes and procedures are difficult to codify and employee turnover can spell disaster.
>
> *Competition with Alternatives*—New ideas and inventions often pose a threat to existing conditions; thus, innovation often prompts resistance and undermining political efforts (Fast, 1976). Within this scenario, being and doing different things requires courage and commitment, if not outright protection, by a significant other.
>
> *Boundary Crossing*—Innovation requires the crossing of boundaries, the combining of two or more ideas, thoughts, products, etc. Consequently, conditions must exist to facilitate the flow of people and ideas across separate entities.

Central to administrativeship is the process of maintaining the *status quo,* of predictability and routinization. This process is essentially distinguished by conditions opposite to the four of innovation outlined above. Thus, administrativeship and entrepreneurship are at odds with each other (Kanter, 1985). One demands managing the old and the same, and the other, managing the new and the different. Conflict and tension are typical byproducts; ineffectiveness may be as well, but is not a necessary consequence. In fact, recognizing and effectively dealing with entrepreneurship and administrativeship in the same organization is essential to success in most firms:

> To be a successful enterprise, we have to do two apparently contradictory things quite well: We have to stay innovative and creative, but at the same time we have to be tightly controlled about certain aspects of our corporate behavior. But I think that what you have to do about paradox is embrace it. So we have the kind of company where certain things are very loose and other things are very tight. The whole art of management is sorting things into the loose pile or the tight pile and then watching them carefully (Mitchell Kapor, CEO, Lotus Development Corporation; *Boston Globe*, 1/27/85).

Perhaps easier said than done. Achieving this balanced loose-tight mix constitutes the essential challenge, and meeting it successfully is aided by an understanding of the structural and human resource management practices required to foster and facilitate entrepreneurship. Although the practices necessary for realizing administrativeship are generally well known to most readers, they are discussed by implication in our consideration of those practices that encourage entrepreneurship.

STRUCTURAL PRACTICES FOR ENTREPRENEURSHIP

In describing structural practices for entrepreneurship, it is essential to keep in mind that:

> Entrepreneurial activity can be depicted as falling into two broad categories: (1) *Identifying and*

fulfilling opportunities within existing activities—the development of new products and processes, improving existing operations, developing new marketing methods—basically innovating effectively within the existing product markets of the firm. (2) *Creating and building new businesses*—those which differ significantly in products, technology, markets, and even in financial characteristics (capital intensity, cost element distribution, inherent balance sheet differences, margins), from the existing businesses of the company (Block, 1985).

These distinctions are critical because of their implications for structural practices. Essentially, the more new and different the nature of the entrepreneurial activity (i.e., the more it is typical of creating and building new businesses distinctively different from existing businesses), the more complete the structure arrangements have to be and the more flexibility is needed in policies and procedures. The more an entrepreneurial activity is new and different, the more there will be uncertainty, knowledge-intensity, and competition with alternatives, and there will be greater need for boundary crossing. Accordingly, varying the degrees of entrepreneurial activity will moderate the extent of structural arrangements and policy and practice flexibility necessary for effectiveness.

Structural Arrangements

At the heart of structural arrangements to promote entrepreneurship is the granting of some degrees of freedom and support to an individual or group of individuals in the organization. Typically, the more different the entrepreneurial activity, the more unique the products developed or produced, and the more unique the industry characteristics compared to the parent organization, the more structural autonomy is necessary. Campbell Soup Company recognized that the soup business is far different than the gourmet food business. Because the lion's share of revenue growth was coming from gourmet foods, Campbell Soup determined that it had to have new structural arrangements:

> Convinced that Campbell was missing the action in the food business, McGovern began looking for inspiration, not from within his own 116-year-old company, but from entrepreneurs like Murray Lender of Lender's Bagel Bakery and Mo Siegel of Celestial Seasonings Inc. "Both those guys taught me a lot," he says. "They had the right feedback systems. They were quick to act. It takes us too long to get things through management."
>
> To overcome that weakness, McGovern broke Campbell into some 50 independent business units—averaging $50 million in sales—and gave each a charter to develop its own products. Each business unit has its own general manager who, as effective chief executive officer, has under him a marketing director, controller, and product development staff.
>
> "McGovern lets the managers play on their own until he hears the glass break," observes one company insider. "Everyone goes out, comes up with ideas, and competes for resources. Each unit is run like an independent company except that McGovern plays the banker" (Kotkin, 1985).

The result of creating highly autonomous but functionally complete business groups has been more innovation:

> In 1984 alone, the company introduced 92 new products, bringing its five-year total to 334—far more than such larger competitors as Beatrice, Nestle, and General Foods. And although not all the new products have been clear successes (some, such as Pepperidge Farm's Star Wars cookies, were notable failures), others have reaped spectacular rewards. Two new products introduced in 1983, Prego Spaghetti Sauce and Le Menu Frozen Dinners, already contribute a combined $450 million a year to Campbell's coffers (Kotkin, 1985).

But companies need not provide structural autonomy to all units of the organization. IBM was successful in forwarding entrepreneurship by creating a single autonomous group in Boca Raton, Florida to develop the PC. Apple Computer did the same with its MacIntosh. Similarly, new units do not necessarily need to be created. Rather, the present structure can be left intact and temporary task forces or a parallel organization can be created (Kanter, 1985).

Although the Campbell Soup and IBM structural arrangements are different from the creation of task forces or parallel organizations in the degree of structural autonomy given to foster and facilitate entrepreneurship, they are similar in the fact they represent official action of top management to *systematically* create innovation. But as Kanter (1985) suggests:

> Innovation and new venture development may originate as a deliberate and official decision of the highest levels of management or they may be the more-or-less "spontaneous" creation of mid-level people who take the initiative to solve a problem in new ways or to develop a proposal for change. Of course, highly successful companies allow both, and even official top management decisions to undertake a development effort benefit from the spontaneous creativity of those below.

Representing a less systematic though not necessarily less successful effort to create innovation is 3M's informal doctrine of employees bootlegging 15% of their time to work on their own projects (Peters and Waterman, 1982). An even less systematic effort is to encourage all employees in the organization to look at their work in new ways, offer suggestions for new and improved ways or products, etc.

The point is that there are many structural arrangements that can be used to further the establishment of entrepreneurship. Moreover, these arrangements vary in the extent to which they foster and facilitate systematic innovation (entrepreneurship). As depicted in Exhibit 1, the more significant and complete the structural arrangement (and granting of autonomy), the more innovation is systematically advanced. While not necessarily always producing more of the new and different, it substantially increases the likelihood of this occurring. Innovation may occur under more modest structural arrangements, but it is apt to occur less frequently and at a less predictable rate. In other words, innovation under more modest structural arrangements is less systematic.

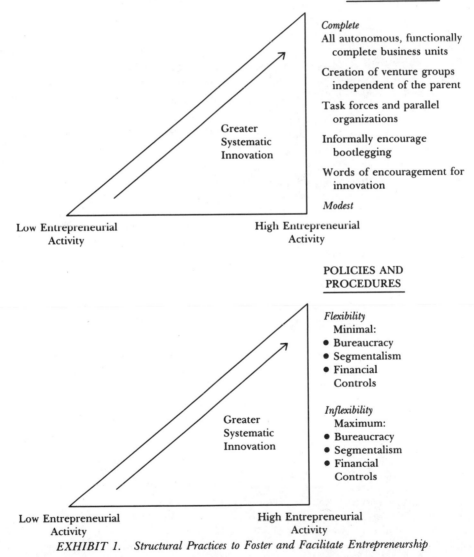

EXHIBIT 1.   *Structural Practices to Foster and Facilitate Entrepreneurship*

Thus, as the structural arrangements go from more modest to more significant and complete, innovation becomes more likely and represents a higher level of entrepreneurial activity. That is, more of the new and different results as structural arrangements go from modest to complete.

Use of an inappropriate structural arrangement for the extent of entrepreneurial activity required is apt to be unnecessary and inefficient. When Levi Strauss' 1984 profits dropped 74% from the preceding year, management knew that it had to get into the faster growing, more entrepreneurial (requiring more innovation) fashion clothes market. The company also knew that it had to view the fashion business much differently. Trouble began, however, with the structural arrangement Levi selected to accommodate its new entrepreneurial business:

The company soon realized that it needed to view the fashion business differently. "We need to be like commandos, special forces, and SWAT teams, and that's different from being the Third Army sweeping across Europe," says Leo Isotalo, who oversees all of Levi's business units.

The company partly blamed its plush campus for lulling managers and designers into complacency. So its new approach to fashion called for shuttling some top managers to the decrepit building, where the group devised marketing, merchandising, and distribution strategies for its fashion lines. Traces of the parent were erased from clothes tags and shipping cartons. "They didn't have to worry about thinking or looking like the division next door," explains Thomas Kasten, an executive vice-president.

But Levi's strategy had faulty seams. The idea that an atmosphere of small cubicles and bare fluorescent light bulbs would stimulate creativity was just that—atmospherics. "They put the people in a dump and just scared them" says one observer. "You can't scare people into creativity."

The company also failed to bring in fresh talent. Employees who understood the jeans market still had no feel for the fast-paced fashion world. And they were far from Manhattan, the nation's fashion capital. As a result, the unit's two lines have been troubled, one so badly that it was pulled off the market for a season (Hyatt, 1985).

In other words, Levi's structural arrangements were too modest. The businesses weren't really given sufficient autonomy and independence from the parent. However:

The lessons haven't been lost on Levi. It recently reached outside to hire fashion designers. And its new unit is based in New York, with few employees drawn from Levi's ranks.

According to Drucker, something similar happened at General Electric:

One is to believe that you can truly innovate within the existing operating unit. I myself made this mistake 30 years ago when I was a consultant on the first major organizational change in American industry, the General Electric reorganization of the early 1950s. I advised top management, and they accepted it, that the general managers would be responsible for current operations as well as for making tomorrow. At the same time, we worked out one of the first systematic compensation plans, and the whole idea of paying people on the basis of their performance in the preceding year came out of that.

The result of it was that for ten years General Electric totally lost its capacity to innovate, simply because tomorrow produces costs for ten years and no return. So, the general manager—not only out of concern for himself, but also out of concern for his group—postponed spending any money for innovation. It was only when the company dropped this compensation plan and at the same time organized the search for the truly new, not just for improvement outside the existing business that G.E. recovered its innovative capacity, and brilliantly. Many companies go after the new and slight today and soon find they have neither (Rutigliano, 1986).

But as shown in Exhibit 1, more is needed to foster and facilitate entrepreneurship than new structural arrangements. Policies and procedures must also be considered, and more specifically, they must become more flexible if systematic innovation is to be realized.

Policy and Procedure Flexibility

More new and different entrepreneurial activity is fostered and facilitated by increased flexibility in a firm's policies and procedures. The policies and procedures particularly relevant to entrepreneurship are those with bureaucracy, segmentalism, and financial processes (Kanter, 1985; Drucker, 1985; Brandt, 1986).

Bureaucracy describes the preciseness and tightness of department arrangements, reporting practices, the chain of command, and rules and procedures as to who does things and how they are to be done. Systematic innovation is strengthened to the extent that the bureaucracy is minimized. Less precise and looser departmental boundaries facilitate the flow of information and ideas so critical to forming new combinations. Less necessity to adhere to the chain of command also facilitates interaction and knowledge exchange. And, less reliance on rules and procedures recognizes the dynamics of knowledge-intense activities so characteristic of innovation.

Closely associated with increasing flexibility by reducing bureaucracy, is reducing segmentalism. Reducing segmentalism and increasing integration across groups, teams, departments, and divisions fosters and facilitates idea, information, and product exchanges (Kanter. 1983a, b; 1985). Reduction of segmentalism occurs as a matter of both top management support and company culture reflect-

ing teamwork and cooperation. It is facilitated by alternations in structural rearrangements from more modest to complete.

Financial processes also need to become more flexible if systematic innovation is to be fostered and facilitated:

> Following the lead of 3M, and now several other major organizations such as Eastman Kodak, an increasing number of companies are setting up special "innovation banks" to fund new ventures or innovations outside of operating budgets. This not only permits a large new venture to be supported inside the company as a separate business, but it also permits many small development activities to be undertaken that would otherwise find no place in a line manager's budget (with its usual requirement for immediate profitability). Efforts that are more experimental, or may take more time to bring returns, or do not fit neatly within existing areas, can still find a home. This is useful not only for those innovations in products or technology that might normally fall within the scope of an R&D operation, but also for numerous other special projects in marketing or information systems or personnel or dealer relations that can themselves net considerable payoffs. A large computer manufacturer has funded innovative organizational improvement projects out of a corporate innovation council (Kanter, 1985).

Other forms of flexibility include allocating portions of budgets to uncommitted projects or uses. This budget slack, provided either with direct funds or employee time, facilitates employee innovation and entrepreneurship. Another form of increased financial flexibility is top management sponsoring as many small and diverse entrepreneurial projects as possible rather than just a few big ones.

In spite of all the structural practices in place for innovation and entrepreneurship, success is not guaranteed even though the cost of implementing these practices could be enormous. In fact, according to Drucker, a big mistake

. . . is believing that money can be used in lieu of good people. It's very common when it comes to the question of how do you staff, that people will say, "We can't spare Joe for the new. What he's doing is so important, we can't take him off it." The result is that companies staff with people they can spare. And whenever I hear, "All we can spare is Joe," I say, "You are staffing by proven incompetence." Unfortunately, that is the most common staffing principle. Organizations then try to make up for this by giving new money. That is the quickest way to kill something—the combination of poor people and generous budget. It's a guarantee of failure. It is the biggest mistake of all large organizations from the Pentagon on down (Rutigliano, 1986).

Thus, there is a charge to attend to staffing issues in fostering and facilitating entrepreneurship. But as is becoming more apparent than ever, when it comes to managing people, one human resource practice such as staffing cannot be examined in isolation. Human resource management practices have to be executed in an integrated fashion in order to systematically stimulate and reinforce needed characteristics and behaviors from employees. Not systematically approaching and designing human resource management practices to fit what the organization needs from its employees is likely to result in ineffective employee behavior (Schuler, 1987). Accordingly, it is useful to examine human resource management practices and determine the ones required to further entrepreneurship.

HUMAN RESOURCE MANAGEMENT PRACTICES FOR ENTREPRENEURSHIP

Human resource management practices in any organization articulate its true culture (Lawler, 1984; Fombrun et al., 1984). The extent to which a company is concerned for the develop-ment of its people is reflected in the amount of money it spends on training and development and the extensiveness of its socialization process. Thus, while stating a culture of concern for employees is important to foster and facilitate entrepreneurship, there must be support from human resource practices consistent with that particular culture and consistent with what's needed from the employees. Key is determining what's needed from employees to be effective at entrepreneurship. Once this is determined, the specific HRM practices that organizations need to utilize to achieve entrepreneurship can be described.

To be effective, organizations need their employees to express particular characteristics. These are essentially general behaviors and attitudes, ways of doing and thinking about things. They are at a level more general than the specific skills, knowledge, and abilities required to perform specific jobs (Schneider, 1985). General employee characteristics that have been identified as important in strategy execution are shown in Exhibit 2.

What determines these characteristics is the strategy or general thrust being pursued by the organization (Gerstein and Reisman, 1983). Different strategies require different employee characteristics. As described by Kanter (1985), what's required from employees in firms striving to be entrepreneurial is quite different from what firms require when pursuing a nonentrepreneurial posture. This results from the inherent needs and qualities that are at the root of these strategies. As indicated earlier, the essence of effective performance under the entrepreneurial strategy is based on employees' ability to manage uncertainty, knowledge-intensity, competition with alternatives, and boundary-crossing.

In Exhibit 2, employee characteristics critical for strategy execution are depicted using descriptions of behavior at either end of a continuum. Consequently, organizations can choose to foster and facilitate highly creative,

EXHIBIT 2.   *General Employee Characteristics For Strategy Execution*

1. Highly Repetitive, Predictable Behavior	————	Highly Creative Innovative Behavior
2. Very Short Term Focus	————	Very Long Term Focus
3. Highly Cooperative, Interdependent Behavior	————	Highly Independent Autonomous Behavior
4. Very Low Concern for Quality	————	Very High Concern for Quality
5. Very Low Concern for Quantity	————	Very High Concern for Quantity
6. Very Low Risk Taking	————	Very High Risk Taking
7. Very High Concern for Process	————	Very High Concern for Results
8. High Preference to Avoid Responsibility	————	High Preference to Assume Responsibility
9. Very Inflexible to Change	————	Very Flexible to Change
10. Very Comfortable with Stability	————	Very Tolerant of Ambiguity and Unpredictability
11. Very Low Task Orientation	————	Very High Task Orientation
12. Very Low Organizational	————	Very High Organizational Identification
13. Primary Focus on Efficiency	————	Primary Focus on Effectiveness

innovative behavior or highly repetitive, predictable behavior. This is true for all the employee characteristics shown in Exhibit 2; however, not all characteristics are equally relevant in executing of all strategies (Schuler et al., 1985). The characteristics most relevant in the successful execution of an entrepreneurial strategy have been identified and described in some detail, [e.g., Brandt (1986); Kanter (1985); Drucker (1985); Pinchot (1984); Brocknaus (1980); Hornaday and Aboud (1971); Miller (1983); Burgelman (1983); Roberts (1980); Peterson (1981); and Maidique (1980)]. These characteristics include:

- Creative, innovative behavior
- Long term focus
- Cooperative, interdependent behavior
- Risk taking
- High concern for results
- Preference to assume responsibility
- Flexibility to change
- Tolerance of ambiguity
- Task orientation
- Focus on effectiveness

Just as the level of entrepreneurial activity varies, so do the needed levels of these characteristics for entrepreneurial strategy execu-tion. The greater the level of entrepreneurial activity, i.e., the more of the new and different that is desired, the more that extreme levels of the above characteristics are needed. With the entrepreneurial strategy, the thrust is idea creation, innovation, and new product development. In firms that are noted for their innovation and new product development, such as 3M and Hewlett-Packard, these comprise the mandatory employee characteristics (Drucker, 1985; Peters and Waterman, 1982; Kanter, 1985; Mortiz, 1984).

Accordingly, to increase the likelihood of systematic innovation, thereby fostering and facilitating entrepreneurship, organizations need to stimulate and reinforce these characteristics via human resource management practices. These are the primary employee characteristics. Based upon them, the HRM practices needed to nurture entrepreneurship can be described and their rationale explained (Schuler, 1987).

Human Resource Management Practice Choices

Central to the notion that human resource management practices can systematically foster and facilitate an organization's strategy are: a) the existence of a menu of choices for each practice, and b) the ability of different choices to stimulate and reinforce different employee characteristics (Schuler, 1987; Schuler et al. 1985).

The menu of choices for the HR practices of planning (including strategic planning and job analysis), staffing, appraising, compensating, and training and development are shown in Exhibit 3. The choices to be selected for promoting entrepreneurship and an entrepreneurial strategy are many. A description of the choices to be made in each practice will illustrate this.

Planning. Entrepreneurial strategy is fostered and facilitated to the extent that planning practices are formal, long term, tight, implicit, broad, integrative, and encourage high employee participation. These planning practices stimulate innovation, willingness to work well and cooperate with others, and get employees to assume responsibility (Angle et al. 1985; Burgelman, 1983; Kanter 1983b; Milkovich et al., 1983; Schuler, 1984). Additionally, calculated risk taking may be facilitated through the use of more broadly written job descriptions that focus more on results than process. Unstructured tasks not easily bound by rigid policies necessitate that employees work by general job descriptions. Objectives and milestone accomplishments (results criteria) should serve as the content of job descriptions. Results criteria as a basis for job analysis force employees to work toward implementing ideas and systems. Oftentimes, their work is unprecedented. In such cases, the establishment of process-centered guidelines is not practical where refinements realized through experience have not yet happened.

Organizations also need to engage in more formal long range human resource planning. A result of more formal planning is Hewlett-Packard's willingness and ability to state and support its human resource policy of "not to be a hire and fire company" (Pet-

ers and Waterman, 1982). An advantage of this type of formalized planning is that it enables a company to provide employees employment security, a facet of human resource management critical for stimulating a long term orientation and moderate risk taking behavior (Peters and Waterman, 1982; Dyer and Heyer, 1984).

Staffing. Entrepreneurial strategy is fostered and facilitated to the extent that staffing practices offer individuals broad paths and multiple ladders, have implicit criteria and open procedures, use external sources, and allow extensive socialization. These staffing practices stimulate employee innovation, cooperation, and longer term focus in the organization (Burgelman, 1983; Cummings, 1984; London and Stumpf, 1982; Maidique and Hayes, 1984; Peters and Waterman, 1982).

An entrepreneurial strategy also requires that employees be flexible and tolerant of ambiguity. Tolerating uncertainty means feeling comfortable with change and unpredictable situations. It implies being adaptable.

Consequently, organizations recruit and select individuals most likely to tolerate ambiguity. Organizations also engage in open staffing procedures to enable individuals to select themselves into more entrepreneurial positions. Individuals cannot simply be selected to manage and lead an organization's venture activity based on previous performance in any functional area, or because there simply is no other person readily available with the requisite skills and knowledge. Peters stresses that an entrepreneur ". . . cannot be 'assigned' or 'appointed'. He must possess the characteristics of an entrepreneur, be a doer—not a thinker or talker—have a clear vision of what he wants to 'create' and volunteer . . ." (de Chambeau and Shays, 1984).

Note that these staffing practices, in part, are the same characteristics stimulated by the planning practices. Essential here is that there be a consistency attained across HRM practices

EXHIBIT 3.   Human Resource Management Practice Menus

Planning Choices
Informal .... Formal
Loose .... Tight
Short term .... Long term
Explicit Analysis .... Implicit Analysis
Narrow Jobs .... Broad Jobs
Segmental Design .... Integrative Design
Low Employee Involvement .... High Employee Involvement

Staffing Choices
Internal Sources .... External Sources
Narrow Paths .... Broad Paths
Single Ladder .... Multiple Ladders
Explicit Criteria .... Implicit Criteria
Limited Socialization .... Extensive Socialization
Closed Procedures .... Open Procedures

Appraising Choices
Loose, Incomplete Integration .... Tight, Complete Integration
Behavioral Criteria .... Results Criteria
Purposes: Development Remedial Maintenance
Low Employee Participation .... High Employee Participation
Short-term Criteria .... Long-Term Criteria
Individual Criteria .... Group Criteria

Compensating Choices
Low Base Salaries .... High Base Salaries
Internal Equity .... External Equity
Few Perks .... Many Perks
Standard, Fixed Package .... Flexible Package
Low Participation .... High Participation
No Incentives .... Many Incentives
Short-term Incentives .... Long-term Incentives
No Employment Security .... High Employment Security
Hierarchical .... Egalitarian

Training and Development
Short Term .... Long Term
Narrow Application .... Broad Application
Spontaneous, Unplanned, Unsystematic .... Planned, Systematic
Individual Orientation .... Group Orientation
Low Participation .... High Participation
Extensive Organizational Structure .... Minimal Organizational Structure

Adapted from R.S. Schuler, Human resource management practice choices. In R.S. Schuler and S.A. Youngblood (Eds.), *Readings in personnel and human resource management.* 3e. St. Paul: West Publishing, 1987.

within a strategy type. A consequence of this is that different HRM practices unavoidably stimulate some of the same characteristics. Similarly, different practices stimulate the opposite characteristics. Therefore, these HRM menu choices need to be made cautiously and systematically.

Appraising. Entrepreneurial strategy is fostered and facilitated to the extent that appraising practices emphasize results criteria, use longer-term criteria, encourage high employee participation, and recognize the accomplishments of groups of individuals. These appraising practices stimulate risk taking, a willingness to assume responsibility, and a longer term orientation (Carroll and Schneier, 1982; Cummings, 1984; George and MacMillan, 1984; Giles and Landauer, 1984; Kanter, 1983a; Roberts and Fusfeld, 1981; Timmons, 1979). At 3M, division managers are appraised on their division's contribution to total profits, not on the merits of individual plans and the processes employed to achieve them (*Business Week*, 1984a). Creating more functionally complete and independent business units also provides the opportunity for managers to assume more responsibility.

The 3M example indicates that while division results serve as the basis of appraising, each division is comprised of functional specialists who have contributed to the division's overall performance. Oftentimes, it is impossible to separate and quantify particular individual contributions. Essentially, an overall contribution cannot easily be divided up into the contributions of each individual. As a consequence, group level performance criteria are appropriate.

Group level criteria as a basis for performance appraisal and compensation are instrumental in creating synergies of corporate entrepreneurs such as are practiced within TRW's venture groups. These HRM practices set the stage for Kanter's proverbial right places: "The right places are the integrative environments that support innovation, encourage the building of coalitions and teams to support and implement visions" (Kanter, 1983a).

Consistent with the idea of performance appraisal based on results, it is useful that a significant portion of compensation be a function of results. Yet, there needs to be an acceptable amount of failure allowed to achieve results. Here there are two major considerations. First, as Frank de Chambeau and E. Michael Shays (1984) believe, "Mistakes, even one big one, are not necessarily reason to cancel a project or dismiss an intrapreneur (corporate entrepreneur). People in new situations make mistakes. The question is whether they learn from them. If they do, they're more valuable to the firm." Second, inherently risky factors generally make it impossible for the entrepreneur to have total control of outcomes. In a report on senior management responsibilities in corporate venturing, Rain Hill Group's Robin George and New York University's Ian MacMillan (1984), imply that results criteria facilitate entrepreneurship since they prompt managers to focus on the distinction ". . . between a situation where the venturer made a poor decision and a situation where the venturer made a good decision with all the limited information available at the time of the decision, but the outcome was poor because the 'ball bounced the wrong way'."

Many of the fruits of entrepreneurial effort may not ripen in the short term (i.e., less than 12 months). A performance appraisal policy based on a predetermined, fixed interval may not be effective. A long-term appraisal policy tailored to the particular situation may be appropriate. For example, with regard to Chesebrough-Ponds' "Polishing Pen," the results of its entrepreneurial efforts were not expected to be realized until the end of 1985 even though the project began in 1983 (*Business Week*, 1984b).

Compensating.   Entrepreneurial strategy is fostered and facilitated to the extent that compensating practices emphasize external equity, are flexible, contain many long-term incentives, encourage high employee participation, offer some employment security, and are administered in a more egalitarian fashion. These compensation practices reinforce the appraising practices quite nicely. Accordingly, they should stimulate and reinforce risk taking, or willingness to assume responsibility and a longer term orientation (Bentson and Schuster, 1983; Hutton, 1985; Lawler, 1984).

Related to a sense of responsibility is the enjoyment of significant rewards resulting from high performance. Jeffrey Timmons, professor of entrepreneurial studies at Babson College, indicates that many corporate entrepreneurs are given profit and loss responsibility for their ventures. To further foster and facilitate a sense of responsibility, companies can provide many compensation benefits such as stock option plans, perquisites, and bonus plans that strengthen commitment to entrepreneurship. In a recent study, McKinsey and Company has found that, "In addition to such extensive stock ownership, financial motivation in the winner companies is stimulated by tying incentives to company performance" (Albertine and Levitt, 1983).

Consistent with a significant period before results may be realized, organizations need to establish long-term financial arrangements to compensate entrepreneurial employees. Employee stock ownership plans and profit sharing plans ensure that employees will be compensated in accordance with the performance of the product or service over its life. Entrepreneurship is also fostered and facilitated by providing choices in compensation. Accordingly, companies need to have flexibility and employee participation in their compensation practices.

Training and Development.   Entrepreneurial strategy is advanced to the extent that training and development practices are characterized by broad applications, emphasize quality of work life, encourage high employee participation, and rely upon minimal organizational structure. These training and development practices should stimulate a willingness to assume responsibility, be innovative, promote a willingness to work with others, and be flexible. These practices also help retain key employees (Beer, 1981; Maidique and Hayes, 1984; de Chambeau and Shays, 1984).

Training programs that enable individuals to keep up with changing technologies and job demands help keep people flexible and willing to tolerate changes. This is aided greatly by some degree of employment security. Thus, individuals who tolerate uncertainty can be brought into the organization and helped to stay. Meanwhile those currently in the organization can be made to feel more comfortable with change and ambiguity.

The entrepreneurial process is an ever changing one requiring continuous data gathering and rapid decision making. Policies and procedures specifying action plans for entrepreneurial conditions cannot be prescribed in advance; to do so would only hinder a correct response. Similarly, requiring several levels of management approval would only hinder a timely response. Consequently, human resource practices fostering spontaneity include more implicit and loosely written job descriptions, a more results oriented performance appraisal system, and some employment security. Structurally, the organization should reflect minimal levels of management and approval. In order to enhance progress at Unimation, Westinghouse has slashed the number of management layers that direct operations. It has discarded rules requiring approval by corporate committees for many major expenditures. "If we need to buy something, we can just go and do it," states Ira Pence, Unimation's research director. As a result, Unimation scientists recently purchased software only a few weeks after the need was realized. Normally, it would have taken a year to receive approval (Levin, 1984).

A summary of all these human resource management practice menu selections to foster and facilitate entrepreneurship, are shown in Exhibit 4.

SUMMARY AND IMPLICATIONS

This discussion of HRM practices and structural practices that foster and facilitate entrepreneurship suggests that entrepreneurship is becoming a more dominant force in society, comprising a significant slice of all business activity (Kanter, 1983a,b). We have seen it thrive outside existing organizational structures, yet many major corporations have initiated action to keep entrepreneurial activity within the organization for two major reasons: 1) To maintain a strong foothold in order to remain competitive; 2) To enhance organizational profitability,

survival, growth, and competitiveness by extending use of existing product lines, diversifying into markets and lines of business in which its efforts are not currently directed, and being pioneers in the development of needed products and services for which no markets previously existed (Pinchot, 1984). The question for corporations then is not whether they should or should not engage in entrepreneurial activity, but rather what can be done to encourage establishment of entrepreneurship.

In addressing the question of what structural practices can be used to foster and facilitate entrepreneurship, it was suggested that organizations need to first consider the desired level of entrepreneurial activity. That is, organizations need to determine exactly how much of the new and different is desired or necessary. The more that is desired, the more organizations need to choose structural practices that are more complete and policies and procedures that are highly flexible.

In addressing the question of what HRM practices can be systematically used to further

EXHIBIT 4.   *Human Resource Management Practices to Foster and Facilitate Entrepreneurship*

PLANNING	STAFFING
Formal	External Sources
Tight	Broad Paths
Long-term	Multiple Ladders
Implicit	Implicit Criteria
Integrative	Extensive Socialization
High Involvement	Open Procedures
APPRAISING	COMPENSATING
Results Criteria	External Equity
High Participation	Flexible Benefits Package
Long-term Criteria	Many Incentives
Group Individual	Some Employment Security
Determined Criteria	Highly Egalitarian

TRAINING & DEVELOPMENT
Broad Application
Quality of Work Life Emphasis
Group Orientation
High Participation
Minimal Organizational Structure

entrepreneurship, several suggestions relevant to each HRM function and activity were suggested. Implied by these suggestions may be the thought that there is a "one best set of structural and HRM practices for entrepreneurship." To the contrary, there are likely to be several different sets of HRM practices for entrepreneurship with the appropriateness of each set dependent upon the level of entrepreneurial activity or the stage of the activity. This is the same with the structural practices. Nevertheless, while these different sets of practices may vary somewhat, they are likely to be rather similar since the requisite employee characteristics for any level or stage of entrepreneurial activity is likely to vary in degree but not in kind (Burgelman, 1983). Consequently, if corporations have several entrepreneurial groups going on simultaneously but in different levels and states of activity, there are likely to be several sets of HRM practices fostering and facilitating entrepreneurship. Companies such as GE, Equitable Life Assurance Society, and Manufacturer's Hanover Trust, with many satellite venture groups have already begun to experience this.

The existence of concomitant sets of HRM practices is also expected to occur in corporations with just one venture or entrepreneurial group. This is because the behaviors and attitudes of employees in the parent organization are likely to be more nonentrepreneurial than those in the venture group. As a result, companies wanting to foster and facilitate just one entrepreneurial group will end up utilizing at least two sets of HRM practices, challenging the HR practitioner with designing, implementing, and managing both. Because of the existence of two or more sets of HRM practices, the HR practitioner will have to manage the likely perceptions of inequity that typically arise when two different sets of practices are employed. As at Manufacturer's Hanover Trust, the personnel group has to work that much harder to explain to employees the dif-ferences in practices. A change in their perceptions may not be immediate, but implementing dual practices will convey that the HRM department understands the situation.

The HR practitioner is also likely to face a much larger challenge in the near future. As Kanter suggests, ". . . sooner or later all U.S. corporations will be forced to develop innovative entrepreneurial structures in order to survive." If interpreted to mean that all corporations as a whole will have to become more entrepreneurial, human resource practitioners will have to begin changing the HRM practices of their parent organizations in the direction of the entrepreneurial groups' needs. Conceived as such, practitioners are in for a future in which HRM practices are constantly being altered and fine tuned to simultaneously stimulate and reinforce a variety of employee behaviors and attitudes, especially those necessary for some degree of entrepreneurship. Without a willingness and ability to do this, the very survival, not to mention profitability and competitiveness, of corporations is at stake.

REFERENCES

"3M's Aggressive New Consumer Drive," *Business Week,* July 16, 1984a, pp. 114, 116, 118, 122.

"How Chesebrough-Ponds Put Nail Polish in a Pen," *Business Week,* October 8, 1984b, pp. 196, 200.

Albertine, J. and Levitt Jr., A. "The Successful Entrepreneur: A Personality Profile," *The Wall Street Journal,* August 29, 1983, p. 12.

Angle, H. L., Manz, C. C., and Van de Ven, A. H. Integrating human resource management and corporate strategy: A preview of the 3M story. *Human Resource Management Journal,* Spring 1985, 51–68.

Beer, M. Performance Appraisal: Dilemmas and Possibilities, *Organizational Dynamics,* Winter 1981, 25–33.

Bentson, M. A., and Schuster, J. R. Executive compensation and employee benefits, In S. J. Carroll and R. S. Schuler (Eds.), *Human resources management in the 1980s.* Washington, D.C.: The Bureau of National Affairs, 1983, pp. 6-1—6-31.

Block, Z. Concepts for corporate entrepreneurs, *The Texas A&M Business Forum,* January 1985.

Brockhaus, R. H. Risk taking propensity of entrepreneurs, *Academy of Management,* September 1980, 509–520.

Brandt, S. C. *Entrepreneuring in established companies.* Homewood, IL: Dow Jones-Irwin, 1986.

Burgelman, R. A. Corporate entrepreneurship and strategic management: Insights from a process study, *Management Science,* December 1983, 1349–1364.

Carroll, Jr., S. J., and Schneier, C. E. *Performance appraisal and review systems.* Glenview, IL.: Scott, Foresman and Company, 1982.

Cummings, L. L. Compensation, culture, and motivation: A systems perspective, *Organizational Dynamics,* Winter 1984, 33–43.

de Chambeau, F., and Shays, E. M. Harnessing entrepreneurial energy within the corporation, *Management Review,* September 1984, 17–20.

Drucker, P. F. *Innovation and entrepreneurship.* New York: Harper & Row, 1985.

Dyer, L., and Heyer, N. D. Human resource planning at IBM, *Human Resource Planning,* VII(3), 1984.

Fast, N. D. The future of industrial new venture departments. *Industrial Marketing Management,* November 1976, 264–273.

Feinberg, A. Inside the entrepreneur, *Venture,* May 1984, 86, 80–83.

Fombrun, C., Tichy, N. M., and Devanna, M. A. *Strategic human resource management.* New York: John Wiley & Sons, 1984.

George, R. and MacMillan, I. C. Corporate Venturing/Senior Management Responsibilities, (working paper, Center for Entrepreneurial Studies, New York University, 1984).

Gerstein, M., and Reisman, H. Strategic selection: Matching executives to business conditions. *Sloan Management Review,* Winter 1983, 33–49.

Giles, R., and Landauer, C. Setting specific standards for appraising creative staffs. *Personnel Administrator,* 1984, 29, 35–47.

Greenwald, J. Earning more than equity. *Venture,* September 1983, p. 60, 62.

Hornaday, J. A., and Aboud, J. Characteristics of successful entrepreneurs. *Personnel Psychology,* Summer 1971, 141–153.

Hutton, T. J. Recruiting the entrepreneurial executive. *Personnel Administrator,* January 1985, 35–36, 38, 40–41.

Hyatt, J. Levi Strauss learns a fitting lesson. *Inc.,* August 1975, 17.

Kanter, R. M. Supporting innovation and venture development in established companies. *Journal of Business Venturing,* Winter 1985, 47–60.

Kanter, R. M. Change masters and the intricate architecture of corporate culture change. *Management Review,* October 1983a, 18–28.

Kanter, R. M. Superstars and lone rangers rescue dull enterprises. *The Wall Street Journal,* January 23, 1984, 22.

Kanter, R. M. *The change masters.* New York: Simon and Schuster, 1983b.

Kotkin, J. The revenge of the Fortune 500, *Inc.,* August 1985. 39–44.

Lawler III, E. E. The strategic design of reward systems. In R. S. Schuler and S. A. Youngblood (Eds.), *Readings in personnel and human resource management,* 2nd edition, St. Paul: West Publishing, 1984, 253–269.

Levin, D. P. Westinghouse move into robotics shows pitfalls of high-tech field. *The Wall Street Journal,* May 14, 1984, 29.

London, M., and Stumpf, S. A. *Managing careers.* Reading, MA: Addison-Wesley Publishing Company, 1982.

Maidique, M. A. Entrepreneurs, champions, and technological innovation. *Sloan Management Review,* Winter 1980, 559–576.

Maidique, M. A., and Hayes, R. H. The art of high-technology management. *Sloan Management Review,* Winter 1984, 17–31.

Milkovich, G. T., Dyer, L., and Mahoney, T. A. HRM planning. In S. J. Carroll and R. S. Schuler (Eds.), *Human resources management in the 1980's.* Washington, D.C.: The Bureau of National Affairs, 1983, pp. 2-1-2-28.

Miller, D. The correlates of entrepreneurship in three types of firms. *Management Science,* July 1983, 770–790.

Moritz, M. *The little kingdom.* New York: William Morrow and Company, Inc., 1984.

Peters, T. A., and Waterman, Jr., R. H. *In search of excellence.* New York: Warner Books, 1982.

Peterson, R. A. Entrepreneurship and organization. In P. Nystrom and W. Starbuck (Eds.), *Handbook of organizational design*. New York: Oxford University Press, 1981, 65–83.

Pinchot III, G. Intrapreneurship: How to top corporate creative energies. *The Mainstream*, 1984, I(2).

Quinn, J. B. Technological innovation, entrepreneurship, and strategy. *Sloan Management Review*, Spring 1979, 20–30.

Roberts, E. B. New ventures for corporate growth. *Harvard Business Review*, July–August 1980, 134–142.

Roberts, E. B., and Fusfeld, A. R. Staffing the innovative technology-based organization. *Sloan Management Review*, Spring 1981, 19–34.

Rutigliano, A. J. Managing the new: An interview with Peter Drucker. *Management Review*, January 1986, 38–41.

Schneider, B. Organizational behavior. *Annual Review of Psychology*, 1985, 36, 573–611.

Schuler, R. S. *Personnel and human resource management*, 2nd edition. St. Paul: West Publishing, 1984.

Schuler, R. S. Human resource management practice choices. In R. S. Schuler and S. A. Youngblood (Eds.), *Readings in personnel and human resource management*, 3rd edition. St. Paul: West Publishing, 1987.

Schuler, R. S., MacMillan, I. C., and Martocchio, J. J. Key strategic questions for human resource management. In W. D. Guth (Ed.), *Handbook of business strategy 1985/1986 yearbook*. Boston: Warren, Gorham and Lamont, 1985.

Timmons, J. A. Careful self-analysis and team assessment can aid entrepreneurs. *Harvard Business Review*, November/December 1979, 198–200, 202, 206.

SECTION
III

Informal Organization and Social Processes

INTRODUCTION AND OVERVIEW

As shown in Section II, managers can use formal organization arrangements such as organizational design, reward systems, and human resource practices to direct and control organizational actions. One way to think about these levers is as a formal control system, with managers able to adjust the direction of the organization through changes in design or systems. But the *formal control system* is not the only important control mechanism available to managers. The informal organization, in terms of culture, norms, and social influence processes, may provide an equally powerful *social control system* that can be shaped by management.

In considering the congruence model, it may be helpful to think about the organization as a *socio-technical system.* The task-formal organizational arrangement axis of the model includes those levers available to managers as part of their formal authority. In this way, actions such as changing the organization's structure or modifying the formal reward system can be thought of as aspects of formal control. The people-informal organizational arrangement axis of the model, or social control system, provides another set of potential levers available to managers for achieving congruence. Ironically, as the readings in Section I by Tom Peters and Hal Leavitt point out, the social control system may be critical to an organization's success but is too often overlooked by managers. It is important to remember that organizations don't accomplish things—people do. In the end, a manager's success is determined by his or her ability to get others to do those things required to accomplish the critical tasks identified in the model.

But what do we mean when we talk about a social control system? In generic terms, control can be thought of as coming from *the individual or group's knowledge that someone who matters cares about what happens and is paying close attention.* When people care about someone, either because they have formal or informal authority, the evidence shows that they are more likely to comply. When the person or group knows that this authority figure is paying attention and cares what happens, control is increased. To be effective, managers must use both formal controls, such as budgeting or performance appraisal systems, and informal methods of control, such as work group norms or persuasion. Section III introduces a set of perspectives for analyzing and managing the social systems side of the model, particularly the informal organization. The readings consider both the underlying social psychological processes and the actions a manager might consider when dealing with developing and influencing individuals and groups in organizations.

READINGS IN SECTION III

Section III is composed of two chapters. The first, Chapter 5, begins with an overview of the foundations of social influence by Berkowitz. This material is important, since it provides the psychological basis for understanding how and why influence processes work. Terry Connolly's piece then succinctly reviews more than forty years of research on how leaders of groups can manage effectively. This review shows chronologically how researchers and practitioners have attempted to understand when certain types of supervisory styles are likely to be appropriate. Salancik and Pfeffer then consider explicitly where power comes from and how it can be used in organizations. With this knowledge as background, Ware then discusses what one needs to be done to develop effective work teams.

Chapter 8 focuses on culture in organizations. Whereas the material in the Chapter 7 is concerned primarily with groups, the Chapter 8 readings examine the process of social control as it relates to the larger organization. O'Reilly begins with a perspective for understanding and analyzing culture in terms of the central norms that may be widely shared and strongly held within an organization or its subunits. He notes how these may be important in helping or hindering the organization's ability to achieve its critical tasks and execute its strategy.

Pascale then describes how some firms notable for their strong cultures socialize their members to create these cultures. Abegglen and Stalk show how Japanese firms engage in similar practices. They argue that the success of the Japanese firm results not from any special characteristics of the Japanese worker or culture but from the system of management practices used, a system that may work in many contexts. Keys and Miller then show that in spite of some of the confusion about what is meant by the term *Japanese management,* there are identifiable underlying factors that seem to be common across organizations and national cultures. Overall, these readings provide a perspective on the informal organization that permits a manager to analyze the congruence between the culture of an organization and the other components of the model.

5

SOCIAL PROCESSES

Imitation, Conformity, and Compliance

Leonard Berkowitz

IMITATION AND MODELING

In some instances an individual follows an-other's actions in the absence of any social pressures. The other person sets an example which is copied in one way or another. Psychologists usually speak of *imitation* when the observer duplicates what he or she sees fairly closely, but they talk about *modeling* when the exemplar's influence is somewhat broader and the observer's action isn't an exact replica of the model's behavior (Bandura, 1969, 1970). Since it is a more extensive concept than imitation, modeling refers to a wider range of processes. The conditions that produce imitation don't necessarily operate in every case of modeling.

Albert Bandura (1969, 1970) at Stanford University is perhaps the leading theorist in this area; he has discussed three kinds of modeling effects: response stimulation (which he terms "response facilitation"), observational learn-

ing, and the lowering of inhibitions. We'll follow his analysis with some modifications.

Response Stimulation

Reflexive Imitation. Researchers tell us that several species of animals have a "monkey see, monkey do" tendency, in which one animal sometimes copies the behavior of another almost reflexively (Tolman, 1968). Human infants imitate the facial expressions of nearby adults in this involuntary manner, and even grown-ups may show this simple copying, as when one person's yawn causes a contagion of yawning throughout a group. Most important, this relatively primitive imitation doesn't involve the transmission of information from the model to the observer. The model's action doesn't explicitly tell the observer, "Do what I do if you want to get a reward." The imitation is largely involuntary and can thus be viewed as an instance of our Theme I, involuntary responses to external events.

I occasionally exhibit this kind of reaction on fall Sunday afternoons when I look at football on TV. Watching a particular player closely, not having any distracting thoughts, and not being engaged in any competing activities, I sometimes dart and lunge along with him as he moves. This reflexive copying of another may not have been learned, although learning can add to and complicate the reaction.

A team of investigators at the University of Texas may have observed such a blend of learned reactions and stimulus-elicited copying as they recorded the behavior of pedestrians at a traffic light (Lefkowitz, Blake, and Mouton, 1955).

At the appropriate time, right after the traffic signal at a busy street corner commanded the pedestrians to "wait," a 31-year-old man (the experimenters' accomplice) disregarded the red light and walked across the street. On some occasions his clothing (business suit, shirt and tie, and highly polished shoes) indicated he had a relatively high social status, whereas at other times he wore soiled and patched work clothes, suggesting that he had a lower status. The violator's apparent social level affected the extent to which the other pedestrians crossed the street with him. As is typical in this kind of situation, the traffic light violator's action probably stimulated some onlookers to move. He started crossing and some other pedestrians automatically did the same thing. But the stimulation effect was greater when the violator seemed to have a high social status. (While only 1 percent of the pedestrians crossed against the traffic when the accomplice hadn't violated the signal, 4 percent of the onlookers disregarded the light when the illegally acting model had low status, and 14 percent crossed when he was well-dressed.) The onlookers may have paid greater attention to the high-status than to the low-status model. Whatever the explanation, in this study one person's movement prompted others to start forward also . . .

The Contagion of Violence. News stories reporting violent crimes can [also] have [an] imitative effect. The widespread publicity produces a contagion of violence as other persons are stimulated to carry out similar actions. In the late nineteenth century the French sociologist Gabriel Tarde described what he called "suggesto-imitative-assaults." Coining what used to be a well-known phrase, he wrote that epidemics of crime "follow the line of the telegraph." That is, news of a spectacular crime in one community suggests the idea to other people, leading to imitative crimes. According to Tarde (1912), the brutal Jack the Ripper murders in London inspired a series of female mutilation cases in other sections of England. Police officials in the United States have offered similar observations. The Chicago Police Department reported, for example, that Richard Speck's murder of 8 nurses in Chicago in July 1966 and Charles Whitman's shooting of 45 people from the University of Texas Tower the next month were followed by an unusually sharp increase in homicides in Chicago (*Look Magazine*, September 19, 1967). Also, that fall an 18-year-old high school senior shot 4 women and a child in an Arizona beauty parlor. He told police afterwards that he had gotten the idea for a mass killing from the news stories of the Speck and Whitman crimes.

Other illustrations of the contagion of violence can also be cited if we classify suicides as violence. Evidence (Phillips, 1974) indicates that suicides increase immediately after a suicide story has been publicized in the newspapers. And the greater the publicity devoted to a suicide story, the greater is the subsequent rise in the suicide rate. When movie actress Marilyn Monroe committed suicide, there was a 12-percent increase in the suicides in the United States and a 10-percent rise in England and Wales in the next month. The ideas and feelings evoked in susceptible people when they see these news stories need not produce only a close imitation; they may end their own lives by any available means. In a careful statistical analysis, Phillips (1978) has demonstrated that widely publicized murder-suicides tend to be followed by a significant increase in private and business airplane crashes. The greater the publicity given to any murder-suicide, the more crashes occurred. Some people with suicidal tendencies are apparently stirred to action by news stories of suicides, so that they may use the opportunity of an airplane flight to kill themselves, even if they take other persons' lives as well. . . . You may recall the television movie *The Doomsday Flight.* . . . The film portrays an attempt to extort money from an airline by threatening to blow up a passenger plane in flight. The showing of this movie in the United States and abroad provoked a rash of hoax telephone calls warning about bombs aboard airlines, and some flights had to be recalled or canceled. Indeed, this happened so regularly each time the film was telecast that the Federal Aviation Administration asked television stations not to air it. Similarly, airplane hijackings have shown a contagion effect (see Figure 1).

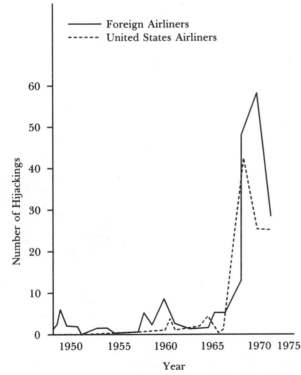

FIGURE 1. *The Number of Airplane Hijackings in the United States and Abroad Between 1947 and 1972*
Courtesy of Albert Bandura.

Besides giving some people ideas they may otherwise not have had (an involuntary reaction), the story provides information: It tells them how they can get money (or some other goal) and just what they have to do to reach this goal.

A good deal of what we know and much of what we do has been acquired through observational learning. We have learned how to get to some locations in our community, play certain games, put on some items of clothing, and carry out at least part of our jobs by watching other persons engage in similar activities. Adults serve as models for children and deliberately or inadvertently teach them how to behave in various situations. Parental actions often speak louder than words. Parents frequently exhort their sons and daughters to work hard, although they themselves seem bent on having an easy time; to be honest, although they themselves try to cheat whenever possible; and to be helpful and considerate toward others, although they themselves are often selfish and inconsiderate. Needless to say, youngsters who see adult hypocrisy frequently copy what their parents do and not what they say (Bryan, 1970).

The influence any model will have depends on several considerations. Observers don't automatically learn every detail of the lesson before them. If the learning is to last, the watchers have to *attend* to the model's action and then *rehearse* what they see. Onlookers won't watch the model carefully, however, if they aren't interested in the activity or if the model isn't attractive or prestigious enough to command their attention. Moreover, observers will probably remember the witnessed action better if they describe or repeat the lesson to themselves as they watch (Bandura, Grusec, & Menlove, 1966; Jeffrey, 1976).

Qualities of Influential Models. The models' characteristics often affect the extent to which their actions are copied, partly by influencing what the observers learn (Bandura, 1969). Especially important is the models' control over the observers' goals (Bandura, Ross, & Ross, 1963; Grusec, 1971; Mischel & Grusec, 1966). If the observers realize that the model can determine whether they will get what they want or whether they'll be punished, they are more likely to look closely at what the model does and to think about his activity, implicitly practicing it, as he performs.

Investigations of the effects of the model's power illustrate how laboratory experiments can throw light on child development. Social scientists have long been interested in *identification*, the process by which a child adopts someone else's qualities and ways of acting.

Bandura et al. (1963) studied identification experimentally by establishing three-person groups composed of two adults and a child to represent the nuclear family—a "father," "mother," and "child." Researchers' accomplices filled the parental roles, whereas the subject—a nursery-school-aged boy or girl—played the part of the offspring. It was quickly apparent that one of the adults—sometimes the man and sometimes the woman—was the powerful member of the "family" and determined who could play with the attractive toys in the room. As the power in the family, this adult dispensed the rewards. The powerful adult rewarded the subject allowing the rewarded individual to have the attractive toys, in some cases and the other adult in other cases. After these conditions had been established, the two adults exhibited distinctively different behaviors while working on another task, and the child was given an opportunity to copy them. Defining "identification" for their purposes as imitation, the psychologists recorded the number of times each child imitated either adult's actions. As Table 1 shows, the children were most likely to copy the powerful adult rather than the less powerful one (the sex of the model didn't have any significant effect). Furthermore, the subjects tended to imitate even a powerful model who had been somewhat frustrating to them.

In Bandura et al.'s study (1963) the subjects carried out the novel behaviors they

TABLE 1.   *Mean Number of Imitative Responses Shown by Children in Reaction to Model's Power and Extent to Which the Model Had Rewarded the Subject*

	Object of Imitation	
Reward Conditions	Powerful Model	Less Powerful Model
When other adult is rewarded	26.88	13.60
When the subject is rewarded	27.46	22.38

Adapted from Ross A. Bandura and S. A. Ross, "A comparative test of the status envy, social power, and secondary reinforcement theories of identificatory learning." *Journal of Abnormal Social Psychology, 67,* 1963, pp. 527–34. Copyright 1963 by the American Psychological Association. Reprinted by permission of the author.

learned, but this is not always the case. People usually don't display the lesson taught to them unless they are also motivated to act. By seeing a violent model we can learn how to be aggressive and even that violence is appropriate behavior in some situations, but we can still restrain ourselves if we think aggression will be punished in the particular setting (Bandura, 1965). Aggressive models can teach others that aggression is sometimes desirable and can even evoke aggressive inclinations (as indicated earlier), but this readiness to carry out the witnessed behavior may not be translated into open action if the observers are strongly inhibited or have good reason to believe that they won't benefit by acting this way or (in the absence of an incentive) if they aren't sufficiently excited as they watch the model's behavior.

The observer's similarity to the model is another important factor affecting the likelihood of imitation. Both children and adults have a greater tendency to copy the actions of someone who is similar to them than of someone who is greatly different (Bandura, 1969). It's easy to see why this should occur. As we watch someone similar to us behave, we're apt to infer that what happens to this individual will also happen to us. We're less likely to make this assumption if we're very different from the person we're observing. If the similar model is rewarded, or at least isn't punished, we're inclined to think our behavior will have the same outcome, and we accordingly imitate the model's behavior.

Bandura (1969) suggested that the most important kind of similarity is *similarity in previous reinforcements.* Let me explain what this concept means. As children grow up, they find that they get the same kind of benefits that certain other persons obtain when they exhibit a given kind of behavior. Susan learns that she and other young girls receive approval when they act like grown-up women in some ways; all of these persons (Susan, other young girls, grown-up women) are thus similarly reinforced for displaying certain actions. This similarity in reinforcement contingencies heightens the chances of imitation, so that Susan will be particularly likely to copy other females. Bussey and Perry (1976) verified this reasoning in an experiment with Australian schoolchildren. When the young boys and girls watched an adult make a series of choices, they were more imitative of the adult in their later choices if they had previously experienced the same reinforcement contingencies as the adult model. That is, when the children saw that both they and the adult had been given the same rewards for doing the same things, they tended to copy the adult's behavior afterwards.

Seeing Others Be Brave. Observational learning of the kind described here can have very powerful effects. As a consequence of the experiences (and reinforcements) we share with others in the course of growing up, we can be profoundly influenced by the things we see happen to other persons. We may react emotionally to the painful treatment someone else receives (Berger, 1962) or get over some of our fears by watching other persons act fearlessly. In one experiment (Bandura, Blanchard, & Ritter, 1969) adults who were very afraid of snakes watched a series of models handle snakes. Where many of the adults hadn't been able to even look at the reptiles, after only two hours of exposure to the fearless models, over 90 percent of the subjects could allow a snake to crawl freely over their hands, neck and arms. Seeing someone else be brave can lessen our own fear.

This effect isn't necessarily a matter of putting up a brave front. Let's say that Daphne Wardle is so frightened of electric shocks that she is upset by even the possibility of a mild electrical tingle on her hands. Now imagine that Daphne sees another woman receive a series of electric shocks of increasing intensity and not show any signs of discomfort. Soon afterwards, when it's Daphne's turn to be shocked, she may be able to take a fairly high level of electric shocks herself, higher than otherwise would have been the case. It's not that Daphne is only trying to look just as good as the other woman and is gritting her teeth in order to withstand the pain. If she is typical of the subjects in two experiments reported by Kenneth Craig (Craig & Neidermeyer, 1974; Craig & Prkachin, 1978), the model's fearless response to the shocks could actually make Daphne experience less pain. The information transmitted by the model's behavior can influence the way that observers interpret their own sensations. To a great extent, our feeling of pain is the result of our interpretations of physical sensations; and these interpretations can be shaped by external events, including the actions of others.

Raising and Lowering Restraints

In addition to stimulating certain responses within us and teaching us something, a model's behavior or its outcome may also affect our attitude toward the kind of conduct we see. As we look at the model and note what happens to her, we get some idea of the likely consequences should we behave the same way. We're not particularly inclined to copy the model's aggressiveness, at least for a while, if we see her punished for being violent; we may be more willing to emulate her if we see that her conduct pays off (Bandura, 1965).

Our moral judgments can also be temporarily influenced by the events we watch. This has been demonstrated repeatedly in research on movie violence, in my own laboratory (Berkowitz & Geen, 1967; Berkowitz & Rawlings, 1963), elsewhere (Hoyt, 1970; Meyer, 1972), and in experiments with juvenile delinquents as well as with college men (Berkowitz, Parke, Leyens, & West, 1974). All of these studies found that angry subjects became more willing to attack the person who had provoked them earlier if they had just seen a movie "bad guy" get the beating he supposedly deserved, than if they had watched "less justified" aggression in which a sympathetic movie character received unwarranted punishment. The events on the screen apparently colored the subjects' judgment of the propriety of their own aggression. "Good" aggression in the film—a scoundrel supposedly getting what was coming to him—meant that they could hurt the scoundrel in their own lives.

Hollywood movies often portray such "good" aggression. As the hero triumphs over the villains, he frequently beats them up, giving them their just desserts. All this is often emotionally satisfying for the audience—justice has been served, an eye has been given for an eye, equity has been attained, bad people have gotten their deserved punishment. But the "warranted" violence on the screen may also induce angry people in the audience to think (for a short while) that their own aggression is also warranted.

CONFORMITY: YIELDING TO OTHERS

In most of the above instances an individual imitated the actions of others with relatively

little thought or, in other cases, with little questioning. The person wasn't under any social pressure and copied others' behavior quite freely. This type of modeling influence should be differentiated from *conformity,* which social psychologists usually define as yielding to group pressure of some sort. When people conform, they change their behavior or beliefs, moving from an earlier way of acting or thinking toward the position advocated by those around them "as a result of real or imagined group pressure" (Kiesler & Kiesler, 1969). Patricia Hearst's conduct right after she joined the Symbionese Liberation Army may be viewed as conformity. Because of the psychological power the terrorists had over her, she may have felt some pressure to conform to her captors' views.

This definition refers to a *change* in behavior or belief, which means that people aren't necessarily conforming when they go along with or act in the same way as others. They could be following a social rule or convention which they accept just because they have grown up in a particular society. When Americans answer the telephone, they usually say "Hello" or give their name, because this is what one does in this type of situation. People can also be conventional in their tastes in home furnishings or clothing. Their choices reflect what they are accustomed to or what they are used to wearing. They haven't given up other tastes or other modes of conduct in response to real or implied pressures.

The Benefits of Conformity

We are especially likely to accede to social pressures when we think it is to our benefit to do so. On these occasions we follow the old political dictum, "If you want to get along, go along." We realize there's something to be gained by conforming to other persons' views and something to be lost if we are different. This is a very commonplace observation, but it's still impressive how widespread is the tendency to conform in order to avoid social costs.

The Asch Experiments. One of the classic demonstrations of people yielding to others can be found in Solomon Asch's research (1958) on conformity, which started in the early 1950s.

Seven male undergraduates listened to the experimenter explain that they were participating in a study of the judgment of perceptual relations. On each trial in the series, the men were told, they would be shown four lines—a standard line and three others of varying lengths. Their task was simply to say which of the latter three lines was the same length as the standard. The experiment began with each subject expressing his judgments aloud. Then, on the third trial, something unexpected happened. To his surprise, subject 6 heard one person after another report that the standard's best match was with line A—which actually appeared somewhat longer than the standard—even though he clearly saw that line C was the closest in length. What should he say when his turn came? The other men were unanimously contradicting the evidence provided by his own senses.

Not realizing that the other undergraduates were the experimenter's confederates and had been instructed to express wrong judgments on certain trials, subject 6 was faced perhaps for the first time in his life with a situation in which he had to decide whether to go along with the group's unanimous judgment or report what his eyes told him was correct. Even though he knew the judgment was incorrect, the typical subject 6 in this study went along with the group on about 4 of the 12 trials in which the majority gave a wrong answer.

This is a graphic case of conformity. The subjects in these experiments seemed to be well aware of the correct answer, yet about one-third of them surrendered to the erroneous majority by voicing the wrong answer. Was it possible that a good portion of those who went along with the majority actually believed that the majority was right? When Asch interviewed his subjects afterwards, many of the conform-

ists claimed that they had thought the majority opinion was probably correct. Since all of the others were in agreement, these subjects said, they suspected something was wrong with their own eyesight. Now, is this the case? Did many of the conformists actually believe the majority judgment was probably right?

An interesting answer to this question is given in a later variation of the Asch experiments. A few years after Asch published the first report of his research, Deutsch and Gerard (1955) repeated the study with some modifications. Most important for our purposes, they established one condition in which subjects could express their estimates anonymously, so that no one else in the group supposedly knew who gave what judgment. This anonymity greatly reduced conformity to the incorrect majority to well below the incidence observed by Asch. Many of the conformists in Asch's initial studies apparently tried to justify their yielding by claiming that they thought the majority was right. They had evidently known the majority was wrong, but went along anyway. Even though the others in the room were strangers whom they might not see again, the yielders publicly conformed to the erroneous majority judgment in order to avoid seeming different.

Types of Conformity. In the words of some social psychologists (Kiesler & Kiesler, 1969), Asch's subjects exhibited *compliance* in going along with the others without a true (or private) acceptance of the group's opinions. If the stimulus had been much more ambiguous, so that these subjects hadn't been so certain of what was right, many more of them would have acceded to the group's judgments and would have believed that the majority was probably correct. Deutsch and Gerard used two now well-known concepts to refer to these different kinds of social influence. Adapting their terminology, we would say that the compliance shown by Asch's conformists arose through *normative social influence;* these persons conformed to the others' view because they thought that it would be to their benefit. Other people's opinions are truly accepted, however, when there is *informational social influence,* and other's views are taken "as evidence about reality."

Independence Versus Rebelliousness. So far we've been talking about distinctions in cases of going along with others. Are there any differentiations we should make when an individual doesn't follow the others around her? In a variation of the Asch procedure (Milgram, 1961), Norwegian and French university students were led to think that other students occasionally differed with them in judging the duration of sounds. The Norwegians were more inclined than the French to yield to the wrong opinions of their peers. But what were the French students doing when they didn't conform? Were they truly independent in the sense of being indifferent to the majority judgment, or did they notice the majority view and decide to rebel against it? We can't tell which reaction occurred in this situation. Truly *independent* people know what others expect of them, but don't use these expectations as a guide for their own behavior; they are indifferent to them. *Rebelliousness*—or what some social psychologists call *anticonformity*—exists when the individual reacts against the group's expectations and moves away from the actions or beliefs it advocates (Hollander & Willis, 1967).

Perhaps we can apply this distinction between independence and rebelliousness to the social scene of the mid-1960s to early 1970s. Although some young men and women prided themselves on their independence, they weren't indifferent to society's rules and conventions, but only rebelled against them. They were self-conscious rebels rather than being quietly and self-confidently independent.

Factors Influencing Compliance

Deviation May Be Dangerous. Compliance basically arises because we realize that we are likely to be punished in some way if we don't conform. The other people around us are apt to hurt us, psychologically or at times even physically, if we depart from their norms, their standards defining what is proper behavior. For example, throughout much of the 1960s long-haired youths were often subjected to scorn and even harassment because many people assumed that the youths rejected other social norms and values besides those concerned with appearance and dress. Workers in industry frequently apply sanctions against others in their group who deviate from the work norms they've informally agreed on (Homans, 1961). I recently heard that a young and still eager janitor at my university had been punched, harried, and generally mistreated by other janitors in his section who thought he worked too hard and did too much.

Even if the majority is in no real danger as a result of the nonconformist's failure to adhere to its standards, such resistance to the group norm can be disturbing. The deviation may cast doubt on the majority's cherished attitudes and values; seeing the "odd man out" cling to his discrepant views, the majority may begin to wonder if their own beliefs are right (Moscovici & Faucheux, 1972). Young married couples with babies who hear their friends insist that they won't have any children may question the wisdom of their own decision to raise a family. Then too, as some writers have pointed out (Kiesler, 1973), people holding the predominant position often regard the norm violator as disturbingly unpredictable. The deviant may be doing something unexpected when she insists on her unusual views, and this unpredictability can be bothersome.

Most of us are aware of these possibilities. We know that we may be punished by being rejected or by not being liked or worse, and we're inclined to comply with others' expectations, especially if these people can give us something we desire.

The Person's Goals. An individual will follow the views of the people around her, even when she doesn't agree with them, if she thinks that compliance will bring her something she wants. On the other hand, if she's basically interested in determining what is the right belief or in defending her own opinion, she may not yield to others' pressure on her to change. She's much more apt to submit if she is concerned with gaining their approval or keeping their goodwill.

Thibaut and Strickland (1956) have demonstrated how a person's goals can affect his reaction to group pressures. Male students at the University of North Carolina were assembled in small groups and required to make complex judgments of physical stimuli. Each subject was induced to become somewhat committed to his initial opinion (by telling him he would have to justify his answers later). Then the experimenter led him to think that the other group members unanimously disagreed with him. At this point the student received written messages, ostensibly from his partners, which put either high, moderate, or low pressure on him to alter his judgment. Cross-cutting this variation, half of the subjects were made to be concerned about the task and about getting the best answer to the problem, while the others were led to be more interested in their social relationships.

The proportion of subjects in each condition who conformed to group pressure is shown in Figure 2. Look first at the responses of those who were primarily interested in getting the best answer to the problem. Being somewhat committed to their own ideas, the more pressure the other persons placed on them, the more likely these subjects were to hold on to their initial beliefs. The subjects who were problem oriented evidently experienced reactance . . . and resented the pressure on them to change; they were apt to cling doggedly to their own views. However, the students who were concerned with their social relationships showed a very different pattern. The greater the pressure the other group members imposed on them, the more likely they were to yield and go along with them.

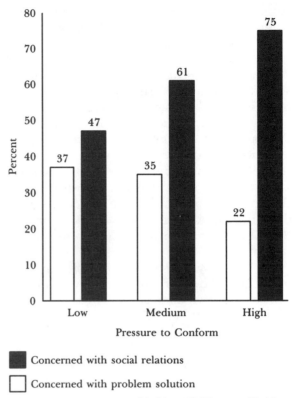

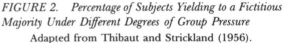
Concerned with social relations

Concerned with problem solution

FIGURE 2. Percentage of Subjects Yielding to a Fictitious Majority Under Different Degrees of Group Pressure
Adapted from Thibaut and Strickland (1956).

Many Americans appear to be equally concerned with their social relationships. When we meet someone new, we usually want to get along with her or even be liked by her. If we aren't strongly committed to a particular attitudinal position, we may be inclined to accede to her opinions, at least overtly, in order to win her acceptance, especially if we know we'll meet again in the future (Lears, et al., 1972).

Many of us especially desire to be accepted after we find that we've expressed deviant views on some issue. Knowing that people are usually suspicious of those who are "different," we may become anxious at learning we've just voiced a minority opinion. If we have another opportunity to state our beliefs (on another issue) right afterwards, we may take care

235

to go along with someone else in order to avoid being frowned on as an oddball (Darley, Moriarty, Darley, & Berscheid, 1974).

The Others' Attractiveness.   While many of us seek the approval of strangers, we are even more intent on keeping the goodwill of those who are attractive to us. We like being with them and would be hurt if they rejected us. The more we care for people, the more apt we are to go along with their views if we know how they want us to act and if they can see what we do (Berkowitz, 1954). Unless we're very sure of these people, we don't want to risk offending them by conspicuously departing from their standards.

There may be personality differences in this regard, however. In connection with the Thibaut and Strickland study, we saw that conformity is heightened when a person is interested in social relationships with others rather than in getting the best answer. Some individuals are preoccupied with having others like them, while other persons mainly want to find out what's right. The former are more inclined to yield to the majority's opinions (McDavid, 1959) and are probably also particularly responsive to the views of people they find attractive. By contrast, people who usually focus on learning the correct solution tend to go along with unattractive people as readily as with those they find attractive (Wilson, 1960).

Social Status and Compliance

Much of what we have been discussing can be translated into power terms. When we learn that other people are important to us because they can either provide us with the rewards we greatly desire or punish us in ways we especially fear (for example, by rejecting us), we come under their control to a considerable extent. They have some power over us. Attractive people have power over us because they control something we want—their approval. An individual's status in a group often determines how

much power the other group members have over him and how much influence he can exert over them.

Low Status.   We are in a very precarious position if we have low status in our group, aren't well accepted by the others, or are afraid that we may be completely excluded. Clinging to our precious foothold in the group—maybe even hoping that we can better our position— we walk the straight and narrow, not daring to deviate openly from the group's standards. We may not even like the other group members because they don't seem to care for us, so that we don't truly adopt their point of view (Dittes & Kelley, 1956). However, such surface compliance comes about when the low-status individual is interested in maintaining or even improving her standing in the group. If we've given up on the others, we won't bother to hide our real opinions and will show our noncompliance (Harvey & Consalvi, 1960).

High Status.   The high-status group member is in a much more fortunate position, especially if his rank is unlikely to change. His status gives him the security to express disagreement if he differs from the majority at any time. Norma Feshbach (1967) assembled four-man groups of fraternity members, seeing that two of the members were among the most popular people in the fraternity (high status) and the other two were relatively unpopular (low status). Moreover, the high- and low-status members had the task of deciding which card of the two presented to them on each trial contained the greater number of dots. Even though incorrect estimates would hurt their group and possibly cost their fraternity a $25 prize, the low-status members were generally reluctant to disagree with the high-status members' incorrect judgments. When each person was misled into thinking that his partners were unanimously wrong, the high-status fraternity members were much more willing to deviate from this view than were their less popular counterparts.

236

There are most likely two interrelated reasons for the high-status fraternity members' feeling that they could safely stand apart from their group. One has to do with differences in power. The highly popular people were undoubtedly aware that their partners needed their approval more than they required these others' goodwill. Then too, groups may actually permit high-status members greater freedom to deviate from the majority position. These persons are often given "idiosyncrasy credit," as Hollander (1958) put it, and allowed to be oddballs.

I suspect that high-status members who occupy a formally designated position symbolizing the group's ideals, such as the President of the United States or the king of England, don't have an idiosyncrasy credit in matters that are important to the group. Indeed, they probably have less freedom to deviate from approved standards in these areas than the average group member. Edward VIII couldn't marry a divorced woman and remain king; and Princess Margaret was discouraged from marrying a divorced man, even though a British commoner could do so without suffering ostracism. The group may hold fairly stringent expectations for certain high-status members on important matters at least, and would be quite annoyed if the high-status people violated these expectations (Wahrman, 1970).

Compliance with Authority

In January 1942 a group of top-level civil servants in the Nazi government met in a suburb of Berlin to coordinate efforts to the Final Solution, Hitler's plan to exterminate the Jews of Europe. Adolf Eichmann, head of the Jewish Office in the German Secret Police, or Gestapo, was impressed by the meeting. Here he was chatting and drinking with high governmental officials, despite his humble background.

There was another reason that made the day . . . unforgettable for Eichmann. Although he had been doing his best right along to help with the Final Solution, he had still harbored some doubts about "such a bloody solution through violence," and these doubts had now been dispelled. "Here now . . . the most prominent people had spoken. . . ." Not only Hitler . . . not just the S.S. or the Party, but the elite of the good old Civil Service were vying and fighting with each other for the honor of taking the lead in these bloody matters. "At that moment, I sensed a kind of Pontius Pilate feeling, for I felt free of all guilt." Who was he to judge? (Arendt, 1963, p. 101)

Eichmann was reassured and led to believe that the plan must be all right, since all these important people agreed on it. As he told the court during his trial in Jerusalem in 1961, his conscience was soothed because "he could see no one, no one at all, who actually was against the Final Solution" (quoted in Arendt, 1963, p. 103). Moreover, even if he had any misgivings in the coming months and years, as millions of Jewish men, women, and children were slaughtered, he could always tell himself that "This was the way things were, this was the new law of the land, based on the Fuhrer's order; whatever he did he did, as far as he could see, as a law-abiding citizen. He did his duty, as he told the [Jerusalem] court over and over again; he not only obeyed orders, he also obeyed the law" (Arendt, 1963, p. 120).

"Following orders" is a defense that the German generals were to repeat again and again after World War II: "I wasn't really responsible for the deaths of those thousands of civilians ruthlessly shot by my soldiers; I was a soldier myself, obeying a superior's orders" (see, for example, Shirer, 1960, p. 380). The Germans aren't the only ones who have tried to excuse or explain their actions in such terms. In every country "good soldiers" have said that if they hurt someone in the performance of their duties, they were absolved of blame because they were only following orders or obeying the law. Hannah Arendt, the author of the book on Eichmann just cited, has maintained that this pattern of behavior is now all too prevalent in our society. Western history, she believes, has produced a type of official who, "for the sake of his pension, his life insurance, the security of his wife and children [is] prepared to do literally anything" (Arendt, 1978). He follows his superiors' orders, partly because he believes they have the right to tell him what to do, but also because he believes compliance is to his benefit.

In some ways, such compliance is part of an age-old problem: the relation of the individual to the authority systems of society, or the conflict between personal freedom and the requirements of the social order. Long before the rise of Nazi Germany, the Greek philosopher Plato asked whether a person is obliged to obey an unjust law. Plato's teacher Socrates had thought there were only a few limited alternatives to obedience to the state and had accepted his society's right to condemn him to death.

The Right to Give Orders. We have now observed that people have sometimes given other persons the right to tell them what to do in some domains of life. In my view, this permission may be an automatic, relatively unthinking, response (Theme I) to persons who carry the symbols of legitimate authority.

The social order is a network of interlocking roles and statuses in which some positions have authority over other roles. Thus, judges can impose fines, parents can legitimately tell children what to do in some situations, teachers can influence their students' activities in the classroom, and employers can properly direct their workers. These expectations hold for subordinates as well as for those exerting power, so that on at least some occasions, most of us think we ought to obey those having recognized authority over us.

Research on Reactions to Legitimate Authority.
A well-known research program conducted by Stanley Milgram (1963), now of the City University of New York, demonstrates how many

United States citizens have learned to follow the dictates of those in authority.

Milgram's male subjects, recruited by newspaper ads, had a much more diverse background than is customary in psychological experiments. They were blue-collar workers, salesmen, businessmen, and professionals between 20 and 50 years of age. Each man thought he was a "teacher" in a learning experiment who had the job of punishing another subject (actually the investigator's accomplice) each time that person made a mistake on the learning task. The teacher was to administer electric shocks as the punishment, increasing the shock intensity regularly as the mistakes continued. The "mistakes" were prearranged so that each subject was required to raise the shock intensity 30 times, supposedly in 15-volt steps, going from 15 to 450 volts, with the last electric switch bearing the sign, "Danger, Severe Shock." If the subject seemed reluctant to proceed with this assignment and was slow to go on to the next shock switch, the watching experimenter instructed him to continue, even though the confederate learner in the next room occasionally pounded the wall and cried out in pain. No one was really shocked, but almost every subject thought he was hurting the person next door (although he had been reassured that there would be "no permanent tissue damage").

All of the subjects complied with the experimenter's orders until they reached the 300-volt level (switch 20), the point at which the learner next door began pounding the wall. Either then or at the next switch, 22 percent refused to continue despite the experimenter's insistence. A few more went a little bit further and then refused to go on. But only a minority resisted the authority of the experimenter; 65 percent obeyed the instructions and steadily increased the punishment they inflicted up to the maximum, and supposedly dangerous, level. They believed they were hurting someone badly, yet they did what they were told.

Other experiments have since determined how our willingness to inflict pain in response to the dictates of authority is affected by various situational conditions. For example, Milgram (1965) found that the investigator's commands became less effective as the victim's suffering was made clearer. While only 35 percent of the subjects refused to follow the experimenter's orders at some point in the procedure when the victim was next door, about 60 percent defied the authority's instructions before they reached the maximum intensity if the victim was in the same room, and 70 percent refused to go all the way if they had to forcibly hold the victim's hand on the shockplate as the shocks were administered. Evidently, it became more difficult for the subjects to hurt someone in compliance with orders when they could readily see the consequences of their acquiescence (also see Tilker, 1970). They couldn't keep punishing the victim severely unless they had a strong respect for the authority or, possibly, a low regard for the victim.

Another factor is also at work here. Notice that subjects showed the greatest resistance to authority when they had to hold the victim down. These men couldn't pass the buck; they couldn't tell themselves that they were passively following orders because they actively contributed to the injury done to the other person. So they had to take some of the blame if they continued. Not wanting to feel personal responsibility for the pain they inflicted, they defied their instructions. Two other experiments—one in West Germany (Mantell, 1971) and the other in the United States (Tilker, 1970)—have shown that many people are reluctant to hurt others if they have to take personal responsibility for their actions. Thus, in the West German study (Mantell, 1971), only 7 percent of the "teachers" gave the maximum shocks when they were told it was up to them to decide whether and how much the "learner" was to be punished. By contrast, in the baseline condition (exactly the same as Milgram's original condition) 85 percent of the subjects administered the maximum punishment.

We can easily translate the research on obedience to authority into terms applicable to our own country. Suppose you were an American soldier in Vietnam in the late 1960s. On patrol in possibly dangerous territory, your platoon enters a small village. Everyone is on edge, even scared. Then your commanding officer orders the platoon to shoot any Vietnamese on sight. What would you do? Would you obey orders?

Unthinking Reactions to Legitimate Authority.

Authorities are obeyed to a very substantial extent because we have learned to give them the right to tell us what to do in certain situations. Much of the time we don't have to be forced to comply. Indeed, coercion is unlikely to hold an organization together for long. If the group is to be stable, its members must submit voluntarily to those in command (Weber, 1947). As the eminent sociologist Robert Nisbet (1970) observed, "For most persons, most of the time, in most places, the authorities they obey are perceived as legitimate authorities. Obedience is willed, or at least not checked, in light of this legitimacy" (p. 140). As one testimonial to the power of legitimacy, the West German version of Milgram's study (Mantell, 1971) demonstrated a drop in subjects' compliance with the experimenter's instructions when his legitimacy was undermined. The subjects accorded him less right to control their actions when they didn't think his job was to tell them what to do.

Since the authority's legitimacy is so important any comprehensive analysis of compliance requires a greater understanding of the sources of legitimacy than we now possess. Why are some people empowered with the right to influence others, and—an especially intriguing question nowadays—why do previously accepted authorities sometimes come under attack so that their areas of influence shrink?

Probably more than any other factor, *collective approval*—the agreement of the group members—legitimates the patterns of dominance and subordination in the group (Blau, 1964). In our society collective approval usually becomes explicit when someone is elected to the authority role. What we often see, then, is that election justifies the adoption of power. We may strongly oppose a politician's candidacy in an election campaign, but if she is elected we usually accept her right to exert the authority of the office. By the same token, when a person in a small work group starts telling the other group members what to do, these people are more apt to feel that he has a right to prescribe behavior for them if he has been elected to the supervisory position than if he has simply usurped this job. And in the former case, group members are also more inclined to adopt the leader's prescriptions as their own beliefs (French & Raven, 1959; Raven & French, 1958): the election has legitimated his influence attempts.

The great sociological theorist Max Weber (1947) has also pointed out that legitimacy is frequently derived from rational considerations. Modern societies tend to regard authorities as legitimate if they operate in a reasonable manner. Thus, the authorities exercise their control on the basis of their knowledge rather than because they have been born into the right family or group. Evan and Zelditch (1961) used this conception in a laboratory analog of a bureaucratic organization. In this experiment college students worked under the guidance of an appointed supervisor, who they were led to believe knew either more, the same, or less about the job than they did. Supervisors should be more expert than their subordinates, and their appointment isn't reasonable (or legitimate) if they know less. In keeping with Weber's view, the students were more disobedient to the supervisor's commands, particularly in hard-to-see ways, if his knowledge was supposedly inferior to theirs. His position was apparently not totally legitimate if it had an illogical basis.

Some Concluding Thoughts.   Authority is not a simple matter, and there is no easy way to eliminate the wrongs committed in authority's name. As long as society continues, some people will violate the trust we place in them or abuse the power given them or hurt other persons if they think their job requires this. But we can't do away with all authority. Even the leading theorists of the anarchist movement thought that some authority was necessary and indispensable (Nisbet, 1970, p. 141). Every social order must have a regulatory system (hopefully one that is humane and just), an agreed-upon conception of what is legitimate authority, and a widespread willingness to comply with the rules laid down in the appropriate, "proper" manner—or else brute force will control how people interact. Maybe, as some writers have suggested and as the founders of the American Republic recognized, it is best to have institutionalized checks and balances in which countervailing authorities press against each other. "Whether authority is in fact limited or total depends upon norms of freedom and authority . . . and also . . . upon the degree to which that authority is checked, limited, challenged, and countervailed by other authorities in the social order" (Nisbet, 1970, p. 135).

TRUE ACCEPTANCE OF OTHERS' STANDARDS

Social Consensus and Informational Influence

Authoritative Opinions.   Most of us not only comply with the dictates of authority, but frequently think that the attitudes or practices advocated by government officials are correct. Throughout the Johnson and Nixon administrations, millions of Americans approved of the Vietnam war because this was the President's policy. Since the government had undertaken to fight this war, many citizens believed that it must be the right thing to do. Similarly, when English university students were told that laws defined certain behaviors as legal (or illegal), their judgments of the moral propriety of these actions were correspondingly affected to a slight but significant degree (Berkowitz & Walker, 1967). Actions certified by legal authority gained in moral rightness, whereas conduct condemned by the laws was regarded more morally improper than it had been before.

Consensus and the Social Definition of Reality.
There are a number of reasons why legitimate authority can validate particular opinions or actions. One possibility has to do with the social consensus implicitly supporting the authority. We're generally aware that duly constituted government ultimately rests upon the approval of the governed. Thus, a law is implicitly right or correct to the extent that it is backed by a widespread social consensus. The obvious defiance of the no-liquor laws of the Prohibition era probably further weakened their effectiveness; people who once thought Prohibition was a good idea no longer backed this policy when they saw that many of their peers disapproved of it.

Adolf Eichmann's belief that the Final Solution was a proper course of action is also a testimony to the power of social consensus. His doubts about "such a bloody solution through violence" were largely obliterated by the agreement of the top-level officials meeting to implement the plan. Not one person disagreed with the proposal, he said, so he thought it must be all right.

In all of these instances the group consensus defined the validity, the correctness, perhaps even the "truth," of the issue. We can look at this in terms of Theme III and say that the agreement among the people in the situation affected any one person's interpretation of the ambiguous stimulation (that it, the nature of the information received). As some social psychologists have stated, the consensus provided a social definition of reality. Social agreement creates reality in many different walks of life and even, to some extent, in the Asch experiment and its later variations. Earlier in this chapter I mentioned the variation of Asch's experiment in which the subjects were permitted to express their views anonymously (Deutsch & Gerard, 1955). Although this procedure reduced the amount of compliance to the erroneous majority opinion, as I reported, a small number of subjects still yielded to the majority view. These few were apparently so lacking in self-confidence that they doubted their own senses in the face of others' unanimity. Questioning themselves, they thought the others might be right since everyone else had the same judgment.

The Sherif Experiment. A classic experiment carried out by Muzafer Sherif (1936) in the mid-1930s illustrates how agreement among the members of a group can define reality. In contrast to the Asch study, where the subject could easily see what was right, the situation was much more ambiguous in Sherif's experiment.

In this investigation, the subject sat in a completely darkened room, along with two other college students, looking at a point of light waving back and forth in the distance. The walls were not visible, nor were there any other physical frames of reference for subjects to use in their task of judging how far the light moved as it followed its erratic course in the darkness. Because the stimulus was so ambiguous, the three people didn't "see" it in exactly the same way at first. After a while, however, their estimates converged. They developed a common perception, a shared way of viewing the light. In the next phase of the experiment the subject was alone in the darkened room, and he again had to say how far the light moved. As he stared at the faint glow, he wondered if the light was acting in the same way as before. Yes it was, he decided. It appeared to be moving just as much as it had in the group session.

Unknown to the subject, however, the light actually was physically stationary at all times and only *seemed* to be moving, an illusion called the "autokinetic effect." The ambiguous stimulus was defined in a certain way by the group, and the subjects then carried the group's definition with them when they were alone. This earlier experience in the group taught them how to view the stimulus.

Social Support May Break Consensus. We can also see the effects of consensus when we look at what happens when the group's unanimity is broken. In Asch's original research the subjects were less likely to yield to the erroneous majority when there was another dissident in the room than when they were alone against the group. Destroying the group's unanimity increased the student's resistance to the pressures of the majority. There are several reasons for this finding. For example, the naive subject may have been less afraid of being ostracized or laughed at if someone else also refused to go along with the group. In addition, the other deviant (who gave his judgments before subject 6 did) might have weakened the group's credibility—the majority opinion seemed less right—and also heightened the individual's confidence in his own belief.

An experiment by Allen and Levine (1969) at the University of Wisconsin shows how the group's credibility is lessened when the members are no longer unanimous.

Using a modification of the Asch procedure devised by Crutchfield, the psychologists placed five people in separate booths. Each subject was told he would be the fifth person in the group to express his answer to the presented problem and that signal lights in his cubicle would let him know how each of the others had re- *sponded. . . . Unknown to the subjects, these lights were actually controlled by the experimenter, who gave each student prearranged information about his partners' views.*

The first three persons answering were always in agreement, and on the 18 critical trials they expressed highly unusual judgments (as determined by prior testing with college students) that were different from the subjects' own opinions. The fourth member's answers varied with the experimental condition. In the social support condition his responses were in complete accord with the subjects' judgments (which had been ascertained previously), while in the extreme dissent condition his answers were even more incorrect than those stated by the erroneous majority. Finally, in the no-support condition the fourth person always went along with the majority. Thus, there were two conditions in which the group consensus was lowered; but only in the first of these treatments, the social support group, did the deviant agree with the subject's own views.

The subjects were given three types of problems—visual (as in the original Asch experiment), information, and opinion. Allen and Levine found that the weakened group consensus in both the social support and extreme dissent conditions significantly reduced the level of conformity to the incorrect majority on the visual and information items, and substantially decreased the yielding to the majority on the opinion items (see Figure 3). However, on the opinion items there was less conformity in the social support than in the extreme dissent treatment.

As Allen and Levine (1969) suggest, most people probably expect complete agreement on factual matters such as the visual and information problems. Should the consensus be less complete, the group is regarded as a defective judge of reality and can be disregarded. In other words, on objective problems it doesn't matter whether others agree with us or if they have another judgment; as long as the group is not unanimous, its credibility is suspect. On more subjective issues, such as opinions, we're not surprised if there's less than

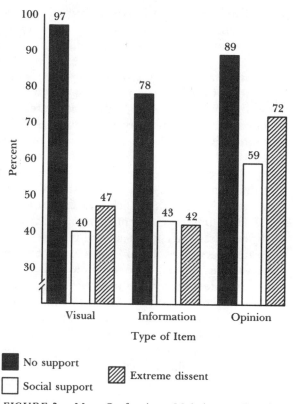

FIGURE 3. *Mean Conformity to Majority as a Function of Type of Item and Type of Support*

Adapted from V. L. Allen and J. M. Levine. "Consensus and conformity," *Journal of Experimental Psychology,* 1969, Vol. 5, pp. 389–399. Copyright 1969 by the American Psychological Association. Reprinted by permission.

perfect agreement. In this case we usually think that the greater the consensus, the greater the probability that the others may be right. But if someone sides with us on such ambiguous issues, we're more confident of our own judgments (Allen & Levine, 1971). Social agreement defines reality primarily in subjective matters for which we know there is no single, unquestioned truth.

Another study indicates that the time at which its consensus is broken can be very important in determining the amount of power the majority will have over the individual. According to Morris and Miller (1975), we are less likely to go along with a majority holding a very

different view if someone else expresses a judgment close to our own ideas before we hear the people in the majority. Then, when it's our turn to offer an opinion, we're more likely to hold on to our own judgment. The other person's initial statement corroborates our own first thoughts, strengthening our confidence in our own views, so that we can withstand the majority's divergent judgment. More strongly convinced of the rightness of our initial opinion because of the support provided by the other person, we don't believe the majority has correctly defined what is real and true. . . .

Influence of the Minority on the Majority

Until now we've focused on the effects of the group on the individual. Two French social psychologists, Moscovici and Faucheux (1972), have pointed out, however, that such a one-sided emphasis neglects the considerable impact that a few determined persons sometimes have on the larger group. Every now and then a small band has triumphed over the many, convincing a once scornful majority to accept ideas it had previously rejected. History has been made by such innovators as Copernicus in astronomy, Luther in religion, and Freud in psychology. If social psychology is to say anything about social innovations, it must consider the minority's influence as well as the majority's power.

Moscovici and his associates (Moscovici & Faucheux, 1972; Moscovici & Nemeth, 1974) have argued that a persistent few can change the prevailing group norms by maintaining their own deviant views consistently, coherently, and forcefully. The minority's continuous and determined pressure raises doubts where certainty existed before. The others begin to wonder if the majority consensus does indeed define what is true or correct, and they open their minds to the ideas they repudiated earlier. Thus, in keeping with our present information-processing theme (Theme III), a determined minority can influence the majority by shaping the majority's understanding. Other investigators have obtained some evidence consistent with this reasoning (see Nemeth & Wachtler, 1974).

Reasonably Self-confident. According to this later research, dedicated dissidents are particularly likely to be convincing when they express their minority views with confidence and with reason. Let's suppose that Daphne Wardle is involved in an argument with the other women in her dormitory and finds herself holding a minority position. Where most of the residents favor one policy, Daphne and one or two others prefer a very different proposal. How can Daphne convince the majority? Well, an experiment by a Swiss psychologist (Mugny, 1975) tells us she should appear firm, but not dogmatic. In this study a group member's minority opinion was less likely to be accepted by the others if he seemed to be rigidly dogmatic rather than reasonably firm. The people in the majority were more inclined to go along with the deviant when he acknowledged that their views were reasonable while arguing for his position. . . . If we want to convince other persons, we're often better off if we don't flatly repudiate their beliefs in a head-on confrontation. But the minority has to seem self-confident; individuals who appear very sure of themselves are especially likely to be influential (Spitzer & Davis, 1978). Charlan Nemeth and her colleagues (Nemeth, Swedlund, & Kanki, 1974; Nemeth & Wachtler, 1974) have demonstrated that dissidents can waver occasionally and still be convincing, as long as their variations don't create an impression of uncertainty. Thus, Daphne Wardle doesn't have to be rigidly consistent if she states her views with confidence.

As I said before, this self-assurance makes the people in the majority question the correctness of their own beliefs and causes them to wonder if the minority isn't right after all. But the minority's persuasiveness is also helped by anything else that adds credence to its position, such as someone's past history of success and even the size of the minority.

Minority Size and the Perceived Correctness of the Minority.   Consider the matter of the minority's size. Would Daphne Wardle be better off in her efforts to convince the majority in her dormitory if she had only a few people on her side or if she had lots of adherents?

Nemeth pointed out that we can expect two different things to happen as the minority gets larger (Nemeth, Wachtler, & Endicott, 1977). For one thing, the majority may assume that the dissidents are less self-confident as their numbers grow. Think of this in attribution theory terms. If a single person holds out as the lone dissenter against the pressure of the majority, we tend to assume this individual must be quite self-confident. The majority thus attributes the deviation to an internal factor, the person's self-assurance. However, the discounting principle may come into play as the minority gets larger. . . . We tend to rule out internal factors as a possible cause of someone's behavior if we can reasonably attribute the action to external circumstances (Kelley, 1972, 1973). This means observers will be less likely to believe that any one deviant is self-confident, the more dissidents there are. The majority assigns the minority's stance to an external factor (the support the dissidents provide each other) and not to internal self-confidence. On the other hand, as Nemeth also noted, increased numbers may also enhance the perceived correctness of the minority position, as when social consensus defines reality in ambiguous matters. The more people there are who share a given opinion, up to some maximum number, the more likely it is that we will think they are probably right (Asch, 1958). Putting all of these findings together, we would expect an increasing minority to be regarded as (1) somewhat less self-confident, but (2) more correct.

Nemeth et al. (1977) examined the effect of the minority's size upon its persuasiveness as a function of the two components of perceived self-confidence and correctness. Undergraduate women were assembled in groups of six naive subjects together with a certain number of the investigators' confederates. Some groups had only one confederate, other groups had two, and some other groups had either three or four confederates. All of the people in the group had to express judgments about the colors of stimuli that were shown to them, but where the naive subjects in the majority were quite sure these stimuli were blue, the confederates adopted the minority position and persisted in labeling the stimuli "blue-green."

The subjects' ratings of the minority at the end of the session are summarized in Table 2. As you can see, the larger the size of the minority, the more correct (competent), but less self-confident, they were thought to be. In this study at least, the minority's perceived correctness was generally more important than their self-assurance in determining their persuasiveness. In general, even though the majority rejected the dissident viewpoint most of the time (the stimulus was much too

TABLE 2. *Reactions of Majority Members to Those in Minority*

	Minority Size			
	1	2	3	4
Number of times minority judgment was adopted*	1.35	1.31	2.25†	1.88
Perceived confidence of minority‡	5.67	5.22	5.29	5.13
Perceived competence of minority†	3.78	4.28	4.42	4.52

*In the control condition containing no confederates, no subject ever gave the response persistently voiced by the confederates.

†This mean is significantly greater than the mean in the 1-confederate condition.

‡There were significant linear trends for these two measures so that we can say there was a regular decrease in the minority's assumed confidence and a regular increase in their perceived competence.

Data from Nemeth et al. (1977).

clear-cut), the naive subjects were somewhat more accepting of the minority judgment, the more people there were in the minority. Despite this finding, other evidence indicates that both the perceived self-confidence and the perceived correctness of the minority contributed to the minority's influence. When the researchers formed a composite index based on the subjects' ratings of both of these qualities, this combination was a better predictor of the minority's influence than either characteristic alone.

If we can generalize from this particular experiment, Daphne would be well advised to seek additional adherents to her cause. The other women might think Daphne and her supporters weren't especially self-confident, but the dissident arguments might appear more valid as the minority grew.

Breaking the Majority's Consensus. Just as the dissidents' consensus can affect the onlookers' estimate of how correct their own opinions are, so can agreement among the majority influence its members' confidence in their own viewpoint. This point has implications for how the minority may go about convincing the majority. What happens, we may ask, if some people desert the majority cause and take up the minority opinion? Kiesler and Pallak's study (1975) indicates that those in the minority should "chip away" at a susceptible member of the majority in order to get her over to their side. The people who remain in the majority aren't going to like the "switcher," according to Kiesler and Pallak, and may even regard her as a renegade, but the switch tends to make the majority lose confidence. "Maybe there's a good reason why that person joined the other side," they think. As their doubts mount, they can be more easily persuaded by the persistent minority.

My impression is that this type of process was at work in the United States during the Vietnam war. As the war continued, quite a few people who initially supported the United States government's policy in Asia began to side with the antiwar protestors. The former supporters' desertion of the majority cause undoubtedly contributed to the majority's growing doubts about the wisdom of continuing the struggle.

SELF-PERCEPTION IN COMPLIANCE

Low Balling the Customer

Joe Arbuthnot received a substantial amount of money as a birthday present and decided to buy a new car. Determined to be a smart customer, he told a salesperson at one of the largest automobile dealerships in the city that he would only buy a new car from that firm if he received a good deal on his present vehicle as a trade-in. The salesperson assured Joe he would get the best trade-in value in town, and Joe chose the new model he wanted. But when Joe sat down to sign the necessary papers for the purchase, the salesperson told Joe that the manager would have to approve the amount offered for Joe's old car. In a little while the salesperson returned and said the manager had rejected the trade-in price. The manager was supposed to have said that the firm wouldn't make enough money on the sale if he paid that much for Joe's old car. If Joe wanted the new automobile he had selected, he would have to spend several hundred dollars more than he had thought just a few minutes earlier.

Joe's experience wasn't unique. He was the victim of "low balling," a reprehensible but widespread practice used by many salespeople, especially in the automobile industry (*Consumer Reports*, May 1974, p. 368). The idea is to get the customer committed to the purchase on the basis of a very favorable deal and then eliminate some of the favorable features after the customer is "hooked." Joe had made his decision after being told he would have to pay only a certain amount of money for the new car. How-

ever, once Joe "bit" and was psychologically committed to the purchase, the salesperson informed him that he would have to spend more. This manipulative technique is frequently effective.

I think we can see why low balling works if we look at it in connection . . . with the self in social behavior. A customer who agrees to make the purchase does two things: (1) He *activates his intentions.* . . . It's not enough just to expect or intend to do something. We also have to think *actively* of carrying out that behavior if the intention is to be translated into action (Leventhal, Singer, & Jones, 1965). Thus, the customer's decision to buy the product could start him moving psychologically toward that goal. (2) As Cialdini, Cacioppo, Bassett, and Miller (1978) have suggested, the decision makes the customer feel *personally committed* to the purchase. From our present point of view, we can say his failure to carry through might then reflect negatively on his self-image. "I agreed to do this and I should be consistent," he may tell himself.

Cialdini et al. (1978) have reported three experiments which testify to the effectiveness of the low-balling technique. These investigations were carried out in naturalistic and artificial settings. We'll discuss their last study, which provides a good example of low balling. Male and female undergraduates serving in the study to gain extra class credit were told that the research required them to take one of two different personality tests, and they were provided with a brief description of the tests. In two conditions (both analogs of the low-balling procedure) the students were informed that they would receive twice as much credit if they worked on one test (call it test A) rather than on the other. And one of these groups was also told the choice was up to the subjects. Needless to say, when the people in this group made their selection right after this, they overwhelmingly preferred test A. The subjects in the second condition had no choice and were instructed to work on test A. After the students in these two conditions had rated their impressions of the personality tests, the experi-

menter supposedly noticed that he had made a mistake and said he wouldn't be able to award the extra credit for test A. Then, whether or not they had been told the choice was up to them, all of the people in these conditions were instructed that they were free to work on either of the two tests. In a third, control condition the experimenter didn't say anything about extra credit for test A. Here too, the subjects were asked which test they wanted to take after they read the description of the tests.

The findings indicated the students typically wanted to carry through with the commitment they had voluntarily undertaken, even when the extra inducement used to win this commitment was withdrawn. Sixty-one percent of the subjects in the choice condition still agreed to do test A, as compared to only 42 percent of those in the no-choice group and 31 percent in the control condition.

Most of the students in the choice group evidently wanted to be consistent. They had freely agreed to carry out the given activity (they thought), and they went through with it. Their self-image would suffer if they changed their mind. Of course, many more subjects would have refused to honor this commitment if they believed they had been tricked into making their decision. In real life, people can stop such manipulation if they realize the salesperson's initial offer may simply be a trick to get them hooked on the line before the attractive inducement is withdrawn.

The Foot in the Door

Low balling is quite similar to another procedure used by salespeople and others. In this second technique the would-be influencer makes a small and fairly reasonable request in order to get a foot in the door. When the unknowing individual complies, the influencer then brings the real major request forward.

Two well-known field experiments by Jonathan Freedman and Scott Fraser (1966) illustrate how effective this procedure can be. In one of these investigations the experimenters started out with a small request. They asked housewives to install a small sign on their lawns urging motorists to drive carefully. Several weeks later, when other interviewers contacted the women and asked them to put up a monstrous sign with the same message, three-quarters of them complied. By contrast, fewer than one-fifth of another group of women who hadn't received the first request agreed to install the large, ugly sign. The researchers had increased their persuasiveness by getting subjects to do them a small favor (the foot in the door) and then asking for a much more substantial favor. This phenomenon isn't limited to cases in which the first and second requests are very similar, such as in putting up signs. Other findings indicate that the tendency to comply can generalize to quite different situations. Freedman and Fraser first asked another group of housewives to sign a petition in favor of keeping their state beautiful. Even though this initial request was different in both form (petition) and topic (state beauty), almost half of the women later agreed to put up the big, ugly safe-driving sign—as against less than one-fifth of the control group.

The foot-in-the-door technique can also be understood in terms of . . . the role of self-concept in social behavior. Freedman and Fraser suggest that when the women complied with the first request they thought of themselves as people who acted responsibly. They were people who did good things such as supporting highway safety or state beautification. When the interviewers came along with the second request, they essentially reminded the women of this self-conception and thus motivated them to live up to this image of themselves.

The issues need not be as socially desirable as those used by Freedman and Fraser for this technique to work. As long as we can induce people to think of themselves in a certain way, we theoretically should be able to have them try to live up to this self-conception. After

Snyder and Cunningham (1975) led some of their subjects to view themselves as people who agreed to reasonable requests, these subjects were inclined to go along with even larger requests of the same nature. The researchers telephoned a sample of Minneapolis residents, soliciting their participation in a telephone survey for a public service organization. Some were asked if they would answer 8 questions in this survey (small request), whereas others were requested to answer a long series of 50 questions. Two days later all of these persons were called back and a moderate favor was solicited for a different organization: Would they answer 30 questions? In comparison with control subjects, for whom no request was made, those who had complied to the previous small request were much more likely to agree (52 percent saying yes). The persons who had been asked to do the much more substantial favor, on the other hand, were much less inclined to comply (22 percent acquiescing). As you can see, as a result of going along with the first small request, the former subjects apparently thought of themselves as the kind of people who would do a reasonable favor for others; and they later acted in keeping with this self-concept, even though the second requester was supposedly someone else.

The findings also tell us something else. The initial request has to be small enough so that the first favor is granted, but not so small that the right kind of self-concept isn't established. If we ask people to do something trivial, they may well agree without viewing themselves as good persons; the action is just too easy. Seligman, Bush, and Kirsch (1976) showed this in a study similar to that of Snyder and Cunningham. Bush and Kirsch's telephone callers first asked for favors of various magnitudes, ranging from very easy to more difficult. Those who complied with the easiest requests weren't inclined to grant the second, more substantial favor two days later. When people grant the first favor, the compliance has to be significant enough that they think of themselves as having done something special.

This research reveals how people can be manipulated through their self-concepts. We often urge those we know to be true to themselves, as if they will become more independent if they live up to their image of themselves. The paradox is that a would-be influencer can alter people's self-concepts (at least temporarily and to some degree), so that people are exploited as they try to adhere to their self-concepts. The persuasion operates through people's desire to be true to themselves.

REFERENCES

Allen, V. L., and Levine, J. M. Consensus and conformity. *Journal of Experimental Psychology*, 1969, *5*, 389–399.

Allen, V. L., and Levine, J. M. Social support and conformity. The role of independent assessment of reality. *Journal of Experimental Social Psychology*, 1971, *7*, 48–58.

Arendt, H. *Eichmann in Jerusalem*. New York: Viking, 1963.

Asch, S. E. Effects of group pressures upon modification and distortion of judgments. In E. E. Maccoby, T. M. Newcomb, and E. L. Hartley (Eds.), *Readings in social psychology*. New York: Holt, Rinehart and Winston, 1958, 174–183.

Bandura, A. Vicarious processes: A case of no-trial learning. In L. Berkowitz (Ed.), *Advances in experimental social psychology, Vol. 2*. New York: Academic Press, 1965.

Bandura, A. *Principles of behavior modification*. New York: Holt, Rinehart and Winston, 1969.

Bandura, A. *Theories of modeling*. New York: Atherton Press, 1970.

Bandura, A., Blanchard, B., and Ritter, B. Relative efficacy of desensitization and modeling approaches for inducing behavioral, affective, and attitudinal changes. *Journal of Personality and Social Psychology*, 1969, *13*, 173–199.

Bandura, A., Grusec, J. E., and Menlove, F. L. Observational learning as a function of symbolization and incentive set. *Child Development*, 1966, *37*, 499–506.

Bandura, A., Ross, D., and Ross, S. A. A comparative test of the status envy, social power, and secondary reinforcement theories of identificatory learning. *Journal of Abnormal Social Psychology*, 1963, *67*, 527–534.

Berger, S. M. Conditioning through vicarious instigation. *Psychological Review*, 1962, *69*, 450–466.

Berkowitz, L. Group standards, cohesiveness and productivity. *Human Relations*, 1954, *7*, 509–519.

Berkowitz, L. Some determinants of impulsive aggression: The role of mediated associations with reinforcements for aggression. *Psychological Review*, 1974, *81*, 165–176.

Berkowitz, L., and Geen, R. G. Stimulus qualities of the target of aggression: A further study. *Journal of Personality and Social Psychology*, 1967, *5*, 364–368.

Berkowitz, L., Parke, R. D., Leyens, J-P., and West, S. G. Reactions of juvenile delinquents to "justified" and "less justified" movie violence. *Journal of Research in Crime and Delinquency*, 1974, *11*, 16–24.

Berkowitz, L., and Rawlings, E. Effects of film violence on inhibitions against subsequent aggression. *Journal of Abnormal and Social Psychology*, 1963, *66*, 405–412.

Berkowitz, L., and Walker, N. Laws and moral judgments. *Sociometry*, 1967, *30*, 410–422.

Blau, P. M. *Exchange and power in social life.* New York: Wiley, 1964.

Bryan, J. H. Children's reactions to helpers: Their money isn't where their mouths are. In J. Macaulay and L. Berkowitz (Eds.), *Altruism and helping behavior.* New York: Academic Press, 1970, 61–73.

Bussey, K., and Perry, D. G. Sharing reinforcement contingencies with a model: A social-learning analysis of similarity effects in imitation research. *Journal of Personality and Social Psychology*, 1976, *34*, 1168–1176.

Cialdini, R. B., Cacioppo, J. T., Bassett, R., and Miller, J. A. Low-ball procedure for producing compliance: Commitment then cost. *Journal of Personality and Social Psychology*, 1978, *36*, 463–476.

Craig, K. D., and Neidermeyer, H. Autonomic correlates of pain thresholds influenced by social modeling. *Journal of Personality and Social Psychology*, 1974, *29*, 246–252.

Craig, K. D., and Prkachin, K. M. Social modeling influences on sensory decision theory and psychophysiological indexes of pain. *Journal of Personality and Social Psychology*, 1978, *36*, 805–815.

Darley, J. M., Moriarty, T., Darley, S., and Berscheid, E. Increased conformity to a fellow deviant as a function of prior deviation. *Journal of Experimental Social Psychology*, 1974, *10*, 211–223.

Deutsch, M., and Gerard, H. B. A study of normative and informational social influences upon individual judgment. *Journal of Abnormal and Social Psychology*, 1955, *51*, 629–636.

Dittes, J. E., and Kelley, H. H. Effects of different conditions of acceptance upon conformity to group norms. *Journal of Abnormal and Social Psychology*, 1956, *53*, 100–107.

Evan, W., and Zelditch, M., Jr. A laboratory experiment on bureaucratic authority. *American Sociological Review*, 1961, *26*, 883–893.

Feshbach, N. D. Nonconformity to experimentally induced group norms of high-status versus low-status members. *Journal of Personality and Social Psychology*, 1967, *6*, 55–63.

Freedman, J. L., and Fraser, S. C. Compliance without pressure: The foot-in-the-door technique. *Journal of Personality and Social Psychology*, 1966, *4*, 195–202.

French, J. R. P., Jr., and Raven, B. The bases of social power. In D. Cartwright (Ed.), *Studies in social power.* Ann Arbor, Mich.: Institute for Social Research, 1959.

Grusec, J. E. Power and the internalization of self-denial. *Child Development*, 1971, *42*, 93–105.

Harvey, O. J., and Consalvi, C. Status and conformity to pressures in informal groups. *Journal of Abnormal and Social Psychology*, 1960, *60*, 182–187.

Hollander, E. P. Conformity, status and idiosyncracy credit. *Psychological Review*, 1958, *65*, 117–127.

Hollander, E. P., and Willis, R. H. Some current issues in the psychology of conformity and nonconformity. *Psychological Bulletin*, 1967, *68*, 62–76.

Homans, G. C. *Social behavior: Its elementary forms.* New York: Harcourt, Brace Jovanovich, 1961.

Hoyt, J. L. Effect of media violence "justification" on

aggression. *Journal of Broadcasting*, 1970, *16*, 455–464.

Jeffery, R. W. The influence of symbolic and motor rehearsal on observational learning. *Journal of Research in Personality*, 1976, *10*, 116–127.

Kelley, H. H. *Causal schemata and the attribution process.* Morristown, NJ.: General Learning Press, 1972.

Kelley, H. H. The process of causal attribution. *American Psychologist*, 1973, *28*, 107–128.

Kiesler, C. A., and Kiesler, S. B. *Conformity.* Reading, Mass.: Addison-Wesley, 1969.

Kiesler, C. A., and Pallak, M. S. Minority influence: The effect of majority reactionaries and defectors, and minority and majority compromisers, upon majority opinion and attraction. *European Journal of Social Psychology*, 1975, *5*, 237–256.

Kiesler, S. B. Preference for predictability or unpredictability as a mediator of reactions to norm violations. *Journal of Personality and Social Psychology*, 1973, *27*, 354–359.

Lefkowitz, M., Blake, R. R., and Mouton, J. S. Status factors in pedestrian violation of traffic signals. *Journal of Abnormal and Social Psychology*, 1955, *51*, 704–706.

Leventhal, H., Singer, R., and Jones, S. Effects of fear and specificity of recommendations upon attitudes and behavior. *Journal of Personality and Social Psychology*, 1965, *2*, 20–29.

Mann, J., Berkowitz, L., Sidman, J., Starr, S., and West, S. Satiation of the transient stimulating effects of erotic films. *Journal of Personality and Social Psychology*, 1974, *30*, 729–735.

Mann, J., Sidman, J., and Starr, S. Effects of erotic films on the sexual behavior of married couples. In *Technical report of the Commission on Obscenity and Pornography, Vol. 8.* Washington, D.C.: U.S. Government Printing Office, 1971, 170–254.

Mantell, D. M. The potential for violence in Germany. *Journal of Social Issues*, 1971, *27*, 101–112.

McDavid, J. W. Personality and situational determinants of conformity. *Journal of Abnormal and Social Psychology*, 1959, *58*, 241–246.

Meyer, T. P. Effects of viewing justified and unjustified real film violence on aggressive behavior. *Journal of Personality and Social Psychology*, 1972, *23*, 21–29.

Milgram, S. Nationality and conformity. *Scientific American*, 1961, *205*, 45–51.

Milgram, S. Behavioral study of obedience. *Journal of Abnormal and Social Psychology*, 1963, *67*, 371–378.

Milgram, S. Some conditions of obedience and disobedience to authority. *Human Relations*, 1965, *18*, 57–75.

Mischel, W., and Grusec, J. Determinants of the rehearsal and transmission of natural and aversive behaviors. *Journal of Personality and Social Psychology*, 1966, *3*, 197–203.

Morris, W. N., and Miller, R. S. The effects of consensus-breaking and consensus-preempting partners on reduction of conformity. *Journal of Experimental Social Psychology*, 1975, *11*, 215–223.

Moscovici, S., and Faucheux, C. Social influence, conformity bias, and the study of active minorities. In L. Berkowitz (Ed.), *Advances in experimental social psychology, Vol. 6.* New York: Academic Press, 1972, 149–202.

Moscovici, S., and Nemeth, C. Social influence. II. Minority influence. In C. Nemeth (Ed.), *Social psychology: Classic and contemporary integrations.* Chicago: Rand McNally, 1974.

Mugny, G. Negotiations, image of the other and the process of minority influence. *European Journal of Social Psychology*, 1975, *5*, 209–228.

Nemeth, C., Swedlund, M., and Kanki, B. Patterning of the minority's responses and their influence on the majority. *European Journal of Social Psychology*, 1974, *4*, 53–64.

Nemeth, C., and Wachtler, J. Creating the perceptions of consistency and confidence: A necessary condition for minority influence. *Sociometry*, 1974, *37*, 529–540.

Nemeth, C., Wachtler, J., and Endicott, J. Increasing the size of the minority: Some gains and some losses. *European Journal of Social Psychology*, 1977, *7*(1), 15–27.

Nisbet, R. A. *The social bond.* New York: Knopf, 1970.

Phillips, D. P. The influence of suggestion on suicide: Substantive and theoretical implications of the Werther effect. *American Sociological Review*, 1974, *39*, 340–354.

Phillips, D. P. Airplane accident fatalities increase after newspaper stories about murder and suicide. *Science*, 1978, *201*, 748–750.

Raven, B. H., and French, J. R. P., Jr. Legitimate power, coercive power, and observability in social influence. *Sociometry*, 1958, *21*, 83–97.

Seligman, C., Bush, M., and Kirsch, K. Relationship between compliance in the foot-in-the-door paradigm and size of the first request. *Journal of Personality and Social Psychology,* 1976, *33,* 517–520.

Sherif, M. *The psychology of social norms.* New York: Harper & Row, 1936.

Shirer, W. L. *The rise and fall of the third reich.* New York: Simon and Schuster, 1960.

Snyder, M., and Cunningham, M. R. To comply or not comply: Testing the self-perception explanation of the "foot-in-the-door" phenomenon. *Journal of Personality and Social Psychology,* 1975, *31,* 64–67.

Spitzer, C. E., and Davis, J. H. Mutual social influence in dynamic groups. *Social Psychology,* 1978, *41,* 24–33.

Tarde, G. *Penal philosophy.* Boston: Little, Brown, 1912.

Thibaut, J. W., and Strickland, L. H. Psychological set and social conformity. *Journal of Personality,* 1956, *25,* 115–129.

Tilker, H. A. Socially responsible behavior as a function of observer responsibility and victim feedback. *Journal of Personality and Social Psychology,* 1970, *14,* 95–100.

Tolman, C. W. The role of the companion in social facilitation of animal behavior. In E. C. Simmel, R. A. Hoppe, and G. A. Milton (Eds.), *Social facilitation and imitative behavior.* Boston: Allyn and Bacon, 1968, 33–54.

Wahrman, R. High status, deviance and sanctions. *Sociometry,* 1970, *33,* 485–504.

Weber, M. *The theory of social and economic organization.* New York: Oxford University Press, 1947.

Wilson, R. S. Personality patterns, source attractiveness, and conformity. *Journal of Personality,* 1960, *28,* 186–199.

Leadership

Terry Connolly

Of all the subjects covered by organizational behavior, leadership is perhaps the most frustrating. We see examples of what we believe to be good or bad leadership around us every day. Sports teams play well or badly, and it seems obvious that it has something to do with the coach or manager. Project groups come up with good or bad designs, and it seems obvious that it has something to do with the project leader. Orchestras play well or badly, apparently as a result of the conductor. Whole corporations raise their profits, or head towards bankruptcy, as chief executives come and go. Leadership, in short, seems to affect every area of life, and in a rather clear-cut way.

Yet, when we sit down to digest what is known about this interesting phenomenon, we come up with a complex and unsatisfactory picture. There is a mountain of research—literally thousands of studies—looking at leadership in all sorts of contexts, from leaders of nations to leaders of small discussion groups, from sports teams to juries. Despite this enormous effort, we still lack satisfactory answers to most of the key questions: What exactly is effective leadership? Can we select, or train, people who will be effective as leaders? How much of a difference does leadership actually make? Can we learn to become more effective as leaders?

For each of these questions we have intriguing, if partial, answers. The available research suggests that leaders do, in fact, make

some difference, though not as much as we might expect. We may be able to raise our own effectiveness as leaders, but, again, not as much as we might hope. We are a long way short of an understanding of effective leadership that would allow us to be effective in every situation, every time. At best, we can hope to raise our batting averages a few points, certainly not to hit home runs off every pitch.

In this chapter, we will summarize some of the major themes in current leadership research, and try to identify those areas that offer some hope of improving our own leadership skills.

APPOINTED AND EMERGENT LEADERS

People become leaders in one of two ways. The most obvious way is by appointment: if you are the *head* of the applied physics branch, the *chair* of the grievance committee, or the *captain* of the lacrosse team, your title indicates that you hold the job of leadership. It is in your job description that you will act as the leader. However, there is a second way by which people become leaders: they emerge as the group operates. In any classroom discussion, someone commonly takes on the role of discussion leader—making notes on the blackboard, directing the traffic of who speaks when, proposing action plans, and making summaries. No one has to appoint such a per-

From *Scientists, Engineers, and Organizations* by Terry Connolly, copyright © 1983. Reprinted by permission of the author.

son. He or she just emerges, generally with at least the tacit consent of the group, to handle these necessary functions. There is no guarantee that the appointed leader and the emergent leader will be the same person, although that is clearly a happy situation when it happens. (In fact, one basic idea of simple democracy is to achieve this end: people choose as official, or appointed, leader someone who has already demonstrated informal, or emergent, leadership skills.)

Which of the "power bases" discussed in Chapter 6 does each of these leaders have available? Appointed leaders have formal, legitimate power; emergent leaders may not. Appointed leaders also have, at least in theory, a wide range of reward and coercive resources on which to draw—pay, promotion, work assignments, firing, etc.—although these may be severely limited by formal procedures or union rules. Emergent leaders also have some reward and coercive powers; their opinions and judgments are valued. A pat on the back from such a person may be a powerful reward and a harsh word a powerful punishment. However, their most important power resource is their referent and expert power, resources that may not be available to the appointed leader at all. Thus, emergent leaders may, in fact, be in fairly powerful positions, while the official, appointed leader may be relatively powerless.

Who becomes an emergent leader? Studies comparing emergent and appointed leaders suggest that:

1. *Overall intelligence is not a large factor.* Both sorts of leaders seem generally to be at or a little above the average intelligence of the group (Stogdill, 1948).
2. *Social skills matter.* Emergent leaders have good social skills much more often than appointed leaders do (Stogdill, 1948).
3. *Situational factors make a difference in the emergence of a leader.* Having strong skills in the specific task facing the group makes emergent leadership more likely (Hollander,

1964; Stogdill, 1974). Good athletes tend to emerge as leaders on the sports field; good scholars tend to emerge as leaders in class discussion.

4. *Some apparently trivial aspects of the situation can affect leadership emergence.* Seating arrangements can make a difference, with those sitting at the ends of a table more likely to emerge as leaders than those sitting on the sides (Strodtbeck and Hook, 1961). Similarly, being at the hub of a communication net makes leadership emergence more likely (Leavitt, 1951).

No single type of person regularly emerges as a leader. Rather, it is a matter of being in the right place, at the right time, with the right skills (both task related and social). This conclusion will recur in the remainder of this chapter, as we turn from the question of who becomes a leader to who becomes an *effective* leader.

EFFECTIVE AND INEFFECTIVE LEADERS

Given that a group has a leader, appointed or emergent, what determines whether or not that leader will be effective? By "effective," we mean here that the group has a task to do or a problem to solve. If the task is performed well under Leader A, and poorly under Leader B, we shall rate Leader A as more effective than Leader B. However, we shall add the stipulation that effective task performance is not achieved at the expense of the long-term viability of the group. A leader who achieves good task results at the cost of low member satisfaction, high internal levels of conflict, or other signs of "wearing out" of the group will not be rated as effective.

A great deal of early leadership research was aimed at identifying personal characteristics, "leadership traits," that distinguished effective leaders from ineffective ones. Are effective leaders more intelligent than ineffective ones? Superior orators? Taller? Of a higher-class upbringing? Each of these, and dozens of others, have been investigated, but the overall results have been meager and confusing. Stogdill (1948), reviewing well over a hundred studies available at the time, summarized his results as follows:

> The findings suggest that leadership is not a matter of passive status, or of the mere possession of some combination of traits. It appears rather to be a working relationship among members of a group, in which the leader acquires status through active participation and demonstration of his capacity for carrying cooperative tasks through to completion. Significant aspects of this capacity for organizing and expediting cooperative effort appear to be intelligence, alertness to the needs and motives of others, and insight into situations, further reinforced by such habits as responsibility, initiative, persistence, and self-confidence. (Stogdill, 1948: p. 69)

In short, it is not just a matter of who you are, but of what you do, and what the situation demands.

Frustration with the "leader trait" approach led to greater research interest in analysis of leader behavior, of situations, and of how these fit together to affect effectiveness. One aspect of leader behavior that has been extensively studied is the extent to which the leader allows participation of the subordinates in making decisions. For example, Tannenbaum and Schmidt (1958) suggested a scale of participation from boss centered to subordinate centered:

Boss-centered leadership   Subordinate-centered leadership

0   1   2   3   4   5   6   7   8   9   10

On this scale, an entirely boss-centered approach (scale value 0) is when the boss makes a decision alone, and merely announces it to the group. In the middle range are such approaches as presenting a tentative decision to the group for suggestions or approval. Scale value 10 indicates an approach where the leader essentially turns the problem over to the group, for them to decide within limits set by the boss. Tannenbaum and Schmidt discuss the factors that might lead one to choose a particular point on this scale to operate. Forces in the leader, forces in the subordinates, and forces in the situation are all considered. However, this discussion is largely paralleled by a more refined model we shall consider in a moment, so we need not review the details here.

An interesting sidelight: Tannenbaum and Schmidt titled their paper "How to Choose a Leadership Pattern." The implication is that there is a choice to be made; moving away from the idea of a fixed set of traits, leaders are thought of as able to act in a variety of different ways. This is at least a questionable assumption. Probably most of us have some region of the spectrum at which we operate most comfortably. In many organizations, subordinates similarly have strong expectations about how leaders should behave. In military organizations, for example, officers' behavior is expected to be at the low end of the scale. In universities, in contrast, deans are expected to create at least an appearance of strong group involvement in such major decisions as hiring and promoting faculty. In both settings, leaders who violate expectations may face difficulties. Thus, both the setting and our personal limitations restrict the leadership styles we may use.

A somewhat more complex way of describing leader behavior emerged from extensive research conducted by a group at Ohio State University (Fleishman and Peters, 1962). From a very large number of measures of particular leader activities, the Ohio State group identified and labelled two important dimensions of how leaders actually behave:

1. *Consideration:* The extent to which the leader is considerate of the subordinates'

feelings, respects their ideas, and develops mutually trusting working relationships with them.

2. *Initiating structure:* The extent to which the leader clarifies and defines the subordinates' work roles, relationships, channels of communication, and ways of getting the job done.

Descriptions of leader behavior in terms of "consideration" and "initiating structure" have come to be the hallmark of Ohio State leadership studies.

Two comments are needed here. First, the two dimensions are considered independent of one another, so that a particular leader may be high on both, low on both, or high on one and low on the other. Second, as has become clear from later research, the two dimensions do not capture all of what leaders do. The dimensions focus on the way the leader sets up the internal workings of the group, in terms of task-oriented ways of operating (initiating structure) and interpersonal ways of operating (consideration). They do not consider important external matters such as the leader's dealings with superiors, with other work groups, or with suppliers of raw materials or necessary information. In short, they describe some important features of the internal operations of the group, as they are affected by the leader.

MODELS OF EFFECTIVE LEADERSHIP

Numerous models of how to be an effective leader have been proposed by different researchers. It is probably fair to say that, at this point, no one of them has emerged as the clear winner in terms of producing the most reliable high-quality leaders. (This, of course, produces heated partisan conflict at meetings of leadership researchers!) Several of the models have been developed into elaborate and expensive training programs, which further complicates dispassionate appraisal of relative strengths and weaknesses.

Virtually all models that are still receiving serious research attention and development are what might be called "situational," "diagnostic," or "contingency" models. That is, they all argue that an effective leader must first undertake a diagnosis of the situation in which (s)he is to operate, and only then select a course of action. Included in the diagnostic phase are different aspects of the situation: characteristics of the task, of the subordinates, and of the leader. Different models suggest different lists of alternatives from which the leader is to choose. Some emphasize degree of participation, others emphasize behaviors in terms of the Ohio State dimensions, and others suggest alternatives of a quite different sort. We shall review a sampling of several of the currently more popular models.

Fiedler's Contingency Model

Fiedler (1967, 1976) has developed a leadership model that has some of the aspects of the old "leadership traits" ideas. In his model, effectiveness is determined by an interaction between a personal characteristic of the leader and a rating of the overall favorableness of the situation in which (s)he is to lead. The personal characteristic is considered to be relatively fixed, so the leader's key diagnostic task is to weigh up the situation and decide whether or not it fits with his or her personality. If it does not, the leader should change the situation or possibly get a replacement who fits the situation better.

The specifics of this model may be summarized as follows:

Diagnostic phase.

Assessing situational favorability. Three factors affect how favorable the situation is for the leader: leader-member relations, task struc-

	Highly favorable	SITUATIONAL FAVORABILITY					Highly unfavorable	
	1	2	3	4	5	6	7	8
Leader-member relations	Good				Poor			
Task structure	High		Low		High		Low	
Position power	Strong	Weak	Strong	Weak	Strong	Weak	Strong	Weak

FIGURE 1   *Determinants of Situational Favorability in Fiedler's Model*

ture, and leader position power. Generally, it is easiest to be a leader when: (1) the group respects, accepts, and trusts the leader; (2) the task is clear and well structured, so everyone knows what to do and how to do it; and (3) the leader has real power (to hire and fire, give raises, or promote). If all three factors are positive, the leader is in a most favorable situation; if all are negative, the situation is most unfavorable. In mixed situations leader-member relations are most important, and position power least important, in determining situational favorability. Figure 1 illustrates this idea.

Assessing the leader's personality. Fiedler's model also assesses the characteristic of the leader known as his or her "Least Preferred Co-worker" (LPC) score. The LPC score is derived from asking the leader to rate the person with whom (s)he has been least able to work well. The questionnaire simply lists sixteen pairs of adjectives, such as:

Uncooperative	1 2 3 4 5 6 7 8	Cooperative
Inefficient	1 2 3 4 5 6 7 8	Efficient
Boring	1 2 3 4 5 6 7 8	Interesting

People who tend to rate their least preferred co-worker low on these dimensions, called "low LPC" people, seem to be showing a pretty harsh, judgmental feeling about the co-worker they are imagining, while those who score high seem to be more forgiving and people oriented. There is some dispute about just what the LPC

measures and whether it really is a stable personality characteristic. Fiedler suggests that it is a measure of whether one is primarily task motivated or relationship motivated. He allows that an individual can be both, but that one or the other characteristic is primary and will emerge in pressure situations. Roughly, then, low LPC scores suggest that the leader is primarily task oriented, while high LPC scores suggest that (s)he is more person oriented.

Effective Choices.   The core of Fiedler's model is the evidence he has accumulated that there is a relationship among situational favorability, the leader's LPC, and group performance. This evidence indicates that:

1. Low LPC leaders do well in the more favorable situations (sectors 1, 2, and 3 in the diagram) and in the least favorable situation (sector 8).
2. High LPC leaders do well in the moderately favorable situations (sectors 4 and 5).
3. There is no relationship between LPC and effectiveness in the remaining two sectors (6 and 7).

Just why these relationships seem to hold is a matter for speculation, but the practical implications are reasonably clear. First, you need to find out what your LPC score is. In Fiedler's view, there is not much you can do to change this, at least in the short run, so to be effective you either have to take on only those leadership situations where your LPC fits, or to try to change the situation into one that fits. This focus on manipulating the situation to fit the leader is unique to Fiedler's approach. Most of the other currently popular models tend to emphasize the relative flexibility of the leader's behavior, treating the situation as basically fixed. Fiedler reminds us that selecting, or changing, the situation to fit our styles is an option that should not be neglected.

Fiedler's model has been criticized on various grounds, including questions as to what exactly the LPC measures, whether or not LPC is stable over time, just *how* it is that LPC and situation interact, and how precisely situations can be diagnosed (see, e.g., Ashour, 1973). In response, Fiedler continues to turn out studies supporting his model and to train managers how to achieve a good match between their LPCs and their situations. He has achieved a measure of practical success, while leaving important questions unresolved. His major contributions have been to force us to look seriously at the situation and whether it can be manipulated. He has also reminded us that the easy assumption that we can change our behaviors readily to fit leadership requirements may not be true.

The Vroom-Yetton Model

The Vroom-Yetton model of leadership (Vroom and Yetton, 1973) focuses on a single aspect of the leader's behavior: the extent to which the leader shares decision-making power with his or her subordinates. "Power sharing" is similar to "degree of participation" in the Tannenbaum and Schmidt scale, discussed earlier. Vroom and Yetton consider the leader as choosing from five possible alternatives along this scale:

Autocratic:
AI: Leader solves the problem alone, using available information.

AII: Leader solves the problem alone, after collecting necessary information from subordinates.

Collaborative:
CI: Leader consults with subordinates individually, gets their ideas and suggestions, then decides alone.

CII: As CI, but consultation takes place in a group meeting.

Group:
GII: Leader chairs group meeting aimed at reaching a consensus decision.

The model suggests that effective leadership results when a suitable style is chosen from this list in light of the requirements of the situation. The diagnostic phase consists of a series of questions aimed at discovering what these requirements are.

Diagnostic phase. In somewhat simplified form, the five key diagnostic questions in the Vroom-Yetton model are:

1. *Is decision quality important?* A decision may be unimportant either because the stakes are small, or because all the alternatives are of equal value. For example, I may not care much where the company picnic is held or who is to represent us at some social function. On the other hand, the choice of the new research director may be very important; but, if the choice is between three excellent candidates, I may still not care which one is chosen.

2. *Do I have adequate information?* Care is needed in making this assessment. We all tend to overestimate our own expertise compared to our subordinates'. A realistic judgment is needed as to whether or not the leader has adequate information.

3. *Is the problem structured?* If information gathering is needed, do I, the leader, know what the necessary information is, and where it can be found?

257

4. *Is there a problem with acceptance of a solution?* This question covers two issues. First, is it essential that the subordinates accept the decision? Second, if it is essential, will they accept a decision made autocratically by me? The leader has an acceptance problem only if acceptance is essential, and autocratic decisions will be resisted. In these circumstances, involving the group may be necessary for effective implementation of the solution.

5. Do my subordinates share my goals? If I delegate the decision to my subordinates, will they use the same choice criteria as I would? If my subordinates share my goals, I will be more prepared to share my power with them than I would otherwise be.

    The leader's answers to these five questions provide a diagnosis of the situation. The remainder of the Vroom-Yetton model links this diagnosis to a choice of one of the five styles listed earlier (AI, AII, CI, CII, and GII). In many situations, the diagnostic questions eliminate some style choices but leave more than one in the "feasible set." A choice can be made from the "feasible set" on other grounds, which we will discuss later.

Effective choices.   It will be convenient to consider three different types of problem, defined by the answers to the first two diagnostic questions listed above. If decision quality does not matter, we shall refer to the problem as a "Type 1." If quality matters and the leader has the relevant information, the problem is "Type 2." If quality matters and the leader does not have the relevant information, the problem is "Type 3."

    Type 1 (quality not a problem): If I, as a leader, do not care which solution is picked, other issues such as availability of information and problem structure do not matter. My only question concerns decision acceptance. If acceptance is not a problem, all five decision styles are still open to me. If, however, acceptance is important, and the group will resist an autocratic decision, then a fully participative style (Style GII) would be the best approach. In summary, for these problems, the leader's decision tree is simple:

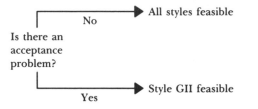

    Type 2 (quality matters; leader has relevant information): Since I have the information, I *can* make the decision if I wish to. On the other hand, some degree of delegation might help acceptance. However, I care about solution quality, so I have to consider whether or not the subordinates share my goals before I turn the problem over to them. This gives four options for these types of problem:

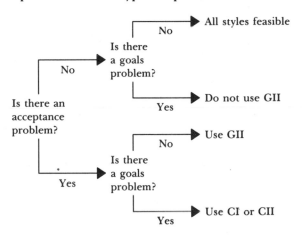

    Type 3 (quality matters; leader does not have relevant information):

a. *Structured problem:* Type 3 problems are the trickiest. Decision quality matters, and the leader has to involve the group somehow, because (s)he does not have the necessary information to make a good decision alone. AI is precluded: I have to consult with the group. But the options leaving me a good deal of control (AII or CI) are still open, since I know where to go for information. My choice, then, turns on the acceptance and goals questions as before:

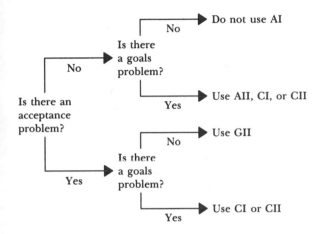

b. *Unstructured problem:* Here we have the same difficulties as above with the extra wrinkle that I do not know where to go for the information. This cuts further my list of options, eliminating both of the modestly participative approaches AII and CI. Striking these, we are left with:

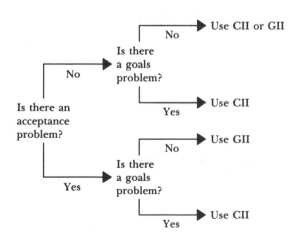

Laying out all possibilities in this way may seem complicated, but the underlying logic is simple. We start with all five possible decision styles and eliminate options as we work through the list of diagnostic questions. If I cannot make the decision on my own, AI is out. If I do not care about what is decided, then I only have to worry about possible problems with acceptance by the subordinates; and this is generally helped by involving them in making the decision. If I need the group's input to make a good decision, I can still be fairly non-participative if I know where to go for information. If not, I am forced to fairly high participation (CII or GII). Finally, turning the problem over to the group is risky if I suspect they will apply criteria counter to mine (or the organization's) in making the decision. If our goals clash, GII is out.

Note that a range of approaches is feasible for several problem types. How do we make this choice? Here Vroom (1976) suggests a final strategy consideration: the trade-off between time and people development. In general, the more participative the decision process, the longer it takes. On the other hand, decision participation allows subordinates to develop their problem-solving skills, to become informed, and to feel more involved in the organization's affairs. When several decision styles are feasible, one can choose on the basis of a tradeoff between time (both speed and work hours) and people development. Thus, the same decision that, in an emergency, has to be handled by style AI might, in more leisurely times, be handled by style GII. Again, the situation shapes the preferred decision approach.

Does the Vroom-Yetton method work? Do leaders following its recommendations really lead more effectively? There is not yet any convincing evidence that they do, though there are some encouraging signs. Vroom (1976) asked managers to describe decisions they felt they had made particularly well—or particularly badly. The decisions reported as successful tended to have been made by procedures that the model would have recommended; the unsuccessful decisions more often were made by methods the model would advise against. In general, managers seemed to vary their styles less from one situation to another than the model would recommend. For example, a manager might use only AII and CI, never using the other styles at all. Vroom also found that managers tend to get subordinate input more often, and delegate authority less often, than the model calls for.

In summary, the Vroom-Yetton model is a complex version of a "contingency theory" of leadership behavior, focusing particularly on the situational factors that should influence the leader's choice of a level of subordinate participation. The logic it uses has some solid support in the research literature, and the model as a whole seems to identify high-percentage approaches, as reported by working managers. There is not, however, any solid body of evidence at this point that leaders trained in these procedures actually end up with better decision processes. The model continues to be developed and may provide more reliable evidence of its soundness in the future.

Consideration/Structuring Models

The Ohio State dimensions of leader behavior—consideration and task structuring—have formed the basis for a number of models of effective leadership. Perhaps the simplest is that popularized by Blake and Mouton (1964), the managerial grid. The basis of the managerial grid is simply the replacement of the two dimensions of *behavior* with measures of a leader's *orientation;* that is, tendencies to act in certain ways, rather than reports of actual behaviors. This allows one to describe a range of management styles:

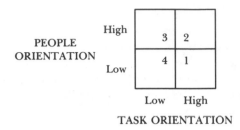

A manager whose style falls in Quadrant 1 is strongly task oriented and not at all people oriented: the tough, cool, all-business taskmaster. A manager who falls in Quadrant 3, in contrast (strong people orientation, low task orientation), would be more the warm, friendly "nice-guy" type. (Blake and Mouton scale each dimension from 1 to 9 so that, for example, the two styles just mentioned would be referred to as "1,9" and "9,1" managers, respectively.)

The basis of managerial grid training is not really a contingency model at all. It simply aims to train all managers, regardless of task and situation, to operate in Quadrant 2, the "high-high" or "9,9" style. This may, in fact, be the most generally useful of the four styles. However, there is serious question whether it is universally appropriate. For example, in simple, routine, high-speed tasks such as those commonly found in manufacturing, Quadrant 1 (task-only) might be more effective. Conversely, a leader of a highly productive group of R&D professionals might be most effective in Quadrant 4, doing little on either task or people dimensions. In short, there is no difficulty finding studies in which "high-high" leaders are effective, nor is there any trouble finding counterexamples.

A review by Kerr and his colleagues (1974) attempted to bring some order into this mixed evidence. In general, leaders who are high on structure tend to have more productive groups, with lower satisfaction. This fits the stereotype of the taskmaster: the work gets done, but grudgingly. Highly considerate leaders tend to have happier groups, but often at the expense of production. (These findings seem to underlie the "myth of the high-high manager"; leaders high on both dimensions could be expected to have the best of both worlds, a group that is both productive and satisfied.) However, these general tendencies are moderated by a number of situational factors:

1. High structuring by the leader seems to have an effect only when such structuring is not already provided by the work. For example, if the task is highly ambiguous or the group members are intolerant of ambiguity, structuring by the leader helps both task performance and satisfaction. If these features are not present, leader structuring does not help performance, and reduces satisfaction.
2. Considerate behavior by the leader improves satisfaction only if the organization is a generally considerate place. Considerate behavior is ineffective in cold, hostile, or inconsiderate organizations.
3. Workers on inherently interesting jobs react less to either dimension of leader activity than do those on boring jobs.

There are, then, fairly clear exceptions to the rule that high-high is the universal best style. Structuring behavior helps performance only if the task is unstructured. Consideration helps satisfaction only if there is no adequate alternative source of satisfaction (such as interesting work). Providing either structure or consideration when not needed is unhelpful and may actively hinder. Studies suggesting that high-high leaders are often effective may thus tell us more about the work people do than about good leadership: if most people are working in ill-structured, uninteresting jobs, high-high leaders may be effective; structuring helps productivity and consideration in-

troduces at least some payoffs interpersonally, which increases satisfaction.

An interesting model, also based on the Ohio State dimensions of leader behavior, has been advanced by Hersey and Blanchard (1969) under the title of "life cycle" or "maturity" theory. Although research support for this approach is not strong, the model provides a clear example of the diagnostic approach we have been exploring, and we therefore review it briefly here. In this approach, the central diagnostic task the leader must face is assessing the "maturity" of the group to the specific task. By "maturity" they mean a rather precise assessment of three things:

1. The extent to which the group has the skills necessary for the task
2. The extent to which the group is ready to take responsibility for accomplishing the task
3. The extent to which the group finds the task inherently satisfying.

A group low on all three characteristics is scored as "immature" while a high score on the three dimensions reflects "maturity."

Life-cycle theory asserts that effective leadership consists of moving successively through the four quadrants of the structure/consideration grid in response to the growing maturity of the group to the task. As an illustration, Hersey and Blanchard suggest an approach to teaching a small child a new skill, e.g., tying shoelaces. Suppose that the initial assessment is that the child is completely "immature" to this task, low on skills, taking responsibility, and inherent interest. What is required, they argue, is an "all task" approach (Quadrant 1 in the earlier diagram). The parent demonstrates, allows the child to practice the skill, and instructs. As the child starts to get the hang of it, the leader (parent) rewards the child with praise and encouragement, maintaining task focus as well (Quadrant 2, or "high-high" behavior). As the child progresses, the parent phases out task instruction, maintaining encouragement (Quadrant 3), and, finally, with the child fully "mature" to this particular task, the parent turns it over to the child entirely (Quadrant 4). Thus the term "life-cycle": the leader's overall task is to move the group or subordinate to full maturity, at which point the leader's task is complete (see Figure 2).

This model is less well developed than several of those we have examined and solid research support is scanty, but it is a useful reminder that the situational assessment demanded by all the models is not a one-time thing. Over time the situation is likely to change, so that new leadership styles are demanded for effectiveness. Leadership style used at one time influences the situation at a later time. Achieving a match between situation and style is a dynamic, continuous task.

The Ohio State dimensions of initiating structure and consideration are two of the best-researched areas of leadership. One or the other, or both, of these dimensions have been found to be associated with leadership effectiveness in many studies, though not always in

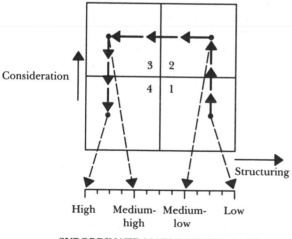

SUBORDINATE MATURITY TO TASK
FIGURE 2. Life-Cycle Theory

the same way. The popular managerial grid training approach has emphasized a universal practice of "high-high" leadership; the evidence suggests that such a style is often, but not always, effective. Other readings of the evidence have led to subtler, more complex situational models, taking into account the nature of the task, the organizational climate, and the changes over time in the maturity of the group to the task.

Path-Goal Theory

The last and in many ways the most satisfactory of the theories of effective leadership we shall consider here is known as path-goal theory (Evans, 1970; House and Mitchell, 1974). This theory draws on much of the earlier research work. It is arranged so that it may be continuously refined and extended as new evidence comes in; and it is firmly based on a well-studied motivation theory, the expectancy theory we examined in an earlier chapter.

The core idea of path-goal theory is that effective leadership consists in increasing the subordinates' motivation toward, and satisfaction in, the performance of their tasks. The leader's task is twofold: "increasing the number and kinds of personal payoffs to subordinates for work-goal attainment" (i.e., the "goals" element), and "making paths to these payoffs easier to travel by clarifying the paths, reducing road blocks and pitfalls, and increasing the opportunities for personal satisfaction en route" (i.e., the "path" element) (House and Mitchell, 1974).

The underlying motivational theory is a version of expectancy theory. It can be sketched as follows:

Engage in → Exert effort → Perform → Receive
the activity   in the activity   successfully   extrinsic
                                               rewards

As before, we assume that people do things they believe to be in their interests. That is, people are more likely to engage in a particular work activity if it is intrinsically interesting or they expect it to lead to other valued payoffs. Similarly, they will be more likely to exert effort in the activity if (1) doing so is likely to lead to good performance and (2) good performance is likely to lead to valued payoffs for them. Path-goal theory argues that the leader has a role to play at each stage in making it more likely that subordinates will choose the paths the leader desires. Let us examine the process step-by-step, and see what the leader might be able to do, and when it is likely to work.

How can the leader make it more likely that the follower will engage in the desired activity?

The leader's prime goal here is to achieve a good match between the individual and the job, either by good initial selection of recruits, or by improved job design or job training.

How can the leader make it more likely that the follower will exert effort in the desired activity?

First, the leader must make it clear just what the desired activity *is* (i.e., path clarification). Clarity may be achieved by instruction and monitoring. Participation in decision making may also help. By participating, the subordinate learns more about the reasons underlying particular path choices, how the activities fit together, and how the achievement of others is dependent on his or her performance. Second, the leader must help the subordinate see the connection between the activities to be performed and the goals to be achieved. Helping the subordinate set clear personal achievement goals, and expressing confidence that (s)he will attain them, both help motivation. The leader can also help by setting priorities and resolving role conflicts. Again, personal support and consideration may help in reducing any tensions and anxieties the subordinate may experience.

All this is aimed at (1) clarifying the subordinate's "path" (i.e., the activities toward which effort is to be directed), and (2) making that path more attractive than others (such as exerting lower levels of effort, or effort directed elsewhere). However, the critical question remains: does the subordinate see effort directed along this path as leading to important personal rewards?

How can the leader make it more likely that the subordinate's efforts will lead to valued rewards?

The focus here is on the subordinate's belief in the connection between effort, successful performance and valued rewards. The leader has various options in trying to enhance this belief. First, the subordinate must feel that successful performance is properly measured. (S)he must receive feedback on how well (s)he is doing, and must agree that the performance measures are reasonable. Second, the subordinate must believe (and it must, in the long run, be true) that achieving good performance is the best-rewarded outcome.

Again, the leader has several options. Training, coaching, and skills development make it more likely that effort will, in fact, lead to improved performance. For most of us there is nothing more frustrating than trying hard at a task and persistently failing because we do not have the necessary skills. Second, good performance feedback requires both that the leader is sufficiently well informed for the assessment to be accurate, and that the leader has the skills to give feedback effectively. The leader must be clear about what exactly the subordinate needs to do to improve performance, and must be non-threatening and supportive in communicating this to the subordinate. Being told that one is performing poorly is threatening, and we tend to close our ears and act defensively. The skilled leader must be able to give feedback without hitting this stone wall.

Finally, the leader has to deliver. Rewards valued by the subordinate must actually result from good performance. This sounds obvious but it is frequently forgotten. For example, across-the-board pay raises violate this requirement, since good and bad performance get rewarded equally. Offering promotions or extra responsibility is not likely to be an effective incentive for a subordinate who does not want them. Indeed, it may be a real disincentive to good performance. To be effective, the rewards offered must be (1) contingent on good performance, and (2) valued by the subordinate.

As we saw in our earlier discussion of motivation (Chapter 4), the leader is not limited to formal organizational rewards such as pay or promotion. (S)he can also provide interpersonal rewards, such as praise and approval; social rewards, such as group recognition and esteem; and outsider feedback (e.g., by establishing client relationships, so that the final impact of good performance is more clearly visible to the subordinate). To the extent that goals are set participatively, good performance may be *self*-rewarding, since the subordinate then feels the goals are personal ones. Leaders who monopolize the limelight may cut off members of their group from receiving rewards in the form of credit or recognition for good work. Allowing credit where it is due is likely both to increase the subordinate's satisfaction in good performance and enhance the leader's reputation for fair and considerate behavior. And a leader who exerts upward influence in the organization is more likely to be able to secure for the group and its members both the resources they need for performing well, and the rewards that such achievement merits.

Note, again, how the various pieces fit together. The basic diagnostic question, coming directly from the expectancy model, is: "What is needed here before this individual will perform well, and feel good about it?" To answer that question, the leader must be sensitive to the differences in interests, abilities, and goals of the group members. Offering large pay bonuses to an individual who lacks the necessary skill to perform, or offering a promotion to a person who would rather have time off, or presenting a weekly "best worker" award that the group regards as insulting, trivial, or not given on merit—all these suggest a leader who either is not clear what (s)he is doing, or who is out of touch with the individuals in the group. The requirement that leaders provide valued, contingent rewards is simply stated, but highly complex to bring about in practice.

OTHER ISSUES

None of the models we have reviewed gives a completely satisfactory account of all the evidence. However, in addition to the debates about which model best fits the data, there are three other, perhaps more fundamental, matters we should mention briefly.

What Causes What?

Each of the approaches we have discussed implies that what the leader does (or is) affects the way the group operates. We should bear in mind that influence can, and probably does, work the other way: the way the group operates influences what the leader does. For example, if your group works well, you may well adopt a looser, friendlier style of supervision than you would if you saw them working poorly. Lowin and Craig (1968) demonstrated exactly this, by having people believe that they were supervising another individual (actually a stooge) who sometimes performed well, sometimes badly. When the stooge performed badly, the supervisors became less considerate, initiated structure more, and supervised more closely. Evidence such as this suggests that followers influence leaders, as well as vice versa. Most teachers, for example, would agree that the class shapes their behavior as much as they shape the class's.

Leaders or Situations?

We have noted that part of what the leader does can be seen as making up for something that is lacking in the situation. For example, if performance feedback is built into the job, there is no need for the leader to provide it. If the job is highly structured (for example, repetitive assembly-line work), then there is no need for the leader to structure the task any further. Indeed, the subordinate may resent it if (s)he does. This substitutability of leader and situation may account for many of the research problems. Sometimes considerate leadership helps, other times it does not. Perhaps the situation is already providing what is needed in the latter case. Steve Kerr and John Jermier (1978) have recently started work on a systematic review of such "substitutes for leadership." Their work certainly resolves some of the puzzles found in previous studies, and promises to enrich our broad understanding of when particular leader actions are, and are not, likely to make an impact.

Is Leadership Real?

Perhaps the broadest attack on the whole leadership notion has been proposed by Calder (1977), who suggests, essentially, that the whole thing is an attributional error, like those we reviewed in Chapter 3. Groups and individuals notice that their work is sometimes better, sometimes worse, and look around for a "cause" to which they can attribute the change. Since everyone believes that leaders have something to do with group performance, we "attribute" the performance change to the leader's actions. Leaders buy into the same belief and so does the organization, since it needs some justification for appointing some people

as leaders, and needs to believe that it is in control of the situation. Thus if the shared belief is that, say, considerate leadership is most effective, the data will tend to bear it out. Conversely, if authoritarian leadership is believed to be effective, the data will confirm this. In this light, leadership behavior, group reactions to different leaders, and the hiring and firing of leaders can all be understood more as a complex ritual of confirming certain beliefs about leaders and their importance than as anything to do with real direct effects of leaders on followers. If we all believe that leaders matter, they will. And if we think good leadership is of a certain kind, the data will "prove" us right. It is worth considering the ritual of firing managers of losing baseball clubs in this light. You cannot fire the whole team, but something has to be done to reassure us that the club is being properly run. Firing the manager is a handy scapegoating device, even if managers do not in fact make much difference.

SUMMARY

As we said at the start of the chapter, leadership is complex, and not yet fully understood. Now that we have looked at the evidence, what are the take-home lessons? First, clearly, we should look very carefully at anyone claiming to have a sure-fire way to lead well. If such a method exists, it certainly has not yet reached the leadership researchers.

But acknowledging that we do not know everything is not the same as saying that we know nothing. There is good evidence that what leaders do makes at least some difference. There is also good evidence that doing the same thing, regardless of the situation, is not likely to be very effective all the time. To be effective, we need to strive for a match between what we do (or are) and the situation in which we find ourselves.

We have reviewed several models of how this match can be achieved. To Fiedler, matching is achieved by knowing our LPC score, and then getting into, or reshaping, situations so that their favorableness matches our LPC. To Vroom and Yetton, we choose from a range of decision-making techniques, some more participative, some less, in light of our evaluation of the need to protect decision quality and ensure acceptance by the group. The various approaches based on the Ohio State dimensions of consideration and initiating structure range from the "one best way," "high-high manager" model promoted by Blake and Mouton to more complex diagnoses based on the situation. Finally, path-goal theory suggests a set of diagnostic questions revolving around what it takes to motivate subordinates, and a set of leader responses aimed at filling the gaps and enhancing the subordinates' motivation.

As throughout the book, then, we see that the answer to "What makes a good leader?" is, "It depends." We have tried to summarize in this chapter some of the key features on which leadership depends, and how. You will certainly be forced, in your own work, to develop a range of leadership methods and a set of diagnostic questions for choosing one or another. You may well be exposed to training based on one or another of the theories reviewed here. This chapter has aimed (1) to sharpen the diagnostic questions you may ask and (2) add to the range of responses you have available. At the least, it should convince you that both elements are necessary. In leadership, if nowhere else, the search for the "one best way" is surely a fool's search.

REFERENCES

Ashour, A.S. "The Contingency Model of Leadership Effectiveness: An Evaluation." *Organizational Behavior and Human Performance* 9 (1973):339–55.

Blake, R.R., and Mouton, J.S. *The Managerial Grid.* Houston: Gulf Publishing, 1964.

Calder, B.J. "An Attribution Theory of Leadership." In *New Directions in Organizational Behavior,* B.M. Staw and G.R. Salancik, eds. Chicago: St. Clair, 1977.

Evan, W.M. "Conflict and Performance in R&D Organizations." *Industrial Management Review* 7 (1965):37–45.

Fiedler, F.E. *A Theory of Leadership Effectiveness.* New York: McGraw-Hill, 1967.

———. "The Leadership Game: Matching the Man to the Situation." *Organizational Dynamics* 4 (1976):6–16.

Fleishman, E.F., and Peters, D.R. "Interpersonal Values, Leadership Attitudes, and Managerial 'Success'." *Personnel Psychology* 15 (1962):127–43.

Hersey, P., and Blanchard, K.H. "Life Cycle Theory of Leadership." *Training and Development Journal* 23 (1969):15–21.

Hollander, E.P. *Leaders, Groups and Influence.* New York: Oxford University Press, 1964.

House, R.J., and Mitchell, T.R. "Path Goal Theory of Leadership." *Journal of Contemporary Business* 5 (1974):81–97.

Kerr, S., Schriesheim, C.A.; Murphy, C.J.; and Stogdill, R.M. "Toward a Contingency Theory of Leadership Based upon the Consideration and Initiating Structure Literature." *Organizational Behavior and Human Performance* 12 (1974):62–82.

Kerr, S., and Jermier, J.M. "Substitutes for Leadership: Their Meaning and Measurement." *Organizational Behavior and Human Performance* 22 (1978):375–403.

Leavitt, H.A. "Some Effects of Certain Communication Patterns on Group Performance." *Journal of Abnormal and Social Psychology* 46 (1951):38–50.

Lowin, A., and Craig, J.R. "The Influence of Level of Performance on Managerial Style: An Object-Lesson in the Ambiguity of Correlational Data." *Organizational Behavior and Human Performance* 3 (1968):440–58.

Stogdill, R.M. "Personal Factors Associated with Leadership: A Survey of the Literature." *Journal of Psychology* 25 (1948):35–71.

———. *Handbook of Leadership.* Glencoe, Ill.: Free Press, 1975.

Strodtbeck, F.L., and Hook, L.H. "The Social Dimensions of a Twelveman Jury Table." *Sociometry* 24 (1961):397–415.

Tannenbaum, R., and Schmidt, W. "How to Choose a Leadership Pattern." *Harvard Business Review* 36 (1958):95–102.

Vroom, V.H. "Can Leaders Learn to Lead?" *Organizational Dynamics* 4 (1976):17–28.

———, and Yetton, P.W. *Leadership and Decision Making.* Pittsburgh, Pa.: University of Pittsburgh Press, 1973.

Who Gets Power—and How They Hold on to It: A Strategic Contingency Model of Power

Gerald R. Salancik

Jeffrey Pfeffer

Power adheres to those who can cope with the critical problems of the organization. As such, power is not a dirty secret, but the secret of success. And that's the path power follows, until it becomes institutionalized—which makes administration the most precarious of occupations.

Power is held by many people to be a dirty word or, as Warren Bennis has said, "It is the organization's last dirty secret."

This article will argue that traditional "political" power, far from being a dirty business, is, in its most naked form, one of the few mechanisms available for aligning an organization with its own reality. However, institutionalized forms of power—what we prefer to call the cleaner forms of power: authority, legitimization, centralized control, regulations, and the more modern "management information systems"—tend to buffer the organization from reality and obscure the demands of its environment. Most great states and insti-

tutions declined, not because they played politics, but because they failed to accommodate to the political realities they faced. Political processes, rather than being mechanisms for unfair and unjust allocations and appointments, tend toward the realistic resolution of conflicts among interests. And power, while it eludes definition, is easy enough to recognize by its consequences—the ability of those who possess power to bring about the outcomes they desire.

The model of power we advance is an elaboration of what has been called strategic-contingency theory, a view that sees power as something that accrues to organizational subunits (individuals, departments) that cope with critical organizational problems. Power is used by subunits, indeed, used by all who have it, to

Reprinted, by permission of the publisher, from *Organizational Dynamics* (Winter 1977). © 1977, American Management Association, New York. All rights reserved.

enhance their own survival through control of scarce critical resources, through the placement of allies in key positions, and through the definition of organizational problems and policies. Because of the processes by which power develops and is used, organizations become both more aligned and more misaligned with their environments. This contradiction is the most interesting aspect of organizational power, and one that makes administration one of the most precarious of occupations.

WHAT IS ORGANIZATIONAL POWER?

You can walk into most organizations and ask without fear of being misunderstood, "Which are the powerful groups or people in this organization?" Although many organizational informants may be *unwilling* to tell you, it is unlikely they will be *unable* to tell you. Most people do not require explicit definitions to know what power is.

Power is simply the ability to get things done the way one wants them to be done. For a manager who wants an increased budget to launch a project that he thinks is important, his power is measured by his ability to get that budget. For an executive vice-president who wants to be chairman, his power is evidenced by his advancement toward his goal.

People in organizations not only know what you are talking about when you ask who is influential but they are likely to agree with one another to an amazing extent. Recently, we had a chance to observe this in a regional office of an insurance company. The office had 21 department managers; we asked ten of these managers to rank all 21 according to the influence each one had in the organization. Despite the fact that ranking 21 things is a difficult task, the managers sat down and began arranging the names of their colleagues and themselves in a column. Only one person bothered to ask, "What do you mean by influence?" When told "power," he responded, "Oh," and went on. We compared the rankings of all ten managers and found virtually no disagreement among them in the managers ranked among the top five or the bottom five. Differences in the rankings came from department heads claiming more influence for themselves than their colleagues attributed to them.

Such agreement on those who have influence, and those who do not, was not unique to this insurance company. So far we have studied over 20 very different organizations—universities, research firms, factories, banks, retailers, to name a few. In each one we found individuals able to rate themselves and their peers on a scale of influence or power. We have done this both for specific decisions and for general impact on organizational policies. Their agreement was unusually high, which suggests that distributions of influence exist well enough in everyone's mind to be referred to with ease—and we assume with accuracy.

WHERE DOES ORGANIZATIONAL POWER COME FROM?

Earlier we stated that power helps organizations become aligned with their realities. This hopeful prospect follows from what we have dubbed the strategic-contingencies theory of organizational power. Briefly, those subunits most able to cope with the organization's critical problems and uncertainties acquire power. In its simplest form, the strategic-contingencies theory implies that when an organization faces a number of lawsuits that threaten its existence, the legal department will gain power and influence over organizational decisions. Somehow other organizational interest groups will recognize its critical importance and confer upon it a status and power never before enjoyed. This influence may extend beyond handling legal matters and into decisions about product design, advertising production, and so on. Such extensions undoubtedly would be accompanied by appropriate, or acceptable, verbal justifications. In time, the head of the legal department may become the head of the corporation, just as in times past the vice-president for marketing had become the president when market shares were a worrisome problem and, before him, the chief engineer, who had made the production line run as smooth as silk.

Stated in this way, the strategic-contingencies theory of power paints an appealing picture of power. To the extent that power is determined by the critical uncertainties and problems facing the organization and, in turn, influences decisions in the organization, the organization is aligned with the realities it faces. In short, power facilitates the organization's adaptation to its environment—or its problems.

We can cite many illustrations of how influence derives from a subunits's ability to deal with critical contingencies. Michael Crozier described a French cigarette factory in which the maintenance engineers had a considerable say in the plantwide operation. After some probing he discovered that the group possessed the solution to one of the major problems faced by the company, that of troubleshooting the elaborate, expensive, and irrascible automated machines that kept breaking down and dumbfounding everyone else. It was the one problem that the plant manager could in no way control.

The production workers, while troublesome from time to time, created no insurmountable problems; the manager could reasonably predict their absenteeism or replace them when necessary. Production scheduling was something he could deal with since, by watching inventories and sales, the demand for cigarettes was known long in advance. Changes in demand could be accommodated by slowing down or speeding up the line. Supplies of tobacco and paper were also easily dealt with through stockpiles and advance orders.

The one thing that management could neither control nor accommodate to, however, was the seemingly happenstance breakdowns. And the foremen couldn't instruct the workers what to do when emergencies developed since the maintenance department kept its records of problems and solutions locked up in a cabinet or in its members' heads. The breakdowns were, in truth, a critical source of uncertainty for the organization, and the maintenance engineers were the only ones who could cope with the problem.

The engineers' strategic role in coping with breakdowns afforded them a considerable say on plant decisions. Schedules and production quotas were set in consultation with them. And the plant manager, while formally their boss, accepted their decisions about personnel in their operation. His submission was to his credit, for without their cooperation he would have had an even more difficult time in running the plant.

Ignoring Critical Consequences

In this cigarette factory, sharing influence with the maintenance workers reflected the plant manager's awareness of the critical contingencies. However, when organizational members are not aware of the critical contingencies they face, and do not share influence accordingly, the failure to do so can create havoc. In one case, an insurance company's regional office was having problems with the performance of one of its departments, the coding department. From the outside, the department looked like a disaster area. The clerks who worked in it were somewhat dissatisfied; their supervisor paid little attention to them, and they resented the hard work. Several other departments were critical of this manager, claiming that she was inconsistent in meeting deadlines. The person most critical was the claims manager. He resented having to wait for work that was handled by her department, claiming that it held up his claims adjusters. Having heard the rumors about dissatisfaction among her subordinates, he attributed the situation to poor supervision. He was second in command in the office and therefore took up the issue with her immediate boss, the head of administrative services. They consulted with the personnel manager and the three of them concluded that the manager needed leadership training to improve her relations with her subordinates. The coding manager objected, saying it was a waste of time, but agreed to go along with the training and also agreed to give more priority to the claims department's work. Within a week after the training, the results showed that her workers were happier but that the performance of her department had decreased, save for the people serving the claims department.

About this time, we began, quite independently, a study of influence in this organization. We asked the administrative services director to draw up flow charts of how the work of one department moved onto the next department. In the course of the interview, we noticed that the coding department began or interceded in the work flow of most of the other departments and casually mentioned to him, "The coding manager must be very influential." He said "No, not really. Why would you think so?" Before we could reply he recounted the story of her leadership training and the fact that things were worse. We then told him that it seemed obvious that the coding department would be influential from the fact that all the other departments depended on it. It was also clear why productivity had fallen. The coding manager took the training seriously and began spending more time raising her workers' spirits than she did worrying about the problems of all the departments that depended on her. Giving priority to the claims area only exaggerated the problem, for their work was getting done at the

expense of the work of the other departments. Eventually the company hired a few more clerks to relieve the pressure in the coding department and performance returned to a more satisfactory level.

Originally we got involved with this insurance company to examine how the influence of each manager evolved from his or her department's handling of critical organizational contingencies. We reasoned that one of the most important contingencies faced by all profit-making organizations was that of generating income. Thus we expected managers would be influential to the extent to which they contributed to this function. Such was the case. The underwriting managers, who wrote the policies that committed the premiums, were the most influential; the claims managers, who kept a lid on the funds flowing out, were a close second. Least influential were the managers of functions unrelated to revenue, such as mailroom and payroll managers. And contrary to what the administrative services manager believed, the third most powerful department head (out of 21) was the woman in charge of the coding function, which consisted of rating, recording, and keeping track of the codes of all policy applications and contracts. Her peers attributed more influence to her than could have been inferred from her place on the organization chart. And it was not surprising, since they all depended on her department. The coding department's records, their accuracy and the speed with which they could be retrieved, affected virtually every other operating department in the insurance office. The underwriters depended on them in getting the contracts straight; the typing department depended on them in preparing the formal contract document; the claims department depended on them in adjusting claims; and accounting depended on them for billing. Unfortunately, the "bosses" were not aware of these dependences, for unlike the cigarette factory, there were no massive breakdowns that made them obvious, while the coding manager, who was a hard-working but quiet person, did little to announce her importance.

The cases of this plant and office illustrate nicely a basic point about the source of power in organizations. The basis for power in an organization derives from the ability of a person or subunit to take or not take actions that are desired by others. The coding manager was seen as influential by those who depended on her department, but not by the people at the top. The engineers were influential because of their role in keeping the plant operating. The two cases differ in these respects: The coding supervisor's source of power was not as widely recognized as that of the maintenance engineers, and she did not use her source of power to influence decisions; the maintenance engineers did. Whether power is used to influence anything is a separate issue. We should not confuse this issue with the fact that power derives from a social situation in which one person has a capacity to do something and another person does not, but wants it done.

POWER SHARING IN ORGANIZATIONS

Power is shared in organizations; and it is shared out of necessity more than out of concern for principles of organizational development or participatory democracy. Power is shared because no one person controls all the desired activities in the organization. While the factory owner may hire people to operate his noisy machines, once hired they have some control over the use of the machinery. And thus they have power over him in the same way he has power over them. Who has more power over whom is a mooter point than that of recognizing the inherent nature of organizing as a sharing of power.

Let's expand on the concept that power

derives from the activities desired in an organization. A major way of managing influence in organizations is through the designation of activities. In a bank we studied, we saw this principle in action. This bank was planning to install a computer system for routine credit evaluation. The bank, rather progressive-minded, was concerned that the change would have adverse effects on employees and therefore surveyed their attitudes.

The principal opposition to the new system came, interestingly, not from the employees who performed the routine credit checks, some of whom would be relocated because of the change, but from the manager of the credit department. His reason was quite simple. The manager's primary function was to give official approval to the applications, catch any employee mistakes before giving approval, and arbitrate any difficulties the clerks had in deciding what to do. As a consequence of his role, others in the organization, including his superiors, subordinates, and colleagues, attributed considerable importance to him. He, in turn, for example, could point to the low proportion of credit approvals, compared with other financial institutions, that resulted in bad debts. Now, to his mind, a wretched machine threatened to transfer his role to a computer programmer, a man who knew nothing of finance and who, in addition, had ten years less seniority. The credit manager eventually quit for a position at a smaller firm with lower pay, but one in which he would have more influence than his redefined job would have left him with.

Because power derives from activities rather than individuals, an individual's or subgroup's power is never absolute and derives ultimately from the context of the situation. The amount of power an individual has at any one time depends, not only on the activities he or she controls, but also on the existence of other persons or means by which the activities can be achieved and on those who determine what ends are desired and, hence, on what activities are desired and critical for the organization. One's own power always depends on other people for these two reasons. Other people, or groups or organizations, can determine the definition of what is a critical contingency for the organization and can also undercut the uniqueness of the individual's personal contribution to the critical contingencies of the organization.

Perhaps one can best appreciate how situationally dependent power is by examining how it is distributed. In most societies, power organizes around scarce and critical resources. Rarely does power organize around abundant resources. In the United States, a person doesn't become powerful because he or she can drive a car. There are simply too many others who can drive with equal facility. In certain villages in Mexico, on the other hand, a person with a car is accredited with enormous social status and plays a key role in the community. In addition to scarcity, power is also limited by the need for one's capacities in a social system. While a racer's ability to drive a car around a 90° turn at 80 mph may be sparsely distributed in a society, it is not likely to lend the driver much power in the society. The ability simply does not play a central role in the activities of the society.

The fact that power revolves around scarce and critical activities, of course, makes the control and organization of those activities a major battleground in struggles for power. Even relatively abundant or trivial resources can become the bases for power if one can organize and control their allocation and the definition of what is critical. Many occupational and professional groups attempt to do just this in modern economies. Lawyers organize themselves into associations, regulate the entrance requirements for novitiates, and then get laws passed specifying situations that require the services of an attorney. Workers had little power in the conduct of industrial affairs until they organized themselves into closed and con-

trolled systems. In recent years, women and blacks have tried to define themselves as important and critical to the social system, using law to reify their status.

In organizations there are obviously opportunities for defining certain activities as more critical than others. Indeed, the growth of managerial thinking to include defining organizational objectives and goals has done much to foster these opportunities. One sure way to liquidate the power of groups in the organization is to define the need for their services out of existence. David Halberstam presents a description of how just such a thing happened to the group of correspondents that evolved around Edward R. Murrow, the brilliant journalist, interviewer, and war correspondent of CBS News. A close friend of CBS chairman and controlling stockholder William S. Paley, Murrow, and the news department he directed, were endowed with freedom to do what they felt was right. He used it to create some of the best documentaries and commentaries ever seen on television. Unfortunately, television became too large, too powerful, and too suspect in the eyes of the federal government that licensed it. It thus became, or at least the top executives believed it had become, too dangerous to have in-depth, probing commentary on the news. Crisp, dry, uneditorializing headliners were considered safer. Murrow was out and Walter Cronkite was in.

The power to define what is critical in an organization is no small power. Moreover, it is the key to understanding why organizations are either aligned with their environments or misaligned. If an organization defines certain activities as critical when in fact they are not critical, given the flow of resources coming into the organization, it is not likely to survive, at least in its present form.

Most organizations manage to evolve a distribution of power and influence that is aligned with the critical realities they face in the environment. The environment, in turn, includes both the internal environment, the shifting situational contexts in which particular decisions get made, and the external environment that it can hope to influence but is unlikely to control.

THE CRITICAL CONTINGENCIES

The critical contingencies facing most organizations derive from the environmental context within which they operate. This determines the available needed resources and thus determines the problems to be dealt with. That power organizes around handling these problems suggests an important mechanism by which organizations keep in tune with their external environments. The strategic-contingencies model implies that subunits that contribute to the critical resources of the organization will gain influence in the organization. Their influence presumably is then used to bend the organization's activities to the contingencies that determine its resources. This idea may strike one as obvious. But its obviousness in no way diminishes its importance. Indeed, despite its obviousness, it escapes the notice of many organizational analysts and managers, who all too frequently think of the organization in terms of a descending pyramid, in which all the departments in one tier hold equal power and status. This presumption denies the reality that departments differ in the contributions they are believed to make to the overall organization's resources, as well as to the fact that some are more equal than others.

Because of the importance of this idea to organizational effectiveness, we decided to examine it carefully in a large midwestern university. A university offers an excellent site for studying power. It is composed of departments with nominally equal power and is administered by a central executive structure much like other bureaucracies. However, at the same time it is a situation in which the departments have clearly defined identities and face diverse external environments. Each department has its own bodies of knowledge, its own institutions, its own sources of prestige and resources. Because the departments operate in different external environments, they are likely to contribute differentially to the resources of the overall organization. Thus a physics department with close ties to NASA may contribute substantially to the funds of the university; and a history department with a renowned historian in residence may contribute to the intellectual credibility or prestige of the whole university. Such variations permit one to examine how these various contributions lead to obtaining power within the university.

We analyzed the influence of 29 university departments throughout an 18-month period in their history. Our chief interest was to determine whether departments that brought more critical resources to the university would be more powerful than departments that contributed fewer or less critical resources.

To identify the critical resources each department contributed, the heads of all departments were interviewed about the importance of seven different resources to the university's success. The seven included undergraduate students (the factor determining size of the state allocations by the university), national prestige, administrative expertise, and so on. The most critical resource was found to be contract and grant monies received by a department's faculty for research or consulting services. At this university, contract and grants contributed somewhat less than 50 percent of the overall budget, with the remainder primarily coming from state appropriations. The importance attributed to contract and grant monies, and the rather minor importance of undergraduate students, was not surprising for this particular university. The university was a major center for graduate education; many of its departments ranked in the top ten of their respective fields. Grant and contract monies were the primary source of discretionary funding available for maintaining these programs of graduate education, and hence for maintaining the university's prestige. The prestige of the university itself was critical both in recruiting able students and attracting top-notch faculty.

From university records it was determined what relative contributions each of the 29 departments made to the various needs of the university (national prestige, outside grants, teaching). Thus, for instance, one department may have contributed to the university by teaching 7 percent of the instructional units, bringing in 2 percent of the outside contracts and grants, and having a national ranking of 20. Another department, on the other hand, may have taught one percent of the instructional units, contributed 12 percent to the grants, and be ranked the third best department in its field within the country.

The question was: Do these different contributions determine the relative power of the departments within the university? Power was measured in several ways; but regardless of how measured, the answer was "Yes." Those three resources together accounted for about 70 percent of the variance in subunit power in the university.

But the most important predictor of departmental power was the department's contribution to the contracts and grants of the university. Sixty percent of the variance in power was due to this one factor, suggesting that the power of departments derived primarily from the dollars they provided for graduate education, the activity believed to be the most important for the organization.

THE IMPACT OF ORGANIZATIONAL POWER ON DECISION MAKING

The measure of power we used in studying this university was an analysis of the responses of the department heads we interviewed. While such perceptions of power might be of interest in their own right, they contribute little to our understanding of how the distribution of power might serve to align an organization with its critical realities. For this we must look to how power actually influences the decisions and policies of organizations.

While it is perhaps not absolutely valid, we can generally gauge the relative importance of a department of an organization by the size of the budget allocated to it relative to other departments. Clearly it is of importance to the administrators of those departments whether they get squeezed in a budget crunch or are given more funds to strike out after new opportunities. And it should also be clear that when those decisions are made and one department can go ahead and try new approaches while another must cut back on the old, then the deployment of the resources of the organization in meeting its problems is most directly affected.

Thus our study of the university led us to ask the following question: Does power lead to influence in the organization? To answer this question, we found it useful first to ask another one, namely: Why should department heads try to influence organizational decisions to favor their own departments to the exclusion of other departments? While this second question may seem a bit naive to anyone who has witnessed the political realities of organizations, we posed it in a context of research on organizations that sees power as an illegitimate threat to the neater rational authority of modern bureaucracies. In this context, decisions are not believed to be made because of the dirty business of politics but because of the overall goals and purposes of the organization. In a university, one reasonable basis for decision making is the teaching workload of departments and the demands that follow from that workload. We would expect, therefore, that departments with heavy student demands for courses would be able to obtain funds for teaching. Another reasonable basis for decision making is quality. We would expect, for that reason, that departments with esteemed reputations would be able to obtain funds both because their quality suggests they might use such funds effectively and because such funds would allow them to maintain their quality. A rational model of bureaucracy intimates, then, that the organizational decisions taken would favor those who perform the stated purposes of the organization—teaching undergraduates and training professional and scientific talent—well.

The problem with rational models of decision making, however, is that what is rational to one person may strike another as irrational. For most departments, resources are a question of survival. While teaching undergraduates may seem to be a major goal for some members of the university, developing knowledge may seem so to others; and to still others, advising governments and other institutions about policies may seem to be the crucial business. Everyone has his own idea of the proper priorities in a just world. Thus goals rather than being clearly defined and universally agreed upon are blurred and contested throughout the organization. If such is the case, then the decisions taken on behalf of the organization as a whole are likely to reflect the goals of those who prevail in political contests, namely, those with power in the organization.

Will organizational decisions always reflect the distribution of power in the organization? Probably not. Using power for influence requires a certain expenditure of effort, time, and resources. Prudent and judicious persons are not likely to use their power needlessly or wastefully. And it is likely that power will be used to influence organizational decisions primarily under circumstances that both require and favor its use. We have examined three conditions that are likely to affect the use of power in organizations: scarcity, criticality, and uncertainty. The first suggests that subunits will try to exert influence when the resources of the organization are scarce. If there is an abundance of resources, then a particular department or a particular individual has little need to attempt influence. With little effort, he can get all he wants anyway.

The second condition, criticality, suggests that a subunit will attempt to influence decisions to obtain resources that are critical to its own survival and activities. Criticality implies that one would not waste effort, or risk being labeled obstinate, by fighting over trivial decisions affecting one's operations.

An office manager would probably balk less about a threatened cutback in copying machine usage than about a reduction in typing staff. An advertising department head would probably worry less about losing his lettering artist than his illustrator. Criticality is difficult to define because what is critical depends on people's beliefs about what is critical. Such beliefs may or may not be based on experience and knowledge and may or may not be agreed upon by all. Scarcity, for instance, may itself affect conceptions of criticality. When slack resources drop off, cutbacks have to be made—those "hard decisions," as congressmen and resplendent administrators like to call them. Managers then find themselves scrapping projects they once held dear.

The third condition that we believe affects the use of power is uncertainty: When individuals do not agree about what the organization should do or how to do it, power and other social processes will affect decisions. The reason for this is simply that, if there are no clear-cut criteria available for resolving conflicts of interest, then the only means for resolution is some form of social process, including power, status, social ties, or some arbitrary process like flipping a coin or drawing straws. Under conditions of uncertainty, the powerful manager can argue his case on any grounds and usually win it. Since there is no real consensus, other contestants are not likely to develop counter arguments or amass sufficient opposition. Moreover, because of his power and their need for access to the resources he controls, they are more likely to defer to his arguments.

Although the evidence is slight, we have found that power will influence the allocations of scarce and critical resources. In the analysis of power in the university, for instance, one of the most critical resources needed by departments is the general budget. First granted by the state legislature, the general budget is later allocated to individual departments by the university administration in response to requests from the department heads. Our analysis of the factors that contribute to a department getting more or less of this budget indicated that subunit power was the major predictor, overriding such factors as student demand for courses, national reputations of departments, or even the size of a department's faculty. Moreover, other research has shown that when the general budget has been cut back or held below previous uninflated levels, leading to monies becoming more scarce, budget allocations mirror departmental powers even more closely.

Student enrollment and faculty size, of course, do themselves relate to budget allocations, as we would expect since they determine a department's need for resources, or at least offer visible testimony of needs. But departments are not always able to get what they need by the mere fact of needing them. In one analysis it was found that high-power departments were able to obtain budget without regard to their teaching loads and, in some cases, actually in inverse relation to their teaching loads. In contrast, low-power departments could get increases in budget only when they could justify the increases by a recent growth in teaching load, and then only when it was far in excess of norms for other departments.

General budget is only one form of resource that is allocated to departments. There are others such as special grants for student fellowships or faculty research. These are critical to departments because they affect the ability to attract other resources, such as outstanding faculty or students. We examined how power influenced the allocations of four resources department heads had described as critical and scarce.

When the four resources were arrayed from the most to the least critical and scarce, we found that departmental power best predicted the allocations of the most critical and scarce resources. In other words, the analysis of how power influences organizational allocations leads to this conclusion: Those subunits most likely to survive in times of strife are those that are more critical to the organization. Their importance to the organization gives them power to influence resource allocations that enhance their own survival.

HOW EXTERNAL ENVIRONMENT IMPACTS EXECUTIVE SELECTION

Power not only influences the survival of key groups in an organization, it also influences the selection of individuals to key leadership positions, and by such a process further aligns the organization with its environmental context.

We can illustrate this with a recent study of the selection and tenure of chief administrators in 57 hospitals in Illinois. We assumed that since the critical problems facing the organization would enhance the power of certain groups at the expense of others, then the leaders to emerge should be those most relevant to the context of the hospitals. To assess this we asked each chief administrator about his professional background and how long he had been in office. The replies were then related to the hospitals' funding, ownership, and competitive conditions for patients and staff.

One aspect of a hospital's context is the source of its budget. Some hospitals, for instance, are run much like other businesses. They sell bed space, patient care, and treatment services. They charge fees sufficient both to cover their costs and to provide capital for expansion. The main source of both their operating and capital funds is patient billings. Increasingly, patient billings are paid for, not by patients, but by private insurance companies. Insurers like Blue Cross dominate and represent a potent interest group outside a hospital's control but critical to its income. The insurance companies, in order to limit their own costs, attempt to hold down the fees allowable to hospitals, which they do effectively from their positions on state rate boards. The squeeze on hospitals that results from fees increasing slowly while costs climb rapidly more and more demands the talents of cost accountants or people trained in the technical expertise of hospital administration.

By contrast, other hospitals operate more like social service institutions, either as government healthcare units (Bellevue Hospital in New York City and Cook County Hospital in Chicago, for example) or as charitable institutions. These hospitals obtain a large proportion of their operating and capital funds, not from privately insured patients, but from government subsidies or private donations. Such institutions rather than requiring the talents of a technically efficient administrator are likely to require the savvy of someone who is well integrated into the social and political power structure of the community.

Not surprisingly, the characteristics of administrators predictably reflect the funding context of the hospitals with which they are associated. Those hospitals with larger proportions of their budget obtained from private insurance companies were most likely to have administrators with backgrounds in accounting and least likely to have administrators whose professions were business or medicine. In contrast, those hospitals with larger proportions of their budget derived from private donations and local governments were most likely to have administrators with business or professional backgrounds and least likely to have accountants. The same held for formal training in hos-

pital management. Professional hospital administrators could easily be found in hospitals drawing their incomes from private insurance and rarely in hospitals dependent on donations or legislative appropriations.

As with the selection of administrators, the context of organizations has also been found to affect the removal of executives. The environment, as a source of organizational problems, can make it more or less difficult for executives to demonstrate their value to the organization. In the hospitals we studied, long-term administrators came from hospitals with few problems. They enjoyed amicable and stable relations with their local business and social communities and suffered little competition for funding and staff. The small city hospital director who attended civic and Elks meetings while running the only hospital within a 100-mile radius, for example, had little difficulty holding on to his job. Turnover was highest in hospitals with the most problems, a phenomenon similar to that observed in a study of industrial organizations in which turnover was highest among executives in industries with competitive environments and unstable market conditions. The interesting thing is that instability characterized the industries rather than the individual firms in them. The troublesome conditions in the individual firms were attributed, or rather misattributed, to the executives themselves.

It takes more than problems, however, to terminate a manager's leadership. The problems themselves must be relevant and critical. This is clear from the way in which an administrator's tenure is affected by the status of the hospital's operating budget. Naively we might assume that all administrators would need to show a surplus. Not necessarily so. Again, we must distinguish between those hospitals that depend on private donations for funds and those that do not. Whether an endowed budget shows a surplus or deficit is less important than the hospital's relations with benefactors. On the other hand, with a budget dependent on patient billing, a surplus is almost essential;

monies for new equipment or expansion must be drawn from it, and without them quality care becomes more difficult and patients scarcer. An administrator's tenure reflected just these considerations. For those hospitals dependent upon private donations, the length of an administrator's term depended not at all on the status of the operating budget but was fairly predictable from the hospital's relations with the business community. On the other hand, in hospitals dependent on the operating budget for capital financing, the greater the deficit the shorter was the tenure of the hospital's principal administrators.

CHANGING CONTINGENCIES AND ERODING POWER BASES

The critical contingencies facing the organization may change. When they do, it is reasonable to expect that the power of individuals and subgroups will change in turn. At times the shift can be swift and shattering, as it was recently for powerholders in New York City. A few years ago it was believed that David Rockefeller was one of the ten most powerful people in the city, as tallied by *New York* magazine, which annually sniffs out power for the delectation of its readers. But that was before it was revealed that the city was in financial trouble, before Rockefeller's Chase Manhattan Bank lost some of its own financial luster, and before brother Nelson lost some of his political influence in Washington. Obviously David Rockefeller was no longer as well positioned to help bail the city out. Another loser was an attorney with considerable personal connections to the political and religious leaders of the city. His talents were no longer in much demand. The persons with more influence were the bankers and union pension fund executors who fed money to the city; community leaders who represent blacks and Spanish-Americans, in contrast, witnessed the erosion of their power bases.

One implication of the idea that power shifts with changes in organizational environments is that the dominant coalition will tend to be that group that is most appropriate for the organization's environment, as also will the leaders of an organization. One can observe this historically in the top executives of industrial firms in the United States. Up until the early 1950s, many top corporations were headed by former production line managers or engineers who gained prominence because of their abilities to cope with the problems of production. Their success, however, only spelled their demise. As production became routinized and mechanized, the problem of most firms became one of selling all those goods they so efficiently produced. Marketing executives were more frequently found in corporate boardrooms. Success outdid itself again, for keeping markets and production steady and stable requires the kind of control that can only come from acquiring competitors and suppliers or the invention of more and more appealing products—ventures that typically require enormous amounts of capital. During the 1960s, financial executives assumed the seats of power. And they, too, will give way to others. Edging over the horizon are legal experts, as regulation and antitrust suits are becoming more and more frequent in the 1970s, suits that had their beginnings in the success of the expansion generated by prior executives. The more distant future, which is likely to be dominated by multinational corporations, may see former secretaries of state and their minions increasingly serving as corporate figureheads.

THE NONADAPTIVE CONSEQUENCES OF ADAPTATION

From what we have said thus far about power aligning the organization with its own realities, an intelligent person might react with a resounding ho-hum, for it all seems too obvious: Those with the ability to get the job done are given the job to do.

However, there are two aspects of power that make it more useful for understanding organizations and their effectiveness. First, the "job" to be done has a way of expanding itself until it becomes less and less clear what the job is. Napoleon began by doing a job for France in the war with Austria and ended up Emperor, convincing many that only he could keep the peace. Hitler began by promising an end to Germany's troubling postwar depression and ended up convincing more people than is comfortable to remember that he was destined to be the savior of the world. In short, power is a capacity for influence that extends far beyond the original bases that created it. Second, power tends to take on institutionalized forms that enable it to endure well beyond its usefulness to an organization.

There is an important contradiction in what we have observed about organizational power. On the one hand we have said that power derives from the contingencies facing an organization and that when those contingencies change so do the bases for power. On the other hand we have asserted that subunits will tend to use their power to influence organizational decisions in their own favor, particularly when their own survival is threatened by the scarcity of critical resources. The first statement implies that an organization will tend to be aligned with its environment since power will tend to bring to key positions those with capabilities relevant to the context. The second implies that those in power will not give up their positions so easily; they will pursue policies that guarantee their continued domination. In short, change and stability operate through the same mechanism, and, as a result, the organization will never be completely in phase with its environment or its needs.

The study of hospital administrators illustrates how leadership can be out of phase with reality. We argued that privately funded hospitals needed trained technical administrators more so than did hospitals funded by donations. The need as we perceived it was matched in most hospitals, but by no means in all. Some organizations did not conform with our predictions. These deviations imply that some administrators were able to maintain their positions independent of their suitability for those positions. By dividing administrators into those with long and short terms of office, one finds that the characteristics of longer-termed administrators were virtually unrelated to the hospital's context. The shorter-termed chiefs on the other hand had characteristics more appropriate for the hospital's problems. For a hospital to have a recently appointed head implies that the previous administrator had been unable to endure by institutionalizing himself.

One obvious feature of hospitals that allowed some administrators to enjoy a long tenure was a hospital's ownership. Administrators were less entrenched when their hospitals were affiliated with and dependent upon larger organizations, such as governments or churches. Private hospitals offered more secure positions for administrators. Like private corporations, they tend to have more diffused ownership, leaving the administrator unopposed as he institutionalizes his reign. Thus he endures, sometimes at the expense of the performance of the organization. Other research has demonstrated that corporations with diffuse ownership have poorer earnings than those in which the control of the manager is checked by a dominant shareholder. Firms that overload their boardrooms with more insiders than are appropriate for their context have also been found to be less profitable.

A word of caution is required about our judgment of "appropriateness." When we argue some capabilities are more appropriate for one context than another, we do so from the perspective of an outsider and on the basis of reasonable assumptions as to the problems the organization will face and the capabilities they will need. The fact that we have been able to predict the distribution of influence and the characteristics of leaders suggests that our reasoning is not incorrect. However, we do not think that all organizations follow the same pattern. The fact that we have not been able to predict outcomes with 100 percent accuracy indicates they do not.

MISTAKING CRITICAL CONTINGENCIES

One thing that allows subunits to retain their power is their ability to name their functions as critical to the organization when they may not be. Consider again our discussion of power in the university. One might wonder why the most critical tasks were defined as graduate education and scholarly research, the effect of which was to lend power to those who brought in grants and contracts. Why not something else? The reason is that the more powerful departments argued for those criteria and won their case, partly because they were more powerful.

In another analysis of this university, we found that all departments advocate selfserving criteria for budget allocation. Thus a department with large undergraduate enrollments argued that enrollments should determine budget allocations, a department with a strong national reputation saw prestige as the most reasonable basis for distributing funds, and so on. We further found that advocating such self-serving criteria actually benefited a department's budget allotments but, also, it paid off more for departments that were already powerful.

Organizational needs are consistent with a current distribution of power also because of a human tendency to categorize problems in familiar ways. An accountant sees problems with organizational performance as cost ac-

countancy problems or inventory flow problems. A sales manager sees them as problems with markets, promotional strategies, or just unaggressive salespeople. But what is the truth? Since it does not automatically announce itself, it is likely that those with prior credibility, or those with power, will be favored as the enlightened. This bias, while not intentionally self-serving, further concentrates power among those who already possess it, independent of changes in the organization's context.

INSTITUTIONALIZING POWER

A third reason for expecting organizational contingencies to be defined in familiar ways is that the current holders of power can structure the organization in ways that institutionalize themselves. By institutionalization we mean the establishment of relatively permanent structures and policies that favor the influence of a particular subunit. While in power, a dominant coalition has the ability to institute constitutions, rules, procedures, and information systems that limit the potential power of others while continuing their own.

The key to institutionalizing power always is to create a device that legitimates one's own authority and diminishes the legitimacy of others. When the "Divine Right of Kings" was envisioned centuries ago it was to provide an unquestionable foundation for the supremacy of royal authority. There is generally a need to root the exercise of authority in some higher power. Modern leaders are no less affected by this need. Richard Nixon, with the aid of John Dean, reified the concept of executive privilege, which meant in effect that what the President wished not to be discussed need not be discussed.

In its simpler form, institutionalization is achieved by designating positions or roles for organizational activities. The creation of a new post legitimizes a function and forces organization members to orient to it. By designating how this new post relates to older, more established posts, moreover, one can structure an organization to enhance the importance of the function in the organization. Equally, one can diminish the importance of traditional functions. This is what happened in the end with the insurance company we mentioned that was having trouble with its coding department. As the situation unfolded, the claims director continued to feel dissatisfied about the dependency of his functions on the coding manager. Thus he instituted a reorganization that resulted in two coding departments. In so doing, of course, he placed activities that affected his department under his direct control, presumably to make the operation more effective. Similarly, consumer-product firms enhance the power of marketing by setting up a coordinating role to interface production and marketing functions and then appoint a marketing manager to fill the role.

The structures created by dominant powers sooner or later become fixed and unquestioned features of the organization. Eventually, this can be devastating. It is said that the battle of Jena in 1806 was lost by Frederick the Great, who died in 1786. Though the great Prussian leader had no direct hand in the disaster, his imprint on the army was so thorough, so embedded in its skeletal underpinnings, that the organization was inappropriate for others to lead in different times.

Another important source of institutionalized power lies in the ability to structure information systems. Setting up committees to investigate particular organizational issues and having them report only to particular individuals or groups, facilitates their awareness of problems by members of those groups while limiting the awareness of problems by the members of other groups. Obviously, those who have information are in a better position to interpret the problems of an organization, re-

gardless of how realistically they may, in fact, do so.

Still another way to institutionalize power is to distribute rewards and resources. The dominant group may quiet competing interest groups with small favors and rewards. The credit for this artful form of cooptation belongs to Louis XIV. To avoid usurpation of his power by the nobles of France and the Fronde that had so troubled his father's reign, he built the palace at Versailles to occupy them with hunting and gossip. Awed, the courtiers basked in the reflected glories of the "Sun King" and the overwhelming setting he had created for his court.

At this point, we have not systematically studied the institutionalization of power. But we suspect it is an important condition that mediates between the environment of the organization and the capabilities of the organization for dealing with that environment. The more institutionalized power is within an organization, the more likely an organization will be out of phase with the realities it faces. President Richard Nixon's structuring of his White House is one of the better documented illustrations. If we go back to newspaper and magazine descriptions of how he organized his office from the beginning in 1968, most of what occurred subsequently follows almost as an afterthought. Decisions flowed through virtually only the small White House staff; rewards, small presidential favors of recognition, and perquisites were distributed by this staff to the loyal; and information from the outside world—the press, Congress, the people on the streets—was filtered by the staff and passed along only if initialed "bh." Thus it was not surprising that when Nixon met war protestors in the early dawn, the only thing he could think to talk about was the latest football game, so insulated had he become from their grief and anger.

One of the more interesting implications of institutionalized power is that executive turnover among the executives who have structured the organization is likely to be a rare event that occurs only under the most pressing crisis. If a dominant coalition is able to structure the organization and interpret the meaning of ambiguous events like declining sales and profits or lawsuits, then the "real" problems to emerge will easily be incorporated into traditional molds of thinking and acting. If opposition is designed out of the organization, the interpretations will go unquestioned. Conditions will remain stable until a crisis develops, so overwhelming and visible that even the most adroit rhetorician would be silenced.

IMPLICATIONS FOR THE MANAGEMENT OF POWER IN ORGANIZATIONS

While we could derive numerous implications from this discussion of power, our selection would have to depend largely on whether one wanted to increase one's power, decrease the power of others, or merely maintain one's position. More important, the real implications depend on the particulars of an organizational situation. To understand power in an organization one must begin by looking outside it—into the environment—for those groups that mediate the organization's outcomes but are not themselves within its control.

Instead of ending with homilies, we will end with a reversal of where we began. Power, rather than being the dirty business it is often made out to be, is probably one of the few mechanisms for reality testing in organizations. And the cleaner forms of power, the institutional forms, rather than having the virtues they are often credited with, can lead the organization to become out of touch. The real trick to managing power in organizations is to ensure somehow that leaders cannot be unaware of the realities of their environments and cannot

avoid changing to deal with those realities. That, however, would be like designing the "self-liquidating organization," an unlikely event since anyone capable of designing such an instrument would be obviously in control of the liquidations.

Management would do well to devote more attention to determining the critical contingencies of their environments. For if you conclude, as we do, that the environment sets most of the structure influencing organizational outcomes and problems, and that power derives from the organization's activities that deal with those contingencies, then it is the environment that needs managing, not power. The first step is to construct an accurate model of the environment, a process that is quite difficult for most organizations. We have recently started a project to aid administrators in systematically understanding their environments. From this experience, we have learned that the most critical blockage to perceiving an organization's reality accurately is a failure to incorporate those with the relevant expertise into the process. Most organizations have the requisite experts on hand but they are positioned so that they can be comfortably ignored.

One conclusion you can, and probably should, derive from our discussion is that power—because of the way it develops and the way it is used—will always result in the organization suboptimizing its performance. However, to this grim absolute, we add a comforting caveat: If any criteria other than power were the basis for determining an organization's decisions, the results would be even worse.

SELECTED BIBLIOGRAPHY

The literature on power is at once both voluminous and frequently empty of content. Some is philosophical musing about the concept of power, while other writing contains popularized palliatives for acquiring and exercising influence. Machiavelli's *The Prince,* if read carefully, remains the single best prescriptive treatment of power and its use. Most social scientists have approached power descriptively, attempting to understand how it is acquired, how it is used, and what its effects are. Mayer Zald's edited collection *Power in Organizations* (Vanderbilt University Press, 1970) is one of the more useful sets of thoughts about power from a sociological perspective, while James Tedeschi's edited book, *The Social Influence Processes* (Aldine-Atherton, 1972) represents the social psychological approach to understanding power and influence. The strategic contingencies's approach, with its emphasis on the importance of uncertainty for understanding power in organizations, is described by David Hickson and his colleagues in "A Strategic Contingencies Theory of Intraorganizational Power" (*Administrative Science Quarterly,* December 1971, pp. 216-229).

Unfortunately, while many have written about power theoretically, there have been few empirical examinations of power and its use. Most of the work has taken the form of case studies. Michel Crozier's *The Bureaucratic Phenomenon* (University of Chicago Press, 1964) is important because it describes a group's source of power as control over critical activities and illustrates how power is not strictly derived from hierarchical position. J. Victor Baldridge's *Power and Conflict in the University* (John Wiley & Sons, 1971) and Andrew Pettigrew's study of computer purchase decisions in one English firm (*Politics of Organizational Decision-Making,* Tavistock, 1973) both present insights into the acquisition and use of power in specific instances. Our work has been more empirical and comparative, testing more explicitly the ideas presented in this article. The study of university decision making is reported in articles in the June 1974, pp. 135-151, and December 1974, pp. 453-473, issues of the *Administrative Science Quarterly,* the insurance firm study in J. G. Hunt and L. L. Larson's collection, *Leadership Frontiers* (Kent State University Press, 1975), and the study of hospital administrator succession will appear in 1977 in the *Academy of Management Journal.*

6

MANAGING ORGANIZATION CULTURE

Corporations, Culture, and Commitment: Motivation and Social Control in Organizations

Charles O'Reilly

Corporate culture is a topic receiving much attention in the business press. A casual glance at the major business journals over the past twelve months finds over fifty references to culture as an important ingredient in an organization's success or failure. For example, an article in *Fortune* (Jan. 2, 1989) describes how the CEO at Black & Decker "transformed an entire corporate culture, replacing a complacent manufacturing mentality with an almost manic, market-driven way of doing things." The success of Food Lion, a $3 billion supermarket chain with an annual growth rate of 37 percent over the past twenty years and yearly returns on equity of 24 percent, is attributed to a culture that emphasizes hard work, simplicity, and frugality (*Fortune*, Aug. 15, 1988). Other well-known firms, such as 3M, Johnson & Johnson, Apple, and Kimberly-Clark, have been frequently praised for their innovative cultures (*Fortune*, June 6, 1988).

Even the success of Japanese firms in the U.S. has been partly attributed to their ability to change the traditional culture developed under American managers. Peters and Waterman (1982, p. 39) report how a U.S. television manufacturing plant under Japanese management reduced its defect rate from 140 to 6, its complaint rate from 70 percent to 7 percent, and the turnover rate among employees from 30 percent to 1 percent, by changing management philosophy and culture. Consider, for example, the situation at the Toyota-managed New United Motors Manufacturing Incorporated (NUMMI) plant in Fremont, California. When General Motors closed this facility in 1982, it was one of the worst plants in the GM assembly division with an 18 percent daily absenteeism rate and a long history of conflictual labor relations. The plant reopened as a joint venture between Toyota and GM in 1983. Over 85 percent of the original labor force was rehired, and workers are still represented by the UAW. Although the technology used is vintage 1970s and the plant is not as automated as many others within GM and Toyota, productivity is almost double that of other GM facilities. In 1987 it took an estimated 20.8 hours to pro-

© [1989] by the Regents of The University of California. Reprinted from the *California Management Review*, Vol. 31, No. 4. By permission of The Regents.

duce a car at NUMMI compared to 40.7 hours in other GM plants and 18.0 hours at Toyota. The quality of the NUMMI automobiles, based on both internal audits and owner surveys, is the highest in the GM system, and absenteeism is at 2 percent rather than the 8 percent found at other GM facilities.

What accounts for this remarkable success? The answer appears to be in the Japanese approach. "At the system's core is a culture in which the assembly line workers maintain their machines, ensure the quality of their work, and improve the production process" (*Fortune*, January 30, 1989). Again the answer to the puzzle of such successes rests, in part, with culture.

But cultures are not always a positive force. They have also been implicated when firms run into difficulties. The CEO of financially-troubled Computerland, William Tauscher, has been restructuring the firm, noting that "a low-cost culture is a must" (*Business Week*, Oct. 10, 1988). Henry Wendt, CEO of SmithKline Beckman has attributed his firm's current difficulties to complacency: "We've been victims of our own success . . . I want to create a new culture" (*Business Week*, Oct. 10, 1988). Similar analyses of culture's contribution to a firm's failure have been made about Sears, Caterpillar, Bank of America, Polaroid, General Motors, and others. Even difficulties in mergers and acquisitions are seen sometimes to reflect cultural conflicts that hinder integration. Examples from industries as diverse as law, electronics, natural resources, and financial services abound. When R.J. Reynolds, with a staff-oriented, conglomerate-style management, joined Nabisco and its more freewheeling, decentralized approach, the CEO Ross Johnson imposed a new culture more in the mold of Standard Brands (*Fortune*, July 18, 1988). Failure to merge two cultures can lead to debilitating conflict, a loss of talent, and an inability to reap the benefits of synergy which often motivates such mergers.

A central theme in all these examples

seems to be that certain cultures can provide a competitive edge by coordinating and motivating people throughout an organization, either by promoting innovation, encouraging high standards of quality and service, or providing for efficiency and cost advantages. As Peters and Waterman concluded, "Above all, the intensity itself, stemming from strongly held beliefs, marks these companies" (1982, p. 16). It is this agreement which, if it is widely shared and strongly held, defines an organization's culture.

But what is really meant by a firm's "culture"? Do all organizations have them? Are they always important? Even if we can identify cultures, do we know enough about how they work to manage them? Four major questions need to be answered: 1) What is culture? 2) From a manager's perspective, when is culture important? 3) What is the process through which cultures are developed and maintained? and, finally, 4) How can cultures be managed?

Our argument is that we do have answers for these questions and that they can help us understand and manage culture in organizations. Essentially strong cultures are seen as developing through the creation of strong norms or social expectations about what is important. These expectations represent a social construction of reality in which employees come to know what is important as well as how to feel and act through the provision of cues from others. When these signals are clear, consistent, and continually reinforced, a strong normative order may develop which can focus people's attention and shape their attitudes and behavior.

To illustrate how this happens we will consider a diverse set of organizations characterized by strong normative orders and high member commitment. The range of organizations that typify strong cultures encompasses not only familiar commercial enterprises, but many Japanese organizations and other high commitment groups, including cults and religious orders. In fact, if one were to arrange these groups in order according to the strength of their culture, one might begin with cults, move to religious groups, Japanese firms, and strong culture organizations, and conclude with typical corporations. The interesting point here is that the manner in which commitment in these organizations is developed and maintained is the same, regardless of the group. As we shall see, the underlying psychological mechanisms are common to all strong culture settings. Only the degree to which some of these mechanisms are used varies. Because the process of developing a strong culture is largely the same regardless of the type of organization, understanding how these processes work can help managers diagnose and shape culture and commitment.

WHAT IS CULTURE?

If culture is to be studied and managed, it is important that we be clear about what is meant by the term. This is not simply an academic issue. Failure to specify clearly what "culture" is can result in confusion, misunderstanding, and conflict about its basic function and importance. If, as is sometimes suggested, (Schwartz & Davis, 1981; Barney, 1986), culture can offer a competitive edge, it is imperative that researchers and practitioners have a precise understanding of what culture is and what it is not. Vagueness only confirms the skeptic's definition of culture as "what is left over after you have forgotten all you definitely set out to learn."

Culture as Control

Before defining culture, let us first think briefly about control in organizations. Clearly little would get done by or in organizations if some control systems were not in place to direct and

coordinate activities. In fact, since organizations are often seen to be efficient and effective solely because control systems operate (Wilkins & Ouchi, 1983; Williamson, 1975), much attention is paid by managers and business schools to designing such systems.

And what is meant by "control"? A generic definition might be: "Control is the knowledge that someone who knows and cares is paying close attention to what we do and can tell us when deviations are occurring." Although broad, this definition can easily encompass traditional formal control systems ranging from planning and budgeting systems to performance appraisals. According to this definition, control systems work when those being monitored are aware that someone who matters, such as a boss or staff department, is paying attention and is likely to note when things are not going as designed. Thus, a budgeting system is effective when people understand that they are being monitored by others who can spot deviations. Several years ago a large toy manufacturer installed, at considerable expense, a management-by-objectives (MBO) performance appraisal system. After a year or so, top management became aware that the system was working well in one part of the organization but not in another. Concerned, they conducted an investigation and discovered the reason for the failure. In the part of the organization where MBO was working well, senior management was enthusiastic and committed. They saw real benefits and conveyed their belief up and down the chain of command. In the part of the organization where the system had failed, senior management saw MBO as another bureaucratic exercise to be endured. Subordinate managers quickly learned to complete the paperwork but ignore the purpose. The lesson here is that a control system, no matter how carefully designed, works only when those being monitored believe that people who matter care about the results and are paying close attention. When Jan Carlzon became head of

SAS Airline, he was concerned about the poor on-time record. To correct this, he personally requested a daily accounting of the on-time status of all flights. In the space of two years, the SAS on-time record went from 83 percent to 97 percent (Carlzon, 1987).

These examples apply easily to our notions of formal control systems (Eisenhardt, 1985). Although less obvious, our definition applies equally well to informal or "social" control systems. In designing formal control systems, we typically attempt to measure either outcomes or behaviors. For example, in hospitals it makes no sense to evaluate the nursing staff by whether patients get well. Instead, control systems rely on assessing behaviors. Are specified medical procedures followed? Are checks made at appropriate times? In other settings, where behavior may not be observable, we then attempt, whenever possible, to measure outcomes. Sales people, for instance, are usually measured on their productivity, because the nature of their job often precludes any effective monitoring of behavior. In some situations, such as retail sales, control systems can be designed that monitor both behaviors (how the customer is addressed, how quickly the order is taken, whether the sales floor is kept stocked) and outcomes (sales volume).

Holding aside the issue of how it feels to be tightly controlled, it is often the case that neither behavior nor outcomes can be adequately monitored (Dornbusch & Scott, 1975). What are the circumstances in which formal control is difficult? Those in which activities are nonroutine and unpredictable, situations that require initiative, flexibility, and innovation. These are precisely the times when organizations are at greatest risk. Such situations can be dealt with, insofar as they can be anticipated, only through the development of social control systems in which people agree on and mutually enforce appropriate standards of behavior.

Culture, then, may be thought of as a potential social control system. When individuals share a common understanding of what is important and what is the appropriate way of responding, a social control system may exist. Interestingly, unlike formal control systems that typically assess outcomes or behaviors only intermittently, social control systems can be much more finely tuned. Return for a moment to our definition of control as "the knowledge that someone who knows and cares is paying close attention." When we care about those with whom we work and have a common set of expectations, we are "under control" whenever we are in their presence. If we want to be accepted, we try to live up to their expectations. In this sense, social control systems can operate more extensively than most formal systems. In addition, our response to being monitored by formal and social control systems may also differ. With formal systems we often have a sense of external constraint which is binding and unsatisfying. With social controls, we paradoxically often feel as though we have great autonomy, even though we are acting in great conformity. Because the sense is one of intrinsic rather than extrinsic control, it may be accompanied by more positive attitudes.

Thus, from a management perspective, culture in the form of shared expectations may be thought of as a social control system. In some situations this form of control may be more appropriate and effective than traditional formal systems. This leads to the question of what culture really is?

Culture Defined

One group of scholars who have long studied culture are the anthropologists. A quick review of their approach turns up definitions such as those offered by Malinowski: "Culture comprises inherited artifacts, goods, technical processes, ideas, habits and values"; and Ruth Benedict: "What really binds men together is their culture—the ideas and standards they have in common." Kroeber and Kluckholm (1952) provide these among 164 different conceptions of culture in the anthropology literature. While these definitions may be useful for an anthropologist about to embark on a study of a group whose language, kinship patterns, religion, and social structure are unknown, they do not seem very helpful for a manager.

Organizational researchers, on the other hand, come closer to defining culture in a practical way. Van Maanen and Barley (1984) describe culture as "the values and expectations which organizational members come to share." Deal and Kennedy (1982, p. 4) claim that culture is "the way we do business around here." While closer to the mark, even these definitions seem a bit too broad to be managerially useful. Howard Schwartz and Stan Davis (1981, p. 33), offer a more practical definition of culture as "a pattern of beliefs and expectations shared by the organization's members. These beliefs and expectations produce norms that powerfully shape the behavior of individuals and groups."

Culture as Normative Order

What Schwartz and Davis are referring to as culture are the central norms that characterize an organization. Norms are expectations about what constitute appropriate or inappropriate attitudes and behaviors, socially created standards that help us interpret and evaluate events. Although their content may vary, norms exist in all societies and, while often unnoticed, are pervasive. For instance, in our society we have rather explicit norms about eye contact and become uncomfortable when these are violated. Consider what happens when someone doesn't look at you while speaking or who continues to look without pause. In organizations we often find peripheral or unimportant norms around such issues as dress or forms of address. The old railroads, for example, required hats for all managers and everyone was addressed with a formal "mister." More important norms often exist for quality, performance, flexibility,

or dealing with conflict. In many organizations, it is impolite to disagree publicly with others. Instead, much behind-the-scenes interaction takes place to anticipate or resolve disputes. In other organizations, there may be norms that legitimate and encourage the public airing of disputes. Intel Corporation, for example, has an explicit policy of "constructive confrontation" that encourages employees to deal with disagreements in an immediate and direct manner.

In this view of culture, the central values and styles that characterize a firm, although they may not be written down, can form the basis for the development of norms that attach approval or disapproval to holding certain attitudes or beliefs and to acting in certain ways. For instance, a fundamental value of aggressiveness or competition, if widely held and supported, may be expressed as a norm that encourages organizational participants to stress winning in competition. Pepsico, for one, encourages competition and punishes failure to compete (*Business Week,* October 27, 1980). Service is a pivotal norm in IBM; innovation is recognized as central in 3M. It is through norms—the expectations shared by group members and the approval or disapproval attached to these expectations—that culture is developed and maintained.

In thinking about culture from this perspective two distinctions need to be kept in mind. First, as Stan Davis (1984) notes, there is an important difference between the guiding beliefs or vision of top management and the daily beliefs or norms held by those at lower levels in a unit or organization. The former reflect top managements' ideas about how things ought to be; the latter define how things actually are. Simply because top managers are in agreement about how they would like the organization to function is no guarantee that their beliefs will be held by others. One CEO spoke at some length about the glowing corporate philosophy that he believed in and felt characterized his firm's culture. After spending some time talking to mid-level managers in the organization, a very different picture emerged. A central norm shared by many of these managers was "Good people don't stay here." It is all too common to find a noble sounding statement of corporate values framed on the wall and a very different and cynical interpretation of this creed among people who have been around long enough to know what is really important.

A second distinction to note about the central norms that may define an organization's culture is that norms can vary on two dimensions: 1) the intensity or amount of approval/disapproval attached to an expectation; and 2) the crystallization or degree of consensus or consistency with which a norm is shared. Figure 1 illustrates how, when analyzing an organization's culture, one may find wide consensus about certain values but no intensity. Everyone understands what top management values, but there is no strong approval or disapproval attached to these beliefs or behaviors—a vacuous norm. Or, it may be that a given norm, such as innovation, can be positively valued in one group (for example, marketing or research and development) and negatively valued in another (say, manufacturing or personnel). There is intensity but no crystallization. Strong cultures exist only when there is both intensity and consensus. The extent to which this is true suggests why it is difficult to develop or change a culture. Organizational members must come to know and share a common set of expectations. These must, in turn, be consistently valued and reinforced across divisions and management levels (Feldman, 1984). Only when this occurs will there be both intensity and consensus. Similarly, a failure to share beliefs or to reward them consistently may lead to vacuous norms, conflicting interpretations, or to microcultures that exist only within subunits.

The good news seems to be that although it is difficult to develop a strong culture, an organization does not have to have very many strongly held values. On the contrary, the evidence seems to be that only a few core values that are critical for the execution of strategy and that help employees identify with the firm seem to characterize such strong-culture firms as Mars, Marriott, Hewlett-Packard, Walmart, and others. What is critical is that these beliefs be widely shared and strongly held; that is, people throughout the organization must be willing to tell one another when a core belief is not being lived up to. Otherwise values such as quality, service, and performance are not meaningful.

The Role of Culture in Promoting Innovation

To illustrate how culture as norms operate, let us consider briefly how culture and innovation may be linked. How is it that firms such as Intel, Hewlett-Packard, Cray Research, 3M, and Johnson & Johnson successfully develop both new products and new ways of doing things (Foster, 1986)? First, it is important to recognize that organizational innovation, defined as "the successful introduction into an applied situation of means and ends that are new to the situation" (Mohr, 1969, p. 112), consists of two component processes: 1) creativity—or the generation of a new way of doing something; and 2) implementation—or the successful introduction of this new idea. We know when innovation has occurred only when both com-

Intensity

	HIGH	LOW
HIGH	Strong culture	Vacuous beliefs
LOW	Value conflict	External control

Consensus

FIGURE 1.

290

ponents are present. Something new was suggested or developed *and* it was actually installed or implemented.

How can culture help or hinder this process? To address this question we need only think which norms, if widely shared and strongly held by members of the organization, would actively promote the generation of new ideas and would help implement new approaches as they were developed. What might these norms be? This question was put to over five hundred managers in firms as diverse as pharmaceuticals, consumer products, computers and semiconductors, and manufacturing. Table 1 contains a summary of norms that they frequently cited.

Several things are notable about this list. First, regardless of the industry or technology, managers invariably identified virtually the same sets of norms as important. While it is certainly true that the process of innovation varies widely from discovering new drugs, to improving oil exploration efforts, building new electronic devices, and developing a better toilet bowl cleaner, the norms that can facilitate these efforts are remarkably consistent. Second, in general these norms all function either to facilitate the process of introducing new ways of doing things and/or to help people implement new ways. For example, when people share the expectation that it is not only permissible but also desirable to challenge the status quo, the likelihood of innovation is increased. At Cray Research, a prime example of a firm that succeeds or fails based on its ability to innovate, creativity and diversity are seen as virtues. Similarly, at Intel Corporation, whose strategy has long been that of a first-mover or innovator, all employees are told to expect conflict and to deal with it directly. The firm's strong belief is that in a creative setting there will always be conflict. Employees are trained in a process called "constructive confrontation"

which helps them deal with and resolve conflict in productive rather than destructive ways. At Johnson & Johnson a similar belief is referred to as "creative conflict."

To appreciate how critical the norms shown in table 1 are to innovation, simply envision an organization that is characterized by norms opposite to those listed. Imagine an organization where failure is punished severely and no recognition or rewards are provided for doing things differently, where the past is venerated and only ideas generated internally are considered worthwhile, where "dumb" ideas are ridiculed and risk-taking is discouraged, and where there is no drive to change and improve things. In this environment, one would be amazed to see any change. Contrast this with an organization like 3M in which a basic financial goal is to generate 25 percent of annual sales from products developed over the last five years. Allen Jacobsen, the CEO, says, "People ask me how do you get people to be innovative. It's simple. You give them responsibility for their own destinies and encourage them to take risks" (*Fortune,* June 6, 1988). The secret to 3M's success isn't in Mr. Jacobsen's words but in the norms that compose the culture. These are widely shared and strongly held because management up and down the line provides the resources and encouragement to sustain them. It is the expectations held by people throughout the company, not just those in research and development, that make 3M and similar firms so innovative.

The important point here is that there is nothing magical or elusive about the culture. One has only to be clear about the specific attitudes and behaviors that are needed, and then to identify the norms or expectations that promote or impede them. In the case of innovation, the dual issues of creativity and implementation are critical, and those norms that help or hinder these define the successful or unsuccessful culture. Similar sets of norms could easily be

TABLE 1   *Norms that Promote Innovation*

A. *Norms to Promote Creativity*
1. Risk Taking
   - Freedom to try things and fail
   - Acceptance of mistakes
   - Allow discussion of "dumb" ideas
   - No punishments for failure
   - Challenge the status quo
   - Forget the past
   - Willingness *not* to focus on the short term
   - Expectation that innovation is part of the job
   - Positive attitudes about change
   - Drive to improve
2. Rewards for Change
   - Ideas are valued
   - Respect for beginning ideas
   - Build into the structure
     - –Budgets –Time –Tools
     - –Resources –Opportunities –Promotions
   - Top management attention and support
   - Celebration of accomplishments
   - Suggestions are implemented
   - Encouragement
3. Openness
   - Open communication and share information
   - Listen better
   - Open access
   - Bright people, strong egos
   - Scanning, broad thinking
   - Force exposure outside the company
   - Move people around
   - Encourage lateral thinking
   - Adopt the customer's perspective
   - Accept criticism
   - Don't be too sensitive
   - Continuous training
   - Intellectual honesty
   - Expect and accept conflict
   - Willingness to consult others

B. *Norms to Promote Implementation*
1. Common Goals
   - Sense of pride in the organization
   - Teamwork
   - Willingness to share the credit
   - Flexibility in jobs, budgets, functional areas
   - Sense of ownership
   - Eliminate mixed messages
   - Manage interdependencies
   - Shared visions and a common direction
   - Build consensus
   - Mutual respect and trust
   - Concern for the whole organization
2. Autonomy
   - Decision-making responsibility at lower levels
   - Decentralized procedures
   - Freedom to act
   - Belief that *you* can have an impact
   - Delegation
   - Quick, flexible decision making
   - Minimize the bureaucracy
3. Belief in Action
   - Don't be obsessed with precision
   - Expectation of action
   - Emphasis on results
   - Meet your commitments
   - Anxiety about timeliness
   - Value getting things done
   - Hard work is expected and appreciated
   - Empower people
   - Emphasis on quality
   - Eagerness to get things done
   - Cut through the bureaucracy

generated in support of quality, service, low cost, and other core values.

WHY CULTURE IS IMPORTANT

The examples provided by a number of authors (Davis, 1984; Deal & Kennedy, 1982; Peters & Waterman, 1982) highlight two reasons why a strong culture may be valuable: 1) the fit of culture and strategy; and 2) the increased commitment by employees to the firm. Both these factors may provide a competitive edge, giving a strong-culture firm an advantage over its competitors.

Strategy and Corporate Culture

Each firm competing in an industry has, implicitly or explicitly, a competitive strategy that dictates how and on what basis the firm attempts to position itself with respect to competitors. Depending on the strategy, different organizational structures and systems may be appropriate (Miles & Snow, 1978). For example, organization theorists have demonstrated that in stable, routine product markets mechanistic or functionally organized firms seem to prosper, while in unstable, complex environments organic forms appear to be more appropriate.

Nadler and Tushman (1980) have characterized the relationships among strategy, structure, and process as outlined in figure 2. In their conceptualization, once a firm's strategy is in effect, it dictates a set of critical tasks or objectives that must be accomplished. Depending on their nature, these critical tasks can best be achieved through congruence among the elements of people, structure, and culture. For example, a decision to compete on innovation rather than price may suggest an appropriate formal structure and control system (the vertical axis in figure 2). Once decided, these fundamental tasks may also imply the types of people required to accomplish the objectives and to fit the structure. In this way, a firm choosing to compete by being the most innovative, as opposed to being the low-cost producer, may require both a different structure and a different mix of people. Importantly, the choice of a strategy also has implications for the informal organization or culture; that is, do the norms of the organization help execute the strategy? Is there a congruency or fit among people, tasks, and structure? What happens when congruence doesn't exist?

Several illustrations may help. Consider the history of AT&T. For most of this century, the Bell System faced a very predictable environment. Their strategy was simple: provide the best quality service to all customers at the lowest cost consistent with the financial health of the firm. In support of this, AT&T was organized along functional lines, had strict control and reward systems emphasizing quality and service, and was composed of people who could be characterized as conservative and service-

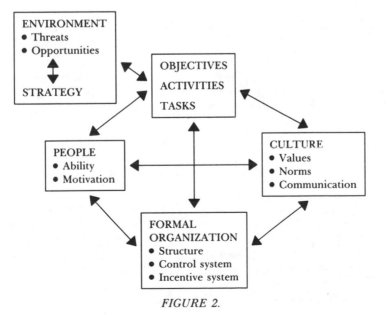

FIGURE 2.

293

oriented (Schlesinger et al., 1987). The culture or norms supported the complex but routine nature of the tasks. The functional organization emphasized teamwork, service, and quality and devalued entrepreneurship, marketing, and change. With deregulation, massive changes occurred. The key to the future was a market-oriented strategy that emphasized a decentralized organization, new reward and control systems, people with new skills, and, if these were to succeed, a culture or normative order that supported these new objectives. Similar challenges confront other deregulated industries, such as banking and transportation.

Another example of the importance of fit to strategy, structure, and culture can be seen in the three major Silicon Valley firms manufacturing integrated circuits (IC's). Although operating in the same product market, Intel, National Semi conductor, and Advanced Micro Devices have each pursued a different strategy, one that has been reflected in their structures and cultures. National Semi conductor has chosen to compete largely as a low-cost manufacturer. It stresses strict cost control, a functional organizational structure, and a strong culture that emphasizes numbers, a lack of frills, and a certain ruthlessness that has earned them the sobriquet of "animals of the valley." Intel, on the other hand, has chosen to compete on product innovation rather than cost. It has a looser formal organization and a culture valuing collegial interaction and the development of new technologies and products. Advanced Micro Devices has chosen a marketing strategy offering very high quality products, often as a second source. Its strength has been in its marketing, and its culture reflects the value placed on selling, service, and quality.

The point is obvious. For a strategy to be successfully implemented, the appropriate culture can be an important asset. Lack of sensitivity to this consideration is most evident when firms change strategies, and often structures, yet fail because the underlying shared values

simply do not support the new approach. For instance, a declaration by the top management of an engineering firm that they are now going to be "market-driven" does not ensure that the new strategy will be successful, no matter how good the planning or correct the decision. People throughout the organization need to understand why the change is important and how it is to be accomplished, and must support the new orientation with their day-to-day approval. A failure to develop new norms supportive of the strategy means that changes will persist only where they are closely monitored and directly rewarded.

For instance, Schwartz and Davis (1981) report how the CEO of a large industrial paint company developed a strategy to move the company toward a more retail-based focus where the volumes and margins were higher. He failed to implement the strategy, however, and was fired. His resignation speech captured some of his frustration when he said, "When you take a 100-year-old company and (try to) change the culture . . . well it takes time." Ironically, his successor was able to implement the original strategy successfully. In another case, a large, integrated electronics firm with a very strong culture built around technical excellence decided to enter the word-processing market. They made equipment that could easily be used as a basis for a word processor. Unfortunately, the culture that made them successful in the design and manufacture of satellites and other sophisticated equipment ultimately sabotaged their efforts to design a word processor. Engineers with a strong ethic of "getting it right" would not release the machine, and the window of opportunity for entry into the market passed, leaving the firm with a $40 million write-off of their investment.

The point here is both simple and important. As firms grow and strategies change, the culture or social control system may also need to be realigned to reflect the new direction. The irony is that long periods of success and a venerated organizational culture may, unwittingly, make the situation worse. With years of success, Kodak and Polaroid had cultures that valued only products developed from within. As competition in the photographic industry shifted and the pace of innovation accelerated, it left both these firms vulnerable. With a tradition of high quality, firms like Caterpillar and John Deere were slow to recognize the need to get their costs down as overseas competition ate into their markets. What defines "service" for IBM developed when mainframe computers were its central product. Is this standard of service appropriate when selling much smaller systems?

Executives need to be sensitive to the social control systems in their organizations. An over-reliance on formal systems and a failure to shape the culture can hinder the execution of otherwise successful strategies.

Culture and Commitment

Independent of the importance of culture for the implementation of strategy, culture can also be critical in developing and maintaining the levels of intensity and dedication that often characterize strong-culture firms. This powerful attachment can be particularly valuable when employees' knowledge is critical for the success of the organization or when very high levels of motivation are required. When IBM bought ROLM, the critical resource was not the existing product line but the design and engineering expertise of ROLM's staff. A failure to gain the commitment of employees during mergers and acquisitions can diminish or destroy the value of the venture. Having a very highly dedicated workforce can offer a significant competitive advantage. Under turbulent or changing conditions, relying on employees who wait to be told exactly what to do can be a liability. How, then, do strong-culture organizations develop the intensity and commitment suggested by a twenty-year veteran of IBM who

was quoted in a *Wall Street Journal* article as saying, "I don't know what a cult is and what it is those bleary-eyed kids selling poppies really do, but I'm probably that deeply committed to the IBM company" (April 7, 1986). To understand this process, we need to understand the psychology underlying commitment and its development. We can then think about how to design systems that foster attachment among employees.

Organizational Commitment. What is meant by the term "organizational commitment"? Without being too academic, it is typically conceived of as an individual's psychological bond to the organization, including a sense of job involvement, loyalty, and a belief in the values of the organization (Mowday, Porter & Steers, 1982). Focusing on the third component, a belief in the values of the organization, O'Reilly and Chatman (1986) have demonstrated that there are actually three processes or stages of commitment: 1) compliance; 2) identification; and 3) internalization. In the first stage, *compliance,* a person accepts the influence of others mainly to obtain something from them, such as pay. Thus, when a person first joins an organization, commitment is usually that of compliance; the new person accepts directions in order to be rewarded.

The second stage is *identification,* in which the individual accepts influence so as to maintain a satisfying, self-defining relationship. Commitment here is based on a desire to continue the association with the organization because it represents something attractive to the person. People feel pride in belonging to the firm.

The final stage of commitment is *internalization,* in which the individual finds the values of the organization to be intrinsically rewarding and congruent with personal values. In this phase the values of the individual and the firm are congruent.

A conception of commitment as developing in this manner is useful for two reasons. First, it allows us to draw upon and to use an extensive body of research showing how commitment can be generated (O'Reilly and Caldwell, 1981; Salancik, 1977). Second, from this perspective it is possible to understand how a variety of organizations, ranging from cults to strong-culture corporations, generate commitment among their members. In fact, these organizations can be categorized based on the type of commitment displayed by members. Cults and religious organizations, for example, typically have members who have internalized the values of the organization and who become "deployable agents," or individuals who can be relied on to go forth and proselytize (Appel, 1983; Gerstel, 1982). Japanese organizations and strong-culture firms are characterized by members who identify strongly with the organization because it stands for something they value (O'Reilly and Chatman, 1986; Ouchi, 1981). In typical corporations, members comply with directions but may have little involvement with the firm beyond self-interest; that is, there is no commitment to the firm beyond that of a fair exchange of effort for money and, perhaps, status.

Understanding that identification and internalization are the bases of commitment that result in the intensity of effort described by Tom Peters allows us to focus on the processes that foster them. Identification and internalization appear to be central to the increased motivation and sense of responsibility shown by members of strong-culture organizations (Ouchi, 1981). Failure to develop this attachment among employees leaves management to rely on compliance-based commitment. This means increased attention to specifying job requirements, designing formal control systems to ensure quality, and accepting the fact that employees' loyalty is predicated solely on a perception of fair exchange. While this type of commitment may be suitable for jobs with well-designed formal control systems, compliance cannot be relied upon when what is required are initiative, flexibility, and innovation. By their very nature these cannot be programmed. Under these circumstances, commitment based on identification and internalization, where employees understand the right thing to do and do it without formal control, is necessary.

HOW IS CULTURE DEVELOPED?

How do people become committed to organizations? Why, for example, would someone choose to join a cult? How do firms such as NUMMI get the incredible levels of productivity from their employees, leading one to say, "I like the new system so much it scares me. I'm scared because it took me eighteen years to realize that I blew it at GM. Now we have a chance to do things a different way . . ." The answer to this puzzle is simultaneously simple and nonobvious. As Jerry Salancik has noted, "Commitment is too easy" (1977), yet it relies on an understanding of human motivation that is counter-intuitive.

Constructing Social Realities

Most discussions of motivation begin with a model that presumes a stable set of individual needs and values (Herzberg et al, 1959; Maslow, 1970) that are seen as shaping expectations, goals, and attitudes. In turn, the latter are presumed to guide behavior and peoples' responses to situations. In Maslow's (1970) theory, for instance, people are assumed to have a hierarchy of needs. The managerial consequence of this view can be seen in our theories of job design (Hackman and Oldham, 1980), in which jobs are meant to take advantage of the growth need strength of the job holders—more enriched jobs offering a higher motivating potential for those with higher levels of growth need strength. But are such theories correct?

The empirical evidence is weak at best (Salancik & Pfeffer, 1978). In spite of numerous efforts to demonstrate the effect of needs and personality, there is little support for the power of individual differences to predict behavior.

Consider the results of two experiments. In the first, Christian seminary students were approached and given one of two requests. In both situations they were asked to walk to a classroom and extemporaneously address a visiting class on the subject of the parable of the Good Samaritan. One set of students were informed that the class was already there and that they should hurry. The others were told that the class would arrive in several minutes. As they walked to the classroom, all subjects passed an old man (the "victim") dressed in shabby clothes and in obvious need of help. The experimenters were interested to see what proportion of Christian seminarians thinking of the Good Samaritan would stop and help this person. Surprisingly, of the subjects who were told to hurry, only 30 percent paid any attention to him (Darley and Batson, 1973). Think about this. Seventy percent of a group of individuals with religious values and in training to be ministers failed to stop. Ninety-five percent of those who were not in a hurry stopped to help.

In another experiment, researchers observed how often students using a campus restroom washed their hands. They discovered that when another person was visible in the restroom, 90 percent washed their hands. When no other person was visible, less than 20 percent did so.

What explains these and other findings (Milgram, 1969)? What often seems to account for behavior are the expectations of others. As individuals we are very susceptible to the informational and normative influence of other people. We pay attention to the actions of others and learn from them. As Bandura (1977) has argued, "In actuality, virtually all learning phenomena resulting from direct experience occur on a vicarious basis by observing other people's behavior and its consequences for them." We watch others and form expectations about how and when we should act.

Yet, we are not sensitive to the degree our world is really a social construction—one that rests on shared agreements. Part of this oversight occurs because of what social psychologists call an attributional error, often referred to as "the actor-observer error" (Shaver, 1975). This refers to an interesting and robust tendency in all of us to attribute the behavior of others to stable, internal, dispositional causes while explaining our own behavior by external factors. When we see someone acting in an unexpected way (for instance, joining a cult), we are quick to try to explain the incident with something about the individual's personality (for example, he or she is easily influenced). When we find ourselves behaving in ways we didn't anticipate (for example, exceeding the speed limit or driving recklessly), we tend not to invoke personality ("I'm aggressive and risk-taking") but blame external causes ("Officer, I'm late for a very important meeting"). This bias can easily lead us to expect that individual motives are operating where they are not. It can also lead us to underestimate the degree to which situations and the expectations of others can constrain and shape behavior. Strong situations, ones in which there are very clear incentives and expectations about what constitutes appropriate attitudes and behavior, can be very powerful. When we care what others think, the power of these norms or social expectations can be heightened.

This argument underscores several of the points made earlier. First, norms or social expectations can be a powerful and pervasive force in organizations. Second, they may constitute an important but overlooked social control system. Third, depending on the content of these norms, an organization's culture can help or hinder the execution of strategy. And finally, a culture may also act to bind or commit people to the organization. Thus, the argument made here is not that all organizations do, or even should, have strong cultures. There may be situations where a strong culture is unnecessary or problematic—for example, when formal controls are precise and effective or when the culture would prohibit needed change. On the other hand, when formal control systems are inadequate, when high commitment is valuable, and when unprogrammed efforts requiring initiative, innovation, and great consistency are demanded, then culture, operating as a social control system, may be the only effective alternative. Under these conditions, executives need explicitly to understand and to manage the organization's culture.

Mechanisms for Developing Culture

With this brief background, we can now sketch out how cultures can be developed and managed in organizations ranging from the sacred to the secular. These organizations all draw on the same underlying psychology to create situations characterized by strong norms that focus people's attention, provide clear guidance about what is important, and provide for group reinforcement of appropriate attitudes and behavior. Four common mechanisms are used to accomplish this. What varies is not what is done but the degree to which these mechanisms are used. In this sense, there is a great deal of similarity in these organizations and in how people feel about them. As we shall see, however, there are also important differences. Let us consider the four mechanisms for shaping culture.

Participation.   The first mechanism that can be critical in developing or changing a culture is systems that provide for participation. These encourage people to be involved and send signals to the individual that he or she is valued. They may range from such formal efforts as quality circles and advisory boards to less formal efforts like suggestion systems, opportunities to meet with top managers, and informal social gatherings. What is important about these processes is that people are encouraged to make incremental choices and to develop a sense of responsibility for their actions. In some cases, such as work design, the specific choices made may be less important for future success than the fact that a chance was provided to make them.

From a psychological perspective, choice is often associated with commitment. When we choose of our own volition to do something, we often feel responsible (Cialdini, 1984). When the choice is volitional, explicit, public, and irrevocable, the commitment is even more binding (Salancik, 1977). For instance, direct sales companies have learned that by getting the customer to fill out the order sheet, they can cut cancellations dramatically. A large number of psychological experiments have convincingly shown that participation can lead to both commitment and enjoyment, even when people are induced to engage in such physically and emotionally stressful activities as eating earthworms and becoming bone marrow donors (Janis and Mann, 1977).

How do organizations use participation? Marc Galanter (1980) has documented how the Moonies use a process of incremental commitment to recruit cult members. Individuals are invited to dinner, convinced to spend the weekend for a seminar, and, in some cases, induced to remain permanently with their new-found "friends." Interestingly, there is no evidence that people who join cults under these circumstances are suffering from any psychopathology. Traditional religious organizations as well often use elaborate systems of incremental choice and participation that lead to greater and greater involvement. Japanese-managed automobile companies in the U.S. also have selection and orientation systems that rely heavily on these approaches, as do notable strong-culture firms.

Management as Symbolic Action. The second mechanism commonly seen in strong-culture organizations is clear, visible action on the part of management in support of the cultural values (Pfeffer, 1981). In organizations, participants typically want to know what is important. One way we gain this information is to watch and listen carefully to those above us. We look for consistent patterns. When top management not only says that something is important but also consistently behaves in ways that support that message, we begin to believe what is said. When David Kearns, the CEO of Xerox, began his quest for improved quality, there was some initial uncertainty about his sincerity. Over time, as the message was repeated again and again, and as resources continued to be devoted to the quality effort, norms developed that raised expectations about the role and importance of quality throughout the corporation (Jacobsen and Hillkirk, 1986).

As Pfeffer has noted (1981), one important function of management is to interpret events for the organization's members. Without a shared meaning, confusion and conflict can result. Managers need to be sensitive to how their actions are viewed. Interpreting (or reinterpreting) history, telling stories, using vivid language, spending time, and being visibly in support of certain positions are all potential ways of shaping an organization's culture. This does not mean that managers need to be charismatic. As Michael Tushman and Elaine Romanelli (1985) have suggested, managers need to engage in acts of "mundane symbolism." By this they refer to activities such as ensuring that suitable amounts of time are allotted to important issues, that questions are continually asked about important topics, and important subjects are put on the agenda and followed up. The appropriate use of symbols and ceremonies may also help. When Jerry Sanders, CEO of Advanced Micro Devices, a semiconductor manufacturer, decided to shift the firm's strategy toward innovation, he not only made substantive changes in budget, positions, and organizational structure, he also used a symbol. As a part of many talks with employees in which he described the need to change, Sanders would also describe the importance of investing in areas others could not easily duplicate—such as proprietary products. He would tell how a poor farmer always needs a cash crop at the end of the year if he is to survive. But if he begins to prosper, a smart farmer begins to plant crops that others might not be able to afford—crops, for example, that take more than a year to come to fruition, crops like asparagus. The notion of asparagus became a visible and important symbol for change within AMD, even to the point where managers would refer to revenues from new proprietary products as "being measured on asparagus."

The point here is not that symbols can substitute for substance or that ceremonies can replace content. Rather, it is that many of the substantive changes that occur in organizations, such as promotions or reorganizations, have multiple meanings and interpretations. Over time, people may lose a clear sense of what the superordinate goals are and why their jobs are important. In strong-culture organizations managers frequently and consistently send signals to help renew understanding. They do so by continually calling attention to what is important, in word and in action.

Information from Others. While clear messages from management are an important determinant of a culture, so too are consistent messages from co-workers. If control comes from the knowledge that someone who matters is paying attention, then the degree to which we care about our co-workers also gives them control over us. Again, the experimental evidence supports this effect. Years ago several researchers conducted an experiment in which subjects were placed in a room to complete a questionnaire. As the subjects worked on their task, smoke began to flow into the room from an air vent. While 75 percent of the subjects who were alone responded by notifying the experimenter of a possible fire, only 38 percent of those in the company of two other subjects did so. When these other two were confederates of the experimenter and deliberately said nothing, only 10 percent of the subjects responded. One conclusion that may be drawn from this and similar experiments is that we often take our cue from others when we are uncertain what to do.

In organizations during periods of crisis or in a new situation, people often look to others for explanations of what to do and how to interpret events. Strong cultures are typically characterized by consensus about these questions. In these settings attempts are often made to ensure a consistency of understanding and to minimize any us-them attitudes between parts of the organization. Strong-culture firms often pride themselves on their equal treatment of all employees. At Mars, for instance, all employees punch a time-clock, and no one has a private secretary. At Gore-Tex, WalMart, Disney, and other firms there are no employees or managers, only associates, team members, and hosts. At NUMMI, Honda, and Nissan there are no private dining rooms for managers, and both managers and workers often wear uniforms. In the Rajneesh Commune, everyone wore purple.

The goal here is to create a strong social construction of reality by minimizing contradictory interpretations. In cults this is often done by isolating the members from family and friends. Other religious organizations encourage extensive involvement in a variety of church activities and meetings. In Japanese firms there is the expectation of after-work socializing. At NUMMI, for instance, each work team is given a semiannual budget to be spent only on team-sponsored activities in which the entire team participates. In corporations, sixty-hour work weeks can also isolate people from competing interpretations. Some electronics firms in Silicon Valley have given employees T-shirts with slogans like "Working 80 hours a week and loving it." With such a time commitment, workers may be as isolated as if they had joined a cult.

Comprehensive Reward Systems.   A final mechanism for promoting and shaping culture is the reward system. Eschewing simple monetary rewards, these systems focus on recognition and approval which can be given more frequently than money. These rewards also stress the intrinsic aspects of the job and of belonging to the organization. Recognition by a boss or coworkers for doing the right thing can be more potent in shaping behavior than an annual bonus. In the words of a popular management book, the trick is to catch someone doing something right and to reward it on the spot. While tokens like scrolls or badges can be meaningless, under the right circumstances they can also be highly valued.

Steven Kerr (1975), in what is now a classic article entitled "On the Folly of Rewarding for A, While Hoping for B," reminds us how easy it is to desire one type of behavior while rewarding another. Often management professes a concern for quality while systematically rewarding only those who meet quantitative goals, regardless of quality. Innovation may be espoused, but even the slightest failure is punished. At its simplest, people usually do what they are rewarded for and do not do what they are punished for. If this is true, and to be taken seriously, then a simple analysis of what gets management's attention should give us a sense of what a culture supports. Who gets promoted, for example. At 3M, one important sign of success is to be associated with the introduction of a new product. If, on the other hand, innovation is espoused but doing things by the book is rewarded, it doesn't take a psychologist to figure out what the culture will value. In fact, if there are inconsistencies between what top management says and what it actually rewards, the likely outcome will be confusion and cynicism.

MANAGING CULTURE

Each of the mechanisms described can affect the development of a shared set of expectations. As shown in figure 3, the process begins with the words and actions of the group's leaders. Even if no explicit statements are made, subordinates will attempt to infer a pattern. If management is credible and communicates consistently, members of the group may begin to develop consistent expectations about what is important. When this consensus is also rewarded, clear norms can emerge.

This process appears to operate across a variety of organizational types, from the extreme examples of cults and religious organizations (Appel, 1983) to Japanese organizations in the United States (Ouchi, 1981) to strong-culture firms (Deal & Kennedy, 1982). All rely on processes that include incremental commitment and public participation, dependence on groups for control of members, and a comprehensive reward system that often uses recognition and approval to enhance group solidarity and to justify actions (Pascale, 1985). Management's role here is to develop the vision and superordinate goals and to reinforce them through credible communication and employee involvement. Emphasis is often placed on keeping groups small enough to ensure that individuals know one another. This promotes the development of the central norms that anchor the culture.

Whether these norms constitute a desirable culture depends on the critical tasks to be accomplished and on the ability of the formal control system to provide sufficient leverage to attain them. If culture is important, four steps can help a manager understand how to manage it.

1. Identify the strategic objectives of the unit. Once identified, specify the short-term objectives and critical actions necessary if the strategic objectives are to be accomplished.
2. Analyze the existing values and norms that characterize the organization. Focus on what people in the unit feel is expected of them by their peers and bosses and what is really rewarded. What does it take to get ahead? What stories are routinely told? Who are the people who exemplify the group? Look for norms that are widely shared and strongly felt.
3. Once these values and norms are identified, look for: a) norms that may hinder the accomplishment of critical tasks; b) norms that would help but are not currently present; and c) conflicts between what is needed and what is currently rewarded.

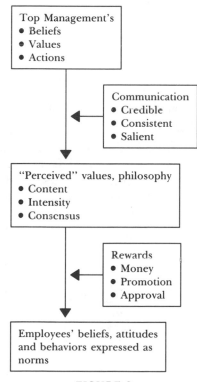

FIGURE 3.

4. When these norms and conflicts are identified, programs can be designed to begin to shape or develop the desired norms. These can draw on the psychological mechanisms discussed previously.

The logic here is straightforward and links culture to those activities critical to the implementation of strategy and the generation of widespread understanding and commitment among the organization's members. Obviously these actions take time and management resources to accomplish. However, to ignore them is to ignore a social control system that may already be operating in the organization. The issue is whether this system is helping or hindering.

SUMMARY

The material presented here offers one perspective on corporate culture (see Ott, 1989, and Schein, 1985, for alternative views). It emphasizes how, from a managerial perspective, culture may be understood in terms of the norms shared by members of the organization. When these expectations are widely shared and strongly held, they may powerfully shape behavior, and in turn, be of great help or harm to the individual or the organization. Management needs to be sensitive to what the central organizational norms are and to how it can affect them. To fail to understand these issues is to ignore the advice of a CEO who said, "We will either be a victim or a successful result of our culture."

REFERENCES

Appel, W. (1983) *Cults in America.* New York: Holt, Rinehart and Winston.

Bandura, A. (1977) *Social Learning Theory.* Englewood Cliffs, NJ: Prentice-Hall.

Barney, J. (1986) "Organizational culture: Can it be a source of sustained competitive advantage?" *Academy of Management Review,*" 656–665.

Carlzon, J. (1987) *Moments of Truth.* Cambridge, MA: Ballinger.

Caildini, R. (1984) *Influence: The New Psychology of Modern Persuasion.* New York: Quill.

Darley, J. and Batson, C. (1973) "From Jerusalem to Jericho: A study of situational and dispositional variables in helping behavior." *Journal of Personality and Social Psychology, 27,* 100–108.

Davis, S. (1984) *Managing Corporate Culture.* Cambridge, MA: Ballinger.

Deal, T. and Kennedy, A. (1982) *Corporate Cultures.* Reading, MA: Addison-Wesley.

Dornbusch, S. and Scott, W.R. (1975) *Evaluation and the Exercise of Authority.* San Francisco, CA: Jossey-Bass.

Eisenhardt, K. (1985) "Control: Organizational and economic approaches." *Management Science, 31,* 134–149.

Feldman, D. (1984) "The development and enforcement of group norms." *Academy of Management Review, 9,* 47–53.

Foster, R. (1986) *Innovation: The Attacker's Advantage.* New York: Summit Books.

Galanter, M. (1980) "Psychological induction into the large group: Findings from a modern religious sect." *American Journal of Psychiatry, 137,* 1574–1579.

Gerstel, D. (1982) *Paradise Incorporated: Synanon.* San Francisco, CA: Presidio Press.

Hackman, J. R. and Oldham, G. (1980) *Work Redesign.* Reading, MA: Addison-Wesley.

Herzberg, F., Mausner, B. and Snyderman, B. (1959) *The Motivation to Work.* New York: John Wiley.

Jacobsen, G. and Hillkirk, J. (1986) *Xerox: American Samurai.* New York: Collier Books.

Janis, I. and Mann, L. (1977) *Decision Making: A Psychological Analysis of Conflict, Choice, and Commitment.* New York: Free Press.

Kerr, S. (1975) "On the folly of rewarding A, while hoping for B." *Academy of Management Journal, 18,* 769–783.

Kroeber, A. and Kluckholm, C. (1952) *Culture: A Critical Review of Concepts and Definitions.* New York: Vintage Books.

Maslow, A. (1970) *Motivation and Personality.* New York: Harper & Row.

Miles, R. and Snow, C. (1978) *Organizational Strategy, Structure, and Process.* New York: McGraw-Hill.

Milgram, S. (1969) *Obedience to Authority.* New York: Harper & Row.

Mohr, L. (1969) "Determinants of innovation in organizations." *American Political Science Review, 63,* 111–126.

Mowday, R., Porter, L. and Steers, R. (1982) *Organizational Linkages: The Psychology of Commitment, Absenteeism, and Turnover.* New York: Academic Press.

Nadler, D. and Tushman, M. (1980) "A model for diagnosing organizational behavior: Applying a congruence perspective." *Organizational Dynamics.*

O'Reilly, C. and Caldwell, D. (1981) "The commitment and job tenure of new employees: Some evidence of post-decisional justification." *Administrative Science Quarterly, 26,* 597–616.

O'Reilly, C. and Chatman, J. (1986) "Organizational commitment and psychological attachment; the effects of compliance, identification and internalization on prosocial behavior." *Journal of Applied Psychology, 71,* 492–499.

Ott, J. S. (1989) *The Organizational Culture Perspective.* Pacific Grove, CA: Brooks-Cole.

Ouchi, W. (1981) *Theory Z.* Reading, MA: Addison-Wesley.

Pascale, R. (1985) "The paradox of corporate culture: Reconciling ourselves to socialization." *California Management Review, 27,* 26–40.

Peters, T. and Waterman, R. H. (1982) *In Search of Excellence: Lessons From America's Best-Run Companies.* New York: Harper & Row.

Pfeffer, J. (1981) Management as symbolic action: The creation and maintenance of organizational paradigms. In L. Cummings and B. Staw (eds.) *Research in Organizational Behavior,* vol. 3. Greenwich, CT: JAI Press.

Salancik, G. (1977) "Commitment is too easy!" *Organizational Dynamics,* (Summer), 62–80.

Salancik, G. and Pfeiffer, J. (1978) "A social information processing approach to job attitudes and task design." *Administrative Science Quarterly, 23,* 224–253.

Schein, E. H. (1985) *Organizational Culture and Leadership.* San Francisco, CA: Jossey-Bass.

Schlesinger, L., Dyer, D., Clough, T. and Landau, D. (1987) *Chronicles of Corporate Change,* Lexington, MA: D.C. Heath.

Schwartz, H. and Davis, S. (1981) "Matching corporate culture and business strategy." *Organizational Dynamics,* 30–48.

Shaver, K. (1975) *An Introduction to Attribution Processes.* Cambridge, MA: Winthrop.

Tushman, M. and Romanelli, E. (1985) "Organizational evolution: A metamorphosis model of convergence and reorientation." In L. Cummings and B. Staw (eds.) *Research in Organizational Behavior,* vol. 7. Greenwich, CT: JAI Press.

Van Maanen, J. and Barley, S. (1984) "Occupational communities: Culture and control in organizations." In B. Staw and L. Cummings (eds.) *Research in Organizational Behavior,* Vol. 6. Greenwich, CT: JAI Press.

Wilkins, A. and Ouchi, W. (1983) "Efficient cultures: Exploring the relationship between culture and organizational performance." *Administrative Science Quarterly, 28,* 468–481.

Williamson, O. (1975) *Markets and Hierarchies.* New York: Free Press.

The Paradox of "Corporate Culture": Reconciling Ourselves to Socialization

Richard Pascale

- An assistant controller at IBM is rehearsed for a stand-up presentation with flip charts—the principal means of formal communication. Each presentation gets "probed"—IBM's secret weapon for training and assessing young professionals. A manager states: "You're so accustomed to being probed you're almost unaware of it. IBM bosses have an uncanny way of pushing, poking, having a follow-up question, always looking for the hidden ball. It's a rigorous kind of self-discipline we impose on ourselves for getting to the heart of problems. It's also management's way of assessing potential and grooming subordinates for the next job. Senior management spends most of its time 'probing.' "[1]

- An MBA joining Bain and Company, the management consulting firm, is surprised by the incredible number of meetings he must attend—company meetings, recruiting meetings, officer meetings, office meetings, case team meetings, and near-mandatory participation on sports teams and attendance at social events. The objective is to build cohesiveness, participation, and close identification with the firm. There are a set of imperatives for working at Bain: "don't compete directly with peers," "make major conceptual contributions without being a prima donna," "demonstrate an ability to build on others' ideas." In aggregate, these features of Bain's culture are viewed as the underpinnings of success—both internally and with clients.[2]

- An applicant for an entry-level position in brand management at Procter and Gamble experiences an exhaustive application and screening process. His or her interviewer is one of an elite cadre who have been selected and trained extensively via lectures, video tapes, films, practice interviews, and role plays. P&G regards this as a crucial task; it predestines the creative and managerial resources on which the institution's future depends. The applicant is interviewed in depth for such qualities as his or her ability to "turn out high volumes of excellent work," "identify and understand problems," and "reach thoroughly substantiated and well reasoned conclusions that lead to action." The applicant receives two interviews and a general knowledge test, before being flown back to Cincinnati for three more one-on-one interviews and a group interview at lunch. Each encounter seeks corroborating evidence of the traits which P&G believes correlate highly with "what counts" for institutional excellence. Notwithstanding the intensity of this screening process, the recruiting team strives diligently to avoid overselling P&G, revealing both its plusses and minuses. P&G actually *facilitates* an applicant's de-selection, believing that no one knows better than the candidate whether the organization meshes with his or her own objectives and values.[3]

- Morgan Guaranty, a bank so profitable and well run that most other bankers use it as a model, competes fiercely for bright and aggressive talent. Once recruited, an extraordinary amount of institutional energy is invested into molding these strong and talented individuals into the Morgan "collegial" style. All employees go through a one year training program that tests their intellect, endurance, and that *requires teamwork* as an essential factor of survival. Constant evaluation assesses interpersonal skills as well as analytical abilities. "The spirit of camaraderie and togetherness" is an explicit objective of entry level indoctrination. Once on the job, frequent rotations provide cross-training and necessitate building an ever-growing network of relationships. Performance evaluations are based not solely upon one's own boss's opinion but upon inputs from every major department with which one interacts. One learns quickly that to succeed one must succeed through the team. Overt political battles are taboo and conflict is resolved directly but never disagreeably. States one officer: "The Morgan traits provide a basic grammar of understanding that enables divergent elements of our organization to speak a common language."[4]

The common thread of these examples is the systematic means by which firms bring new members into their culture. The technical term is "socialization." It encompasses the process of being made a member of a group, learning the ropes, and being taught how one must communicate and interact to get things done. Mention the term "socialization" and a variety of unsavory images come to mind. Some equate it to the teaching of socialism—an incorrect interpretation—but even when correctly understood as the imposition of social conformity, the concept makes most of us cringe. Americans, dedicated by constitution and conviction to the full expression of individuality, regard "socialization" as alien and vaguely sinister. This taboo causes us to undermanage the forces for cohesion in organizations.

The debate between "individuality" and "socialization," like politics or religion, evokes a strong emotional response. Due perhaps to our hypersensitivity to the topic, most corporations avoid the issue. Most American managers know relatively little about the precise process through which strong culture firms "socialize." There is little written on the subject. Business schools give the subject a passing wink. In fact, business schools find themselves in a particular dilemma since, in extolling management as a profession, they foster the view that a cadre of "professional managers" can move from firm to firm with generic skills that enable them to be effective in each. This runs squarely against the requirements of a strong culture. MIT's Edgar Schein states: "I believe that management education, particularly graduate (business schools), are increasingly attempting to train professionals, and in this process are socializing the students to a set of professional values which are, in fact, in a severe and direct conflict with typical organizational values."[5] It is not surprising that many businesses have become disenchanted with MBAs in line management positions because of their tendency to skip from one firm to the next. It is certainly of interest that most strong culture firms, if they hire MBAs at all, insist on starting them from the ground up and promote exclusively from within. There are no significant MBA programs in Japan—and Japanese students earning MBAs in the U.S. are sent primarily for language skills and the cross-cultural experience.[6]

Consider the fad that currently surrounds the subject of "organizational culture." Many adherents lose enthusiasm when brought face-to-face with the stark reality that "creating a strong culture" is a nice way of saying that an organization's members have to be more comprehensively socialized. Most American firms are culturally permissive. We are guided by a philosophy—initially articulated by Locke, Hobbes, and Adam Smith—which holds that individuals who are free to choose make the most efficient decisions. The independence of the parts makes a greater sum. Stemming from this tradition, American organizations allow members to do their own thing to a remarkable degree. Trendy campaigns "to become a strong culture" encounter resistance when an organization's members are asked to give up their idiosyncrasies and some of their individuality for the common good. The end result is usually the status quo.

Of course, some firms do openly worry about their "culture." Many, however, often err on the side of fostering "pseudo-cultures." (There are numerous examples in Silicon Valley.) Issuing "company creeds" or hosting rituals like "Friday night beer busts" may project the aura of corporate culture; but such elements alone do not facilitate organizational effectiveness. Real changes in style cannot prevail without a carefully thought through and interlocking socialization process.

The crux of the dilemma is this: We are intellectually and culturally opposed to the manipulation of individuals for organizational purposes. At the same time, a certain degree of social uniformity enables organizations to work better. The less we rely on informal social controls, the more we must inevitably turn to formal financial controls and bureaucratic procedures. U.S. firms that have perfected and systematized their processes of socialization tend to be a disproportionate majority of the great self-sustaining firms which survive from one generation to the next. Virtually none of these companies discuss "socialization" directly. It occurs as an exercise of the left hand—something that just happens "as the way we do things around here." When we examine any particular aspect (e.g., how the firm recruits, the nature of its entry level training, its reward systems, and so forth), little stands out as unusual. But when the pieces are assembled, what emerges in firms as different as AT&T is from P&G, as Morgan Guaranty is from IBM or Delta Airlines, is an awesome internal consistency which powerfully shapes behavior.

STEPS OF SOCIALIZATION

It is time to take socialization out of the closet. If some degree of socialization is an inescapable necessity for organizational effectiveness, the challenge for managers is to reconcile this with the American insistence upon retaining the latitude for independent action. The solution is neither mind control nor manipulation. It is neither necessary nor desirable to oscilate from extreme individualism to extreme conformity. We can learn from those who have mastered the process. A practical middle road is available. Strong culture firms that have sustained themselves over several generations of management reveal remarkable consistency across seven key steps.

Step One:
Careful selection of entry-level candidates. Trained recruiters use standardized procedures and seek specific traits that tie to success in the business. Never oversell a new recruit. Rely heavily on the informed applicant deselecting himself if the organization doesn't fit with his personal style and values.

The earlier Procter and Gamble illustration captures the crucial aspect.[7] Recruitment is the organizational equivalent of "romance." Hiring someone is like marriage—and a broken engagement is preferable to a messy divorce. Recruiters are expected to get deeper than first impressions. Their skill and intuition are developed by intensive training. A great deal of thought is given to articulating precisely and concretely the traits that count. The format for recording these traits is standardized. From the recruit's point of view, the extensive screening sends a signal: "You've got to be special to join." The screening process causes one to reveal oneself and causes most to wonder if they are good enough to get in. This increases receptivity for the second stage.

Step Two:

Humility-inducing experiences in the first months on the job precipitate self-questioning of prior behavior, beliefs, and values. A lowering of individual self-comfort and self-complacency promotes openness toward accepting the organization's norms and values.

Most strong culture companies get the new hire's attention by pouring on more work than can possibly be done. IBM and Morgan Guaranty socialize extensively through training where "you work every night until 2:00 a.m. on your own material and then help others."[8] Procter and Gamble achieves the same result via "upending experiences," sometimes requiring a new recruit to color in a sales territory map—a task for which the novitiate is clearly overqualified.[9] These experiences convey a metamessage: "While you're smart in some ways, you're in kindergarten as far as what you know about this organization." One learns to be humble. Humility tends to flourish under certain conditions; especially long hours of intense work that bring you to your limits. When vulnerability is high, one also becomes close to one's colleagues—and cohesiveness is intensi-

fied in pressure-cooker environments where little opportunity is given to re-establish social distance and regain one's bearings. At the investment banking firm Morgan Stanley, one is expected to work 12-to-14 hour days and most weekends. Lunches are confined to the firm cafeteria and limited to thirty minutes; trainees are censured for taking lunch outside.[10] Near identical patterns of long hours, exhausting travel schedules, and extensive immersion in case work are true at the major consulting firms and law practices. Socialization is a little like exercise—it's easier to reconcile yourself to it when you're young.

Step Three:

In-the-trenches training leads to mastery of one of the core disciplines of the business. Promotion is inescapably tied to a proven track record.

The first phase of socialization aims to attract the right trainees predisposed toward the firm's culture. The second instills enough humility to evoke self-examination; this facilitates "buying in" to the firm's values. Increasingly, the organizational culture becomes the relevant universe of experience. Having thus opened one's mind to the company's way of doing business, the task is now to cement this new orientation. The most effective method for doing so is via extensive and carefully reinforced field experience. While IBM hires some MBAs and a few older professionals with prior work experience, almost all go through the same training and start at the same level. It takes six years to grow an IBM marketing representative, twelve years for a controller. McKinsey consultants and Morgan Stanley analysts must likewise earn their way up from the ranks. The gains from such an approach are cumulative. When all trainees understand there is one step by step career path, it reduces politics. There is no quick way to jump ranks and reach the top. Because the evaluation process has a long time horizon, short term behavior is counterproductive. Cutting corners catches up with you. Relationships, staying power and a consistent proven track record are the inescapable requirements of advancement. Those advancing, having been grown from within, understand the business not as financial abstraction but as a hands on reality. Senior managers can communicate with those at the lowest ranks in the "short hand" of shared experience.

Step Four:
Meticulous attention is given to systems measuring operational results and rewarding individual performance. Systems are comprehensive, consistent, and triangulate particularly on those aspects of the business that are tied to competitive success and corporate values.

Procter and Gamble measures three "what counts" factors that have been found to drive brand success. These factors are Building Volume; Building Profit; and Planned Change (defined as changes which simply put, increase effectiveness or otherwise add satisfaction to a job).[11] Operational measures track these factors using Nielsen market share indices as well as traditional financial yardsticks. All performance appraisals are tied to milestones which impact on these factors. Promotions are determined by success against these criteria—plus successful demonstration of management skills.

Another example of comprehensive, consistent, and interlocking systems are those used at IBM to track adherence to its value of "respecting the decency of the individual." This is monitored via climate surveys; "Speak up!" (a confidential suggestion box); open door procedures; skip-level interviews; and numerous informal contacts between senior-level managers and employees.[12] The Personnel Department moves quickly when any downward changes are noted in the above indices. In addition, managers are monitored for percent performance ap-

praisals completed on time and percent of employees missing the required one week a year of training. All first-level managers receive an intensive two-week course in people management and each managerial promotion results in another week-long refresher. These systems provide a near "fail-safe" network of checks and double checks to ensure adherence to IBM's core value of respecting individual dignity.

Included in IBM's mechanisms for respecting the individual is a device known as the "Penalty Box."[13] Often a person sent to the "penalty box" has committed a crime against the culture—for example, harsh handling of a subordinate, overzealousness against the competition, gaming the reporting system. Most penalty box assignments involve a lateral move to a less desirable location—a branch manager in Chicago might be moved to a nebulous staff position at headquarters. For an outsider, penalty box assignments look like normal assignments, but insiders know they are off the track. Penalty boxes provide a place for people while the mistakes they've made or the hard feelings they've created are gradually forgotten—and while the company looks for a new useful position. The mechanism is one among numerous things IBM does that lend credence to employees' beliefs that the firm won't act capriciously and end a career. In the career of strong, effective managers, there are times when one steps on toes. The penalty box is IBM's "half-way house" enabling miscreants to contemplate their errors and play another day. (Don Estridge, maverick pioneer of IBM's success in personal computers and currently head of that division, came from the penalty box.)

Step Five:
Careful adherence to the firm's transcendent values. Identification with common values enables employees to reconcile personal sacrifices necessitated by their membership in the organization.[14]

Of all the steps this is perhaps most essential. It is the foundation of trust between organization and individual. Values also serve as the primary safeguard against our great fear that highly socialized organizations will degenerate into an Orwellian nightmare.[15] Much of our resistance to socialization stems from the suspicion that corporations are fundamentally amoral and their members, once socialized, will pursue inappropriate goals. There are, in fact, significant checks and balances in American society against the extremes of social manipulation. Government, the media, and various other stakeholders such as consumers, environmentalists, and unions become powerfully vocal when corporations cross the line of decorum. And of the great self-sustaining institutions, all over a half century old, little evidence exists of major transgressions despite their strongly socialized cultures. These corporations avoid the undesirable extremes by continually recommitting themselves to shared values that keep them in tune with society.

Placing one's self "at the mercy" of an organization imposes real costs. There are long hours of work, missed weekends, bosses one has to endure, criticism that seems unfair, job assignments and rotations that are inconvenient or undesirable. The countervailing force for commitment under these circumstances is the organization's set of transcendent values which connect *its* purpose with significant higher-order human values—such as serving mankind, providing a first-class product for society, or developing people. Prior to joining Delta Airlines, candidates hear endlessly about the "Delta family feeling." Numerous anecdotes illustrate that Delta's values require sacrifices: management takes pay cuts during lean times; senior flight attendants and pilots voluntarily work fewer hours per week in order to avoid laying off more junior employees.[16] Candidates who accept employment with Delta tend to accept this quid pro quo, believing that the restrictions on individual action comprise a reasonable trade-off. In effect, Delta's family philosophy is deemed worthy enough to make their sacrifices worthwhile. The organization, in turn, needs to honor its values and continually reaffirm their importance. To the outsider, the fuss IBM makes over "respecting the dignity of the individual," the intensity with which Delta Airlines expresses "the Delta family feeling," may seem like overzealousness. But for those within, these values represent a deeply felt mission. Their credibility and constancy is essential to the socialization transaction.

Step Six:

Reinforcing folklore provides legends and interpretations of watershed events in the organization's history that validate the firm's culture and its aims. Folklore reinforces a code of conduct for "how we do things around here."

All firms have their stories. The difference among firms that socialize well is that the morals of the stories all tend to "point north." Procter and Gamble fires one of their best brand managers for overstating the features of a product. The moral: ethical claims come ahead of making money. Morgan Stanley canonizes partners with legendary skills at "cutting a deal." One of the richest legacies of folklore was found within the former Bell system where numerous stories and anecdotes extolled employees who made sacrifices to keep the phones working.

The Bell folklore was so powerful and widely shared that when natural disaster struck, all elements of a one million member organization were able to pull together, cut corners, violate procedures, make sacrifices against measurement criteria—all in the interest of restoring phone service. This occurred despite extensive bureaucratic obstacles and illustrates how folklore, when well understood, can legitimize special channels for moving an organization in a hurry.[17]

309

Step Seven:
Consistent role models and consistent traits are associated with those recognized as on the fast track.

Nothing communicates so powerfully to younger professionals within an organization than having peers or superiors who share common qualities and who are formally or informally recognized as winners. Far more can be taught by examples than can ever be conveyed in a classroom. The protégé watches the role model make presentations, handle conflict, write memos—and replicates as closely as possible the traits that seem to work most effectively.

Strong culture firms regard role models as the most powerful ongoing "training program" available. Because other elements of the culture are consistent, those emerging as role models are consistent. Morgan Stanley carefully selects its high-potential cadre for the combination of energy, aggressiveness, and team play that the organization requires.[18] Procter and Gamble exhibits extraordinary consistency among its brand managers across traits such as tough mindedness, motivational skills, enormous energy, and ability to get things done through others.[19]

Unfortunately most firms leave the emergence of role models to chance. Some on the fast track seem to be whizzes at analysis, others are skilled with people, others seem astute at politics: the result for those below is confusion as to what it *really* takes to succeed. The set of companies, formerly parts of the Bell System, have a strong need to become more market oriented and aggressive. Yet the Bell culture continues to discriminate against candidates for the high-potential list who, against the backdrop of the older monopoly culture, are "too aggressive."[20]

The seven dimensions of socialization, while not surprising when examined individually, tend to be overlooked and undermanaged. Many companies can point to isolated aspects

of their organizational practices that follow these patterns but rarely is each of the seven factors managed as a concerted and well-coordinated effort. Rarer yet is the firm where all seven hang together. Indeed, it is *consistency* across all seven elements of socialization process that results in a strong cohesive culture that lasts over time.

THE CASE FOR SOCIALIZATION

All organizations require a certain degree of order and consistency. To achieve this, they either utilize *explicit* procedures and formal controls or *implicit* social controls. Great firms tend to do an artful job of blending both. American firms, in aggregate, tend to rely on formal controls. The result is that management often appears to be over-steering, rigid, and bureaucratic. A United Technologies executive states: "I came from the Bell system. Compared to AT&T, this is a weak culture and there is little socialization. But, of course there is still need for controls. So they put handcuffs on you, shackle you to every nickel, track every item of inventory, monitor every movement in production, and head count. They control you by balance sheet."[21]

An inordinate amount of energy in American companies is invested in fighting "the system." (We often find ourselves playing games to work around it.) When an organization instills a strong, consistent set of implicit understandings, it is effectively establishing a common law to supplement its statutory laws. This enables us to interpret formal systems in the context for which they were designed, to use them as tools rather than straitjackets. An IBM manager states: "Socialization acts as a fine-tuning device; it helps us make sense out of the procedures and quantitative measures. Any number of times I've been faced with a situation where the right thing for the measurement system was 'X' and the right thing for IBM was 'Y'. I've always been counselled to tilt toward what was right for IBM in the long term and what was right for our people. They pay us a lot to do that. Formal controls, without coherent values and culture are too crude a compass to steer by."[22]

Organizations that socialize effectively manage a lot of internal ambiguity. This tends to free up time and energy; more goes toward getting the job done and focusing on external things like the competition and the customer. "At IBM you spend 50% of your time managing the internal context," states a former IBMer, now at ITT, "at most companies it's more like 75%."[23] A marketing manager at Atari states: "You can't imagine how much time and energy around here goes into politics. You've got to determine who's on first base this month in order to figure out how to obtain what you need to get the job done. There are no rules. There are no clear values. Bushnell and Kassar stood for diametrically opposite things. Your bosses are constantly changing. I've had 4 in 18 months. We're spread out over 43 buildings over a 20-mile radius and we're constantly reorganizing. All this means that you never have time to develop a routine way for getting things done at the interface between your job and the next guy's. Without rules for working with one another, a lot of people get hurt, get burned out, are never taught the 'Atari way' of doing things because there isn't an 'Atari way.' "[24]

The absence of cultural rules makes organizational life capricious. This is so because success as middle and senior managers not only requires managing the substance of the business, but increasingly involves managing one's role and relationships. When social roles are unclear, no one is speaking the same language; communication and trust break down. Remember, the power to get things done in corporations seldom depends on formal titles and formal authority alone. In great measure, it depends on a person's track record and reputation, knowledge, and a network of relationships. In effect, the power to implement change and execute effectively relies heavily on one's *social* currency, something a person accumulates over time. Strong culture firms *empower* employees helping them build this social currency by providing continuity and clarity. Organizations which do not facilitate this process incur a cost.

Continuity and clarity also yield great dividends in reducing career anxiety. The ebbs and flows of career fortunes attract close scrutiny in organizations. Mixed signals surrounding such things as rewards, promotions, career paths, criteria for being on the "fast track" or a candidate for termination, inevitably generate a lot of gossip, game playing, and counter productive expenditure of energy. Some might feel that these elements can be entirely resolved by the explicit provisions in the policy manual. Fact is, many of the criteria of success for middle and senior level positions are implicit. It is almost impossible to articulate in writing the nuances and shared understandings that govern the rise or demise of executives. The rules tend to be communicated and enforced via relatively subtle cues. When the socialization process is weak, the cues tend to be poorly or inconsistently communicated.[25]

Look carefully at career patterns in most companies. Ambitious professionals strive to learn the ropes but there are as many "ropes" as there are individuals who have, by one means or another, made their way to the top. So one picks an approach and if by coincidence it coincides with how your superiors do things, you're on the fast track. Far more prevalent, however, the approach that works with one superior is offensive to another. "As a younger manager, I was always taught to touch bases and solicit input before moving ahead," a manager of a Santa Clara electronics firm states, "It always worked. But at a higher level with a different boss, my base touching was equated with 'being political.' Unfortunately, the organization doesn't forewarn you when it changes signals. A lot of good people leave owing to misunderstandings over things of this kind. The human cost in weakly socialized organizations tends to go unrecognized."[26]

What about the cost of conformity? A senior vice-president of IBM states: "Conformity among IBM employees has often been described as stultifying in terms of dress, behavior, and lifestyle. There is, in fact, strong pressure to adhere to certain norms of superficial behavior, and much more intensely to the three tenets of the company philosophy—1) respect for the dignity of the individual, 2) providing first-rate customer service, and 3) excellence. These are the bench marks. Between them there is wide latitude for divergence in opinions and behavior." A Procter and Gamble executive adds: "There is a great deal of consistency around here in how certain things are done and these are rather critical to our sustained success. Beyond that, there are very few hard and fast rules. People on the outside might portray our culture as imposing lock-step uniformity. It doesn't feel rigid when you're inside. It feels like it accommodates you. And best of all, you know the game you're in—you know whether you're playing soccer or football; you can find out very clearly what it takes to succeed and you can bank your career on that."[27]

It is useful to distinguish between norms that are central to the core factors that drive business success and social conventions that signal commitment and belonging. The former set is most essential as it ensures consistency around certain crucial activities that link to a firm's strategy. At IBM, people, customers, and excellence have priority. As noted earlier, IBM's format for stand-up presentations and its style of "probing" are seen as vital to keeping the culture on its toes. Bain, Morgan Guaranty, and Procter & Gamble each imposes variations on this theme.

The second set of norms are, in effect, organizational equivalents of a handshake. They are social conventions that make it easier for people to be comfortable with one another. One need not observe all of them, but as some conventions count more than others, one strives to reassure the organization that one is on the team. The important aspect of this second set of social values is that, like a handshake, they are usually not experienced as oppressive. Partly, this is because adherence is only skin deep. (Most of us don't feel our individualism is compromised by shaking hands.) In addition, these social conventions are usually self-evident to prospective members and self-selection eliminates many whose integrity would be violated by observing them.

MISCONCEPTIONS

The aim of socialization is to establish a base of attitudes, habits, and values that foster cooperation, integrity, and communication. The most frequently advanced objection is that the companies who do so will lose innovativeness over the long haul. The record does not bear this out. Many of the companies who socialize most extensively are the ones that have lasted over many generations—at least prima facie evidence of sufficient innovation to cope with the changing environment. Further consider 3M or Bell Labs. Both socialize extensively and both are highly innovative institutions—and they remain so by fostering social rules that *reward* innovation. Another misconception is that socialization necessarily occurs at the expense of maintaining a desirable amount of internal competition. Again, IBM, P&G, major consulting firms, law practices, and outstanding financial institutions like Morgan Stanley are illustrations of strong culture firms where internal competition tends to be healthy but intense. There is, of course, an ever present danger of strong culture firms becoming incestuous and myopic—the "General Motors syndrome." Most opponents of socialization rally around this argument. But what is learned from the firms that have avoided these pitfalls is that they consciously minimize the downside of socialization by cultivating *obsessions*—not just *any* obsession, but ones that serve to continually wrench attention from internal matters to the world outside. The four most common "obsessions" are quality, competition, customer service, and productivity. Each demands an external focus and serves as a built-in way of maintaining vigilance. Positive examples are McDonald's obsessive concern for quality control, Toyota's for productivity, IBM's for cus-

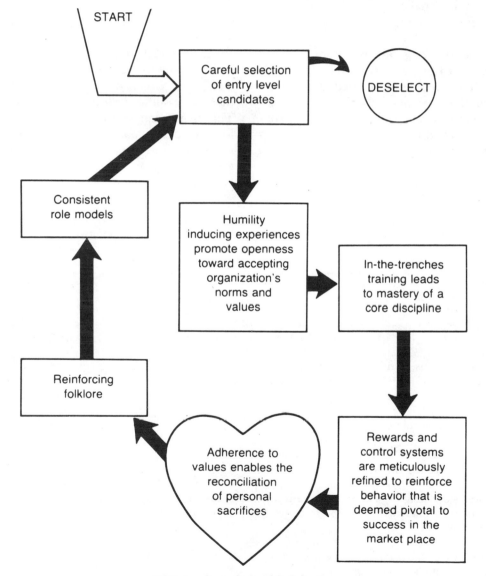

BOX 1. Seven Steps of Socialization

tomer service, and Morgan Stanley's for competition. These "obsessions" contribute to a lot of fire drills and are regarded as overkill by some. But they also serve as an organizational equivalent of calisthenics. They maintain organizational alertness and muscle tone for the day when real change is required. It should be noted that organizations which tend to be obsessive over internal matters, such as Delta's with "the family feeling," may be riding for a fall.[28]

The underlying dilemma of socialization is so sensitive to core American values that it is seldom debated. When discussed, it tends toward a polarized debate—especially from members of the media and academics who, as a subset of the U.S. population, tend to be among the most preoccupied with individualism and individual rights. A central premise of this essay is that such polarization generates more heat than light. We will do better if we can advance beyond the extremes of the argument.

Revolutions begin with an assault on awareness. It is time to deal more clear-mindedly with this crucial aspect of organizational effectiveness. Between our *espoused* individualism and the *enacted* reality in most great companies lies a zone where organizational and individual interests overlap. If we can come to grips with our ambivalence about socialization we will undoubtedly make our organizations more effective. Equally important, we can reduce the human costs that arise today as many stumble along ineffectually on careers within companies that lack a sufficient foundation of social rules. This insufficiency is only partly the result of ignorance. In equal measure it derives from our instinctive resistance to social controls—even when some measure of them may be in our own best interest.

BOX 2.   Compute Your "Socialization" Score

Respond to the items below as they apply to the handling of professional employees. Upon completion, compute the total score. For comparison, scores for a number of strong, intermediate, and weak culture firms are to be found below.

	Not True of This Company				Very True of This Company
1. Recruiters receive at least one week of intensive training.	1	2	3	4	5
2. Recruitment forms identify several key traits deemed crucial to the firm's success, traits are defined in concrete terms and interviewer records specific evidence of each trait.	1	2	3	4	5
3. Recruits are subjected to at least four in-depth interviews.	1	2	3	4	5
4. Company actively facilitates de-selection during the recruiting process by revealing minuses as well as plusses.	1	2	3	4	5
5. New hires work long hours, are exposed to intensive training of considerable difficulty and/or perform relatively menial tasks in the first months.	1	2	3	4	5
6. The intensity of entry level experience builds cohesiveness among peers in each entering class.	1	2	3	4	5

	Not True of This Company			Very True of This Company
7. All professional employees in a particular discipline begin in entry level positions regardless of prior experience or advanced degrees.	1	2	3	4	5
8. Reward systems and promotion criteria require mastery of a core discipline as a precondition of advancement.	1	2	3	4	5
9. The career path for professional employees is relatively consistent over the first six to ten years with the company.	1	2	3	4	5
10. Reward systems, performance incentives, promotion criteria and other primary measures of success reflect a high degree of congruence.	1	2	3	4	5
11. Virtually all professional employees can identify and articulate the firm's shared values (i.e., the purpose or mission that ties the firm to society, the customer or its employees).	1	2	3	4	5
12. There are very few instances when actions of management appear to violate the firm's espoused values.	1	2	3	4	5
13. Employees frequently make personal sacrifices for the firm out of commitment to the firm's shared values.	1	2	3	4	5
14. When confronted with trade-offs between systems measuring short-term results and doing what's best for the company in the long term, the firm usually decides in favor of the long-term.	1	2	3	4	5
15. This organization fosters mentor-protégé relationships.	1	2	3	4	5
16. There is considerable similarity among high potential candidates in each particular discipline.	1	2	3	4	5

Compute your score: _____

For comparative purposes:

	Scores	
Strongly Socialized Firms.........	65–80	.... IBM, P&G, Morgan Guaranty
	55–64	.... ATT, Morgan Stanley, Delta Airlines
	45–54	.... United Airlines, Coca Cola
	35–44	.... General Foods, Pepsi Co.
	25–34	.... United Technologies, ITT
Weakly Socialized Firms	Below 25	.... Atari

REFERENCES

1. Interview with Skip Awalt, Director of Management Development, IBM, Armonk, NY, May 26, 1982.

2. Interviews with Bain Consultants, 1983. Also, see: "Those Who Can't, Consult," *Harpers* (November 1982), pp. 8–17.

3. N. Kaible, Recruitment and Socialization at Procter and Gamble, Stanford Graduate School of Business, Case II S-BP-236, May 1984.

4. Interviews with professional staff, Morgan Guaranty Trust, New York, 1982.

5. Edgar H. Schein, "Organizational Socialization," in Kolb, Rubin, and McIntire, eds. *Organizational Psychology* (Englewood Cliffs, NJ: Prentice Hall, 1974), pp. 1–15.

6. Richard Pascale and Anthony Athos, *The Art of Japanese Management* (New York, NY: Simon & Schuster, 1981).

7. Kaible, op. cit., pp. 2–6.

8. Interview with recent trainees of IBM's sales development program, Palo Alto, CA, May 1982.

9. Kaible, op. cit., p. 10.

10. Interviews with professional staff, Morgan Stanley, New York, March 1983.

11. Kaible, op. cit., p. 16. *See also* "Readiness Criteria for Promotion to Assistant Brand Manager," unpublished P&G internal document #0689A, pp. 1–2.

12. Interview with Skip Awalt, IBM, op. cit. *See also* T. Rohan, "How IBM Stays Non Union," *Industry Week*, November 26, 1979, pp. 85–96.

13. Interviews with IBM managers, Palo Alto, CA, April 13, 1983. *See also* N. Foy, *The Sun Never Gets on IBM.*

14. See Pascale and Athos, op. cit., Chapter Seven.

15. See for example Zimbardo, "To Control a Mind," *The Stanford Magazine* (Winter 1983), pp. 59–64.

16. J. Guyon, "Family Feeling at Delta Creates Loyal Workers," *Wall Street Journal,* July 17, 1980, p. 13.

17. Interviews with executives of AT&T, Basking Ridge, NJ, February 1982.

18. Interview with professional staff, Morgan Guaranty, Palo Alto, CA, April 1983.

19. Kaible, op. cit., p. 16.

20. Interview with line executives, of Northwestern Bell, Omaha, NE, March 1982.

21. Interview with executives, Pratt & Whitney Division, United Technologies, NY, January 1981.

22. Interview with IBM Marketing and Production managers, Palo Alto, CA, op. cit.

23. Ibid.

24. Interview with product development managers, Atari, Santa Clara, CA, April 1983.

25. Pascale and Athos, op. cit., Chapters 3 & 4.

26. Interview with a production manager of Rolm, Santa Clara, CA, January 1983.

27. Interview with IBM marketing and production managers, Palo Alto, CA, op. cit.

28. M. Loeb, "Staid Delta Air Tries to Stem Losses by Following Other Carriers' Moves," *Wall Street Journal,* July 10, 1983.

Whose Company Is It?

James Abegglen

George Stalk

A PHRASE much used in Japan is *Nihonteki keiei,* or Japanese-style management, referring to what the Japanese see as considerable differences between Japanese management methods and those commonly used in the West. The differences cited are usually those having to do with personnel practices—career job security, unions that include all the employees of the company, pay and promotion systems heavily weighted toward seniority, and group approaches to decision making. There is now considerable pride in this Japanese-style management.

The basis for pride is apparent as Japanese productivity levels continue to rise rapidly. Reporting OECD data on productivity growth from 1964 to 1983, *The Economist* noted that "the old truth remains: the pace of economic growth depends largely on the growth of each worker's output. Among industrial countries, the big winner by far is still Japan. Though its productivity grew more slowly in the 1970s than in the 1960s, it is still rising as quickly as West German productivity did at its postwar fastest."[1]

Not only are the Japanese working effectively, but they are working long hours. Hours worked per person annually declined in every major industrial country from 1975 to 1982, except in Japan, where they increased over the period. This was despite steadily increasing income and living standard levels in Japan. The Japanese worker puts in an average of more than 2,000 hours per year, while the average in Great Britain and Sweden is less than 1,500.

There are many other indicators of a higher level of worker commitment. Absentee rates in Japan are lower than in other major countries. Days lost to industrial disputes are fewer than in any other industrial nation except West Germany. Suggestion systems for productivity improvements are in place in almost all Japanese companies, with quite extraordinary rates of participation. Quality Control Circles, which organize workers to study and deal with production problems on their own initiative and time, and their high level of participation and output are the envy of Western managements.

Indeed, there are so many of these indicators of a work force that is more dedicated and concerned than others that the conclusion of a real difference in performance is inescapable. Many Japanese attribute the difference to national characteristics—diligence; a preference for working hard; a sense of loyalty to the group. There may well be aspects of Japanese society and Japanese character that contribute to their impressive performance, but the causes may also lie in more basic and universally relevant explanations.

The kaisha have dealt effectively with the fundamental problem of all organizations, that of tying together the interests of the individuals that make up the organization with the interests of the organization as a whole. The kaisha system of management has gone farther than others to minimize conflicting interests and to integrate each of the members of the group into a whole that works in the common interest. This achievement results not from special diligence, loyalty, or other special characteristics of individual Japanese. Rather, it results from a total system of employment and corporate governance that combines to produce exceptional results. The system is, as a whole, unique to Japan, and perhaps could only have taken shape in the context of Japanese society. But it is a system whose elements can be introduced into any management system given adequate understanding, conviction, and effort.

DOES THE SHAREHOLDER OWN THE JAPANESE COMPANY?

Whose company is it? In the West, as in Japan, the answer provided by legal convention is clear. The company belongs to the shareholders, to those who provide the capital that makes the company possible. Because the company belongs to the shareholders, benefits accruing to the company from successful performance belong to the shareholder who has undertaken the risk of investment.

With ownership separate from the management of corporations, the board of directors represents the interests of the shareholder-owners. Thus, in U.S. companies, directors are named to the board from outside the company in the majority of cases. A strong chief executive of the company may well control board membership and build a friendly and relatively accommodating board. Nonetheless, the board is expected to maintain surveillance of company affairs, and step in as necessary in cases of mismanagement (even though the precise legal responsibilities of the board members remain unclear).

This has also come to mean generally that the U.S. shareholder is to receive a significant share of profits in the form of dividend payments. While a few companies, like Digital Equipment Corporation, retain earnings and do not pay dividends in order to command less expensive capital, most U.S. companies view a dividend payout rate of about 50 percent of earnings as appropriate. Dividends are taken to be a sign of successful operations and competent management. Share price is strongly influenced by the rate and level of dividends paid.

In order to help ensure that management works in the interests of the shareholders and to link the interests of management with that of the shareholders, profit-related bonus plans for management (and stock options and similar plans to reward management for improved earnings and increased share price) have become widespread and even recognized in U.S. tax codes. As Western stock markets tend to be highly sensitive to trends in earnings per share, management has a strong motive to maintain steady improvement in earnings, even on a quarterly basis. A faltering in earnings trends lowers share price, which lowers the value of stock options and similar compensation programs of management. Management is expected to maintain earnings trends and provide increasing rewards to shareholders. This pattern is so familiar and accepted in the West, especially in the United States, that it is taken for granted as the natural and proper state of corporate affairs.

The Western corporate pattern might be described as an alliance of senior management and shareholders to optimize current earnings from the company to mutual benefit. The company becomes a vehicle for profit optimization, or, at worst, for profit maximization. Implicit is the view that the success of the company depends critically on a single executive or small group of executives. Thus, if they achieve success through their individual efforts their compensation should be appropriately increased. Not surprisingly then, lower ranking employees, especially as represented by their trade unions, also seek to optimize, and in fact seek to maximize their share of current earnings. In this process, the company becomes an organization external to the interests of its members, to be used to further their earnings advantage to the maximum.

Against this pattern as it has developed in the West, the common stock shareholder of the Japanese company is more in the position of a preferred shareholder in a Western company. Having made an investment that is at risk, the shareholder is entitled to a return on that investment. Therefore dividends are paid, but not as a percent of earnings but as a percent of the par value of shares in the company.

Dividend yields as a percent of market value of Japanese shares are low, typically only one to two percent. Nevertheless, it is critically important that the dividend be paid, and Japanese companies in some earnings trouble have been known to borrow to cover the dividend payment and thus meet the investor's expectations and maintain their ability to raise equity funds.

Yet, when the shareholder's claim to a return on his investment is met by the Japanese company, the shareholder has little or no further voice in corporate affairs. The board of directors of the Japanese company consists almost entirely of inside board members, that is, of the senior management of the company. They achieve board member status as they move up in the executive ranks; they are career employees. To the extent that they might be seen as representatives of a constituency, their constituency is the career employees of the company itself. In a few of the companies that are members of the traditional groups of companies, such as NEC as a member of the Sumitomo group, there will be an occasional outside director representing and symbolic of group membership. In cases where the company has become deeply obligated to a commercial bank, and the bank feels at some risk, it may well second an executive to serve as financial officer in the company and sit on the board. But in no event are outside directors either a majority, or even truly outsiders to the company.

A recent and colorful case was an interesting exception to these rules of continuity and control from inside the company. Shigeru Okada was dismissed as president of the Mitsukoshi Department Store through the offices of an outside director. Mitsukoshi has long been Japan's most prestigious department store group, the proper place to buy gifts for special occasions. It was also once the largest retail operation in Japan, losing that pride of place with the onslaught of supermarket chains. Its special prestige stems largely from its being the source of the fortunes of the Mitsui family, the initial firm in what became the Mitsui Group, once Japan's largest combination of companies.

Okada assumed the presidency of Mitsukoshi in the early 1970s, and soon established a reputation as both a flamboyant and a one-man operator. His one-man style was evident as executives began to leave the company for other firms (in itself very unusual) and his flamboyance was displayed in his rental of the Versailles Palace for a night, with guests flown to Paris to celebrate the fame and position of Mitsukoshi.

The trigger for Okada's downfall in 1982 was a store-sponsored display of Persian treasures, many of gold, and many of which turned out to be fakes produced in a workshop not far from Tokyo. With the press in full outcry, management rose up and removed him, reportedly by a unanimous vote of the sixteen directors, on the grounds of the ruinous inventory position of the store. Most of the excess, unsaleable inventory had been supplied to the store by companies organized by Okada's mistress. This proved the last straw in a long sequence of mismanagement.

The Okada case is of interest in this discussion in two regards. First, it has been widely reported as the first in recollected Japanese history where a chief executive has been voted out of office by his board of directors in direct confrontation. In itself, the rarity of this case supports the view of succession, continuity, and lack of shareholder control as being the Japanese pattern.

Second, other players in this drama are of interest. The coup that unseated Okada was engineered by Goro Koyama, retired executive of and still advisor to the Mitsui Bank. Koyama served on the Mitsukoshi board as banker and group representative and arranged the overturn to defend the good name of the Mitsui Group, as well as to defend the financial interests of its bank and department store. Even so, some reports indicated that the actual vote to dismiss Okada was close, despite the appearance of unanimity.

A final observation on the Mitsukoshi case is important. Okada's successor was not an outsider brought in to clean up the situation, nor a bank executive sent to defend the interests of the Mitsui Bank. The successor was another company officer who had been running Mitsukoshi's Nagoya store, and thus was not involved with Okada's operations. For all of the drama, the final note was the continuity and integrity of the organization.

Along with the pattern of inside directors, with no specific shareholder representation on the board, goes a quite different approach to dividend payments in the case of the Japanese company. As noted, dividends are paid as a percent of par value of shares. This means that a highly profitable company can meet its dividend requirements with only a small percent of its total earnings. Most of its earnings will be available for reinvestment in the company. To meet the same dividend requirement, a less profitable company must pay out a large share of its earnings in dividends.

In 1984, Matsushita Electric Industries, the world's largest appliance company and highly profitable, paid out less than ten percent of its earnings in dividends, retaining the balance for reinvestment. As one consequence, Matsushita has been growing in sales nearly 15 percent a year and doing so without incurring the risks and costs of bank borrowings. Conversely, Toshiba, in a less favorable market position and therefore less profitable, paid out nearly 50 percent of its earnings in dividends and has a 2:1 debt-to-equity ratio, borrowing heavily to maintain a growth rate of less than 10 percent per year. The Japanese approach to dividends is a powerful factor in separating corporate winners and losers in the Japanese economy. The winners are able to become very strong companies indeed.

With the shareholder in the position of investor rather than controller, and with dividends not critical to share price, Japanese management has developed a different view of the importance of share price. In the survey presented in chapter 7 regarding corporate objectives of U.S. and Japanese managements, U.S. executives ranked return on investment as their first objective and share price second. In reviewing these survey findings with U.S. executives, there is usually agreement that these are the top two objectives for U.S. management, though there are some who argue that share price is the first objective, even taking precedence over profitability. In the same survey, of the nine corporate objectives presented for rating, Japanese executives rated share price as the least important objective in managing their companies. Few cited share price as an objective of their company at all. The survey data do not provide an explanation of this result. Several explanations are possible: first, that Japanese executives simply do not care about the price of their company's shares. Few Japanese executives hold significant amounts of shares and because treasury shares owned by the company cannot be held, there are no stock option programs in Japan, or even similar plans such as "phantom stock" for executives. Second, Japanese shareholders have little voice in corporate affairs, so again perhaps share price need not rank as a corporate objective. Perhaps this is the explanation of the seeming indifference of the Japanese executives surveyed to the price of company shares as an objective in managing their companies.

A third explanation is also possible. Perhaps Japanese managers believe that if their companies achieve market share and profitability targets, and continue to grow through introducing new products that allow the cycle of market share and profit to be repeated, the stock market will recognize their performance by supporting the shares of the company, thus leading to higher share price. In this view of objectives, a high and increasing share price is not an objective of the company, but is rather the consequence of good management of those companies that get their basic objectives right, and work to achieve them.

There is a real competitive advantage in this pattern of shareholder relations for the successful Japanese competitor. Managements of the kaisha are freed from the tyranny of accountants, and from the terrible pressures throughout the U.S. organizations for steady improvement in earnings per share. It is rational for U.S. managers to be preoccupied with short-term earnings. Their job security depends on it, because the board, the top executives, and the shareholders demand steady earnings improvements. Moreover, their per-

sonal income and estate depend on it, because their principal potential asset is likely to be in the form of options and other plans dependent on stock price. Earnings can always be improved in the short term by sacrificing those expenses and investments that build long-term position. The Japanese manager is able to look further into the future and is freer to do what is necessary to ensure a successful future. This is possible only because of the system the Japanese executive operates in, not from any natural tendency to take the longer view. At the same time, the shorter time horizon of the U.S. executive is a function of the system he operates in, and is not necessarily from a lack of understanding or concern over the company's future.

During the 1950s and 1960s period of very rapid growth of the Japanese economy, with capital in short supply, something of the role of the Western common stock holder was played by the banks of Japan. Most investment funds came not from equity or retained earnings but from bank borrowings. Furthermore, most of these were short-term loans that were "evergreen," or regularly renewed. Under these circumstances, it was hardly surprising that the main supplier of funds—the banks—became significant factors in corporate decision making.

With greatly increased liquidity in the Japanese economy, and with stronger company balance sheets, this system has changed. Banks must now solicit attractive borrowers, and find themselves providing funds to the weaker companies, in which their powers remain considerable. The most successful of Japan's companies work to maintain good relations with key banks, but are hardly under bank control. The leading companies have little debt, and they can choose their bank sources. Companies like Kubota (a major manufacturer of farm machinery) and Hitachi are careful to balance their banking business between two or more banks, rather than relying on one main bank. By recent law, bank shareholdings in companies will soon be limited to a maximum of 5 percent. The conclusion is that dependence on a bank is no more to the liking of Japanese management than management in other countries, and for leading Japanese companies no longer a significant issue.

A rather similar situation has developed with respect to Japan's historically important groups of companies, the former *zaibatsu,* or giant holding companies, like the Mitsubishi, Mitsui, and Sumitomo groups. Members of these groups are often large and important companies in their industries. Impressive maps of group memberships and affiliations are often drawn up by observers of Japanese industry. There are some industries—housing and related equipment is a good example—where group membership and affiliation is crucial to success, because the important customers are for the most part group members.

Yet, when a list is made of the companies that have led the growth and success of the postwar Japanese economy, few are group members. Toyota, Honda, Hino, and Suzuki in vehicles; Kubota in farm machinery; Shiseido, Kao, and Lion in personal products; Hitachi, Sharp, Sanyo, Matsushita, and Sony in electronics; Shionogi and Fujisawa in pharmaceuticals; and Fuji Film, Canon, Ricoh, and Seiko are neither group members, nor bank dependent. Some have become so large and successful that through subsidiaries and affiliates they now control groups of their own. They are highly independent companies, with recent entrepreneurial origins. They are the kaisha that have succeeded in the sectors of fast-changing consumer markets and high technology.

Companies in the traditional groups are large, ponderous, and slow moving. Their businesses are mostly in declining industries. By an irony of history, these group companies have major positions in those raw material processing and heavy industries that are now in trouble in Japan. In sectors that require a good deal of

long-term financing, that have long engineering lead times, and that often require good government relations—the export of industrial plants would be an example—the group member companies remain strong. Where the technology changes fast, and where the market changes fast, they do not do well. The trading companies of the groups, with which the manufacturing companies have been so closely associated, are also a troubled group of companies.

There are exceptions: NEC, a high technology leader, is a Sumitomo group member; Kirin, with the leading domestic share in beer, is a member of the Mitsubishi group. But the exceptions are few. Furthermore, whether traditional or bank or trading company-centered, these groups are in no sense centrally controlled or closely coordinated. All things being equal—quality, price, and delivery—a group member will be favored in purchase decisions. But because things are often not equal, group affiliation does not provide a captive market nor assured support. Group membership may be an important starting point, but it will more often than not be irrelevant to corporate policy and business decisions.

It is interesting to see references in the Japanese business press to the Morgan group, Mellon group, or Rockefeller group of U.S. companies, and to IBM's close government-business relationship, inferred from the flow of personnel between that company and Washington. These misconceptions parallel the U.S. tendency to see plots and plotters in the Japanese business community. There are some plots, and some plotters, and some feelings of paranoia—on both sides—are not neurotic. They must be kept in proper proportion, however, on both sides.

In sum, the shareholder in the kaisha is in the position of an investor, but is in no operational sense in control of the company. With adequate return on investment, the shareholder's role is largely ended. Furthermore, it is no longer useful nor accurate to view the kaisha as being under the thumb of their banks, soliciting borrowings and deferring to bank judgment on decisions. The successful kaisha are as free of bank control as are their Western counterparts. Finally, describing the kaisha as group members and thereby under some form of control from that membership is of limited value. Those kaisha that have led the postwar international competitive thrust are generally separate from Japan's traditional groupings of companies, and operate independently.

HOW THE MONEY IS DISTRIBUTED

If the shareholders' control is limited, and banks and groups have little influence on the most successful kaisha, perhaps it is possible for the chief executive officers of these companies to operate essentially without check. A useful way of examining this possibility is to look into the pattern of compensation in the kaisha.

With increasing debate over levels of executive compensation in U.S. companies, the pattern of compensation in the Japanese company provides both an interesting contrast and a measure of some basic differences between the kaisha and Western companies. In 1982, Nikkeiren, the Japan Federation of Employers Associations, reviewed the differences in compensation between the presidents of large Japanese companies and newly employed college graduates in those companies (see table 1). In the prewar period, in the late 1920s, the spread in total cash compensation between the newly employed and the top ranking officer was one hundred times more for the latter. In those halcyon days of low income taxes, both pre-tax and post-tax differences were of the same magnitude. In the postwar period, the difference in compensation has been steadily diminishing, and on an after-tax basis is now only eight times less.

The level of pay of the lower ranks of the Japanese companies has been rising much more rapidly than the level of pay of the top executives, a thousand-times increase for the new entrants compared with a hundred times increase for the top executives. Not only has the disparate spread in compensation narrowed, but it is also clear from the Nikkeiren report that the pre-tax annual compensation level at the top of the Japanese company is low—about $100,000. This generally low level of pay for Japanese top management is borne out by

TABLE 1. *Annual Cash Compensation of Company Presidents and Newly Hired Employees (in yen)*

Year		President Compensation	New Employee Compensation (Male, College Graduates)	Difference
1927	Pre-tax	165,000	1,500	110.0x
	After-tax	151,000	1,500	100.6x
1963	Pre-tax	6,082,000	257,900	23.6x
	After-tax	3,013,000	252,500	11.9x
1973	Pre-tax	15,676,700	825,500	19.0x
	After-tax	7,181,400	797,400	9.0x
1980	Pre-tax	23,593,000	1,623,000	14.5x
	After-tax	11,543,000	1,546,000	7.5x

Source: **Rodo Mondai Kenkyo Iinkai Hokoku** (Report of the Research Committee on Labor Problems). *Senshinkoku Byo ni Ochuranai Tameni* (In Order not to Succumb to the Advanced Nations Disease) (Tokyo: Nihon Keieisha Dantai Renmev [Federation of Japanese Managers Associations, 1982]), p. 6.

other reports; for example, *Fortune* of 19 March 1984 reported on "salaries of Japanese chairmen and presidents, which range from $50,000 to $250,000 depending on company size." *Fortune* also commented on U.S. executive salaries. "In 1982 at least 85 American chief executives earned more than $1 million. In contrast, the highest paid foreign bosses rarely earned more than $500,000."[2] *Business Week,* reporting on 1983 executive compensation levels in the United States noted that there were twenty-five U.S. chief executive officers with total annual compensation of more than $2.3 million.[3]

There are Japanese who report very high levels of income—farmers benefiting from the leap in postwar land prices, individuals with substantial shareholdings, baseball players, film stars, and the like. The executives of the kaisha do not join this happy group on the basis of their salaried compensation.

The large differences in salaries between the executives of the kaisha and those of U.S. companies cannot be explained on the basis of profits—as has been seen, the top companies in both economies enjoy similar levels of profitability. They also cannot be explained in terms of greater perquisites of office paid one group compared with the other. The Japanese executive's generous expense accounts, company-provided housing, Mercedes and driver, luxurious office, and deferred retirement impress

foreign visitors with the benefits of his position. However, the U.S. executive also has his or her expense account, a jet plane or helicopter, company apartment, deferred compensation, special insurance program, golden parachute protection against dismissal if the company is taken over, and special retirement benefits. It is not clear which group of executives does better; perquisites do not begin to close the compensation gap.

The differences in executive compensation cannot be explained in terms of low overall levels of pay in Japan either. Studies of relative levels of workers' pay indicate that the average Japanese worker is well remunerated compared to workers in other advanced countries. Reports by the OECD indicate that the typical Japanese worker was about as well paid in 1982 as was the U.S. worker, even with the distortions from an over-valued dollar, and was considerably better off in after-tax take-home pay than the workers in the United States, as well as those in West Germany, France, and Great Britain (see table 2)

In evaluating the data in the OECD report, it is clear that they differ from the usual reports of "average wages." The 1983 average wage per hour in manufacturing in Japan was about the same as in West Germany, higher than in Britain or France but only two-thirds of the U.S. average hourly wage in manufacturing.

TABLE 2.   Annual Earnings of a Typical Worker,* 1982 (in U.S. dollars)

	Annual Gross Earnings ($)	Payments to Government ($)	Cash Transfers from Government	Disposable Income ($)
Japan	17,099	$1,966	—	15,133
U.S.	17,136	3,587	—	13,549
West Germany	14,918	4,027	$742	11,633
Great Britain	13,070	3,781	996	10,285
France	10,458	1,418	2,436	11,476

*Male, manufacturing sector worker with two-child family, wife not working.
Source: The 1982 Tax/Benefit Position of a Typical Worker in OECD Member Countries. (Paris: Organization for Economic Cooperation and Development, 1983), p. 8.

Three factors make for the difference between "average wage" and "annual earnings of a typical worker." First, the Japanese worker puts in a good many more hours, part of them at overtime rates. Second, the average encompasses all workers, including temporary workers and women, who in Japan are lower paid. Third, seniority weighs heavily on the Japanese pay scale. Thus a "typical worker" in Japan—on closer examination than is possible through the use of averages—turns out to do very well relative to foreign counterparts.

The pattern of relatively high pay to lower ranked employees is not limited to Japanese manufacturing workers. The Union Bank of Switzerland reported on the earnings of several different categories of employees, including production department managers in large manufacturing firms in different cities. In table 3, the disposable income of the Tokyo department manager is higher than in other major economies. The disposable income advantage at this level in the company is also about 10

TABLE 3. *Earnings of Department Managers (in U.S. dollars)*

	Gross Earnings per Year*	Net Earnings after Taxes and Social Service Contributions†
Tokyo	$41,600	$30,700
New York	46,500	28,000
Paris	31,600	21,100
Dusseldorf	31,400	20,600
Stockholm	28,900	13,000
London	16,700	11,600

*Technical manager of a production department in a sizable company (more than 100 employees) of the metal working industry, completed professional training with many years of experience in the firm: about 40 years old, married, no children.

†Including all supplements such as additional monthly salaries, bonuses, and vacation money.

SOURCE: *Prices and Earnings Around the Globe, 1982—UBS Publications on Business Banking and Monetary Problems,* vol 81 (Zurich: Union Bank of Switzerland, 1982), p. 40.

percent. In terms of pre-tax income, the Tokyo manager is behind the New York manager, though well ahead of counterparts in other major industrial cities.

These data help make clearer the indication of a compression in the range of company compensation that the earlier Nikkeiren data in this chapter—on the spread from CEO to newly hired graduate—suggested. Both within the kaisha, and in comparison with compensation levels in other countries, the lower ranks of the kaisha do well and the higher ranks do not do as well in total cash compensation.

It should also be noted that the kaisha provide perquisites in terms of housing support, commuting allowances, access to vacation facilities, family allowances, and the like at all levels of employee. This suggests that the proportion of compensation provided through perquisites is similar at all levels of the kaisha and does not work to broaden the range of total compensation from the bottom ranks to the top.

Put simply, the employees of the Japanese company share more equally in the cash benefits available from the company than is the case in other countries. The Nikkeiren report states, "Rather than seeking increased personal income, the objective of the [Japanese] executive is the growth and development of the enterprise."[4] Given that by all reasonable measures, Japanese executives, and indeed the Japanese in general, show a considerable interest in increased personal income, this statement has a rather sanctimonious air about it. Surveys of executive attitudes indicate that Japanese executive pay levels are set with a conscious awareness of the need to stay within reasonable ranges with regard to other levels of compensation in the kaisha. Organizational pressures work to limit executive pay at least as much as do self-sacrificing impulses by the executives themselves.

There is an interesting parallel in this to

the pattern of income distribution in Japan as a whole. Income distribution in Japan, while far from equal, is more nearly equal than in most countries:

> Depending on which of the measures [of income] is preferred, three countries (Australia, Japan and Sweden) would seem to record the lowest degree of inequality for a post-tax distribution. At the other end of the scale, France is consistently ranked as the country with the most unequal distribution. The rankings given by pre-tax inequality are not very different. Australia and Japan, in that order, rank as the least unequal countries on most measures. And France is joined by the United States at the opposite end of the scale.[5]

The conclusion seems inescapable that some part of the cause of the political stability of postwar Japan is a consequence of this relative equality in income distribution. Not only have incomes been rising rapidly, but the sharing of the total has been reasonably equitable. Similarly, in the Japanese company, income distribution is more nearly equal than in companies in the other major industrialized countries. It seems likely that within a corporate organization, all else being equal, a relative equity in distribution of benefits results in a higher degree of integration and sense of common purpose.

One feature of the kaisha's compensation system that deserves special attention in terms of its potential for application in other systems is bonus payments. Generally, about one-third of total annual compensation is paid in the form of a semiannual bonus, paid out at the traditional gift-giving seasons at mid-year and year-end. In the case of very successful firms, bonuses are paid that are the equivalent of a full year's basic compensation.

The bonus has many advantages for the kaisha. It is a deferred payment system, allowing the company use of the cash until the bonus is paid. Through increasing the bonus rather than base compensation, those allowances including retirement benefits that are a function of base pay can be held down. From a national point of view, the bonus has served as a major factor in bringing about the high rate of savings from the Japanese household. There is a clear-cut tendency to live within the base monthly pay and a propensity to save at the time of bonus payments.

In terms of managing the company, the bonus payment system has a further advantage. It is, in principle at least, and in practice to a good degree, a payment made contingent on the continuing adequate financial performance of the company. The bonus is paid at all levels of the kaisha, and can be reduced when circumstances demand without forcing the company to consider reducing the total labor force.

This, of course, is not the bonus system that Detroit made notorious—bonuses paid executives while negotiating with the union for reductions in total worker compensation. This is a company-wide system, in which all levels of the management and work force participate. Reductions in bonus affect all, proportionately equally, as do increases. Given all of its potential advantages, it is clear why the kaisha use a bonus system, but it is not clear why the system has not been more widely adopted in other countries. If bonuses serve to motivate management personnel, they presumably would serve the same function in motivating workers on the shop floor.

Still another feature of the compensation system in Japan conveys something of the nature of labor relations within the kaisha. This is the approach to wage-cut negotiations with the union and work force. When a Japanese company is in deep trouble, it can cut its temporary and part-time workers. There are no contracts or other constraints against reducing that part of total labor cost. The next step is to limit bonus payments. Following this, the next step will be to seek to reduce wages. At this point the general pattern is for management to announce across-the-board cuts in executive compensation. Having made these cuts, management, then and only then, approaches the union to open discussions of possible wage reductions.

This pattern was followed recently by Mitsubishi Corporation, Japan's largest general trading company, with annual sales of $85 billion. Like nearly all of the general trading companies, Mitsubishi Corporation's financial performance had been deteriorating for some years. Labor costs are an especially large part of total costs in the trading business and Mitsubishi Corporation was forced to act to lower labor costs of its regular work force. The first step in the process was the announcement of a 20 percent salary cut by the management of the company, preparatory to negotiations for a wage reduction across the company.

There is a common theme in these several compensation patterns. The kaisha provide more equal compensation throughout their organizations than is the case for companies in other countries. Extremes of compensation are avoided, and thereby a good deal of anger and conflict within the organization is presumably avoided. A good part of compensation at all levels is in the form of a bonus, proportionately equal for all employees, with some minor differentiation for individual performance. This provides a reward system for all that is tied to total performance of the organization, rather than to the performance of an individual in it. It also provides a cushion against a downturn in the economy or for the company. Finally, when the company is in trouble, the top executives of the organization sacrifice their compensation first, before asking for sacrifices from the rest of the employees.

This system of compensation assumes that the organization is a unit in which all members share in its success or failure. In terms of its compensation system, the kaisha is a more integrated and egalitarian organization than most companies in the West. The competitive advantages that are in part a result of these facts are reflected in the productivity performances of its members—to a considerable degree, the company belongs to its employees.

THE BASES FOR THE KAISHA'S INTEGRATION

Just as the kaisha have been shaped by the fast-growing and fast-changing economic environment of Japan, so have they been shaped by their social environment. Japan's is a notably group-centered society, with far less emphasis on individualism as a value than in the West. The Confucian ethic, with its emphasis on respect for rank and age, has provided much of the value system. The view of the family as paradigm for nation and for organization has carried over to the postwar business organization as well.

The three main elements of what has come to be called "Japanese-style management" are career employment security, a system of pay and promotion based on seniority in the firm, and the enterprise union system whereby all employees of the corporation belong to a single union with no differentiation by job skills. Each of these elements is worth examining, as they affect the capability of the kaisha as competitors, and as they affect the nature of the company itself. The high quality of the Japanese labor force has been noted earlier. It is in the recruiting, training, motivating, and organizing of this work force that Japanese-style management comes into play.

Career Employment
The Japanese system of career-long employment, which applies only to men, has several key elements. First, the employee is hired directly from school, rather than from an open job market. Second, he is hired for his general

characteristics and abilities, rather than for a particular skill or a particular job. Third, he is expected to remain with the company for a life-long career, and in turn expects not to be laid-off or discharged.

The consequences of this pattern of employment are profound. In terms of selection of new employees, the company needs to exercise considerable care, for a recruiting error is not easily corrected and has long and expensive consequences. Thus, academic examinations of the candidate, personal interviews, and investigations of the individual and family background are well warranted.

From the new employee's point of view, great care is also needed in deciding where to apply for employment. His commitment is not for a single, particular job, but for a career. The best performing companies can recruit the best students into employment. The best students seek out the company that appears to have the most promising long-term prospects. Allocation of the labor force from an overall economic point of view is thus made highly efficient, with the most able young people tending to move from school into the faster-growing and most promising sectors of the economy.

There is a real exchange of obligations in this process of selection. The individual is taking considerable risk in linking his future fortunes with those of the company. The company for its part is obliging itself to care for the recruit for his entire career. This concept is only meaningful when in fact the company is prepared to make real sacrifices on behalf of its employee, and is willing to incur losses when it is necessary to protect the individual's job security. The crisis of 1974, when the real growth rate of the economy plunged in a single year from 9 percent to minus one percent, provided a severe test. Japan's corporations as a whole showed losses in that terrible year, yet pay increases fully covered the explosive inflation, going up an average of nearly 30 percent in only one year. There were no significant lay-offs or discharge of permanent employees. The mutual obligation was real, not a matter of lip service.

All too often the U.S. company will piously announce that "our employees are our most valuable asset," and promptly waste that asset with sudden plant closings, "head count programs," or arbitrary staff dismissals to demonstrate the power of the new chief executive. These things simply do not happen in the kaisha. It is hardly surprising that as a result the kaisha's employees show a greater degree of commitment to the company than is customarily the case in the United States.

It is in the context of the exchange of commitments between employee and employer that the notion of the kaisha as family becomes a meaningful one. The leaders of the kaisha can speak, and do, of entry into the company as being born again into another family. Furthermore, rather like the family, there is a real socialization process that takes place following entry into the Japanese company. The first years of employment are largely a process of initiation—moving between departments to learn the nature of the company's activities, its history and its culture, as well as learning job skills. The employee may reside in a company dormitory, and will certainly focus not only working hours but social hours as well on relationships in the company. The employee will not be differentiated from others in his age cohort in these first years, in terms of rank or pay. The first differentiations will be slight and gradual. The indoctrination will be thorough; the calibration of the employee's skills and abilities will be fine; mutual knowledge of members of the organization, and of each others' strengths and weaknesses will become detailed.

It is in this employment process that the kaisha becomes a different social institution than the corporation in the West. Involvement is more total; options are more limited; commitments are more difficult to revoke. The West has institutions that share these patterns—religious orders, professional armies, professional bureaucracies. Western corporations are rarely among them.

In the ideology of Japanese management, this employment pattern is held out as the proper one, as the ideal model to be emulated. As the pattern of employment of major Japanese corporations, it is the pattern that the Western firm operating in Japan is expected to adhere to (and deviation from which will prove costly).

There is, however, a sizable part of the Japanese labor force that is not involved in this system. Women are expected to—and usually do—end their period of initial employment at marriage or on the birth of the first child, perhaps reentering the labor force later. Also, some part of the labor force of many large companies is made up of temporary employees, often seasonally hired, who are outside this system unless or until they become regular employees. Finally, small firms with limited resources will aspire to follow the permanent employment system, but may find it uneconomical to do so. They will, however, be expected by employees to adhere to it within the limits of their resources.

It has been suggested that some 30 percent of the Japanese labor force is covered by the system of permanent employment, but it appears that this estimate derives from the fact that 30 percent of the labor force is unionized. The system is by no means coterminous with unionization. An accurate estimate of the proportion of labor force included in the system is not possible both because of the pervasiveness of the concept of permanent employment and because of gray zones where its application is uncertain.

There are real costs and competitive disadvantages to the system. Compared to U.S. companies in particular, the Japanese work force cannot quickly be adjusted to downturns in demand. The kaisha have to depend on reduction first of temporary workers, then on a reduction in subcontracted work, then pulling that work back into the plants of the company, then offering special retirement allowances to encourage workers to withdraw from the work force, and finally allowing attrition to do its work. Only in acute crisis, only after exhausting other approaches, and only with full agreement of the union and work force, can actual layoffs or dismissals take place.

Even short of crises, there are immobility costs. Both NEC and Fujitsu report that some 10 to 15 percent of their electronics workforce is redundant, despite the fact that these firms continue to hire new recruits at a rapid pace. What is happening is that there is an accumulation of less-than-competent staff that these kaisha find redundant but cannot discharge.

A further cost of the system is the extreme difficulty of bringing about acquisitions or mergers. The kaisha in a real sense belongs to all its employees. By law, merger or acquisition is possible only with the unanimous consent of all its directors, who with few exceptions are career employees. Sale of the company has about it the sense of buying and selling people, with implications of immorality and social irresponsibility. Merger raises nearly insoluble problems of combining two entrenched work forces, and under Japanese conditions of employment offers little scope for concentration of facilities and reduction of work force.

As a result, the Japanese economy suffers from the fact that mergers are very difficult to bring about even in fragmented industries with facilities that are not world-scale. Despite years of effort, the several Mitsubishi group companies in the distressed chemical fertilizer industry have not been able to merge, even given their common group affiliation. Personnel barriers are too great to allow merger. Yet merger of these and other companies in industries in trouble would make very good economic sense.

For the kaisha themselves, the difficulties of merger and acquisition pose special problems in terms of diversification. In the West, entry into a new business area can be greatly facilitated by acquiring a firm already in the new sector. The kaisha confronted with a mature or declining business must grow its way out of the problem by internal diversification efforts—a more risky and time-consuming route—though perhaps a route that in the long-run, if successful, makes for more secure diversification.

In any event, the career employment system has its costs to the kaisha. Again, there is a trade-off—the kaisha trade flexibility in personnel management for maximizing employee involvement and commitment to the company. Their Western competitors choose the opposite.

In many of these employment patterns, the situation of the Japanese company is not greatly different from that of firms in West European economies, who are similarly restrained, often by law, from arbitrary work force reduction. However, in the Japanese case, the system has been embraced by management, and is used as a positive factor in building personnel relations. Full advantage is taken by the kaisha in identifying the interests of the work force with those of the company, and using the system as a basis for increasing motivation and morale of the work force. European firms tend to incur the penalties of the system, without exploiting its potential strengths.

Seniority Pay and Promotion: A System Under Pressure

Closely related to the practice of career employment, and the second characteristic of "Japanese-style management" is the importance of length of service with the kaisha in determining pay and promotion. The linkage to career employment is a natural one—if the kaisha have responsibility for the career of the individual, then compensation needs to in-

crease as the individual's responsibilities increase. Japan remains, in important respects, an age-graded society, and the concept of compensation and position being determined by age is deemed appropriate. When the employee is hired directly from school, age and length of service become parallel, and seniority becomes an appropriate basis for reward.

The competitive effects of a seniority system in the context of career employment have been powerful. The fast-growing industry or company is hiring large numbers of new staff members. In the Japanese case, these are necessarily younger people. The result of high levels of hiring is to reduce the average age of the work force. As average age declines, so then does average wage level. Whatever forces were responsible for rapid growth are now reinforced by a wage advantage. The slower growing company, hiring few if any people, is experiencing a steady increase in the average age of its work force. Its competitive disadvantage is reinforced by rising wage rate levels.

It is a unique feature of standard information on the kaisha that the average age of the work force, reported separately by male and female workers, is published along with the usual financial data on the company. Most Western companies would probably not have the data available, much less consider it important information. For the kaisha, age data are an important index of the competitive position of the company.

The seniority-based pay system has come under considerable pressure in recent years, however. With slower overall economic growth, the economic advantages of the system have lessened. Moreover, as life expectancy has lengthened, the earlier retirement age of fifty-five has been extended. The average retirement age from large companies will soon reach sixty.

Pay increases granted automatically with each additional year of service become more and more costly as seniority increases. Therefore, a number of experiments are underway in various kaisha, seeking to flatten the wage curve at some earlier point. The rationale is that family and other responsibilities lessen past the mid-forties, and therefore a flattening of the wage increase curve need not work a hardship. This is the sector of Japanese employment practices that is most liable to change in the near future.

Promotion is also a function of age in the Japanese firm, being provided within a predictable and narrow age range. Not everyone gets promoted—the escalator cannot carry everyone to the top floor—but promotion will rarely if ever take place until adequate seniority has been attained.

Western businessmen are prone to overestimate the frustrations that this seniority-weighted system engenders in young (especially Western-trained) Japanese. For many of these young people, the frustrations early in their career are real. There appears to be increasing mobility from job to job. Yet the frustrations appear to diminish sharply as the system begins to reward the young person reaching the early thirties. Further, few of the complainers feel a sense of frustration so extreme as to cause them to risk the security their job provides by hazarding a new career in another, especially Western, company.

Seniority-weighted pay and promotion systems are by no means peculiar to Japan. Most societies have some degree of age-grading, and most personnel systems pay some respect to length of service in their reward systems. It is the degree of weighting, the systemization of the seniority factor, and its pervasiveness as a major issue in the Japanese company that warrants giving it place in the complex of Japanese-style management.

The Unions

The third aspect of Japanese-style management is the enterprise union, which includes all employees of the company with no differentiation as to skills or job category. As an employee is promoted to a management position, he ceases being a union member. Nearly one in six of the major kaisha executives have been executives of the company's union. The trade union and the kaisha are coterminous in that the worker does not have a separate skill identification outside of or differentiated from his job assignment in the company. The union does not exist as an entity separate from, or with an adversarial relationship to, the company. The union includes all company members, and only company members. Its future and the kaisha's are identical.

Not surprisingly, there has been little interest in the issue of co-determination, of demands that the union and management share executive authority. The notion of co-determination implies basic differences in objectives between company and union, an adversarial interaction, and a need for the union (and workers) to have better knowledge of and control over company affairs. This confrontation of interests and objectives is far less likely to happen given the kaisha's enterprise union system.

The linking of the fate of union and company puts limits on the extent to which the union is prepared to risk damaging the economic situation of the company. Employees have no illusions that management is entirely benign; union membership is seen as a counterweight to potential abuses of management authority. However, damage to the company risks damage to the employees' own interests in a clear and immediate sense. Thus, the wearing of armbands with "solidarity" written on them is a meaningful statement to management of worker and union purpose, as is a lunch hour demonstration, or an after-hours protest meeting.

An especially high economic value of the enterprise union system results from the fact that the union structure poses no barriers to the movement of worker from one job to another. Unlike the situation where workers are organized by skills or job categories, there is no institutional restraint within the kaisha against reassigning workers to the limits of their capabilities. This fact is an important balancing factor to the limited mobility of Japanese workers between companies, which by itself would impose an economic cost in restricting the efficient allocation of the labor resource.

In addition, the enterprise union system means that the kaisha deal with a single negotiating unit. In an adversarial context this might provide exceptional power to the union, but this is mitigated for the kaisha by the identity of union and management interests in preserving and strengthening the company. It means that the kaisha are free of the plague of jurisdictional disputes and multiple union bargaining situations so common in the West.

The union in Japan is important, but its organizational pattern raises the question of why Western managements, instead of resisting unionization of the work force, do not work to encourage the formation of a union with which management can cooperate. It is a curious fact that the Western company in Japan often resists formation of a union, from its Western experience. The best move would be to encourage early formation of a union in the Japanese subsidiary and facilitate communications with the work force, ensuring that the union could be dealt with in a constructive fashion. Rather than taking this initiative, Western management in Japan usually attempts to forestall unionization. As a result, when the number of employees reaches a certain size, usually about 200, professional organizers, often of a distinctly leftist persuasion, organize a union that management finds difficult or impossible to deal with.

It needs to be noted that the influence of the trade union in Japan as elsewhere appears to be diminishing. The year 1984 marked the thirtieth anniversary of Japan's unique approach to wage negotiations, the *shunto,* or spring struggle, a pattern of settlement of wage negotiations during a concentrated period in March and April of each year. The anniversary was observed with widespread comment that the *shunto* is losing its meaning. Settlements are being reached at reasonable levels, without disputes, with general agreement that wage increases should reflect productivity improvements plus inflation.

As in the United States, the proportion of the work force in Japan that is organized into unions is declining. It is now 30 percent in Japan, compared with 20 percent in the United States, in contrast to more than 40 percent in Western Europe. As the Japanese company shifts further toward the tertiary sector—toward services and away from manufacturing—this trend will continue and union influence, both in the workplace and in national politics, is likely to slowly but steadily diminish.

In Japan, the three features of Japanese-style management, career employment, seniority-based pay and promotion, and the enterprise union, are referred to as the "three pillars" of the system. The three are mutually reinforcing, and as a system, the results are remarkable. To a degree unmatched by any other organizational system, the *kaisha* of Japan have achieved an identification of corporate and individual interests. This is not the result of some special inclination of the workers of Japan toward feelings of loyalty, or toward diligence, or toward hard work. It is the result of a system that imposes close identification of corporate and individual interests. The costs of confrontation are minimized. Investments made in training of staff can be fully amortized over the career of the employee. Thus, the company can invest in the individual—in recruiting, training, and retraining—to the limit of its resources. The individual in return has every reason to work on behalf of the company, without concern over arbitrary discharge or capricious abortion of his career. The company can call for, and reasonably expect, levels of effort and quality of output that are only exceptionally available in most other employment systems.

The kaisha becomes in a real sense the property of the people who make it up. It will not be sold, in whole or in part, without the specific approval of all of its directors, acting on behalf of all of its employees. Earnings of the company go first as a return to investors, with the entire balance going to ensure the company's future and thus ensure the future of its employees. The kaisha is not simply an economic institution, but is a deeply social institution, working out its destiny in a competitive economic environment.

THE PROCESS OF DECISION MAKING

In discussing Japanese-style management, some reference needs be made to the issue of decision making, and differences in the process between the kaisha and Western companies, if only because the topic is so often raised. There is a general view that the kaisha have a special approach to decision making, consensual in nature to an exceptional extent, as symbolized by the formal *ringi seido,* in which a memorandum summarizing the decision is circulated and signed by all concerned.

Much attention has also been paid to the informal, predecision processes of discussion and accommodation of views, called in Japanese *nemawashi.* The kaisha are felt to take a relatively long time to arrive at a decision as these informal and formal processes are worked through, but are seen as able to implement decisions very rapidly once a formal decision is arrived at.

This is no doubt a reasonable description of the usual Japanese decision-making process. It is self-evident that the organization of

the kaisha, with tight integration of individuals into the group and an emphasis on group values and behavior, would emphasize group-centered decisions as well. The entire culture of the kaisha mitigates against the spectacular individual making his way against odds and general opinion and finally drawing the group after him. (Japanese politics are similarly free from this man-on-horseback model.)

The problem with this characterization is that it sets up a polarity between all Western decisions made rapidly by an individual and all Japanese decisions made slowly by groups. Neither extreme describes either universe very well. Japan has its occasional one-man companies. Not all Japanese decisions are long drawn-out ones. Indeed, the Western negotiator who believes negotiations with a Japanese company are taking a long time has probably been politely refused and is unable to comprehend the fact.

Many Western organizations have elaborate procedures for study and review before decisions are made, and it is a rare and usually unsuccessful Western executive who fails to sound out his or her organization informally before making a decision. The usual contrast between cultures in terms of decision making seems not to be a very useful one. One might conclude that the culture of most kaisha will ensure group discussion before decisions are made, with the corollary that responsibility for any decision tends to be shared, and that all concerned understand and act on their role in implementation once it is made.

WHEN WILL THE EMPLOYMENT SYSTEM CHANGE?

The system of organization and personnel relations of the *kaisha* is not an old system in its present, integrated form. Essentially a product of elements of earlier systems and of the conditions prevailing after World War II, it dates from around 1950. It is a product of a special set of circumstances, history, and events coming together in a particular social and cultural setting. As such, it is liable to change, if and as it becomes dysfunctional under the pressure of changed needs and conditions.

Western journalists are given to writing periodic articles on how the Japanese employment system is changing, based on anecdotal reports or rumors of changes. Some job changes have always taken place between Japanese companies, and continue to; the occasional exception in no way negates the rule, nor signals an end to the general pattern. The Japanese system of employment has proved to be quite durable, through periods of high growth and no growth, in flourishing industries and declining industries. It offers very real advantages to both employees and to the kaisha. It is not surprising therefore that it has survived periods of difficulty.

Viewed in terms of individual motivation, the Japanese system of employment is a trade-off of opportunity for security. It provides security above all, at the loss of opportunity for unusually high reward. It is often remarked by Westerners that security has a high value for the Japanese, and that preference for security against opportunity and risk can be inferred not only from occupational and job preferences but from savings and consumption patterns, as well as political choices.

A security preference is usual for most Japanese, which is not surprising. Until quite recently Japan was a very poor country. The long period of war, the experience of total defeat, and the desperate conditions of the early postwar period would alone make a preference for security over risk entirely understandable. Seen from a historical view, there has been in Japan the sense of a country limited in land, terribly poor in resources, and subject to an exceptionally unpredictable and violent geographic environment. It is not surprising that under these conditions there would be a need to husband limited resources and invest those resources carefully. A strong preference for security over risk would be a natural response.

But as these conditions are changing in important ways, it would not be surprising to find that the security-risk trade-off is also changing, with young people prepared to take career chances their parents did not. Patience with and satisfaction from seniority-based pay and promotion systems would then be likely to wear thin, and the opportunity to change jobs might appear to be a reasonable exchange for the security of the present job.

Changes in attitudes and values may well erode the system over time, but are likely to work slowly. More immediately, the system is under real and continuing economic pressure. It has been the case from the earliest applications of the system that companies in declining industries in Japan, facing a steady falling off of demand, come under severe pressures. As noted earlier, these companies have an aging work force, and thus rising wage levels. The technological level of their work force tends to become obsolete as young graduates are no longer hired. As the age cohorts remaining in the work force move up in seniority, their promotion opportunities dwindle as growth stops and younger workers are not hired. Titles indicating career progress must be created to preserve an illusion of advance.

From point of the economy the results are entirely beneficial. Pressures on declining sectors are increased, accelerating their decline. The labor force shifts to growth sectors, as young people are drawn into the growth industries. Pressure on companies in the declining industries to find growth in new products is intense.

Just such a picture was presented by one of Japan's major shipbuilding companies in a recent study. Its employment peaked in 1973, and fell off sharply after that bulge in employment. Those hired in 1973 are now in their mid-thirties, moving inexorably, like a pig in a python, in age and in wage cost, their morale little improved by a proliferation of titles that are empty of the substance of authority or responsibility. A very hard fate for the company, its employees and its shareholders, but very sound for the economy. The company is being driven out of shipbuilding and toward new kinds of engineering businesses out of desperation—but to Japan's overall advantage.

Yet under the pressures of lower eco-

nomic growth and of automation, this pattern and this problem is no longer limited to Japanese companies in declining sectors. Figure 1 shows the age structure of one of Japan's largest, best-managed, and fastest growing electronics companies. One would have expected hiring to continue at a high level in this company, and the age bulge problem to be nonexistent. In fact, until about ten years ago, the age pattern was perfect—a smooth triangular pattern, with hirings increasing, average age declining, and all the resulting advantages. But

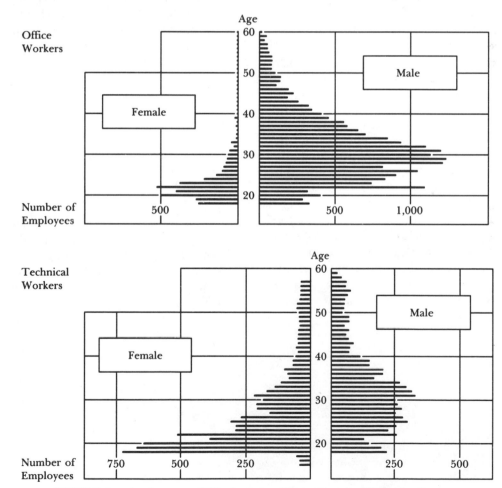

FIGURE 1. *Age Structure of Employees in a Major Japanese Electronics Company*

even in this fast growth sector, hirings of male workers has dropped off steadily and sharply in recent years. Female workers do not present a problem, as they tend to leave the company as they marry, or have children, and generally therefore do not pose a problem in terms of long employment. But the pattern for male workers is an ominous one.

It is worth noting that table 1 was available from the company in essentially the form shown in a matter of minutes after requesting it. It was in the personnel department's computer in chart form. Similarly, the shipbuilding company's age structure data were immediately available upon request. This fact is itself a measure of the importance of the problem to the kaisha management.

A survey of a number of major Japanese companies reveals a similar pattern of age structure. The electronics company's personnel manager predicted that the effect would be an end to the current Japanese system of employment by the end of the current decade. The general view is that the seniority-based pay and promotion system will need to give way to a job- and output-based system, but that security of employment will continue.

It seems likely that the benefits to the kaisha of the current system, and the system's fit to the attitudes and expectations of employees, are such that Japan's employment system will change only slowly—and not necessarily in the individualistic, confrontational and, in human terms, costly U.S. or Western system. However, just as the retirement pattern has already changed, so changes in the compensation system are underway and likely to continue. The enterprise union and career employment security are likely to give way last, and continue longest in the manufacturing sector. It may well be that in the service sector, where the emphasis is likely to be on specific professional skills, and where the organizational unit is smaller and more mobile, employment practices will be more individualistic and the employee more mobile. In manufacturing, however, the kaisha have developed a powerful and effective approach to dealing with the human problems of the organization. The approach is not likely to change quickly in significant fashion.

NOTES

1. *The Economist,* 20 October 1984, p. 107.
2. Lisa Miller Mesdag, "Are You Underpaid?" *Fortune,* 19 March 1984, pp. 15–19.
3. "Executive Pay: The Top Earners," *Business Week,* 7 May 1984, pp. 60–65.
4. *Senshinkoku Byo ni Ochiiranai Tameni,* p. 10.
5. Malcolm Sawyer, "Income Distribution in OEGD Countries," in *OECD Economic Outlook, Occasional Studies.* (Paris: Organization for Economic Cooperation and Development, July 1976), p. 16.

The Japanese Management Theory Jungle

J. Bernard Keys

Thomas Miller

Many competing hypotheses have been advanced to account for the apparent effectiveness of Japanese management practices. The present review of some of the leading theories attempts to classify and clarify the state of knowledge of Japanese management. Although each theory may be correct as a partial explanation of Japan's success, no single conceptualization has captured the complexity of Japan's managerial achievement. Further development of integrated, internally consistent models is needed.

In response to Japan's impressive business performance over the last decade, the mystique of Japanese management has been addressed by a deluge of books and articles. The perceived superiority of management practices in Japan has been the subject of intensive inquiry by both the academic and the executive communities. Researchers' efforts to unlock this mystery have revealed a multitude of factors presumed to account for the excellence of Japanese management, but the most striking results perhaps are the diversity of factors cited and the disagreement over the causes of this success.

Competing hypotheses abound, ranging from the "Seven S" theory of Pascale and Athos (1981) about a unique Japanese management style to the "bottom line" explanation that stresses the Japanese focus on long term operating results. Some observers believe that excellence in Japanese management springs primarily from an emphasis on human resource development. Others maintain that the source of Japanese success is not found in social practices, but rather in the profound understanding of the intricacies of the decision making process. Several researchers laud the effective use of employee quality circles as the key element of Japanese success. Still others claim that Japanese expertise in technological developments and in manufacturing management is the basis of their effectiveness. Yet another school of thought attributes Japanese achievement to their mastery of the use of statistical quality control applications.

To those attempting to comprehend the

From *Academy of Management Review* (1984), Volume 9, Number 2. Reprinted by permission.

Note: Portions of this paper were presented at the 42nd Annual Meeting of the Academy of Management, New York, 1982. The authors acknowledge Harold Koontz (1961), author of the classic paper, "The Management Theory Jungle."

Japanese phenomenon, it appears that a dense jungle of confusion has grown up consisting of conflicting "theories" (using the term broadly), each of which offers hope as an explanation for the apparent superiority of the Japanese system of management. The jungle of Japanese theories is reminiscent of the "mental entanglement" that characterized American management theories in the 1950s, addressed in a classic article by Harold Koontz (1961). The purpose of this paper is to classify and to clarify the state of knowledge of Japanese management.

THE JUNGLE OF THEORIES

Manufacturing Management

Robert H. Hayes (1981) conducted his research by visiting and studying several plants of six Japanese companies. He finds the answer to Japanese superiority in their excellent manufacturing management: clean facilities, responsible employees, little or no inventories on the plant floor made possible by the absence of work stoppages, almost no rejected products, and "just-in-time" materials arrival. He discovered a remarkable absence of crisis management in the plant and excellent maintenance of equipment. Hayes captures the essence of Japanese manufacturing management in the old Japanese proverb: "pursuing the last grain of rice in the corner of the lunchbox." He points out that the Japanese are never satisfied with the quality of their products even when the defect rate is at an unbelievable 1 percent, nor are they satisfied as long as any defect exists in the manufacturing operation. Hayes believes that technological advantages in Japan stem not from superior technology per se, but from the Japanese insistence on building their own process equipment in-house, which they in turn match with skilled employees trained in-house. They will not accept the compromise of a ma-

chine developed for several "users, and therefore several uses."

Further support for the manufacturing management theory is provided by Wheelwright (1981), who states that Japan's impressive accomplishments in manufacturing result chiefly from the effective integration of operations policy and manufacturing strategy. In marked contrast to the Japanese, the author cites the common American tendency to treat product quality and production planning as "swing factors" that can be traded off in order to meet the production output deadline. Thus, an American manager may deliver a product that, although functionally acceptable, does not meet the quality specifications. In reporting their impressions after visiting the plants of three Japanese companies—Tokyo Sanyo Electric, Toshita Tsurumi Works, and Yokogaua Electric Works, General Electric manufacturing executives agreed that the critical differences between Japanese and American manufacturing were not really cultural and environmental, but rather were related to basic manufacturing policy and practice. Observers reported a high degree of cleanliness and organization with orderly and timely flow of materials through the production system. They commented that although Americans have the necessary knowledge of effective manufacturing processes, they have lacked the discipline to implement them fully (Wheelwright, 1981). Wheelwright concludes that Japan's "truly impressive discipline and consistency in manufacturing operations" is the result of "a deliberate, thorough, and painstakingly developed way of thinking about the day-to-day management of production" (1981, p. 68). In other words, he holds that the Japanese have become so efficient chiefly because of excellent manufacturing practices. However, in interpreting these observations in order to isolate causes, an alternative hypothesis should be recognized: orderly production operations may be the *result* of the effective practice of management rather than the *cause* of manufacturing efficiency.

Quality Circle

A common theme in the literature on the effectiveness of Japanese management is their development and utilization of "quality control circles" or just "quality circles," as they are now commonly called (Cole, 1980; Rehder, 1981; Takeuchi, 1981; Yager, 1980). Although there are many variations of quality circles in practice, nearly all are structured as a relatively small group of employees who meet together to discuss and develop solutions for work problems relating to quality, productivity, or cost.

In many respects, quality circles are rooted in the work of the humanistic behavioral scientists such as Chris Argyris, Douglas McGregor, and Rensis Likert, who have long emphasized the significance of employee participation to effective management. Schooled in these behavioral techniques, the Japanese borrowed and adapted them to their organizations. However, it appears that the Japanese found their organizations more receptive to this form of participation than have American managers. Cole (1980) argues that Japanese managers have more fully accepted the fundamental premise of participative management—that employees are capable of contributing and desire to contribute to organizational requirements of a supportive supervisory climate and that the commitment of sufficient time for the participative process may be better satisfied in Japanese industry than in the United States.

Thus, the quality circle theory ascribes the effectiveness of Japanese management to an in-depth application of the participation concept, which apparently has resulted in improved productivity through higher levels of motivation, greater sharing of decision making, stronger employee commitment, and increased job satisfaction. In an extensive review of quality circles, Munchus (1983) concluded that they

have been successful in widely diversified cultures, but that the results of their use in the United States are still open to question. Matsushita Electric, for example, uses them widely in Japan but does not consider the American worker suited to such activity.

Statistical Quality Control

In the 1950s the Japanese focused on upgrading the quality level of their manufactured products in an effort to reverse the notion that "made in Japan" signaled inferior merchandise. As with the development of quality circles, the expertise came largely from consultants in America—in particular from W. Edwards Deming and J. M. Juran, who lectured widely on the development and utilization of statistics and quality control techniques. The Japanese quickly embraced and effectively implemented the popular techniques developed in the United States, including zero defects and value engineering, and have become dedicated to the gospel of quality (Takeuchi, 1981). The Japanese appreciation for Deming's work is evidenced by his receipt of the Second Order Medal of the Sacred Treasure from Japan's Emperor Hirohito.

Of course, productivity is closely related to quality, and in Japan there is a fervent interest in "doing it right the first time." Deming argues that quality cannot be increased by inspection, and using men and machines to separate good products from bad is not the answer. The quality capability must be built into the production process. In comparing Japanese and American management, Deming (1980) argues that Americans learned the techniques too, but the Japanese took them seriously.

Long Term, Bottom Line

Peter Drucker suggests that the real reason for Japanese superiority springs from their focus on long term objectives. Large U.S. institutional investors, such as the pension funds, he laments, tend to reject firms that do not show strong performance in such short term measures as quarterly earnings per share. Thus, high technology companies are reluctant to "plow back money long term" for fear of adverse effects of their price earnings ratios. The market, he believes, has become far too sensitive to short term fluctuations (Flanigan, 1981).

A similar theme is echoed by William Anderson (1981), chairman and chief executive officer of National Cash Register Corporation. He cautions that American managers must look "beyond this month's sales report and this year's financial performance" and begin to evaluate both employee and organizational achievements from a long term prospective. The clear implication is that U.S. management should adopt criteria that look five years ahead, not just a month ahead.

Further evidence of the long planning horizon of Japanese management is the tradition of lifetime employment, resulting in a worker spending his entire career with one firm. For example, the average job tenure at Fujitsu is 13 years; the average job tenure in the United States is 3.6 years (Nakayama, 1980). While providing essentially a guaranteed job to the worker, the longevity of employment encourages extensive investment in employee training and development and promotes employee loyalty and esprit de corps, as evidenced by the company songs and exercise programs in many of the large plants. The nearly complete job security also reduces costs of turnover and subsequent recruitment. But, perhaps most important, the worker's assurance of economic security greatly reduces one's resistance to technological change that enables methods changes to be implemented more easily. Drucker maintains that this willingness to accept change and to embrace opportunities for productivity gains might be "the most important secret of the Japanese economy" (1971, p. 116). In sharp contrast, the typical American worker in a union-ized firm has been conditioned to resist change, fearing both real and imagined threats to his/her economic security.

However, a key point in evaluating the unionization issue should be noted. In Japan, employees belong to company unions rather than craft unions; thus they could not readily change companies if they wished to do so. The strong company affiliation makes it easy to shift employees from plant to plant within the same company (Tanaka, 1981). These employer advantages are enhanced by the strong feeling of security promoted by the Japanese lifetime employment concept. Drucker recently commented that lifetime employment, which restricts labor mobility and the threat of strikes, has rendered the union powerless in the private sector, almost an "organ of management" (1982, p. 26).

It should be recognized that the Japanese management focus on long term profitability is feasible, in part, because of the supportive role of the Japanese government. The comments of Reddy and Rao are revealing: "The Japanese government has been pursuing economic growth with a passion that American government has reserved for fighting communism" (1982, p. 5). The close relationship between business and government has been characterized as "Japan, Inc.," suggesting the behavior of a superconglomerate (Drucker, 1981). Indeed, some argue that Japan's economic success is related chiefly to the unique business-government relationship fostered by the Ministry of International Trade and Industry (MITI). As noted by Tsurumi (1981), government policies through tax incentives and other assistance programs are directed to rewarding the firms fulfilling the goals that support industrial growth and national stability. A related factor enabling business to focus its attention on the civilian product market is the low level of national resources committed to defense expenditures in Japan, a much publicized criticism by American producers.

Decision Making

At first glance, the consensus decision process of the Japanese appears to be simply an application of the American concept of participative management. Ouchi (1981) states that a consensus has been reached when there is agreement on a single alternative and when there is a mutual understanding of views of the participants and when there is support for the decision, whether one preferred it or not, because it was determined in an open and fair manner. However, Ouchi argues that even this degree of participation does not approach the Japanese concept of consensus decision making, in which an important decision such as where to put a new plant or changing a production process would involve all who would likely be affected by it, perhaps 60 to 80 people. Ouchi further notes that two or three persons would have the task of discussing the decision with the affected employees and repeating this process when significant changes arise. Although this process is very time consuming, when the decision is finally determined, the support for it is nearly unanimous.

Howard and Teramoto (1981), professors in Great Britain and Tokyo, respectively, argue strongly that the most important difference in American and Japanese management involves the subtle differences in decision making. The word in the Japanese vocabulary that describes decision making is "nemawashi," which refers to the "political" processes by which an unofficial understanding is reached before any final decision is made on a particular matter. The literal meaning of nemawashi is "the process of planting a tree, i.e., implanting its roots into the soil so it can grow." The authors believe that it perfectly describes the appropriate process of practical decision making in any culture.

To the Western observer, the consensus decision making process may appear to be exceedingly inefficient, but this attitude fails to give proper consideration to the implementation of the decision. In defense of the Japanese decision making practice, it is advanced that a consensus decision, though mediocre, can yield better outcomes than an imposed decision, though brilliant, because of the support of employees, their knowledge of the decision parameters, and their commitment to successful execution of the decisions. Further, the considerable time that goes into defining the issue reduces the risk that a preconceived solution will prevent proper definition of the problem, a criterion of decision making practices of American managers (Kobayashi, 1970).

Attempts at Integrated Models of Japanese Management

Several students of the Japanese management process have gone beyond the search for the single-factor explanation in their efforts to develop more comprehensive theories. Three of these notable efforts will be reviewed briefly.

Seven S Richard Pascale and Anthony Athos (1981) utilize in their model the framework of seven management variables developed by McKinsey & Company. The seven variables of S's are superordinate goals, strategy, structure, systems, staff, skills, and style. These are the "levers" of organizational and management functions with which executives can influence large complex organizations. Superordinate goals function as the unifying elements that tie together the various activities and interests of organizational members.

According to Pascale and Athos, the variables can be divided into "hard S's" and "soft S's." The hard S's, presumably the more impersonal and institutional factors, are strategy, structure, and systems. In contrast, the soft S's, dealing more with human values and interpersonal issues, are staff (the concern for having the right sort of people to do the work), skills (training and developing people to do what is needed), and style (the manner in which management handles subordinates, peers, and superiors). The authors' chief research instrument included interviews and observations of the styles of chief executive officers in the United States and Japan—in particular, the Matsushita Corporation and ITT.

Pascale and Athos maintain that U.S. management is very similar to Japan on all the hard S's of strategy, structure, and system, but that Japan has advantages in the soft S's of staff, skills, and style. These advantages stem largely from the Japanese culture, which differs in its approach to ambiguity, uncertainty, imperfection, and interdependence. The authors discuss at length how the Japanese manager in communicating with others has learned to make the most of ambiguity, indirection, subtle cues, trust, interdependence, uncertainty, implicit messages, and management of process, as opposed to the U.S. managerial norm of striving for complete openness, explicitness, and directness in order to minimize ambiguity and uncertainty. Unfortunately, the authors support their theory only with broad generalizations drawn from comparisons of the chief executive officer of Matsushita Corporation and ITT's Geneen.

Organizational William Ouchi (1981) summarizes his work in what has become the best selling book on Japanese management, *Theory Z.* Instead of emphasizing the differences in the styles of leaders of key organizations in the United States and Japan, Ouchi focused in his writing on the organizations, themselves. He first describes the ideal Japanese organizational model, which he used as a "foil" against which to compare and understand the American model. The Japanese organization is characterized by lifetime employment, slow evaluation and promotion, nonspecialized career paths, implicit control mechanisms, collective decision making, collective responsibility, and holistic concern for employees. In sharp contrast,

features of American organizations include short term employment, rapid evaluation and promotion, specialized career paths, explicit control mechanisms, individual decision making, individual responsibility, and segmented concern for workers.

Ouchi also argues that the characteristics of Japanese management have derived from their culture—a culture woven interdependently because of collective rice farming and crowded conditions causing Japan to be very ripe for industrialization. In contrast, the American culture has developed from the spirit of individualism of an expanding frontier, a culture less conducive to industrialization.

Ouchi and Jaeger (1978), like Pascale and Athos, point out that the Japanese style is not culture bound, however. Many Japanese firms, with little adaptation, have transported their successful operations to the United States. Theory Z, then, becomes the modified model, which includes the best of the Japanese and American models. Theory Z emphasizes long, but not lifetime, employment; consensual decision making, as in Japan; individual responsibility as opposed to the Japanese emphasis on collective responsibility; slow evaluation and promotion as in Japan; implicit control (Japanese) but with explicit measures (American); moderately specialized career paths (a compromise); and a holistic concern for employees, as in Japan (Ouchi & Jaeger, 1978).

Ouchi's theory has not been immune to criticism. In his review of *Theory Z,* for example, Gibney sharply challenges Ouchi's assertion that Japanese organizations can be so readily typified and understood from the few cases cited by Ouchi: "Ouchi has given us a chrome-plated collection of hasty generalizations, slogan-type writing, and dimestore business sociology, based on what one might call a modified dartboard technique of research" (1981, p. 17).

A thoughtful, incisive critique of Theory Z is provided by Sullivan (1983), who develops an anti-theory Z "descriptive" conceptualization that contrasts sharply with Ouchi's "prescriptive" model. Anti-theory Z acknowledges the existence of life-time employment, nonspecialized careers, and automatic promotions, but suggests that these are cultural, historical factors rather than managerially initiated incentives. Further, Sullivan hypothesizes that these conditions produce some minimally competent managers who, when promoted automatically, must depend heavily on subordinates. The resultant consensus decisions and sharing of responsibility may stem more from necessity than from intimacy, involvement, and trust. Thus, consensus decisions and collective responsibility protect bureaucratic, hierarchical relationships, which, he proposes, exist in some Japanese firms. In addition, Sullivan argues that Theory Z does not, as Ouchi claims, emanate from humanistic management. Instead, Sullivan contends that Theory Z derives from the "industrial clan" values of Durkheim (1902/1933) that promote and sustain a regulated social order as opposed to the self-interest of individuals.

Human Resource Hatvany and Pucik (1981) have conceptualized a model of Japanese management that focuses on the maximization of human resource development. Emphasizing the use of an integrated system of management, the authors' model rests on the implementation of three interrelated strategies: development of an internal labor market, articulation of a company philosophy stressing cooperation and teamwork, and utilization of a well-defined socialization process for hiring and integrating new employees into the company.

The unique element of Japanese management highlighted by Hatvany and Pucik is the internal labor market, which derives from the lifetime employment syndrome discussed earlier. Japanese firms hire males after graduation, with the expectation of retaining them for a lifetime. This security of male employment is assisted by using female and part time workers in order to adjust the size of the workforce to current economic conditions, by underpaying workers in the early stages of their careers in favor of compensation in later years, and by slow career path movement. The Japanese utilize an intensive socialization process designed to foster a "company man" identity.

Many specific techniques are utilized by the Japanese to promote and reinforce their management system. Broad knowledge of company operations is fostered by job rotation, slow promotion, and the lifetime employment. Company policies and assignments tend to build group cohesiveness and teamwork and emphasize the importance of the collective interests of the group, rather than the individual's own interests. Employee evaluation encompasses both performance factors and workers' attitudes and behaviors. Open communications are fostered by extensive face-to-face communications (the absence of private offices, even for high ranking managers) and by the frequency with which foremen and senior plant managers tend to visit workers on the plant floor. Use of consultative decision making practices is another supporting technique of Hatvany and Pucik's model. The final element in their model is management's expression of concern for employees enhanced by extensive company sponsored cultural, athletic, and recreational activities.

In contrast to the above model, Cole (1971) cautions that Western knowledge of the blue-collar worker in Japan is still shallow and laden with stereotypes of limited validity. He claims that the vision of the Japanese worker as always polite and unemotional differs sharply from the gregarious, spontaneous, openly expressive workers in the Tokyo plant he observed. The character of the Japanese worker is further explicated by Tsurumi (1981), who maintains that politeness, hard work, orientation toward group activity, and loyalty to management are no more inborn traits of the Japanese than of Canadians and Americans. Although a popular view of Japanese work groups touts their strong cohesiveness and the benefits of consensus decision making, Cole warns that this emphasis masks the strong competition within Japanese society. Such competition reveals itself in efforts to cultivate favor with superiors through flattery or politicking, which can result in conflicts within the work group. Further, Cole questions the authenticity of Japanese employee security through lifetime employment, noting that there are many devices employers can use to get employees to quit that fall short of actually firing them.

Yazaburo Mogi, first executive vice president of the Kikkoman soy sauce plant at Waleworth, Wisconsin, cautions that "the Japanese seniority system, while it offers security and creates a harmonious atmosphere conducive to good results, may also reduce incentives to do good work" ("How the Japanese Manage," 1981, p. 103). Rejecting the "myth" of the Japanese as "supermen" and the conclusion that Japan's industrial success is linked to the uniqueness of Japanese human factors or "the spirit of its workers," Blotnick argues that it would be as correct to link Japan's success to "the coercive, regimented side of its society," which Americans would "hardly want to emulate" (1981, p. 132).

The transfer of strong family ties to industry has fostered several interesting phenomena. Tanaka (1981) reports that employees tend to hire "total persons," and employees tend to become totally immersed in the organization for which they work. Because the company becomes a surrogate for the family, work takes on the same ethos as a contribution to the family—loyalty, sincerity, and so on. The company's (family's) prosperity becomes more important than individual prosperity, and work for the company—not leisure—becomes the essence of life.

SOURCES OF ENTANGLEMENT IN THE JUNGLE

Many differences in the Japanese style of management and Western styles can be attributed to sharp differences in the respective cultures rather than to management practices (Schein, 1981). The common thread about which Japanese life has developed is "intimacy," which has evolved from the dictates of collective farming, little available land space, and the need to construct homes that offered little privacy. The family cultural forces are transferred to business firms, reinforcing compliance of behavior and promoting high performance (Cao, 1981). In strong opposition to this style, which promotes close social relations, American life has developed around rugged individualism and independence (Ouchi, 1981), which has grown out of the developing frontier and a land intensive economy rather than a labor intense one. Thus, the cultural focus on the groups' interests, as opposed to the individual's, is strongly imbedded in Japanese workers in contrast to their American counterparts.

Several environmental and structural factors seem to offer Japanese management an advantage over the United States. Most Japanese employees who are union members belong to company unions. Of the directors of major corporations, 16 percent are former union officials (Janger & Berenkein, 1981). Unions and management tend to form a strong productive partnership, paving the way for easy introduction of labor-saving devices. The influence of such "macro" factors as MITI, extensive capital investment, modest defense expenditures, lower wage rates, and the relatively undervalued yen have been slighted as causal factors of Japan's economic success when compared to the much publicized managerial prowess of the Japanese. Further, Vogel has argued that the Japanese educational environment is the foundation of its economic achievement: "If any single factor explains the Japanese success, it is the group-directed quest for knowledge" (1982 p. 65). Perhaps this quest arises in the very competitive school systems and is reinforced by the close relationships among academic performance, schools attended and job placement.

Nearly all of the confrontations faced by Japanese firms arise from consumer or environmental issues. Rarely does protest involve issues such as feminism, investment policy, wages, or living and working conditions. For protests that do arise, litigation is quite uncommon (Japan has half the population of the United States, but only 11,000 lawyers). Nor is shareholder pressure a viable alternative for special interest groups; 90 percent of all directors are "inside" directors employed by the company (Janger & Berenkein, 1981).

A further source of confusion is the tendency toward oversimplification in explaining the effectiveness of Japanese management. It is doubtful that a one-factor or two-factor theory of management such as "decision making" or "quality control" can account fully for a country's economic achievements. Surely a group of complex forces taken together delineate the dimensions of Japanese management experience. A related element of confusion is the difficulty of distinguishing causation from correlation. Sullivan (1983) bases his anti-theory Z on such an argument.

Another caveat to the student of Japanese management concerns the tendency toward overgeneralization of the "Japanese management" mystique. Research on Japanese management practices has focused primarily on large, highly visible firms in the automotive and electronics industries. What of the experience of the smaller firms and businesses engaged in retailing, agriculture, chemicals, or in the service industries such as banking and finance? Can one characterize the management practices of an entire nation from such a small and nonrepresentative sample? Although Ouchi and Pascale and Athos have highlighted dramatic differences between Japanese and Ameri-

can management practices, it is doubtful that the few firms cited truly represent the norms of "Japanese" and "American" management. The excellent productivity and quality of Japanese manufacturing in such mass production industries as automobiles, household appliances, and steel are well recognized, but one should not conclude that the Japanese enjoy superiority over international competitors in all industrial efforts. As noted by Tsurumi:

> Japanese industries do not outperform American, Canadian and other foreign counterparts . . . in agriculture, aircraft, nonferrous metals, and some advanced telecommunications equipment. In the fields of organic and non-organic chemicals, pharmaceuticals, large-scale computers and large earth-moving equipment, American firms lead the Japanese by a substantial margin (1981, p. 7).

The need for additional research to resolve inconsistencies and conflicts is clear. True, insights and understandings are developing, but much of the evidence is andecdotal or is so narrowly based that accurate conclusions must necessarily be tentative. Although these results are to be expected, given the youthful state of research on Japanese industrial sciences, some observers have been unable to resist drawing broad conclusions that are appealing in their simplicity but are unwarranted by the research data.

COMMON FACTORS IN THE THEORIES AND MODELS—A MENTAL FACTOR ANALYSIS

Although the positions of the writers above present different views and perspectives on Japanese management success that have contributed to the "entanglement," there appear to be underlying factors at the heart of the Japanese system that foster the development of the various management theories and models. First, Japanese managers seem to be oriented to a longer planning horizon than their American counterparts. Second, Japanese firms are more inclined to accept a lifetime commitment and holistic concern for their employees. Finally, the Japanese appear more strongly committed to the concept of collective responsibility than individual accountability. These three factors are explored as integrating concepts in interrelating the streams of Japanese management thought presented above.

A suggested pattern of causality among the underlying factors of long run planning horizon, commitment to lifetime employment, and collective responsibility and a summary of outcomes characterizing Japanese management are shown in Figure 1. The authors contend that these underlying factors may be chiefly responsible for the development of the elements of the Japanese system of management and that these are rooted in the Japanese culture. Although a model of perfect causality

is not claimed, the tentative pattern of causality in Figure 1 relates and summarizes much of the existing evidence.

Long Run Planning Horizon

Once management commits itself to planning for the long run rather than focusing on short run maximization, certain benefits are likely to follow. Management is allocated more time to develop objectives and implementation plans. The longer planning horizon is conducive to the generation of interpersonal relationships that foster mutual understandings and implicit goals. Furthermore, the time frame of all plans—short run, intermediate, and long term—tends to lengthen, and immediate pressures tend to diminish. Deliberate planning and communication exhibits itself in orderliness and diligence of implementation of production operations and in the integration of manufacturing strategy and operations policy. There is time to produce customized in-house process equipment, and, perhaps more importantly, the

Underlying Factors   *Management Practices*

Long-Run Planning Horizon

Commitment to Lifetime Employment

Collective Responsibility

- Commitment to sufficient time to manage
- Diligence in implementation of plans
- Discipline and order in work
- Sufficient time to implement concepts and systems
- Development of an integrated organizational philosophy
- Growth of implicit control systems
- Atticulation of company philosophy
- Executive investment in employee training and development
- Socialization process in hiring and integration
- Reduced turnover and high loyalty
- Nonspecialized career paths
- Development of internal labor markets
- Emphasis on soft S's—staff, skills, style
- Company unions rather than craft unions
- Emphasis on teamwork and cooperation
- Consensus decision making
- Participative management
- Trust and interdependence
- Quality circles

FIGURE 1.   *Fundamental Factors Underlying Japanese Management Practices: A Suggested Pattern of Causality*[a]
[a]Overlapping lines represent shadings of dual causality. The authors acknowledge that some of the resultant practices may, in turn, reinforce the underlying factors, suggesting two-way causality.

long tenure of employees provides time to select employees whose skills match the equipment or to train those whose skills do not.

The impact of the long planning horizon on Japanese industry is further evidenced in the activities of the Ministry of Trade and Industry, which provide a supportive, stable environment for the industries that are responsive to expressed national economic goals. The predictability of public policy toward business and industry permits an easier organizational commitment to long term strategies rather than a penchant for short run expediencies.

The success in Japan of quality circles, statistical quality control, and consensus decision making also is facilitated by the long term focus. Often the lack of success with these approaches in the United States has not been because they are faulty in theory or concept, but rather because they have been implemented poorly. Poor implementation usually means too hastily introduced. However, given sufficient time for employers to become comfortable with these new approaches, and with co-workers, many implicit control systems and corrective adjustments arise to prevent the failure of these complex managerial concepts and systems.

Commitment to Lifetime Employment

The mutual commitment of Japanese management and the employee to lifetime employment appears to underlie a number of the celebrated Japanese management practices. The mutual awareness created by the investment of the two parties permits long term efforts in training and development. It also encourages rotational training programs outside one's specialized field and, perhaps most importantly, as cited by Drucker, promotes the acceptance of changes in work methods and technology that enhance productivity. (This approach contrasts sharply with an American tendency to reap short term benefits from new employees with entry-level skills by retaining them in a job until they leave the organization.)

The recruitment and selection process is approached differently when one hires for a lifetime rather than the short term. More emphasis must be given to the socialization factors—the "fit" of the employee to the organization, one's satisfaction with the company philosophy, one's relationships with peer groups at work, the acceptance of management style, and so on. Indeed, hiring may be based more on social factors than on entry skills, because the latter will be utilized less.

The intensive socialization of the Japanese firm's efforts to inculcate the culture of the organization in employees—through such extensive ritualistic practices as employee calisthenics, singing the company song, after-hours group activities, and company sponsored vacations—help develop and sustain long term commitment and loyalty to the organization. The holistic concern that is evidenced for employees and their families may be viewed as a sensible effort to safeguard the employer's substantial investment in human resources and further bond the employees to the organization.

The long term commitment and concern for employees and the consequent familial relationship promote trust and support of organizational leadership. Unlike the employee who is likely to remain with an employer (and a boss) for a short time, the Japanese system promotes accommodation and unity of interest. Knowing the extended nature of the employment practice, the worker is less inclined to engage in major confrontations or conflicts that would damage the long term superior-subordinate relationship. One would expect communications to be more gentle, subtle, implicit, and "family oriented."

Finally, a commitment to lifetime employment with holistic concern for employees is likely to produce a balanced, reciprocal psychological contract calling for a "company" type of identity. The employer's side of the contract is likely to include more participation of employees in the decision making process. When one has remained with a company long enough "to belong," the person also is more likely to be "consulted" on important matters affecting the company.

Emphasis on Collective Responsibility

According to most writers, Japanese management shuns individual accountability and credit in preference for collective or group responsibility and rewards. If true, organizations managed by such persons would place heavy emphasis on the values of teamwork and cooperation. Decisions more often would be made collectively or, more likely, nemawashi style. Participative management or consensus management would not be a style that most managers forced on themselves, but rather would be a natural way of engaging in the collective sharing of responsibility.

The present phenomena of quality circles and consensus decision making are rooted in the Japanese cultural traditions emphasizing interdependence, collaboration, and cooperation. The apparent subordination of the individual's needs and interests to those of the group has strong precedent in the Japanese culture. The willing acceptance of one's role in the organization reflects the traditional commitment to the priority of collective action. The emphasis on collective responsibility fosters a congruence of goals among employees and management, which is bolstered further by lifetime, two-way contracts between them.

The presence of a hard-working, orderly workforce can be related to the orientation to collective responsibility of the Japanese. When coupled with a high degree of goal congruence between employer and employee, the emergence of cohesive, productive, disciplined work groups is not surprising. The impressive performance of the Japanese work force, particularly their high productivity and exceptional quality levels, reasonably derives from those underlying conditions that support vigorous implementation of high output standards and superior quality control systems.

CLEARING A PATH THROUGH THE JUNGLE

From a review of the research findings on Japanese managerial success, one is reminded of Porter's (1962) parable of the spindle, in which the proverbial specialists, called on to solve a problem, all found the answer deeply imbedded in their own particular expertise. On greater reflection, however, it is proposed that the writers probably are not biased in their analyses, but rather are unable to fully grasp the intricacies of the data to describe adequately Japan's industrial success. For, as noted, in addition to the host of management-based theories proposed as explanations for Japanese achievements, alternative theories built on government and environmental models, for example, "Japan Inc.," have been hypothesized. Thus, they are reacting not only as did the scientists in the parable of the spindle, but also as did the blind men in the fable in which they describe the elephant. You will recall that one felt the knee of the elephant and described it as a tree-like creature; another felt the tusk and likened it to a spear; and a third felt the tail and insisted that it was small and round like a rope.

Perhaps all of the theorists are correct in attributing some Japanese excellence to the area of Japan's industry that they have examined. Maybe the Japanese, in their obsession to redeem the honor of their country after World War II and in their quest for world respect in industry, have produced excellence in many areas of the process of management. If so, it should not be surprising that existing research efforts have failed to capture adequately the essence of Japanese management effectiveness. Further, it seems unlikely that additional research seeking single-factor or dual-factor explanations of the Japanese success will be more successful; the panacea will continue to be elusive. Also, the jungle warfare among management theorists cited by Koontz in 1961 is not lacking among students of Japanese management today. For there exists a tendency to discount or discredit rival hypotheses or conceptualizations that are incompatible with one's own.

Of what value are the present theories in the jungle? It is argued that they are of considerable value as long as researchers and organization development implementors recognize that elements of Japanese management do not stand alone, but rather they require supporting cultural and environmental frameworks to be effective. As in most new systems of management, practice must precede research, and research must initially address small segments of the implementation. For the organization contemplating adoption of the Japanese system, Chung and Gray (1982) stress that extensive preparation and commitment is necessary, pointing out that an adoption will not work unless the organization is willing to change its whole philosophy of organizing people. In a similar vein, England (1982) presents evidence to suggest that the social and institutional framework of American industry is inimicable to the tenets of Ouchi's Theory Z, and this will limit its adoption by firms in the United States.

Perhaps the most fruitful approach for uncovering tracks in the Japanese management theory jungle will be to build models that reflect the "system" of Japanese management—the interdependencies of the political, economic, social, and religious variables with management practices. What appears to be most needed is the development of integrated, internally consistent models that encompass the evaluation and the context of Japanese management practices, rather than focusing on the techniques or concepts in isolation. Present understanding of Japanese management is limited by the narrow comprehension of the environment in which it exists—societal norms and values, educational and socialization processes, and the interfaces of business, government, and labor. Armed with a better understanding of the interrelationships of the elements of the Japanese management system, one will be better equipped to address the issues of emulation, adaptation, and implementation in American enterprises. When one attempts to traverse a jungle, a complete understanding of the terrain is helpful.

REFERENCES

Anderson, W. S. Meeting the Japanese economic challenge. *Business Horizons,* 1981, 24(2), 56–62.

Blotnick, S. Supermen? *Forbes,* August 17, 1981, pp. 132–133.

Cao, A. D. The Japanese challenge in the 1980's: A sociocultural interpretation. *Mid-South Business Journal.* 1981, 2(1), 7–14.

Chung, K. H., & Gray, M. A. Can we adopt the Japanese methods of human resources management? *Personnel Administrator,* 1982, 28(5), 41–46, 80.

Cole, R. E. *Japanese blue collar: The changing tradition.* Berkeley, Cal.: University of California Press, 1971.

Cole, R. E. Learning from the Japanese: Prospects and pitfalls. *Management Review,* 1980, 69(9), 22–28, 38–42.

Deming, W. E. What can American manufacturers learn from the Japanese? *Iron Age,* October 6, 1980, p. 51.

Drucker, P. F. What we can learn from Japanese management. *Harvard Business Review,* 1971, 49(2), 110–122.

Drucker, P. F. Behind Japan's success. *Harvard Business Review,* 1981, 59(1), 83–90.

Drucker, P. Are unions becoming irrelevant? *Wall Street Journal,* September 22, 1982, p. 26.

Durkheim, E. Preface. In *The division of labor in society.* 2nd ed. New York: Macmillan Co., 1933, 1–31. (Originally published, 1902).

England, G. W. Japanese and American management: Theory Z and beyond. Unpublished paper, University of Oklahoma, 1982.

Flanigan, J. The wrong bottom line. *Forbes,* May 25, 1981, pp. 42, 46.

Gibney, F. B. Now it's time to imitate the Japanese. *Pacific Basin Quarterly,* 1981, 6, 17–18.

Hatvany, N., & Pucik, V. An integrated management system: Lessons from the Japanese experience. *Academy of Management Review,* 1981, 6, 469–480.

Hayes, R. H. Why Japanese factories work. *Harvard Business Review,* 1981, 59(4), 57–66.

How the Japanese manage in the U.S. *Fortune,* June 15, 1981, 97–98, 102–103.

Howard, N., & Teramoto, Y. The really important difference between Japanese and western management. *Management International Review,* 1981, 21, 19–30.

Janger, A. R. & Berenkein, R. E. *External challenges to management decisions: A growing international problem.* The Conference Board. Report no. 808, 1981, 48–68.

Kobayashi, S. The creative organization—A Japanese experiment. *Personnel,* 1970, 47(6), 8–17.

Koontz, H. The management theory jungle. *Journal of the Academy of Management,* 1961, 4(3), 174–188.

Munchus, G. Employer-employee based quality circles in Japan: Human resource policy implications for American firms. *Academy of Management Review,* 1983, 8, 255–261.

Nakayama, N. The United States and Japan: Some management contrasts. *Computers and People,* 1980, 29, 8–10.

Ouchi, W. C. Theory Z: How American business can meet the Japanese challenge. Reading, Mass.: Addison-Wesley, 1981.

Ouchi, W. C., & Jaeger, A. M. Type Z organization: Stability in the midst of mobility. *Academy of Management Review,* 1978, 3, 305–314.

Pascale, R. T., & Athos, A. G. *The art of Japanese management.* New York: Simon and Schuster, 1981.

Porter E. H. The parable of the spindle. *Harvard Business Review,* 1962, 40(3), 58–66.

Reddy, A. C., & Rao, C. P. Japanese marketing: Underlying reasons for its success. *Mid-South Business Journal,* 1982, 2(1), 3–6.

Rehder, R. R. What American and Japanese managers are learning from each other. *Business Horizons,* 1981, 24(2), 63–70.

Schein, E. H. Does Japanese management style have a message for American managers? *Sloan Management Review,* 1981, 23(1), 55–67.

Sullivan, J. J. A critique of theory Z. *Academy of Management Review,* 1983, 8, 132–142.

Takeuchi, H. Productivity: Learning from the Japanese. *California Management Review,* 1981, 23(4), 5–18.

Tanaka, F. J. Lifetime employment in Japan. *Challenge,* 1981, 24(4), 23–29.

Tsurumi, Y. Productivity: The Japanese approach. *Pacific Basin Quarterly,* 1981, 6, 7–11.

Vogel, E. F. *Japan as number one: Lessons for America.* New York: Harper & Row, 1979. Quoted in L. A. Bryan, Jr., The Japanese and the American first-line supervisor. *Training and Development Journal,* 1982, 36(1), 65.

Wheelwright, S. C. Japan—Where operations really are strategic. *Harvard Business Review,* 1981, 59(4), 67–74.

Yager, E. Quality circle: A tool for the 80's. *Training and Development Journal,* 1980, 34(8), 60–62.

SECTION
IV

Understanding and Managing Individual Behavior

INTRODUCTION AND OVERVIEW

The previous section stressed the importance of considering social control systems as well as formal ones. Organizational culture was seen as one such vehicle. But how does the individual with unique competencies and motivation fit into this process and the larger congruence model? This section considers the role of the individual in the organizational context—both from the standpoint of what guides and motivates individual behavior and how situations can subtly but importantly shape individual perceptions and responses.

Understanding both individual motivation and the impact of the organizational context is particularly important for managers. Much of the past research on individual behavior has focused almost exclusively on explaining individual perceptions and motivation without close attention to the setting. While these are certainly important aspects of management, much of the early research ignored the powerful impacts that the context can have on shaping behavior in organizations. Since managers are typically not trained as psychologists or clinicians, they often have much less leverage over others' personal traits than they do over the context, such as rewards, goals, job design, and the information available. These elements may offer the manager several powerful ways to shape individual behavior.

To understand how these processes work, it is first important that we fully appreciate several of the points raised by Berkowitz in Section III. While it is certainly true that each of us as an individual is partly motivated by internal needs and drives, we are also more sensitive than we may realize to external cues that focus our attention and guide our behavior. We may be too quick to attribute the behavior of others to stable, internal causes and underestimate the power of situational influences. The readings in this section encourage a

351

consideration of both. As managers, it is important to appreciate the individual's needs and motives as well as how elements of the situation can affect individual motivation and behavior. By paying close attention to both, the person and the situation, the astute manager may be much better able to diagnose and harness the energies of others than by concentrating only on the person.

READINGS IN SECTION IV

Section IV has two chapters. The first, Chapter 7, offers some overall perspectives for understanding individual behavior in organizational settings. The first reading, by Rosenhan, poses a fundamental question: which makes a bigger difference in understanding behavior in organizations, the individual or the context? The critical point here is the importance of seeing individual behavior in context, not assuming, as we sometimes do, that the world is largely an objective place with a clear consensus about what is real and unreal. In the second reading, Lawler offers an overview of drives, needs, and outcomes and how they can be understood in organizations. Nadler and Lawler then provide a diagnostic view of motivation using an expectancy theory approach. While these two readings adopt a person-centered perspective, the Salancik reading calls attention to the situation as a source of motivation. Salancik shows how individuals may find themselves committed to unanticipated actions, not because of individual needs but simply because of the way the situation is structured. Taken as a group, these readings point to how important it is for managers to analyze and shape both individual needs and situational constraints.

Chapter 8 contains three readings that illustrate how managers can use their knowledge of individuals and situations to effectively motivate people. Hackman and Oldham consider job design as one mechanism for motivation and demonstrate how this approach can be used. Latham and Locke offer another alternative, goal setting. They show how the simple process of systematically setting specific, difficult goals can be used to increase performance. In the final reading, Ralph Katz examines how the relationship between motivation and performance can change depending on how long one has been in a job or group. Taken as a whole, the readings in this section offer a way to understand individual behavior in organizations as well as a variety of techniques to actually increase motivation.

7

UNDERSTANDING INDIVIDUAL BEHAVIOR

On Being Sane in Insane Places

David Rosenhan

If sanity and insanity exist, how shall we know them?

The question is neither capricious nor itself insane. However much we may be personally convinced that we can tell the normal from the abnormal, the evidence is simply not compelling. It is commonplace, for example, to read about murder trials wherein eminent psychiatrists for the defense are contradicted by equally eminent psychiatrists for the prosecution on the matter of the defendant's sanity. More generally, there are a great deal of conflicting data on the reliability, utility, and meaning of such terms as "sanity," "insanity," "mental illness," and "schizophrenia." Finally, as early as 1934, Benedict suggested that normality and abnormality are not universal. What is viewed as normal in one culture may be seen as quite aberrant in another. Thus, notions of nor-

mality and abnormality may not be quite as accurate as people believe they are.

To raise questions regarding normality and abnormality is in no way to question the fact that some behaviors are deviant or odd. Murder is deviant. So, too, are hallucinations. Nor does raising such questions deny the existence of the personal anguish that is often associated with "mental illness." Anxiety and depression exist. Psychological suffering exists. But normality and abnormality, sanity and insanity, and the diagnoses that flow from them may be less substantive than many believe them to be.

At its heart, the question of whether the sane can be distinguished from the insane (and whether degrees of insanity can be distinguished from each other) is a simple matter: do the salient characteristics that lead to diagnoses reside in the patients themselves or in the environments and contexts in which observers find them? From Bleuler, through Kretschmer, through the formulators of the recently revised *Diagnostic and Statistical Manual* of the American

Reprinted from *Science*, 1973 (Jan. 19), *179*, 250–258, with permission of the author and the American Association for the Advancement of Science. Copyright 1973 by the American Association for the Advancement of Science.

Psychiatric Association, the belief has been strong that patients present symptoms, that those symptoms can be categorized, and, implicitly, that the sane are distinguishable from the insane. More recently, however, this belief has been questioned. Based in part on theoretical and anthropological considerations, but also on philosophical, legal, and therapeutic ones, the view has grown that psychological categorization of mental illness is useless at best and downright harmful, misleading, and pejorative at worst. Psychiatric diagnoses, in this view, are in the minds of the observers and are not valid summaries of characteristics displayed by the observed.

Gains can be made in deciding which of these is more nearly accurate by getting normal people (that is, people who do not have, and have never suffered, symptoms of serious psychiatric disorders) admitted to psychiatric hospitals and then determining whether they were discovered to be sane and, if so, how. If the sanity of such pseudopatients were always detected, there would be prima facie evidence that a sane individual can be distinguished from the insane context in which he is found. Normality (and presumably abnormality) is distinct enough that it can be recognized wherever it occurs, for it is carried within the person. If, on the other hand, the sanity of the pseudopatients were never discovered, serious difficulties would arise for those who support traditional modes of psychiatric diagnosis. Given that the hospital staff was not incompetent, that the pseudopatient had been behaving as sanely as he had been outside of the hospital, and that it had never been previously suggested that he belonged in a psychiatric hospital, such an unlikely outcome would support the view that psychiatric diagnosis betrays little about the patient but much about the environment in which an observer finds him.

This article describes such an experiment. Eight sane people gained secret admission to twelve different hospitals. Their diagnostic experiences constitute the data of the first part of this article; the remainder is devoted to a description of their experiences in psychiatric institutions. Too few psychiatrists and psychologists, even those who have worked in such hospitals, know what the experience is like. They rarely talk about it with former patients, perhaps because they distrust information coming from the previously insane. Those who have worked in psychiatric hospitals are likely to have adapted so thoroughly to the settings that they are insensitive to the impact of that experience. And while there have been occasional reports of researchers who submitted themselves to psychiatric hospitalization, these researchers have commonly remained in the hospitals for short periods of time, often with the knowledge of the hospital staff. It is difficult to know the extent to which they were treated like patients or like research colleagues. Nevertheless, their reports about the inside of the psychiatric hospital have been valuable. This article extends those efforts.

PSEUDOPATIENTS AND THEIR SETTINGS

The eight pseudopatients were a varied group. One was a psychology graduate student in his 20s. The remaining seven were older and "established." Among them were three psychologists, a pediatrician, a psychiatrist, a painter, and a housewife. Three pseudopatients were women, five were men. All of them employed pseudonyms, lest their alleged diagnoses embarrass them later. Those who were in mental health professions alleged another occupation in order to avoid the special attentions that might be accorded by staff, as a matter of courtesy or caution, to ailing colleagues. With the exception of myself (I was the first pseudopatient and my presence was known to the hospital administrator and chief psychologist and, so far as I can tell, to them alone), the presence of pseudopatients and the nature of the research program were not known to the hospital staffs.

The settings were similarly varied. In order to generalize the findings, admission into a variety of hospitals was sought. The twelve hospitals in the sample were located in five different states on the East and West coasts. Some were old and shabby, some were quite new. Some were research-oriented, others not. Some had good staff-patient ratios, others were quite understaffed. Only one was a strictly private hospital. All of the others were supported by state or federal funds or, in one instance, by university funds.

After calling the hospital for an appointment, the pseudopatient arrived at the admissions office complaining that he had been hearing voices. Asked what the voices said, he replied that they were often unclear, but as far as he could tell they said "empty," "hollow," and "thud." The voices were unfamiliar and were of the same sex as the pseudopatient. The choice of these symptoms was occasioned by their apparent similarity to existential symptoms. Such symptoms are alleged to arise from painful concerns about the perceived meaninglessness of one's life. It is as if the hallucinating person were saying, "My life is empty and hollow." The choice of these symptoms was also determined by the *absence* of a single report of existential psychoses in the literature.

Beyond alleging the symptoms and falsifying name, vocation, and employment, no further alterations of person, history, or circumstances were made. The significant events of the pseudopatient's life history were presented as they had actually occurred. Relationships with parents and siblings, with spouse and children, with people at work and in school, consistent with the aforementioned exceptions, were described as they were or had been. Frustrations and upsets were described along with joys and satisfactions. These facts are impor-

tant to remember. If anything, they strongly biased the subsequent results in favor of detecting sanity, since none of their histories or current behaviors were seriously pathological in any way.

Immediately upon admission to the psychiatric ward, the pseudopatient ceased simulating *any* symptoms of abnormality. In some cases, there was a brief period of mild nervousness and anxiety, since none of the pseudopatients really believed that they would be admitted so easily. Indeed, their shared fear was that they would be immediately exposed as frauds and greatly embarrassed. Moreover, many of them had never visited a psychiatric ward; even those who had, nevertheless had some genuine fears about what might happen to them. Their nervousness, then, was quite appropriate to the novelty of the hospital setting, and it abated rapidly.

Apart from that short-lived nervousness, the pseudopatient behaved on the ward as he "normally" behaved. The pseudopatient spoke to patients and staff as he might ordinarily. Because there is uncommonly little to do on a psychiatric ward, he attempted to engage others in conversation. When asked by staff how he was feeling, he indicated that he was fine, that he no longer experienced symptoms. He responded to instructions from attendants, to calls for medication (which was not swallowed), and to dining-hall instructions. Beyond such activities as were available to him on the admissions ward, he spent his time writing down his observations about the ward, its patients, and the staff. Initially these notes were written "secretly," but as it soon became clear that no one much cared, they were subsequently written on standard tablets of paper in such public places as the dayroom. No secret was made of these activities.

The pseudopatient, very much as a true psychiatric patient, entered a hospital with no foreknowledge of when he would be discharged. Each was told that he would have to get out by his own devices, essentially by convincing the staff that he was sane. The psychological stresses associated with hospitalization were considerable, and all but one of the pseudopatients desired to be discharged almost immediately after being admitted. They were, therefore, motivated not only to behave sanely but to be paragons of cooperation. That their behavior was in no way disruptive is confirmed by nursing reports, which have been obtained on most of the patients. These reports uniformly indicate that the patients were "friendly," "cooperative," and "exhibited no abnormal indications."

THE NORMAL ARE NOT DETECTABLY SANE

Despite their public "show" of sanity, the pseudopatients were never detected. Admitted, except in one case, with a diagnosis of schizophrenia, each was discharged with a diagnosis of schizophrenia "in remission." The label "in remission" should in no way be dismissed as a formality, for at no time during any hospitalization had any question been raised about any pseudopatient's simulation. Nor are there any indications in the hospital records that the pseudopatient's status was suspect. Rather, the evidence is strong that, once labeled schizophrenic, the pseudopatient was stuck with that label. If the pseudopatient was to be discharged, he must naturally be "in remission"; but he was not sane, nor, in the institution's view, had he ever been sane.

The uniform failure to recognize sanity cannot be attributed to the quality of the hospitals, for, although there were considerable variations among them, several are considered excellent. Nor can it be alleged that there was simply not enough time to observe the pseudopatients. Length of hospitalization ranged from seven to fifty-two days, with an average of nineteen days. The pseudopatients were not, in fact, carefully observed, but this failure clearly speaks more to traditions within psychiatric hospitals than to lack of opportunity.

Finally, it cannot be said that the failure to recognize the pseudopatients' sanity was due to the fact that they were not behaving sanely. While there was clearly some tension present in all of them, their daily visitors could detect no serious behavioral consequences—nor, indeed, could other patients. It was quite common for the patients to "detect" the pseudopatients' sanity. During the first three hospitalizations, when accurate counts were kept, 35 of a total of 118 patients on the admissions ward voiced their suspicions, some vigorously. "You're not crazy. You're a journalist or a professor [referring to the continual note taking]. You're checking up on the hospital." While most of the patients were reassured by the pseudopatient's insistence that he had been sick before he came in but was fine now, some continued to believe that the pseudopatient was sane throughout his hospitalization. The fact that the patients often recognized normality when staff did not raises important questions.

Failure to detect sanity during the course of hospitalization may be due to the fact that physicians operate with a strong bias toward what statisticians call the type 2 error (see Scheff, 1966). This is to say that physicians are more inclined to call a healthy person sick (a false positive, type 2) than a sick person healthy (a false negative, type 1). The reasons for this are not hard to find: it is clearly more dangerous to misdiagnose illness than health. Better to err on the side of caution, to suspect illness even among the healthy.

But what holds for medicine does not hold equally well for psychiatry. Medical illnesses, while unfortunate, are not commonly pejorative. Psychiatric diagnoses, on the contrary, carry with them personal, legal, and social stigmas. It was therefore important to see whether the tendency toward diagnosing the sane insane could be reversed. The following experiment was arranged at a research and teaching hospital whose staff had heard these findings but doubted that such an error could occur in their hospital. The staff was informed that, at some time during the following three months, one or more pseudopatients would attempt to be admitted into the psychiatric hospital. Each staff member was asked to rate each patient who presented himself at admissions or on the ward according to the likelihood that the patient was a pseudopatient. A ten-point scale was used, with a 1 and 2 reflecting high confidence that the patient was a pseudopatient.

Judgments were obtained on 193 patients who were admitted for psychiatric treatment. All staff who had had sustained contact with or primary responsibility for the patient-attendants, nurses, psychiatrists, physicians, and psychologists—were asked to make judgments. Forty-one patients were alleged, with high confidence, to be pseudopatients by at least one member of the staff. Twenty-three were considered suspect by at least one psychiatrist. Nineteen were suspected by one psychiatrist *and* one other staff member. Actually, no genuine pseudopatient (at least from my group) presented himself during this period.

The experiment is instructive. It indicates that the tendency to designate sane people as insane can be reversed when the stakes (in this case, prestige and diagnostic acumen) are high. But what can be said of the nineteen people who were suspected of being "sane" by one psychiatrist and another staff member? Were these people truly "sane," or was it rather the case that in the course of avoiding the type 2 error the staff tended to make more errors of the first sort—calling the crazy "sane"? There is no way of knowing. But one thing is certain: any diagnostic process that lends itself so readily to massive errors of this sort cannot be a very reliable one.

THE STICKINESS OF PSYCHODIAGNOSTIC LABELS

Beyond the tendency to call the healthy sick—a tendency that accounts better for diagnostic behavior on admission than it does for such behavior after a lengthy period of exposure—the data speak to the massive role of labeling in psychiatric assessment. Having once been labeled schizophrenic, there is nothing the pseudopatient can do to overcome the tag. The tag profoundly color others' perceptions of him and his behavior.

From one viewpoint, these data are hardly surprising, for it has long been known that elements are given meaning by the context in which they occur. Gestalt psychology made this point vigorously, and Asch (1946, 1952) demonstrated that there are "central" personality traits (such as "warm" versus "cold") which are so powerful that they markedly color the meaning of other information in forming an impression of a given personality. "Insane," "schizophrenic," "manic-depressive," and "crazy" are probably among the most powerful of such central traits. Once a person is designated abnormal, all of his other behaviors and characteristics are colored by that label. Indeed, that label is so powerful that many of the pseudopatients' normal behaviors were overlooked entirely or profoundly misinterpreted. Some examples may clarify this issue.

Earlier I indicated that there were no changes in the pseudopatient's personal history and current status beyond those of name, employment, and, where necessary, vocation. Otherwise, a veridical description of personal history and circumstances was offered. Those circumstances were not psychotic. How were they made consonant with the diagnosis of psychosis? Or were those diagnoses modified in such a way as to bring them into accord with the circumstances of the pseudopatient's life, as described by him?

As far as I can determine, diagnoses

were in no way affected by the relative health of the circumstances of a pseudopatient's life. Rather, the reverse occurred: the perception of his circumstances was shaped entirely by the diagnosis. A clear example of such translation is found in the case of a pseudopatient who had had a close relationship with his mother but was rather remote from his father during his early childhood. During adolescence and beyond, however, his father became a close friend, while his relationship with his mother cooled. His present relationship with his wife was characteristically close and warm. Apart from occasional angry exchanges, friction was minimal. The children had rarely been spanked. Surely there is nothing especially pathological about such a history. Indeed, many readers may see a similar pattern in their own experiences, with no markedly deleterious consequences. Observe, however, how such a history was translated in the psychopathological context, this from the case summary prepared after the patient was discharged.

> This white 39-year-old male . . . manifests a long history of considerable ambivalence in close relationships, which begins in early childhood. A warm relationship with his mother cools during his adolescence. A distant relationship to his father is described as becoming very intense. Affective stability is absent. His attempts to control emotionality with his wife and children are punctuated by angry outbursts and, in the case of the children, spankings. And while he says that he has several good friends, one senses considerable ambivalence embedded in those relationships also.

The facts of the case were unintentionally distorted by the staff to achieve consistency with a popular theory of the dynamics of a schizophrenic reaction (Rosenthal and Jacobson, 1968). Nothing of an ambivalent nature had been described in relations with parents, spouse, or friends. To the extent that ambivalence could be inferred, it was probably not

greater than is found in all human relationships. It is true the pseudopatient's relationships with his parents changed over time, but in the ordinary context that would hardly be remarkable—indeed, it might very well be expected. Clearly, the meaning ascribed to his verbalizations (that is, ambivalence, affective instability) was determined by the diagnosis: schizophrenia. An entirely different meaning would have been ascribed if it were known that the man was "normal."

All pseudopatients took extensive notes publicly. Under ordinary circumstances, such behavior would have raised questions in the minds of observers, as, in fact, it did among patients. Indeed, it seemed so certain that the notes would elicit suspicion that elaborate precautions were taken to remove them from the ward each day. But the precautions proved needless. The closest any staff member came to questioning these notes occurred when one pseudopatient asked his physician what kind of medication he was receiving and began to write down the response. "You needn't write it," he was told gently. "If you have trouble remembering, just ask me again."

If no questions were asked of the pseudopatients, how was their writing interpreted? Nursing records for three patients indicate that the writing was seen as an aspect of their pathological behavior. "Patient engages in writing behavior" was the daily nursing comment on one of the pseudopatients who was never questioned about his writing. Given that the patient is in the hospital, he must be psychologically disturbed. And given that he is disturbed, continuous writing must be a behavioral manifestation of that disturbance, perhaps a subset of the compulsive behaviors that are sometimes correlated with schizophrenia.

One tacit characteristic of psychiatric diagnosis is that it locates the sources of aberration within the individual and only rarely within the complex of stimuli that surrounds him. Consequently, behaviors that are stimulated by the environment are commonly misattributed to the patient's disorder. For example, one kindly nurse found a pseudopatient pacing the long hospital corridors. "Nervous, Mr. X?" she asked. "No, bored," he said.

The notes kept by pseudopatients are full of patient behaviors that were misinterpreted by well-intentioned staff. Often enough, a patient would go "berserk" because he had, wittingly or unwittingly, been mistreated by, say, an attendant. A nurse coming upon the scene would rarely inquire even cursorily into the environmental stimuli of the patient's behavior. Rather, she assumed that his upset derived from his pathology, not from his present interactions with other staff members. Occasionally, the staff might assume that the patient's family (especially when they had recently visited) or other patients had stimulated the outburst. But never were the staff found to assume that one of themselves or the structure of the hospital had anything to do with a patient's behavior. One psychiatrist pointed to a group of patients who were sitting outside the cafeteria entrance half an hour before lunchtime. To a group of young residents he indicated that such behavior was characteristic of the oral-acquisitive nature of the syndrome. It seemed not to occur to him that there were very few things to anticipate in a psychiatric hospital besides eating.

A psychiatric label has a life and an influence of its own. Once the impression has been formed that the patient is schizophrenic, the expectation is that he will continue to be schizophrenic. When a sufficient amount of time has passed, during which the patient has done nothing bizarre, he is considered to be in remission and available for discharge. But the label endures beyond discharge, with the unconfirmed expectation that he will behave as a schizophrenic again. Such labels, conferred by mental health professionals, are as influential on the patient as they are on his relatives and friends, and it should not surprise anyone that

the diagnosis acts on all of them as a self-fulfilling prophecy (see Rosenthal and Jacobson, 1968). Eventually, the patient himself accepts the diagnosis, with all of its surplus meanings and expectations, and behaves accordingly.

The inferences to be made from these matters are quite simple. Much as Zigler and Phillips (1961) have demonstrated that there is enormous overlap in the symptoms presented by patients who have been variously diagnosed, so there is enormous overlap in the behaviors of the sane and the insane. The sane are not "sane" all of the time. We lose our tempers "for no good reason." We are occasionally depressed or anxious, again for no good reason. And we may find it difficult to get along with one or another person—again for no reason that we can specify. Similarly, the insane are not always insane. Indeed, it was the impression of the pseudopatients while living with them that they were sane for long periods of time—that the bizarre behaviors upon which their diagnoses were allegedly predicated constituted only a small fraction of their total behavior. If it makes no sense to label ourselves permanently depressed on the basis of an occasional depression, then it takes better evidence than is presently available to label all patients insane or schizophrenic on the basis of bizarre behaviors or cognitions. It seems more useful, as Mischel (1968) has pointed out, to limit our discussions to *behaviors,* the stimuli that provoke them, and their correlates.

It is not known why powerful impressions of personality traits, such as "crazy" or "insane," arise. Conceivably, when the origins of and stimuli that give rise to a behavior are remote or unknown, or when the behavior strikes us as immutable, trait labels regarding the *behaver* arise. When, on the other hand, the origins and stimuli are known and available, discourse is limited to the behavior itself. Thus, I may hallucinate because I am sleeping, or I may hallucinate because I have ingested a peculiar drug. These are termed sleep-induced hallucinations, or dreams, and drug-induced hallucinations, respectively. But when the stimuli to my hallucinations are unknown, that is called craziness, or schizophrenia—as if that inference were somehow as illuminating as the others.

THE EXPERIENCE OF PSYCHIATRIC HOSPITALIZATION

The term *mental illness* is of recent origin. It was coined by people who were humane in their inclinations and who wanted very much to raise the station of (and the public's sympathies toward) the psychologically disturbed from that of witches and "crazies" to one that was akin to the physically ill. And they were at least partially successful, for the treatment of the mentally ill *has* improved considerably over the years. But while treatment has improved, it is doubtful that people really regard the mentally ill in the same way that they view the physically ill. A broken leg is something one recovers from, but mental illness allegedly endures forever. A broken leg does not threaten the observer, but a crazy schizophrenic? There is by now a host of evidence that attitudes toward the mentally ill are characterized by fear, hostility, aloofness, suspicion, and dread. The mentally ill are society's lepers.

That such attitudes infect the general population is perhaps not surprising, only upsetting. But that they affect the professionals—attendants, nurses, physicians, psychologists, and social workers—who treat and deal with the mentally ill is more disconcerting, both because such attitudes are self-evidently pernicious and because they are unwitting. Most mental health professionals would insist that they are sympathetic toward the mentally ill, that they are neither avoidant nor hostile. But it is more likely that an exquisite ambivalence characterizes their relations with psychiatric patients, such that their avowed impulses are only part of their entire attitude. Negative attitudes are there too and can easily be detected. Such attitudes should not surprise us. They are the natural offspring of the labels patients wear and the places in which they are found.

Consider the structure of the typical psychiatric hospital. Staff and patients are strictly segregated. Staff have their own living space, including their dining facilities, bathrooms, and assembly places. The glassed quarters that contain the professional staff, which the pseudopatients came to call "the cage," sit out on every dayroom. The staff emerge primarily for caretaking purposes—to give medication, to conduct a therapy or group meeting, to instruct or reprimand a patient. Otherwise, staff keep to themselves, almost as if the disorder that afflicts their charges is somehow catching.

So much is patient-staff segregation the rule that, for four public hospitals in which an attempt was made to measure the degree to which staff and patients mingle, it was necessary to use "time out of the staff cage" as the operational measure. While it was not the case that all time spent out of the cage was spent mingling with patients (attendants, for example, would occasionally emerge to watch television in the dayroom), it was the only way in which one could gather reliable data on time for measuring.

The average amount of time spent by attendants outside of the cage was 11.3 percent (range, 3 to 52 percent). This figure does not represent only time spent mingling with patients, but also includes time spent on such chores as folding laundry, supervising patients while they shave, directing ward cleanup, and sending patients to off-ward activities. It was the relatively rare attendant who spent time talking with patients or playing games with them. It proved impossible to obtain a "percent mingling time" for nurses, since the amount of time they spent out of the cage was too brief. Rather, we counted instances of emergence from the cage. On the average, daytime nurses emerged from the cage 11.5 times per shift, including instances when they left the ward entirely (range, 4 to 39 times). Late afternoon and night nurses were even less available, emerging on the average 9.4 times per shift (range, 4 to 41 times). Data on early morning nurses, who arrived usually after midnight and departed at 8 A.M., are not available because patients were asleep during most of this period.

Physicians, especially psychiatrists, were even less available. They were rarely seen on the wards. Quite commonly, they would be seen only when they arrived and departed, with the remaining time being spent in their offices or in the cage. On the average, physicians emerged on the ward 6.7 times per day (range, 1 to 17 times). It proved difficult to make an accurate estimate in this regard, since physicians often maintained hours that allowed them to come and go at different times.

The hierarchical organization of the psychiatric hospital has been commented on before (Stanton and Schwartz, 1954), but the latent meaning of that kind of organization is worth noting again. Those with the most power have least to do with patients, and those with the least power are most involved with them. Recall, however, that the acquisition of role-appropriate behaviors occurs mainly through the observation of others, with the most powerful having the most influence. Consequently, it is understandable that attendants not only spend more time with patients than do any other members of the staff—that is required by their station in the hierarchy—but also, insofar as they learn from their superiors' behavior, spend as little time with patients as they can. Attendants are seen mainly in the cage, which is where the models, the action, and the power are.

I turn now to a different set of studies, these dealing with staff response to patient-initiated contact. It has long been known that the amount of time a person spends with you can be an index of your significance to him. If he initiates and maintains eye contact, there is reason to believe that he is considering your requests and needs. If he pauses to chat or actually stops and talks, there is added reason to infer that he is individuating you. In four hospitals, the pseudopatient approached the staff member with a request which took the following form: "Pardon me, Mr. [or Dr. or Mrs.] X, could you tell me when I will be eligible for grounds privileges?" (or ". . . when I will be presented at the staff meeting?" or ". . . when I am likely to be discharged?"). While the content of the question varied according to the appropriateness of the target and the pseudopatient's (apparent) current needs, the form was always a courteous and relevant request for information. Care was taken never to approach a particular member of the staff more than once a day, lest the staff member become suspicious or irritated. In examining these data, remember that the behavior of the pseudopatients was neither bizarre nor disruptive. One could indeed engage in good conversation with them.

The data for these experiments are shown in Table 1, separately for physicians (column 1) and for nurses and attendants (column 2). Minor differences between these four institutions were overwhelmed by the degree to which staff avoided continuing contacts that patients had initiated. By far their most common response consisted of either a brief response to the question, offered while they were "on the move" and with head averted, or no response at all.

The encounter frequently took the following bizarre form: (pseudopatient) "Pardon me, Dr. X. Could you tell me when I am eligible for grounds privileges?" (physician) "Good morning, Dave. How are you today?" (Moves off without waiting for a response.)

It is instructive to compare these data with data recently obtained at Stanford University. It has been alleged that large and eminent universities are characterized by faculty who

361

TABLE 1. *Self-Initiated Contact by Pseudopatients with Psychiatrists and Nurses and Attendants, Compared to Contact with Other Groups*

| | Psychiatric Hospitals | | University Campus (Nonmedical) | University Medical Center | | |
| | | | | Physicians | | |
Contact	(1) Psychiatrists	(2) Nurses and Attendants	(3) Faculty	(4) "Looking for a Psychiatrist"	(5) "Looking for an Internist"	(6) No Additional Comment
Responses						
Moves on, head averted (%)	71	88	0	0	0	0
Makes eye contact (%)	23	10	0	11	0	0
Pauses and chats (%)	2	2	0	11	0	10
Stops and talks (%)	4	0.5	100	78	100	90
Mean number of questions answered (out of 6)	[a]	[a]	6	3.8	4.8	4.5
Respondents (No.)	13	47	14	18	15	10
Attempts (No.)	185	1,283	14	18	15	10

[a]Not applicable.

are so busy that they have no time for students. For this comparison, a young lady approached individual faculty members who seemed to be walking purposefully to some meeting or teaching engagement and asked them the following six questions:

1. "Pardon me, could you direct me to Encina Hall?" (at the medical school: ". . . to the Clinical Research Center?").
2. "Do you know where Fish Annex is?" [There is no Fish Annex at Stanford.]
3. "Do you teach here?"
4. "How does one apply for admission to the college?" (at the medical school: ". . . to the medical school?").
5. "Is it difficult to get in?"
6. "Is there financial aid?"

Without exception, as can be seen in Table 1 (column 3), all of the questions were answered. No matter how rushed they were, all respondents not only maintained eye contact but stopped to talk. Indeed, many of the respondents went out of their way to direct or take the questioner to the office she was seeking, to try to locate "Fish Annex," or to discuss with her the possibilities of being admitted to the university.

Similar data, also shown in Table 1 (columns 4, 5, and 6), were obtained in the hospital. Here, too, the young lady came prepared with six questions. After the first question, however, she remarked to eighteen of her respondents (column 4), "I'm looking for a psychiatrist," and to fifteen others (column 5). "I'm looking for an internist." Ten other respondents received no inserted comment (column 6). The general degree of cooperative responses is considerably higher for these university groups than it was for pseudopatients in psychiatric hospitals. Even so, differences are apparent within the medical school setting. Once having indicated that she was looking for a psychiatrist, the degree of coop-

eration elicited was less than when she sought an internist.

POWERLESSNESS AND DEPERSONALIZATION

Eye contact and verbal contact reflect concern and individuation; their absence, avoidance and depersonalization. The data I have presented do not do justice to the rich daily encounters that grew up around matters of depersonalization and avoidance. I have records of patients who were beaten by staff for the sin of having initiated verbal contact. During my own experience, for example, one patient was beaten in the presence of other patients for having approached an attendant and told him, "I like you." Occasionally, punishment meted out to patients for misdemeanors seemed so excessive that it could not be justified by the most radical interpretations of psychiatric canon. Nevertheless, they appeared to go unquestioned. Tempers were often short. A patient who had not heard a call for medication would be roundly excoriated, and the morning attendants would often wake patients with "Come on, you m—f—s, out of bed!"

Neither anecdotal nor "hard" data can convey the overwhelming sense of powerlessness which invades the individual as he is continually exposed to the depersonalization of the psychiatric hospital. It hardly matters *which* psychiatric hospital—the excellent public ones and the very plush private hospital were better than the rural and shabby ones in this regard, but, again, the features that psychiatric hospitals had in common overwhelmed by far their apparent differences.

Powerlessness was evident everywhere. The patient is deprived of many of his legal rights by dint of his psychiatric commitment. He is shorn of credibility by virtue of his psychiatric label. His freedom of movement is restricted.

He cannot initiate contact with the staff but may only respond to such overtures as they make. Personal privacy is minimal. Patient quarters and possessions can be entered and examined by any staff member, for whatever reason. His personal history and anguish is available to any staff member (often including the "grey lady" and "candy striper" volunteer) who chooses to read his folder, regardless of their therapeutic relationship to him. His personal hygiene and waste evacuation are often monitored. The water closets may have no doors.

At times, depersonalization reached such proportions that pseudopatients had the sense that they were invisible, or at least unworthy of account. Upon being admitted, I and other pseudopatients took the initial physical examinations in a semipublic room, where staff members went about their own business as if we were not there.

On the ward, attendants delivered verbal and occasionally serious physical abuse to patients in the presence of other observing patients, some of whom (the pseudopatients) were writing it all down. Abusive behavior, on the other hand, terminated quite abruptly when other staff members were known to be coming. Staff are credible witnesses. Patients are not.

A nurse unbuttoned her uniform to adjust her brassiere in the presence of an entire ward of viewing men. One did not have the sense that she was being seductive. Rather, she didn't notice us. A group of staff persons might point to a patient in the dayroom and discuss him animatedly, as if he were not there.

One illuminating instance of depersonalization and invisibility occurred with regard to medications. All told, the pseudopatients were administered nearly 2,100 pills, including Elavil, Stelazine, Compazine, and Thorazine, to name but a few. (That such a variety of medications should have been administered to patients presenting identical symptoms is itself worthy of note.) Only two were swallowed. The rest were either pocketed or deposited in the toilet. The pseudopatients were not alone in this. Although I have no precise records on how many patients rejected their medications, the pseudopatients frequently found the medications of other patients in the toilet before they deposited their own. As long as they were cooperative, their behavior and the pseudopatients' own in this matter, as in other important matters, went unnoticed throughout.

Reactions to such depersonalization among pseudopatients were intense. Although they had come to the hospital as participant observers and were fully aware that they did not "belong," they nevertheless found themselves caught up in and fighting the process of depersonalization. Some examples: a graduate student in psychology asked his wife to bring his textbooks to the hospital so he could "catch up on his homework"—this despite the elaborate precautions taken to conceal his professional association. The same student, who had trained for quite some time to get into the hospital and who had looked forward to the experience, "remembered" some drag races that he had wanted to see on the weekend and insisted that he be discharged by that time. Another pseudopatient attempted a romance with a nurse. Subsequently, he informed the staff that he was applying for admission to graduate school in psychology and was very likely to be admitted, since a graduate professor was one of his regular hospital visitors. The same person began to engage in psychotherapy with other patients—all of this as a way of becoming a person in an impersonal environment.

THE SOURCES OF DEPERSONALIZATION

What are the origins of depersonalization? I have already mentioned two. First are attitudes held by all of us toward the mentally ill—including those who treat them—attitudes characterized by fear, distrust, and horrible expectations on the one hand, and benevolent intentions on the other. Our ambivalence leads, in this instance as in others, to avoidance.

Second, and not entirely separate, the hierarchical structure of the psychiatric hospital facilitates depersonalization. Those who are at the top have least to do with patients, and their behavior inspires the rest of the staff. Average daily contact with psychiatrists, psychologists, residents, and physicians combined ranged from 3.9 to 25.1 minutes, with an overall mean of 6.8 (six pseudopatients over a total of 129 days of hospitalization). Included in this average are time spent in the admissions interview, ward meetings in the presence of a senior staff member, group and individual psychotherapy contacts, case presentation conferences, and discharge meetings. Clearly, patients do not spend much time in interpersonal contact with doctoral staff. And doctoral staff serve as models for nurses and attendants.

There are probably other sources. Psychiatric installations are presently in serious financial straits. Staff shortages are pervasive, staff time at a premium. Something has to give, and that something is patient contact. Yet, while financial stresses are realities, too much can be made of them. I have the impression that the psychological forces that result in depersonalization are much stronger than the fiscal ones and that the addition of more staff would not correspondingly improve patient care in this regard. The incidence of staff meetings and the enormous amount of record keeping on patients, for example, have not been as substantially reduced as has patient contact. Priorities exist, even during hard times. Patient contact is not a significant priority in the traditional psychiatric hospital, and fiscal pressures do not account for this. Avoidance and depersonalization may.

Heavy reliance upon psychotropic medication tacitly contributes to depersonalization by convincing staff that treatment is indeed being conducted and that further patient contact may not be necessary. Even here, however, caution needs to be exercised in understanding the role of psychotropic drugs. If patients were powerful rather than powerless, if they were viewed as interesting individuals rather than diagnostic entities, if they were socially significant rather than social lepers, if their anguish truly and wholly compelled our sympathies and concerns, would we not *seek* contact with them, despite the availability of medications? Perhaps for the pleasure of it all?

THE CONSEQUENCES OF LABELING AND DEPERSONALIZATION

Whenever the ratio of what is known to what needs to be known approaches zero, we tend to invent "knowledge" and assume that we understand more than we actually do. We seem unable to acknowledge that we simply don't know. The needs for diagnosis and remediation of behavioral and emotional problems are enormous. But rather than acknowledge that we are just embarking on understanding, we continue to label patients "schizophrenic," "manic-depressive," and "insane," as if in those words we had captured the essence of understanding. The facts of the matter are that we have known for a long time that diagnoses are often not useful or reliable, but we have nevertheless continued to use them. We now know that we cannot distinguish insanity from sanity. It is depressing to consider how that information will be used.

Not merely depressing, but frightening. How many people, one wonders, are sane but not recognized as such in our psychiatric institutions? How many have been needlessly stripped of their privileges of citizenship, from the right to vote and drive to that of handling their own accounts? How many have feigned insanity in order to avoid the criminal consequences of their behavior, and, conversely, how many would rather stand trial than live interminably in a psychiatric hospital—but are wrongly thought to be mentally ill? How many have been stigmatized by well-intentioned, but nevertheless erroneous, diagnoses? On the last point, recall again that a "type 2 error" in psychiatric diagnosis does not have the same consequences it does in medical diagnosis. A diagnosis of cancer that has been found to be in error is cause for celebration. But psychiatric diagnoses are rarely found to be in error. The label sticks, a mark of inadequacy forever.

Finally, how many patients might be "sane" outside the psychiatric hospital but seem insane in it—not because craziness resides in them, as it were, but because they are responding to a bizarre setting, one that may be unique to institutions which harbor nether people? Goffman (1961) calls the process of socialization to such institutions "mortification"—an apt metaphor that includes the processes of depersonalization that have been described here. And while it is impossible to know whether the pseudopatients' responses to these processes are characteristic of all inmates—they were, after all, not real patients—it is difficult to believe that these processes of socialization to a psychiatric hospital provide useful attitudes or habits of response for living in the "real world."

SUMMARY AND CONCLUSIONS

It is clear that we cannot distinguish the sane from the insane in psychiatric hospitals. The hospital itself imposes a special environment in which the meanings of behavior can easily be misunderstood. The consequences to patients hospitalized in such an environment—the powerlessness, depersonalization, segregation, mortification, and self-labeling—seem undoubtedly countertherapeutic.

I do not, even now, understand this problem well enough to perceive solutions. But two matters seem to have some promise. The first concerns the proliferation of community mental health facilities, of crisis intervention centers, of the human potential movement, and of behavior therapies that, for all of their own problems, tend to avoid psychiatric labels, to focus on specific problems and behaviors, and to retain the individual in a relatively non-pejorative environment. Clearly, to the extent that we refrain from sending the distressed to insane places, our impressions of them are less likely to be distorted. (The risk of distorted perceptions, it seems to me, is always present, since we are much more sensitive to an individual's behaviors and verbalizations than we are to the subtle contextual stimuli that often promote them. At issue here is a matter of magnitude. And, as I have shown, the magnitude of distortion is exceedingly high in the extreme context that is a psychiatric hospital.)

The second matter that might prove promising speaks to the need to increase the sensitivity of mental health workers and researchers to the *Catch 22* position of psychiatric patients. Simply reading materials in this area will be of help to some such workers and researchers. For others, directly experiencing the impact of psychiatric hospitalization will be of enormous use. Clearly, further research into the social psychology of such total institutions will both facilitate treatment and deepen understanding.

I and the other pseudopatients in the psychiatric setting had distinctly negative reactions. We do not pretend to describe the subjective experiences of true patients. Theirs may be different from ours, particularly with the passage of time and the necessary process of adaptation to one's environment. But we can and do speak to the relatively more objective indices of treatment within the hospital. It could be a mistake, and a very unfortunate one, to consider that what happened to us derived from malice or stupidity on the part of the staff. Quite the contrary, our overwhelming impression of them was of people who really cared, who were committed, and who were uncommonly intelligent. Where they failed, as they sometimes did painfully, it would be more accurate to attribute those failures to the environment in which they, too, found themselves than to personal callousness. Their perceptions and behavior were controlled by the situation, rather than being motivated by a malicious disposition. In a more benign environment, one that was less attached to global diagnosis, their behaviors and judgments might have been more benign and effective.

REFERENCES

Asch, S. E. "Forming Impressions of Personality." *Journal of Abnormal and Social Psychology,* 1946, *41,* 258–290.

Asch, S. E. *Social Psychology.* Englewood Cliffs, N.J.: Prentice-Hall, 1952.

Benedict, R. "Anthropology and the Abnormal." *Journal of General Psychology,* 1934, *10,* 59–80.

Goffman, E. *Asylums.* New York: Doubleday, 1961.

Mischel, W. *Personality and Assessment.* New York: Wiley, 1968.

Rosenthal, R., and Jacobson, L. *Pygmalion in the Classroom.* New York: Holt, Rinehart and Winston, 1968.

Scheff, T. J. *Being Mentally Ill: A Sociological Theory.* Chicago: Aldine, 1966.

Stanton, A. H., and Schwartz, M. S. *The Mental Hospital: A Study of Institutional Participation in Psychiatric Illness and Treatment.* New York: Basic Books, 1954.

Zigler, E., and Phillips, L. "Psychiatric Diagnosis and Symptomatology." *Journal of Abnormal and Social Psychology,* 1961, *63,* 69–75.

Drives, Needs, and Outcomes

Edward Lawler

For centuries, psychologists and philosophers have tried to explain why some objects or outcomes seem to be desired by people while others are not. The concepts of instinct, drive, intrinsic motives, functional autonomy, derived motives, and many others have been used to explain this phenomenon. This chapter will review many of these concepts and present an integrated view of present knowledge about why certain outcomes are desirable or attractive to people.

An adequate explanation of why certain outcomes are desirable must deal with three separate but interrelated questions.

1. What is it about the nature of individuals that causes outcomes to become desirable to them?
2. What general classes or groups of outcomes do people find desirable or undesirable?
3. What factors influence the desirability of outcomes, that is, how does the desirability of outcomes change over time and why do individuals differ in the importance they attach to various outcomes?

Unless the second and third questions are answered, it is impossible to predict the kind of behavior choices a person will make. Although

the answer to the first question is not needed in order to predict behavior, most theorists have found that answering it is a prerequisite to answering questions two and three. That is, these theorists have found it necessary to make assumptions about what causes outcomes to be important in the first place in order to make statements about the kinds of outcomes people value and the things that are likely to influence the attractiveness of outcomes.

Our first question has typically been answered by a set of assumptions about man's internal state. For example, some theorists have assumed that man has homeostatic drives, others have talked of instincts, while still others have talked of learned drives. The second question has been answered by the development of a number of need or outcome classification systems. Some of these systems assume only two classes of needs while others assume more than 20. The third question has been answered in many different ways. Maslow (1943), for example, has theorized that needs are arrayed in a hierarchy such that the lower-level needs have to be satisfied before the higher-level needs come into play. Other psychologists have stressed that learned associations can cause change in the attractiveness of outcomes.

Not every theory that has dealt with the attractiveness of outcomes has attempted to answer all of these questions. In fact, some theories have dealt essentially with only one of the questions. For example, in his discussion of the competence motive, White (1959) is concerned with establishing the existence of that motive. He does not present a general classification of motives, nor does he make statements about what influences the importance of other motives. As we discuss the various theories dealing with the attractiveness of outcomes, it is important to note which of the three questions are answered and which are ignored.

Let us now turn to a consideration of some of the more prominent theories.

HISTORICAL APPROACHES

Prior to the 1940s three theoretical approaches to explaining why outcomes are valued dominated the thinking in psychology. The first two, instinct theory and hedonism, do not make scientifically testable predictions of what outcomes people will seek. The third, drive theory, represents an attempt to develop a theory that does make testable predictions.

Instinct Theory

Charles Darwin was the first to call the attention of the scientific world to the possibility that much of human and animal behavior may be determined by instincts. He thought that many "intelligent" actions were inherited, and he provided a number of examples from his research on animals to support this view. William James, Sigmund Freud, and William McDougall developed the instinct doctrine as an important concept in their psychological theories. Some theorists thought of instincts as mechanical and automatic rather than as conscious motivators of behavior, but McDougall, who developed the most exhaustive taxonomy of instincts, thought of them as purposive, inherited, goal-seeking tendencies.

McDougall (1908) wrote that "we may then define an instinct as an inherited or innate psycho-physical disposition that determines the possessor to perceive and pay attention to objects of a certain class, to experience an emotional excitement of a particular quality on perceiving such an object, and to act in regard to it in a particular manner, or at least to experience an impulse to such action" (p. 39). Thus, the "pugnacity instinct" was an instinct that manifested itself in fighting when the organism was exposed to appropriate stimuli. At first McDougall thought he could account for all behavior in terms of about a dozen instincts. However, as time progressed he added more and more instincts to his list so that by 1932 his list included 19 instincts. Other psychologists added more, so that by the 1920s the list of instincts totaled nearly 6,000, including the "instinct to avoid eating apples in one's own orchard" (Murray, 1964, p. 6).

In a sense, instinct theory died of its own weight. As more and more instincts were stated, psychologists began to question the explanatory usefulness of the approach. To say that an animal fights because of the instinct of pugnacity or that an individual takes a job because he has an instinct to work is merely to give a redundant description of the observed behavior that adds nothing to our understanding of why the behavior took place. The tendency of some psychologists to add a new instinct to explain each new behavior that was observed also weakened the theory. As instinct theory developed, it seemed to provide unsatisfactory answers to all of our questions. It said that heredity determined which goals or outcomes organisms would seek (which was incomplete and misleading) and that people's goals consisted of the objects they sought (a circular definition). Thus, instinct theory did not allow for the prediction of which outcomes would be sought; it allowed only for the *post hoc* explanation of why certain goals were sought. Instinct theory also failed to provide a useful classification of the type of outcomes people sought. The original list of instincts was too short and the later ones were so long that they proved use-less.

Hedonism

The origins of most contemporary conceptions of motivation can be traced to the principle of hedonism (Atkinson, 1964). In turn, hedonism can be traced to the original writings of the English utilitarians. The central assumption is that behavior is directed toward outcomes that provide pleasure and away from those that produce pain. In every situation people strive to obtain those goals or outcomes that provide the most pleasure. Despite its simplicity and popularity, the principle of hedonism fails to answer any of our three questions adequately. Nothing is said about why certain things give pleasure while others don't. There is no specification of the types of outcomes that are pleasurable or painful or even how these outcomes can be determined in advance for a particular individual. Any kind of behavior can be explained after the fact by postulating that particular outcomes were sources of either pain or pleasure. Finally, nothing is said about how the attractiveness of outcomes may be modified by experience or environmental circumstances. In short, the hedonistic assumption has no real empirical content leading to predictions of behavior and, thus, it is untestable.

Despite the fact that hedonism can be described as circular and lacking in content, its influence on psychology has been extensive. As one psychologist stated, "the study of motivation by psychologists has largely been directed toward filling in the missing empirical content in hedonism" (Vroom, 1964, p. 10). It is certainly true that almost all modern theories assume that people direct their behavior toward outcomes that they find pleasurable and away from those that they find unattractive. However, most modern theories do attempt to overcome the circularity of hedonism. They specify in advance how attractive specific outcomes will be to particular individuals and they develop models that predict when the attractiveness of outcomes will change.

Drive Theory

Drive theory developed partially as a reaction to instinct theory and hedonism. It is in the tradition of hedonism, but it is more closely tied to empirical events and therefore more testable. In 1918, R. S. Woodworth published a little book entitled *Dynamic Psychology* in which he advanced the view that psychologists should study what induces people to behave in particular ways. He referred to this inducement as drive, and the concept of drive soon replaced the concept of instinct in the psychologist's glossary of important terms. Later, the term "drive" took on a very precise meaning in the writings of C. L. Hull (1943). He assumed that all behavior is motivated by either primary or secondary drives. According to Hull, the primary drives were biologically based; they represented states of homeostatic imbalance. Hull's position was that:

> The major primary needs or drives are so ubiquitous that they require little more than to be mentioned. They include the need for foods of various sorts (hunger), the need for water (thirst), and need for air, the need to avoid tissue injury (pain), the need to maintain an optimal temperature, the need to defecate, the need to micturate, the need for rest (after protracted exertion), the need for sleep (after protracted wakefulness), and the need for activity (after protracted inaction). The drives concerned with the maintenance of the species are those which lead to sexual intercourse and the need represented by nest building and care of the young [pp. 59–60].

In Hull's theory, outcomes become rewards when they are able to reduce primary drives and thereby reduce homeostatic imbalance and the tension that occurs when organisms are in a state of ecological deprivation. Thus, food is a reward to a hungry person and water is a reward to a thirsty person. Hull also stressed that drive strength can be increased by deprivation and reduced as needs become satisfied. Thus, the hungrier a person gets, the more he desires food; but as he eats food, he becomes less hungry and his desire diminishes. Although Hull assumed that all rewards and drives are ultimately based on the reduction of primary drives, he recognized that certain secondary drives and rewards could develop—or be "learned"—if in the past they were associated with food or other primary rewards. Thus, money is a secondary reward because it is often associated with food and other primary rewards. Social approval becomes a reward for children who are praised for eating well, or dressing themselves, and so on. According to Hull's view, most of the rewards used by work organizations would be considered secondary rewards.

Hull's theory represents a significant advance over the previous theories of motivation. It gives a clear-cut answer to the question of what objects or outcomes have value—that is, objects or outcomes that either reduce primary, biologically based drives or have been related to outcomes that do. It also provides a classification of drives that is still commonly used (it divides them into primary and secondary drives, and it specifies what the primary drives are). Finally, it says that deprivation increases drive strength, whereas obtaining the desired outcomes reduces drive strength. Thus, Hull's theory has answers to all three of our questions. But the real significance of Hull's theory rests in the fact that it is empirically testable. Since it specifies in detail the relationship between such measurable things as deprivation, drive, and learning, the theory can be tested, and it has spawned a large number of research studies.

At this point it is safe to say that these studies have found Hull's theory to be inadequate in a number of important respects. The most important shortcomings have to do with the ability of the theory to explain motivation that is not based on primary drives. Hull's basic point about organisms' possessing certain primary drives that become stronger with deprivation and weaker with satisfaction still seems valid. What does not seem valid is his argument that all secondary motives are learned on the basis of primary physiological or homeostatic drives.

There is no solid evidence that drives can be learned on the basis of their association with positive drives such as hunger and thirst (Cravens and Renner, 1970). There is evidence that organisms will work for rewards that have been associated with the reduction of a primary drive if the primary drive is present. However, when the primary drive is not present, there seems to be no "acquired" drive to obtain the reward. For example, in the classic experiments of Wolfe (1936) and Cowles (1937), chimpanzees learned to associate tokens with the acquisition of food. Initially, the chimps learned to operate an apparatus that required lifting a weight to obtain grapes. They continued to operate it when the only visible reward was a token that had been associated with the grapes. However, they didn't seem to develop an acquired need for tokens, since they were willing to work to obtain the tokens only as long as they were hungry and the tokens led to something they desired—that is, food. Hence, it is difficult to see how Hull's explanation can help us understand why workers continue to work for more money even when their basic needs are satisfied.

More damaging to Hull's view than the evidence on the failure of animals to acquire learned drives is the great amount of evidence indicating that people and animals are attracted to many outcomes that do not seem to be directly related to primary needs. Rats will learn mazes in order to explore novel environments, monkeys will solve puzzles even though they receive no extrinsic rewards, and people will work simply in order to develop their skills and abilities and to increase their competence. These and many other phenomena cannot be explained easily by drive theory.

CONTEMPORARY APPROACIIES

Recently, many psychologists have rejected thc emphasis of drive theory on primary drives and have argued that people have many needs. This argument has come particularly from those psychologists who are interested in studying human behavior. As we shall see, they have proposed a number of needs that do not seem to be directly related to homeostatic imbalance, organism survival, or species survival. This recent work on motivation has produced two somewhat different approaches.

Researchers in one group have focused on establishing the existence of one or two human motives that they consider to be particularly important. Thus, McClelland has focused on the achievement motive and White has focused on the competence motive. They have not tried to develop complex need, or motive, classification systems. In other words, they have not tried to answer our second question. They have contented themselves with trying to understand why one set or type of outcomes is attractive to people. Other researchers have tried to develop need, or motive, classification systems in an attempt to predict which kinds of outcomes will be attractive to people. Murray's (1938) list of needs and Maslow's (1943) statement of a need hierarchy are examples of this approach. But before we consider these classification systems, we need to look at some of the needs that have been proposed as necessary additions to the primary drives observed by Hull.

The Affiliation Motive

A number of researchers have presented evidence to show that an affiliation motive exists. They have shown that social interaction is attractive to people and that it is particularly likely to occur under certain conditions. For example, Schachter (1959) has shown that people seek the companionship of others when they are anxious and confused about their motives. In Schachter's work, college students faced with the prospect of being shocked were given the opportunity to be with another person. The subjects under such anxiety were more likely to accept invitations to be with others than were subjects who were not under such anxiety. This result occurred even when the subjects were not permitted to talk to the person they were to be with. Other research suggests that people are likely to seek social interaction at times when they are doubting their self-esteem.

Harlow (1958) has presented some interesting evidence suggesting that the social motive may be innate. As part of his work with monkeys he raised some infant monkeys, providing them with two surrogate mothers in place of their natural mothers. One surrogate mother consisted of a cylinder of wire mesh with an opening in the center of the "breast" for a bottle. The other was similarly shaped but was covered with cotton terry cloth. In the experiment, baby monkeys were placed in cages containing the two "mothers." Half were fed from the cloth mother, the other half from the wire mother. According to drive theory, the monkeys who were fed by the wire mother should have become attached to the wire mother because it provided the drive reduction—that is, the milk. However, it did not work out that way. The monkeys who were fed on the wire mother spent most of their time clinging to the cloth mother. Thus, it appears that monkeys develop their attachment to their mothers based on contact comfort rather than on primary-drive reduction.

However, the important point for us about the research on the need for social contact is not whether this need is innate or acquired but that it exists in most adult human beings. It clearly is an important motivation—one that has a significant impact on behavior in organizations. Many organizations have discovered—to their sorrow—that jobs that do not provide opportunities for social contact have higher turnover and absenteeism rates because employees simply cannot stand the isolation. Frequently, unnecessary social isolation results from mechanical and architectural designs that do not consider employees' needs for social relationships.

Need for Equity

People want to be treated fairly. They observe what happens to other people and if they receive either "too much" or "too little" in comparison to other people it makes them uncomfortable. For example, one study showed that dissatisfaction with promotion was highest in Army units where promotion rates were high. Why? Because the individuals who weren't promoted in these units felt unfairly treated. Adams (1963, 1965) has developed a theory that makes a number of interesting predictions about the effects of wage inequity on work output, work quality, and attitudes toward work. Although this theory is a general theory of social inequity, it has been tested largely with respect to the effects of wage inequity, and it has some interesting things to say about how equity may affect the attractiveness of rewards. Its predictions seem to be particularly relevant to understanding the effects of offering various sizes of pay increases and the effects of paying different wage rates.

Adams (1965) defines inequity as follows:

Inequity exists for Person when he perceives that the ratio of his outcomes to inputs and the ratio of Other's outcomes to Other's inputs are unequal. This may happen either (a) when he and Other are in a direct exchange relationship or (b) when both are in an exchange relationship with a third party, and Person compares himself to Other [p. 280].

Outcomes in the job situation include pay, fringe benefits, status, the intrinsic interest of the job, and so on. Inputs include how hard the person works, his education level, his general qualifications for the job, and so on. It must be remembered that what determines the equity of a particular input-outcome balance is the individual's perception of what he is giving and receiving; this cognition may or may not correspond to an observer's perception or to reality.

Equity theory states that the presence of inequity will motivate an individual to reduce inequity and that the strength of the motivation to reduce inequity varies directly with the perceived magnitude of the imbalance experienced between inputs and outcomes. Feelings of inequity can be produced in a variety of ways and in a variety of situations. Adams has studied inequity produced by overpayment. His research suggests that overpayment is less attractive to employees than equitable payment is. There is evidence, for example, that when a person is paid on a piece rate and feels overpaid, he will reduce his productivity in order to reduce the amount of pay he receives. The important thing for this discussion about the research on equity theory is that people tend to seek equity in their work activities, which can affect their job behavior.

Activity and Exploration

Too little stimulation is very uncomfortable for humans. In one study, college students were employed at $20 a day to stay in a low stimulation environment (Bexton, Heron, & Scott, 1954). They were asked to remain for as many days as they could, lying on a cot in a lighted, partially sound-deadened room. They wore translucent goggles, gloves, and cardboard cuffs that minimized tactile stimulation. An air conditioner provided a noise that blocked out other sounds, and the students rested their heads on a U-shaped pillow. After a certain period—usually filled with sleeping—the subjects found this situation impossible to tolerate and asked to leave the experiment. Rarely did a subject endure it for as long as 2 days despite the fact that the pay was relatively high. Other studies have reported similar results, stressing that under these conditions people seem to develop a hunger for stimulation and action leading to such responses as touching the fingers together and twitching the muscles.

Research by Scott (1969) has shown that the results are very similar when people are given repetitive tasks to perform. They develop a negative attitude toward the task, and, as time goes on, they take more breaks and try in many ways to vary their behavior. As we shall see, this finding has direct implications for the design of jobs in organizations.

Other studies have shown that both people and animals seek out opportunities to experience novel situations. Butler (1953) has shown that monkeys will learn to push open a window for no reward other than being able to see what is going on in a room, and they will keep doing it. Butler has also shown that the strength of the drive for novel stimulation can be increased by deprivation. An experiment by Smock and Holt (1962) has shown that if children are given a chance to control what they see on a television screen, they will look at objects that offer complex stimuli rather than unconflicting, simple stimuli.

Many studies of rats have shown that they will learn certain behaviors in order to experience novel stimuli. In one experiment, rats preferred a goal box that contained objects to an empty goal box. Miles (1958) found that kittens would learn things when the reward was simply the opportunity to explore a room.

There is much evidence that humans and animals will try to solve puzzles simply because of the stimulation provided by working on them. Harlow (1953) has shown that monkeys will persist in solving puzzles for many days. One monkey, who was presented with a square peg and a round hole, persisted for months in trying to get the two to fit together. (The monkey finally died of perforated ulcers.)

Several theorists have suggested that the results of both the stimulus-deprivation studies and the studies of novel-stimulus environments can be explained by considering how novelty affects stimulus attractiveness (Berlyne, 1967). According to activation theory, people become used to a certain level and pattern of stimulation from the environment. For some people this adaptation level may be a relatively low level of stimulation; for others it may be a rather high level. Regardless of where a person's level of adaptation is, however, psychologists hypothesize that deviation from it will have a strong impact on the person. Slight deviations will be experienced as pleasurable and rewarding while large deviations will be experienced as noxious and dissatisfying. Figure 1 illustrates this point graphically. According to this approach, the subjects in the stimulus-deprivation experiment were uncomfortable because the situation fell too far below the adaptation level. The animals who wanted to explore new things were attracted to them because these new things represented stimulus situations that were somewhat above their adaptation levels. Presumably if the stimulus situations had been too far above their adaptation levels, the animals would have avoided them, and indeed there is evidence that both animals and people fear situations that are very unfamiliar to them.

One of the problems with activation theory is that it can be very difficult to measure in advance what a person's adaptation level is. Still, the theory and its related research provide some interesting evidence to support the point

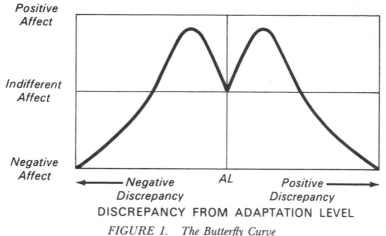

FIGURE 1.   *The Butterfly Curve*

From R. N. Haber, "Discrepancy from Adaptation Level as a Source of Affect."
Journal of Experimental Psychology, 1958, 56, 370–75. Copyright 1958 by the
American Psychological Association. Reproduced by permission.

that not all drives or needs are either primary or learned on the basis of primary drives. It is hard to see how people's reactions to different levels of stimulation can be explained by reference to a drive that has been learned on the basis of a primary drive.

Achievement

The achievement motive has been extensively studied by D. C. McClelland. It is defined by McClelland (1951, 1961) as a desire to perform in terms of a standard of excellence or as a desire to be successful in competitive situations. McClelland stresses that achievement motivation is present in most people but that the amount people have depends on a number of things, including how they were treated during childhood. One study has shown that high-need-achievement people tend to come from families where high demands were made for independence and performance at an early age. Their mothers evaluated their accomplishments favorably and rewarded them liberally.

McClelland measures the strength of people's achievement motive by scoring their responses to a series of pictures. The pictures are shown to individuals who are asked to write a five-minute story about what is going on in the picture. The stories are scored on the basis of how frequently achievement-oriented themes are mentioned (for example, "He will try his best to succeed"). The following is an example of a story showing a young boy in the foreground and a hazy representation of an operation in the background.

> A boy is dreaming of being a doctor. He can see himself in the future. He is hoping that he can make the grade. It is more or less a fantasy. The boy has seen many pictures of doctors in books, and it has inspired him. He will try his best and hopes to become the best doctor in the country. He can see himself as a very important doctor. He is performing a very dangerous operation. He can see himself victorious and is proud of it. He gets world renown for it. He will become the best doctor in the U.S.. He will be an honest man, too. His name will go down in medical history as one of the greatest men [Atkinson, 1958, p. 193].

McClelland's research has shown that under certain conditions achievement motivation can be an important motivator of good performance in work organizations. When achievement motivation is operating, good job performance becomes very attractive to people; as a result, the motivation to perform well is higher. Achievement motivation typically does not operate when people are performing routine or boring tasks where no competition is involved. However, when challenge and competition are involved, achievement motivation can stimulate good performance. A study by French (1955) clearly illustrates this point. In French's study, Officer Candidate School cadets performed a simple task under three different sets of instructions. Under the "relaxed" instructions the subjects were told that the experimenter was merely interested in determining what kinds of scores people make on the test. The "task-motivated" instructions said that the task was a measure of people's ability to deal rapidly with new materials. The "extrinsically motivated" instructions said that the best performers could leave while the others had to continue performing. Performance was highest under the "task-motivated" instructions and lowest under the "relaxed" instructions. Subjects with high need for achievement performed better on the "task-motivated" instructions but not under the two other kinds of instructions.

Other studies also support the view that people can be motivated simply by a drive to achieve. For example, Alper (1946) gave two groups of subjects a list of nonsense syllables to learn. Only one group was told it was an intelligence test. A test given 24 hours later showed that the "intelligence test" group remembered more of what they had learned. McClelland (1961) showed that successful people in competitive occupations tend to be universally high in achievement motivation. For example, he showed that successful managers from countries such as the United States, Italy, and India tend to be high in achievement motivation.

Overall, the research on achievement motivation suggests that such motivation is most likely to be present when moderately challenging tasks have to be performed (where about a 50–50 chance of success exists), in competitive situations, in situations where performance is perceived to depend upon some important or valued skill, and in situations where performance feedback is given. The research also suggests that people with a high need for achievement tend to seek out situations in which they can achieve, and they tend to find successful performance attractive once they are in these situations. These points have important implications for the design of jobs in organizations and for the kinds of people that are attracted to jobs in different types of work situations.

Judging from the research cited earlier on the effects of child rearing on the strength of need for achievement, it seems certain that achievement motivation is a partly learned drive. McClelland in fact argues that it is differentially present in certain cultures precisely because child-rearing practices differ. However, even though achievement motivation is a learned drive, it is hard to see how it could develop because of the primary drives. There may be some relationship here, since success often helps people to obtain primary rewards, such as food; but it is hard to see how the primary drive approach can explain the fact that early independence training leads to a strong need for achievement. Thus, even though achievement is a learned drive, it seems that it is only partially learned on the basis of primary drives.

Competence

Robert W. White (1959) has argued for the existence of a competence motive. He uses competence to refer to an organism's capacity to interact effectively with its environment. In organisms capable of little learning, competence is considered to be innate; however, competence in man—that is, his fitness to interact with the environment—is slowly attained through prolonged feats of learning. The human learning that is needed to gain competence is characterized by high persistence and a strong goal orientation. Because of this dedication to learning, White argues that it is necessary to treat competence as having a motivation aspect that is separate from motivation derived from primary drives or instincts. He presents considerable evidence of organisms trying to cope with their environment seemingly for no other reason than that they want to master it. As White notes, there are repeated references in psychological literature.

> . . . to the familiar series of learned skills which starts with sucking, grasping, and visual exploration and continues with crawling and walking, acts of focal attention and perception, memory, language and thinking, anticipation, the exploring of novel places and objects, effecting stimulus changes in the environment, manipulating and exploiting the surroundings, and achieving higher levels of motor and mental coordination. . . . Collectively they are sometimes referred to as mechanisms . . . but on the whole we are not accustomed to cast a single name over the diverse feats whereby we learn to deal with the environment. . . . I now propose that we gather the various kinds of behavior just mentioned, all of which had to do with effective interaction with the environment, under the general heading of competence . . . it is necessary to make competence a motivational concept; there is a competence motivation [1959, pp. 317–318].

White argues that competence motivation is aroused when people are faced with somewhat new situations and wanes when a situation has been explored and mastered to the point at which it no longer presents a challenge.

There is an obvious similarity between White's view of when competence motivation is aroused and the activation theorists' view of how stimulus novelty affects motivation. Both argue for high motivation when somewhat novel situations are encountered. White's theory is also very closely related to the theory of achievement motivation, since both talk of man's need to perform adequately. In fact, White says that achievement may be one outcome of competence motivation. White's theory has some interesting implications for the design of jobs in organizations. It suggests that if presented with the right task people can be motivated to perform effectively without the use of extrinsic rewards such as pay and promotion. However, once the task is mastered, competence motivation will disappear. It is also interesting to note that White, like other recent theorists, argues that the competence motive is not based on any primary drive. Although he does not say exactly where it comes from, he does imply that man's desire to be competent is innate.

Self-Actualization

In the last thirty years a number of psychologists have introduced concepts into their theories that have to do with people's need to grow and develop. Table 1 lists some of these theo-

TABLE 1. *List of Theorists Classified as Emphasizing Self-actualization, and the Term Each Uses*

Kurt Goldstein (1939): Self-actualization
Erich Fromm (1941): The productive orientation
Prescott Lecky (1945): The unified personality; self-consistency
Donald Snygg and Arthur Combs (1949): The preservation and enhancement of the phenomenal self
Karen Horney (1950): The real self and its realization
David Riesman (1950): The autonomous person
Carl Rogers (1951): Actualization, maintenance, and enhancement of the experiencing organism
Rollo May (1953): Existential being
Abraham Maslow (1954): Self-actualization
Gordon W. Allport (1955): Creative becoming

Adapted from Cofer, C. N., and Appley, M. H., *Motivation: Theory and Research.* Copyright © 1964 by John Wiley & Sons, Inc.

rists and their concepts. The work of Maslow has had by far the greatest impact on the thinking concerned with motivation in organizations. Maslow uses the term "self-actualization" to describe the need people have to grow and develop. According to him, it is the "desire for self-fulfillment, namely . . . the tendency [for a person] to become actualized in what he is potentially . . . the desire to become more and more of what one is, to become everything that one is capable of becoming . . ." (1954, pp. 91–92). Maslow stresses that not all people function on the self-actualization level. He then goes on to describe the characteristics of people who are motivated by self-actualization. According to him, much of the self-actualizing person's behavior is motivated solely by the sheer enjoyment he obtains from using and developing his capacities. He does not necessarily behave in accordance with extrinsic goals or rewards. For him, the goal is simply to behave in a certain way or experience a certain feeling. Maslow makes the point like this:

> . . . we must construct a profoundly different psychology of motivation for self-actualizing people, e.g., expression motivation or growth motivation, rather than deficiency motivation. Perhaps it will be useful to make a distinction between living and preparing to live. Perhaps the concept of motivation should apply only to non-self-actualizers. Our subjects no longer strive in the ordinary sense, but rather develop. They attempt to grow to perfection and to develop more and more fully in their own style. The motivation of ordinary men is a striving for the basic need gratifications that they lack. But self-actualizing people in fact lack none of these gratifications; and yet they have impulses. They work, they try, and they are ambitious, even though in an unusual sense. For them motivation is just character growth, character expression, maturation, and development; in a word self-actualization [p. 211].*

---

*From *Motivation and Personality* (2nd ed.) by A. H. Maslow. Copyright © 1970 by Harper & Row, Publishers, Inc.

Thus, like White and others, Maslow is careful to say that all motivation is not tied to the primary drives. Maslow also stresses that people will work to obtain outcomes that are intrinsic, such as feelings of growth. He completely rejects the view that valued outcomes have to be related to such extrinsic rewards as food and water. Maslow probably goes further than any of the other theorists we have reviewed in stressing the differences between motivation based on primary drives and motivation that is independent of primary drives. He says that, unlike motivation based on primary drives, motivation based on growth needs does not decrease as the needs become satisfied. Quite to the contrary, Maslow argues that as people experience growth and self-actualization they simply want more. In his view, obtaining growth creates a desire for more growth, whereas obtaining food decreases one's desire for food.

Maslow argues that the concept of self-actualization can explain a significant amount of the motivation in organizations. He states that, particularly at the managerial level, many people are motivated by a desire to self-actualize. There is a considerable amount of evidence to support this point. In one study, managers rated the need for self-actualization as their most important need (Porter, 1964). In addition, most large organizations abound with training and development programs designed to help people develop their skills and abilities. Sometimes people do enter these programs in the hope of obtaining a raise or promotion, but on other occasions they do it only because it contributes to their self-development. There is also evidence of people seeking more challenging jobs for no other reason than to develop themselves.

An interesting contrast to Maslow's work on self-actualization is provided by the work of existential psychologists such as Allport (1955) and Rogers (1961). They too talk of people being motivated by desires that are not related to obtaining rewards such as money and status.

However, they give less emphasis to the development of skills and abilities and the achievement of goals than does Maslow, and they give more emphasis to new experiences as a way of learning about one's self. Rogers, for example, talks of people being motivated "to be that self which one truly is." He emphasizes self-discovery and the importance of being open to experience. Perhaps because they don't emphasize skill development and accomplishments as much as Maslow, the existential psychologists have not had much impact on the research of psychologists interested in work organizations. This is unfortunate, and it is important to remember that at times people may be motivated by nothing more than self-discovery and a desire to experience.

Need-Classification Theories

Numerous lists and classifications of needs have been presented by psychologists. One of the most important is Henry A. Murray's (1938) list of "psychogenic" or "social" needs. This list, which contains more than 20 motives, was arrived at on the basis of the study of a number of "normal" people. Although Murray's list has been very influential in the field of psychology, it has not been applied very much to the study of motivation in organizations, probably because its length greatly reduces its usefulness. Like the early lists of instincts, it is so long that there is almost a separate need for each behavior people demonstrate. A look at Table 2, which lists some of Murray's needs, may help the reader gain an impression of the nature of the problem. The issue is not whether Murray has identified separate kinds of behavior (he has) but whether these behaviors might not be better dealt with by a more parsimonious list of needs.

Maslow's hierarchical classification of needs has been by far the most widely used classification system in the study of motivation in organizations. Maslow differs from Murray in two important ways: first, his list is shorter; second, he argues that needs are arranged in a hierarchy.

Maslow's (1943, 1954, 1970) hierarchical model is composed of a five-level classification of human needs and a set of hypotheses about how the satisfaction of these needs affects their importance.

The five need categories are as follows:

1. *Physiological needs,* including the need for food, water, air, and so on.
2. *Safety needs,* or the need for security, stability, and the absence from pain, threat, or illness.
3. *Belongingness and love needs,* which include a need for affection, belongingness, love, and so on.
4. *Esteem needs,* including both a need for personal feelings of achievement or self-esteem and also a need for recognition or respect from others.
5. *The need for self-actualization,* a feeling of self-fulfillment or the realization of one's potential.

More important than the definition of these five need groups, however, is the *process* by which each class of needs becomes important or active. According to Maslow, the five need categories exist in a hierarchy of prepotency such that the lower or more basic needs are inherently more important (prepotent) than the higher or less basic needs. This means that before any of the higher-level needs will become important, a person's physiological needs must be satisfied. Once the physiological needs have been satisfied, however, their strength or importance decreases, and the next-higher-level need becomes the strongest motivator of behavior. This process of "increased satisfaction / decreased importance / increased importance of the next higher need" repeats itself until the highest level of the hierarchy is reached. Maslow has proposed in later revisions of his theory (1968, 1970) that at the highest level of the hierarchy a reversal occurs

TABLE 2.   *Murray's List of Needs.*

Social Motive	Brief Definition
Abasement	To surrender. To comply and accept punishment. To apologize, confess, atone. Self-depreciation. Masochism.
Achievement	To overcome obstacles, to exercise power, to strive to do something difficult as well and as quickly as possible.
Affiliation	To form friendships and associations. To greet, join, and live with others. To cooperate and converse sociably with others. To love. To join groups.
Aggression	To assault or injure an other. To murder. To belittle, harm, blame, accuse or maliciously ridicule a person. To punish severely. Sadism.
Autonomy	To resist influence or coercion. To defy an authority or seek freedom in a new place. To strive for independence.
Blamavoidance	To avoid blame, ostracism or punishment by inhibiting asocial or unconventional impulses. To be well-behaved and obey the law.
Counteraction	Proudly to refuse admission of defeat by restriving and retaliating. To select the hardest tasks. To defend one's honor in action.
Defendance	To defend oneself against blame or belittlement. To justify one's actions. To offer extenuations, explanations and excuses. To resist "probing."
Deference	To admire and willingly follow a superior allied other. To cooperate with a leader. To serve gladly.
Dominance	To influence or control others. To persuade, prohibit, dictate. To lead and direct. To restrain. To organize the behavior of a group.
Exhibition	To attract attention to one's person. To excite, amuse, stir, shock, thrill others. Self-dramatization.
Harmavoidance	To avoid pain, physical injury, illness and death. To escape from a dangerous situation. To take precautionary measures.
Infavoidance	To avoid failure, shame, humiliation, ridicule. To refrain from attempting to do something that is beyond one's powers. To conceal a disfigurement.
Nurturance	To nourish, aid or protect a helpless other. To express sympathy. To "mother" a child.
Order	To arrange, organize, put away objects. To be tidy and clean. To be scrupulously precise.
Play	To relax, amuse oneself, seek diversion and entertainment. To "have fun," to play games. To laugh, joke and be merry. To avoid serious tension.
Rejection	To snub, ignore or exclude an other. To remain aloof and indifferent. To be discriminating.
Sentience	To seek and enjoy sensuous impressions.
Sex	To form and further an erotic relationship. To have sexual intercourse.
Succorance	To seek aid, protection or sympathy. To cry for help. To plead for mercy. To adhere to an affectionate, nurturant parent. To be dependent.
Understanding	To analyze experience, to abstract, to discriminate among concepts, to define relations, to synthesize ideas.

From H. A. Murray, *Explorations in Personality.* New York: Oxford, 1938.

in the satisfaction-importance relationship. He states that for self-actualization, increased satisfaction leads to *increased* need strength. "Gratification breeds increased rather than decreased motivation, heightened rather than lessened excitement" (1968, p. 30).

In short, individual behavior is motivated by an attempt to satisfy the need that is *most important* at that point in time. Further, the strength of any need is determined by its position in the hierarchy and by the degree to which it and all lower needs have been satisfied. Maslow's theory predicts a dynamic, step-by-step, causal process of human motivation in which behavior is governed by a continuously changing (though predictable) set of "important" needs. An increase (change) in the satisfaction of the needs in one category *causes* the strength of these needs to decrease, which results in an increase in the importance of the needs at the next-higher level. Maslow does say that the hierarchy of needs is not a rigidly fixed order that is the same for all individuals. Especially in the case of needs in the middle of the hierarchy, the order varies somewhat from person to person. However, this view clearly states that physiological needs are the most prepotent and that self-actualization needs are usually the least.

Two other need-hierarchy theories have been stated. One is by Langer (1937)—predating Maslow's—and another by Alderfer (1969). Alderfer's (1972) theory is the best developed of these two theories. Alderfer argues for three levels of needs: existence, relatedness, and growth. Like Maslow, he argues that the satisfaction of a need influences its importance and the importance of higher-level needs. He agrees with Maslow's hypothesis that the satisfaction of growth needs makes them more important rather than less important to people; however, he also hypothesizes that the lack of satisfaction of higher-order needs can lead to lower-order needs becoming more important to people. He then argues that the importance of any need is influenced by the satisfaction /

frustration of the needs above and below it in the hierarchy. He also assumes that all needs can be simultaneously active; thus, prepotency does not play as major a role in his theory as it does in Maslow's.

From the point of view of the three questions we asked at the beginning of the chapter, the hierarchical theories of Maslow and Alderfer provide rather complete answers to the last two questions. These theories make specific statements about what outcomes people will value (outcomes that satisfy whatever need or needs are active). They also make specific predictions about what will influence the attractiveness of various outcomes—for example, satisfaction of relevant needs including those lower on the hierarchy. They provide less complete answers to our first question, since they are not clear on why needs originate. They do, however, imply that the lower-order needs are innate and that the higher-order needs are present in most people and will appear if not blocked from appearing.

The hierarchical concept has received a great deal of attention among those interested in organizations. This interest is undoubtedly because the concept, if valid, provides a powerful tool for predicting how the importance of various outcomes will change in response to certain actions by organizations. It also can provide some important clues concerning what is likely to be important to employees. It suggests, for example, that as people get promoted in organizations and their lower-level needs become satisfied, they will become concerned with self-actualization and growth. It also suggests that if a person's job security is threatened, he will abandon all else in order to protect it. Finally, it suggests that an organization can give an employee enough of the lower-level rewards, such as security, but that it cannot give him enough growth and development. Thus, as employees receive more valued outcomes from organizations, they will *want* more; although the nature of what they want may change from things that satisfy their lower-order needs to things that satisfy their higher-order needs. As more than one manager has noted, "we have given our employees good working conditions, high pay, and a secure future. Now they want more interesting jobs and a chance to make more decisions. Won't they ever be satisfied?" Need hierarchy suggests that they won't!

AN APPROACH TO OUTCOME ATTRACTIVENESS

The approaches of Maslow, McClelland, and others are useful in thinking about motivation in organizations. They clearly indicate a number of important points that need to be included in any approach that tires to deal with the issue of why certain outcomes are attractive to people. However, there are still many questions. The rest of this chapter will be concerned with answering these questions and with developing an approach to explaining outcome attractiveness.

Drives, Needs, Motives, or Just Outcomes?

All of the theorists discussed so far have assumed that outcomes are attractive to a person because of some drive, motive, or need the person has. On the other hand, Vroom (1964) has taken a different approach. He does not use the terms drive, need, or motive in his theory. He simply says that outcomes have value if they lead to other valued outcomes. Nothing is said about what causes people to value those other outcomes nor about what other outcomes are likely to be valued. Although it does solve the problem of trying to understand why individual outcomes are attractive, a theory that deals with the problem as Vroom's does sacrifices predictive power, in contrast to a theory of needs that

states in advance what outcomes are likely to be valued and what affects their value.

A theory of needs can make some predictions—such as when outcomes will be important and what will be the effects of certain events—that Vroom's theory cannot make. For example, if it is known that pay is important to an individual because it leads to prestige, Vroom's theory can only predict that, as prestige outcomes become less important, so will pay. On the other hand, a need theory such as Maslow's can make further predictions. It can predict what conditions will affect the importance of prestige outcomes—that is, satisfaction of esteem needs or lower-level needs—and can then predict what the effect of a number of factors, such as a promotion, will be on the importance of pay.

The issue of whether needs are innate or learned is an important one; but since we are dealing with adults whose need structures are already developed, it is not crucial for us. This issue is important for us only in the sense that it might provide information about how common it is for people to have a need. Innate needs should be present in a greater proportion of the society than learned needs. Of course, at this point no one seriously argues that any needs other than the basic ones are either purely learned or purely innate. Still, it does seem that the needs that are lower on Maslow's hierarchy are more innate and, therefore, more universally present than are those that are at the top of the hierarchy.

For our purposes a theory of needs does not have to specify why people have needs, since it can say something about the needs people have and the conditions under which certain needs operate without doing this. All it has to say is that certain outcomes can be grouped together because when one is sought the others are no longer sought. People often have several groups of such outcomes. The groups can be called "needs," and, if the same ones are sought by most people, then it is reasonable to speak of a "human need" for the group of outcomes. Perhaps it should be added that before a group of outcomes is called a need the outcomes should be sought as ends in themselves rather than as instruments for obtaining other outcomes. For example, food outcomes are sought as an end in themselves, and thus we speak of a *need* for food; a big office is not an end in itself, and thus cannot be called a need. Once it is decided that people have needs, the question is "how many needs?".

How Many Needs?

Interestingly, theorists defining different categories of human needs usually don't disagree over which specific outcomes are likely to be goals for people, but they do disagree on what kinds of needs lead to outcomes taking on goal characteristics. Psychologists have argued that people have from three to several hundred needs. Part of the reason for this variance rests in the way needs are defined. Originally, the criterion was simple; needs or drives were only said to exist when it could be established that a physiological basis could be found for the attractiveness of the outcomes sought by a person.

The recent research on higher-level needs has clearly shown this approach to be too restrictive. A suggested alternative is to use the term "need" to refer to clusters of outcomes that people seek as ends in themselves. This definition, however, does not solve the problem of how to determine what constitutes a valid cluster. Different foods provide a simple example of the problem. Various food objects can be grouped together in the sense that when a person wants one he often wants the others and when he gets enough of one he may lose interest in the others. Thus, we can say that people have a need for meat rather than saying that people have a need for roast beef or steak. By thinking in terms of outcome clusters such as the one just described, we move to a more general level and begin to group outcomes more parsimoniously. The question that arises now, however, is where to stop. That is, at what level of abstraction or generality should we stop grouping outcomes. Should we, for example, stop at the level of meat or put all food outcomes together and speak of a need for food, since food objects are somewhat similar in attractiveness as shown in Figure 2. The former is a tighter cluster in the sense that the attractiveness of different kinds of meat is probably more closely related than is the attractiveness of meat to the attractiveness of fruit. However, there are still tighter clusters (different kinds of steak), and thus there is no final answer to the question of how tight a cluster should be.

It is also possible to go to a higher level of abstraction and combine food outcomes with water and oxygen and call this combination an existence need (see Figure 3). This existence need includes all the outcomes that people need to sustain life. The criterion for grouping at this level is different from the criterion stated earlier (when one outcome is sought the other will be sought, and when one is obtained the attractiveness of the other is affected). The grouping in Figure 3 is based on the fact that all the outcomes have a common property: they are necessary for existence. Unlike the cluster shown in Figure 2, the attractiveness of one is not necessarily related to the other. Using this system, we would say that people desire food objects because of a basic need to exist; whereas, if we operated at a lower level, we would say people desire food objects because of a need for nourishment. A somewhat similar grouping problem occurs with achievement, self-actualization, and competence. Although it is possible to say that these concepts each represent separate needs, they also overlap in many respects. They all focus on the attractiveness to people of dealing effectively with challenging problems. Thus, they can be grouped and la-

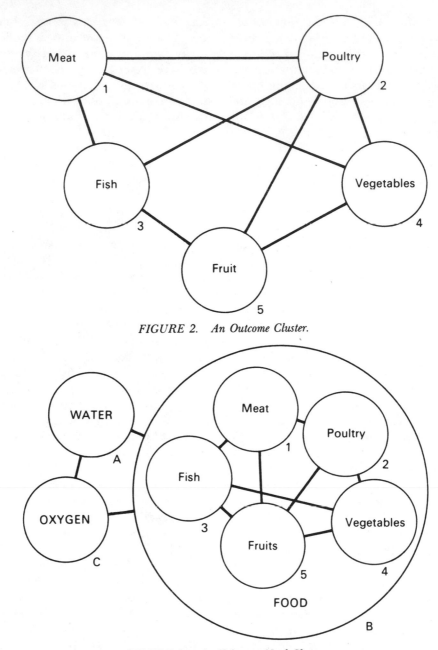

FIGURE 2.   An Outcome Cluster.

FIGURE 3.   An Existence-Need Cluster.

beled as "a need for competence and growth" or they can be treated separately.

Ultimately, the best approach to categorizing needs is that which allows the greatest prediction of behavior in organizations. Unfortunately, at the moment there is not enough research evidence to allow us to state conclusively which listing of needs leads to the greatest predictability. Because of this lack of evidence, the best approach would seem to be grouping only those outcomes that have a strong empirical relationship to each other. By this condition we mean those outcomes that can be observed to have common degrees of attractiveness to people. Using this criterion and thinking in terms of organizations, the following needs can be identified:

1. A number of existence needs—primarily sex, hunger, thirst, and oxygen.
2. A security need.
3. A social need.
4. A need for esteem and reputation.
5. An autonomy or freedom need.
6. A need for competence and self-actualization.

Is There a Need Hierarchy?

Now that we have identified a specific set of human needs, we must consider whether these needs should be arranged in a hierarchy. What does the evidence show about the existence of a need hierarchy?

There is strong evidence to support the view that unless existence needs are satisfied, none of the higher-order needs will come into play. There is also evidence that unless security needs are satisfied, people will not be concerned with higher-order needs. One report shows that subjects kept in a state of hunger think of little else than food (Keys, Brozek, Henschel, Mickelsen, & Taylor, 1950). Similar data is available in the literature on brainwashing and concentration camps (Lawler & Suttle, 1972).

There is, however, very little evidence to support the view that a hierarchy exists above the security level. Thus, it probably is not safe to assume more than a two-step hierarchy with existence and security needs at the lowest level and all the higher-order needs at the next level. This line of thinking leads to the prediction that

unless these lower-order needs are satisfied, the others will not come into play. However, which higher-order needs come into play after the lower ones are satisfied and in what order they will come into play cannot be predicted. If anything, it seems that most people are simultaneously motivated by several of the same-level needs. On the other hand, people do not seem to be simultaneously motivated by needs from the two different levels. One person might, for example, be motivated by social and autonomy needs, while another might be motivated by hunger and thirst. Once a need appears, it does seem to persist until it is satisfied or the satisfaction of the lower-order needs is threatened. The one exception to this rule is the need for self-actualization and competence. Unlike the other needs, evidence shows that this need does not appear to be satiable and, thus, is not likely to cease to be important unless the satisfaction of one of the lower-level needs is threatened.

Can Outcomes Satisfy More Than One Need?

There is a considerable amount of research evidence indicating that some outcomes are relevant to the satisfaction of more than one need. That is, when these outcomes are obtained they affect the attractiveness of more than one cluster of outcomes. A classic example is pay (Lawler, 1971). Pay appears to have the ability to satisfy not only existence needs but also security and esteem needs. For example, Lawler and Porter (1963) report that the more a manager is paid, the higher is his security- and esteem-need satisfaction. This statement means that when a person is trying to satisfy either security or esteem needs, pay will be important. It is not difficult to see why pay has the ability to satisfy a number of needs. Pay can be used to buy articles, such as food, that satisfy existence needs, and high pay also earns a certain amount of esteem and respect in our society.

How Important Are Different Needs?

Literally hundreds of studies have tried to measure the importance of different needs and outcomes to employees. Some idea of the importance of different needs can be obtained by looking at the data collected by Porter (1964), which appears in Figure 4. These data show that for over 1,900 managers sampled the higher-order needs are clearly the most important. Other data from the study show that the managers are most satisfied with the lower-order needs. Thus, it follows that these lower-order needs should be the least important. Whether this same concern with higher-order need satisfaction exists at the lower levels in organizations is not clear. The data presented in Figure 4 show that higher-order needs do seem to be somewhat less important to lower-level managers than to higher-level managers. Other data suggest that pay and certain lower-level needs are rated as more important by workers than by managers (Porter & Lawler, 1965). Dubin (1956), for example, argues that the work place

is not a central part of the life of most industrial workers and that it is unwise to expect the workers to be concerned with fulfilling their higher-order needs within the context of their jobs.

Figure 5 shows the average ratings of the importance of job factors in a large number of studies (16 studies and 11,000 employees). Most of these studies were done on non-managerial employees. It shows job security and intrinsic job interest to be the most important factors to the employees. Lawler (1971) reviewed 43 studies in which pay was rated and found that its average rating was third. This is an interesting finding, but, like other findings that are based on employee ratings of how important various needs and job characteristics are, it must be interpreted very cautiously. These ratings are difficult for people to make and are strongly influenced by how the questions are worded. Thus, it is impossible to reach any strong conclusions about which job factors are the most important. Perhaps the most significant thing to remember from these studies

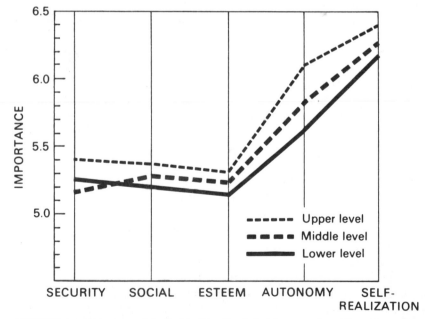

FIGURE 4.   *Importance Attached to Five Needs by Managers from Three Organization Levels*

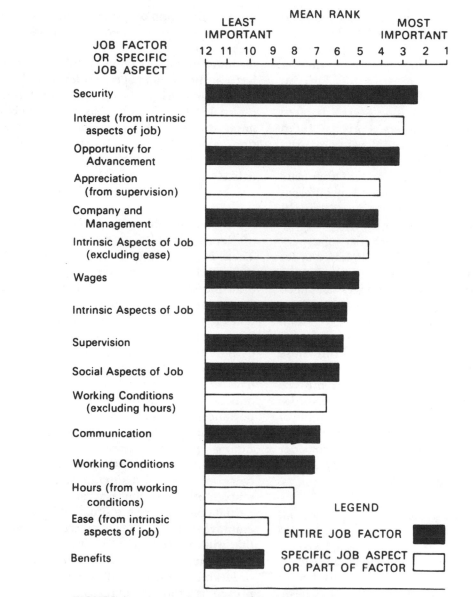

FIGURE 5. *Average Importance of Factors in Employee Attitude (Compiled from 16 studies, including over 11,000 employees)*

From Herzberg et al., *Job Attitudes: Review of Research and Opinion.* Copyright 1957 by the Psychological Service of Pittsburgh. Reprinted by permission.

is that employees rate a number of factors as very important. Some of these factors seem to be most strongly related to lower-order needs, while others are related to higher-order needs.

Individual Differences in Need Strength

Large differences clearly exist in the goals and needs people have, and these differences must

387

be considered when viewing individual motivation in organizations. For example, Lawler reports that in about ¼ of the cases he analyzed, pay was rated as first in importance, while in many other cases it was rated sixth or lower in importance. Because of these differences a pay system that will motivate one person is often seen as irrelevant by others. Porter's (1963) data show that managers at different organization levels differ in the degree to which they are motivated by higher-order needs. Other data show that managers are motivated by different needs; some managers are motivated by self-actualization, while others are motivated by autonomy. There is also evidence that some people seem to be fixated on such lower-order needs as security.

Many individual differences in need strength are understandable if we relate them to personal characteristics and situations. Hulin and Blood (1968), for example, point out that urban workers have different values from those of rural workers. Urban workers seem to be more alienated from work and apparently are less concerned with fulfilling higher-order needs on the job. For an interesting example of the type of individual profile that can be drawn from the research on need strength, consider the profile of a person to whom money is likely to be very important (Lawler, 1971).

> The employee is a male, young (probably in his twenties); his personality is characterized by low self-assurance and high neuroticism; he comes from a small town or farm background; he belongs to few clubs and social groups, and he owns his own home and probably is a Republican and a Protestant [p. 51].

In summary then, there are significant individual differences among employees in the importance of different needs and outcomes. These differences are not surprising; in fact, many are predictable from what has been said about how the importance of needs is affected by the satisfaction of needs and by certain child-rearing experience. There is also evidence that these individual differences are related in meaningful ways to a number of organizational factors, such as management level, and to personal characteristics, such as age, sex, and education level. This point has some interesting implications for the management of organizations, since it means that it is possible to identify those people for whom a particular reward is likely to be important.

How Changeable Is the Importance of Needs?

There is evidence to indicate that some things can and do influence the importance of needs. Still, the evidence suggests that organizations have relatively little influence over how important various outcomes will be to their members. The importance of needs is determined partly by hereditary factors and partly by childhood experiences—things over which organizations have no control. Organizations can influence only two of the factors that determine need importance: need satisfaction and need arousal. Satisfaction influences importance, and organizational practices strongly influence satisfaction. Achievement motivation can be aroused by certain tasks and situations, as can competence motivation. Since organizations do have partial control over the situation in which their employees work, they can create conditions that will arouse certain needs. However, these needs must be present in the individual in order to be aroused, and whether the needs are present is a function of many things beyond the control of the organization.

Probably the best opportunity organizations have to influence the needs of their employees is provided by the selection process. Since need importance is relatively fixed and it is possible to identify people who are high on particular needs, organizations can select people who have the kinds of need-strength patterns they want. This would seem to be a much better approach than trying to change people's needs once they join the organization. This point also has some interesting implications for managers who have to motivate employees. It suggests that rather than trying to change the needs of their subordinates, managers should concentrate on placing people in jobs where their need structure is appropriate. The motivation system that is used must fit the needs of the person or it will not work. If pay is not important to an employee, he or she will never be motivated by a pay-incentive system.

Has There Been an Overall Change in the Relative Importance of Needs?

Many writers (for example, Roszak, 1969) have speculated that the strength of the various needs in the population has been changing over the past 60 years. They argue that only recently has a significant proportion of the population been concerned with needs such as self-actualization and autonomy. (And it is interesting to note that only recently have psychologists been concerned with needs such as self-actualization.) The concept of man as a self-actualizing organism is essentially a development of the 1960s.

Two reasons are generally advanced for the emergence of higher-order needs. First, there is the rising level of education in our society; approximately 40 percent of the high school graduates in the United States go to college. Second, the standard of living has constantly increased so that fewer and fewer people are concerned with satisfying their existence needs and, thus, can focus on satisfying their higher-order needs.

Unfortunately, there is very little evidence to either support or disprove the view that the strength of needs is changing. To test this view adequately we would have to compare need-strength data collected 60 years ago from a random population sample with data col-lected recently. Unfortunately, such data do not exist. There are, however, some data that can be said to support the view that higher-order needs have become more important. We've already seen that there is evidence to support a two-step hierarchy. If we accept the fact that the standard of living is higher, then, on the basis of a two-step hierarchy, this higher standard of living supports the view that higher-order needs probably are more important. In addition, Porter's (1962) data show that younger managers place greater importance on self-actualization than older managers do. This could, of course, be simply a function of age, but it could also be due to the higher education level of these younger managers and the fact that they never experienced a depression.

There is also some direct evidence that higher-educated people are more concerned with self-actualization. Finally, there is the fact that the idea of self-actualization has gained fairly wide attention in our society. It now seems "in" to talk about self-actualization; and, as we pointed out, the concept of "self-actualization" is now prominent in psychology. Although this evidence is only indirect, it does support the view that concern with self-actualization has increased recently. In summary, although there is little direct data to support the view, it probably is true that, in general, people are somewhat more concerned with satisfying higher-order needs than they used to be.

SUMMARY AND CONCLUSIONS

The following statements summarize the major points that have been made so far about human needs.

1. Needs can be thought of as groups of outcomes that people seek.
2. Man's needs are arranged in a two-level hierarchy. At the lowest level are existence

and security needs; at the other level are social, esteem, autonomy, and self-actualization needs.

3. The higher-level needs will appear only when the lower-level ones are satisfied.

4. All needs except self-actualization are satiable, and as needs become satisfied they decrease in importance.

5. A person can be motivated by more than one need at a given point in time and will continue to be motivated by a need until either it is satisfied or satisfaction of the lower-order needs is threatened.

Thus, we have answered two of the three questions asked at the beginning of the chapter. A classification system for needs has been developed, and statements have been made about what influences the importance of needs. No conclusions have been reached about why people develop needs or about whether needs are innate or learned because these questions don't seem to be answerable at this time.

REFERENCES

Adams, J. S. Toward an understanding of inequity. *Journal of Abnormal Psychology.* 1963, **67,** 422–436.

Adams, J. S. Injustice in social exchange. In L. Berkowitz (Ed.), *Advances in experimental social psychology.* Vol. 2. New York: Academic Press, 1965.

Alderfer, C. P. An empirical test of a new theory of human needs. *Organizational Behavior and Human Performance,* 1969, **4,** 142–175.

Alderfer, C. P. *Existence, relatedness, and growth: Human needs in organizational settings.* New York: The Free Press, 1972.

Allport, G. W. *Becoming: Basic considerations for a psychology of personality.* New Haven: Yale University Press, 1955.

Alper, T. G. Task-orientation vs. ego-orientation in learning and retention. *American Journal of Psychology,* 1946, **38,** 224–238.

Atkinson, J. W. Towards experimental analysis of human motivation in terms of motives, expectancies, and incentives. In J. W. Atkinson (Ed.), *Motives in fantasy, action, and society.* Princeton, N.J.: Van Nostrand Reinhold, 1958.

Atkinson, J. W. *An introduction to motivation.* Princeton, N.J.: Van Nostrand Reinhold, 1964.

Berlyne, D. E. Arousal and reinforcement. In D. Levine (Ed.), *Nebraska symposium on motivation.* Lincoln: University of Nebraska Press, 1967.

Bexton, W. H., Heron, W., & Scott, T. H. Effects of decreased variation in the sensory environment. *Canadian Journal of Psychology,* 1954, **8,** 70–76.

Butler, R. A. Discrimination learning by rhesus monkeys to visual-exploration motivation. *Journal of Comparative and Physiological Psychology.* 1953, **46,** 95–98.

Cofer, C. N., & Appley, M. H. *Motivation: Theory and research.* New York: John Wiley & Sons, 1964.

Cowles, J. T. Food tokens as incentives for learning by chimpanzees. *Comparative Psychology Monograph,* 1937, **14** (No. 71).

Cravens, R. W., & Renner, K. E. Conditioned appetitive drive states: Empirical evidence and theoretical status *Psychological Bulletin,* 1970, **73,** 212–220.

Dubin, R. Industrial workers' worlds: A study of the "central life interests" of industrial workers. *Social Problems,* 1956, **3,** 131–142.

French, E. G. Some characteristics of achievement motivation. *Journal of Experimental Psychology,* 1955, **50,** 232–236.

Fromm, E. *Escape from freedom.* New York: Rinehart & Winston, 1941.

Goldstein, K. *The organism.* New York: American Book, 1939.

Haber, R. N. Discrepancy from adaptation level as a source of affect. *Journal of Experimental Psychology,* 1958, **56,** 370–375.

Hall, C. S., & Lindzey, G. *Theories of personality.* New York: John Wiley & Sons, 1957.

Harlow, H. F. Mice, monkeys, men, and motives. *Psychological Review,* 1953, **60,** 23–32.

Harlow, H. F. The nature of love. *American Psychologist.* 1958, **13,** 673–685.

Herzberg, F., Mausner, B., Peterson, R. O., & Capwell, D. F. *Job attitudes: Review of research and opinion.* Pittsburgh: Psychological Service of Pittsburgh, 1957.

Horney, K. *Neurosis and human growth.* New York: W. W. Norton, 1950.

Hulin, C. L., & Blood, M. R. Job enlargement, individual differences, and worker responses. *Psychological Bulletin,* 1968, **69,** 41–55.

Hull, C. L. *Principles of behavior.* New York: Appleton-Century-Crofts, 1943.

Keys, A., Brozek, J., Henschel, A., Mickelsen, O., & Taylor, H. *The biology of human starvation.* Minneapolis: University of Minnesota Press, 1950. 2 vols.

Langer, W. C. *Psychology and human living.* New York: Appleton-Century-Crofts, 1937.

Lawler, E. E. *Pay and organizational effectiveness: A psychological view.* New York: McGraw-Hill, 1971.

Lawler, E. E., & Porter, L. W. Perceptions regarding management compensation. *Industrial Relations,* 1963, **3,** 41–49.

Lawler, E. E. & Suttle, J. L. A causal correlational test of the need hierarchy concept. *Organizational Behavior and Human Performance,* 1972, **7,** 265–287.

Lecky, P. *Self-consistency: A theory of personality.* New York: Island Press, 1945.

McClelland, D. C. Measuring motivation in phantasy: The achievement motive. In H. Guetzkow (Ed.), *Groups, leadership, and men.* Pittsburgh: Carnegie Press, 1951.

McClelland, D. C. *The achieving society.* Princeton: Van Nostrand Reinhold, 1961.

McDougall, W. *An introduction to social psychology.* London: Methuen & Co., 1908.

Maslow, A. H. A theory of human motivation. *Psychological Review, 1943,* **50,** 370–396.

Maslow, A. H. *Motivation and personality.* New York: Harper & Row, 1954.

Maslow, A. H. *Toward a psychology of being.* (2nd ed.) Princeton, N.J.: Van Nostrand Reinhold, 1968.

Maslow, A. H. *Motivation and personality.* (2nd ed.) New York: Harper & Row, 1970.

May, R. *Man's search for himself.* New York: W. W. Norton, 1953.

Miles, R. C. Learning in kittens with manipulatory, exploratory, and food incentives. *Journal of Comparative and Physiological Psychology,* 1958, **51,** 39–42.

Murray, E. J. *Motivation and emotion.* Englewood Cliffs, N.J.: Prentice-Hall, 1964.

Murray, H. A. *Explorations in personality.* New York: Oxford University Press, 1938.

Porter, L. W. Job attitudes in management: I. Perceived deficiencies in need fulfillment as a function of job level. *Journal of Applied Psychology,* 1962, **46,** 375–384.

Porter, L. W. Job attitudes in management: II. Perceived importance of needs as a function of job level. *Journal of Applied Psychology,* 1963, **47,** 141–148.

Porter, L. W. *Organizational patterns of managerial job attitudes.* New York: American Foundation for Management Research, 1964.

Porter, L. W., & Lawler, E. E., Properties of organization structure in relation to job attitudes and job behavior. *Psychology Bulletin,* 1965, 64, 23–51.

Rogers, C. R., *On becoming a person.* Boston: Houghton Mifflin, 1961.

Roszak, T., *The making of a counter culture.* Garden City, New York: Doubleday, 1969.

Schachter, S., *The psychology of affiliation.* Stanford, Calif.: Stanford University Press, 1959.

Scott, W. E., The behavioral consequences of repetitive task design: Research and theory. In L. L. Cummings & W. E. Scott (Eds.), *Readings in organizational behavior and human performance.* Homewood, Ill.: Richard D. Irwin, 1969.

Smock, C. D., & Holt, B. G., Children's reactions to novelty: An experimental study of "curiosity motivation," *Child Development.* 1962, 33, 631–642.

Vroom, V. H., *Work and Motivation,* New York: John Wiley & Sons, 1964.

White, R. W., Motivation reconsidered: The concept of competence. *Psychological Review,* 1959, 66, 297–333.

Wolfe, J. B., Effectiveness of token-rewards for chimpanzees. *Comparative Psychology Monograph,* 1936, 12, 15.

Motivation: A Diagnostic Approach

David Nadler

Edward Lawler

What makes some people work hard while others do as little as possible?
How can I, as a manager, influence the performance of people who work for me?
Why do people turn over, show up late to work, and miss work entirely?

These important questions about employees' behavior can only be answered by managers who have a grasp of what motivates people. Specifically, a good understanding of motivation can serve as a valuable tool for *understanding* the causes of behavior in organizations, for *predicting* the effects of any managerial action, and for *directing* behavior so that organizational and individual goals can be achieved.

EXISTING APPROACHES

During the past twenty years, managers have been bombarded with a number of different approaches to motivation. The terms associated with these approaches are well known—"human relations," "scientific management," "job enrichment," "need hierarchy," "self-actualization," etc. Each of these approaches has something to offer. On the other

hand, each of these different approaches also has its problems in both theory and practice. Running through almost all of the approaches with which managers are familiar are a series of implicit but clearly erroneous assumptions.

Assumption 1: All Employees Are Alike Different theories present different ways of looking at people, but each of them assumes that all employees are basically similar in their makeup: Employees all want economic gains, or all want a pleasant climate, or all aspire to be self-actualizing, etc.

Assumption 2: All Situations Are Alike Most theories assume that all managerial situations are alike, and that the managerial course of action for motivation (for example, participation, job enlargement, etc.) is applicable in all situations.

Assumption 3: One Best Way Out of the other two assumptions there emerges a basic principle that there is "one best way" to motivate employees.

When these "one best way" approaches are tried in the "correct" situation they will work. However, all of them are bound to fail in some situations. They are therefore not adequate managerial tools.

A NEW APPROACH

During the past ten years, a great deal of research has been done on a new approach to looking at motivation. This approach, frequently called "expectancy theory," still needs further testing, refining, and extending. However, enough is known that many behavioral scientists have concluded that it represents the most comprehensive, valid, and useful approach to understanding motivation. Further, it is apparent that it is a very useful tool for understanding motivation in organizations.

The theory is based on a number of specific assumptions about the causes of behavior in organizations.

Assumption 1: Behavior Is Determined by a Combination of Forces in the Individual and Forces in the Environment Neither the individual nor the environment alone determines behavior. Individuals come into organizations with certain "psychological baggage." They have past experiences and a developmental history which has given them unique sets of needs, ways of looking at the world, and expectations about how organizations will treat them. These all influence how individuals respond to their work environment. The work environment provides structures (such as a pay system or a supervisor) which influence the behavior of people. Different environments tend to produce different behavior in similar people just as dissimilar people tend to behave differently in similar environments.

Assumption 2: People Make Decisions about Their Own Behavior in Organizations While there are many constraints on the behavior of individuals in organizations, most of the behavior that is observed is the result of individuals' conscious decisions. These decisions usually fall into two categories. First, individuals make decisions about *membership behavior*—coming to work, staying at work, and in other ways being a member of the organization. Second, individuals make decisions about the amount of *effort* they will direct *towards performing their jobs.* This includes decisions about how hard to work, how much to produce, at what quality, etc.

Assumption 3: Different People Have Different Types of Needs, Desires and Goals Individuals differ on what kinds of outcomes (or rewards) they desire. These differences are not random; they can be examined systematically by an understanding of the differences in the strength of individuals' needs.

Assumption 4: People Make Decisions among Alternative Plans of Behavior Based on Their Perceptions (Expectancies) of the Degree to Which a Given Behavior will Lead to Desired Outcomes In simple terms, people tend to do those things which they see as leading to outcomes (which can also be called "rewards") they desire and avoid doing those things they see as leading to outcomes that are not desired.

In general, the approach used here views people as having their own needs and mental maps of what the world is like. They use these maps to make decisions about how they will behave, behaving in those ways which their mental maps indicate will lead to outcomes that will satisfy their needs. Therefore, they are inherently neither motivated nor unmotivated; motivation depends on the situation they are in, and how it fits their needs.

THE THEORY

Based on these general assumptions, expectancy theory states a number of propositions about the process by which people make decisions about their own behavior in organizational settings. While the theory is complex at first view, it is in fact made of a series of fairly straightforward observations about behavior. (The theory is presented in more technical terms in Appendix A.) Three concepts serve as the key building blocks of the theory:

Performance-Outcome Expectancy Every behavior has associated with it, in an individual's mind, certain outcomes (rewards or punishments). In other words, the individual believes or expects that if he or she behaves in a certain way, he or she will get certain things.

Examples of expectancies can easily be described. An individual may have an expectancy that if he produces ten units he will receive his normal hourly rate while if he produces fifteen units he will receive his hourly pay rate plus a bonus. Similarly an individual may believe that certain levels of performance will lead to approval or disapproval from members of her work group or from her supervisor. Each performance can be seen as leading to a number of different kinds of outcomes and outcomes can differ in their types.

Valence Each outcome has a "valence" (value, worth, attractiveness) to a specific individual. Outcomes have different valences for different individuals. This comes about because valences result from individual needs and perceptions, which differ because they in turn reflect other factors in the individual's life.

For example, some individuals may value an opportunity for promotion or advancement because of their needs for achievement or power, while others may not want to be promoted and leave their current work group because of needs for affiliation with others.

Similarly, a fringe benefit such as a pension plan may have great valence for an older worker but little valence for a young employee on his first job.

Effort-Performance Expectancy Each behavior also has associated with it in the individual's mind a certain expectancy or probability of success. This expectancy represents the individual's perception of how hard it will be to achieve such behavior and the probability of his or her successful achievement of that behavior.

For example, you may have a strong expectancy that if you put forth the effort, you can produce ten units an hour, but that you have only a fifty-fifty chance of producing fifteen units an hour if you try.

Putting these concepts together, it is possible to make a basic statement about motivation. In general, the motivation to attempt to behave in a certain way is greatest when:

a. The individual believes that the behavior will lead to outcomes (performance-outcome expectancy)
b. The individual believes that these outcomes have positive value for him or her (valence)
c. The individual believes that he or she is able to perform at the desired level (effort-performance expectancy)

Given a number of alternative levels of behavior (ten, fifteen, and twenty units of production per hour, for example) the individual will choose that level of performance which has the greatest motivational force associated with it, as indicated by the expectancies, outcomes, and valences.

In other words, when faced with choices about behavior, the individual goes through a process of considering questions such as, "Can I perform at that level if I try?" "If I perform at that level, what will happen?" "How do I feel about those things that will happen?" The individual then decides to behave in that way which seems to have the best chance of producing positive, desired outcomes.

A General Model

On the basis of these concepts, it is possible to construct a general model of behavior in organizational settings (see Figure 1). Working from left to right in the model, motivation is seen as the force on the individual to expend effort. Motivation leads to an observed level of effort by the individual. Effort, alone, however, is not enough. Performance results from a combination of the effort that an individual puts forth *and* the level of ability which he or she has (reflecting skills, training, information, etc.) Effort thus combines with ability to produce a given level of performance. As a result of performance, the individual attains certain outcomes. The model indicates this relationship in a dotted line, reflecting the fact that sometimes people perform but do not get desired outcomes. As this process of performance-reward occurs, time after time, the actual events serve to provide information which influences the individual's perceptions (particularly expectancies) and thus influences motivation in the future.

Outcomes, or rewards, fall into two major categories. First, the individual obtains outcomes from the environment. When an individual performs at a given level he or she can receive positive or negative outcomes from supervisors, coworkers, the organization's rewards systems, or other sources. These environmental rewards are thus one source of outcomes for the individual. A second source of outcomes is the individual. These include outcomes which occur purely from the performance of the task itself (feelings of accomplishment, personal worth, achievement, etc.). In a sense, the individual gives these rewards to himself or herself. The environment cannot give them or take them away directly; it can only make them possible.

Supporting Evidence

Over fifty studies have been done to test the validity of the expectancy-theory approach to predicting employee behavior.[1] Almost without exception, the studies have confirmed the predictions of the theory. As the theory predicts, the best performers in organizations tend to see a strong relationship between performing their jobs well and receiving rewards they value. In addition they have clear performance goals and feel they can perform well. Similarly, studies using the expectancy theory to predict how people choose jobs also show that individuals tend to interview for and actually take

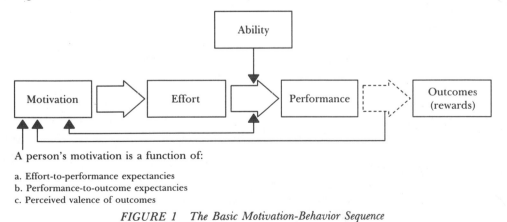

A person's motivation is a function of:

a. Effort-to-performance expectancies
b. Performance-to-outcome expectancies
c. Perceived valence of outcomes

FIGURE 1   The Basic Motivation-Behavior Sequence

those jobs which they feel will provide the rewards they value. One study, for example, was able to correctly predict for 80 percent of the people studied which of several jobs they would take.[2] Finally, the theory correctly predicts that beliefs about the outcomes associated with performance (expectancies) will be better predictors of performance than will feelings of job satisfaction since expectancies are the critical causes of performance and satisfaction is not.

Questions about the Model

Although the results so far have been encouraging, they also indicate some problems with the model. These problems do not critically affect the managerial implications of the model, but they should be noted. The model is based on the assumption that individuals make very rational decisions after a thorough exploration of all the available alternatives and on weighing the possible outcomes of all these alternatives. When we talk to or observe individuals, however, we find that their decision processes are frequently less thorough. People often stop considering alternative behavior plans when they find one that is at least moderately satisfying, even though more rewarding plans remain to be examined.

People are also limited in the amount of information they can handle at one time, and therefore the model may indicate a process that is much more complex than the one that actually takes place. On the other hand, the model does provide enough information and is consistent enough with reality to present some clear implications for managers who are concerned with the question of how to motivate the people who work for them.

Implications for Managers

The first set of implications is directed toward the individual manager who has a group of people working for him or her and is concerned

with how to motivate good performance. Since behavior is a result of forces both in the person and in the environment, you as manager need to look at and diagnose both the person and the environment. Specifically, you need to do the following:

Figure out what outcomes each employee values
As a first step, it is important to determine what kinds of outcomes or rewards have valence for your employees. For each employee you need to determine "what turns him or her on." There are various ways of finding this out, including (a) finding out employees' desires through some structured method of data collection, such as a questionnaire, (b) observing the employees' reactions to different situations or rewards, or (c) the fairly simple act of asking them what kinds of rewards they want, what kind of career goals they have, or "what's in it for them." It is important to stress here that it is very difficult to change what people want, but fairly easy to find out what they want. Thus, the skillful manager emphasizes diagnosis of needs, not changing the individuals themselves.

Determine what kinds of behavior you desire
Managers frequently talk about "good performance" without really defining what good performance is. An important step in motivating is for you yourself to figure out what kinds of performances are required and what are adequate measures or indicators of performance (quantity, quality, etc.). There is also a need to be able to define those performances in fairly specific terms so that observable and measurable behavior can be defined and subordinates can understand what is desired of them (e.g., produce ten products of a certain quality standard—rather than only produce at a high rate).

Make sure desired levels of performance are reachable   The model states that motivation is determined not only by the performance-to-outcome expectancy, but also by the effort-to-performance expectancy. The implication of this is that the levels of performance which are set as the points at which individuals receive desired outcomes must be reachable or attainable by these individuals. If the employees feel that the level of performance required to get a reward is higher than they can reasonably achieve, then their motivation to perform well will be relatively low.

Link desired outcomes to desired performances
The next step is to directly, clearly, and explicitly link those outcomes desired by employees to the specific performances desired by you. If your employee values external rewards, then the emphasis should be on the rewards systems concerned with promotion, pay, and approval. While the linking of these rewards can be initiated through your making statements to your employees, it is extremely important that employees see a clear example of the reward process working in a fairly short period of time if the motivating "expectancies" are to be created in the employees' minds. The linking must be done by some concrete public acts, in addition to statements of intent.

If your employee values internal rewards (e.g., achievement), then you should concentrate on changing the nature of the person's job, for he or she is likely to respond well to such things as increased autonomy, feedback, and challenge, because these things will lead to a situation where good job performance is inherently rewarding. The best way to check on the adequacy of the internal and external reward system is to ask people what their perceptions of the situation are. Remember it is the perceptions of people that determine their motivation, not reality. It doesn't matter for example whether you feel a subordinate's pay is related to his or her motivation. Motivation will be present only if the subordinate sees the relationship. Many managers are misled about the behavior of their subordinates because they

rely on their own perceptions of the situation and forget to find out what their subordinates feel. There is only one way to do this: ask. Questionnaires can be used here, as can personal interviews. (See Appendix B for a short version of a motivation questionnaire.)

Analyze the total situation for conflicting expectancies Having set up positive expectancies for employees, you then need to look at the entire situation to see if other factors (informal work groups, other managers, the organization's reward systems) have set up conflicting expectancies in the minds of the employees. Motivation will only be high when people see a number of rewards associated with good performance and few negative outcomes. Again, you can often gather this kind of information by asking your subordinates. If there are major conflicts, you need to make adjustments, either in your own performance and reward structure, or in the other sources of rewards or punishments in the environment.

Make sure changes in outcomes are large enough In examining the motivational system, it is important to make sure that changes in outcomes or rewards are large enough to motivate significant behavior. Trivial rewards will result in trivial amounts of effort and thus trivial improvements in performance. Rewards must be large enough to motivate individuals to put forth the effort required to bring about significant changes in performance.

Check the system for its equity The model is based on the idea that individuals are different and therefore different rewards will need to be used to motivate different individuals. On the other hand, for a motivational system to work it must be a fair one—one that has equity (not equality). Good performers should see that they get more desired rewards than do poor performers, and others in the system should see that also. Equity should not be confused with a system of equality where all are rewarded equally, with no regard to their performance. A system of equality is guaranteed to produce low motivation.

Implications for Organizations

Expectancy theory has some clear messages for those who run large organizations. It suggests how organizational structures can be designed so that they increase rather than decrease levels of motivation of organization members. While there are many different implications, a few of the major ones are as follows:

Implication 1: The design of pay and reward systems   Organizations usually get what they reward, not what they want. This can be seen in many situations, and pay systems are a good example.[3] Frequently, organizations reward people for membership (through pay tied to seniority, for example) rather than for performance. Little wonder that what the organization gets is behavior oriented towards "safe," secure employment rather than effort directed at performing well. In addition, even where organizations do pay for performance as a motivational device, they frequently negate the motivational value of the system by keeping pay secret, therefore preventing people from observing the pay-to-performance relationship that would serve to create positive, clear, and strong performance-to-reward expectancies. The implication is that organizations should put more effort into rewarding people (through pay, promotion, better job opportunities, etc.) for the performances which are desired, and that to keep these rewards secret is clearly self-defeating. In addition, it underscores the importance of the frequently ignored performance evaluation or appraisal process and the need to evaluate people based on how they perform clearly defined specific behaviors, rather than on how they score on ratings of general traits such as "honesty," "cleanliness," and

other, similar terms which frequently appear as part of the performance appraisal form.

Implication 2: The design of tasks, jobs, and roles   One source of desired outcomes is the work itself. The expectancy-theory model supports much of the job enrichment literature, in saying that by designing jobs which enable people to get their needs fulfilled, organizations can bring about higher levels of motivation.[4] The major difference between the traditional approaches to job enlargement or enrichment and the expectancy-theory approach is the recognition by the expectancy theory that different people have different needs and, therefore, some people may not want enlarged or enriched jobs. Thus, while the design of tasks that have more autonomy, variety, feedback, meaningfulness, etc., will lead to higher motivation in some, the organization needs to build in the opportunity for individuals to make choices about the kind of work they will do so that not everyone is forced to experience job enrichment.

Implication 3: The importance of group structures   Groups, both formal and informal, are powerful and potent sources of desired outcomes for individuals. Groups can provide or withhold acceptance, approval, affection, skill training, needed information, assistance, etc. They are a powerful force in the total motivational environment of individuals. Several implications emerge from the importance of groups. First, organizations should consider the structuring of at least a portion of rewards around group performance rather than individual performance. This is particularly important where group members have to cooperate with each other to produce a group product or service, and where the individual's contribution is often hard to determine. Second, the organization needs to train managers to be aware of how groups can influence individual behavior and to be sensitive to the kinds of expectancies which informal groups set up and their conflict or consistency with the expectancies that the organization attempts to create.

Implication 4: The supervisor's role   The immediate supervisor has an important role in creating, monitoring, and maintaining the expectancies and reward structures which will lead to good performance. The supervisor's role in the motivation process becomes one of defining clear goals, setting clear reward expectancies, and providing the right rewards for different people (which could include both organizational rewards and personal rewards such as recognition, approval, or support from the supervisor). Thus, organizations need to provide supervisors with an awareness of the nature of motivation as well as the tools (control over organizational rewards, skill in administering those rewards) to create positive motivation.

Implication 5: Measuring motivation   If things like expectancies, the nature of the job, supervisor-controlled outcomes, satisfaction, etc., are important in understanding how well people are being motivated, then organizations need to monitor employee perceptions along these lines. One relatively cheap and reliable method of doing this is through standardized employee questionnaires. A number of organizations already use such techniques, surveying employees' perceptions and attitudes at regular intervals (ranging from once a month to once every year-and-a-half) using either standardized surveys or surveys developed specifically for the organization. Such information is useful both to the individual manager and to top management in assessing the state of human resources and the effectiveness of the organization's motivational systems.[5] (Again, see Appendix B for excerpts from a standardized survey.)

Implication 6: Individualizing organizations   Expectancy theory leads to a final general implication about a possible future direction for the design of organizations. Because different people have different needs and therefore have different valences, effective motivation must come through the recognition that not all employees are alike and that organizations need to be flexible in order to accommodate individual differences. This implies the "building in" of choice for employees in many areas, such as reward systems, fringe benefits, job assignments, etc., where employees previously have had little say. A successful example of the building in of such choice can be seen in the experiments at TRW and the Educational Testing Service with "cafeteria fringe-benefits plans" which allow employees to choose the fringe benefits they want, rather than taking the expensive and often unwanted benefits which the company frequently provides to everyone.[6]

SUMMARY

Expectancy theory provides a more complex model of man for managers to work with. At the same time, it is a model which holds promise for the more effective motivation of individuals and the more effective design of organizational systems. It implies, however, the need for more exacting and thorough diagnosis by the manager to determine (a) the relevant forces in the individual, and (b) the relevant forces in the environment, both of which combine to motivate different kinds of behavior. Following diagnosis, the model implies a need to act—to develop a system of pay, promotion, job assignments, group structures, supervision, etc.—to bring about effective motivation by providing different outcomes for different individuals.

Performance of individuals is a critical issue in making organizations work effectively. If a manager is to influence work behavior and performance, he or she must have an understanding of motivation and the factors which influence an individual's motivation to come to work, to work hard, and to work well. While simple models offer easy answers, it is the more complex models which seem to offer more promise. Managers can use models (like expectancy theory) to understand the nature of behavior and build more effective organizations.

APPENDIX A: THE EXPECTANCY THEORY MODEL IN MORE TECHNICAL TERMS

A person's motivation to exert effort towards a specific level of performance is based on his or her perceptions of associations between actions and outcomes. The critical perceptions which contribute to motivation are graphically presented in Figure 2. These perceptions can be defined as follows.

a. The effort-to-performance expectancy $(E \rightarrow P)$: This refers to the person's subjective probability about the likelihood that he or she can perform at a given level, or that effort on his or her part will lead to successful performance. This term can be thought of as varying from 0 to 1. In general, the less likely a person feels that he or she can perform at a given level, the less likely he or she will be to try to perform at that level. A person's $E \rightarrow P$ probabilities are also strongly influenced by each situation and by previous experience in that and similar situations.

b. The performance-to-outcomes expectancy $(P \rightarrow O)$ and valence (V): This refers to a combination of a number of beliefs about what the outcomes of successful performance will be and the value or attractiveness of these outcomes to the individual. Valence is considered to vary from $+1$ (very desirable) to -1 (very undesirable) and the performance-to-outcomes probabilities vary from $+1$ (performance sure to lead to outcome) to 0 (performance not related to outcome). In general, the more likely a person feels that performance will lead to va-

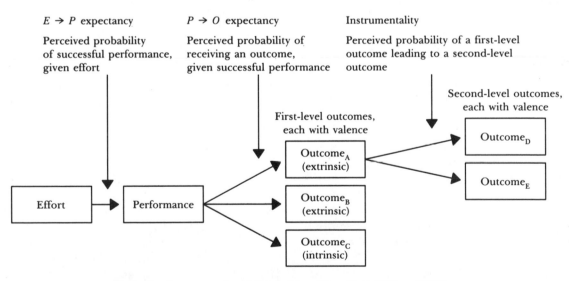

Motivation is expressed as follows: $M = [E \rightarrow P] \times \Sigma[(P \rightarrow O)(V)]$

FIGURE 2.   Major Terms in Expectancy Theory

lent outcomes, the more likely he or she will be to try to perform at the required level.

c. Instrumentality: As Figure 3-2 indicates, a single level of performance can be associated with a number of different outcomes, each having a certain degree of valence. Some outcomes are valent because they have direct value or attractiveness. Some outcomes, however, have valence because they are seen as leading to (or being "instrumental" for) the attainment of other "second level" outcomes which have direct value or attractiveness.

d. Intrinsic and extrinsic outcomes: Some outcomes are seen as occurring directly as a result of performing the task itself and are outcomes which the individual thus gives to himself (i.e., feelings of accomplishment, creativity, etc.). These are called "intrinsic" outcomes. Other outcomes that are associated with performance are provided or mediated by external factors (the organization, the supervisor, the work group, etc.). These outcomes are called "extrinsic" outcomes.

Along with the graphic representation of these terms presented in Figure 2, there is a simplified formula for combining these perceptions to arrive at a term expressing the relative level of motivation to exert effort towards performance at a given level. The formula expresses these relationships:

a. The person's motivation to perform is determined by the $P \to O$ expectancy multiplied by the valence (V) of the outcome. The valence of the first order outcome subsumes the instrumentalities and valences of second order outcomes. The relationship is multiplicative since there is no motivation to perform if either of the terms is zero.

b. Since a level of performance has multiple outcomes associated with it, the products of all probability-times-valence combinations are added together for all the outcomes that are seen as related to the specific performance.

c. This term (the summed $P \to O$ expectancies times valences) is then multiplied by the $E \to P$ expectancy. Again the multiplicative relationship indicates that if either term is zero, motivation is zero.

d. In summary, the strength of a person's motivation to perform effectively is influenced by (1) the person's belief that effort can be converted into performance, and (2) the net attractiveness of the events that are perceived to stem from good performance.

So far, all the terms have referred to the individual's perceptions which result in motivation and thus an intention to behave in a certain way. Figure 3 is a simplified representation of the total model, showing how these intentions get translated into actual behavior.[7] The model envisions the following sequence of events:

a. First, the strength of a person's motivation to perform correctly is most directly reflected in his or her effort—how hard he or she works. This effort expenditure may or may not result in good performance, since at least two factors must be right if effort is to be converted into performance. First, the person must possess the necessary abilities in order to perform the job well. Unless both ability and effort are high, there cannot be good performance. A second factor is the person's perception of how his or her effort can best be converted into performance. It is assumed that this perception is learned by the individual on the basis of previous experience in similar situations. This "how to do it" perception can obviously vary widely in accuracy,

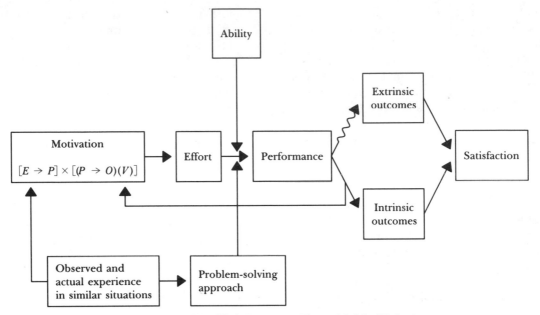

FIGURE 3.   Simplified Expectancy-Theory Model of Behavior

and—where erroneous perceptions exist—performance is low even though effort or motivation may be high.

b.   Second, when performance occurs, certain amounts of outcomes are obtained by the individual. Intrinsic outcomes, not being mediated by outside forces, tend to occur regularly as a result of performance, while extrinsic outcomes may or may not accrue to the individual (indicated by the wavy line in the model).

c.   Third, as a result of the obtaining of outcomes and the perceptions of the relative value of the outcomes obtained, the individual has a positive or negative affective response (a level of satisfaction or dissatisfaction).

d.   Fourth, the model indicates that events which occur influence future behavior by altering the $E{\rightarrow}P$, $P{\rightarrow}O$, and V perceptions. This process is represented by the feedback loops running from actual behavior back to motivation.

APPENDIX B: MEASURING MOTIVATION USING EXPECTANCY THEORY

Expectancy theory suggests that it is useful to measure the attitudes individuals have in order to diagnose motivational problems. Such measurement helps the manager to understand why employees are motivated or not, what the strength of motivation is in different parts of the organization, and how effective different rewards are for motivating performance. A short version of a questionnaire used to measure motivation in organizations is included here.[8] Basically, three different questions need to be asked (see Tables 1, 2, and 3).

Using the Questionnaire Results

The results from this questionnaire can be used to calculate a *work-motivation score*. A score can be calculated for each individual and scores can be combined for groups of individuals. The

TABLE 1. **Question 1:** *Here are some things that could happen to people if they do their jobs* especially well. *How likely is it that each of these things would happen if you performed your job* especially well?

		Not at all Likely		Somewhat Likely		Quite Likely		Extremely Likely
a	You will get a bonus or pay increase	(1)	(2)	(3)	(4)	(5)	(6)	(7)
b	You will feel better about yourself as a person	(1)	(2)	(3)	(4)	(5)	(6)	(7)
c	You will have an opportunity to develop your skills and abilities	(1)	(2)	(3)	(4)	(5)	(6)	(7)
d	You will have better job security	(1)	(2)	(3)	(4)	(5)	(6)	(7)
e	You will be given chances to learn new things	(1)	(2)	(3)	(4)	(5)	(6)	(7)
f	You will be promoted or get a better job	(1)	(2)	(3)	(4)	(5)	(6)	(7)
g	You will get a feeling that you've accomplished something worthwhile	(1)	(2)	(3)	(4)	(5)	(6)	(7)
h	You will have more freedom on your job	(1)	(2)	(3)	(4)	(5)	(6)	(7)
i	You will be respected by the people you work with	(1)	(2)	(3)	(4)	(5)	(6)	(7)
j	Your supervisor will praise you	(1)	(2)	(3)	(4)	(5)	(6)	(7)
k	The people you work with will be friendly with you	(1)	(2)	(3)	(4)	(5)	(6)	(7)

TABLE 2. **Question 2:** *Different people want different things from their work. Here is a list of things a person could have on his or her job. How* important *is each of the following to you?*

		Moderately Important or Less			Quite Important		Extremely Important
	How Important Is . . . ?						
a	The amount of pay you get	(1)	(2)	(3)	(4)	(5)	(6)	(7)
b	The chances you have to do something that makes you feel good about yourself as a person	(1)	(2)	(3)	(4)	(5)	(6)	(7)
c	The opportunity to develop your skills and abilities	(1)	(2)	(3)	(4)	(5)	(6)	(7)
d	The amount of job security you have	(1)	(2)	(3)	(4)	(5)	(6)	(7)
	How Important Is . . . ?						
e	The chances you have to learn new things	(1)	(2)	(3)	(4)	(5)	(6)	(7)
f	Your chances for getting a promotion or getting a better job	(1)	(2)	(3)	(4)	(5)	(6)	(7)
g	The chances you have to accomplish something worthwhile	(1)	(2)	(3)	(4)	(5)	(6)	(7)
h	The amount of freedom you have on your job	(1)	(2)	(3)	(4)	(5)	(6)	(7)
	How Important Is . . . ?						
i	The respect you receive from the people you work with	(1)	(2)	(3)	(4)	(5)	(6)	(7)
j	The praise you get from your supervisor	(1)	(2)	(3)	(4)	(5)	(6)	(7)
k	The friendliness of the people you work with	(1)	(2)	(3)	(4)	(5)	(6)	(7)

TABLE 3.   **Question 3:** *Below you will see a number of pairs of factors that look like this:*

Warm weather→sweating   (1) (2) (3) (4) (5) (6) (7)

You are to indicate by checking the appropriate number to the right of each pair how often it is true for *you* personally that the first factor leads to the second on *your job.* Remember, for each pair, indicate how often it is true by checking the box under the response which seems most accurate.

	Never		Sometimes		Often		Almost Always
a Working hard → high productivity	(1)	(2)	(3)	(4)	(5)	(6)	(7)
b Working hard → doing my job well	(1)	(2)	(3)	(4)	(5)	(6)	(7)
c Working hard → good job performance	(1)	(2)	(3)	(4)	(5)	(6)	(7)

procedure for obtaining a work-motivation score is as follows:

a. For each of the possible positive outcomes listed in questions 1 and 2, multiply the score for the outcome on question 1 ($P \to O$ expectancies) by the corresponding score on question 2 (valences of outcomes). Thus, score 1a would be multiplied by score 2a, score 1b by score 2b, etc.

b. All of the 1 times 2 products should be added together to get a total of all expectancies times valences _____.

c. The total should be divided by the number of pairs (in this case, eleven) to get an average expectancy-times-valence score _____.

d. The scores from question 3 ($E \to P$ expectancies) should be added together and then divided by three to get an average effort-to-performance expectancy score _____.

e. Multiply the score obtained in step c (the average expectancy times valence) by the score obtained in step d (the average $E \to P$ expectancy score) to obtain a total work-motivation score _____

Additional Comments on the Work-Motivation Score

A number of important points should be kept in mind when using the questionnaire to get a work-motivation score. First, the questions presented here are just a short version of a larger and more comprehensive questionnaire. For more detail, the articles and publications referred to here and in the text should be consulted. Second, this is a general questionnaire. Since it is hard to anticipate in a general questionnaire what may be valent outcomes in each situation, the individual manager may want to add additional outcomes to questions 1 and 2. Third, it is important to remember that questionnaire results can be influenced by the feelings people have when they fill out the questionnaire. The use of the questionnaire as outlined above assumes a certain level of trust between manager and subordinates. People filling out questionnaires need to know what is going to be done with their answers and usually need to be assured of the confidentiality of their responses. Finally, the research indicates that, in many cases, the score obtained by simply averaging all the responses to question 1 (the $P \to O$ expectancies) will be as useful as the fully calculated work-motivation score. In each situation, the manager should experiment and find out whether the additional information in questions 2 and 3 aid in motivational diagnosis.

NOTES

1. For reviews of the expectancy theory research see Mitchell, T. R. Expectancy models of job satisfaction, occupational preference and effort:

A theoretical methodological, and empirical appraisal. *Psychological Bulletin,* 1974, **81,** 1053–1077. For a more general discussion of expectancy theory and other approaches to motivation see Lawler, E. E. *Motivation in work organizations,* Belmont Calif.: Brooks/Cole, 1973.

2. Lawler, E. E., Kuleck, W. J., Rhode, J. G., & Sorenson, J. E. Job choice and post-decision dissonance. *Organizational Behavior and Human Performance,* 1975, 13, 133–145.

3. For a detailed discussion of the implications of expectancy theory for pay and reward systems, see Lawler, E. E. *Pay and organizational effectiveness: A psychological view.* New York: McGraw-Hill, 1971.

4. A good discussion of job design with an expectancy theory perspective is in Hackman, J. R., Oldham, G. R., Janson, R., & Purdy, K. A new strategy for job enrichment. *California Management Review,* Summer, 1975, p. 57.

5. The use of questionnaires for understanding and changing organizational behavior is discussed in Nadler, D. A. *Feedback and organizational development: Using data-based methods.* Reading, Mass.: Addison-Wesley, 1977.

6. The whole issue of individualizing organizations is examined in Lawler, E. E. The individualized organization: Problems and promise. *California Management Review,* 1974, **17**(2), 31–39.

7. For a more detailed statement of the model see Lawler, E. E. Job attitudes and employee motivation: Theory, research and practice. *Personnel Psychology,* 1970, 23, 223–237.

8. For a complete version of the questionnaire and supporting documentation see Nadler, D. A., Cammann, C., Jenkins, G. D., & Lawler, E. E. (Eds.) *The Michigan organizational assessment package* (Progress Report II). Ann Arbor: Survey Research Center, 1975.

Commitment and the Control of Organizational Behavior and Belief

Gerald R. Salancik

Most articles on organizational commitment extol the virtues of commitment. In them, you will find that the committed employee is the happy employee, the success of the organization is a matter of its members sacrificing their time and effort, and commitment to the values of the organization gives meaning to a person's life. In them commitment enhances productivity, assures quality in the final product, and guarantees the flow of adaptive innovation. In them, you will find, in short, a lot of nonsense mixed with a lot of common sense. But from them your understanding of commitment may not be enhanced. . . .

The view of commitment we present in this paper is one which is grounded in behavior and the implications of behavior in one situation for behavior in another. The view derives primarily from the model of commitment developed by Kiesler (1971), with intellectual roots going back to Festinger (1957; 1964) and Lewin (1947). We borrow considerably from Kiesler's work, and deviate in significant ways. As a working definition, "commitment is the binding of the individual to behavioral acts" (Kiesler and Sakumura, 1966). The important words are "binding" and "acts."

To act is to commit oneself. A person may talk about how important it is to keep the population growth rate down, but to be sterilized is to give eloquent, unshakeable force to the statement. An adulterer may proclaim unrelenting devotion to a lover, but to give up children, home, and joint bank accounts is to put meaning into the proclamation. Thus, at a minimum, a concept of commitment implies that behavior, or action, be a central focus.

DETERMINANTS OF COMMITMENT

While action is a necessary ingredient in commitment, all behaviors are not equally committing. There are degrees of commitment. A statement of a belief or attitude is a less committing action than the signing of a petition in favor of the belief, which in turn is less committing than actively advocating the belief to a hostile or skeptical audience.

The degree of commitment derives from the extent to which a person's behaviors are binding. Four characteristics of behavioral acts make them binding, and hence determine the extent of commitment: explicitness; revocability; volition; and publicity. The first is the *explicitness* or deniability of the act, and concerns the extent to which an action can be said to have taken place. Two contributors to explicitness are the observability of the act and the unequivocality of the act. Some acts are not observable and we may know them only by inference from assumed consequences. You leave a dollar bill on a checkout counter, turn away for a moment, then find it missing. The consequence is obvious, but do you know if the customer next to you took it or if it was carried away by a draft from the open door? Acts themselves can be equivocal, forgotten, or otherwise intractable. A person who says, "I sometimes think . . ." is behaving more equivocally than one who says, "I think. . . ."

A second characteristic of behavior affecting commitment is the *revocability* or reversibility of the action. Some actions are like trials. We try them out, see how they fit with us, and if they don't suit us we change our minds and do something else. Few actions are really irreversible. Even a vasectomy can be undone. Promises can be made and broken. Jobs can be quit. Marriages can be dissolved; engagements, broken. Contracts can be torn up. On the other hand, some actions are permanent and having occurred, they cannot be undone. They are committing. Slapping someone in the face can be excused, forgiven, forgotten or reciprocated, but it cannot be taken back. Consumption of food or drink may be regretted but not reversed. Pulling the trigger of a loaded gun pointed at a friend commits all to its gross reality.

The explicitness and irrevocability of an act link action to an indelible reality. *Volition,* a third characteristic of committing behaviors, links action to the individual. This is one of the more difficult characteristics of human action to define precisely, and is frequently associated with such concepts as freedom and personal responsibility. What makes definition difficult is that all human action is both free and constrained, being done under one's own volition and in response to contingencies. Even the most seemingly free and personal action can be

perceived as constrained. Artists and writers, such as Dostoevski and George Bernard Shaw, describe their acts of creation as the result of compulsions and external forces. And even the most seemingly constrained acts can be considered free. A person with a gun to his head ultimately is free to choose, whether to comply or accept the consequences of noncompliance. The perception of volition, moreover, can vary with the consequences that follow acts. A manager who takes a decision which turns out to be a disaster for his firm may make every effort to divest himself of responsibility. And one can observe in the annual reports of most corporations the following simple relationship. When sales increase from the previous year, the annual report points out how management's ingenious investments and development programs are paying off; when, the next year, sales decrease, an astounding downturn in the economy is lugubriously noted.

Despite difficulties in developing a precise concept of volition, volition wields powerful influences on the attitudes and behaviors of people, at least in Western culture. Some major characteristics found to relate to the degree of perceived volition of action are: (1) choice; (2) the presence of external demands for action; (3) the presence of extrinsic bases for action; and (4) the presence of other contributors to action. Thus a person who works hard in order to make a lot of money is not perceived as having as much volition as a person who works hard for nothing. A person who works hard because his superior stands over him constantly is not perceived as having as much volition as one who does as much on his own. With regard to choice, a person who buys a Ford because that is the only car available for sale is not perceived as having as much volition as one who passes over a hundred other models to make the same purchase. . . .

A fourth characteristic of action affecting commitment is the *publicity* or publicness of the act. This characteristic links the action into a social context. While all action and behavior is by definition observable, publicity refers to the extent to which others know of the action and the kinds of persons who know of it. Some audiences are unimportant to us, as are their observations of our behavior. One of the simplest ways to commit yourself to a course of action is to go around telling all your friends that you are definitely going to do something. You will find yourself bound by your own statements. The same commitment will not develop from proclamations to strangers you meet on trains. The publicity of one's action places the action in a social context which is more or less binding and, as we shall describe, contributes to directing the effect of those behaviors on subsequent behaviors. . . .

COMMITMENT TO ORGANIZATIONS

A careless interpretation of the consistency assumption might lead one to infer that having chosen to join an organization or to do a job, individuals will be willing to stay with it and be quite satisfied. After all, one implication of taking a job is that the person likes it. Choice, however, is not enough. The choice itself must be committing. The person must be bound to this choice. . . .

Sacrifice and Initiation Rites

Some organizations prefer not to leave a member's commitment to the happenstance of his own decision process. Corporations frequently publicize the decisions of their new managers. The *Wall Street Journal* is crammed with advertisements by companies announcing that a particular individual has joined their firm, an act giving instant status to the manager's new role. Friends and past associates call in their congratulations and set into motion a climate of

expectation that he is part of that firm. In recent years, insurance companies have been taking full spreads in such magazines as *Time* and *Newsweek* to publish the pictures of their sales personnel. Western Electric has done the same with television scans of their employees working on the job. For a few hundred dollars, an individual is identified with the organization. Next-door neighbors rush to ask, "Say, is this you?" One implication of the advertisement to both the employee and his friends is that the company really cares about its employees, and as a consequence it becomes more and more difficult to complain about it to friends. Harvard Business School uses a particularly effective method of maintaining long-term commitment from its graduates. Entering MBAs are immediately assigned to a group of classmates. This class does everything together from then on. They live in the same dormitories, hear the same lectures, and take the same exams. Virtually everything is scheduled for the class as a whole. Within each class, individuals are identified by namecards so that everyone knows the name of everyone else and is referred to by name in classroom discussions. Twenty years later, when the individuals have long departed the ivy-draped halls, the social network created there continues to operate. One of the things it is used for is to drum donations to the "B School," as it is fondly called.

In addition to advertising a person's commitment, some organizations take pains to make sure the individual is aware he has made a decision. Like the experiments with a well-constructed social psychological choice manipulation, the new employer commits the beginner: "Now, we want to be sure you're taking this job because you want to. We know you've given up a lot to come here and we're grateful. You left your home, your old friends. It must have been very difficult for you. And the salary we're offering, while more than you were making, is never enough to compensate for that."

The idea of giving up something to join

the organization is one exploited in many ways. A common form is the initiation rites which still persist in college fraternities and sororities, fraternal clubs like the Masons or Elks, prisons, military organizations, revolutionary cadres, communal living experiments, police academies and religious organizations, orders and cults. An important part of the initiation process is the forcing of a sacrifice, in which members are asked to give up something as a price of membership (Kanter, 1968). College fraternities require pledges to do hours of push-ups, to take verbal abuse, to have their privileges restricted, to accept subservient roles; in the end, those who endure love it. The effect is obvious. The individual in order to give meaning to his sacrifices is left to conclude they were made because of his devotion to the organization, a conclusion made more likely by his public pledge to enter the organization out of his own choosing. Other organizations have less colorful forms of sacrifice. Exclusive country clubs require their new members to make large initial donations in addition to yearly fees. The donations themselves provide for no services, and members pay for almost all services. But having given up an initial thousand, or a few thousand dollars, members feel a certain compulsion to spend $3.00 for a martini at the club's bar rather than half that at a public lounge.

Investments and Tenure

Many organizations do not exploit the idea of sacrifice as a price of membership. Instead they emphasize the instrumental or exchange bases for participation. Members are hired rather than invited into the organization. Commitment under such circumstances will obviously be more difficult.

Studies on commitment to organizations that emphasize the instrumental bases for membership—work organizations—have consistently found two factors as most reliably re-

lated to commitment. The two factors are position in the organization and tenure with the organization. Study after study on the issue comes down to: People with good jobs are willing to stay in them, and, the longer a person has been with an organization, the more he wants to stay. Unfortunately, most of the studies were done in such ways that it is difficult, and in many cases impossible, to interpret the meaning of the findings.

The relationship of tenure to organizational commitment is predictable from the model of commitment presented in this chapter and has been discussed in a related manner. Howard Becker (1960) suggested that individuals build up commitment over time through certain "side-bets" they make in the organization. One obvious form of accumulation investments in an organization is the build-up of pension benefits and credits over the course of a lifetime. Until recently, such employee benefits, often called the "golden padlock," were not transferable from one organization to another. If an individual terminated in one organization, he lost some of his future wealth or security and had to begin accumulating it again in another organization. The costs of leaving the organization thus increase the longer one's involvement and one becomes more and more likely to continue where one is.

Regardless of financial investments, mobility also declines with tenure in an organization. As time goes by, one becomes less employable. And one's expertise becomes increasingly specific to one's current organization. Some organizations purposely manipulate the costs of leaving for some individuals. Universities will promote some of their assistant professors at rapid rates, making it more costly for other organizations to entice them away. Some business organizations will give young managers attractive positions unusual for their age, knowing it would be difficult for them to obtain equivalent offers elsewhere and also knowing it is cheaper to buy their commitment at an early age than it would be when they become industry hot-shots. . . .

WORK ENVIRONMENTS AND ORGANIZATIONAL COMMITMENT

Thus far we have discussed commitment to the organization as the result of the constraints on an individual's ability to leave the organization, and the extent to which the individual himself has made a definite and committing choice. In reading this over, one gets the feeling that commitment to an organization is an entrapment: an individual is either cut off from other alternatives because no one else wants him or because his own situation doesn't allow him to change it. Thus, individuals rarely make job changes involving moves when their children are entrenched in a school. In all, it is a rather negative view of commitment. You are committed because the facts of your life have bound you.

What about more positive features? Do people become committed to their jobs because they are attracted to them and find them enjoyable? The research on this issue is unimpressive. Much is based on termination interviews which find that workers who quit say they quit because they didn't like the job or the pay. Having taken so decisive a step, it would be rather amusing to find them saying that they loved the job. Studies attempting to predict employee turnover or absenteeism from prior reports of job satisfaction have been notoriously unsuccessful from a practical point of view; that is, the studies report statistically reliable relationships of so low a magnitude that they predict little about behavior. Even superior measurement techniques do poorly (Newman, 1974).

The typical relationship found between job attitudes and turnover or absenteeism is clouded by other factors. We have already discussed that one of these factors is the tenure of the employee. Job satisfaction increases with age and tenure, as does commitment to the organization (see Grupp and Richards, 1975; Organ and Greene, 1974; Gow, Clark, and Dossett, 1974 for illustrative studies). Where investigators have bothered to make the necessary causal analyses, they have found that the change is a "real" one and not simply a function of changes in position, jobs, or salary (Stagner, 1975). As a person becomes more experienced in what he does he becomes more able to cope with the negative and positive features of his job. . . .

Commitment and Job Features

Despite the rather unpredictable relationship between job attitudes, absenteeism, turmoil, and turnover, the model of commitment presented here does suggest that certain features of a person's job situation will affect his commitment. In general, any characteristic of a person's job situation which reduces his felt responsibility will reduce his commitment. As for the relationship between commitment and satisfaction, our own view is that enjoyment is more likely to follow commitment than the reverse.

Many characteristics of job situations can affect a person's perception of responsibility. Some positions simply carry more responsibility, and persons in higher positions tend to be more committed. Similarly, some jobs offer more discretion and self-determination to their occupants, and it has been found that employees in autonomous positions generally have more favorable attitudes than those with little freedom to decide how to do their jobs (Hackman and Lawler, 1971; Hackman and Oldham, 1974).

In addition to the job and the freedom it permits, the manner by which the job is supervised or monitored can affect perceptions of responsibility. The supervisor who stands over a subordinate provides an excuse for the subordinate's behavior. When unpleasant aspects of the job become apparent, rather than coping with them, and finding some joy in the job, the subordinate can attribute his endurance to the supervisor's tenacious pressure. Lepper and Greene (1975) found that surveillance deteriorates interest in a task. Zanna (1970) found that when students are led to believe they worked very hard for a nasty supervisor, they enjoyed the task more than when they worked very hard for a nice supervisor. When they work for a nice person they attribute their effort to their liking for him, not the job. This would be an unrealistic attribution to a nasty boss, so they like the job more.

If a supervisor merely stands by without taking an active part in determining the subordinate's behavior, his presence may serve to reinforce the subordinate's felt responsibility. Maguire and Ouchi (1975) found that close output supervision improves employee satisfaction but that close behavioral supervision does not. Monitoring and providing an individual with feedback about his work performance can increase a person's felt responsibility. The person, knowing his outcomes and knowing his outcomes are known by others, may become more aware that the outcomes are his responsibility. Hackman and Oldham (1974) found worker's perception of responsibility was in part a function of feedback about their performance. While the precise effects of various supervisory conditions on commitment have not been well studied, we would expect that high output monitoring coupled with low behavioral control would lead to the greatest felt responsibility on the part of the worker. Whether or not these conditions will lead to greater satisfaction, would depend on whether or not the worker can handle the task. Maguire and Ouchi (1975) found more satisfaction among monitored workers who could do their jobs without depending on others (i.e., low interdependence), than those who could not.

Commitment also derives from the relation of an employee's job to those of others in the organization. Some jobs are rather isolated and can be done independently of other jobs in the organization. It has been found that jobs which are not integrated with the work activities of others tend to be associated with less favorable attitudes (Shepherd, 1973). Gow, Clark and Dossett (1974), for instance, find that telephone operators who quit tend to be those who are not integrated into the work group. Work integration can affect commitment by the fact that integrated jobs are likely to be associated with salient demands from others in the organization. If a person has a job which affects the work of others in the organization, it is likely that those others will communicate their expectations for performance of that job. Such expectations can be committing in that the other people implicitly or explicitly hold the person accountable for what he does. Earlier we mentioned that when individuals did not know what was expected of them they tended to be less committed to the organization. One reason an individual will not know what is expected is because no one is telling him. In general, we would expect that anything which contributes to creating definite expectations for a person's behavior would enhance his felt responsibility, and hence commitment. Integration may be one such contributor.

Perhaps the most pervasive condition of a job which affects commitment is its instrumentality, the fact that work is a means to some other end. While all jobs in industrial and commercial organizations are done in exchange for salary, there are perhaps great variations in the extent to which the instrumental basis for the work is salient or not. In general, we would expect that when the instrumental basis for work is salient it will reduce a person's felt responsibility. The attribution, "I am doing this job only for the money," should inhibit commitment. A similar point was raised by Ingham (1970), who analyzed absenteeism and turnover in light engineering firms in Bradford, England. Observing that larger organizations had more absenteeism (but lower turnover), he argued that workers were attracted to large firms because of the higher pay offered, but that this instrumental orientation led to little personal involvement with the organization. . . .

There is far too little empirical work on the nature of commitment to jobs, and how features of the work situation lead to or detract from feelings of personal responsibility for work. Much more detailed accountings of the particulars of job situations need to be made.

REFERENCES

Becker, H. S. Notes on the concept of commitment. *American Journal of Sociology,* 1960, 66, 32–40.

Festinger, L. *A theory of cognitive dissonance.* Stanford, Calif.: Stanford University Press, 1957.

Festinger, L. *Conflict, decision, and dissonance.* Stanford, Calif.: Stanford University Press, 1964.

Gow, J. S., Clark, A. W., & Dossett, G. S. A path analysis of variables influencing labour turnover. *Human Relations,* 1974, 27, 703–19.

Hackman, J. R., & Lawler, E. E. Employee reactions to job characteristics. *Journal of Applied Psychology,* 1971, 55, 259–86.

Hackman, J. R., & Oldham, G. R. Motivation through the design of work: Test of a theory. Technical Report no. 6, Administrative Sciences, Yale University, 1974.

Ingham, G. K. *Size of industrial organizations and worker behavior.* Cambridge: Cambridge University Press, 1970.

Kanter, R. M. Commitment and social organizations. *American Sociological Review,* 1968.

Kiesler, C. A. *The psychology of commitment: Experiments linking behavior to belief.* New York: Academic Press, 1971.

Kiesler, C. A., & Sakumura, J. A test of a model for commitment. *Journal of Personality and Social Psychology,* 1966, 3, 349–53.

Lepper, M. R., Greene, D., & Nisbett, R. E. Undermining children's intrinsic interest with extrinsic rewards: A test of the "overjustification" hypothesis. *Journal of Personality and Social Psychology,* 1973, 28, 129–37.

Lewin, K. Group decision and social change. In T. M. Newcomb and E. L. Hartley (Eds.), *Readings in social psychology.* New York: Holt, Rinehart & Winston, 1947, pp. 330–44.

Maguire, M. A., & Ouchi, W. Organizational control and work satisfaction. Research Paper no. 278, Graduate School of Business, Stanford University, 1975.

Newman, J. E. Predicting absenteeism and turnover: A field comparison of Fishbein's model and traditional job attitude measures. *Journal of Applied Psychology,* 1974, 59, 610–15.

Organ, D. W., & Greene, N. The perceived purposefulness of job behavior: Antecedents and consequences. *Academy of Management Journal,* 1974, 17, 69–78.

Stagner, R. Boredom on the assembly line: Age and personality variables. *Industrial Gerontology,* 1975, 21, 23–44.

Zanna, M. P. Attitude inference in a low choice setting. Ph.D. dissertation, Yale University, 1970.

8

MANAGING INDIVIDUAL BEHAVIOR

A New Strategy for Job Enrichment

J. Richard Hackman

Greg Oldham

Robert Janson

Kenneth Purdy

Practitioners of job enrichment have been living through a time of excitement, even euphoria. Their craft has moved from the psychology and management journals to the front page and the Sunday supplement. Job enrichment, which began with the pioneering work of Herzberg and his associates, originally was intended as a means to increase the motivation and satisfaction of people at work—and to improve productivity in the bargain.[1-5] Now it is being acclaimed in the popular press as a cure for problems ranging from inflation to drug abuse.

Much current writing about job enrichment is enthusiastic, sometimes even messianic, about what it can accomplish. But the hard questions of exactly what should be done to improve jobs, and how, tend to be glossed over. Lately, because the harder questions have not been dealt with adequately, critical winds have begun to blow. Job enrichment has been described as yet another "management fad," as "nothing new," even as a fraud. And reports of job-enrichment failures are beginning to appear in management and psychology journals.

This article attempts to redress the excesses that have characterized some of the recent writings about job enrichment. As the technique increases in popularity as a management tool, top managers inevitably will find themselves making decisions about its use. The intent of this paper is to help both managers and behavioral scientists become better able to make those decisions on a solid basis of fact and data.

Succinctly stated, we present here a new strategy for going about the redesign of work. The strategy is based on three years of collaborative work and cross-fertilization among the authors—two of whom are academic researchers and two of whom are active practitioners in job enrichment. Our approach is new, but it has been tested in many organizations. It draws on the contributions of both management practice and psychological theory, but it is firmly in the middle ground between them. It builds on and complements previous work by Herzberg and others, but provides for the first time a set of tools for *diagnosing* existing jobs—and a map for translating the diagnostic results into specific action steps for change.

What we have, then, is the following:

1. A theory that specifies when people will get personally "turned on" to their work. The theory shows what kinds of jobs are most likely to generate excitement and commitment about work, and what kinds of employees it works best for.
2. A set of action steps for job enrichment based on the theory, which prescribe in concrete terms what to do to make jobs more motivating for the people who do them.
3. Evidence that the theory holds water and that it can be used to bring about measurable—and sometimes dramatic—improvements in employee work behavior, in job satisfaction and in the financial performance of the organizational unit involved.

THE THEORY BEHIND THE STRATEGY

What Makes People Get Turned on to Their Work?

For workers who are really prospering in their jobs, work is likely to be a lot like play. Con-

sider, for example, a golfer at a driving range, practicing to get rid of a hook. His activity is *meaningful* to him; he has chosen to do it because he gets a "kick" from testing his skills by playing the game. He knows that he alone is *responsible* for what happens when he hits the ball. And he has *knowledge of the results* within a few seconds.

Behavioral scientists have found that the three "psychological states" experienced by the golfer in the above example also are critical in determining a person's motivation and satisfaction on the job.

1. *Experienced meaningfulness:* The individual must perceive his work as worthwhile or important by some system of values he accepts.
2. *Experienced responsibility:* He must believe that he personally is accountable for the outcomes of his efforts.
3. *Knowledge of results:* He must be able to determine, on some fairly regular basis, whether or not the outcomes of his work are satisfactory.

When these three conditions are present, a person tends to feel very good about himself when he performs well. And those good feelings will prompt him to try to continue to do well—so he can continue to earn the positive feelings in the future. That is what is meant by "internal motivation"—being turned on to one's work because of the positive internal feelings that are generated by doing well, rather than being dependent on external factors (such as incentive pay or compliments from the boss) for the motivation to work effectively.

What if one of the three psychological states is missing? Motivation drops markedly. Suppose, for example, that our golfer has settled in at the driving range to practice for a couple of hours. Suddenly a fog drifts in over the range. He can no longer see if the ball starts to tail off to the left a hundred yards out. The satisfaction he got from hitting straight down the middle—and the motivation to try to correct something whenever he didn't—are both gone. If the fog stays, it's likely that he soon will be packing up his clubs.

The relationship between the three psychological states and on-the-job outcomes is illustrated in Figure 1. When all three are high, then internal work motivation, job satisfaction, and work quality are high, and absenteeism and turnover are low.

What Job Characteristics Make It Happen?

Recent research has identified five "core" characteristics of jobs that elicit the psychological states described above.[6–8] These five core job dimensions provide the key to objectively mea-

suring jobs and to changing them so that they have high potential for motivating people who do them.

Toward Meaningful Work. Three of the five core dimensions contribute to a job's meaningfulness for the worker:

1. Skill variety—the degree to which a job requires the worker to perform activities that challenge his skills and abilities. When even a single skill is involved, there is at least a seed of potential meaningfulness. When several are involved, the job has the potential of appealing to more of the whole person, and also of avoiding the monotony of performing the same task repeatedly, no matter how much skill it may require.

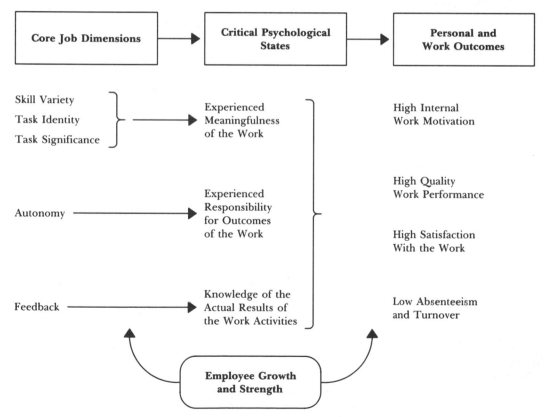

FIGURE 1.   Relationships Among Core Job Dimensions, Critical Psychological States, and On-the-job Outcomes

2. Task identity—the degree to which the job requires completion of a "whole" and identifiable piece of work—doing a job from beginning to end with a visible outcome. For example, it is clearly more meaningful to an employee to build complete toasters than to attach electrical cord after electrical cord, especially if he never sees a completed toaster. (Note that the whole job, in this example, probably would involve greater skill variety as well as task identity.)

3. Task significance—the degree to which the job has a substantial and perceivable impact on the lives of other people, whether in the immediate organization or the world at large. The worker who tightens nuts on aircraft brake assemblies is more likely to perceive his work as significant than the worker who fills small boxes with paper clips—even though the skill levels involved may be comparable.

Each of these three job dimensions represents an important route to experienced meaningfulness. If the job is high in all three, the worker is quite likely to experience his job as very meaningful. It is not necessary, however, for a job to be very high in all three dimensions. If the job is low in any one of them, there will be a drop in overall experienced meaningfulness. But even when two dimensions are low the worker may find the job meaningful if the third is high enough.

Toward Personal Responsibility.   A fourth core dimension leads a worker to experience increased responsibility in his job. This is *autonomy,* the degree to which the job gives the worker freedom, independence, and discretion in scheduling work and determining how he will carry it out. People in highly autonomous jobs know that they are personally responsible for successes and failures. To the extent that their autonomy is high, then, how the work goes will be felt to depend more on the individual's own efforts and initiatives—rather than on detailed instructions from the boss or from a manual of job procedures.

Toward Knowledge of Results.   The fifth and last core dimension is *feedback.* This is the degree to which a worker, in carrying out the work activities required by the job, gets information about the effectiveness of his efforts. Feedback is most powerful when it comes directly from the work itself—for example, when a worker has the responsibility for gauging and otherwise checking a component he has just finished, and learns in the process that he has lowered his reject rate by meeting specifications more consistently.

The Overall 'Motivating Potential' of a Job.   Figure 1 shows how the five core dimensions combine to affect the psychological states that are critical in determining whether or not an employee will be internally motivated to work effectively. Indeed, when using an instrument to be described later, it is possible to compute a "motivating potential score" (MPS) for any job. The MPS provides a single summary index of the degree to which the objective characteristics of the job will prompt high internal work motivation. Following the theory outlined above, a job high in motivating potential must be high in at least one (and hopefully more) of the three dimensions that lead to experienced meaningfulness and high in both autonomy and feedback as well. The MPS provides a quantitative index of the degree to which this is in fact the case (see Appendix for detailed formula). As will be seen later, the MPS can be very useful in diagnosing jobs and in assessing the effectiveness of job-enrichment activities.

Does the Theory Work for Everybody?

Unfortunately not. Not everyone is able to become internally motivated in his work, even

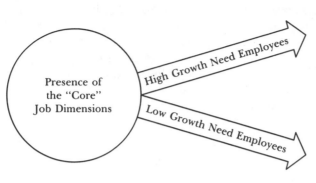

High Internal Motivation
High Growth Satisfaction
High Quality Performance
Low Absenteeism & Turnover

Risk of "over-stretching"
the individual, possible
balking at the job

FIGURE 2.   The Moderating Effect of Employee Growth-Need Strength

when the motivating potential of a job is very high indeed.

Research has shown that the *psychological needs* of people are very important in determining who can (and who cannot) become internally motivated at work. Some people have strong needs for personal accomplishment, for learning and developing themselves beyond where they are now, for being stimulated and challenged, and so on. These people are high in "growth-need strength."

Figure 2 shows diagrammatically the proposition that individual growth needs have the power to moderate the relationship between the characteristics of jobs and work outcomes. Many workers with high growth needs will turn on eagerly when they have jobs that are high in the core dimensions. Workers whose growth needs are not so strong may respond less eagerly—or, at first, even balk at being "pushed" or "stretched" too far.

Psychologists who emphasize human potential argue that everyone has within him at least a spark of the need to grow and develop personally. Steadily accumulating evidence shows, however, that unless that spark is pretty strong, chances are it will get snuffed out by one's experiences in typical organizations. So, a person who has worked for twenty years in stultifying jobs may find it difficult or impossible to become internally motivated overnight when given the opportunity.

We should be cautious, however, about creating rigid categories of people based on their measured growth-need strength at any particular time. It is true that we can predict from these measures who is likely to become internally motivated on a job and who will be less willing or able to do so. But what we do not know yet is whether or not the growth-need "spark" can be rekindled for those individuals who have had their growth needs dampened by years of growth-depressing experience in their organizations.

Since it is often the organization that is responsible for currently low levels of growth desires, we believe that the organization also should provide the individual with the chance to reverse that trend whenever possible, even if that means putting a person in a job where he may be "stretched" more than he wants to be. He can always move back later to the old job—and in the meantime the embers of his growth needs just might burst back into flame, to his surprise and pleasure, and for the good of the organization.

FROM THEORY TO PRACTICE: A TECHNOLOGY FOR JOB ENRICHMENT

When job enrichment fails, it often fails because of inadequate *diagnosis* of the target job

417

and employees' reactions to it. Often, for example, job enrichment is assumed by management to be a solution to "people problems" on the job and is implemented even though there has been no diagnostic activity to indicate that the root of the problem is in fact how the work is designed. At other times, some diagnosis is made—but it provides no concrete guidance about what specific aspects of the job require change. In either case, the success of job enrichment may wind up depending more on the quality of the intuition of the change agent—or his luck—than on a solid base of data about the people and the work.

In the paragraphs to follow, we outline a new technology for use in job enrichment which explicitly addresses the diagnostic as well as the action components of the change process. The technology has two parts: (1) a set of diagnostic tools that are useful in evaluating jobs and people's reactions to them prior to change—and in pinpointing exactly what aspects of specific jobs are most critical to a successful change attempt; and (2) a set of "implementing concepts" that provide concrete guidance for action steps in job enrichment. The implementing concepts are tied directly to the diagnostic tools; the output of the diagnostic activity specifies which action steps are likely to have the most impact in a particular situation.

The Diagnostic Tools

Central to the diagnostic procedure we propose is a package of instruments to be used by employees, supervisors, and outside observers in assessing the target job and employees' reactions to it.[9] These instruments gauge the following:

1. The objective characteristics of the jobs themselves, including both an overall indication of the "motivating potential" of the job as it exists (that is, the MPS score) and the score of the job on each of the five core

dimensions described previously. Because knowing the strengths and weaknesses of the job is critical to any work-redesign effort, assessments of the job are made by supervisors and outside observers as well as the employees themselves—and the final assessment of a job uses data from all three sources.

2. The current levels of motivation, satisfaction, and work performance of employees on the job. In addition to satisfaction with the work itself, measures are taken of how people feel about other aspects of the work setting, such as pay, supervision, and relationships with coworkers.

3. The level of growth-need strength of the employees. As indicated earlier, employees who have strong growth needs are more likely to be more responsive to job enrichment than employees with weak growth needs. Therefore, it is important to know at the outset just what kinds of satisfactions the people who do the job are (and are not) motivated to obtain from their work. This will make it possible to identify which persons are best to start changes with and which may need help in adapting to the newly enriched job.

What then, might be the actual steps one would take in carrying out a job diagnosis using these tools? Although the approach to any particular diagnosis depends upon the specifics of the particular work situation involved, the sequence of questions listed below is fairly typical.

Step 1. Are Motivation and Satisfaction Central to the Problem?   Sometimes organizations undertake job enrichment to improve the work motivation and satisfaction of employees when in fact the real problem with work performance lies elsewhere—for example, in a poorly designed production system, in an error-prone computer, and so on. The first step is to examine the scores of employees on the motivation and satisfaction portions of the diagnostic instrument. (The questionnaire taken by the employees is called the Job Diagnostic Survey and will be referred to hereafter as the JDS.) If motivation and satisfaction are problematic, the change agent would continue to Step 2; if not, he would look to other aspects of the work situation to identify the real problem.

Step 2. Is the Job Low in Motivating Potential?

To answer this question, one would examine the motivating potential score of the target job and compare it to the MPS's of other jobs to determine whether or not *the job itself* is a probable cause of the motivational problems documented in Step 1. If the job turns out to be low on the MPS, one would continue to Step 3; if it scores high, attention should be given to other possible reasons for the motivational difficul-

ties (such as the pay system, the nature of supervision, and so on).

Step 3. What Specific Aspects of the Job Are Causing the Difficulty?

This step involves examining the job on each of the five core dimensions to pinpoint the specific strengths and weaknesses of the job as it is currently structured. It is useful at this stage to construct a "profile" of the target job, to make visually apparent where improvements need to be made. An illustrative profile for two jobs (one "good" job and one job needing improvement) is shown in Figure 3.

Job A is an engineering maintenance job and is high on all of the core dimensions; the MPS of this job is a very high 260. (MPS scores can range from 1 to about 350; an "average" score would be about 125.) Job enrichment

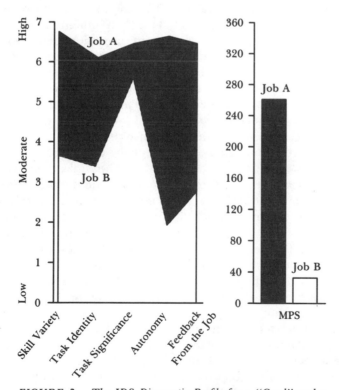

FIGURE 3.   The JDS Diagnostic Profile for a "Good" and a "Bad" Job

419

would not be recommended for this job; if employees working on the job were unproductive and unhappy, the reasons are likely to have little to do with the nature or design of the work itself.

Job B, on the other hand, has many problems. This job involves the routine and repetitive processing of checks in the "back room" of a bank. The MPS is 30, which is quite low—and indeed, would be even lower if it were not for the moderately high task significance of the job. (Task significance is moderately high because the people are handling large amounts of other people's money, and therefore the quality of their efforts potentially has important consequences for their unseen clients.) The job provides the individuals with very little direct feedback about how effectively they are doing it; the employees have little autonomy in how they go about doing the job; and the job is moderately low in both skill variety and task identity.

For Job B, then, there is plenty of room for improvement—and many avenues to examine in planning job changes. For still other jobs, the avenues for change often turn out to be considerably more specific: for example, feedback and autonomy may be reasonably high, but one or more of the core dimensions that contribute to the experienced meaningfulness of the job (skill variety, task identity, and task significance) may be low. In such a case, attention would turn to ways to increase the standing of the job on these latter three dimensions.

Step 4. How "Ready" Are the Employees for Change? Once it has been documented that there is need for improvement in the job—and the particularly troublesome aspects of the job have been identified then it is time to begin to think about the specific action steps which will be taken to enrich the job. An important factor in such planning is the level of growth needs of the employees, since employees high on growth needs usually respond more readily to

job enrichment than do employees with little need for growth. The JDS provides a direct measure of the growth-need strength of the employees. This measure can be very helpful in planning how to introduce the changes to the people (for instance, cautiously versus dramatically), and in deciding who should be among the first group of employees to have their jobs changed.

In actual use of the diagnostic package, additional information is generated which supplements and expands the basic diagnostic questions outlined above. The point of the above discussion is merely to indicate the kinds of questions which we believe to be most important in diagnosing a job prior to changing it. We now turn to how the diagnostic conclusions are translated into specific job changes.

The Implementing Concepts

Five "implementing concepts" for job enrichment are identified and discussed below.[10] Each one is a specific action step aimed at improving both the quality of the working experience for the individual and his work productivity. They are (1) forming natural work units; (2) combining tasks; (3) establishing client relationships; (4) vertical loading; (5) opening feedback channels.

The links between the implementing concepts and the core dimensions are shown in Figure 4—which illustrates our theory of job enrichment, ranging from the concrete action steps through the core dimensions and the psychological states to the actual personal and work outcomes.

After completing the diagnosis of a job, a change agent would know which of the core dimensions were most in need of remedial attention. He could then turn to Figure 4 and select those implementing concepts that specifically deal with the most troublesome parts of the existing job. How this would take place in practice will be seen below.

420

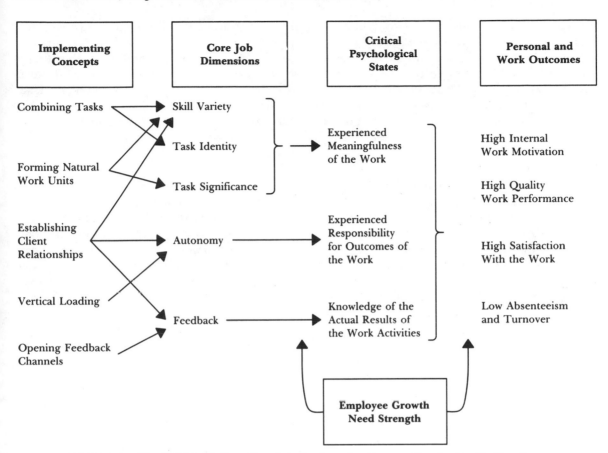

FIGURE 4.   The Full Model: How Use of the Implementing Concepts Can Lead to Positive Outcomes

Forming Natural Work Units.   The notion of distributing work in some logical way may seem to be an obvious part of the design of any job. In many cases, however, the logic is one imposed by just about any consideration except job-holder satisfaction and motivation. Such considerations include technological dictates, level of worker training or experience, "efficiency" as defined by industrial engineering, and current workload. In many cases the cluster of tasks a worker faces during a typical day or week is natural to anyone *but* the worker.

For example; suppose that a typing pool (consisting of one supervisor and ten typists) handles all work for one division of a company. Jobs are delivered in rough draft or dictated

form to the supervisor, who distributes them as evenly as possible among the typists. In such circumstances the individual letters, reports, and other tasks performed by a given typist in one day or week are randomly assigned. There is no basis for identifying with the work or the person or department for whom it is performed, or for placing any personal value upon it.

The principle underlying natural units of work, by contrast, is "ownership"—a worker's sense of continuing responsibility for an identifiable body of work. Two steps are involved in creating natural work units. The first is to identify the basic work items. In the typing pool, for example, the items might be "pages to

421

be typed." The second step is to group the items in natural categories. For example, each typist might be assigned continuing responsibility for all jobs requested by one or several specific departments. The assignments should be made, of course, in such a way that workloads are about equal in the long run. (For example, one typist might end up with all the work from one busy department, while another handles jobs from several smaller units.)

At this point we can begin to see specifically how the job-design principles relate to the core dimensions (cf. Figure 4). The ownership fostered by natural units of work can make the difference between a feeling that work is meaningful and rewarding and the feeling that it is irrelevant and boring. As the diagram shows, natural units of work are directly related to two of the core dimensions: task identity and task significance.

A typist whose work is assigned naturally rather than randomly—say, by departments—has a much greater chance of performing a whole job to completion. Instead of typing one section of a large report, the individual is likely to type the whole thing, with knowledge of exactly what the product of the work is (task identity). Furthermore, over time the typist will develop a growing sense of how the work affects coworkers in the department serviced (task significance).

Combining Tasks.   The very existence of a pool made up entirely of persons whose sole function is typing reflects a fractionalization of jobs that has been a basic precept of "scientific management." Most obvious in assembly-line work, fractionalization has been applied to non-manufacturing jobs as well. It is typically justified by efficiency, which is usually defined in terms of either low costs or some time-and-motion type of criteria.

It is hard to find fault with measuring efficiency ultimately in terms of cost-effectiveness. In doing so, however, a manager should

be sure to consider *all* the costs involved. It is possible, for example, for highly fractionalized jobs to meet all the time-and-motion criteria of efficiency, but if the resulting job is so unrewarding that performing it day after day leads to high turnover, absenteeism, drugs and alcohol, and strikes, then productivity is really lower (and costs higher) than data on efficiency might indicate.

The principle of combining tasks, then, suggests that whenever possible existing and fractionalized tasks should be put together to form new and larger modules of work. At the Medfield, Massachusetts plant of Corning Glass Works the assembly of a laboratory hot plate has been redesigned along the lines suggested here. Each hot plate now is assembled from start to finish by one operator, instead of going through several separate operations that are performed by different people.

Some tasks, if combined into a meaningfully large module of work, would be more than an individual could do by himself. In such cases, it is often useful to consider assigning the new, larger task to a small *team* of workers—who are given great autonomy for its completion. At the Racine, Wisconsin plant of Emerson Electric, the assembly process for trash disposal appliances was restructured this way. Instead of a sequence of moving the appliance from station to station, the assembly now is done from start to finish by one team. Such teams include both men and women to permit switching off the heavier and more delicate aspects of the work. The team responsible is identified on the appliance. In case of customer complaints, the team often drafts the reply.

As a job-design principle, task combination, like natural units of work, expands the task identity of the job. For example, the hot-plate assembler can see and identify with a finished product ready for shipment, rather than a nearly invisible junction of solder. Moreover, the more tasks that are combined into a single worker's job, the greater the variety of skills he must call on in performing the job. So task combination also leads directly to greater skill variety—the third core dimension that contributes to the overall experienced meaningfulness of the work.

Establishing Client Relationships. One consequence of fractionalization is that the typical worker has little or no contact with (or even awareness of) the ultimate user of his product or service. By encouraging and enabling employees to establish direct relationships with the clients of their work, improvements often can be realized simultaneously on three of the core dimensions. Feedback increases because of additional opportunities for the individual to receive praise or criticism of his work outputs directly. Skill variety often increases because of the necessity to develop and exercise one's interpersonal skills in maintaining the client relationship. And autonomy can increase because the individual often is given personal responsibility for deciding how to manage his relationships with the clients of his work.

Creating client relationships is a three-step process. First, the client must be identified. Second, the most direct contact possible between the worker and the client must be established. Third, criteria must be set up by which the client can judge the quality of the product or service he receives. And whenever possible, the client should have a means of relaying his judgments directly back to the worker.

The contact between worker and client should be as great as possible and as frequent as necessary. Face-to-face contact is highly desirable, at least occasionally. Where that is impossible or impractical, telephone and mail can suffice. In any case, it is important that the performance criteria by which the worker will be rated by the client must be mutually understood and agreed upon.

Vertical Loading. Typically the split between the "doing" of a job and the "planning" and "controlling" of the work has evolved along with horizontal fractionalization. Its rationale, once again, has been "efficiency through specialization." And once again, the excess of specialization that has emerged has resulted in unexpected but significant costs in motivation, morale, and work quality. In vertical loading, the intent is to partially close the gap between the doing and the controlling parts of the job—and thereby reap some important motivational advantages.

Of all the job-design principles, vertical loading may be the single most crucial one. In some cases, where it has been impossible to implement any other changes, vertical loading alone has had significant motivational effects.

When a job is vertically loaded, responsibilities and controls that formerly were reserved for higher levels of management are added to the job. There are many ways to accomplish this:

1. Return to the job holder greater discretion in setting schedules, deciding on work methods, checking on quality, and advising or helping to train less experienced workers.
2. Grant additional authority. The objective should be to advance workers from a position of no authority or highly restricted authority to positions of reviewed, and eventually, near-total authority for their own work.
3. Time management. The job holder should have the greatest possible freedom to decide when to start and stop work, when to break, and how to assign priorities.
4. Troubleshooting and crisis decisions. Workers should be encouraged to seek problem solutions on their own, rather than calling immediately for the supervisor.
5. Financial controls. Some degree of knowledge and control over budgets and other financial aspects of a job can often be

highly motivating. However, access to this information frequently tends to be restricted. Workers can benefit from knowing something about the costs of their jobs, the potential effect upon profit, and various financial and budgetary alternatives.

When a job is vertically loaded it will inevitably increase in *autonomy*. And as shown in Figure 4, this increase in objective personal control over the work will also lead to an increased feeling of personal responsibility for the work, and ultimately to higher internal work motivation.

Opening Feedback Channels. In virtually all jobs there are ways to open channels of feedback to individuals or teams to help them learn whether their performance is improving, deteriorating, or remaining at a constant level. While there are numerous channels through which information about performance can be provided, it generally is better for a worker to learn about his performance directly as he does his job—rather than from management on an occasional basis.

Job-provided feedback usually is more immediate and private than supervisor-supplied feedback, and it increases the worker's feelings of personal control over his work in the bargain. Moreover, it avoids many of the potentially disruptive interpersonal problems that can develop when the only way a worker has to find out how he is doing is through direct messages or subtle cues from the boss.

Exactly what should be done to open channels for job-provided feedback will vary from job to job and organization to organization. Yet in many cases the changes involve simply removing existing blocks that isolate the worker from naturally occurring data about performance—rather than generating entirely new feedback mechanisms. For example:

1. Establishing direct client relationships often removes blocks between the worker and natural external sources of data about his work.

2. Quality-control efforts in many organizations often eliminate a natural source of feedback. The quality check on a product or service is done by persons other than those responsible for the work. Feedback to the workers—if there is any—is belated and diluted. It often fosters a tendency to think of quality as "someone else's concern." By placing quality control close to the worker (perhaps even in his own hands), the quantity and quality of data about performance available to him can dramatically increase.

3. Tradition and established procedure in many organizations dictate that records about performance be kept by a supervisor and transmitted up (not down) in the organization hierarchy. Sometimes supervisors even check the work and correct any errors themselves. The worker who made the error never knows it occurred—and is denied the very information that could enhance both his internal work motivation and the technical adequacy of his performance. In many cases it is possible to provide standard summaries of performance records directly to the worker (as well as to his superior), thereby giving him personally and regularly the data he needs to improve his performance.

4. Computers and other automated operations sometimes can be used to provide the individual with data now blocked from him. Many clerical operations, for example, are now performed on computer consoles. These consoles often can be programmed to provide the clerk with immediate feedback in the form of a CRT display or a printout indicating that an error has been made. Some systems even have been programmed to provide the operator with a positive feedback message when a period of error-free performance has been sustained.

Many organizations simply have not recognized the importance of feedback as a motivator. Data on quality and other aspects of performance are viewed as being of interest only to management. Worse still, the *standards* for acceptable performance often are kept from workers as well. As a result, workers who would be interested in following the daily or weekly ups and downs of their performance, and in trying accordingly to improve, are deprived of the very guidelines they need to do so. They are like the golfer we mentioned earlier, whose efforts to correct his hook are stopped dead by fog over the driving range.

THE STRATEGY IN ACTION: HOW WELL DOES IT WORK?

So far we have examined a basic theory of how people get turned on to their work; a set of core dimensions of jobs that create the conditions for such internal work motivation to develop on the job; and a set of five implementing concepts that are the action steps recommended to boost a job on the core dimensions and thereby increase employee motivation, satisfaction, and productivity.

The remaining question is straightforward and important: *Does it work?* In reality, that question is twofold. First, does the theory itself hold water, or are we barking up the wrong conceptual tree? And second, does the change strategy really lead to measurable differences when it is applied in an actual organizational setting?

This section summarizes the findings we have generated to date on these questions.

Is the Job-Enrichment Theory Correct?

In general, the answer seems to be yes. The JDS instrument has been taken by more than 1,000 employees working on about 100 diverse jobs

in more than a dozen organizations over the last two years. These data have been analyzed to test the basic motivational theory—and especially the impact of the core job dimensions on worker motivation, satisfaction, and behavior on the job. An illustrative overview of some of the findings is given below.[11]

1. People who work on jobs high on the core dimensions are more motivated and satisfied than are people who work on jobs that score low on the dimensions. Employees with jobs high on the core dimensions (MPS scores greater than 240) were compared to those who held unmotivating jobs (MPS scores less than 40). As shown in Figure 5, employees with high MPS jobs were higher on (a) the three psychological states, (b) internal work motivation, (c) general satisfaction, and (d) "growth" satisfaction.

2. Figure 6 shows that the same is true for measures of actual behavior at work—absenteeism and performance effectiveness—although less strongly so for the performance measure.

3. Responses to jobs high in motivating potential are more positive for people with weak needs for growth. In Figure 7 the linear relationship between the motivating potential of a job and employees' level of internal work motivation is shown, separately for people with high versus low growth needs as measured by the JDS. While both groups of employees show increases in internal motivation as MPS increases, the *rate* of increase is significantly greater for the group of employees who have strong needs for growth.

How Does the Change Strategy Work in Practice?

The results summarized above suggest that both the theory and the diagnostic instrument work when used with real people in real organizations. In this section, we summarize a job-

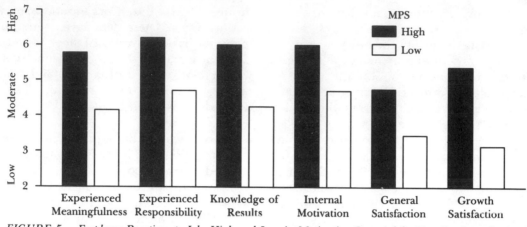

FIGURE 5.   *Employee Reactions to Jobs High and Low in Motivating Potential for Two Banks and a Steel Firm*

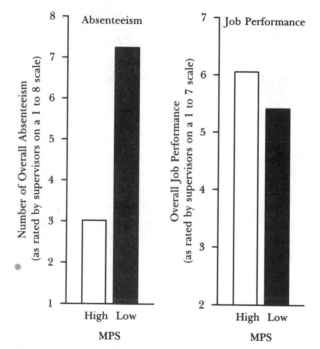

FIGURE 6.   *Absenteeism and Job Performance for Employees with Jobs High and Low in Motivating Potential*

enrichment project conducted at The Travelers Insurance Companies, which illustrates how the change procedures themselves work in practice.

The Travelers project was designed with two purposes in mind. One was to achieve im-provements in morale, productivity, and other indicators of employee well-being. The other was to test the general effectiveness of the strat-egy for job enrichment we have summarized in this article.

The work group chosen was a keypunch-

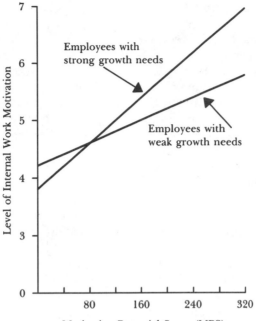

FIGURE 7. *Relationship Between the Motivating Potential of a Job and the Internal Work Motivation of Employees (Shown Separately for Employees with Strong versus Weak Growth-Need Strength)*

ing operation. The group's function was to transfer information from printed or written documents onto punched cards for computer input. The work group consisted of ninety-eight keypunch operators and verifiers (both in the same job classification), plus seven assignment clerks. All reported to a supervisor who, in turn, reported to the assistant manager and manager of the data-input division.

The size of individual punching orders varied considerably, from a few cards to as many as 2,500. Some work came to the work group with a specified delivery date, while other orders were to be given routine service on a predetermined schedule.

Assignment clerks received the jobs from the user departments. After reviewing the work for obvious errors, omissions, and legibility problems, the assignment clerk parceled out the work in batches expected to take about one hour. If the clerk found the work not suitable for punching it went to the supervisor, who either returned the work to the user department or cleared up problems by phone. When work went to operators for punching, it was with the instruction, "Punch only what you see. Don't correct errors, no matter how obvious they look."

Because of the high cost of computer time, key-punched work was 100 percent verified—a task that consumed nearly as many man-hours as the punching itself. Then the cards went to the supervisor, who screened the jobs for due dates before sending them to the computer. Errors detected in verification were assigned to various operators at random to be corrected.

The computer output from the cards was sent to the originating department, accompanied by a printout of errors. Eventually the printout went back to the supervisor for final correction.

A great many phenomena indicated that the problems being experienced in the work group might be the result of poor motivation. As the only person performing supervisory functions of any kind, the supervisor spent most of his time responding to crisis situations, which recurred continually. He also had to deal almost daily with employees' salary grievances or other complaints. Employees frequently showed apathy or outright hostility toward their jobs.

Rates of work output, by accepted work-measurement standards, were inadequate. Error rates were high. Due dates and schedules frequently were missed. Absenteeism was higher than average, especially before and after weekends and holidays.

The single, rather unusual exception was turnover. It was lower than the company-wide average for similar jobs. The company has attributed this fact to poor job market in the base period just before the project began, and to an older, relatively more settled work force—made up, incidentally, entirely of women.

The Diagnosis.   Using some of the tools and techniques we have outlined, a consulting team from the Management Services Department and from Roy W. Walters & Associates concluded that the keypunch-operator's job exhibited the following serious weaknesses in terms of the core dimensions.

1. Skill variety: there was none. Only a single skill was involved—the ability to punch adequately the data on the batch of documents.
2. Task identity: virtually nonexistent. Batches were assembled to provide an even workload, but not whole identifiable jobs.
3. Task significance: not apparent. The key-punching operation was a necessary step in providing service to the company's custom-

ers. The individual operator was isolated by an assignment clerk and a supervisor from any knowledge of what the operation meant to the using department, let alone its meaning to the ultimate customer.

4. Autonomy: none. The operators had no freedom to arrange their daily tasks to meet schedules, to resolve problems with the using department, or even to correct, in punching, information that was obviously wrong.
5. Feedback: none. Once a batch was out of the operator's hands, she had no assured chance of seeing evidence of its quality or inadequacy.

Design of the Experimental Trial.   Since the diagnosis indicated that the motivating potential of the job was extremely low, it was decided to attempt to improve the motivation and productivity of the work group through job enrichment. Moreover, it was possible to design an experimental test of the effects of the changes to be introduced: the results of changes made in the target work group were to be compared with trends in a control work group of similar size and demographic makeup. Since the control group was located more than a mile away, there appeared to be little risk of communication between members of the two groups.

A base period was defined before the start of the experimental trial period, and appropriate data were gathered on the productivity, absenteeism, and work attitudes of members of both groups. Data also were available on turnover; but since turnover was already below average in the target group, prospective changes in this measure were deemed insignificant.

An educational session was conducted with supervisors, at which they were given the theory and implementing concepts and actually helped to design the job changes themselves. Out of this session came an active plan consisting of about twenty-five change items that would significantly affect the design of the target jobs.

The Implementing Concepts and the Changes.

Because the job as it existed was rather uniformly low on the core job dimensions, all five of the implementing concepts were used in enriching it.

1. Natural units of work. The random batch assignment of work was replaced by assigning to each operator continuing responsibility for certain accounts—either particular departments or particular recurring jobs. Any work for those accounts now always goes to the same operator.
2. Task combination. Some planning and controlling functions were combined with the central task of keypunching. In this case, however, these additions can be more suitably discussed under the remaining three implementing concepts.
3. Client relationships. Each operator was given several channels of direct contact with clients. The operators, not their assignment clerks, now inspect their documents for correctness and legibility. When problems arise, the operator, not the supervisor, takes them up with the client.
4. Feedback. In addition to feedback from client contact, the operators were provided with a number of additional sources of data about their performance. The computer department now returns incorrect cards to the operators who punched them, and operators correct their own errors. Each operator also keeps her own file of copies of her errors. These can be reviewed to determine trends in error frequency and types of errors. Each operator receives weekly a computer printout of her errors and productivity, which is sent to her directly, rather than given to her by the supervisor.
5. Vertical loading. Besides consulting directly with clients about work questions,

operators now have the authority to correct obvious coding errors on their own. Operators may set their own schedules and plan their daily work, as long as they meet schedules. Some competent operators have been given the option of not verifying their work and making their own program changes.

Results of the Trial.

The results were dramatic. The number of operators declined from ninety-eight to sixty. This occurred partly through attrition and partly through transfer to other departments. Some of the operators were promoted to higher-paying jobs in departments whose cards they had been handling—something that had never occurred before. Some details of the results are given below.

1. Quantity of work. The control group, with no job changes made, showed an increase in productivity of 8.1 percent during the trial period. The experimental group showed an increase of 39.6 percent.
2. Error rates. To assess work quality, error rates were recorded for about forty operators in the experimental group. All were experienced, and all had been in their jobs before the job-enrichment program began. For two months before the study, these operators had a collective error rate of 1.53 percent. For two months toward the end of the study, the collective error rate was 0.99 percent. By the end of the study the number of operators with poor performance had dropped from 11.1 percent to 5.5 percent.
3. Absenteeism. The experimental group registered a 24.1 percent decline in absences. The control group, by contrast, showed a 29 percent increase.
4. Attitudes toward the job. An attitude survey given at the start of the project showed that the two groups scored about average,

429

and nearly identically, in nine different areas of work satisfaction. At the end of the project the survey was repeated. The control group showed an insignificant 0.5 percent improvement, while the experimental group's overall satisfaction score rose 16.5 percent.

5. Selective elimination of controls. Demonstrated improvements in operator proficiency permitted them to work with fewer controls. Travelers estimates that the reduction of controls had the same effect as adding seven operators—a saving even beyond the effects of improved productivity and lowered absenteeism.

6. Role of the supervisor. One of the most significant findings in the Travelers experiment was the effect of the changes on the supervisor's job, and thus on the rest of the organization. The operators took on many responsibilities that had been reserved at least to the unit leaders and sometimes to the supervisor. The unit leaders, in turn, assumed some of the day-to-day supervisory functions that had plagued the supervisor. Instead of spending his days supervising the behavior of subordinates and dealing with crises, he was able to devote time to developing feedback systems, setting up work modules and spearheading the enrichment effort—in other words, managing. It should be noted, however, that helping supervisors change their own work activities when their subordinates' jobs have been enriched is itself a challenging task. And if appropriate attention and help are not given to supervisors in such cases, they rapidly can become disaffected—and a job-enrichment "backlash" can result.[12]

Summary. By applying work-measurement standards to the changes wrought by job enrichment—attitude and quality, absenteeism, and selective administration of controls—Travelers was able to estimate the total dollar impact of the project. Actual savings in salaries and machine rental charges during the first year totaled $64,305. Potential savings by further application of the changes were put at $91,937 annually. Thus, by almost any measure used—from the work attitudes of individual employees to dollar savings for the company as a whole—The Travelers test of the job-enrichment strategy proved a success.

CONCLUSIONS

In this article we have presented a new strategy for the redesign of work in general and for job enrichment in particular. The approach has four main characteristics:

1. It is grounded in a basic psychological theory of what motivates people in their work.

2. It emphasizes that planning for job changes should be done on the basis of *data* about the jobs and the people who do them—and a set of diagnostic instruments is provided to collect such data.

3. It provides a set of specific implementing concepts to guide actual job changes, as well as a set of theory-based rules for selecting *which* action steps are likely to be most beneficial in a given situation.

4. The strategy is buttressed by a set of findings showing that the theory holds water, that the diagnostic procedures are practical and informative, and that the implementing concepts can lead to changes that are beneficial both to organizations and to the people who work in them.

We believe that job enrichment is moving beyond the stage where it can be considered "yet another management fad." Instead, it represents a potentially powerful strategy for change that can help organizations achieve their goals for higher quality work—and at the same time further the equally legitimate needs of contemporary employees for a more meaningful work experience. Yet there are pressing questions about job enrichment and its use that remain to be answered.

Prominent among these is the question of employee participation in planning and implementing work redesign. The diagnostic tools and implementing concepts we have presented are neither designed nor intended for use only by management. Rather, our belief is that the effectiveness of job enrichment is likely to be enhanced when the tasks of diagnosing and changing jobs are undertaken *collaboratively* by management and by the employees whose work will be affected.

Moreover, the effects of work redesign on the broader organization remain generally uncharted. Evidence now is accumulating that when jobs are changed, turbulence can appear in the surrounding organization—for example, in supervisory-subordinate relationships, in pay and benefit plans, and so on. Such turbulence can be viewed by management either as a problem with job enrichment, or as an opportunity for further and broader organizational development by teams of managers and employees. To the degree that management takes the latter view, we believe, the oft-espoused goal of achieving basic organizational change through the redesign of work may come increasingly within reach.

The diagnostic tools and implementing concepts we have presented are useful in deciding on and designing basic changes in the jobs themselves. They do not address the broader issues of who plans the changes, how they are carried out, and how they are followed up. The way these broader questions are dealt with, we believe, may determine whether job enrichment will grow up—or whether it will die an early and unfortunate death, like so many other fledgling behavioral-science approaches to organizational change.

APPENDIX

For the algebraically inclined, the Motivating Potential Score is computed as follows

$$MPS = \left| \frac{\frac{Skill\ Variety + Task\ Identity + Task\ Significance}{3}}{X\ Autonomy \qquad\qquad X\ Feedback} \right|$$

It should be noted that in some cases the MPS score can be *too* high for positive job satisfaction and effective performance—in effect overstimulating the person who holds the job. This paper focuses on jobs which are toward the low end of the scale—and which potentially can be improved through job enrichment.

Acknowledgments

The authors acknowledge with great appreciation the editorial assistance of John Hickey in the preparation of this paper, and the help of Kenneth Brousseau, Daniel Feldman, and Linda Frank in collecting the data that are summarized here. The research activities reported were supported in part by the Organizational Effectiveness Research Program of the Office of Naval Research, and the Manpower Administration of the U.S. Department of Labor, both through contracts to Yale University.

NOTES

1. F. Herzberg; B. Mausner; and B. Snyderman; *The Motivation to Work* (New York: John Wiley & Sons, 1959).
2. F. Herzberg, *Work and the Nature of Man* (Cleveland: World, 1966).
3. F. Herzberg, "One More Time: How Do You Motivate Employees?" *Harvard Business Review* (1968): 53–62.
4. W. J. Paul, Jr.; K. B. Robertson; and F. Herz-

berg, "Job Enrichment Pays Off." *Harvard Business Review* (1969): 61–78.

5. R. N. Ford, *Motivation Through the Work Itself* (New York: American Management Association, 1969).

6. A. N. Turner and P. R. Lawrence, *Industrial Jobs and the Worker* (Cambridge, Mass.: Harvard Graduate School of Business Administration, 1965).

7. J. R. Hackman and E. E. Lawler, "Employee Reactions to Job Characteristics," *Journal of Applied Psychology Monograph* (1971): 259–86.

8. J. R. Hackman and G. R. Oldham, *Motivation Through the Design of Work: Test of a Theory,* Technical Report No. 6, Department of Administrative Sciences, Yale University, 1974.

9. J. R. Hackman and G. R. Oldham, "Development of the Job Diagnostic Survey," *Journal of Applied Psychology* (1975): 159–70.

10. R. W. Walters and Associates, *Job Enrichment for Results* (Cambridge, Mass.: Addison-Wesley, 1975).

11. Hackman and Oldham, "Development of the Job Diagnostic Survey."

12. E. E. Lawler III; J. R. Hackman; and S. Kaufman, "Effects of Job Redesign: A Field Experiment," *Journal of Applied Social Psychology* (1973): 49–62.

Goal Setting—
A Motivational Technique That Works

Gary Latham

Edwin Locke

The problem of how to motivate employees has puzzled and frustrated managers for generations. One reason the problem has seemed difficult, if not mysterious, is that motivation ultimately comes from within the individual and therefore cannot be observed directly. Moreover, most managers are not in a position to change an employee's basic personality structure. The best they can do is try to use incentives to direct the energies of their employees toward organizational objectives.

Money is obviously the primary incentive, since without it few if any employees would come to work. But money alone is not always enough to motivate high performance. Other incentives, such as participation in decision making, job enrichment, behavior modification, and organizational development, have been tried with varying degrees of success. A large number of research studies have shown, however, that one very straightforward technique—goal setting—is probably not only more effective than alternative methods, but may be the major mechanism by which these other incentives affect motivation. For example, a recent experiment on job enrichment

demonstrated that unless employees in enriched jobs set higher, more specific goals than do those with unenriched jobs, job enrichment has absolutely no effect on productivity. Even money has been found most effective as a motivator when the bonuses offered are made contingent on attaining specific objectives.

THE GOAL-SETTING CONCEPT

The idea of assigning employees a specific amount of work to be accomplished—a specific task, a quota, a performance standard, an objective, or a deadline—is not new. The task concept, along with time and motion study and incentive pay, was the cornerstone of scientific management, founded by Frederick W. Taylor more than 70 years ago. He used his system to increase the productivity of blue collar workers. About 20 years ago the idea of goal setting reappeared under a new name, management by objectives, but this technique was designed for managers.

In a 14-year program of research, we have found that goal setting does not necessarily have to be part of a wider management system to motivate performance effectively. It can be used as a technique in its own right.

LABORATORY AND FIELD RESEARCH

Our research program began in the laboratory. In a series of experiments, individuals were assigned different types of goals on a variety of simple tasks—addition, brainstorming, assembling toys. Repeatedly it was found that those assigned hard goals performed better than did people assigned moderately difficult or easy goals. Furthermore, individuals who had specific, challenging goals out-performed those who were given such vague goals as to "do your best." Finally, we observed that pay and performance feedback led to improved performance only when these incentives led the individual to set higher goals.

While results were quite consistent in the laboratory, there was no proof that they could be applied to actual work settings. Fortunately, just as Locke published a summary of the laboratory studies in 1968, Latham began a separate series of experiments in the wood products industry that demonstrated the practical significance of these findings. The field studies did not start out as a validity test of a laboratory theory, but rather as a response to a practical problem.

In 1968, six sponsors of the American Pulpwood Association became concerned about increasing the productivity of independent loggers in the South. These loggers were entrepreneurs on whom the multimillion-dollar companies are largely dependent for their raw material. The problem was twofold. First, these entrepreneurs did not work for a single company; they worked for themselves. Thus they were free to (and often did) work two days one week, four days a second week, five half-days a third week, or whatever schedule they preferred. In short, these workers could be classified as marginal from the standpoint of their productivity and attendance, which were considered highly unsatisfactory by conventional company standards. Second, the major approach taken to alleviate this problem had been to develop equipment that would make the industry less dependent on this type of worker. A limitation of this approach was that many of the logging supervisors were unable to obtain the financing necessary to purchase a small tractor, let alone a rubber-tired skidder.

Consequently, we designed a survey that would help managers determine "what makes these people tick." The survey was conducted orally in the field with 292 logging supervisors. Complex statistical analyses of the data identified three basic types of supervisor. One type stayed on the job with their men, gave them instructions and explanations, provided them with training, read the trade magazines, and had little difficulty financing the equipment they needed. Still, the productivity of their units was at best mediocre.

The operation of the second group of supervisors was slightly less mechanized. These supervisors provided little training for their workforce. They simply drove their employees to the woods, gave them a specific production goal to attain for the day or week, left them alone in the woods unsupervised, and returned at night to take them home. Labor turnover was high and productivity was again average.

The operation of the third group of supervisors was relatively unmechanized. These leaders stayed on the job with their men, provided training, gave instructions and explanations, and in addition, set a specific production goal for the day or week. Not only was the crew's productivity high, but their injury rate was well below average.

Two conclusions were discussed with the managers of the companies sponsoring this study. First, mechanization alone will not increase the productivity of logging crews. Just as the average tax payer would probably commit more mathematical errors if he were to try to use a computer to complete his income tax return, the average logger misuses, and frequently abuses, the equipment he purchases (for example, drives a skidder with two flat tires, doesn't change the oil filter). This increases not only the logger's downtime, but also his costs which, in turn, can force him out of business. The second conclusion of the survey was that setting a specific production goal combined with supervisory presence to ensure goal commitment will bring about a significant increase in productivity.

These conclusions were greeted with the standard, but valid, cliché, "Statistics don't prove causation." And our comments regarding the value of machinery were especially irritating to these managers, many of whom had received degrees in engineering. So one of the companies decided to replicate the survey in order to check our findings.

The company's study placed each of 892 independent logging supervisors who sold wood to the company into one of three categories of supervisory styles our survey had identified—namely, (1) stays on the job but does not set specific production goals; (2) sets specific production goals but does not stay on the job; and (3) stays on the job and sets specific production goals. Once again, goal setting, in combination with the on-site presence of a supervisor, was shown to be the key to improved productivity.

TESTING FOR THE HAWTHORNE EFFECT

Management may have been unfamiliar with different theories of motivation, but it was fully aware of one label—the Hawthorne effect. Managers in these wood products companies remained unconvinced that anything so simple as staying on the job with the men and setting a specific production goal could have an appreciable effect on productivity. They pointed out that the results simply reflected the positive effects any supervisor would have on the work

unit after giving his crew attention. And they were unimpressed by the laboratory experiments we cited—experiments showing that individuals who have a specific goal solve more arithmetic problems or assemble more tinker toys than do people who are told to "do your best." Skepticism prevailed.

But the country's economic picture made it critical to continue the study of inexpensive techniques to improve employee motivation and productivity. We were granted permission to run one more project to test the effectiveness of goal setting.

Twenty independent logging crews who were all but identical in size, mechanization level, terrain on which they worked, productivity, and attendance were located. The logging supervisors of these crews were in the habit of staying on the job with their men, but they did not set production goals. Half the crews were randomly selected to receive training in goal setting; the remaining crews served as a control group.

The logging supervisors who were to set goals were told that we had found a way to increase productivity at no financial expense to anyone. We gave the ten supervisors in the training group production tables developed through time-and-motion studies by the company's engineers. These tables made it possible to determine how much wood should be harvested in a given number of manhours. They were asked to use these tables as a guide in determining a specific production goal to assign their employees. In addition, each sawhand was given a tallymeter (counter) that he could wear on his belt. The sawhand was asked to punch the counter each time he felled a tree. Finally, permission was requested to measure the crew's performance on a weekly basis.

The ten supervisors in the control group—those who were not asked to set production goals—were told that the researchers were interested in learning the extent to which productivity is affected by absenteeism and injuries. They were urged to "do your best" to maximize the crew's productivity and attendance and to minimize injuries. It was explained that the data might be useful in finding ways to increase productivity at little or no cost to the wood harvester.

To control for the Hawthorne effect, we made an equal number of visits to the control group and the training group. Performance was measured for 12 weeks. During this time, the productivity of the goal-setting group was significantly higher than that of the control group. Moreover, absenteeism was significantly lower in the groups that set goals than in the groups who were simply urged to do their best. Injury and turnover rates were low in both groups.

Why should anything so simple and inexpensive as goal setting influence the work of these employees so significantly? Anecdotal evidence from conversations with both the loggers and the company foresters who visited them suggested several reasons.

Harvesting timber can be a monotonous, tiring job with little or no meaning for most workers. Introducing a goal that is difficult, but attainable, increases the challenge of the job. In addition, a specific goal makes it clear to the worker what it is he is expected to do. Goal feedback via the tallymeter and weekly recordkeeping provide the worker with a sense of achievement, recognition, and accomplishment. He can see how well he is doing now as against his past performance and, in some cases, how well he is doing in comparison with others. Thus the worker not only may expend greater effort, but may also devise better or more creative tactics for attaining the goal than those he previously used.

NEW APPLICATIONS

Management was finally convinced that goal setting was an effective motivational technique for increasing the productivity of the independent woods worker in the South. The issue now raised by the management of another wood products company was whether the procedure could be used in the West with company logging operations in which the employees were unionized and paid by the hour. The previous study had involved employees on a piece-rate system, which was the practice in the South.

The immediate problem confronting this company involved the loading of logging trucks. If the trucks were unloaded, the company lost money. If the trucks were overloaded, however, the driver could be fined by the Highway Department and could ultimately lose his job. The drivers opted for underloading the trucks.

For three months management tried to solve this problem by urging the drivers to try harder to fill the truck to its legal net weight, and by developing weighing scales that could be attached to the truck. But this approach did not prove cost effective, because the scales continually broke down when subjected to the rough terrain on which the trucks traveled. Consequently, the drivers reverted to their former practice of underloading. For the three months in which the problem was under study the trucks were seldom loaded in excess of 58 to 63 percent of capacity.

At the end of the three-month period, the results of the previous goal-setting experiments were explained to the union. They were told three things—that the company would like to set a specific net weight goal for the drivers, that no monetary reward or fringe benefits other than verbal praise could be expected for improved performance, and that no one would be criticized for failing to attain the goal. Once again, the idea that simply setting a specific goal would solve a production problem seemed too incredible to be taken seriously by the union. However, they reached an agreement that a difficult, but attainable, goal of 94 percent of the truck's legal net weight would be assigned to the drivers, provided that no one could be reprimanded for failing to attain the goal. This latter point was emphasized to the company foremen in particular.

Within the first month, performance increased to 80 percent of the truck's net weight. After the second month, however, performance decreased to 70 percent. Interviews with the drivers indicated that they were testing management's statement that no punitive steps would be taken against them if their performance suddenly dropped. Fortunately for all concerned, no such steps were taken by the foremen, and performance exceeded 90 percent of the truck's capacity after the third month. Their performance has remained at this level to this day, seven years later.

The results over the nine-month period during which this study was conducted saved the company $250,000. This figure, determined by the company's accountants, is based on the cost of additional trucks that would have been required to deliver the same quantity of logs to the mill if goal setting had not been implemented. The dollars-saved figure is even higher when you factor in the cost of the additional diesel fuel that would have been consumed and the expenses incurred in recruiting and hiring the additional truck drivers.

Why could this procedure work without the union's demanding an increase in hourly wages? First, the drivers did not feel that they were really doing anything differently. This, of course, was not true. As a result of goal setting, the men began to record their truck weight in a pocket notebook, and they found themselves bragging about their accomplishments to their peers. Second, they viewed goal setting as a challenging game: "It was great to beat the other guy."

Competition was a crucial factor in bringing about goal acceptance and commitment in this study. However, we can reject the hypothesis that improved performance resulted solely from competition, because no spe-

cial prizes or formal recognition programs were provided for those who came closest to, or exceeded, the goal. No effort was made by the company to single out one "winner." More important, the opportunity for competition among drivers had existed before goal setting was instituted; after all, each driver knew his own truck's weight, and the truck weight of each of the 36 other drivers every time he hauled wood into the yard. In short, competition affected productivity only in the sense that it led to the acceptance of, and commitment to, the goal. It was the setting of the goal itself and the working toward it that brought about increased performance and decreased costs.

PARTICIPATIVE GOAL SETTING

The inevitable question always raised by management was raised here: "We know goal setting works. How can we make it work better?" Was there one best method for setting goals? Evidence for a "one best way" approach was cited by several managers, but it was finally concluded that different approaches would work best under different circumstances.

It was hypothesized that the woods workers in the South, who had little or no education, would work better with assigned goals, while the educated workers in the West would achieve higher productivity if they were allowed to help set the goals themselves. Why the focus on education? Many of the uneducated workers in the South could be classified as culturally disadvantaged. Such persons often lack self-confidence, have a poor sense of time, and are not very competitive. The cycle of skill mastery, which in turn guarantees skill levels high enough to prevent discouragement, doesn't apply to these employees. If, for example, these people were allowed to participate in goal setting, the goals might be too difficult or they might be too easy. On the other hand, participation for the educated worker was considered critical in effecting maximum goal acceptance. Since these conclusions appeared logical, management initially decided that no research was necessary. This decision led to hours of further discussion.

The same questions were raised again and again by the researchers. What if the logic were wrong? Can we afford to implement these decisions without evaluating them systematically? Would we implement decisions regarding a new approach to tree planting without first testing it? Do we care more about trees than we do about people? Finally, permission was granted to conduct an experiment.

Logging crews were randomly appointed to either participative goal setting, assigned (nonparticipative) goal setting, or a do-your-best condition. The results were startling. The uneducated crews, consisting primarily of black employees who participated in goal setting, set significantly higher goals and attained them more often than did those whose goals were assigned by the supervisor. Not surprisingly, their performance was higher. Crews with assigned goals performed no better than did those who were urged to do their best to improve their productivity. The performance of white, educationally advantaged workers was higher with assigned rather than participatively set goals, although the difference was not statistically significant. These results were precisely the opposite of what had been predicted.

Another study comparing participative and assigned goals was conducted with typists. The results supported findings obtained by researchers at General Electric years before. It did not matter so much *how* the goal was set. What mattered was *that* a goal was set. The study demonstrated that both assigned and participatively set goals led to substantial improvements in typing speed. The process by which these gains occurred, however, differed in the two groups.

In the participative group, employees in-

sisted on setting very high goals regardless of whether they had attained their goal the previous week. Nevertheless, their productivity improved—an outcome consistent with the theory that high goals lead to high performance.

In the assigned-goal group, supervisors were highly supportive of employees. No criticism was given for failure to attain the goals. Instead, the supervisor lowered the goal after failure so that the employee would be certain to attain it. The goal was then raised gradually each week until the supervisor felt the employee was achieving his or her potential. The result? Feelings of accomplishment and achievement on the part of the worker and improved productivity for the company.

These basic findings were replicated in a subsequent study of engineers and scientists. Participative goal setting was superior to assigned goal setting only to the degree that it led to the setting of higher goals. Both participative and assigned-goal groups outperformed groups that were simply told to "do your best."

An additional experiment was conducted to validate the conclusion that participation in goal setting may be important only to the extent that it leads to the setting of difficult goals. It was performed in a laboratory setting in which the task was to brainstorm uses for wood. One group was asked to "do your best" to think of as many ideas as possible. A second group took part in deciding, with the experimenter, the specific number of ideas each person would generate. These goals were, in turn, assigned to individuals in a third group. In this way, goal difficulty was held constant between the assigned-goal and participative groups. Again, it was found that specific, difficult goals—whether assigned or set through participation—led to higher performance than did an abstract or generalized goal such as "do your best." And, when goal difficulty was held constant, there was no significant difference in the performance of those with assigned as compared with participatively set goals.

FIGURE 1. Representative Field Studies of Goal-Setting

Researcher(s)	Task	Duration of Study or of Significant Effects	Percent of Change in Performance[a]
Blumenfeld & Leidy	Servicing soft drink coolers	Unspecified	+27
Dockstader	Keypunching	3 mos.	+27
Ivancevich	Skilled technical jobs	9 mos.	+15
Ivancevich	Sales	9 mos.	+24
Kim and Hamner	5 telephone service jobs	3 mos.	+13
Latham and Baldes	Loading trucks	9 mos.[b]	+26
Latham and Yukl	Logging	2 mos.	+18
Latham and Yukl	Typing	5 weeks	+11
Migliore	Mass production	2 years	+16
Umstot, Bell, and Mitchell	Coding land parcels	1–2 days[c]	+16

[a]Percentage changes were obtained by subtracting pre-goal-setting performance from post-goal-setting performance and dividing by pre-goal-setting performance. Different experimental groups were combined where appropriate. If a control group was available, the percentage figure represents the difference of the percentage changes between the experimental and control groups. If multiple performance measures were used, the median improvement on all measures was used. The authors would like to thank Dena Feren and Vicki McCaleb for performing these calculations.

[b]Performance remained high for seven years.

[c]Simulated organization.

These results demonstrate that goal setting in industry works just as it does in the laboratory. Specific, challenging goals lead to better performance than do easy or vague goals, and feedback motivates higher performance only when it leads to the setting of higher goals.

It is important to note that participation is not only a motivational tool. When a manager has competent subordinates, participation is also a useful device for increasing the manager's knowledge and thereby improving decision quality. It can lead to better decisions through input from subordinates.

A representative sample of the results of field studies of goal setting conducted by Latham and others is shown in Figure 28-1. Each of these ten studies compared the performance of employees given specific challenging goals with those given "do best" or no goals. Note that goal setting has been successful across a wide variety of jobs and industries. The effects of goal setting have been recorded for as long as seven years after the onset of the program, although the results of most studies have been followed up for only a few weeks or months. The median improvement in performance in the ten studies shown in Figure 1 was 17 percent.

A CRITICAL INCIDENTS SURVEY

To explore further the importance of goal setting in the work setting. Dr. Frank White conducted another study in two plants of a high-technology, multinational corporation on the East Coast. Seventy-one engineers, 50 managers, and 31 clerks were asked to describe a specific instance when they were especially productive and a specific instance when they were especially unproductive on their present jobs. Responses were classified according to a reliable coding scheme. Of primary interest here are the external events perceived by employees as being responsible for the high-productivity and low-productivity incidents. The results are shown in Figure 2.

The first set of events—pursuing a specific goal, having a large amount of work, working under a deadline, or having an uninterrupted routine—accounted for more than half the high-productivity events. Similarly, the converse of these—goal blockage, having a small amount of work, lacking a deadline, and suffering work interruptions—accounted for nearly 60 percent of the low-productivity events. Note that the first set of four categories all are relevant to goal setting and the second set to a lack of goals or goal blockage. The goal category itself—that of pursuing an attainable goal or goal blockage—was the one most frequently used to describe high- and low-productivity incidents.

The next four categories, which are more pertinent to Frederick Herzberg's motivator-hygiene theory—task interest, responsibility, promotion, and recognition—are

less important, accounting for 36.8 percent of the high-productivity incidents (the opposite of these four categories accounted for 19.1 percent for the lows). The remaining categories were even less important.

Employees were also asked to identify the responsible agent behind the events that had led to high and low productivity. In both cases, the employees themselves, their immediate supervisors, and the organization were the agents most frequently mentioned.

The concept of goal setting is a very simple one. Interestingly, however, we have gotten two contradictory types of reaction when the idea was introduced to managers. Some claimed it was so simple and self-evident that everyone, including themselves, already used it. This, we have found, is not true. Time after time we have gotten the following response from subordinates after goal setting was introduced: "This is the first time I knew what my supervisor expected of me on this job." Conversely, other managers have argued that the

FIGURE 2.   *Events Perceived as Causing High and Low Productivity*

Event	Percent of Times Event Caused	
	High Productivity	Low Productivity
Goal pursuit/Goal blockage	17.1	23.0
Large amount of work/Small amount of work	12.5	19.0
Deadline or schedule/No deadline	15.1	3.3
Smooth work routine/Interrupted routine	5.9	14.5
Intrinsic/Extrinsic factors	50.6	59.8
Interesting task/Uninteresting task	17.1	11.2
Increased responsibility/Decreased responsibility	13.8	4.6
Anticipated promotion/Promotion denied	1.3	0.7
Verbal recognition/Criticism	4.6	2.6
People/Company conditions	36.8	19.1
Pleasant personal relationships/Unpleasant personal relationships	10.5	9.9
Anticipated pay increase/Pay increase denied	1.3	1.3
Pleasant working conditions/Unpleasant working conditions	0.7	0.7
Other (Miscellaneous)	—	9.3

$N = 152$ in this study by Frank White.

idea would not work, precisely *because* it is so simple (implying that something more radical and complex was needed. Again, results proved them wrong.

But these successes should not mislead managers into thinking that goal setting can be used without careful planning and forethought. Research and experience suggest that the best results are obtained when the following steps are followed:

Setting the Goal

The goal set should have two main characteristics. First, it should be specific rather than vague: "Increase sales by 10 percent" rather than "Try to improve sales." Whenever possible, there should be a time limit for goal accomplishment: "Cut costs by 3 percent in the next six months."

Second, the goal should be challenging yet reachable. If accepted, difficult goals lead to better performance than do easy goals. In contrast, if the goals are perceived as unreachable, employees will not accept them. Nor will employees get a sense of achievement from pursuing goals that are never attained. Employees with low self-confidence or ability should be given more easily attainable goals than those with high self-confidence and ability.

There are at least five possible sources of input, aside from the individual's self-confidence and ability, that can be used to determine the particular goal to set for a given individual.

The scientific management approach pioneered by Frederick W. Taylor uses time and motion study to determine a fair day's work. This is probably the most objective technique available, but it can be used only where the task is reasonably repetitive and standardized. Another drawback is that this method often leads to employee resistance, especially in cases where the new standard is substantially higher than previous performance and where rate changes are made frequently.

More readily accepted, although less scientific than time and motion study, are standards based on the average past performance of employees. This method was used successfully in some of our field studies. Most employees consider this approach fair but, naturally, in cases where past performance is far below capacity, beating that standard will be extremely easy.

Since goal setting is sometimes simply a matter of judgment, another technique we have used is to allow the goal to be set jointly by supervisor and subordinate. The participative approach may be less scientific than time and motion study, but it does lead to ready acceptance by both employee and immediate superior in addition to promoting role clarity.

External constraints often affect goal setting, especially among managers. For example, the goal to produce an item at a certain price may be dictated by the actions of competitors, and deadlines may be imposed externally in line with contract agreements. Legal regulations, such as attaining a certain reduction in pollution levels by a ceratin date, may affect goal setting as well. In these cases, setting the goal is not so much the problem as is figuring out a method of reaching it.

Finally, organizational goals set by the board of directors or upper management will influence the goals set by employees at lower levels. This is the essence of the MbO process.

Another issue that needs to be considered when setting goals is whether they should be designed for individuals or for groups. Rensis Likert and a number of other human relations experts argue for group goal setting on grounds that it promotes cooperation and team spirit. But one could argue that individual goals better promote individual responsibility and make it easier to appraise individual performance. The degree of task interdependence involved would also be a factor to consider.

Obtaining Goal Commitment

If goal setting is to work, then the manager must ensure that subordinates will accept and remain committed to the goals. Simple instruction backed by positive support and an absence of threats or intimidation were enough to ensure goal acceptance in most of our studies. Subordinates must perceive the goals as fair and reasonable and they must trust management, for if they perceive the goals as no more than a means of exploitation, they will be likely to reject the goals.

It may seem surprising that goal acceptance was achieved so readily in the field studies. Remember, however, that in all cases the employees were receiving wages or a salary (although these were not necessarily directly contingent on goal attainment). Pay in combination with the supervisor's benevolent authority and supportiveness were sufficient to bring about goal acceptance. Recent research indicates that whether goals are assigned or set participatively, supportiveness on the part of the immediate superior is critical. A supportive manager or supervisor does not use goals to threaten subordinates, but rather to clarify what is expected of them. His or her role is that of a helper and goal facilitator.

As noted earlier, the employee gets a feeling of pride and satisfaction from the experience of reaching a challenging but fair performance goal. Success in reaching a goal also tends to reinforce acceptance of future goals. Once goal setting is introduced, informal competition frequently arises among the employees. This further reinforces commitment and may lead employees to raise the goals spontaneously. A word of caution here, however. We do not recommend setting up formal competition, as this may lead employees to place individual goals ahead of company goals. The emphasis should be on accomplishing the task, getting the job done, not "beating" the other person.

When employees resist assigned goals, they generally do so for one of two reasons. First, they may think they are incapable of reaching the goal because they lack confidence, ability, knowledge, and the like. Second, they may not see any personal benefit—either in terms of personal pride or in terms of external rewards like money, promotion, recognition—in reaching assigned goals.

There are various methods of overcoming employee resistance to goals. One possibility is more training designed to raise the employee's level of skill and self-confidence. Allowing the subordinate to participate in setting the goal—deciding on the goal level—is another method. This was found most effective among uneducated and minority group employees, perhaps because it gave them a feeling of control over their fate. Offering monetary bonuses or other rewards (recognition, time off) for reaching goals may also help.

The last two methods may be especially useful where there is a history of labor-management conflict and where employees have become accustomed to a lower level of effort than currently considered acceptable. Group incentives may also encourage goal acceptance, especially where there is a group goal, or when considerable cooperation is required.

Providing Support Elements

A third step to take when introducing goal setting is to ensure the availability of necessary support elements. That is, the employee must be given adequate resources—money, equipment, time, help—as well as the freedom to utilize them in attaining goals, and company policies must not work to block goal attainment.

Before turning an employee loose with these resources, however, it's wise to do a quick check on whether conditions are optimum for reaching the goal set. First, the supervisor must

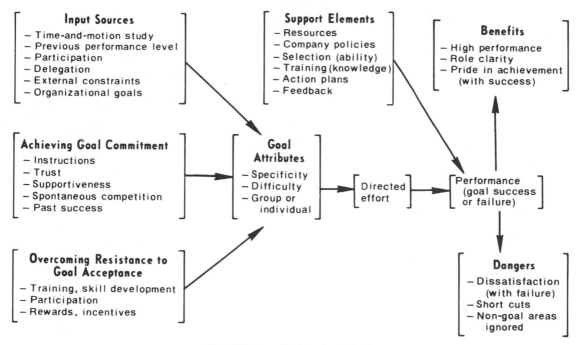

FIGURE 3. Goal-Setting Model

make sure that the employee has sufficient ability and knowledge to be able to reach the goal. Motivation without knowledge is useless. This, of course, puts a premium on proper selection and training and requires that the supervisor know the capabilities of subordinates when goals are assigned. Asking an employee to formulate an action plan for reaching the goal, as in MbO, is very useful, as it will indicate any knowledge deficiencies.

Second, the supervisor must ensure that the employee is provided with precise feedback so that he will know to what degree he's reaching or falling short of his goal and can thereupon adjust his level of effort or strategy accordingly. Recent research indicates that, while feedback is not a sufficient condition for improved performance, it is a necessary condition. A useful way to present periodic feedback is through the use of charts or graphs that plot performance over time.

Elements involved in taking the three steps described are shown in Figure 3, which illustrates in outline form our model of goal setting.

CONCLUSION

We believe that goal setting is a simple, straightforward, and highly effective technique for motivating employee performance. It is a basic technique, a method on which most other methods depend for their motivational effectiveness. The currently popular technique of behavior modification, for example, is mainly goal setting plus feedback, dressed up in academic terminology.

However, goal setting is no panacea. It will not compensate for underpayment of employees or for poor management. Used incorrectly, goal setting may cause rather than solve problems, If, for example, the goals set are unfair, arbitrary, or unreachable, dissatisfaction and poor performance may result. If difficult goals are set without proper quality controls, quantity may be achieved at the expense of quality. If pressure for immediate results is exerted without regard to how they are attained, short-term improvement may occur at the expense of long-run profits. That is, such pressure often triggers the use of expedient and ultimately costly methods—such as dishonesty, high-pressure tactics, postponing of maintenance expenses, and so on—to attain immediate results. Furthermore, performance goals are more easily set in some areas than in others. It's all too easy, for example, to concentrate on setting readily measured production goals and ignore employee development goals. Like any other management tool, goal setting works only when combined with good managerial judgment.

Managing Careers: The Influence of Job and Group Longevities

Ralph Katz

Any serious consideration of organizational careers must eventually explore the dynamics through which the concerns, abilities, and experiences of individual employees combine and mesh with the demands and requirements of their employing work environments. How do employees' needs for security, equitable rewards, and opportunities for advancement and self-development, for example, interact with the needs of organizations for ensured profitability, flexibility, and innovativeness? More important, how should they interact so that both prescription sets are filled satisfactorily?

Further complexity is added to this "matching" process with the realization that interactions between individuals and organizations are not temporally invariant but can shift significantly throughout workers' jobs, careers, and life cycles. As employees pass from one phase in their work lives to the next, different concerns and issues are emphasized; and the particular perspectives that result produce different behavioral and attitudinal combinations within their job settings. Over time, therefore, employees are continuously revising and adjusting their perspectives toward their organi-

zations and their roles in them. And it is the perspective that one has formulated at a particular point in time that gives meaning and direction to one's work and to one's career.

Because the effectiveness of a given organizational unit ultimately depends on the combined actions and performances of its membership, we must begin to examine more systematically the impact of such varying perspectives on the predilections of unit members for particular kinds of activities, interactions, and collective judgments. Clearly, a better understanding of the substantive nature of such dispositions and behavioral tendencies will help clarify accommodation processes between organizations and individuals so that eventual problems can be dealt with to their mutual benefits. To accomplish such objectives, however, we need to develop more process-oriented frameworks for analyzing the diverse kinds of concerns and associated behaviors that tend to preoccupy and characterize employees as they proceed through their respective jobs, project groups, and organizational careers.

"Managing Careers: The Influence of Job and Group Longevities," by Ralph Katz, in *Career Issues in Human Resource Management,* edited by Ralph Katz, pp. 154–181, copyright 1982. Reprinted by permission of Prentice-Hall, Inc., Englewood Cliffs, NJ.

A MODEL OF JOB LONGEVITY

Based on some recent findings in the areas of job satisfaction and task redesign, Katz (1980) has been working to develop a more general theory for describing how employees' perspectives unfold and change as they journey through their own discrete sequences of job situations. In particular, a three-transitional stage model of job longevity has been proposed to illustrate how certain kinds of concerns might change in importance according to the actual length of time an employee has been working in a given job position. Generally speaking, each time an employee is assigned to a new job position within an organization, either as a recent recruit or through transfer or promotion, the individual enters a relatively brief but nevertheless important "socialization" period. With increasing familiarity about his or her new job environment, however, the employee soon passes from socialization into the "innovation" stage, which, in turn, slowly

shifts into a "stabilization" state as the individual gradually adapts to extensive job longevity, (i.e., as the employee continues to work in the same overall job for an extended period of time). Table 1 summarizes the sequential nature of these three stages by comparing some of the different kinds of issues affecting employees as they cycle through their various job positions.[1]

Socialization

As outlined under the initial socialization stage, employees entering new job positions are concerned primarily with reality construction, building more realistic understandings of their unfamiliar social and task environments. In formulating their new perspectives, they are busily absorbed with problems of establishing and

TABLE 1.   *A Model of Job Longevity*

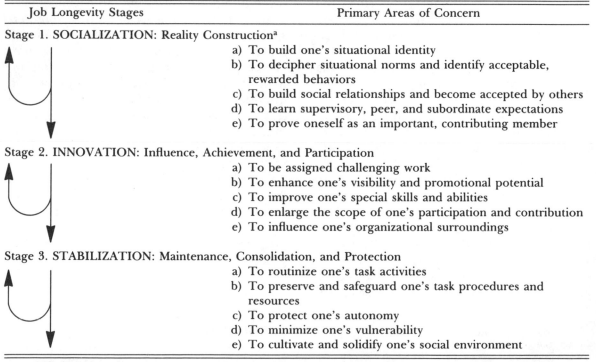

Job Longevity Stages	Primary Areas of Concern
Stage 1. SOCIALIZATION: Reality Construction[a]	a) To build one's situational identity
	b) To decipher situational norms and identify acceptable, rewarded behaviors
	c) To build social relationships and become accepted by others
	d) To learn supervisory, peer, and subordinate expectations
	e) To prove oneself as an important, contributing member
Stage 2. INNOVATION: Influence, Achievement, and Participation	a) To be assigned challenging work
	b) To enhance one's visibility and promotional potential
	c) To improve one's special skills and abilities
	d) To enlarge the scope of one's participation and contribution
	e) To influence one's organizational surroundings
Stage 3. STABILIZATION: Maintenance, Consolidation, and Protection	a) To routinize one's task activities
	b) To preserve and safeguard one's task procedures and resources
	c) To protect one's autonomy
	d) To minimize one's vulnerability
	e) To cultivate and solidify one's social environment

[a]The listed items are not meant to be exhaustive; rather they are intended to illustrate both the domain and the range of issues within each stage.

clarifying their own situational roles and identities and with learning all the attitudes and behaviors that are appropriate and expected within their new job settings. Estranged from their previous work environments and supporting relationships, newcomers must construct situational definitions that allow them to understand and interpret the myriad of experiences associated with their new organizational memberships. They need, for example, to learn the customary norms of behavior, decipher how reward systems actually operate, discover supervisory expectations, and more generally learn how to function meaningfully within their multiple group contexts (Schein, 1978). Through information communicated by their new "significant others," newcomers learn to develop perceptions of their own roles and skills that are both supported within their new surroundings and which permit them to organize their activities and interactions in a meaningful fashion. As pointed out by Hughes (1958) in his discussion of "reality shock," when new employees suddenly discover that their somewhat "overglorified" work-related expectations are neither realistic nor mutually shared by their boss or co-workers, they are likely to feel disenchanted and will experience considerable pressure to either redefine more compatible expectations or terminate from their work settings.

The importance of such a "breaking-in" period has long been recognized in discussions of how social processes affect recent organizational hires trying to make sense out of their newfound work experiences. What is also important to recognize is that veteran employees must also relocate or "resocialize" themselves following their displacements into new job positions within their same organizations (Wheeler, 1966). Just as organizational newcomers have to define and interpret their new territorial domains, veteran employees must also restructure and reformulate perceptions regarding their new social and task realities.[2] As they assume new organizational positions

and enter important new relationships, veterans must learn to integrate their new perceptions and experiences with prior organizational knowledge in order to develop fresh situational perspectives, including perceptions about their own self-images and their images of other organizational members.

Such perceptual revisions are typically necessary simply because work groups and other organizational subunits are often highly differentiated with respect to their idiosyncratic sets of norms, beliefs, perceptions, time perspectives, shared language schemes, goal orientations, and so on (Lawrence and Lorsch, 1967). As communications and interactions within an organizational subunit continue to take place or intensify, it is likely that a more common set of understandings about the subunit and its environment will develop through informational social influence. Such shared meanings and awarenesses not only provide the subunit's members with a sense of belonging and identity but will also demarcate the subunit from other organizational entities (Pfeffer, 1981). Consequently, as one shifts job positions and moves within the organization, one is likely to encounter and become part of a new set of groups with their correspondingly different belief systems and perspectives about themselves, their operations, and their operating environments. It is in this initial socialization period, therefore, that organizational employees, and newcomers in particular, learn not only the technical requirements of their new job assignments but also the interpersonal behaviors and social attitudes that are acceptable and necessary for becoming a true contributing member.

Since employees in the midst of socialization are strongly motivated to reduce ambiguity by creating order out of their somewhat vague and unfamiliar surroundings, it becomes clear why a number of researchers have discovered organizational newcomers being especially concerned with psychological safety and

447

security and with clarifying their new situational identities (Kahn et al., 1964; Hall and Nougaim, 1968). In a similar vein, Schein (1971) suggests that to become accepted and to prove one's competence represent two major problems that newcomers and veterans must face before they can function comfortably within their new job positions. It is these kinds of concerns that help to explain why Katz (1978a) discovered that during the initial months of their new job positions, employees are not completely ready to respond positively to all the challenging characteristics of their new task assignments. Instead, they appear most responsive to job features that provide a sense of personal acceptance and importance as well as a sense of proficiency through feedback and individual guidance.[3] Van Maanen's (1975) study of urban police socialization also demonstrated that for about the first three or four months of their initial job assignments, police recruits are busily absorbed in the process of changing and solidifying their own self- and job-related perceptions as they finally come to know the actual attitudes and behaviors of their veteran counterparts.

How long this initial socialization period lasts, therefore, probably depends on how long it takes employees to feel accepted and competent within their new work environments. Not only is the length of such a time period greatly influenced by the abilities, needs, and prior experiences of individual workers and influenced as well by the clarity and usefulness of the interpersonal interactions that take place, but it also probably differs significantly across occupations. Based on the retrospective answers of his hospital employee sample, for example, Feldman (1977) reports that on the average, accounting clerks, registered nurses, and engineering tradesmen reporting feeling accepted after one, two, and four months, respectively although they did not feel completely competent until after three, six, and eight months, respectively. Generally speaking, one might

posit that the length of one's initial socialization period varies positively with the level of complexity within one's job and occupational requirements, ranging perhaps from as little as a month or two on very routine, programmed-type jobs to as much as a year or more on very skilled, unprogrammed-type jobs, as in the engineering and scientific professions. With respect to engineering, for example, it is generally recognized that a substantial socialization period is often required before engineers can fully contribute within their new organizational settings, using their particular knowledge and technical specialties. Thus, even though one might have received an excellent education in mechanical engineering principles at a university or college, one must still figure out from working and interacting with others in the setting how to be an effective mechanical engineer at Westinghouse, DuPont, or Proctor and Gamble.[4]

Innovation

With time, interaction, and increasing familiarity, employees soon discover how to function appropriately in their jobs and to feel sufficiently secure in their perceptions of their workplace. Individual energies can now be devoted more toward task performance and accomplishment instead of being expended on learning the previously unfamiliar social knowledge and skills necessary to makes sense out of one's work-related activities and interactions. As a result, employees become increasingly capable of acting in a more responsive, innovative, and undistracted manner.

The movement from socialization to the innovation stage of job longevity implies that employees no longer require much assistance in deciphering their new job and organizational surroundings. Having adequately constructed their own situational definitions during the socialization period, employees are now freer to participate within their own conceptions of organizational reality. They are now able to divert their attention from an initial emphasis on psychological safety and acceptance to concerns for achievement and influence. Thus, what becomes progressively more pertinent to employees as they proceed from socialization to the innovation stage are the opportunities to participate and grow within their job settings in a very meaningful and responsible manner.

The idea of having to achieve some reasonable level of psychological safety and security in order to be fully responsive to challenges in the work setting is very consistent with Kuhn's (1963) concept of "creative tensions." According to Kuhn, it is likely that only when conditions of *both* stability and challenge are present can the creative tensions between them generate considerable innovative behavior. Growth theorists such as Maslow (1962) and Rogers (1961) have similarly argued that the presence of psychological safety is one of the chief prerequisites for self-direction and individual responsiveness. For psychological safety to occur, however, individuals must be able to understand and attach sufficient meaning to the vast array of events, interactions, and information flows involving them throughout their workdays. Of particular importance to growth theorists is the idea that employees must be able to expect positive results to flow from their individual actions. Such a precondition implies that employees must have developed sufficient knowledge about their new job situations in order for there to be enough predictability for them to take appropriate kinds of actions.[5]

A similar point of view is taken by Staw (1977) when he argues that if employees truly expect to improve their overall job situations, they must first learn to predict their most relevant set of behavioral-outcome contingencies before they try to influence or increase their control over them. One must first construct a reasonably valid perspective about such contingencies before one can sensibly strive to manage them for increasingly more favorable out-

comes. In short, there must be sufficient awareness of one's environment, sufficient acceptance and competence within one's setting, and sufficient openness to new ideas and experiences in order for employees to be fully responsive to the "richness" of their job demands.

Stabilization

As employees continue to work in their same overall job settings for a considerable length of time, without any serious disruption or displacement, they may gradually proceed from innovation to stabilization in the sense of shifting from being highly involved in and receptive to their job demands to becoming progressively unresponsive. For the most part, responsive individuals prefer to work at jobs they find stimulating and challenging and in which they can self-develop and grow. With such kinds of activities, they are likely to inject greater effort and involvement into their tasks which, in turn, will be reflected in their performances (Hackman and Oldham, 1975; Katz, 1978b). It seems reasonable to assume, however, that in time even the most challenging job assignments and responsibilities can appear less exciting and more habitual to jobholders who have successfully mastered and become increasingly accustomed to their everyday task requirements. With prolonged job longevity and stability, therefore, it is likely that employees' perceptions of their present conditions and of their future possibilities will become increasingly impoverished. They may begin essentially to question the value of what they are doing and where it may lead. If employees cannot maintain, redefine, or expand their jobs for continual challenge and growth, the substance and meaning of their work begins to deteriorate. Enthusiasm wanes, for what was once challenging and exciting may no longer hold much interest at all.

At the same time, it is also important to

mention that if an individual is able to increase or even maintain his or her own sense of task challenge and excitement on a given job for an extended period of time, then instead of moving toward stabilization, the process might be the reverse (i.e., continued growth and innovation). As before, the extent to which an individual can maintain his or her responsiveness on a particular job strongly depends on the complexity of the underlying tasks as well as on the individual's own capabilities, needs, and prior experiences. With respect to individual differences, for example, Katz's (1978b) findings suggest that employees with high growth needs are able to respond to the challenging aspects of their new jobs sooner than employees with low growth needs. At the same time, however, high-order-need employees might not retain their responsiveness for as long a job period as employees with low-growth-need strength.

It should also be emphasized that in addition to job longevity, many other contextual factors can affect a person's situational perspective strongly enough to influence the level of job interest as one continues to work in a given job position over a long period of time. New technological developments, rapid growth and expansion, the sudden appearance of external threats, or strong competitive pressures could all help sustain or even enhance an individual's involvement in his or her job-related activities. On the other hand, having to work closely with a group of unresponsive peers might shorten an individual's responsive period on that particular job rather dramatically. Clearly, the reactions of individuals are not only influenced by psychological predispositions and personality characteristics but also by individuals' definitions of and interactions with their overall situational settings (Homans, 1961; Salancik and Pfeffer, 1978).

Generally speaking, however, as tasks become progressively less stimulating to employees with extended job longevity, they can either leave the setting or remain and adapt to their present job situations (Argyris, 1957). In moving from innovation to stabilization, it is suggested that employees who continue to work in their same overall job situations for long periods of time gradually succeed in adapting to such steadfast employment by becoming increasingly indifferent and unresponsive to the challenging task features of their job assignments (Katz, 1978a). In the process of adaptation, they may also redefine what they consider to be important, most likely by placing relatively less value on intrinsic kinds of work issues. The findings of Kopelman (1977) and Hall and Schneider (1973) suggest, for example, that when individuals perceive their opportunities for intrinsic-type satisfactions and challenges to be diminishing, they begin to match such developments by placing less value on such types of expectations. And as employees come to care less about the intrinsic nature of the actual work they do, the greater their relative concern for certain contextual features, such as salary, benefits, vacations, friendly coworkers, and compatible supervision.

The passage from innovation to stabilization is not meant to suggest that job satisfaction necessarily declines with long-term job longevity. On the contrary, it is likely that in the process of adaptation, employees' expectations have become adequately satisfied as they continue to perform their familiar duties in their normally acceptable fashions. If aspirations are defined as a function of the disparity between desired and expected (Kiesler, 1978), then as long as what individuals desire is reasonably greater than what they can presently expect to attain, there will be energy for change and achievement. On the other hand, when employees arrive at a stage where their chances for future growth and challenges in their jobs are perceived to be remote, then as they adapt, it is likely that existing situations will become accepted as the desired and aspirations for growth and change will have been reduced. As a result, the more employees come to accept their present circumstances, the stronger the tendency to keep the existing work environment fairly stable. Career interests and aspirations may become markedly constricted, for in a sense, adapted employees may simply prefer to enjoy rather than try to add to their present job accomplishments.

Underpinning the descriptive changes represented by the stabilization stage is the basic idea that over time individuals try to organize their work lives in a manner that reduces the amount of stress they must face and which is also low in uncertainty (Pfeffer, 1980; Staw, 1977). Weick (1969) also relies on this perspective when he contends that employees seek to "enact" their environments by directing their activities toward the establishment of a workable level of certainty and clarity. In general, one might argue that employees strive to bring their work activities into a state of equilibrium where they are more capable of predicting events and of avoiding potential conflicts.[6]

Given such developmental trends, it seems reasonable that with considerable job longevity, most employees have been able to build a work pattern that is familiar and comfortable, a pattern in which routine and precedent play a relatively large part. According to Weick (1969), as employees establish certain structures of interlocked behaviors and relationships, these patterns will in time become relatively stable simply because they provide certainty and predictability to these interlinked employees. It is further argued here that as individuals adapt to their long-term job tenure and become progressively less responsive to their actual task demands, they will come to rely more on these established modes of conduct to complete their everyday job requirements. Most likely, adapted employees feel safe and comfortable in such stability, for its keeps them feeling secure and confident in what they do, yet requires little additional vigilance or effort. In adapting to extended job longevity, therefore, employees become increasingly content and ensconced in their customary ways of doing things, in their comfortable routines and interactions, and in their familiar sets of task demands and responsibilities.

If change or uncertainty is seen by individuals in the stabilization period as particularly disruptive, then the preservation of familiar routines and patterns of behavior is likely to be of prime concern. Given such a disposition, adapted employees are probably less receptive toward any change or toward any information that might threaten to disturb their developing sense of complacency. Rather than striving to enlarge the scope of their job demands, they may be more concerned with maintaining their comfortable work environments by protecting themselves from sources of possible interference, from activities requiring new kinds of attention, or form situations that might reveal their shortcomings. Adapted employees, for example, might seek to reduce uncertainty in their day-to-day supervisory dealings perhaps by solidifying their attractiveness through ingratiating kinds of behavior (Wortman and Linsenmeier, 1977) or perhaps by isolating themselves from such supervisory contacts (Pelz and Andrews, 1966). Or they might seek to reduce uncertainty by trying to safeguard their personal allocations of resources and rewards through the use of standardized practices and policies. Whatever the specific behaviors that eventually emerge in a given setting, it is likely that employees who have become unresponsive to the challenging features of their assigned tasks will strongly resist events threatening to introduce uncertainty into their work environments.

One of the best examples of the effects of such long-term stability can still be found in Chinoy's (1955) classic interviews of automobile factory workers. Chinoy discovered that although almost 80% of the workers had wanted to leave their present jobs at one time or another, very few could actually bring themselves to leave. Most of the workers were simply unwilling to give up the predictability and comfortableness of their presently familiar routines and cultivated relationships for the uncertainties of a new job position.

SITUATIONAL VERSUS INDIVIDUAL CONTROL

In presenting this three-stage model of job longevity, I have tried to describe some of the major concerns affecting employees as they enter and adapt to their particular job positions. Of course, the extent to which any specific individual is affected by these issues depends on the particular perceptual outlook that has been developed over time through job-related activities and through role-making processes with other individuals, including supervisors, subordinates, and peers (Weick, 1969; Graen, 1976). Employees, as a result, learn to cope with their particular job and organizational environments through their interpretations of relevant work experiences as well as their expectations and hopes of the future. To varying degrees, then, situational perspectives are derivatives of both retrospective and prospective processes, in that they are built and shaped through knowledge of past events and future anticipations.

One of the more important aspects of the socialization process, however, is that the information and knowledge previously gathered by employees from their former settings are no longer sufficient or necessarily appropriate for interpreting or understanding their new organizational domains. Newcomers, for instance, have had only limited contact within their new institutional surroundings from which to construct their perceptual views. Similarly, the extent to which veterans who are assuming new job positions can rely on their past organizational experiences and perspectives to function effectively within their new work set-

tings can also be rather limited, depending of course on their degrees of displacement.

Essentially, individuals in the midst of socialization are trying to navigate their way through new and unfamiliar territories without the aid of adequate or even accurate perceptual maps. During this initial period, therefore, they are typically more malleable and more susceptible to change (Schein, 1968). In a sense, they are working under conditions of high "situational control" in that they must depend on other individuals within their new situations to help them define and interpret the numerous activities taking place around them. The greater their unfamiliarity or displacement within their new organizational areas, the more they must rely on their situations to provide the necessary information and interactions by which they can eventually construct their own perspectives and reestablish new situational identities. And it is precisely this external need or "situational dependency" that enables these individuals to be more easily influenced during their socialization processes through social interactions (Salancik and Pfeffer, 1978; Katz, 1980).

As employees become increasingly cognizant of their overall job surroundings, however, they also become increasingly capable of relying on their own perceptions for interpreting events and executing their everyday task requirements. In moving from socialization into the innovation or stabilization stage, employees have succeeded in building a sufficiently robust situational perspective, thereby freeing themselves to operate more self-sufficiently within their familiar work settings. They are now working under conditions of less "situational" but more "individual" control, in the sense that they are now better equipped to determine for themselves the importance and meaning of the various events and information flows surrounding them. Having established their own social and task supports, their own perceptual outlooks, and their own situational identities, they become less easily changed and less easily manipulated. As pointed out by Schein (1973), when individuals no longer have to balance their situational perspectives against the views of significant others within their settings, they become less susceptible to change and situational influences. Thus, movement through the three stages of job longevity can also be characterized, as shown in Figure 1, by relative shifts to more individual and less situational control.

As the locus of "control" shifts with increasing job longevity and individuals continue to stabilize their situational definitions, other important behavioral tendencies could also materialize. In particular, strong biases could develop in the way individuals select and interpret information, in their cognitive abilities to generate new options and strategies creatively, and in their willingness to innovate or implement alternative courses of action. Table 2 outlines in more detail some of the specific possibilities within each of these three general areas. Furthermore, it is the capacity either to prevent or overcome these kinds of tendencies that is so important to the long-term success of organizations; for, over time, each of these trends could lead to less effective performance and decision-making outcomes.

Problem-Solving Processes

It has been argued throughout this paper that as employees gradually adapt to prolonged periods of job longevity, they may become less receptive toward any change or innovation threatening to disrupt significantly their comfortable and predictable work practices and patterns of behavior. Individuals, instead, are more likely to develop reliable and effective routine responses (i.e., standard operating procedures) for dealing with their frequently encountered tasks in order to ensure predictability, coordination, and economical information processing. As a result, there may develop over time increasing rigidity in one's problem-solving activities—a kind of functional fixedness that reduces the individual's capacity for flexibility and openness to change. Responses and decisions are made in their fixed, normal patterns while novel situations requiring responses that do not fit such established molds are either ignored or forced into these molds. New or changing situations either trigger responses of old situations or trigger no responses at all. It becomes, essentially, a work world characterized by the phrase "business as usual."

Furthermore, as individuals continue to work by their well-established problem-solving

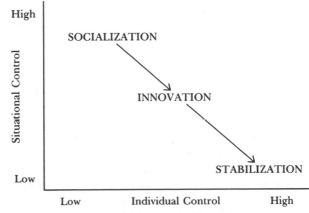

FIGURE 1. *Situational versus Individual Control Along the Job-Longevity Continuum*

TABLE 2.   *Representative Trends Associated With Long-term Job Longevity*

Problem-solving processes
  Increased rigidity
  Increased commitment to established practices
    and procedures
  Increased mainlining of strategies

Information processes
  Increased insulation from critical areas
  Increased selective exposure
  Increased selective perception

Cognitive processes
  Increased reliance on own experiences and
    expertise
  Increased narrowing of cognitive abilities
  Increased homophyly

sent courses of action can become even stronger—often to the extent that these competing alternatives are never reconsidered.[7] In fact, individuals can become overly preoccupied with the survival of their particular approaches, protecting them against fresh approaches or negative evaluations. Much of their energy becomes directed toward "mainlining their strategies," that is, making sure their specific solution approaches are selected and followed. Research by Janis and Mann (1977) and Staw (1980) has demonstrated very convincingly just how strongly committed individuals can become to their problem-solving approaches and decisions, even in the face of adverse information, especially if they feel personally responsible for such strategies.

strategies and procedures, the more committed they may become to such existing methods. Commitment is a function of time, and the longer individuals are called upon to follow and justify their problem-solving approaches and decisions, the more ingrained they are likely to become. Drawing from his work on decision making, Allison (1971) strongly warns that increasing reliance on regularized practices and procedures can become highly resistant to change, since such functions become increasingly grounded in the norms and basic attitudes of the organizational unit and in the operating styles of its members. Bion (1961) and Argyris (1969) even suggest that it may be impossible for individuals to break out of fixed patterns of activity and interpersonal behavior without sufficiently strong outside interference or help.

With extended job tenure, then, problem-solving activities can become increasingly guided by consideration of methods and programs that have worked in the past. Moreover, in accumulating this experience and knowledge, alternative ideas and approaches were probably considered and discarded. With such refutations, however, commitments to the pre-

Information Processes

One of the potential consequences of developing this kind of "status-quo" perspective with respect to problem-solving activity is that employees may also become increasingly insulated from outside sources of relevant information and important new ideas. As individuals become more protective of and committed to their current work habits, the extent to which they are willing or even feel they need to expose themselves to new or alternative ideas, solution strategies, or constructive criticisms becomes progressively less and less. Rather than becoming more vigilant about events taking place outside their immediate work settings, they may become increasingly complacent about external environmental changes and new technological developments.

In addition to this possible decay in the amount of external contact and interaction, there may also be an increasing tendency for individuals to communicate only with those whose ideas are in accord with their current interests, needs, or existing attitudes. Such a tendency is referred to as selective exposure. Generally speaking, there is always the tendency for individuals to communicate with those who are most like themselves (Rogers and Shoemaker, 1971). With increasing adaptation to long-term job longevity and stability, however, this tendency is likely to become even stronger. Thus, selective exposure may increasingly enable these individuals to avoid information and messages that might be in conflict with their current practices and dispositions.

One should also recognize, of course, that under these kinds of circumstances, any outside contact or environmental information that does become processed by these long-tenured individuals might not be viewed in the most open and unbiased fashion. Janis and Mann (1977), for example, discuss at great length the many kinds of cognitive defenses and distortions commonly used by individuals in processing outside information in order to support, maintain, or protect certain decisional policies and strategies. Such defenses are often used to argue against any disquieting information and evidence in order to maintain self-esteem, commitment, and involvement. In particular, selective perception is the tendency to interpret information and communication messages in terms favorable to one's existing attitudes and beliefs. And it is this combination of increasing insulation, selective exposure, and selective perception that can be so powerful in keeping critical information and important new ideas and innovations from being registered.

Cognitive Processes

As individuals become more comfortable and secure in their long-tenured work environments, their desire to seek out and actively internalize new knowledge and new developments may begin to deteriorate. Not only may they become increasingly isolated from outside sources of information, but their willingness to accept or pay adequate attention to the advice and ideas of fellow experts may become less and less. Unlike the socialization period in which individuals are usually very attentive to sources of expertise and influence within their new job settings, individuals in the stabilization stage have probably become significantly less receptive to such information sources. They may prefer, instead, to rely on their own accumulated experience and wisdom and consequently are more apt to dismiss the approaches, advice, or critical comments of others. As a result, adapted employees may be especially defensive with regard to critical evaluations and feedback messages, whether they stem from sources of outside expertise or from internal supervision.

It should also not be surprising that with increasing job stability one is more likely to become increasingly specialized, that is, moving from broadly defined capabilities and solution approaches to more narrowly defined interests and specialties. Without new challenges and opportunities, the diversity of skills and of ideas generated are likely to become narrower and narrower. And as individuals welcome information from fewer sources and are exposed to fewer alternative points of view, the more constricted their cognitive abilities can become. Essentially, there can be a narrowing of one's cognitive processes, resulting in a more restricted perspective of one's situation, coupled with a more limited set of coping responses. Such a restricted outlook, moreover can be very detrimental to the organization's overall effectiveness, for it could lead at times to the screening out of some vitally important environmental information cues.

Homophyly refers to the degree to which interacting individuals are similar with respect to certain attributes, such as beliefs, values, education, and social status (Rogers and Shoemaker, 1971). Not only is there a strong tendency for individuals to communicate with those who are most like themselves, but it is also likely that continued interaction can lead to greater homophyly in knowledge, beliefs, and problem-solving behaviors and

455

perceptions (Burke and Bennis, 1961; Pfeffer, 1980). The venerable proverb "birds of a feather flock together" makes a great deal of sense, but it may be just as sensible to say that "when birds flock together, they become more of a feather." Accordingly, as individuals stabilize their work settings and patterns of communication, a greater degree of homophyly is likely to have emerged between these individuals and those with whom they have been interacting over the long tenure period. And any increase in homophyly could lead in turn to further stability in the communications of the more homophilous pairs, thereby increasing their insulation from heterophilous others. Thus, it is possible for the various trends to feed on each other. Finally, it should be mentioned that although individuals may be able to coordinate and communicate with homophilous partners more effectively and economically, such interactions are also more likely to yield less creative and innovative outcomes (Pelz and Andrews, 1966).

Longevity and Performance

These problem-solving, informational, and cognitive tendencies, of course, can be very serious in their consequences, perhaps even fatal. Much depends, however, on the nature of the work being performed and on the extent to which such trends actually transpire. The performances of individuals working on fairly routine, simple tasks in a rather stable organizational environment, for example, may not suffer as a result of these trends, for their own knowledge, experiences, and abilities become sufficient. Maintaining or improving on one's routine behaviors is all that is required—at least for as long as there are no changes and no new developments. However, as individuals function in a more rapidly changing environment and work on more complex tasks requiring greater levels of change, creativity, and informational vigilance, the effects of these long-

term longevity trends are likely to become significantly more dysfunctional.

GROUP LONGEVITY

The degree to which any of these previously described trends actually materializes for any given individual depends, of course, on the overall situational context. Individuals' perceptions and responses do not take place in a social vacuum but develop over time as they continue to interact with various aspects of their job and organizational surroundings (Crozier, 1964; Katz and Van Maanen, 1977). And in any job setting one of the most powerful factors affecting individual perspectives is the nature of the particular group or project team in which one is a functioning member (Schein, 1978; Katz and Kahn, 1978).

Ever since the well-known Western Electric Studies (Cass and Zimmer, 1975), much of our research in the social sciences has been directed toward learning just how strong group associations can be in influencing individual member behaviors, motivations, and attitudes (Asch, 1956; Shaw, 1971; Katz, 1977). From the diffusion of new innovations (Robertson, 1971) to the changing of meat consumption patterns to less desirable but more plentiful cuts (Lewin, 1965) to the implementation of job enrichment (Hackman, 1978), group processes and effects have been extremely critical to more successful outcomes. The impact of groups on individual responses is substantial, if not pervasive, simply because groups mediate most of the stimuli to which their individual members are subjected while fulfilling their everyday task and organizational requirements. Accordingly, whether individuals experiencing long-term job longevity enter the stabilization period and become subjected to the tendencies previously described may strongly depend on the particular reinforcements, pressures, and behavioral norms encountered within their immediate project or work groups (Likert, 1967; Weick, 1969).

Generally speaking, as members of a project group continue to work together over an extended period of time and gain experience with one another, their patterns of activities are likely to become more stable, with individual role assignments becoming more well-defined and resistant to change (Bales, 1955; Porter et al., 1975). Emergence of the various problem-solving, informational, and cognitive trends, therefore, may be more a function of the average length of time the group members have worked together (i.e., group longevity) rather than varying according to the particular job longevity of any single individual. A project group, then, might either exacerbate or ameliorate the various trends (e.g., insulation from outside developments and expertise), just as previous studies have shown how groups can enforce or amplify certain standards and norms of individual behavior (e.g., Seashore, 1954; Stoner, 1968). Thus, it may be misleading to investigate the responses and reactions of organizational individuals as if they functioned as independent entities; rather, it may be more insightful to examine the distribution of responses as a function of different project teams, especially when project teams are characterized by relatively high levels of group longevity.

NOTES

1. For a more extensive discussion of the job-longevity model, see Katz (1980). In the current presentation, the term "stabilization" is used in place of "adaptation" since individuals are in effect adapting to their job situations in all three stages, albeit in systematically different ways.

2. The extent to which a veteran employee actually undergoes socialization depends on how displaced the veteran becomes in undertaking his or her new job assignment. Generally speaking, the more displaced veterans are from their previously familiar task requirements and interpersonal associations, the more intense the socialization experience.

3. After comparing the socialization reactions of veterans and newcomers, Katz (1978a) suggests that newcomers may be especially responsive to interactional issues involving personal acceptance and "getting on board," whereas veterans may be particularly concerned with reestablishing their sense of competency in their newly acquired task assignments.

4. One of the factors contributing to the importance of this socialization period lies in the realization that engineering strategies and solutions within organizations are often not defined in very generalizeable terms but are peculiar to their specific settings (Allen, 1977; Katz and Tushman, 1979). As a result, R&D project groups in different organizations may face similar problems yet may define their solution approaches and parameters very differently. And it is precisely because technical problems are typically expressed in such "localized" terms that engineers must learn how to contribute effectively within their new project groups.

5. It is also interesting to note that in discussing his career-anchor framework, Schein (1978) points out that career anchors seem to represent a stable concept around which individuals are able to organize experiences and direct activities. Furthermore, it appears from Schein's research that it is within this area of stability that individuals are most likely to self-develop and grow.

6. There are, of course, alternative arguments, such as in activation theory (Scott, 1966), suggesting that people do in fact seek uncertainty, novelty, or change. The argument here, however, is that as individuals adapt and become increasingly indifferent to the task challenges of their jobs, it is considerably more likely that they will strive to reduce uncertainty and maintain predictability rather than the reverse.

7. As shown by Allen's (1966) research on parallel project efforts, such reevaluations can be very important in reaching more successful outcomes.

REFERENCES

Allison, G.T. *Essence of Decision: Explaining the Cuban Missile Crisis.* Boston: Little, Brown, 1971.

Argyris, C. *Personality and Organization.* New York: Harper Torch Books, 1957.

Argyris, C. "The incompleteness of social psychological theory: examples from small group, cognitive consistency and attribution research." *American Psychologist,* 1969, *24,* 893–908.

Asch, S.E. "Studies of independence and conformity: a minority of one against a unanimous majority." *Psychological Monographs,* 1956, *70.*

Bales, R.F. "Adaptive and integrative changes as sources of strain in social systems." In A.P. Hare, E.F. Borgatta, and R.F. Bales, eds., *Small Groups: Studies in Social Interaction.* New York: Knopf, 1955, pp. 127–31.

Bion, W.R. *Experiences in Groups.* New York: Basic Books, 1961.

Burke, R.L., and Bennis, W.G. "Changes in perception of self and others during human relations training." *Human Relations,* 1961, *14,* 165–82.

Cass, E.L., and Zimmer, F.G. *Man and Work in Society.* New York: Van Nostrand Reinhold, 1975.

Chinoy, E. *Automobile Workers and the American Dream.* Garden City, N.Y.: Doubleday, 1955.

Crozier, M. *The Bureaucratic Phenomenon.* Chicago: University of Chicago Press, 1964.

Feldman, D. "The role of initiation activities in socialization." *Human Relations,* 1977, *30,* 977–90.

Graen, G. "Role-making processes within complex organizations." In M.D. Dunnette, ed., *Handbook of Industrial and Organizational Psychology,* Chicago: Rand McNally, 1976.

Hackman, J.R. "The design of self managing work groups." In B. King, S. Streufert, and F. Fielder, eds., *Managerial Control and Organizational Democracy.* New York: Wiley, 1978.

Hackman, J.R., and Oldham, G.R. "Development of the job diagnostic survey." *Journal of Applied Psychology,* 1975, *60,* 159–70.

Hall, D.T. *Careers in Organizations.* Pacific Palisades, Calif.: Goodyear, 1976.

Hall, D.T., and Nougaim, K.E. "An examination of Maslow's need hierarchy in an organizational setting." *Organizational Behavior and Human Performance,* 1968, *3,* 12–35.

Hall, D.T., and Schneider, B. *Organizational Climates and Careers.* New York: Seminar Press, 1973.

Homans, G.C. *Social Behavior: Its Elementary Forms.* New York: Harcourt, Brace and World, 1961.

Hughes, E.C. *Men and Their Work.* Glencoe, Ill.: Free Press, 1958.

Janis, I.L., and Mann, L. *Decision Making.* New York: Free Press, 1977.

Kahn, R.L., Wolfe, D.M., Quinn, R.P., Snoek, J.D., and Rosenthal, R.A. *Organizational Stress: Studies on Role Conflict and Ambiguity.* New York: Wiley, 1964.

Katz, D., and Kahn, R.L. *The Social Psychology of Organizations.* New York: Wiley, 1978.

Katz, R. "The influence of group conflict on leadership effectiveness." *Organizational Behavior and Human Performance,* 1977, *20,* 265–86.

Katz, R. "Job longevity as a situational factor in job satisfaction." *Administrative Science Quarterly,* 1978a, *10,* 204–23.

Katz, R., "The influence of job longevity on employee reactions to task characteristics." *Human Relations,* 1978b, *31,* 703–25.

Katz, R. "Time and work: toward an integrative perspective." In B. Staw and L.L. Cummings, eds., *Research in Organizational Behavior,* Vol. 2. Greenwich, Conn.: JAI Press, 1980, 81–127.

Katz, R., and Allen, T. "Investigating the not-invented-here syndrome." In A. Pearson, ed., *Industrial R&D Strategy and Management,* London: Basil Blackwell Press, 1981.

Katz, R., and Tushman, M. "Communication patterns, project performance and task characteristics: an empirical evaluation and integration in an R&D setting." *Organizational Behavior and Human Performance,* 1979, *23,* 139–62.

Katz, R., and Van Maanen, J. "The loci of work satisfaction: job, interaction, and policy." *Human Relations,* 1977, *30,* 469–86.

Kaufman, H.G. *Obsolescence of Professional Career Development.* New York: AMACOM, 1974.

Kiesler, S. *Interpersonal Processes in Groups and Organizations.* Arlington Heights, Ill.: AHM Publishers, 1978.

Kopelman, R.E. "Psychological stages of careers in engineering: an expectancy theory taxonomy." *Journal of Vocational Behavior,* 1977, *10,* 270–86.

Kuhn, T.S. *The Structure of Scientific Revolutions.* Chicago: University of Chicago Press, 1963.

Lawrence, P.R., and Lorsch, J.W. *Organizational and Environment.* Boston: Harvard Business School, 1967.

Lewin, K. "Group decision and social change." In H. Proshansky and B. Seidenberg, eds., *Basic Studies in Social Psychology.* New York: Holt, Rinehart, and Winston, 1965, pp. 423–36.

Likert, R. *The Human Organization.* New York: McGraw-Hill, 1967.

Maslow, A. *Toward a Psychology of Being.* Princeton, N.J.: D. Van Nostrand, 1962.

Pelz, A., and Andrews, F.M. *Scientists in Organizations.* New York: Wiley, 1966.

Pfeffer, J. "Management as symbolic action: the creation and maintenance of organizational paradigms." In L.L. Cummings and B. Staw, eds., *Research in Organizational Behavior,* Vol. 3. Greenwich, Conn.: JAI Press, 1981.

Porter, L.W., Lawler, E.E., and Hackman, J.R. *Behavior in Organizations.* New York: McGraw-Hill, 1975.

Robertson, T.S. *Innovative Behavior and Communication.* New York: Holt, Rinehart and Winston, 1971.

Rogers, C.R. *On Becoming a Person.* Boston: Houghton Mifflin, 1961.

Rogers, E.M., and Shoemaker, F.F. *Communication of Innovations: A Crosscultural Approach.* New York: Free Press, 1971.

Salancik, G.R., and Pfeffer, J. "A social information processing approach to job attitudes and task design." *Administrative Science Quarterly,* 1978, *23,* 224–53.

Schein, E.H. "Organizational socialization and the profession of management." *Industrial Management Review,* 1968, *9,* 1–15.

Schein, E.H. "The individual, the organization, and the career: a conceptual scheme." *Journal of Applied Behavioral Science,* 1971, *7,* 401–26.

Schein, E.H. "Personal change though interpersonal relationships." In W.G. Bennis, D.E. Berlew, E.H. Schein, and F.I. Steele, eds., *Interpersonal Dynamics: Essays and Readings on Human Interaction.* Homewood, Ill.: Dorsey Press, 1973.

Schein, E.H. *Career Dynamics.* Reading, Mass.: Addison-Wesley, 1978.

Scott, W.E., "Activation theory and task design." *Organizational Behavior and Human Performance,* 1966, *1,* 3–30.

Seashore, S.F. "Group cohesiveness in the industrial work group." Ann Arbor, Mich.: Survey Research Center, University of Michigan, 1954.

Shaw, M.E. *Group Dynamics: The Psychology of Small Group Behavior.* New York: McGraw-Hill, 1971.

Staw, B. "Motivation in organizations: toward synthesis and redirection." In B. Staw and G.R. Salancik, eds., *New Directions in Organizational Behavior.* Chicago: St. Clair Press, 1977.

Staw, B. "Rationality and justification in organizational life." In B. Staw and L.L. Cummings, eds., *Research in Organizational Behavior,* Vol. 2. Greenwich, Conn.: JAI Press, 1980, pp. 45–80.

Stoner, J.A. "Risky and cautious shifts in group decisions: the influence of widely held values." *Journal of Experimental Social Psychology,* 1968, *4,* 442–59.

Tushman, M., and Katz, R. "External communication and project performance: an investigation into the role of gatekeepers." *Management Science,* 1980, *26,* 1071–1085.

Van Maanen, J. "Police socialization." *Administrative Science Quarterly,* 1975, *20,* 207–28.

Weick, K.E. *The Social Psychology of Organizing.* Reading, Mass.: Addison-Wesley, 1969.

Wortman, C.B., and Linsenmeier, J. "Interpersonal attraction and techniques of ingratiation in organizational settings." In B. Staw and G.R. Salancik, eds., *New Directions in Organizational Behavior.* Chicago: St. Clair Press, 1977.

Organization Adaptation and Change

INTRODUCTION AND OVERVIEW

The past four sections have focused on organization statics. We have stressed building an internally consistent social and technical system to get today's work done. If important problems exist, however, the congruence model pushes the manager to engage in systematic diagnosis, which in turn leads to interventions to get at root organization causes. The need to manage organization change may be driven by organization problem-solving efforts. Organization change may also be required in successful organizations that face changing competitive requirements. For example, regulatory changes or an oil shortage may require widespread organizational changes even in the most successful firms.

Managing organization change is difficult, however. Successful organizations have an inherent drive toward stability and increasing rigidity. As organizations grow and age, internal forces for stability stunt a firm's ability to learn. This organizational propensity toward greater inertia is a double-edged sword. Inertia is functional as long as strategy is appropriate and the organization is effective. However, organization inertia cuts the other way if (and when) environmental conditions shift and/or when performance crisis conditions erupt. An organization's capacity to learn and adapt may be reduced as a consequence of internal congruence and past success. If environmental conditions change, today's success may sow the seeds of tomorrow's crisis; today's vigilance often leads to tomorrow's complacency; today's commitment may lead to tomorrow's resistance to change.

Managers face a paradox. Congruence is at once a source of short-term effectiveness as well as long-term inertia. This section confronts this dilemma as we focus on organization adaptation and change. Building on the Leavitt, Greiner, Burgelman, and Miles and Snow readings in prior sections, this section and Section VI suggest that an important managerial task is to build organizations that retain their ability to learn and unlearn as environmental conditions change.

461

A theme in these last sections is the importance of maintaining a balance between organization stability and change. Those most effective managers (at least in turbulent environments) are those that can manage through relatively long periods of incremental change, even as they prepare their organizations for discontinuous change in response to external threats. If environmental conditions change sharply, then management needs to create a fundamentally different organization that can build on its past even as it confronts a completely different present. Under these paradoxical conditions, the manager's role is not unlike that of an artist; creativity, charisma, balance, and vision are critical at these junctures in organization evolution.

Given the complex and unstable environments within which managers work, multiple skills may be required in order for a manager to be successful over time. The engineer's skills are necessary in choosing structures, controls, cultures, and individuals to get today's work done. Political skills are required to shape and build the coalitions necessary to get things done and decisions implemented in mixed-motive settings. Finally, the artist's skills are required to handle the paradoxes and dilemmas faced by managers as they struggle to meet today's deadlines and tomorrow's competitive requirements. This section focuses, then, on the roots of inertia, organization evolution and adaptation, and the management of both incremental and discontinuous change. Section VI picks up the issue of executive leadership and managing organizations over time.

READINGS IN SECTION V

Morison's history of naval gunfire through the turn of the century is a brilliant discussion of the sources and consequences of organization inertia. Where Morison describes the roots of inertia, Tushman, Newman, and Romanelli focus on organization adaptation. They present an approach to organization adaptation that hinges on periods of incremental change punctuated by discontinuous, system-wide, organization change. Their article underscores the role of the executive team in steering a balance between stability and change; between learning and unlearning. Our next two articles discuss implementing strategic change. Nadler, building on the congruence model, presents several ideas on how to implement organization change. Allaire and Firosutu discuss different types of strategic change and different implementation procedures for each type.

9

ORGANIZATION ADAPTATION AND CHANGE

Gunfire at Sea: A Case Study of Innovation

Elting Morison

In the early days of the last war when armaments of all kinds were in short supply, the British, I am told, made use of a venerable field piece that had come down to them from previous generations. The honorable past of this light artillery stretched back, in fact, to the Boer War. In the days of uncertainty after the fall of France, these guns, hitched to trucks, served as useful mobile units in the coast defense. But it was felt that the rapidity of fire could be increased. A time-motion expert was, therefore, called in to suggest ways to simplify the firing procedures. He watched one of the gun crews of five men at practice in the field for some time. Puzzled by certain aspects of the procedures, he took some slow-motion pictures of the soldiers performing the loading, aiming, and firing routines.

When he ran these pictures over once or twice, he noticed something that appeared odd to him. A moment before the firing, two members of the gun crew ceased all activity and came to attention for a three-second interval extending throughout the discharge of the gun. He summoned an old colonel of artillery, showed him the pictures and pointed out this strange behavior. What, he asked the colonel, did it mean. The colonel, too, was puzzled. He asked to see the pictures again. "Ah," he said when the performance was over, "I have it. They are holding the horses."

This story, true or not, and I am told it is true, suggests nicely the pain with which the human being accommodates himself to changing conditions. The tendency is apparently involuntary and immediate to protect oneself against the shock of change by continuing in the presence of altered situations the familiar habits, however incongruous, of the past.

Yet, if human beings are attached to the known, to the realm of things as they are, they also, regrettably for their peace of mind, are incessantly attracted to the unknown and things as they might be. As Ecclesiastes glumly

From *Men, Machines and Modern Times* by Elting Morison, copyright 1977 by MIT Press. Reprinted by permission.

pointed out, men persist in disordering their settled ways and beliefs by seeking out many inventions.

The point is obvious. Change has always been a constant in human affairs; today, indeed, it is one of the determining characteristics of our civilization. In our relatively shapeless social organization, the shifts from station to station are fast and easy. More important for our immediate purpose, America is fundamentally an industrial society in a time of tremendous technological development. We are thus constantly presented with new devices or new forms of power that in their refinement and extension continually bombard the fixed structure of our habits of mind and behavior. Under such conditions, our salvation, or at least our peace of mind, appears to depend upon how successfully we can in the future become what has been called in an excellent phrase a completely "adaptive society."

It is interesting, in view of all this, that so little investigation, relatively, has been made of the process of change and human responses to it. Recently, psychologists, sociologists, cultural anthropologists, and economists have addressed themselves to the subject with suggestive results. But we are still far from a full understanding of the process and still further from knowing how we can set about simplifying and assisting an individual's or a group's accommodation to new machines or new ideas.

With these things in mind, I thought it might be interesting and perhaps useful to examine historically a changing situation within a society; to see if from this examination we can discover how the new machines or ideas that introduced the changing situation developed; to see who introduces them, who resists them, what points of friction or tension in the social structure are produced by the innovation, and perhaps why they are produced and what, if anything, may be done about it. For this case study the introduction of continuous-aim firing in the United States Navy has been selected.

The system, first devised by an English officer in 1898, was introduced in our Navy in the years 1900 to 1902.

I have chosen to study this episode for two reasons. First, a navy is not unlike a society that has been placed under laboratory conditions. Its dimensions are severely limited; it is beautifully ordered and articulated; it is relatively isolated from random influences. For these reasons the impact of change can be clearly discerned, the resulting dislocations in the structure easily discovered and marked out. In the second place, the development of continuous-aim firing rests upon mechanical devices. It therefore presents for study a concrete, durable situation. It is not like many other innovating reagents—a Manichean heresy, or Marxism, or the views of Sigmund Freud—that can be shoved and hauled out of shape by contending forces or conflicting prejudices. At all times we know exactly what continuous-aim firing really is. It will be well now to describe, as briefly as possible, what it really is. This will involve a short investigation of certain technical matters. I will not apologize, as I have been told I ought to do, for this preoccupation with how a naval gun is fired. For one thing, all that follows is understandable only if one understands how the gun goes off. For another thing, a knowledge of the underlying physical considerations may give a kind of elegance to the succeeding investigation of social implications. And now to the gun and the gunfire.

The governing fact in gunfire at sea is that the gun is mounted on an unstable platform, a rolling ship. This constant motion obviously complicates the problem of holding a steady aim. Before 1898 this problem was solved in the following elementary fashion. A gun pointer estimated the range of the target, ordinarily in the nineties about 1600 yards. He then raised the gun barrel to give the gun the elevation to carry the shell to the target at the estimated range. This elevating process was accomplished by turning a small wheel on the gun mount that operated the elevating gears. With the gun thus fixed for range, the gun pointer peered through open sights, not unlike those on a small rifle, and waited until the roll of the ship brought the sights on the target. He then pressed the firing button that discharged the gun. There were by 1898, on some naval guns, telescope sights which naturally greatly enlarged the image of the target for the gun pointer. But these sights were rarely used by gun pointers. They were lashed securely to the gun barrel, and, recoiling with the barrel, jammed back against the unwary pointer's eye. Therefore, when used at all, they were used only to take an initial sight for purposes of estimating the range before the gun was fired.

Notice now two things about the process. First of all, the rapidity of fire was controlled by the rolling period of the ship. Pointers had to wait for the one moment in the roll when the sights were brought on the target. Notice also this: There is in every pointer what is called a "firing interval"—that is, the time lag between his impulse to fire the gun and the translation of this impulse into the act of pressing the firing button. A pointer, because of this reaction time, could not wait to fire the gun until the exact moment when the roll of the ship brought the sights onto the target; he had to will to fire a little before, while the sights were off the target. Since the firing interval was an individual matter, varying obviously from man to man, each pointer had to estimate from long practice his own interval and compensate for it accordingly.

These things, together with others we need not here investigate, conspired to make gunfire at sea relatively uncertain and ineffective. The pointer, on a moving platform, estimating range and firing interval, shooting while his sight was off the target, became in a sense an individual artist.

In 1898, many of the uncertainties were removed from the process and the position of the gun pointer radically altered by the introduction of continuous-aim firing. The major change was that which enabled the gun pointer to keep his sight and gun barrel on the target throughout the roll of the ship. This was accomplished by altering the gear ratio in the elevating gear to permit a pointer to compensate for the roll of the vessel by rapidly elevating and depressing the gun. From this change another followed. With the possibility of maintaining the gun always on the target, the desirability of improved sights became immediately apparent. The advantages of the telescope sight as opposed to the open sight were for the first time fully realized. But the existing telescope sight, it will be recalled, moved with the recoil of the gun and jammed back against the eye of the gunner. To correct this, the sight was mounted on a sleeve that permitted the gun barrel to recoil through it without moving the telescope.

These two improvements in elevating gear and sighting eliminated the major uncertainties in gunfire at sea and greatly increased the possibilities of both accurate and rapid fire.

You must take my word for it, since the time allowed is small, that this changed naval gunnery from an art to a science, and that gunnery accuracy in the British and our Navy increased, as one student said, 3000% in six years. This does not mean much except to suggest a great increase in accuracy. The following comparative figures may mean a little more. In 1899 five ships of the North Atlantic Squadron fired five minutes each at a lightship hulk at the conventional range of 1600 yards. After twenty-five minutes of banging away, two hits had been made on the sails of the elderly vessel. Six years later one naval gunner made fifteen hits in one minute at a target 75 by 25 feet at the same range—1600 yards; half of them hit in a bull's-eye 50 inches square.

Now with the instruments (the gun, elevating gear, and telescope), the method, and the results of continuous-aim firing in mind, let us turn to the subject of major interest: how was the idea, obviously so simple an idea, of continuous-aim firing developed, who introduced it into the United States Navy, and what was its reception?

The idea was the product of the fertile mind of the English officer Admiral Sir Percy Scott. He arrived at it in this way while, in 1898, he was the captain of H.M.S. *Scylla.* For the previous two or three years he had given much thought independently and almost alone in the British Navy to means of improving gunnery. One rough day, when the ship, at target practice, was pitching and rolling violently, he walked up and down the gun deck watching his gun crews. Because of the heavy weather, they were making very bad scores. Scott noticed, however, that one pointer was appreciably more accurate than the rest. He watched this man with care, and saw, after a time, that he was unconsciously working his elevating gear back and forth in a partially successful effort to compensate for the roll of the vessel. It flashed through Scott's mind at that moment that here was the sovereign remedy for the problem of inaccurate fire. What one man could do partially and unconsciously perhaps all men could be trained to do consciously and completely.

Acting on this assumption, he did three things. First, in all the guns of the *Scylla,* he changed the gear ratio in the elevating gear, previously used only to set the gun in fixed position for range, so that a gunner could easily elevate and depress the gun to follow a target throughout the roll. Second, he rerigged his telescopes so that they would not be influenced by the recoil of the gun. Third, he rigged a small target at the mouth of the gun, which was moved up and down by a crank to simulate a moving target. By following this target as it moved and firing at it with a subcaliber rifle rigged in the breech of the gun, the pointer could practice every day. Thus equipped, the ship became a training ground for gunners. Where before the good pointer was an individual artist, pointers now became trained techni-

cians, fairly uniform in their capacity to shoot. The effect was immediately felt. Within a year the *Scylla* established records that were remarkable.

At this point I should like to stop a minute to notice several things directly related to, and involved in, the process of innovation. To begin with, the personality of the innovator. I wish there were time to say a good deal about Admiral Sir Percy Scott. He was a wonderful man. Three small bits of evidence must here suffice, however. First, he had a certain mechanical ingenuity. Second, his personal life was shot through with frustration and bitterness. There was a divorce and a quarrel with that ambitious officer Lord Charles Beresford, the sounds of which, Scott liked to recall, penetrated to the last outposts of empire. Finally, he possessed, like Swift, a savage indignation directed ordinarily at the inelastic intelligence of all constituted authority, especially the British Admiralty.

There are other points worth mention here. Notice first that Scott was not responsible for the invention of the basic instruments that made the reform in gunnery possible. This reform rested upon the gun itself, which as a rifle had been in existence on ships for at least forty years; the elevating gear, which had been, in the form Scott found it, a part of the rifled gun from the beginning; and the telescope sight, which had been on shipboard at least eight years. Scott's contribution was to bring these three elements appropriately modified into a combination that made continuous-aim firing possible for the first time. Notice also that he was allowed to bring these elements into combination by accident, by watching the unconscious action of a gun pointer endeavoring through the operation of his elevating gear to correct partially for the roll of his vessel. Scott, as we have seen, had been interested in gunnery; he had thought about ways to increase accuracy by practice and improvement of existing machinery; but able as he was, he had not been able to produce on his own initiative and by his own thinking the essential idea and modify instruments to fit his purpose. Notice here, finally, the intricate interaction of chance, the intellectual climate, and Scott's mind. Fortune (in this case, the unaware gun pointer) indeed favors the prepared mind, but even fortune and the prepared mind need a favorable environment before they can conspire to produce sudden change. No intelligence can proceed very far above the threshold of existing data or the binding combinations of existing data.

All these elements that enter into what may be called "original thinking" interest me as a teacher. Deeply rooted in the pedagogical mind often enough is a sterile infatuation with "inert ideas"; there is thus always present in the profession the tendency to be diverted from the *process* by which these ideas, or indeed any ideas, are really produced. I well remember with what contempt a class of mine which was reading Leonardo da Vinci's *Notebooks* dismissed the author because he appeared to know no more mechanics than, as one wit in the class observed, a Vermont Republican farmer of the present day. This is perhaps the expected result produced by a method of instruction that too frequently implies that the great generalizations were the result, on the one hand, of chance—an apple falling in an orchard or a teapot boiling on the hearth—or, on the other hand, of some towering intelligence proceeding in isolation inexorably toward some prefigured idea, like evolution, for example.

This process by which new concepts appear, the interaction of fortune, intellectual climate, and the prepared imaginative mind, is an interesting subject for examination offered by any case study of innovation. It was a subject as Dr. Walter Cannon pointed out, that momentarily engaged the attention of Horace Walpole, whose lissome intelligence glided over the surface of so many ideas. In reflecting upon the part played by chance in the development of new concepts, he recalled the story of the three princes of Serendip who set out to find some interesting object on a journey through their realm. They did not find the particular object of their search, but along the way they discovered many new things simply because they were looking for *something*. Walpole believed this intellectual method ought to be given a name, in honor of the founders, serendipity; and serendipity certainly exerts a considerable influence in what we call original thinking. There is an element of serendipity, for example, in Scott's chance discovery of continuous-aim firing in that he was, and had been, looking for some means to improve his target practice and stumbled upon a solution by observation that had never entered his head.

Serendipity, while recognizing the prepared mind, does tend to emphasize the role of chance in intellectual discovery. Its effect may be balanced by an anecdote that suggests the contribution of the adequately prepared mind. There has recently been much posthaste and romage in the land over the question of whether there really was a Renaissance. A scholar has recently argued in print that since the Middle Ages actually possessed many of the instruments and pieces of equipment associated with the Renaissance, the Renaissance could be said to exist as a defined period only in the mind of the historians such as Burckhardt. This view was entertainingly rebutted by the historian of art Panofsky, who pointed out that although Robert Grosseteste indeed did have a very rudimentary telescope, he used it to examine stalks of grain in a field down the street. Galileo, a Renaissance intelligence, pointed his telescope at the sky.

Here Panofsky is only saying in a provocative way that change and intellectual advance are the products of well-trained and well-stored inquisitive minds, minds that relieve us of "the terrible burden of inert ideas by throwing them into a new combination." Educators, nimble in the task of pouring the old wine of our heritage into the empty vessels that appear before them, might give thought to how to develop such independent, inquisitive minds.

But I have been off on a private venture of my own. Now to return to the story, the introduction of continuous-aim firing. In 1900 Percy Scott went out to the China Station as commanding officer of H.M.S. *Terrible*. In that ship he continued his training methods and his spectacular successes in naval gunnery. On the China Station he met up with an American junior officer, William S. Sims. Sims had little of the mechanical ingenuity of Percy Scott, but the two were drawn together by temperamental similarities that are worth noticing here. Sims had the same intolerance for what is called spit and polish and the same contempt for bureaucratic inertia as his British brother officer. He had for some years been concerned, as had Scott, with what he took to be the inefficiency of his own Navy. Just before he met Scott, for example, he had shipped out to China in the brand new pride of the fleet, the battleship *Kentucky*. After careful investigation and reflection he had informed his superiors in Washington that she was "not a battleship at all—but a crime against the white race." The spirit with which he pushed forward his efforts to reform the naval service can best be stated in his own words to a brother officer: "I am perfectly willing that those holding views differing from mine should continue to live, but with every fibre of my being I loathe indirection and shiftiness, and where it occurs in high place, and is used to save face at the expense of the vital interests of our great service (in which silly people place such a childlike trust), I want that man's blood and I will have it no matter what it costs me personally."

From Scott in 1900 Sims learned all there was to know about continuous-aim firing. He modified, with the Englishman's active assistance, the gear on his own ship and tried out the new system. After a few months' training, his experimental batteries began making remarkable records at target practice. Sure of the usefulness of his gunnery methods, Sims then turned to the task of educating the Navy at large. In thirteen great official reports he documented the case for continuous-aim firing, supporting his arguments at every turn with a mass of factual data. Over a period of two years, he reiterated three principal points: first, he continually cited the records established by Scott's ships, the *Scylla* and the *Terrible*, and supported these with the accumulating data from his own tests on an American ship; second, he described the mechanisms used and the training procedures instituted by Scott and himself to obtain these records; third, he explained that our own mechanisms were not generally adequate without modification to meet the demands placed on them by continuous-aim firing. Our elevating gear, useful to raise or lower a gun slowly to fix it in position for the proper range, did not always work easily and rapidly enough to enable a gunner to follow a target with his gun throughout the roll of the ship. Sims also explained that such few telescope sights as there were on board our ships were useless. Their cross wires were so thick or coarse they obscured the target, and the sights had been attached to the gun in such a way that the recoil system of the gun plunged the eyepiece against the eye of the gun pointer.

This was the substance not only of the first but of all the succeeding reports written on the subject of gunnery from the China Station. It will be interesting to see what response these met with in Washington. The response falls roughly into three easily identifiable stages.

First stage: At first, there was no response. Sims had directed his comments to the Bureau of Ordnance and the Bureau of Navigation; in both bureaus there was dead silence. The thing—claims and records of continuous-aim firing—was not credible. The reports were simply filed away and forgotten. Some indeed, it was later discovered to Sims's delight, were half-eaten-away by cockroaches.

Second stage: It is never pleasant for any

man's best work to be left unnoticed by superiors, and it was an unpleasantness that Sims suffered extremely ill. In his later reports, beside the accumulating data he used to clinch his argument, he changed his tone. He used deliberately shocking language because, as he said, "They were furious at my first papers and stowed them away. I therefore made up my mind I would give these later papers such a form that they would be dangerous documents to leave neglected in the files." To another friend he added, "I want scalps or nothing and if I can't have 'em I won't play."

Besides altering his tone, he took another step to be sure his views would receive attention. He sent copies of his reports to other officers in the fleet. Aware as a result that Sims's gunnery claims were being circulated and talked about, the men in Washington were then stirred to action. They responded, notably through the Chief of the Bureau of Ordnance, who had general charge of the equipment used in gunnery practice, as follows: (1) our equipment was in general as good as the British; (2) since our equipment was as good, the trouble must be with the men, but the gun pointer and the training of gun pointers were the responsibility of the officers on the ships; and most significant (3) continuous-aim firing was impossible. Experiments had revealed that five men at work on the elevating gear of a six-inch gun could not produce the power necessary to compensate for a roll of five degrees in ten seconds. These experiments and calculations demonstrated beyond peradventure or doubt that Scott's system of gunfire was not possible.

This was the second stage—the attempt to meet Sims's claims by logical, rational rebuttal. Only one difficulty is discoverable in these arguments; they were wrong at important points. To begin with, while there was little difference between the standard British equipment and the standard American equipment, the instruments on Scott's two ships, the *Scylla* and the *Terrible,* were far better than the standard equipment on our ships. Second, all the men could not be trained in continuous-aim firing until equipment was improved throughout the fleet. Third, the experiments with the elevating gear had been ingeniously contrived at the Washington Navy Yard—on solid ground. It had, therefore, been possible to dispense in the Bureau of Ordnance calculation with Newton's first law of motion, which naturally operated at sea to assist the gunner in elevating or depressing a gun mounted on a moving ship. Another difficulty was of course that continuous-aim firing was in use on Scott's and some of our own ships at the time the Chief of the Bureau of Ordnance was writing that it was a mathematical impossibility. In every way I find this second stage, the apparent resort to reason, the most entertaining and instructive in our investigation of the responses to innovation.

Third stage: The rational period in the counterpoint between Sims and the Washington men was soon passed. It was followed by the third stage, that of name-calling—the *argumentum ad hominem.* Sims, of course, by the high temperature he was running and by his calculated over-statement, invited this. He was told in official endorsements on his reports that there were others quite as sincere and loyal as he and far less difficult; he was dismissed as a crackbrained egotist; he was called a deliberate falsifier of evidence.

The rising opposition and the character of the opposition were not calculated to discourage further efforts by Sims. It convinced him that he was being attacked by shifty, dishonest men who were the victims, as he said, of insufferable conceit and ignorance. He made up his mind, therefore, that he was prepared to go to any extent to obtain the "scalps" and the "blood" he was after. Accordingly, he, a lieutenant, took the extraordinary step of writing the President of the United States, Theodore Roosevelt, to inform him of the remarkable records of Scott's ships, of the inadequacy of our own gunnery routines and records, and of the refusal of the Navy Department to act. Roosevelt, who always liked to respond to such appeals when he conveniently could, brought Sims back from China late in 1902 and installed him as Inspector of Target Practice, a post the naval officer held throughout the remaining six years of the Administration. And when he left, after many spirited encounters we cannot here investigate, he was universally acclaimed as "the man who taught us how to shoot."

With this sequence of events (the chronological account of the innovation of continuous-aim firing) in mind, it is possible now to examine the evidence to see what light it may throw on our present interest: the origins of and responses to change in a society.

First, the origins. We have already analyzed briefly the origins of the idea. We have seen how Scott arrived at his notion. We must now ask ourselves, I think, why Sims so actively sought, almost alone among his brother officers, to introduce the idea into his service. It is particularly interesting here to notice again that neither Scott nor Sims invented the instruments on which the innovation rested. They did not urge their proposal, as might be expected, because of pride in the instruments of their own design. The telescope sight had first been placed on shipboard in 1892 by Bradley Fiske, an officer of great inventive capacity. In that year Fiske had even sketched out on paper the vague possibility of continuous-aim firing, but his sight was condemned by his commanding officer, Robley D. Evans, as of no use. In 1892 no one but Fiske in the Navy knew what to do with a telescope sight any more than Grosseteste had known in his time what to do with a telescope. And Fiske, instead of fighting for his telescope, turned his attention to a range finder. But six years later Sims, following the tracks of his brother officer, took over and became the engineer of the revolution. I would suggest, with some reservations, this explanation: Fiske, as an inventor, took his pleasure in

great part from the design of the device. He lacked not so much the energy as the overriding sense of social necessity that would have enabled him to *force* revolutionary ideas on the service. Sims possessed this sense. In Fiske, who showed rare courage and integrity in other professional matters not intimately connected with the introduction of new weapons of his own design, we may here find the familiar plight of the engineer who often enough must watch the products of his ingenuity organized and promoted by other men. These other promotional men when they appear in the world of commerce are called entrepreneurs. In the world of ideas they are still entrepreneurs. Sims was one, a middle-aged man caught in the periphery (as a lieutenant) of the intricate webbing of a precisely organized society. Rank, the exact definition and limitation of a man's capacity at any given moment in his career, prevented Sims from discharging all his exploding energies into the purely routine channels of the peacetime Navy. At the height of his powers he was a junior officer standing watches on a ship cruising aimlessly in friendly foreign waters. The remarkable changes in systems of gunfire to which Scott introduced him gave him the opportunity to expend his energies quite legitimately against the encrusted hierarchy of his society. He was moved, it seems to me, in part by his genuine desire to improve his own profession but also in part by rebellion against tedium, against inefficiency from on high, and against the artificial limitations placed on his actions by the social structure, in his case, junior rank.

Now having briefly investigated the origins of the change, let us examine the reasons for what must be considered the weird response we have observed to this proposed change. Why this deeply rooted, aggressive, persistent hostility from Washington that was only broken up by the interference of Theodore Roosevelt? Here was a reform that greatly and demonstrably increased the fighting effectiveness of a service that maintains itself almost exclusively to fight. Why then this refusal to accept so carefully documented a case, a case proved incontestably by records and experience? Why should virtually all the rulers of a society so resolutely seek to reject a change that so markedly improved its chances for survival in any contest with competing societies? There are the obvious reasons that will occur to all of you—the source of the proposed reform was an obscure, junior officer 8000 miles away; he was, and this is a significant factor, criticizing gear and machinery designed by the very men in the bureaus to whom he was sending his criticisms. And furthermore, Sims was seeking to introduce what he claimed were improvements in a field where improvements appeared unnecessary. Superiority in war, as in other things, is a relative matter, and the Spanish-American War had been won by the old system of gunnery. Therefore, it was superior even though of the 9500 shots fired at various but close ranges, only 121 had found their mark.

These are the more obvious, and I think secondary or supporting, sources of opposition to Sims's proposed reforms. A less obvious cause appears by far the most important one. It has to do with the fact that the Navy is not only an armed force; it is a society. Men spend their whole lives in it and tend to find the definition of their whole being within it. In the forty years following the Civil War, this society had been forced to accommodate itself to a series of technological changes—the steam turbine, the electric motor, the rifled shell of great explosive power, case-hardened steel armor, and all the rest of it. These changes wrought extraordinary changes in ship design, and, therefore, in the concepts of how ships were to be used; that is, in fleet tactics, and even in naval strategy. The Navy of this period is a paradise for the historian or sociologist in search of evidence bearing on a society's responses to change.

To these numerous innovations, producing as they did a spreading disorder throughout a service with heavy commitments to formal organization, the Navy responded with grudging pain. For example, sails were continued on our first-line ships long after they ceased to serve a useful purpose mechanically, but like the holding of the horses that no longer hauled the British field pieces, they assisted officers over the imposing hurdles of change. To a man raised in sail, a sail on an armored cruiser propelled through the water at 14 knots by a steam turbine was a cheering sight to see.

This reluctance to change with changing conditions was not limited to the blunter minds and less resilient imaginations in the service. As clear and untrammeled an intelligence as Alfred Thayer Mahan, a prophetic spirit in the realm of strategy, where he was unfettered by personal attachments of any kind, was occasionally at the mercy of the past. In 1906 he opposed the construction of battleships with single-caliber main batteries—that is, the modern battleship—because, he argued, such vessels would fight only at great ranges. These ranges would create in the sailor what Mahan felicitously called "the indisposition to close." They would thus undermine the physical and moral courage of a commander. They would, in other words, destroy the doctrine and the spirit, formulated by Nelson a century before, that no captain could go very far wrong who laid his ship alongside an enemy. The fourteen-inch rifle, which could place a shell upon a possible target six miles away, had long ago annihilated the Nelsonian doctrine. Mahan, of course, knew and recognized this fact; he was, as a man raised in sail, reluctant only to accept its full meaning, which was not that men were no longer brave, but that 100 years after the battle of the Nile they had to reveal their bravery in a different way.

Now the question still is, why this blind reaction to technological change, observed in the continuation of sail or in Mahan's contentions or in the opposition to continuous-aim firing? It is wrong to assume, as it is frequently

SECTION V   Organization Adaptation and Change

assumed by civilians, that it springs exclusively from some causeless Bourbon distemper that invades the military mind. There is a sounder and more attractive base. The opposition, where it occurs, of the soldier and the sailor to such change springs from the normal human instinct to protect oneself, and more especially, one's way of life. Military organizations are societies built around and upon the prevailing weapons systems. Intuitively and quite correctly the military man feels that a change in weapon portends a change in the arrangements of his society. Think of it this way. Since the time that the memory of man runneth not to the contrary, the naval society has been built upon the surface vessel. Daily routines, habits of mind, social organization, physical accommodations, conventions, rituals, spiritual allegiances have been conditioned by the essential fact of the ship. What then happens to your society if the ship is displaced as the principal element by such a radically different weapon as the plane? The mores and structure of the society are immediately placed in jeopardy. They may, in fact, be wholly destroyed. It was the witty cliché of the twenties that those naval officers who persisted in defending the battleship against the apparently superior claims of the carrier did so because the battleship was a more comfortable home. What, from one point of view, is a better argument? There is, as everyone knows, no place like home. Who has ever wanted to see the old place brought under the hammer by hostile forces whether they hold a mortgage or inhabit a flying machine?

This sentiment would appear to account in large part for the opposition to Sims; it was the product of an instinctive protective feeling, even if the reasons for this feeling were not overt or recognized. The years after 1902 proved how right, in their terms, the opposition was. From changes in gunnery flowed an extraordinary complex of changes: in shipboard routines, ship design, and fleet tactics. There was, too, a social change. In the days when gun-

nery was taken lightly, the gunnery officer was taken lightly. After 1903, he became one of the most significant and powerful members of a ship's company, and this shift of emphasis naturally was shortly reflected in promotion lists. Each one of these changes provoked a dislocation in the naval society, and with man's troubled foresight and natural indisposition to break up classic forms, the men in Washington withstood the Sims onslaught as long as they could. It is very significant that they withstood it until an agent from outside, outside and above, who was not clearly identified with the naval society, entered to force change.

This agent, the President of the United States, might reasonably and legitimately claim the credit for restoring our gunnery efficiency. But this restoration by *force majeure* was brought about at great cost to the service and men involved. Bitternesses, suspicions, wounds were made that it was impossible to conceal and were, in fact, never healed.

Now this entire episode may be summed up in five separate points:

1. The essential idea for change occurred in part by chance but in an environment that contained all the essential elements for change and to a mind prepared to recognize the possibility of change.
2. The basic elements, the gun, gear, and sight, were put in the environment by other men, men interested in designing machinery to serve different purposes or simply interested in the instruments themselves.
3. These elements were brought into successful combination by minds not interested in the instruments for themselves but in what they could do with them. These minds were, to be sure, interested in good gunnery, overtly and consciously. They may also, not so consciously, have been interested in the implied revolt that is present in the support of all change. Their temperaments and careers indeed support this

view. From gunnery, Sims went on to attack ship designs, existing fleet tactics, and methods of promotion. He lived and died, as the service said, a stormy petrel, a man always on the attack against higher authority, a rebellious spirit; a rebel, fighting in excellent causes, but a rebel still who seems increasingly to have identified himself with the act of revolt against constituted authority.

4. He and his colleagues were opposed on this occasion by men who were apparently moved by three considerations: honest disbelief in the dramatic but substantiated claims of the new process, protection of the existing devices and instruments with which they identified themselves, and maintenance of the existing society with which they were identified.

5. The deadlock between those who sought change and those who sought to retain things as they were was broken only by an appeal to superior force, a force removed from and unidentified with the mores, conventions, devices of the society. This seems to me a very important point. The naval society in 1900 broke down in its effort to accommodate itself to a new situation. The appeal to Roosevelt is documentation for Mahan's great generalization that no military service should or can undertake to reform itself. It must seek assistance from outside.

Now with these five summary points in mind, it may be possible to seek, as suggested at the outset, a few larger implications from this story. What, if anything, may it suggest about the general process by which any society attempts to meet changing conditions?

There is, to begin with, a disturbing inference half-concealed in Mahan's statement that no military organization can reform itself. Certainly civilians would agree with this. We all know now that war and the preparation for war

are too important, as Clemenceau said, to be left to the generals. But as I have said before, military organizations are really societies, more rigidly structured, more highly integrated, than most communities, but still societies. What then if we make this phrase to read, "No society can reform itself"? Is the process of adaptation to change, for example, too important to be left to human beings? This is a discouraging thought, and historically there is some cause to be discouraged. Societies have not been very successful in reforming themselves, accommodating to change, without pain and conflict.

This is a subject to which we may well address ourselves. Our society especially is built, as I have said, just as surely upon a changing technology as the Navy of the nineties was built upon changing weapon systems. How then can we find the means to accept with less pain to ourselves and less damage to our social organization the dislocations in our society that are produced by innovation? I cannot, of course, give any satisfying answer to these difficult questions. But in thinking about the case study before us, an idea occurred to me that at least might warrant further investigation by men far more qualified than I.

A primary source of conflict and tension in our case study appears to lie in this great word I have used so often in the summary, the word "identification." It cannot have escaped notice that some men identified themselves with their creations—sights, gun, gear, and so forth—and thus obtained a presumed satisfaction from the thing itself, a satisfaction that prevented them from thinking too closely on either the use or the defects of the thing; that others identified themselves with a settled way of life they had inherited or accepted with minor modification and thus found their satisfaction in attempting to maintain that way of life unchanged; and that still others identified themselves as rebellious spirits, men of the insurgent cast of mind, and thus obtained a satisfaction from the act of revolt itself.

This purely personal identification with a concept, a convention, or an attitude would appear to be a powerful barrier in the way of easily acceptable change. Here is an interesting primitive example. In the years from 1864 to 1871 ten steel companies in this country began making steel by the new Bessemer process. All but one of them at the outset imported from Great Britain English workmen familiar with the process. One, the Cambria Company, did not. In the first few years those companies with British labor established an initial superiority. But by the end of the seventies, Cambria had obtained a commanding lead over all competitors. The President of Cambria, R. W. Hunt, in seeking a cause for his company's success, assigned it almost exclusively to the labor policy. "We started the converter plant without a single man who had ever seen even the outside of a Bessemer plant. We thus had willing pupils with no prejudices and no reminiscences of what they had done in the old country." The Bessemer process, like any new technique, had been constantly improved and refined in this period from 1864 to 1871. The British laborers of Cambria's competitors, secure in the performance of their own original techniques, resisted and resented all change. The Pennsylvania farm boys, untrammeled by the rituals and traditions of their craft, happily and rapidly adapted themselves to the constantly changing process. They ended by creating an unassailable competitive position for their company.

How then can we modify the dangerous effects of this word "identification"? And how much can we tamper with this identifying process? Our security—much of it, after all—comes from giving our allegiance to something greater than ourselves. These are difficult questions to which only the most tentative and provisional answers may here be proposed for consideration.

If one looks closely at this little case history, one discovers that the men involved were the victims of *severely limited* identifications. They were presumably all part of a society dedicated to the process of national defense, yet they persisted in aligning themselves with separate parts of that process—with the existing instruments of defense, with the existing customs of the society, or with the act of rebellion against the customs of the society. Of them all the insurgents had the best of it. They could, and did, say that the process of defense was improved by a gun that shot straighter and faster, and since they wanted such guns, they were unique among their fellows, patriots who sought only the larger object of improved defense. But this beguiling statement, even when coupled with the recognition that these men were right and extremely valuable and deserving of respect and admiration—this statement cannot conceal the fact that they were interested too in scalps and blood, so interested that they made their case a militant one and thus created an atmosphere in which self-respecting men could not capitulate without appearing either weak or wrong or both. So these limited identifications brought men into conflict with each other, and the conflict prevented them from arriving at a common acceptance of a change that presumably, as men interested in our total national defense, they would all find desirable.

It appears, therefore, if I am correct in my assessment, that we might spend some time and thought on the possibility of enlarging the sphere of our identifications from the part to the whole. For example, those Pennsylvania farm boys at the Cambria Steel Company were, apparently, much more interested in the manufacture of steel than in the preservation of any particular way of making steel. So I would suggest that in studying innovation, we look further into this possibility: the possibility that any group that exists for any purpose—the family, the factory, the educational institution—might begin by defining for itself its grand object and see to it that that grand object is communicated to every member of the group. Thus defined and communicated, it might serve as a unifying agent against the disruptive local allegiances of the inevitable smaller elements that compose any group. It may also serve as a means to increase the acceptability of any change that would assist in the more efficient achievement of the grand object.

There appears also a second possible way to combat the untoward influence of limited identifications. We are, I may repeat, a society based on technology in a time of prodigious technological advance, and a civilization committed irrevocably to the theory of evolution. These things mean that we believe in change; they suggest that if we are to survive in good health we must, in the phrase that I have used before, become an "adaptive society." By the word "adaptive" is meant the ability to extract the fullest possible returns from the opportunities at hand: the ability of Sir Percy Scott to select judiciously from the ideas and material presented both by the past and present and to throw them into a new combination. "Adaptive," as here used, also means the kind of resilience that will enable us to accept fully and easily the best promises of changing circumstances without losing our sense of continuity or our essential integrity.

We are not yet emotionally an adaptive society, though we try systematically to develop forces that tend to make us one. We encourage the search for new inventions; we keep the mind stimulated, bright, and free to seek out fresh means of transport, communication, and energy; yet we remain, in part, appalled by the consequences of our ingenuity, and, too frequently, try to find security through the shoring up of ancient and irrelevant conventions, the extension of purely physical safeguards, or the delivery of decisions we ourselves should make into the keeping of superior authority like the state. These solutions are not necessarily un-

natural or wrong, but they historically have not been enough, and I suspect they never will be enough to give us the serenity and competence we seek.

If the preceding statements are correct, they suggest that we might give some attention to the construction of a new view of ourselves as a society which in time of great change identified with and obtained security and satisfaction from the wise and creative accommodation to change itself. Such a view rests, I think, upon a relatively greater reverence for the mere *process* of living in a society than we possess today, and a relatively smaller respect for and attachment to any special *product* of a society, a product either as finite as a bathroom fixture or as conceptual as a fixed and final definition of our Constitution or our democracy.

Historically such an identification with *process* as opposed to *product,* with adventurous selection and adaptation as opposed to simple retention and possessiveness, has been difficult to achieve collectively. The Roman of the early republic, the Italian of the late fifteenth and early sixteenth century, or the Englishman of Elizabeth's time appears to have been most successful in seizing the new opportunities while conserving as much of the heritage of the past as he found relevant and useful to his purpose.

We seem to have fallen on times similar to theirs, when many of the existing forms and schemes have lost meaning in the face of dramatically altering circumstances. Like them we may find at least part of our salvation in identifying ourselves with the adaptive process and thus share with them some of the joy, exuberance, satisfaction, and security with which they went out to meet their changing times.

I am painfully aware that in setting up my historical situation for examination I have, in a sense, artificially contrived it. I have been forced to cut away much, if not all, of the connecting tissue of historical evidence and to present you only with the bare bones and even with only a few of the bones. Thus, I am also aware, the episode has lost much of the subtlety, vitality, and attractive uncertainty of the real situation. There has, too, in the process, been inevitable distortion, but I hope the essential if exaggerated truth remains. I am also aware that I have erected elaborate hypotheses on the slender evidence provided by the single episode. My defense here is only that I have hoped to suggest possible approaches and methods of study and also possible fruitful areas of investigation in a subject that seems to me of critical importance in the life and welfare of our changing society.

Convergence and Upheaval: Managing the Unsteady Pace of Organization Evolution

Michael Tushman

William Newman

Elaine Romanelli

A snug fit of external opportunity, company strategy, and internal structure is a hallmark of successful companies. The real test of executive leadership, however, is in maintaining this alignment in the face of changing competitive conditions.

Consider the Polaroid or Caterpillar corporations. Both firms virtually dominated their respective industries for decades, only to be caught off guard by major environmental changes. The same strategic and organizational factors which were so effective for decades became the seeds of complacency and organization decline.

Recent studies of companies over long periods show that the most successful firms maintain a workable equilibrium for several years (or decades), but are also able to initiate and carry out sharp, widespread changes (referred to here as reorientations) when their environments shift. Such upheaval may bring renewed vigor to the enterprise. Less successful firms, on the other hand, get stuck in a particular pattern. The leaders of these firms either do not see the need for reorientation or they are unable to carry through the necessary frame-breaking changes. While not all reorientations succeed, those organizations which do not initiate reorientations as environments shift underperform.

This article focuses on reasons why for long periods most companies make only incremental changes, and why they then need to make painful, discontinuous, system-wide shifts. We are particularly concerned with the role of executive leadership in managing this pattern of convergence punctuated by upheaval. Here are four examples of the convergence/upheaval pattern:

· Founded in 1915 by a set of engineers from MIT, the General Radio Company was es-

© [1986] by the Regents of the University of California. Reprinted from the *California Management Review,* vol. 29, No. 1. By permission of The Regents.

The authors thank Donald Hambrick and Kathy Harrigan for insightful comments and the Center for Strategy Research and the Center for Research on Innovation and Entrepreneurship at the Graduate School of Business, Columbia University for financial support

tablished to produce highly innovative and high-quality (but expensive) electronic test equipment. Over the years, General Radio developed a consistent organization to accomplish its mission. It hired only the brightest young engineers, built a loose functional organization dominated by the engineering department, and developed a "General Radio culture" (for example, no conflict, management by consensus, slow growth). General Radio's strategy and associated structures, systems, and people were very successful. By World War II, General Radio was the largest test-equipment firm in the United States.

After World War II, however, increasing technology and cost-based competition began to erode General Radio's market share. While management made numerous incremental changes, General Radio remained fundamentally the same organization. In the late 1960s, when CEO Don Sinclair initiated strategic changes, he left the firm's structure and systems intact. This effort at doing new things with established systems and procedures was less than successful. By 1972, the firm incurred its first loss.

In the face of this sustained performance decline, Bill Thurston (a long-time General Radio executive) was made President. Thurston initiated system-wide changes. General Radio adopted a more marketing-oriented strategy. Its product line was cut from 20 different lines to 3; much more emphasis was given to product-line management, sales, and marketing. Resources were diverted from engineering to revitalize sales, marketing, and production. During 1973, the firm moved to a matrix structure, increased its emphasis on controls and systems, and went outside for a set of executives to help Thurston run this revised General Radio. To perhaps more formally symbolize these changes and

the sharp move away from the "old" General Radio, the firm's name was changed to GenRad. By 1984, GenRad's sales exploded to over $200 million (vs. $44 million in 1972).

After 60 years of convergent change around a constant strategy, Thurston and his colleagues (many new to the firm) made discontinuous system-wide changes in strategy, structure, people, and processes. While traumatic, these changes were implemented over a two-year period and led to a dramatic turnaround in GenRad's performance.

- Prime Computer was founded in 1971 by a group of individuals who left Honeywell. Prime's initial strategy was to produce a high-quality/high-price minicomputer based on semiconductor memory. These founders built an engineering-dominated, loosely structured firm which sold to OEMs and through distributors. This configuration of strategy, structure, people, and processes was very successful. By 1974, Prime turned its first profit; by 1975, its sales were more than $11 million.

In the midst of this success, Prime's board of directors brought in Ken Fisher to reorient the organization. Fisher and a whole new group of executives hired from Honeywell initiated a set of discontinuous changes throughout Prime during 1975–1976. Prime now sold a full range of minicomputers and computer systems to OEMs and end-users. To accomplish this shift in strategy, Prime adopted a more complex functional structure, with a marked increase in resources to sales and marketing. The shift in resources away from engineering was so great that Bill Poduska, Prime's head of engineering, left to form Apollo Computer. Between 1975–1981, Fisher and his colleagues consolidated and incrementally adapted structure, systems, and processes to better accomplish the new strategy. During this convergent period, Prime grew dramatically to over $260 million by 1981.

In 1981, again in the midst of this continuing sequence of increased volume and profits, Prime's board again initiated an upheaval. Fisher and his direct reports left Prime (some of whom founded Encore Computer), while Joe Henson and a set of executives from IBM initiated wholesale changes throughout the organization. The firm diversified into robotics, CAD/CAM, and office systems; adopted a divisional structure; developed a more market-driven orientation; and increased controls and systems. It remains to be seen how this "new" Prime will fare. Prime must be seen, then, not as a 14-year-old firm, but as three very different organizations, each of which was managed by a different set of executives. Unlike General Radio, Prime initiated these discontinuities during periods of great success.

· The Operating Group at Citibank prior to 1970 had been a service-oriented function for the end-user areas of the bank. The Operating Group hired high school graduates who remained in the "back-office" for their entire careers. Structure, controls, and systems were loose, while the informal organization valued service, responsiveness to client needs, and slow, steady work habits. While these patterns were successful enough, increased demand and heightened customer expectations led to ever decreasing performance during the late 1960s.

In the face of severe performance decline, John Reed was promoted to head the Operating Group. Reed recruited several executives with production backgrounds, and with this new top team he initiated system-wide changes. Reed's vision was to transform the Operating Group from a *service-*oriented back office to a *factory* producing high-quality products. Con-

sistent with this new mission, Reed and his colleagues initiated sweeping changes in strategy, structure, work flows, controls, and culture. These changes were initiated concurrently throughout the back office, with very little participation, over the course of a few months. While all the empirical performance measures improved substantially, these changes also generated substantial stress and anxiety within Reed's group.

· For 20 years, Alpha Corporation was among the leaders in the industrial fastener industry. Its reliability, low cost, and good technical service were important strengths. However, as Alpha's segment of the industry matured, its profits declined. Belt-tightening helped but was not enough. Finally, a new CEO presided over a sweeping restructuring: cutting the product line, closing a plant, trimming overhead; then focusing on computer parts which call for very close tolerances, CAD/CAM tooling, and cooperation with customers on design efforts. After four rough years, Alpha appears to have found a new niche where convergence will again be warranted.

These four short examples illustrate periods of incremental change, or convergence, punctuated by discontinuous changes throughout the organization. Discontinuous or "frame-breaking" change involves simultaneous and sharp shifts in strategy, power, structure, and controls. Each example illustrates the role of executive leadership in initiating and implementing discontinuous change. Where General Radio, Citibank's Operating Group, and Alpha initiated system-wide changes only after sustained performance decline, Prime proactively initiated system-wide changes to take advantage of competitive/technological conditions. These patterns in organization evolution are not unique. Upheaval, sooner or later, follows convergence if a company is to survive; only a farsighted minority of firms initiate upheaval prior to incurring performance declines.

The task of managing incremental change, or convergence, differs sharply from managing frame-breaking change. Incremental change is compatible with the existing structure of a company and is reinforced over a period of years. In contrast, frame-breaking change is abrupt, painful to participants, and often resisted by the old guard. Forging these new strategy-structure-people-process consistencies and laying the basis for the next period of incremental change calls for distinctive skills.

Because the future health, and even survival, of a company or business unit is at stake, we need to take a closer look at the nature and consequences of convergent change and of differences imposed by frame-breaking change. We need to explore when and why these painful and risky revolutions interrupt previously successful patterns, and whether these discontinuities can be avoided and/or initiated prior to crisis. Finally, we need to examine what managers can and should do to guide their organizations through periods of convergence and upheaval over time.

firms in diverse industries for at least 20 years per firm (e.g., Miller and Friesen[2]). Another research program conducted by researchers at Columbia, Duke, and Cornell Universities is tracking the history of large samples of companies in the minicomputer, cement, airlines, and glass industries. This research program builds on earlier work (e.g., Greiner[3]) and finds that most successful firms evolve through long periods of convergence punctuated by frame-breaking change.

The following discussion is based on the history of companies in many different industries, different countries, both large and small organizations, and organizations in various stages of their product class's life-cycle. We are dealing with a widespread phenomenon—not just a few dramatic sequences. Our research strongly suggests that the convergence/upheaval pattern occurs within departments (e.g., Citibank's Operating Group), at the business-unit level (e.g., Prime or General Radio), and at the corporate level of analysis (e.g., the Singer, Chrysler, or Harris Corporations). The problem of managing both convergent periods and upheaval is not just for the CEO, but necessarily involves general managers as well as functional managers.

THE RESEARCH BASE

The research which sparks this article is based on the abundant company histories and case studies. The more complete case studies have tracked individual firms' evolution and various crises in great detail (e.g., Chandler's seminal study of strategy and structure at Du Pont, General Motors, Standard Oil, and Sears[1]). More recent studies have dealt systematically with whole sets of companies and trace their experience over long periods of time.

A series of studies by researchers at McGill University covered over 40 well-known

PATTERNS IN ORGANIZATIONAL EVOLUTION: CONVERGENCE AND UPHEAVAL

Building on Strength: Periods of Convergence

Successful companies wisely stick to what works well. At General Radio between 1915 and 1950, the loose functional structure, committee management system, internal promotion practices, control with engineering, and the high-quality, premium-price, engineering mentality all worked together to provide a highly congruent system. These internally consistent patterns in strategy, structure, people, and processes served General Radio for over 35 years.

Similarly, the Alpha Corporation's customer driven, low-cost strategy was accomplished by strength in engineering and production and ever more detailed structures and systems which evaluated cost, quality, and new product development. These strengths were epitomized in Alpha's chief engineer and president. The chief engineer had a remarkable talent for helping customers find new uses for industrial fasteners. He relished solving such problems, while at the same time designing fasteners that could be easily manufactured. The president excelled at production—producing dependable, low-cost fasteners. The pair were role models which set a pattern which served Alpha well for 15 years.

As the company grew, the chief engineer hired kindred customer-oriented application engineers. With the help of innovative users, they developed new products, leaving more routine problem-solving and incremental change to the sales and production departments. The president relied on a hands-on manufacturing manager and delegated financial matters to a competent treasurer-controller. Note how well the organization reinforced Alpha's strategy and how the key people fit the organization. There was an excellent fit between strategy and structure. The informal structure also fit well—communications were open, the simple mission of the company was widely endorsed, and routines were well understood.

As the General Radio and Alpha examples suggest, convergence starts out with an effective dovetailing of strategy, structure, people, and processes. For other strategies or in other industries, the particular formal and informal systems might be very different, but still a winning combination. The formal system includes decisions about grouping and linking resources as well as planning and control systems, rewards and evaluation procedures, and human resource management systems. The informal system includes core values, beliefs, norms, communication patterns, and actual decision-making and conflict resolution patterns. It is the whole fabric of structure, systems, people, and processes which must be suited to company strategy.[4]

As the fit between strategy, structure, people, and processes is never perfect, convergence is an ongoing process characterized by incremental change. Over time, in all companies studied, two types of converging changes were common: fine-tuning and incremental adaptations.

- *Converging Change: Fine-Tuning*—Even with good strategy-structure-process fits, well-run companies seek even better ways of exploiting (and defending) their missions. Such effort typically deals with one or more of the following:

  - *Refining* policies, methods, and procedures.
  - Creating *specialized units and linking mechanisms* to permit increased volume and increased attention to unit quality and cost.
  - *Developing personnel* especially suited to the present strategy—through improved selection and training, and tailoring reward systems to match strategic thrusts.
  - Fostering individual and group *commitments* to the company mission and to the excellence of one's own department.
  - Promoting *confidence* in the accepted norms, beliefs, and myths.
  - *Clarifying* established roles, power, status, dependencies, and allocation mechanism.

481

The fine-tuning fills out and elaborates the consistencies between strategy, structure, people, and processes. These incremental changes lead to an ever more interconnected (and therefore more stable) social system. Convergent periods fit the happy, stick-with-a-winner situations romanticized by Peters and Waterman.[5]

• *Converging Change: Incremental Adjustments to Environmental Shifts*—In addition to fine-tuning changes, minor shifts in the environment will call for some organizational response. Even the most conservative of organizations expect, even welcome, small changes which do not make too many waves.

A popular expression is that almost any organization can tolerate a "ten-percent change." At any one time, only a few changes are being made; but these changes are still compatible with the prevailing structures, systems, and processes. Examples of such adjustments are an expansion in sales territory, a shift in emphasis among products in the product line, or improved processing technology in production.

The usual process of making changes of this sort is well known: wide acceptance of the need for change, openness to possible alternatives, objective examination of the pros and cons of each plausible alternative, participation of those directly affected in the preceding analysis, a market test or pilot operation where feasible, time to learn the new activities, established role models, known rewards for positive success, evaluation, and refinement.

The role of executive leadership during convergent periods is to reemphasize mission and core values and to delegate incremental decisions to middle-level managers. Note that the uncertainty created for people affected by such changes is well within tolerable limits. Opportunity is provided to anticipate and learn what is new, while most features of the structure remain unchanged.

The overall system adapts, but it is not transformed.

Converging Change: Some Consequences— For those companies whose strategies fit environmental conditions, convergence brings about better and better effectiveness. Incremental change is relatively easy to implement and ever more optimizes the consistencies between strategy, structure, people, and processes. At AT&T, for example, the period between 1913 and 1980 was one of ever more incremental change to further bolster the "Ma Bell" culture, systems, and structure all in service of developing the telephone network.

Convergent periods are, however, a double-edged sword. As organizations grow and become more successful, they develop internal forces for stability. Organization structures and systems become so interlinked that they only allow compatible changes. Further, over time, employees develop habits, patterned behaviors begin to take on values (e.g., "service is good"), and employees develop a sense of competence in knowing how to get work done within the system. These self-reinforcing patterns of behavior, norms, and values contribute to increased organizational momentum and complacency and, over time, to a sense of organizational history. This organizational history—epitomized by common stories, heroes, and standards—specifies "how we work here" and "what we hold important here."

This organizational momentum is profoundly functional as long as the organization's strategy is appropriate. The Ma Bell and General Radio culture, structure, and systems—and associated internal momentum—were critical to each organization's success. However, if (and when) strategy must change, this momentum cuts the other way. Organizational history is a source of tradition, precedent, and pride which are, in turn, anchors to the past. A proud history often restricts vigilant problem solving and may be a source of resistance to change.

When faced with environmental threat, organizations with strong momentum

· may not register the threat due to organization complacency and/or stunted external vigilance (e.g., the automobile or steel industries), or
· if the threat is recognized, the response is frequently heightened conformity to the status quo and/or increased commitment to "what we do best."

For example, the response of dominant firms to technological threat is frequently increased commitment to the obsolete technology (e.g., telegraph/telephone; vacuum tube/transistor; core/semiconductor memory). A paradoxical result of long periods of success may be heightened organizational complacency, decreased organizational flexibility, and a stunted ability to learn.

Converging change is a double-edged sword. Those very social and technical consistencies which are key sources of success may also be the seeds of failure if environments change. The longer the convergent period, the greater these internal forces for stability. This momentum seems to be particularly accentuated in those most successful firms in a product class (for example, Polaroid, Caterpillar, or U. S. Steel), in historically regulated organizations (for example, AT&T, GTE, or financial service firms), or in organizations that have been traditionally shielded from competition (for example, universities, not-for-profit organizations, government agencies and/or services).

On Frame-Breaking Change

Forces Leading to Frame-Breaking Change —What, then, leads to frame-breaking change? Why defy tradition? Simply stated, frame-breaking change occurs in response to or, better yet, in anticipation of major environmental changes—changes which require more than incremental adjustments. The need for discontinuous change springs from one or a combination of the following:

· *Industry Discontinuities*—Sharp changes in legal, political, or technological conditions shift the basis of competition within industries. *Deregulation* has dramatically transformed the financial services and airlines industries. *Substitute product technologies* (such as jet engines, electronic typing, microprocessors) or *substitute process technologies* (such as the planar process in semiconductors or float-glass in glass manufacture) may transform the bases of competition within industries. Similarly, the emergence of industry standards, or *dominant designs* (such as the DC-3, IBM 360, or PDP-8) signal a shift in competition away from product innovation and towards increased process innovation. Finally, *major economic changes* (e.g., oil crises) and *legal shifts* (e.g., patent protection in biotechnology or trade/regulator barriers in pharmaceuticals or cigarettes) also directly affect bases of competition.
· *Product-Life-Cycle Shifts*—Over the course of a product class lifecycle, different strategies are appropriate. In the emergence phase of a product class, competition is based on product innovation and performance, where in the maturity stage, competition centers on cost, volume, and efficiency. Shifts in patterns of demand alter key factors for success. For example, the demand and nature of competition for minicomputers, cellular telephones, wide-body aircraft, and bowling alley equipment was transformed as these products gained acceptance and their product classes evolved. Powerful international competition may compound these forces.

- *Internal Company Dynamics*—Entwined with these external forces are breaking points within the firm. Sheer size may require a basically new management design. For example, few inventor-entrepreneurs can tolerate the formality that is linked with large volume; even Digital Equipment Company apparently has outgrown the informality so cherished by Kenneth Olsen. Key people die. Family investors may become more concerned with their inheritance taxes than with company development. Revised corporate portfolio strategy may sharply alter the role and resources assigned to business units or functional areas. Such pressures especially when coupled with external changes, may trigger frame-breaking change.

Scope of Frame-Breaking Change —Frame-breaking change is driven by shifts in business strategy. As strategy shifts so too must structure people, and organizational processes. Quite unlike convergent change, frame-breaking reforms involve discontinuous changes throughout the organization. These bursts of change do not reinforce the existing system and are implemented rapidly. For example, the system-wide changes at Prime and General Radio were implemented over 18–24-month periods, where as changes in Citibank's Operating Group were implemented in less than five months. Frame-breaking changes are revolutionary changes *of* the system as opposed to incremental changes *in* the system.

The following features are usually involved in frame-breaking change:

- *Reformed Mission and Core Values*—A strategy shift involves a new definition of company mission. Entering or withdrawing from an industry may be involved; at least the way the company expects to be outstanding is altered. The revamped AT&T is a conspicuous example. Success on its new course calls for a strategy based on competition, aggressiveness, and responsiveness, as well as a revised set of core values about how the firm competes and what it holds as important. Similarly, the initial shift at Prime reflected a strategic shift away from technology and towards sales and marketing. Core values also were aggressively reshaped by Ken Fisher to complement Prime's new strategy.

- *Altered Power and Status*—Frame-breaking change always alters the distribution of power. Some groups lose in the shift while others gain. For example, at Prime and General Radio, the engineering functions lost power, resources, and prestige as the marketing and sales functions gained. These dramatically altered power distributions reflect shifts in bases of competition and resource allocation. A new strategy must be backed up with a shift in the balance of power and status.

- *Reorganization*—A new strategy requires a modification in structure, systems, and procedures. As strategic requirements shift, so too must the choice of organization form. A new direction calls for added activity in some areas and less in others. Changes in structure and systems are means to ensure that this reallocation of effort takes place. New structures and revised roles deliberately break business-as-usual behavior.

- *Revised Interaction Patterns*—The way people in the organization work together has to adapt during frame-breaking change. As strategy is different, new procedures, work flows, communication networks, and decision-making patterns must be established. With these changes in work flows and procedures must also come revised norms, informal decision-making/conflict-resolution procedures, and informal roles.

- *New Executives*—Frame-breaking change also involves new executives, usually brought in from outside the organization (or business unit) and placed in key managerial positions. Commitment to the new mission, energy to overcome prevailing inertia, and freedom from prior obligations are all needed to refocus the organization. A few exceptional members of the old guard may attempt to make this shift, but habits and expectations of their associations are difficult to break. New executives are most likely to provide both the necessary drive and an enhanced set of skills more appropriate for the new strategy. While the overall number of executive changes is usually relatively small, these new executives have substantial symbolic and substantive effects on the organization. For example, frame-breaking changes at Prime, General Radio, Citibank, and Alpha Corporation were all spearheaded by a relatively small set of new executives from outside the company or group.

Why All at Once? —Frame-breaking change is revolutionary in that the shifts reshape the entire nature of the organization. Those more effective examples of frame-breaking change were implemented rapidly (e.g., Citibank, Prime, Alpha). It appears that a piecemeal approach to frame-breaking changes gets bogged down in politics, individual resistance to change, and organizational inertia (e.g., Sinclair's attempts to reshape General Radio). Frame-breaking change requires discontinuous shifts in strategy, structure, people, and processes concurrently—or at least in a short period of time. Reasons for rapid, simultaneous implementation include:

- *Synergy* within the new structure can be a powerful aid. New executives with a fresh mission, working in a redesigned organization with revised norms and values, backed up with power and status, provide strong reinforcement. The pieces of the revitalized organization pull together, as opposed to piecemeal change where one part of the new organization is out of synch with the old organization.

- *Pockets of resistance* have a chance to grow and develop when frame-breaking change is implemented slowly. The new mission, shifts in organization, and other frame-breaking changes upset the comfortable routines and precedent. Resistance to such fundamental change is natural. If frame-breaking change is implemented slowly, then individuals have a greater opportunity to undermine the changes and organizational inertia works to further stifle fundamental change.

- Typically, there is a *pent-up need for change.* During convergent periods, basic adjustments are postponed. Boat-rocking is discouraged. Once constraints are relaxed, a variety of desirable improvements press for attention, the exhilaration and momentum of a fresh effort (and new team) make difficult moves more acceptable. Change is in fashion.

- Frame-breaking change is an inherently *risky and uncertain venture.* The longer the implementation period, the greater the period of uncertainty and instability. The most effective frame-breaking changes initiate the new strategy, structure, processes, and systems rapidly and begin the next period of stability and convergent change. The sooner fundamental uncertainty is removed, the better the chances of organizational survival and growth. While the pacing of change is important, the overall time to implement frame-breaking change will be contingent on the size and age of the organization.

Patterns in Organization Evolution —This historical approach to organization evolution focuses on convergent periods punctuated by reorientation—discontinuous, organization-wide upheavals. The most effective firms take advantage of relatively long convergent periods. These periods of incremental change build on and take advantage of organization inertia. Frame-breaking change is quite dysfunctional if the organization is successful and the environment is stable. If, however, the organization is performing poorly and/or if the environment changes substantially, framebreaking change is the only way to realign the organization with its competitive environment. Not all reorientations will be successful (e.g., People Express' expansion and up-scale moves in 1985–86). However, inaction in the face of performance crisis and/or environmental shifts is a certain recipe for failure.

Because reorientations are so disruptive and fraught with uncertainty, the more rapidly they are implemented, the more quickly the organization can reap the benefits of the following convergent period. High-performing firms initiate reorientations when environmental conditions shift and implement these reorientations rapidly (e.g., Prime and Citibank). Low-performing organizations either do not reorient or reorient all the time as they root around to find an effective alignment with environmental conditions.

This metamorphic approach to organization evolution underscores the role of history and precedent as future convergent periods are all constrained and shaped by prior convergent periods. Further, this approach to organization evolution highlights the role of executive leadership in managing convergent periods *and* in initiating and implementing frame-breaking change.

EXECUTIVE LEADERSHIP AND ORGANIZATION EVOLUTION

Executive leadership plays a key role in reinforcing system-wide momentum during convergent periods and in initiating and imple-

menting bursts of change that characterize strategic reorientations. The nature of the leadership task differs sharply during these contrasting periods of organization evolution.

During convergent periods, the executive team focuses on *maintaining* congruence and fit within the organization. Because strategy, structure, processes, and systems are fundamentally sound, the myriad of incremental substantive decisions can be delegated to middle-level management, where direct expertise and information resides. The key role for executive leadership during convergent periods is to reemphasize strategy, mission, and core values and to keep a vigilant eye on external opportunities and/or threats.

Frame-breaking change, however, requires direct executive involvement in all aspects of the change. Given the enormity of the change and inherent internal forces for stability, executive leadership must be involved in the specification of strategy, structure, people, and organizational processes *and* in the development of implementation plans. During frame-breaking change, executive leadership is directly involved in *reorienting* their organizations. Direct personal involvement of senior management seems to be critical to implement these system-wide changes (e.g., Reed at Citibank or Iacocca at Chrysler). Tentative change does not seem to be effective (e.g., Don Sinclair at General Radio).

Frame-breaking change triggers resistance to change from multiple sources change must overcome several generic hurdles, including:

- Individual opposition, rooted in either anxiety or personal commitment to the status quo, is likely to generate substantial individual resistance to change.
- Political coalitions opposing the upheaval may be quickly formed within the organization. During converging periods a political equilibrium is reached. Frame-breaking up-

sets this equilibrium; powerful individuals and/or groups who see their status threatened will join in resistance.

- Control is difficult during the transition. The systems, roles, and responsibilities of the former organization are in suspension; the new rules of the game—and the rewards—have not yet been clarified.
- External constituents—suppliers, customers, regulatory agencies, local communities, and the like—often prefer continuation of existing relationships rather than uncertain moves in the future.

Whereas convergent change can be delegated, frame-breaking change requires strong, direct leadership from the top as to where the organization is going and how it is to get there. Executive leadership must be directly involved in: motivating constructive behavior, shaping political dynamics, managing control during the transition period, and managing external constituencies. The executive team must direct the content of frame-breaking change *and* provide the energy, vision, and resources to support, and be role models for, the new order. Brilliant ideas for new strategies, structures, and processes will not be effective unless they are coupled with thorough implementation plans actively managed by the executive team.[6]

When to Launch an Upheaval

The most effective executives in our studies foresaw the need for major change. They recognized the external threats and opportunities, and took bold steps to deal with them. For example, a set of minicomputer companies (Prime, Rolm, Datapoint, Data General, among others) risked short-run success to take advantage of new opportunities created by technological and market changes. Indeed, by acting before being forced to do so, they had more time to plan their transitions.[7]

Such visionary executive teams are the exceptions. Most frame-breaking change is postponed until a financial crisis forces drastic action. The momentum, and frequently the success, of convergent periods breeds reluctance to change. This commitment to the status quo, and insensitivity to environmental shocks, is evident in both the Columbia and the McGill studies. It is not until financial crisis shouts its warning that most companies begin their transformation.

The difference in timing between pioneers and reluctant reactors is largely determined by executive leadership. The pioneering moves, in advance of crisis, are usually initiated by executives within the company. They are the exceptional persons who combine the vision, courage, and power to transform an organization. In contrast, the impetus for a tardy break usually comes from outside stakeholders; they eventually put strong pressure on existing executives—or bring in new executives—to make fundamental shifts.

Who Manages the Transformation

Directing a frame-breaking upheaval successfully calls for unusual talent and energy. The new mission must be defined, technology selected, resources acquired, policies revised, values changed, organization restructured, people reassured, inspiration provided, and an array of informal relationships shaped. Executives already on the spot will probably know most about the specific situation, but they may lack the talent, energy, and commitment to carry through an internal revolution.

As seen in the Citibank, Prime, and Alpha examples, most frame-break-ing upheavals are managed by executives brought in from outside the company. The Columbia research program finds that externally recruited executives are more than three times more likely to initiate frame-breaking change than existing executive teams. Frame-breaking change was coupled with CEO succession in more than 80 percent of the cases. Further, when frame-breaking change was combined with executive succession, company performance was significantly higher than when former executives stayed in place. In only 6 of 40 cases we studied did a current CEO initiate and implement multiple frame-breaking changes. In each of these six cases, the existing CEO made major changes in his/her direct reports, and this revitalized top team initiated and implemented frame-breaking changes (e.g., Thurston's actions at General Radio).[8]

Executive succession seems to be a powerful tool in managing framebreaking change. There are several reasons why a fresh set of executives are typically used in company transformations. The new executive team brings different skills and a fresh perspective. Often they arrive with a strong belief in the new mission. Moreover, they are unfettered by prior commitments linked to the status quo; instead, this new top team symbolizes the need for change. Excitement of a new challenge adds to the energy devoted to it.

We should note that many of the executives who could not, or would not, implement frame-breaking change went on to be quite successful in other organizations—for example, Ken Fisher at Encore Computer and Bill Podusk at Apollo Computer. The stimulation of a fresh start and of jobs matched to personal competence applies to individuals as well as to organizations.

Although typical patterns for the when and who of frame-breaking change are clear—wait for a financial crisis and then bring in an outsider, along with a revised executive team, to revamp the company—this is clearly less than satisfactory for a particular organization. Clearly, some companies benefit from transforming themselves before a crisis forces them to do so, and a few exceptional executives have the vision and drive to reorient a business which they nurtured during its preceding period of convergence. The vital tasks are to manage incremental change during convergent periods; to have the vision to initiate and implement framebreaking change prior to the competition; and to mobilize an executive team which can initiate and implement both kinds of change.

CONCLUSION

Our analysis of the way companies evolve over long periods of time indicates that the most effective firms have relatively long periods of convergence giving support to a basic strategy, but such periods are punctuated by upheavals—concurrent and discontinuous changes which reshape the entire organization. Managers should anticipate that when environments change sharply:

- Frame-breaking change cannot be avoided. These discontinuous organizational changes will either be made proactively or initiated under crisis/turnaround condition.
- Discontinuous changes need to be made in strategy, structure, people, and processes concurrently. Tentative change runs the risk of being smothered by individual, group, and organizational inertia.
- Frame-breaking change requires direct executive involvement in all aspects of the change, usually bolstered with new executives from outside the organization.
- There are no patterns in the sequence of frame-breaking changes, and not all strategies will be effective. Strategy and, in turn, structure, systems, and processes must meet industry-specific competitive issues.

Finally, our historical analysis of organizations highlights the following issues for executive leadership:

- Need to manage for balance, consistency, or fit during convergent period.
- Need to be vigilant for environmental shifts in order to anticipate the need for frame-breaking change.
- Need to effectively manage incremental as well as frame-breaking change.
- Need to build (or rebuild) a top team to help initiate and implement frame-breaking change.
- Need to develop core values which can be used as an anchor as organizations evolve through frame-breaking changes (e.g., IBM, Hewlett-Packard).
- Need to develop and use organizational history as a way to infuse pride in an organization's past and for its future.
- Need to bolster technical, social, and conceptual skills with visionary skills. Visionary skills add energy, direction, and excitement so critical during frame-breaking change.

Effectiveness over changing competitive conditions requires that executives manage fundamentally different kinds of organizations and different kinds of change. The data are consistent across diverse industries and countries, an executive team's ability to proactively initi- ate and implement frame-breaking change *and* to manage convergent change seem to be important factors which discriminate between organizational renewal and greatness versus complacency and eventual decline.

REFERENCES

1. A. Chandler, *Strategy and Structure* (Cambridge, MA: MIT Press, 1962).
2. D. Miller and P. Friesen, *Organizations: A Quantum View* (Englewood Cliffs, NJ: Prentice-Hall, 1984).
3. L. Greiner, "Evolution and Revolution as Organizations Grow," *Harvard Business Review* (July/August 1972), pp. 37–46.
4. D. Nadler and M. Tushman, *Strategic Organization Design* (Homewood, IL: Scott Foresman, 1986).
5. T. Peters and R. Waterman, *In Search of Excellence* (New York, NY: Harper and Row, 1982).
6. Nadler and Tushman, op. cit.
7. For a discussion of preemptive strategies, see I. MacMillan, "Delays in Competitors' Responses to New Banking Products," *Journal of Business Strategy*, 4 (1984): 58–65.
8. M. Tushman and B. Virany, "Changing Characteristics of Executive Teams in an Emerging Industry," *Journal of Business Venturing* (1986).

Concepts for the Management of Organization Change

David Nadler

Bringing about major change in a large and complex organization is a difficult task. Policies, procedures, and structures need to be altered. Individuals and groups have to be motivated to continue to perform in the face of major turbulence. People are presented with the fact that the "old ways," which include familiar tasks, jobs, procedures, and structures are no longer applicable. Political behavior frequently becomes more active and more intense. It is not surprising, therefore, that the process of effectively implementing organizational change has long been a topic that both managers and researchers have pondered. While there is still much that is not understood about change in complex organizations, the experiences and research of recent years do provide some guidance to those concerned with implementing major changes in organizations. This paper is designed to provide some useful concepts to aid in understanding the dynamics of change and to help in the planning and managing of major organizational changes. The paper is organized into several sections. We will start with a brief discussion of a model of organizational behavior. This discussion is necessary since it is difficult to think about changing organizations without some notion of why they work the way they do in the first place. Second, we will define

what we mean by organizational change and identify criteria for the effective management of change. Third, we will discuss some of the basic problems of implementing change. In the last section, we will list some specific methods and tools for effective implementation of organizational changes.

A VIEW OF ORGANIZATIONS

There are many different ways of thinking about organizations and the patterns of behavior that occur within them. During the past two decades, there has emerged a view of organizations as complex open social systems (Katz & Kahn, 1966), mechanisms which take input from the larger environment and subject that input to various transformation processes that result in output.

As systems, organizations are seen as composed of interdependent parts. Change in one element of the system will result in changes in other parts of the system. Similarly, organizations have the property of equilibrium; the system will generate energy to move towards a state of balance. Finally, as open systems, organizations need to maintain favorable transactions of input and output with the environment in order to survive over time.

While the systems perspective is useful,

systems theory by itself may be too abstract a concept to be a usable tool for managers. Thus, a number of organizational theorists have attempted to develop more pragmatic theories or models based on the system paradigm. There are a number of such models currently in use. One of these will be employed here.

The particular approach, called a *Congruence Model of Organizational Behavior* (Nadler & Tushman, 1977; 1979) is based on the general systems model. In this framework, the major inputs to the system of organizational behavior are the *environment* which provides constraints, demands and opportunities, the *resources* available to the organization, and the *history* of the organization. A fourth input, and perhaps the most crucial, is the organization's *strategy*. Strategy is the set of key decisions about the match of the organization's resources to the opportunities, constraints, and demands in the environment within the context of history.

The output of the system is, in general, the effectiveness of the organization's performance, consistent with the goals of strategy. Specifically, the output includes *organizational performance,* as well as *group performance* and *individual behavior and affect* which, of course, contribute to organizational performance.

The basic framework thus views the organization as being the mechanism that takes inputs (strategy and resources in the context of history and environment) and transforms them into outputs (patterns of individual, group, and organizational behavior). This view is portrayed in figure 1.

The major focus of organizational analysis is therefore the transformation process. The model conceives of the organization as being composed of four major components. The first component is the *task* of the organization, or the work to be done and its critical characteristics. The second component is composed of the *individuals* who are to perform organizational tasks. The third component includes all of the *formal organizational arrangements,* including various structures, processes, systems, etc. which are designed to motivate and facilitate individuals in the performance of organizational tasks. Finally, there is a set of *informal organizational arrangements,* which are usually neither planned nor written, but which tend to emerge over time. These include patterns of communication, power and influence, values and norms, etc. which characterize how an organization actually functions.

How do these four components (task,

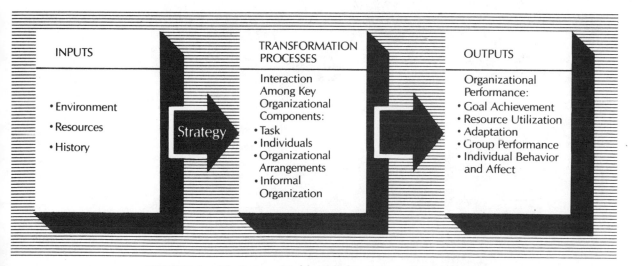

FIGURE 1. The Systems Model Applied to Organizational Behavior

individuals, organizational arrangements, and the informal organization) relate to one another? The relationship among components is the basic dynamic of the model. Each component can be thought of as having a relationship with each other component. Between each pair, then, we can think of a relative degree of consistency, congruence, or "fit." For example, if we look at the type of work to be done (task) and the nature of the people available to do the work (individuals) we could make a statement about the congruence between the two by seeing whether the demands of the work are consistent with the skills and abilities of the individuals. At the same time we would compare the rewards that the work provides to the needs and desires of the individuals. By looking at these factors, we would be able to assess how congruent the nature of the task was with the nature of the individuals in the system.

In fact, we could look at the question of congruence among all the components, or in terms of all six of the possible relationships among them (see Fig 2). The basic hypothesis of the model is therefore that *organizations will be most effective when their major components are congruent with each other.* To the extent that organizations face problems of effectiveness due to management and organizational factors, these problems will stem from poor fit, or lack of congruence, among organizational components.

This approach to organizations is thus a contingency approach. There is not one best organization design, or style of management, or method of working. Rather, different patterns of organization and management will be most appropriate in different situations. The model recognizes the fact that individuals, tasks, strategies, and environments may differ greatly from organization to organization.

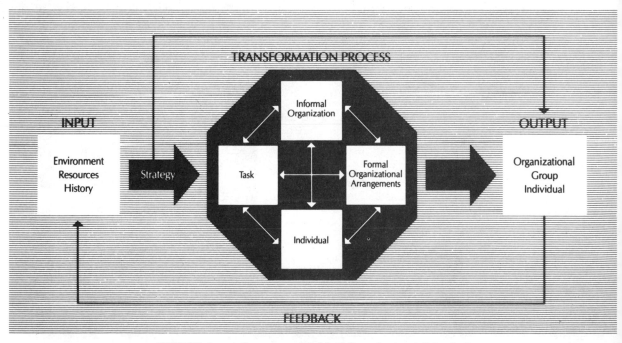

FIGURE 2.   *A Congruence Model of Organizational Behavior**
*From Nadler & Tushman, 1979

THE TASK OF IMPLEMENTING CHANGE

Having briefly presented some concepts that underlie our thinking about organizations, the question of change can now be addressed. Managers are frequently concerned about implementing organizational changes. Often changes in the environment necessitate organizational change. For example, factors related to competition, technology, or regulation, shift and thus necessitate changes in organizational strategy. If a new strategy is to be executed, then the organization and its various subunits (departments, groups, divisions, etc.) must perform tasks that may be different from those previously performed. Building on the organizational model presented above, this means that modification may need to be made in organizational arrangements, individuals and the informal organization.

Typically, implementing a change involves moving an organization to some desired future state. As illustrated in figure 3, we can think of changes in terms of transitions (Beckhard & Harris, 1977). At any point in time, the organization exists in a current state (A). The current state describes how the organization functions prior to the change. The future state (B) describes how the organization should be functioning in the future. It is the state that ideally would exist after the change. The period between A and B can be thought of as the transition state (C). In its most general terms, then, the effective management of change involves developing an understanding of the current state (A), developing an image of a desired future state (B), and moving the organization

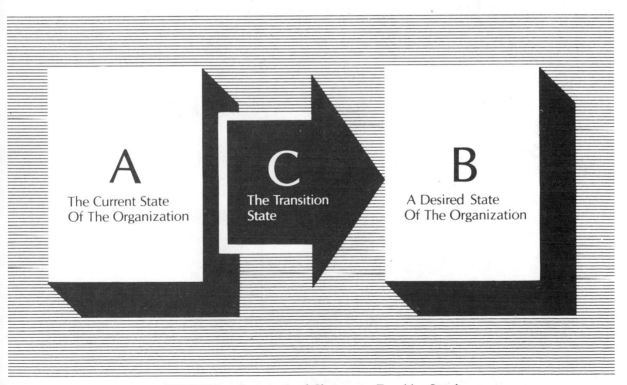

FIGURE 3.   *Organizational Change as a Transition State**
*Adapted from Beckhard & Harris, 1977.

from A through a transition period to B (Beck-hard & Harris, 1977).

Major transitions usually occur in response to changes in the nature of organizational inputs or outputs. Most significant changes are in response to or in anticipation of environmental or strategic shifts, or problems of performance. In terms of the congruence model, a change occurs when managers determine that the configuration of the components in the current state is not effective and the organization must be reshaped. Often this means a rethinking and redefining of the organization's task followed by changes in other components to support that new task (see figure 4).

What constitutes effective management of these changes? There are several criteria to consider. Building on the transition framework presented above, organizational change is effectively managed when:

1. The organization is moved from the current state to the future state.
2. The functioning of the organization in the future state meets expectations; i.e., it works as planned.
3. The transition is accomplished without undue cost to the organization.
4. The transition is accomplished without undue cost to individual organizational members.

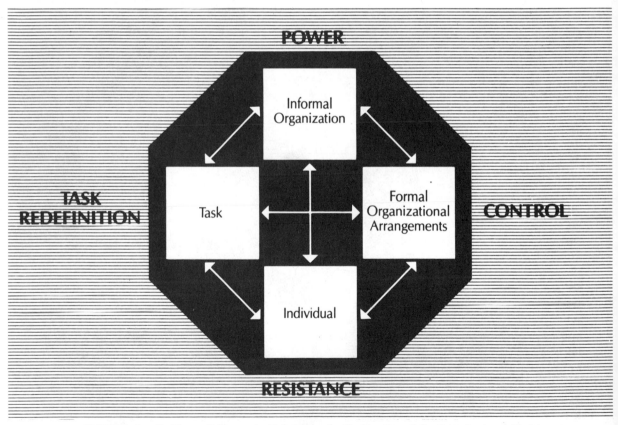

FIGURE 4.   *Problems of Change in Relation to the Components of the Organizational Model*

Of course, not every organizational change can be expected to meet these criteria, but such standards provide a target for planning change. The question is how to manage the way in which the change is implemented so as to maximize the chances that the change will be effective. Experience has shown that the way that a change is implemented can influence the effectiveness of the transition as much as the content of that change.

PROBLEMS IN IMPLEMENTING CHANGE

Experience and research have shown that the process of creating change is more difficult than it might seem. It is tempting to think of an organization as a large machine where parts can be replaced at will. On the contrary, the task of changing the behavior of organizations, groups and individuals has turned out to be a difficult and often frustrating endeavor.

Using the organizational model presented above, we can envision how organizations, as systems, are resistant to change. The forces of equilibrium tend to work to cancel out many changes. Changing one component of an organization may reduce its congruence with other components. As this happens, energy develops in the organization to limit, encapsulate, or revise the change.

The first issue in many changes is to diagnose the current system to identify the source of problems (or opportunities for improvement). In a large organization, this frequently leads to a rethinking of strategy, and a redefinition of the organization's task or work. For example, AT&T examines the environment and determines that it needs to change the primary orientation of its strategy, and thus, its task from service towards marketing.

The analysis of strategy and redefinition of task is an important step in changing an organization. On the other hand, many of the most troublesome problems of changing organizations occur not in the strategic/task shift, but in the implementation of the organizational transition to support the change in the nature of the strategy and the work. More specifically, any major organizational change presents three major problems which must be dealt with.

First is the problem of *resistance* to change (Watson, 1969; Zaltman & Duncan, 1977). Any individual faced with a change in the organization in which he/she works may be resistant for a variety of reasons. People have need for a certain degree of stability or security; change presents unknowns which cause anxiety. In addition, a change that is imposed on an individual reduces his/her sense of autonomy or self-control. Furthermore, people typically develop patterns for coping with or managing the current structure and situation. Change means that they will have to find new ways of managing their own environments—ways that might not be as successful as those currently used. In addition, those who have power in the current situation may resist change because it threatens that power. They have a vested interest in the status quo. Finally, individuals may resist change for ideological reasons; they truly believe that the way things are done currently is better than the proposed change. Whatever the source, individual resistance to change must be overcome for implementation of a change to be successful.

A second problem is that of organizational *control*. Change disrupts the normal course of events within an organization. It thus disrupts and undermines existing systems of management control, particularly those developed as part of the formal organizational arrangements. Change may make those systems irrelevant and/or inappropriate. As a result, during a change, it may become easy to lose control of the organization. As goals, structures, and people shift, it becomes difficult to monitor performance and make corrections as in normal control processes.

A related problem is that most formal organizational arrangements are designed for stable states, not transition states. Managers become fixated on the future state (B) and assume that all that is needed is to design the most effective organizational arrangements for the future. They think of change from A to B as simply a mechanical or procedural detail. The problems created by the lack of concern for the transition state are compounded by the inherent uniqueness of it. In most situations, the management systems and structures developed to manage A or B are simply not appropriate or adequate for the management of C. They are steady state management systems, designed to run organizations already in place, rather than transitional management systems.

The third problem is *power*. Any organization is a political system made up of different individuals, groups, and coalitions competing for power (Tushman, 1977; Salancik & Pfeffer, 1977).

Political behavior is thus a natural and expected feature of organizations. This occurs in both states A and B. In state C (transition), however, these dynamics become even more intense as the old order is dismantled and a new order emerges. This happens because any significant change poses the possibility of upsetting or modifying the balance of power among groups. The uncertainty created by change creates ambiguity, which in turn tends to increase the probability of political activity (Thompson & Tuden, 1959). Individuals and groups may take action based on their perception of how the change will affect their relative power position in the organization. They will try to influence where they will sit in the organization that emerges from the transition, and will be concerned about how the conflict of the transition period will affect the balance of power in the future state. Finally, individuals and groups

may engage in political action because of their ideological position on the change—it may be inconsistent with their shared values or image of the organization (Pettigrew, 1972).

In some sense, each of these problems is related primarily to one of the components of the organization (see figure 4). Resistance relates to the individual component, getting people to change their behavior. Control concerns the design of appropriate organizational arrangements for the transition period. Power relates to the reactions of the informal organization to change. Therefore, if a change is to be effective, all three problems—resistance, control, and power—must be addressed.

GUIDELINES FOR IMPLEMENTING CHANGE

The three basic problems that are inherent in change each lead to a general implication for the management of change (see figure 5).

The implication of the resistance problem is the need to *motivate changes* in behavior by individuals. This involves overcoming the natural resistance to change that emerges, and getting individuals to behave in ways consistent with both the short-run goals of change and the long-run organizational strategy.

The implication of the control problem is the need to *manage the transition*. Organizational arrangements must be designed and used to ensure that control is maintained during and after the transition. They must be specifically appropriate to the transition period rather than to the current or future state.

Finally, the implication of the power issue is the need to *shape the political dynamics of change* so that power centers develop that support the change, rather than block it (Pettigrew, 1975).

Each of these general implications suggests specific actions that can be taken to im-

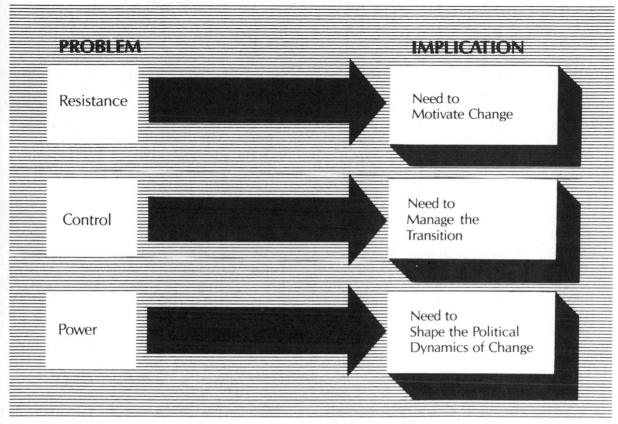

FIGURE 5. *Problems of Change and Implications for Change Management*

prove the chances of achieving an effective change. A number of action steps can be identified for each of the three implications.

Action Steps to Motivate Change

The first action step is to *identify and surface dissatisfaction with the current state.* As long as people are satisfied with the current state, they will not be motivated to change; people need to be "unfrozen" out of their inertia in order to be receptive to change (Lewin, 1947; Bennis et al, 1973). The greater the pain and dissatisfaction with the current state, the greater the motivation to change and the less the resistance to change. As a consequence, the management of change may require the creation of pain and dissatisfaction with the status quo. Dissatisfaction most commonly results from information concerning some aspect of organizational performance which is different from either desired or expected performance. Discrepancies can therefore be used to create dissatisfaction. As a result, data can be an important tool to initiate a process of change (Nadler, 1977).

The second action step is to build in *participation* in the change. One of the most consistent findings in the research on change is that participation in the change tends to reduce resistance, build ownerships of the change, and thus motivate people to make the change work (Coch & French, 1948; Vroom, 1964; Kotter & Schlesinger, 1979). Participation also facilitates the communication of information about what the change will be and why it has come about. Participation may also lead to obtaining new information from those participating, information that may enhance the effectiveness of the change or the future state.

On the other hand, participation has costs since it involves relinquishing control, takes time, and may create conflict. For each situation, different degrees of participation may be most effective (Vroom & Yetton, 1973). Participation may involve work on diagnosing the present situation, in planning change, in implementing change, or in combinations of the above. Participation may also vary in the specific devices that are used, ranging from large-scale data collection to sensing groups, to questionnaires, to cross unit committees, etc.

A third action step is to build in *rewards* for the behavior that is desired both during the transition state and in the future state. Our understanding of motivation and behavior in organizations suggests that people will tend to be motivated to behave in ways that they perceive as leading to desired outcomes (Vroom, 1964; Lawler, 1973). This implies that both formal and informal rewards must be identified and tied to the behavior that is needed, both for the transition and for the future state. The most frequent problem is that organizations expect individuals to behave in certain ways (particularly in a transition) while rewarding them for other conflicting behaviors (Kerr, 1975). In particular, rewards such as bonuses, pay systems, promotion, recognition, job assignment, and status symbols all need to be carefully examined during major organizational changes and restructured to support the direction of the transition.

Finally, people need to be provided with the *time and opportunity to disengage from the present state.* Change frequently creates feelings of loss, not unlike a death. People need to mourn for the old system or familiar way of doing things. This frequently is manifested in the emergence of stories or myths about the "good old days,"

even when those days weren't so good. The process of dealing with a loss and going through mourning takes time, and those managing change should take this into account. This factor underscores the need to provide information about the problems of the status quo and also to plan for enough time in advance of a change to allow people to deal with the loss and prepare for it.

Action Steps to Manage the Transition

One of the first and most critical steps for managing the transition state is to *develop and communicate a clear image of the future.* (Beckhard & Harris, 1977). Resistance and confusion frequently develop during an organizational change because people are unclear about what the future state will be like. Thus the goals and purposes of the change become blurred, and individual expectancies get formed on the basis of information that is frequently erroneous. In the absence of a clear image of the future, rumors develop, people design their own fantasies, and they act on them. Therefore, as clear an image as possible of the future state should be developed to serve as a guideline, target, or goal. In particular, a written statement or description of the future state may be of value in clarifying the image. Similarly, it is important to communicate information to those involved in the change, including what the future state will be like, how the transition will come about, why the change is being implemented, and how individuals will be affected by the change. This communication can be accomplished in a variety of ways, ranging from written communications to small group meetings, large briefing sessions, video-taped presentations, etc.

A second action step for managing the transition involves the use of *multiple and consistent leverage points.* If, building on the model presented above, an organization is made up of components which are interdependent, then the successful alteration of organizational behavior patterns must involve the use of multiple leverage points, or modifications in the larger set of components which shape the behavior of the organization and the people in it (Nadler & Tichy, 1980). Structural change, task change, change in the social environment, as well as changes in individuals themselves are all needed to bring about significant and lasting changes in the patterns of organizational behavior. Changes that are targeted at individuals and social relations (such as training, group interventions, etc.) tend to fade out quickly with few lasting effects when done in isolation (Porter, Lawler & Hackman, 1975). On the other hand, task and structural changes alone, while powerful and enduring, frequently produce unintended and dysfunctional consequences (see, for example, literature on control systems; e.g., Lawler & Rhode, 1976). Change which is in the direction intended and which is lasting therefore requires the use of multiple leverage points to modify more than a single component. Similarly, the changes have to be structured so that they are consistent; the training of individuals, for example, should dovetail with new job descriptions, rewards systems, or reporting relationships. In the absence of consistency, changes run the risk of creating new "poor fits" among organizational components. The result is either an abortive change, or decreases in organizational performance.

The third action step involves a number of different activities. *Organizational arrangements for the transition* need to be explicitly considered, designed, and used. As mentioned earlier, the organizational arrangements that function in either the present or future state are typically steady state designs, rather than designs for use in managing the transition state. The whole issue of developing structures to manage the transition has been discussed in depth elsewhere (see Beckhard & Harris, 1977), but a number of the most important elements should be mentioned here. In particular, the following organizational arrangements are important for managing the change:

A. A Transition Manager Someone should be designated as the manager of the organization for the transition state. This person may be a member of management, a chief executive, or someone else, but frequently it is difficult for one person to manage the current state, prepare to manage the future state, and simultaneously manage the transition. This person should have the power and authority needed to make the transition happen, and should be appropriately linked to the steady state managers, particularly the future state manager.

B. Resources for the Transition Major transitions involve potentially large risks for organizations. Given this, they are worth doing well and it is worth providing the needed resources to make them happen effectively. Resources such as personnel, dollars, training expertise, consultative expertise, etc. must be provided for the transition manager.

C. Transition Plan A transition is a movement from one state to another. To have that occur effectively, and to measure and control performance, a plan is needed with benchmarks, standards of performance, and similar features. Implicit in such a plan is a specification of the responsibilities of key individuals and groups.

D. Transition Management Structures Frequently it is difficult for a hierarchy to manage the process of change itself. As a result, it may be necessary to develop other structures or use other devices outside the regular organizational structure during the transition management period. Special task forces, pilot projects, experimental units, etc. need to be designed and employed for this period (see again Beckhard & Harris, 1977 for a discussion of these different devices).

The final action step for transition management involves developing *feedback mech-*

anisms to provide transition managers with information on the effectiveness of the transition and provide data on areas which require additional attention or action. There is a huge amount of anecdotal data about senior managers ordering changes and assuming those changes were made, only to find out to their horror that the change never occurred. Such a situation develops because managers lack feedback devices to tell them whether actions have been effective or not. During stable periods, effective managers tend to develop various ways of eliciting feedback. During the transition state, however, these mechanisms often break down due to the turbulence of the change, or because of the natural inclination not to provide "bad news." Thus, it becomes important for transition managers to develop multiple, redundant, and sensitive mechanisms for generating feedback about the transition. Devices such as surveys, sensing groups, consultant interviews, etc. as well as informal communication channels need to be developed and used during this period.

Action Steps for Shaping the Political Dynamics of Change

If an organization is a political system composed of different groups competing for power, then the most obvious action step involves *ensuring or developing the support of key power groups.* For a change to occur successfully, a critical mass of power groups has to be assembled and mobilized in support of the change. Those groups that may oppose the change have to in some way be compensated for or have their effects neutralized. Not all power groups have to be intimately involved in the change. Some may support the change on ideological grounds, while others may support the change because it enhances their own power position. With other groups, they will have to be included in the planning of the change so that their participation will motivate them, or co-opt them (Selznick, 1949). Still others may have to

be dealt with by bargaining or negotiations. The main point is that the key groups who may be affected by the change need to be identified, and strategies for building support among a necessary portion of those groups need to be developed and carried out (Sayles, 1979).

A major factor affecting the political terrain of an organization is the behavior of key and powerful leaders. Thus a second major action step involves *using leader behavior to generate energy in support of the change.* Leaders can mobilize groups, generate energy, provide models, manipulate major rewards, and do many other things which can affect the dynamics of the informal organization. Sets of leaders working in coordination can have a tremendously powerful impact on the informal organization. Thus leaders need to think about using their own behavior to generate energy (see House, 1976 on charismatic leadership) as well as to build on the support and behavior of other leaders (both formal and informal) within the organization.

The third action step involves *using symbols and language to create energy* (Peters, 1978; Pfeffer, 1980). By providing a language to describe the change and symbols that have emotional impact, it is possible to create new power centers or to bring together power centers under a common banner. Language is also important in defining an ambiguous reality. If, for example, a change is declared a success then it may become a success in the perception of others.

Finally, there is the need to *build in stability.* Organizations and individuals can only stand so much uncertainty and turbulence. An overload of uncertainty may create dysfunctional effects, as people may begin to panic, engage in extreme defensive behavior, and become irrationally resistant to any new change proposed. The increase of anxiety created by constant change thus has its costs. One way of dealing with this is to provide some sources of stability (structures, people, physical locations, etc. that stay the same) that serve as "anchors" for people to hold onto and provide a means for definition of the self in the midst of turbulence. While too many anchors can encourage resistance, it is important to provide some stability. More importantly, it is necessary to communicate the stability. People may not take comfort from something that is stable if they are unsure of its stability. Thus those aspects of the organization that will not change during a transition period need to be identified and communicated to organization members.

SUMMARY

This paper has attempted to identify some of the problems and issues of bringing about changes in complex organizations. At the same time, a number of general and specific action steps have been suggested. To understand how to change organizational behavior, we need a tool to understand how it occurs in the first place. The model used here (Nadler & Tushman, 1977; 1979) suggests that any change will encounter three general problems: resistance, control, and power. The general implication is the need to motivate change, manage the transition, and shape the political dynamics of change. For each of these three general implications, a number of specific action steps have been identified (see figure 6 below).

Obviously, each of these action steps will be more or less critical (and more or less feasi-

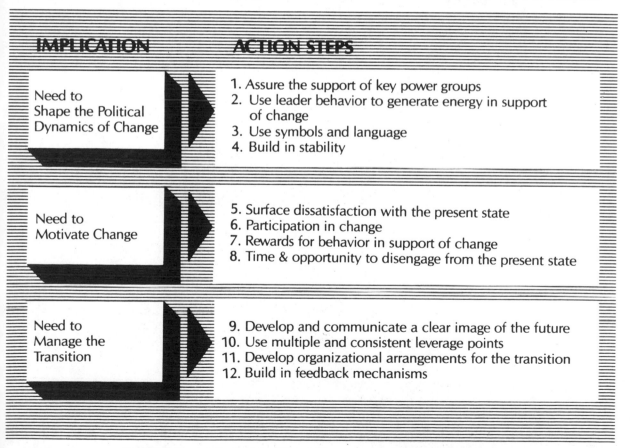

IMPLICATION	ACTION STEPS
Need to Shape the Political Dynamics of Change	1. Assure the support of key power groups 2. Use leader behavior to generate energy in support of change 3. Use symbols and language 4. Build in stability
Need to Motivate Change	5. Surface dissatisfaction with the present state 6. Participation in change 7. Rewards for behavior in support of change 8. Time & opportunity to disengage from the present state
Need to Manage the Transition	9. Develop and communicate a clear image of the future 10. Use multiple and consistent leverage points 11. Develop organizational arrangements for the transition 12. Build in feedback mechanisms

FIGURE 6. *Implications for Change Management and Related Action Steps*

IMPLEMENTATION ANALYSIS GUIDE

	IMPLEMENTATION PRACTICES	RATING	COMMENTS/EXPLANATION
SHAPING POLITICAL DYNAMICS	1. Getting the support of key power groups.		
	2. Using leader behavior to support the direction of change.		
	3. Using symbols and language.		
	4. Building in stability.		
MOTIVATING CHANGE	5. Creating dissatisfaction with the status quo.		
	6. Participation in planning and/or implementing change.		
	7. Rewarding needed behavior in transition and future states.		
	8. Providing time and opportunity to disengage from current state.		
MANAGING THE TRANSITION	9. Developing and communicating a clear image of the future state.		
	10. Using multiple and consistent leverage points.		
	11. Using transition management structures.		
	12. Building in feedback and evaluation of the transition.		

Rating is an assessment of the
general quality of action in
each implementation practice area.
Scale for ratings is — — — — — — —

5 = Very good
4 = Good
3 = Fair
2 = Poor
1 = Very Poor

SUMMARY RATINGS

Motivation   Transition   Political   Overall

ble) in different situations. Thus students of organization and managers alike need to be diagnostic in their approach to the problems of managing change. Each situation, while reflecting general patterns, has unique characteristics, based on its own differences of individuals, history, and situation. Thus specific variants of the action steps need to be developed for specific situations. To do this, managers need diagnostic models to understand problems, as well as guidelines for implementing changes, as presented here. Together, these two types of tools can be powerful aids in building and maintaining effective organizations.

REFERENCES

Beckhard, R. & Harris, R. *Organizational transitions.* Reading, Massachusetts: Addison-Wesley, 1977.

Bennis, W.G., Berlew, D.E., Schein, E.H. & Steele, F.I. *Interpersonal dynamics: Essays and readings on human interaction.* Homewood, Ill.: Dorsey Press, 1973.

Coch, L. & French, J.R.P., Jr. Overcoming resistance to change. *Human Relations,* 1948, **11,**512–532.

House, Robert J. A 1976 theory of charismatic leadership (mimeo). Faculty of Management Studies, University of Toronto, 1976.

Katz, D. & Kahn, R.L. *The social psychology of organizations.* New York: John Wiley & Sons, 1966.

Kerr, S. On the folly of rewarding A while hoping for B. *Academy of Management Journal,* December, 1975, 769–783.

Kotter, J.P. & Schlesinger, L.A. Choosing strategies for change. Harvard Business Review, 1979 (March-April), 106–114.

Lawler, E.E. *Motivation in work organizations.* Belmont, California: Wadsworth Publishing Co., 1973.

Lawler, E.E. & Rhode, J.G. *Information and control in organizations.* Santa Monica, California: Goodyear, 1976.

Lewin, K. Frontiers in group dynamics. *Human Relations,* 1947, **1,** 5–41.

Nadler, D.A. & Tushman, M.L. A congruence model for diagnosing organizational behavior. In D.A. Nadler, M.L. Tushman & N.G. Hatvany (eds.). *Approaches to Managing Organizational Behavior: Models, readings, and cases.* Boston: Little, Brown, 1981.

Nadler, D.A. *Feedback and organization development: Using data based methods.* Reading, Massachusetts: Addison-Wesley, 1977.

Nadler, D.A. & Tushman, M.L. A congruence model for diagnosing organizational behavior. In D. Kolb, I. Rubin, & J. McIntyre. *Organizational Psychology: A book of readings.* (3rd edition), Englewood Cliffs, N.J.: Prentice-Hall, 1979.

Nadler, D.A. & Tichy, N.M. The limitations of traditional intervention technology in health care organizations. In N. Margulies & J. Adams (eds.) *Organization development in health care organizations.* Reading, Mass: Addison-Wesley, 1980.

Peters, T.J. Symbols, patterns, and settings: An optimistic case for getting things done. *Organizational Dynamics,* 1978 (Autumn), 3–23.

Pettigrew, A. *The politics of organizational decision-making.* London: Tavistock Press, 1972.

Pettigrew, A. Towards a political theory of organizational intervention. *Human Relations,* 1978, **28,** 191–208.

Pfeffer, J. Management as symbolic action: The creation and maintainance of organizational paradigms. In L.L. Cummings & B.M. Staw (eds.) *Research in organizational behavior* (Vol. 3), JAI Press, 1980.

Porter, L.W., Lawler, E.E. & Hackman, J.R. *Behavior in organizations,* New York: McGraw-Hill, 1975.

Salancik, G.R. & Pfeffer, J. Who gets power and how they hold on to it: A strategic-contingency model of power. *Organizational Dynamics,* 1977 (Winter), 3–21.

Sayles, L.R. *Leadership: what effective managers really do and how they do it.* McGraw-Hill, 1979.

Selznick, P. *TVA and the Grass Roots.* Berkley: University of California Press, 1949.

Thompson, J.D. & Tuden, A. Strategies, structures and processes of organizational decision. In J.D. Thompson et al (eds.). *Comparative studies in ad-*

ministration. Pittsburgh: University of Pittsburgh Press, 1959.

Tushman, M.L. A political approach to organizations: a review and rationale. *Academy of Management Review,* 1977, **2,** 206–216.

Vroom, V.H. *Work and motivation.* New York: Wiley, 1964.

Vroom, V.H. and Yetton, P.W. Leadership and decision making. Pittsburgh: University of Pittsburgh Press, 1973.

Watson, G. Resistance to change. In W.G. Bennis, K.F. Benne & R. Chin (eds.) *The planning of change.* New York: Holt, Rinehart, Winston, 1969.

Zaltman, G. & Duncan, R. *Strategies for planned change.* New York: John Wiley, 1977.

How to Implement Radical Strategies in Large Organizations

Yvan Allaire

Mihaela Firsirotu

Carrying out a radical strategy in a large firm is the acid test of corporate leadership. Yet, there are no models available to prepare and guide leaders to take unprecedented actions. The authors in this article address this issue and propose a framework for devising and implementing strategies that are discontinuous with the organization's present course of action. The framework considers four types of radical strategies: reorientation, turnaround, revitalization, and transformation.

The business press has recently chronicled many corporations that are experiencing momentous shifts in strategic orientation. Reference is often made to a corporation's market repositioning, acquisitions and divestitures, structural changes, etc. However, when reporting on such major strategic changes, the press has also begun to emphasize the softer dimensions, such as values, culture, and mind-sets. Thus, it is not entirely accidental that the topic of corporate culture has become a popular issue at a time when many corporations are experiencing major overhauls. Culture, and its resistance to change, provides an explanation for the insuperable difficulties a firm encounters when it attempts to shift its strategic direction.

Not only has the "right" corporate culture become the essence and foundation of corporate excellence, but it is also claimed that the success or failure of needed corporate reforms hinges on management's sagacity and ability to change the firm's driving culture *in time* and *in tune* with required changes in formal strategies, structures, and management systems.

But while such observations are relevant, even though they are sometimes simplistic or faddish, they fail to inform corporate leaders on two critical issues:

1. What different types of radical strategies are available? And do different strategies call for different implementation procedures? For example, there has to be a difference between a radical strategy to turn around a moribund firm and a strategy to shift a corporation's resources to totally new markets and industries; or a strategy to

prepare a healthy organization for major changes in its industry.

2. What lessons have been learned from the experience of corporations that have attempted, succeeded, or failed at radical strategies? Are there emerging frameworks, models, bits of wisdom that can guide corporate leaders facing such a task?

This article addresses these two issues by proposing clear, operational distinctions among four types of radical strategies: reorientation, turnaround, revitalization, and transformation. These four, well-demarcated radical change situations, which all call for very different actions, flow from a simple diagnosis of how the firm *fits* in its present and future environments. We then go on to describe a framework for thinking about, devising, and implementing strategies that are discontinuous with the organization's present course of action.

FOUR CASE SITUATIONS

No radical strategy will ever occur if the corporation's leadership is not convinced of the need for dramatic actions. Therefore, a critical first step is for a firm to arrive at an appropriate diagnosis of how the firm fits in its present environment. A prescription prevalent in the business policy and strategy field has been the need for fit[1] or alignment[2] between the firm's strategy and its environment. Still, this wise, but trite, prescription can be made more potent if more of a distinction were made between present and future environments: an assessment of

a corporation's fit and adjustment to its *present* and *future* environments will reveal one of four possible situations, which are described below.

Case I: Harmony and Continuity
In this first case, the firm's strategy is well adjusted to its present environment, which results in the firm's sound economic performance. The future is an evolutionary, predictable version of the present, for which the firm will prepare in an incremental manner. In other words, the preferred state of affairs, whenever attainable, is for a firm to have a harmonious fit in its present environment while making synchronized, gradual changes to meet anticipated future requirements (see Figure 1).

Still, managers, and, for that matter, most people, have a strong tendency to cling to this approach even when there are warning signals indicating that a new approach is needed for the firm to cope with the future. (To the extent that the firm's management is not deluding itself into believing that a Case I strategy is the proper diagnosis, the textbook prescriptions and techniques for good management formulated for just such conditions are relevant and useful.)

A company's harmonious fit to present and future environments is most easily achieved in periods of easy economic growth and tranquil technology. However, periods of economic upheaval or economic transformation may disrupt and threaten the status quo of large businesses. If this happens, the business environment becomes "discontinuous," and becomes increasingly characterized by radical changes in the rules of the game. It is as if, in

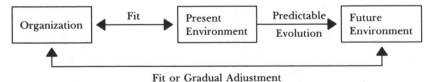

Fit or Gradual Adjustment

FIGURE 1.   Case I: Harmony and Continuity

an ongoing game of chess, one of the players or some outside authority were to decree suddenly changes in the rules that govern the moves of chess pieces. Much of the players' past chess experience (and the hundreds of books offering advice on how to play chess) would automatically become obsolete. In the final analysis, if an organization finds that it has to adjust to radically changed circumstances, the Case I scenario is inappropriate, and even dangerous.

Case II: Preemptive Adjustment or Temporary Misfit

Preemptive Adjustment In this case, the firm is not well adjusted to its present market circumstances, which results in its immediate unsatisfactory performance. However, it is anticipated that the future will be fundamentally different from the present situation. The environment is expected to undergo a sudden breach of continuity or a sharp change from present conditions and trends: the firm is prepared and ready to reap rich rewards when this happens (see Figure 2).

A good illustration of this case is provided by Citibank's expenditures on technology and product development, which resulted in poor performances for some years in its retail banking operations. Nonetheless, this orientation has presently placed the firm in a favorable strategic position as deregulation of the banking industry has begun to take effect and radically change the competitive and market environments. Another example is MCI Communications. Its quixotic challenge at AT&T in

the long-distance telephone market has been made more significant by successive changes in the regulations of the telecommunications industry in the U.S.

Also included in this category are innovating firms that propose radically new products to presently unreceptive or undeveloped markets. Genentech's early foray in the gene-splicing and biotechnology field is a good example. Firms in this situation, if they are persistent and if their resources are sufficient, may eventually be vindicated; on the other hand, it may be that their ventures were ill-timed and ill-conceived.

Temporary Misfit Transient, short-lived phenomena may perturb the organization's present environment, thereby creating havoc and misalignment for the firm. Nonetheless, the future could bring a return to normal circumstances to which the organization will be well adjusted. The organization will then resume its past acceptable level of economic performance. Although this scenario may be plausible, it may also be one of wishful thinking, or what Abernathy, Clark, and Kantrow call the "transient economic misfortune" school of thought.[3]

The prevalence of this type of unfounded rationale is particularly evident in industries that are coming to the end of their growth cycle. For example, the leveling off in sales of kerosene heaters, cross-country ski equipment, video games, snowmobiles, and personal computers was characteristically attributed to transient phenomenon, such as bad weather or bad economic conditions. However, it was believed that as soon as these conditions returned to normal, sales would again surge at

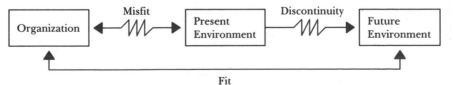

FIGURE 2. *Case II: Preemptive Adjustment or a Temporary Misfit*

their previous rate. Of course, this did not happen. In these cases, sticking to this strategy was damaging as it led to a postponement of the kind of actions required to adjust these businesses to new realities.

Case III: Transformation or Reorientation

Here, the firm is well adjusted to its present environment and turns in strong, respectable performances. However, its management foresees a future environment that is quite different from the prevailing one as a result of demographic, technological, regulatory, or competitive changes. To cope with, and thrive in, these upcoming circumstances, the organization must undergo a fundamental change (see Figure 3).

Transformation Classic examples of major strategic *transformations* that have restructured whole industries include Boeing's shift to the production of jet engine commercial airplanes and IBM's immense wager on the integrated circuit technology of the 360. More recently, current and anticipated dramatic changes in computer markets and technology have called for major modifications of strategy at IBM and Digital Equipment. In the latter case, K.C. Olsen, Digital's president, "embarked upon a radical transformation of his engineering-oriented company into a tough, market-driven competitor."[4]

At Black and Decker, painful competition from Japanese manufacturers has led the company to bet its future on a "global" market strategy that requires a major transformation of the corporation.[5] The management of Beatrice Foods has also voiced its intention to "transform the sprawling food, consumer, and industrial products holding company into a consolidated marketing giant on the order of Procter & Gamble Co."[6]

In Canada, the Bank of Montreal has undertaken a major transformation of its structures and modes of operation. It is preparing for (and ushering in) an emerging banking environment that is thought to call for radically different operating technologies, management systems, and banking philosophy.[7]

The breakup of AT&T along with the heroic efforts of some of its components (Western Electric, Bell Labs, AT&T Information Systems, etc.) to shift from a regulated telephone monopoly environment to a competitive market context is perhaps the most striking example of a large-scale attempt at strategic transformation.[8]

Transformations may also result from a firm's resolve to change the "center of gravity" of the corporation.[9] For example, Monsanto's move downstream from commodity chemicals to proprietary, patented products illustrates a transformation strategy.[10] The displacement of a corporation's center of gravity often means that new skills and radically different modes of operation and styles of management must be brought into the organization in a short period of time. This kind of transformation may result in a company that is temporarily misaligned with its present environment.

Reorientation A reorientation scenario is one where a company, in anticipation of stagnation and even decline as its present markets mature,

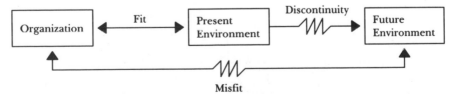

FIGURE 3. *Case III: Transformation or Reorientation*

may *reorient* its resources into more attractive markets and industries. The business press is full of accounts of companies that are searching for renewed vitality through reorientation strategies. Below is a list of organizations that either have reoriented or are in the process of reorienting their operations.

- General Electric's shift from traditional electric products to high technology (computer services, factory automation);[11]
- Sears, Roebuck and American Express's invasion of the financial services market;[12]
- Philip Morris's aggressive entry into the beer industry (through Miller) and into the soft drink industry (through Seven-Up);
- Eaton's shift from reliance on trucks and other vehicle parts to electronics, factory automation machinery, and fluid power systems;[13]
- Pillsbury's shift to fast food and restaurant chains;[14]
- Gould's move from battery operations— the very foundation of the corporation which it recently and symbolically sold— to the production and selling of electronic equipment. Gould Inc. now operates fifty-seven electronic plants in eleven countries;
- Imasco's (a large Canadian cigarette manufacturer) move into the United States' fast food restaurants and retail drug stores;[15]
- Philip's shift to high-tech products;[16]
- Cincinnati Milacron's shift from metal bender to supplier of new robotic technology;[17]
- U.S. Steel's redeployment of assets (Marathon Oil, etc.);[18]

- Singer's expansion into aerospace;[19] and
- Johnson & Johnson's recent emphasis on high-tech medical hardware.[20]

Because the environments in which these firms presently operate do not provide a future with sufficient prospects for growth and profitability, they are seeking to move voluntarily to market environments offering more promise and potential. In such a reorientation of activities, the firm must manage a breach, or discontinuity, between its present and future state.

Case IV: Turnaround and Revitalization

The firm in this case is misaligned with its present environment: its performance may range from mediocre to dismal. Furthermore, the company is ill-equipped to meet the future (see Figure 4). The business press reverberates with stories of dramatic efforts of companies salvaging and turning around large organizations, such as Chrysler, Massey-Ferguson, International Harvester, American Motors, Montgomery Ward, AM International, Geico, Clark Equipment, A&P, Braniff, Pan-Am, Boise Cascade, Allis-Chalmers, Dome Petroleum, Eastern Airlines, and Western Union.

But whether the situation calls for *revitalization* or *turnaround* actions hinges on the severity of the problems. There is, for example, a difference between a Burrough's or a Westinghouse's lackadaisical profit performance, sagging market share, and groping adjustment to changing markets on the one hand and, on the other hand, a Chrysler Massey-Ferguson, or

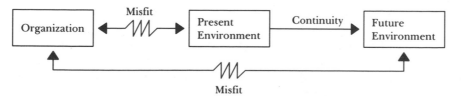

FIGURE 4. *Case IV: Turnaround and Revitalization*

International Harvester on the brink of bankruptcy.

A company is in a *turnaround* situation if it has experienced such grave losses that its very survival is at stake if improvements are not achieved swiftly. However, a corporation may not be in any immediate danger but may show mediocre or below average results, calling for a *revitalization* of its performance in the marketplace. Recent examples of businesses undergoing a revitalization are Prudential-Bache Securities,[21] Continental Corp.,[22] Corning Glass,[23] Burroughs,[24] Goodyear,[25] Sears's retailing division,[26] J.C. Penney,[27] Westinghouse,[28] and Sherwin-Williams.[29]

A FRAMEWORK TO DEVISE AND IMPLEMENT RADICAL STRATEGIES

Leaders faced with the challenge of transforming, reorienting, revitalizing, or turning around a large corporation will find few relevant models or useful prescriptions to guide their actions. Instead, they will most likely fret about culture and about how to create and sustain the kind of values they should want for their organizations. They may even be bullied by popular infatuation into a "search for excellence" that promotes specific and contingent observations as universal and compelling management principles.[30]

Based on the experiences of many leaders who assumed the role of corporate revolutionaries, we have devised a framework for implementing radical strategies. The framework is broken down into six basic steps: (1) making a proper diagnosis; (2) formulating a meta-strategy for radical change; (3) assessing the company's culture and structure; (4) defining the goals of the company's culture and structure; (5) proposing a broad agenda for radical change; and (6) stabilizing the organization.

Step 1: Making a Proper Diagnosis

Perhaps the most pernicious role of a corporation's present culture and structure is in its shaping a *corporate mind-set* that makes its leaders and managers immune or oblivious to signals of danger.

For example, a leadership persuaded of its Case I situation of harmony, continuity, and incremental adjustments may be right. However, the leaders may be deluding themselves or they may be impervious to indications of dramatic industry changes. They may even deny the reality of their present difficulties and shortcomings, and they may cling to a Case II diagnosis of a transient, self-correcting phenomenon, thereby attributing the company's poor performance to factors beyond their control. They may, therefore, feel that no radical actions are called for on their part.

Obviously, the first step in implementing any radical strategy is to make sure that the diagnosis of the firm's state of adjustment to its present environment and its preparedness for future circumstances is based on a tough, lucid, and unbiased assessment. Radical strategies must be considered if the leadership concludes, on the basis of that assessment, that it must either transform, reorient, revitalize, or turn around the corporation. Each of these strategies has its own particular dynamics and set of considerations. Although the contents and rate of change will reflect each company's particularities, these four radical strategies (in particular, turnaround, revitalization, and transformation) should unfold in a pattern of steps and actions, sometimes sequential but often overlapping and concurrent.

The Four Radical Strategies

Reorientation   Of the four radical strategies, reorientation is the easiest to implement. If a reorientation calls for the gradual divestment of present businesses and the acquisition of businesses in new fields—as General Electric and Gould are doing—corporate management would acquire the cultures and structures of the newly acquired firms. On the other hand, if a reorientation calls for the addition of new businesses to a mature, but profitable business—as Philip Morris, Pillsbury, and Imasco have done—the culture and structure of these businesses should not be disturbed if they are functioning well. Nevertheless, there are a few pitfalls that a company should be aware of when implementing a reorientation strategy:

Corporate Management's Mind-set.

The fundamental requirement of a successful reorientation is corporate leaders' awareness that they are entering new territories, and, therefore, that their past experiences and specific skills may be of limited relevance, if not totally inadequate. It is tempting, but dangerous, to assume that what has made their companies successful in their present businesses will also make them successful in other industries. Such an attitude is sometimes reinforced by leaders emphasizing the similarities between the new and old businesses. For example, General Foods bungled in the fast food business (with Burger Chef) precisely because it first attempted to have this totally new business managed by people from its old business.

This trap is particularly dangerous when a corporation moves into new fields incrementally. For example, the chief executive of Johnson & Johnson challenged *Business Week*'s cover story that stated that J&J would have to change its corporate culture as it moved more and more into high-tech medical hardware.[31] In his letter to *BW*, Mr. Burke retorted, "It is well known that Johnson & Johnson has been a high-technology company for decades. . . ."[32] Obviously, J&J's leadership diagnosed the situation as a Case I scenario (continuity), whereas *Business Week* concluded that it was a Case III situation (reorientation).

The Lure of Efficiency through Integration.

Even though corporate management may consciously acknowledge that a newly acquired or a newly formed business is different from the existing mature business, it may be tempted to integrate some of the new business's functions with the old one in order to take advantage of the cost savings. This temptation must be resisted, however, for the old business's culture may permeate the new business, thereby making it increasingly difficult for the new business to adjust to its own competitive environment. Woolworth is a case in point. When Woolworth, a successful, but mature variety store business, formed the discount store Woolco, it decided to integrate some of Woolco's functions (in particular, purchasing) with Woolworth's operations. This led to Woolco's ultimate failure in part because its operations were permeated by Woolworth's "five-and-dime" thinking. In contrast, Kresge managed its successful K mart division as a completely autonomous business.[33]

A successful reorientation, therefore, calls for a corporate leadership that *knows it does not know* how to run the new businesses it is either acquiring or forming. Every attempt should be made to keep the cultures and structures of both the new and old businesses separate and distinct.

Turnaround When a corporation's very survival is threatened, its leaders must carry out emergency actions that will stave off bankruptcy and buy them the time required to implement a radical strategy. The leadership must quickly find a new, more suitable market strategy that offers a compelling long-term solution to the firm's present plight. Often what is required to get the firm out of its rut is a new top management team that will challenge taken-for-granted "facts" and assumptions. Such a crisis provides top management with a formidable tool to carry out changes that would otherwise be impossible. However, the level of stress among managers and employees must be monitored and managed. Too much stress may well lead to counterproductive actions (e.g., rash decisions).

Revitalization   Before a revitalization strategy can be implemented, an organization must first come to terms with two pervasive issues: (1) that there is no immediate evidence of crisis or threat to the firm's survival; and (2) that mediocre performances are often justified by putting the blame on external factors that are thought to be beyond the control of management. Given this backdrop, it is up to corporate leaders to make a looming crisis tangible and to make known the dangers that the corporation faces. The leaders must make the case vivid and persuasive. Corporate management must also develop a sense of control and responsibility for the firm's performance.

Transformation   Of all the radical strategies, transformation requires the most demanding and skillful leadership. What is needed is a genuine revolution initiated by a leader with a *vision* of the corporation's future and the *will* to achieve it. However, the typical scenario is one where the corporation's present performance is satisfactory—maybe even excellent—and thus there is no impetus and no obvious justification for change.

Transformation strategy also involves other risks. Top management frequently makes the mistake of focusing exclusively on the structural aspects of change and of assuming implicitly that an appropriate culture will emerge quickly and inevitably from the new structural arrangements. In addition, in the course of transforming the organization to meet impending changes, top management may bring about a misalignment that is similar to a Case II misfit situation. Corporate management must be aware that some degree of confusion and disarray among employees and clients may be un-

avoidable during the process of transformation and, therefore, may result in a lower level of economic performance for a period of time.

Step 2: Formulating a Meta-strategy for Radical Change

To achieve radical change, the organization should be instilled with the new strategies, structures and systems, and supporting values deemed necessary to make such a change successful. Obviously, the leader, who is usually the CEO, must be able to distance himself or herself from the ongoing operations in order to set in motion the processes of change. This means that when present or anticipated events indicate that change in an organization's culture and structure is necessary, the leader must be able to formulate a *strategy* to implement a radically different strategy in the organization. This strategy is known as a meta-strategy.

The leader's meta-strategy is unwritten and communicated to very few people, at least in its early stages of implementation. At the beginning, the meta-strategy may consist of a leader's tentative search for broad goals and directions. He or she will then set up or activate multiple (internal and external) channels to consult and discuss the goals and orientations.

When a leader becomes convinced—the sooner the better—that particular goals and directions are appropriate, he or she will then take the necessary steps to broaden support for the chosen direction through a well-thought-out sequence of symbolic actions and structural changes. The leader's meta-strategy will reflect some hard thinking and firm conclusions about the kind of values that should be built into the organization. However, this does not mean that the leader should hold corporatewide seminars on the "culture we should have." (Culture is in the realm of feelings and sentiments, and does not develop well under clinical observation.) Rather, the meta-strategy process is a formal, well-mapped-out strategy that leads to a new, formal, explicit strategy for the organization. In this way, the organization's future is dependent upon the quality of this present leadership's meta-strategy.

Presently, the business press is full of sagas of leaders going about the task of major corporate overhauls. The accounts of these struggles and our own research of specific cases lead to a firm conclusion: radical strategies have been successfully implemented only where corporate leaders were equipped with an effective meta-strategy.

Step 3: Assessing the Corporation's Present Culture and Structure

The objective here is to understand the organization as a sociocultural system, to chart the socialization that the corporation actually provides, and to get at the organization's mind-set. If the leaders emerge from the ranks of the corporation, this step requires that they examine the values, beliefs, and mind-sets (including their own) imparted by the organization. On the other hand, if the leaders are newcomers, this step calls for their fast and sensitive learning of the organization's tangible *and* occult properties. In either case, the process may be helped by finding answers to the following questions:

· What are the tacit background assumptions and expectations in the corporation? Where do they come from?
· What are the values and frames of mind that flow from the particular nature of the industry? How did the industry's peculiar technology, regulations, labor-management relations, nature of competition, and economics shape the beliefs and behavior of the organization? These factors almost always play a critical role in shaping the mind-set of a corporation. Yet, this factor is generally overlooked in the recent crop of books and articles on corporate culture, which

tends to view culture merely as the product of past or present charismatic leaders.

· What stories, legends, myths circulate concerning the corporation's history, its past and present leaders? How are its successes and misfortunes explained?
· What are valued behavior, promotion paths, and critical skills for success in the corporation?
· What reinforcement of present culture is afforded by recruitment, training, promotion, organization structures, management systems?
· What is the implicit or explicit process of socialization in the corporation? Who are the role models? What cues and messages are conveyed to new employees? What values are communicated in training sessions?
· What is the degree of employee involvement in the corporation? Is there widespread commitment or calculative, limited participation on the part of management and employees? Are there groups (divisions, departments, etc.) with a subculture substantially at odds with the rest of the corporation?

The end product of this inquiry should be a statement of the basic values, assumptions, or expectations that have emerged from the organization's particular history, leadership, and contingency factors and that are supported by present-day management policies and practices. Below are brief examples of the set of assumptions that deeply permeated the operations of two large corporations.

AT&T. W. Brooke Tunstall, assistant vice president of AT&T, found that AT&T's operations were deeply influenced by the following:[34]

· AT&T's role is to provide the best universal service at the lowest possible cost in a regulated environment;

- AT&T must be "one system," "one policy" throughout the organization to fulfill its role;
- AT&T is a three-legged stool: it must achieve a fair balance in the treatment of its employees, customers, and shareholders;
- operational efficiency, technical skills, and a high level of effort to create a favorable regulatory climate are the keys for success; and
- AT&T is a big family that cares for its employees.

Canadian National. In her study of Canadian National (CN), a state-owned railway company (now diversified to a large extent), Firsirotu discovered the assumptions underlying the corporation:[35]

- CN has a public service responsibility to Canadian communities;
- independence from government interference is a necessary condition of successful operation;
- CN has a degree of control over its market environments;
- revenues for commercial viability are to a large extent dependent upon regulatory and political decisions and orders;
- costing expertise and technical skills are critical to success in the corporation;
- long-range financial planning is essential to successful management of the corporation;
- additional volume of business is always good and will be sought through pricing actions rather than through better service offerings; and
- CN is a big, patriarchal family with a top-down flow of authority and wisdom.

These two studies are instructive in that:

- they identify two sets of assumptions that have their roots in their respective industry's character, not in charismatic leader-

ship. These assumptions are quite functional for the industry and context in which these organizations are operating; however, they would (and did) become very burdensome in different markets and context (e.g., AT&T in communication/information systems, or CN in the trucking business);
- some assumptions may be conflicting, even mutually exclusive (e.g., independence from government and viability that depends upon political decisions), thereby creating tensions, variations in emphasis, and different means of reconciliation at various turns in the organization's history; and
- these values and assumptions are shared and supported with different intensity in different parts of the organization. For instance, the union's leadership at CN is suspicious of the "big family" concept, but it stresses at every opportunity the "public service" role of CN as a functional rampart against the cutbacks and rationalizations that a strictly commercial role would impose on CN.

Step 4: Defining the Goals of a Company's Culture and Structure

A leader aiming to radically change the corporation must set up processes that lead to some definition of the company's goals in terms of its culture and structure. What would the transformed, revitalized, or turned-around corporation look like? What values, expectations, and assumptions are consistent with, and indeed necessary to, the effective implementation of the firm's changed strategic posture and new operating requirements? This determination must be respectful of the factors that have shaped the corporation and that continue to influence its development. Thus, in attempting to change an organization's culture and structure, the leadership should heed the following observations.

Coherence with Contingency Factors. The values, strategies, and management systems that are proposed for the corporation should have an increasingly *functional* role in ensuring the survival and success of the firm as well as providing rewards to its employees. If contingency factors (e.g., regulations, competition, technology) are *not* changing, the proposed culture must build on the assumptions and expectations that flow from these factors. For example, despite repeated attempts, it has proven very difficult to instill a "marketing orientation" in banking firms operating in a regulated environment where the critical tasks, and, therefore, skills, consist of credit rationing, that is, of deciding which loan supplicants would be favored.

It will also be futile to, say, exhort the employees of a regulated monopoly offering a public service and requiring large capital investments to become "close to the customer," to show a "bias for action," to manage with "simple form and lean staff," and to preach "autonomy and entrepreneurship." The requirements for success, imposed by the economics and regulations of these industries, are pushing very hard in another direction, and attempts by management to install a culture that works against these forces will, therefore, be counterproductive.

However, when changes in contingency factors *do* occur, it is management's responsibility to ensure that these factors are quickly made visible to the organization's members and that these mutations are used as levers in working out changes in the organization's values and mind-set.

Multiple Linkages with the Present Culture. In the process of reviving or transforming a corporation, the leader must strive to preserve, emphasize, and build upon aspects of the present culture that are positive and compatible. The leader may even propose a culture that is a modernized version of old values and traditions that once made the corporation successful.

For example, Pistner, the CEO of Montgomery Ward, until very recently, declared his intentions of "replacing Ward's post-office mentality" and to "return to the homely, honest virtues that made Montgomery Ward a powerful retailing force fifty or seventy years ago."[36] Similarly, Warren, the CEO of the newly formed Canada Post Corporation, proposed to postal employees a return to the proud values of reliable service that once upon a time made their work honorable and respected in the community.[37]

A present culture may exhibit inherent contradictions in values and assumptions which the proposed culture should then either build on, emphasizing some assumptions or values and downgrading others, or propose a novel reconciliation of these contradictions. Finally, aspects of a present culture and structure that are antagonistic to the proposed culture and structure should be identified and opposed directly. For example, in the overhaul of a Canadian bank, it was found that any reduction in the number of branches was resisted because the size of the network had become a measure of the institution's success and importance. Having recognized this, the leadership marshaled arguments in direct attack of that belief.

Step 5: Proposing a Broad Agenda for Radical Change

Figure 5 offers a useful schema for this step. The *aim* of radical strategies is to bring about required major changes in the structure—new goals and market strategies and new organizational designs and systems. But the *challenge* of radical strategies is to bring about the changes in culture and individual mind-sets deemed necessary to support and reinforce the changes in structure. If this is not achieved, structural changes will be ineffective, or even, counterproductive. However, it should be emphasized

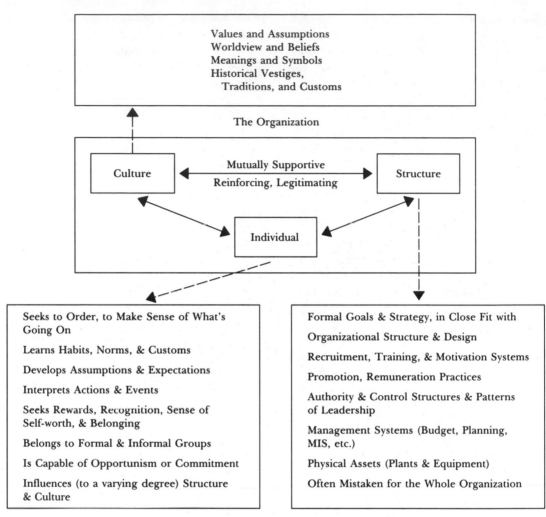

FIGURE 5.   A Schematic View of the Organization

that the three dimensions of any organization (culture, structure, individuals) are not to be changed through the same mechanisms.

Table 1 summarizes the issues raised by radical, discontinuous, strategic change. It underlines the fact that management has a high degree of control on structural variables (formal goals, strategy, design, management systems). These may be changed at moderate to high speed, through the application of good *technical,* analytical management and competent *political* management of internal coalitions.

In addition, if structural changes are legitimated by the present culture, management can implement such changes swiftly and easily.

However, when it comes to changes in cultural properties of the firm, management has, at best, only a moderate degree of control. Changes at that level tend to be slow and must be effected in part through *symbolic* management, accompanied by suitable structural reinforcements.[38] In order for this to happen, management must understand and make a conscious attempt to channel the complex so-

TABLE 1.   *Dynamics of Strategic Change*

The Organization	Degree of Control by Management	Rate of Change	Mode of Change
Structure	High	Moderate to high	Political & technical management plus cultural legitimacy
Culture	Low to moderate	Low to moderate	Symbolic management supported by structural changes
Individual	Low to moderate	Low to moderate	Conversion through replacement, training, reeducation & restructuring of assumptions & worldviews

cial processes through which symbols, meanings, and values are created.

Effective changes in culture and structure must be carried out in a well-coordinated sequence of actions, which mutually reinforce, legitimate, and aim to cognitively reorient and restructure the mind-sets of management and employees. In the process, some tension between culture and structure is inevitable as changes at one level are not rooted in the other. However, this tension must be calibrated so that it does not reach a point where the linkage is severed and the present culture becomes antagonistic to the new structure. The resulting confusion, disarray, and disorientation among the members of the organization would be most disruptive.

To guard against a cultural clash, individual members should be provided with powerful symbolic materials and tangible structural evidence of a new corporate order. These should contain a compelling explanation of the corporation's present problems and future actions, as well as clear messages about the modes and norms of behavior that will be successful and rewarded henceforth. This agenda for radical change would typically include political and symbolic actions as well as recruiting change agents.

Political Actions. (1) Broaden the political support for radical actions; (2) raise the level of dissatisfaction and discomfort with the present situation; (3) sensitize key actors to the need for change. If necessary, use outside consultants or research results to underline the risk of the present course and to offer a compelling case for change. For example, when Pistner took over as CEO of Montgomery Ward, he prepared a dramatic document that he called, "A Charter for Survival." Pistner wrote, "Survival is the right word. It implies that the company is in trouble and that its future is in doubt unless drastic measures are taken. The trouble is real, and an immediate change must be made."[39]

Symbolic Actions. (1) Communicate forcefully a new image that captures the *external strategy and proposed culture* to be implemented; (2) use all available media channels to disseminate them (in-house journals, orientation sessions, training). Here the leader should become the articulate embodiment of the new goals, directions, and values. For example, Smith of GM is synthesizing the new spirit he wants in the corporation by embodying "the 3 Rs— risk, responsibility, and rewards."[40] Similarly, Sullivan of Borden is trying to capture in an acronym, ROSE (return on shareholder's equity), his target for a revitalized company: "He sent ties with a ROSE logo to the top 200 managers. . . . He instituted incentive programs to reward executives for meeting financial goals, including bonuses tied in part to ROSE. . . ."[41]

Change Agents. (1) Identify or recruit, train, and disseminate throughout the organizations change agents who are favorable to the new orientation and who explain and propagandize it; (2) maintain a liaison relationship.

Step 6: Stabilizing the Organization

During periods of transition, more than any other time, the members of the organization will be looking out for signals—watching for clues, inferring intents and motives—to see which way the organization is going. Any discrepancy between the leadership's words and deeds will be spotted. Furthermore, any contradictory or ambiguous signal can sidetrack or slow down the process of change. For example, at AT&T, the former IBM executive Archie McGill had become the symbolic embodiment of the utility company's resolve to become an effective marketer and competitor in the information systems field. The ups and downs of his career at AT&T were interpreted as evidence of the leadership's real intentions concerning this new orientation. For this reason, his recent departure from AT&T created confusion and uncertainty, a feeling that the new style and spirit of management that had sprung up in parts of the corporation might be quickly uprooted.[42]

Therefore, when stabilizing the organization, the following steps should be taken: (1) ratify and reinforce the emerging worldview in the organization with public decisions and announcements by promoting persons identified with the new vision; (2) establish tight consistency and coherence between words and actions; (3) use tactical decisions to support fundamental changes in orientation; (4) control and channel socialization processes; and (5) ensure that recruitment, selection, and training of employees are consistent with the new orientation.

CONCLUSION

Implementing a radical strategy in a large organization has proved to be an immensely difficult task, the acid test of a leader's skills. The difficulty of the task is compounded by a great deal of confusion about the very meaning of radical change and the paucity of models to guide management in such endeavors. However, we feel that the concepts and guidelines offered in this article provide a useful framework to think about and devise radical strategies and to manage strategic discontinuities.

Of course, in these matters, nothing can replace a leader's intuitions, his or her experience, and natural skills. Nevertheless, these necessary attributes will work better when they are supported by a clear understanding of how one should go about transforming a social system and of how a corporation can be radically changed.

REFERENCES

1. See A.D. Chandler, *Strategy and Structure* (Cambridge, MA: MIT Press, 1962).
2. See J. Thompson, *Organizations in Action* (New York: McGraw-Hill, 1967).
3. See W.J. Abernathy, K.B. Clark, and A.M. Kantrow, *Industrial Renaissance: Producing a Competitive Future for America* (New York: Basic Books, 1983).
4. See "A New Strategy for No. 2 in Computers: Will Digital Equipment Corp.'s Massive Overhaul Pay Off?" *Business Week,* 2 May 1983.
5. See "Black and Decker's Gamble on Globalization," *Fortune,* 14 May 1984.
6. See "Slimming Down: Beatrice Foods Moves to Centralize Business to Reverse Its Decline," *Wall Street Journal,* 27 September 1983.
7. See G.L. Reuber, "Bits, Bytes, and Banking," *Business Quarterly,* Spring 1983.
8. See: W.B. Tunstall, "Cultural Transition at AT&T," *Sloan Management Review,* Fall 1983, pp. 15–26; "Culture Shock Is Shaking the Bell

System," *Business Week*, 26 September 1983; "AT&T Manager Finds His Effort to Galvanize Sales Meets Resistance," *Wall Street Journal*, 16 December 1983; A. van Auw, *Heritage and Destiny: Reflections on the Bell System Transition* (New York: Praeger, 1983); P. Drucker, "Beyond the Bell Breakup," *The Public Interest 77*, Fall 1984.

9. See J.R. Galbraith, "Strategy and Organization Planning," *Human Resource Management 22*, Spring-Summer 1983.

10. See "Monsanto Slowly but Deliberately Shifts Emphasis to Research. Patented Products," *Wall Street Journal*, 13 January 1983.

11. See "The $5-Billion Man: Pushing the New Strategy at GE," *Fortune*, 18 April 1983.

12. See "Financial Forays: Sears Expansion Brings Increased Competition to Bankers and Brokers," *Wall Street Journal*, 12 October 1981.

13. See "Eaton: Spinning Its Wheels on the Road to High-Tech Profits," *Business Week*, 28 March 1983.

14. See J.B. Quinn, *Strategies for Change* (Homewood, IL: Irwin, 1980).

15. See "La Mauvaise Annee des Autres, une Autre Annee Record Chez Imasco," *Commerce*, July 1983.

16. See "Philip's High-Tech Crusade," *Business Week*, 18 July 1983.

17. See "High-Tech Track: Cincinnati Milacron, Mainly a Metal-Bender, Now Is a Robot Maker," *Wall Street Journal*, 7 April 1983.

18. See "Rousing a Giant: David Roderick Tries to Recast U.S. Steel by Redeploying Assets," *Wall Street Journal*, 7 February 1983.

19. See "Singer: Sewing Machines Finally Take a Backseat as It Expands into Aerospace," *Business Week*, 13 June 1983.

20. See "Changing a Corporate Culture: Can Johnson & Johnson Go from Band-Aids to High Tech?" *Business Week*, 14 May 1984.

21. See: "New Bache Chief Pushes a Host of Changes, Including New Name, to Lift Firm's Image," *Wall Street Journal*, 29 October 1982; "After a Year, Prudential's Takeover of Bache Mostly Causing Problems," *Wall Street Journal*, 16 July 1982.

22. See "Continental Corp. Still Drifts despite Moves to Reorganize, Lift Its Insurance Earnings," *Wall Street Journal*, 19 April 1983.

23. See "With New Chairman, Corning Tries to Get Tough and Revive Earnings," *Wall Street Journal*, 22 April 1983.

24. See "Burroughs Tightens Up and Aims for IBM, but Many New Obstacles Stand in the Way," *Wall Street Journal*, 20 July 1982.

25. See "Driving Ahead: Chief's Style and Ideas Help to Keep Goodyear No. 1 in the Radial Age," *Wall Street Journal*, 18 January 1983.

26. See "Sears' Overdue Retailing Revival," *Fortune*, 4 April 1983.

27. See "J.C. Penney Goes After Affluent Shoppers, but Store's New Image May Be Hard to Sell," *Wall Street Journal*, 15 February 1983.

28. See "Operation Turnaround: How Westinghouse's New CEO Plans to Fire Up an Old-Line Company," *Business Week*, 5 December 1983.

29. See "Sherwin-Williams Makes Big Turnaround under Chairman's Aggressive Leadership," *Wall Street Journal*, 14 December 1983.

30. Quinn has provided a review of the tactics and processes used by leaders in their efforts to carry out far-reaching changes in organizations. See Quinn (1980).

31. See *Business Week* (14 May 1984).

32. See *Business Week* (18 June 1984).

33. See "Counter Strategy, Woolworth, Defeated in Discounting, Aims at Specialty Markets," *Wall Street Journal*, 3 November 1983.

34. See Tunstall (Fall 1983).

35. See M. Firsirotu, "Strategic Turnaround as Cultural Revolutions," (unpublished Ph.D. thesis, McGill University, Montreal, Canada, 1984).

36. See "Weak Chain: Mobil Grows Impatient for Profit Turnaround at Montgomery Ward," *Wall Street Journal*, 16 February 1983.

37. See P.M. Warren, "Canada Post Corporation's President: Address to the Canadian Club" (Montreal, Canada, March 28, 1984).

38. See T.J. Peters, "Symbols, Patterns, and Settings: An Optimistic Case for Getting Things Done," *Organizational Dynamics*, 1978.

39. See *Wall Street Journal* (16 February 1983).

40. See "GM's Unlikely Revolutionist," *Fortune*, 19 March 1984.

41. See "Borden: Putting the Shareholder First Starts to Pay Off," *Business Week*, 2 April 1984.

42. See *Business Week* (26 September 1983).

Executive Leadership: Does It Matter?

INTRODUCTION AND OVERVIEW

In the introduction we noted that several themes run through the readings, including (1) the need for a *strategic perspective,* (2) a concern for *managerial problem solving,* (3) attention to the paradox of *managing for short-run efficiency and long-term adaptability,* (4) the need to continually *manage organizational change,* and (5) the importance of *building and maintaining an executive team.* As these themes have been picked up and amplified in the different sections of the book, one refrain has echoed again and again: the necessity for executive vision and leadership. Whether it is the incremental change of increasing congruence required to get better and better at a set of tasks or the frame-breaking, discontinuous change required by major environmental shifts, it remains clear that the impetus for continuous improvement and change must come from senior management. The levers that may make such change possible are contained in the congruence model. But how can this be done?

The role of the chief executive and the top management team is not an easy one to analyze and understand. Why is it that some organizations weather periods of trauma and prosper, while others fail? What are the critical competencies possessed by successful leaders? Are different leaders better under certain circumstances? The answers to these questions are critical for the success of individuals as well as organizations. The readings in this section address these issues and emphasize again the importance of understanding the need for congruence.

READINGS IN SECTION VI

The first article asks an obvious question with a not-so-obvious answer: does executive leadership make a difference? Pfeffer reviews the leadership research and argues that what most of us consider as successful "leadership" may be more of retrospective justification than planned, purposeful action. Nadler and Tushman provide a resolution to this paradox. They describe how successful chief executives manage in both the short term and the long term. The potential solutions they discuss, including the importance of the top management team, are echoed and elaborated on by Kouzes and Posner, who remind us again of the importance of emotion and commitment in the process.

Next Donald Hambrick discusses how the requirements for the top management team can be assessed and fitted to the strategic requirements. The last reading, by Kets de Vries and Miller, raises an important but seldom considered ramification of executive leadership: the possibility that executives with strong personalities may also develop organizations in their images—and sometimes both the leader and the organization may be neurotic.

10

EXECUTIVE LEADERSHIP: DOES IT MATTER?

The Ambiguity of Leadership

Jeffrey Pfeffer

Leadership has for some time been a major topic in social and organizational psychology. Underlying much of this research has been the assumption that leadership is casually related to organizational performance. Through an analysis of leadership styles, behaviors, or characteristics (depending on the theoretical perspective chosen), the argument has been made that more effective leaders can be selected or trained or, alternatively, the situation can be configured to provide for enhanced leader and organizational effectiveness.

Three problems with emphasis on leadership as a concept can be posed: (*a*) ambiguity in definition and measurement of the concept itself; (*b*) the question of whether leadership has discernible effects on organizational outcomes; and (*c*) the selection process in succession to leadership positions, which frequently uses organizationally irrelevant criteria and which has implications for normative theories of leadership. The argument here is that leadership is of interest primarily as a phenomenological construct. Leaders serve as symbols for

representing personal causation of social events. How and why are such attributions of personal effects made? Instead of focusing on leadership and its effects, how do people make inferences about and react to phenomena labeled as leadership (5)?

THE AMBIGUITY OF THE CONCEPT

While there have been many studies of leadership, the dimensions and definition of the concept remain unclear. To treat leadership as a separate concept, it must be distinguished from other social influence phenomena. Hollander and Julian (24) and Bavelas (2) did not draw distinctions between leadership and other processes of social influence. A major point of the Hollander and Julian review was that leadership research might develop more rapidly if more general theories of social influence were incorporated. Calder (5) also argued that there is no unique content to the construct of leadership that is not subsumed under other, more general models of behavior.

From *Academy of Management Review,* January 1977. Reprinted by permission.

Kochan, Schmidt, and DeCotiis (33) attempted to distinguish leadership from related concepts of authority and social power. In leadership, influence rights are voluntarily conferred. Power does not require goal compatibility—merely dependence—but leadership implies some congruence between the objectives of the leader and the led. These distinctions depend on the ability to distinguish voluntary from involuntary compliance and to assess goal compatibility. Goal statements may be retrospective inferences from action (46, 53) and problems of distinguishing voluntary from involuntary compliance also exist (32). Apparently there are few meaningful distinctions between leadership and other concepts of social influence. Thus, an understanding of the phenomena subsumed under the rubric of leadership may not require the construct of leadership (5).

While there is some agreement that leadership is related to social influence, more disagreement concerns the basic dimensions of leader behavior. Some have argued that there are two tasks to be accomplished in groups—maintenance of the group and performance of some task or activity—and thus leader behavior might be described along these two dimensions (1, 6, 8, 25). The dimensions emerging from the Ohio State leadership studies—consideration and initiating structure—may be seen as similar to the two components of group maintenance and task accomplishment (18).

Other dimensions of leadership behavior have also been proposed (4). Day and Hamblin (10) analyzed leadership in terms of the closeness and punitiveness of the supervision. Several authors have conceptualized leadership behavior in terms of the authority and discretion subordinates are permitted (23, 36, 51). Fiedler (14) analyzed leadership in terms of the least-preferred-co-worker scale (LPC), but the meaning and behavioral attributes of this dimension of leadership behavior remain controversial.

The proliferation of dimensions is partly a function of research strategies frequently employed. Factor analysis on a large number of items describing behavior has frequently been used. This procedure tends to produce as many factors as the analyst decides to find and permits the development of a large number of possible factor structures. The resultant factors must be named and further imprecision is introduced. Deciding on a summative concept to represent a factor is inevitably a partly subjective process.

Literature assessing the effects of leadership tends to be equivocal. Sales (45) summarized leadership literature employing the authoritarian-democratic typology and concluded that effects on performance were small and inconsistent. Reviewing the literature on consideration and initiating structure dimensions, Korman (34) reported relatively small and inconsistent results, and Kerr and Schriesheim (30) reported more consistent effects of the two dimensions. Better results apparently emerge when moderating factors are taken into account, including subordinate personalities (50), and situational characteristics (23, 51). Kerr, et al. (31) list many moderating effects grouped under the headings of subordinate considerations, supervisor considerations, and task considerations. Even if each set of considerations consisted of only one factor (which it does not), an attempt to account for the effects of leader behavior would necessitate considering four-way interactions. While social reality is complex and contingent, it seems desirable to attempt to find more parsimonious explanations for the phenomena under study.

THE EFFECTS OF LEADERS

Hall asked a basic question about leadership: Is there any evidence on the magnitude of the effects of leadership (17, p. 248)? Surprisingly, he could find little evidence. Given the resources that have been spent studying, selecting, and training leaders, one might expect that the question of whether or not leaders matter would have been addressed earlier (12).

There are at least three reasons why it might be argued that the observed effects of leaders on organizational outcomes would be small. First, those obtaining leadership positions are selected, and perhaps only certain limited styles of behavior may be chosen. Second, once in the leadership position, the discretion and behavior of the leader are constrained. And third, leaders can typically affect only a few of the variables that may impact organizational performance.

Homogeneity of Leaders

Persons are selected to leadership positions. As a consequence of this selection process, the range of behaviors or characteristics exhibited by leaders is reduced, making it more problematic to discover empirically an effect of leadership. There are many types of constraints on the selection process. The attraction literature suggests that there is a tendency for persons to like those they perceive as similar (3). In critical decisions such as the selections of persons for leadership positions, compatible styles of behavior probably will be chosen.

Selection of persons is also constrained by the internal system of influence in the organization. As Zald (56) noted, succession is a critical decision, affected by political influence and by environmental contingencies faced by the organization. As Thompson (49) noted, leaders may be selected for their capacity to deal with various organizational contingencies. In a study of characteristics of hospital administrators, Pfeffer and Salancik (42) found a relationship between the hospital's context and the characteristics and tenure of the administrators. To the extent that the contingencies and power distribution within the organization remain stable, the abilities and behaviors of those selected into leadership positions will also remain stable.

Finally, the selection of persons to leadership positions is affected by a self-selection process. Organizations and roles have images, providing information about their character. Persons are likely to select themselves into organizations and roles based upon their preferences for the dimensions of the organizational and role characteristics as perceived through these images. The self-selection of persons would tend to work along with organizational selection to limit the range of abilities and behaviors in a given organizational role.

Such selection processes would tend to increase homogeneity more within a single organization than across organizations. Yet many studies of leadership effect at the work group level have compared groups within a single organization. If there comes to be a widely shared, socially constructed definition of leadership behaviors or characteristics which guides the selection process, then leadership activity may come to be defined similarly in various organizations, leading to the selection of only those who match the constructed image of a leader.

Constraints on Leader Behavior

Analyses of leadership have frequently presumed that leadership style or leader behavior was an independent variable that could be selected or trained at will to conform to what research would find to be optimal. Even theorists who took a more contingent view of appropriate leadership behavior generally assumed that with proper training appropriate behavior could be produced (51). Fiedler (13), noting how hard it was to change behavior, suggested changing the situational characteristics rather than the person, but this was an unusual suggestion in the context of prevailing literature which suggested that leadership style was something to be strategically selected according to the variables of the particular leadership theory.

But the leader is embedded in a social system, which constrains behavior. The leader has a role set (27), in which members have expectations for appropriate behavior and persons make efforts to modify the leader's behavior. Pressures to conform to the expectations of peers, subordinates, and superiors are all relevant in determining actual behavior.

Leaders, even in high-level positions, have unilateral control over fewer resources and fewer policies than might be expected. Investment decisions may require approval of others, while hiring and promotion decisions may be accomplished by committees. Leader behavior is constrained by both the demands of others in the role set and by organizationally prescribed limitations on the sphere of activity and influence.

External Factors

Many factors that may affect organizational performance are outside a leader's control, even if he or she were to have complete discretion over major areas of organizational decisions. For example, consider the executive in a construction firm. Costs are largely determined by operation of commodities and labor markets; and demand is largely affected by interest rates, availability of mortgage money, and economic conditions which are affected by governmental policies over which the executive has little control. School superintendents have little control over birth rates and community economic development, both of which profoundly affect school system budgets. While the leader may react to contingencies as they arise, or may be a better or worse forecaster, in accounting for variation in organizational outcomes, he or she may account for relatively little compared to external factors.

Second, the leader's success or failure may be partly due to circumstances unique to the organization but still outside his or her control. Leader positions in organizations vary in terms of the strength and position of the organization. The choice of a new executive does not fundamentally alter a market and financial position that has developed over years and affects the leader's ability to make strategic changes and the likelihood that the organization will do well or poorly. Organizations have relatively enduring strengths and weaknesses. The choice of a particular leader for a particular position has limited impact on these capabilities.

Empirical Evidence

Two studies have assessed the effects of leadership changes in major positions in organizations. Lieberson and O'Connor (35) examined 167 business firms in 13 industries over a 20-year period, allocating variance in sales, profits, and profit margins to one of four sources: year (general economic conditions), industry, company effects, and effects of changes in the top executive position. They concluded that compared to other factors, administration had a limited effect on organizational outcomes.

Using a similar analytical procedure, Salancik and Pfeffer (44) examined the effects of mayors on city budgets for 30 U.S. cities. Data on expenditures by budget category were collected for 1951–1968. Variance in amount and proportion of expenditures was apportioned to the year, the city, or the mayor. The mayoral effect was relatively small, with the city accounting for most of the variance, although the mayor effect was larger for expenditure categories that were not as directly connected to important interest groups. Salancik and Pfeffer argued that the effects of the mayor were limited both by absence of power to control many of the expenditures and tax sources, and by construction of policies in response to demands from interests in the environment.

If leadership is defined as a strictly interpersonal phenomenon, the relevance of these two studies for the issue of leadership effects becomes problematic. But such a conceptualization seems unduly restrictive and is certainly inconsistent with Selznick's (47) conceptualization of leadership as strategic management and decision making. If one cannot observe differences when leaders change, then what does it matter who occupies the positions or how they behave?

Pfeffer and Salancik (41) investigated the extent to which behaviors selected by first-line supervisors were constrained by expectations of others in their role set. Variance in task and social behaviors could be accounted for by role-set expectations, with adherence to various demands made by role-set participants a function of similarity and relative power. Lowin and Craig (37) experimentally demonstrated that leader behavior was determined by the subordinate's own behavior. Both studies illustrate that leader behaviors are responses to the demands of the social context.

The effect of leadership may vary depending upon level in the organizational hierarchy, while the appropriate activities and behaviors may also vary with organizational level (26, 40). For the most part, empirical studies of leadership have dealt with first-line supervisors or leaders with relatively low organizational status (17). If leadership has any impact, it should be more evident at higher organizational levels or where there is more discretion in decisions and activities.

THE PROCESS OF SELECTING LEADERS

Along with the suggestion that leadership may not account for much variance in organizational outcomes, it can be argued that merit or ability may not account for much variation in hiring and advancement of organizational personnel. These two ideas are related. If competence is hard to judge, or if leadership competence does not greatly affect organizational outcomes, then other person-dependent criteria may be sufficient. Effective leadership styles may not predict career success when other variables such as social background are controlled.

Belief in the importance of leadership is frequently accompanied by belief that persons occupying leadership positions are selected and trained according to how well they can enhance the organization's performance. Belief in a leadership effect leads to development of a set of activities oriented toward enhancing leadership effectiveness. Simultaneously, persons managing their own careers are likely to place emphasis on activities and developing behaviors that will enhance their own leadership skills, assuming that such a strategy will facilitate advancement.

Research on the bases for hiring and promotion has been concentrated in examination of academic positions (e.g., 7, 19, 20). This is possibly the result of availability of relatively precise and unambiguous measures of performance, such as number of publications or citations. Evidence on criteria used in selecting and advancing personnel in industry is more indirect.

Studies have attempted to predict either the compensation or the attainment of general management positions of MBA students, using personality and other background information (21, 22, 54). There is some evidence that managerial success can be predicted by indicators of ability and motivation such as test scores and grades, but the amount of variance explained is typically quite small.

A second line of research has investigated characteristics and backgrounds of persons attaining leadership positions in major organizations in society. Domhoff (11), Mills (38), and Warner and Abbeglin (52) found a strong preponderance of persons with upper-class backgrounds occupying leadership positions. The implication of these findings is that studies of graduate success, including the success of MBA's, would explain more variance if the family background of the person were included.

A third line of inquiry uses a tracking model. The dynamic model developed is one in which access to elite universities is affected by social status (28) and, in turn, social status and attendance at elite universities affect later career outcomes (9, 43, 48, 55).

Unless one is willing to make the argument that attendance at elite universities or coming from an upper-class background is perfectly correlated with merit, the evidence suggests that succession to leadership positions is not strictly based on meritocratic criteria. Such a conclusion is consistent with the inability of studies attempting to predict the success of MBA graduates to account for much variance, even when a variety of personality and ability factors are used.

Beliefs about the bases for social mobility are important for social stability. As long as persons believe that positions are allocated on meritocratic grounds, they are more likely to be satisfied with the social order and with their position in it. This satisfaction derives from the belief that occupational position results from application of fair and reasonable criteria and that the opportunity exists for mobility if the person improves skills and performance.

If succession to leadership positions is determined by person-based criteria such as social origins or social connections (16), then efforts to enhance managerial effectiveness with the expectation that this will lead to career success divert attention from the processes of stratification actually operating within organizations. Leadership literature has been implicitly aimed at two audiences. Organizations were told how to become more effective, and persons were told what behaviors to acquire in order to become effective and, hence, advance in their careers. The possibility that neither organizational outcomes nor career success are related to leadership behaviors leaves leadership research facing issues of relevance and importance.

THE ATTRIBUTION OF LEADERSHIP

Kelley conceptualized the layman as:

> an applied scientist, that is, as a person concerned about applying his knowledge of causal relationships in order to exercise control of his world (29, p. 2).

Reviewing a series of studies dealing with the attributional process, he concluded that persons were not only interested in understanding their world correctly, but also in controlling it.

> The view here proposed is that attribution processes are to be understood not only as a means of providing the individual with a veridical view of his world, but as a means of encouraging and maintaining his effective exercise of control in that world (29, p. 22).

Controllable factors will have high salience as candidates for causal explanation, while a bias toward the more important causes may shift the attributional emphasis toward causes that are not controllable (29, p. 23). The study of attribution is a study of naive psychology—an examination of how persons make sense out of the events taking place around them.

If Kelley is correct that individuals will tend to develop attributions that give them a feeling of control, then emphasis on leadership may derive partially from a desire to believe in the effectiveness and importance of individual action, since individual action is more controllable than contextual variables. Lieberson and O'Connor (35) made essentially the same point in introducing their paper on the effects of top management changes on organizational performance. Given the desire for control and a feeling of personal effectiveness, organizational outcomes are more likely to be attributed to individual actions, regardless of their actual causes.

Leadership is attributed by observers. Social action has meaning only through a phenomenological process (46). The identification of certain organizational roles as leadership positions guides the construction of meaning in the direction of attributing effects to the actions of those positions. While Bavelas (2) argued that the functions of leadership, such as task accomplishment and group maintenance, are shared throughout the group, this fact provides no simple and potentially controllable focus for attributing causality. Rather, the identification of leadership positions provides a simpler and more readily changeable model of reality. When causality is lodged in one or a few persons rather than being a function of a complex set of interactions among all group members, changes can be made by replacing or influencing the occupant of the leadership position. Causes of organizational actions are readily identified in this simple causal structure.

Even if, empirically, leadership has little effect, and even if succession to leadership positions is not predicated on ability or performance, the belief in leadership effects and meritocratic succession provides a simple causal framework and a justification for the structure of the social collectivity. More importantly, the beliefs interpret social actions in terms that indicate potential for effective individual intervention or control. The personification of social causality serves too many uses to be easily overcome. Whether or not leader behavior actually influences performance or effectiveness, it is important because people believe it does.

One consequence of the attribution of causality to leaders and leadership is that leaders come to be symbols. Mintzberg (39), in his discussion of the roles of managers, wrote of the symbolic role, but more in terms of attendance at formal events and formally representing the organization. The symbolic role of leadership is more important than implied in such a description. The leader as a symbol provides a target for action when difficulties occur, serving as a scapegoat when things go wrong. Gamson and Scotch (15) noted that in baseball, the firing of the manager served a scapegoating purpose. One cannot fire the whole team; yet when performance is poor, something must be done. The firing of the manager conveys to the world and to the actors involved that success is the result of personal actions and that steps can and will be taken to enhance organizational performance.

The attribution of causality to leadership may be reinforced by organizational actions, such as the inauguration process, the choice process, and providing the leader with symbols and ceremony. If leaders are chosen by using a random number table, persons are less likely to believe in their effects than if there is an elaborate search or selection process followed by an elaborate ceremony signifying the changing of control, and if the leader then has a variety of perquisites and symbols that distinguish him or her from the rest of the organization. Construction of the importance of leadership in a given social context is the outcome of various social processes, which can be empirically examined.

Since belief in the leadership effect provides a feeling of personal control, one might argue that efforts to increase the attribution of causality to leaders would occur more when it is more necessary and more problematic to attribute causality to controllable factors. Such an argument would lead to the hypothesis that the more the *context* actually effects organizational outcomes, the more efforts will be made to ensure attribution to *leadership*. When leaders really do have effects, it is less necessary to engage in rituals indicating their effects. Such rituals are more likely when there is uncertainty and unpredictability associated with the organization's operations. This results both from the desire to feel control in uncertain situations and from the fact that in ambiguous contexts it is easier to attribute consequences to leadership without facing possible disconfirmation.

The leader is, in part, an actor. Through statements and actions, the leader attempts to reinforce the operation of an attribution process which tends to vest causality in that position in the social structure. Successful leaders, as perceived by members of the social system, are those who can separate themselves from organizational failures and associate themselves with organizational successes. Since the meaning of action is socially constructed, this involves manipulation of symbols to reinforce the desired process of attribution. For instance, if a manager knows that business in his or her division is about to improve because of the economic cycle, the leader may, nevertheless, write recommendations and undertake actions and changes that are highly visible and that will tend to identify his or her behavior closely with the division. A manager who perceives impending failure will attempt to associate the division and its policies and decisions with others, particularly persons in higher organizational positions, and to disassociate himself or herself from the division's performance, occasionally even transferring or moving to another organization.

CONCLUSION

The theme of this article has been that analysis of leadership and leadership processes must be contingent on the intent of the researcher. If the interest is in understanding the causality of social phenomena as reliably and accurately as possible, then the concept of leadership may be a poor place to begin. The issue of the effects of leadership is open to question. But examination of situational variables that accompany more or less leadership effect is a worthwhile task.

The more phenomenological analysis of leadership directs attention to the process by which social causality is attributed and focuses on the distinction between causality as perceived by group members and causality as assessed by an outside observer. Leadership is associated with a set of myths reinforcing a social construction of meaning which legitimates leadership role occupants, provides belief in potential mobility for those not in leadership roles, and attributes social causality to leadership roles, thereby providing a belief in the effectiveness of individual control. In analyzing leadership, this mythology and the process by which such mythology is created and supported should be separated from analysis of leadership as a social influence process, operating within constraints.

REFERENCE NOTES

1. Bales, R. F. *Interaction process analysis: A method for the study of small groups.* Reading, Mass.: Addison-Wesley, 1950.
2. Bavelas, Alex. Leadership: Man and function, *Administrative Science Quarterly,* 1960, 4:491–98.
3. Berscheid, Ellen, and Walster, Elaine. *Interpersonal attraction.* Reading, Mass.: Addison-Wesley, 1969.
4. Bowers, David G., and Seashore, Stanley E. Predicting organizational effectiveness with a four-factor theory of leadership, *Administrative Science Quarterly,* 1966, 11:238–63.
5. Calder, Bobby J. An attribution theory of leadership, in B. Staw and G. Salancik (eds.), *New directions in organizational behavior.* Chicago: St. Clair Press, 1976, in press.
6. Cartwright, Dorwin C., and Zander, Alvin. *Group dynamics: Research and theory,* 3d ed. Evanston, Ill.: Row, Peterson, 1960.
7. Cole, Jonathan R., and Cole, Stephen. *Social stratification in science.* Chicago: University of Chicago Press, 1973.
8. Collins, Barry E., and Guetzkow, Harold. *A so-*

cial psychology of group processes for decision making. New York: Wiley, 1964.

9. Collins, Randall. Functional and conflict theories of stratification, *American Sociological Review,* 1971, 36:1002–19.

10. Day, R. C., and Hamblin, R. L. Some effects of close and punitive styles of supervision. *American Journal of Sociology,* 1964, 69:499–510.

11. Domhoff, G. William. *Who rules America?* Englewood Cliffs, N.J.: Prentice-Hall, 1967.

12. Dubin, Robert. Supervision and productivity: Empirical findings and theoretical considerations, in R. Dubin, G. C. Homans, F. C. Mann, and D. C. Miller (eds.), *Leadership and productivity.* San Francisco: Chandler Publishing Co., 1965, pp. 1–50.

13. Fiedler, Fred E. Engineering the job to fit the manager, *Harvard Business Review,* 1965, 43:115–22.

14. Fiedler, Fred E. *A theory of leadership effectiveness.* New York: McGraw-Hill, 1967.

15. Gamson, William A., and Scotch, Norman A. Scapegoat in Baseball, *American Journal of Sociology,* 1964, 70:69–72.

16. Granovetter, Mark. *Getting a job.* Cambridge, Mass.: Harvard University Press, 1974.

17. Hall, Richard H. *Organizations: Structure and process.* Englewood Cliffs, N.J.: Prentice-Hall, 1972.

18. Halpin, A. W., and Winer, J. A factorial study of the leader behavior description questionnaire, in R. M. Stogdill and A. E. Coons (eds.), *Leader behavior: Its description and measurement.* Columbus, Ohio: Bureau of Business Research, Ohio State University, 1957, pp. 39–51.

19. Hargens, L. L. Patterns of mobility of new Ph.D.'s among American academic institutions, *Sociology of Education,* 1969, 42:18–37.

20. Hargens, L. L., and Hagstrom, W. O. Sponsored and contest mobility of American academic scientists, *Sociology of Education,* 1967, 40:24–38.

21. Harrell, Thomas W. High earning MBA's, *Personnel Psychology,* 1972, 25:523–30.

22. Harrell, Thomas W., and Harrell, Margaret S. Predictors of management success. *Stanford University Graduate School of Business, Technical Report no. 3 to the Office of Naval Research.*

23. Heller, Frank, and Yukl, Gary. Participation, managerial decision making, and situational variables, *Organizational Behavior and Human Performance,* 1969, 4:227–41.

24. Hollander, Edwin P., and Julian, James W. Contemporary trends in the analysis of leadership processes. *Psychological Bulletin,* 1969, 71:387–97.

25. House, Robert J. A path-goal theory of leader effectiveness, *Administrative Science Quarterly,* 1971, 16:321–38.

26. Hunt, J. G. Leadership-style effects at two managerial levels in a simulated organization, *Administrative Science Quarterly,* 1971, 16:476–85.

27. Kahn, R. L., Wolfe, D. M., Quinn, R. P., and Snock, J. D. *Organizational stress: Studies in role conflict and ambiguity.* New York: Wiley, 1964.

28. Karabel, J., and Astin, A. W. Social class, academic ability, and college "quality," *Social Forces,* 1951, 53:381–98.

29. Kelley, Harold H. *Attribution in social interaction.* Morristown, N.J.: General Learning Press, 1971.

30. Kerr, Steven, and Schriesheim, Chester. Consideration, initiating structure and organizational criteria—An update of Korman's 1966 review," *Personnel Psychology,* 1974, 27:555–68.

31. Kerr, S., Schriesheim, C., Murphy, C. J., and Stogdill, R. M. Toward a contingency theory of leadership based upon the consideration and initiating structure literature, *Organizational Behavior and Human Performance,* 1974, 12:62–82.

32. Kiesler, C., and Kiesler, S. *Conformity.* Reading, Mass.: Addison-Wesley, 1969.

33. Kochan, T. A., Schmidt, S. M., and DeCotiis, T. A. Superior-subordinate relations: Leadership and headship, *Human Relations,* 1975, 28:279–94.

34. Korman, A. K. Consideration, initiating structure, and organizational criteria—A review, *Personnel Psychology,* 1966, 19:349–62.

35. Lieberson, Stanley, and O'Connor, James F. Leadership and organizational performance: A study of large corporations, *American Sociological Review,* 1972, 37:117–30.

36. Lippitt, Ronald. An experimental study of the effect of democratic and authoritarian group atmospheres, *University of Iowa Studies in Child Welfare,* 1940, 16:43–195.

37. Lowin, A., and Craig, J. R. The influence of level of performance on managerial style: An experimental object-lesson in the ambiguity of correlational data, *Organizational Behavior and Human Performance,* 1968, 3:440–58.

38. Mills, C. Wright. The American business elite: A collective portrait, in C. W. Mills, *Power, politics and people.* New York: Oxford University Press, 1963, pp. 110–39.

39. Mintzberg, Henry. *The nature of managerial work.* New York: Harper and Row, 1973.

40. Nealey, Stanley M., and Blood, Milton R. Leadership performance of nursing supervisors at two organizational levels, *Journal of Applied Psychology,* 1968, 52:414–42.

41. Pfeffer, Jeffrey, and Salancik, Gerald R. Determinants of supervisory behavior: A role set analysis, *Human Relations,* 1975, 28:139–54.

42. Pfeffer, Jeffrey, and Salancik, Gerald R. Organizational context and the characteristics and tenure of hospital administrators, *Academy of Management Journal,* 1977, 20 in press.

43. Reed, R. H., and Miller, H. P. Some determinants of the variation in earnings for college men, *Journal of Human Resources,* 1970, 5:117–90.

44. Salancik, Gerald R., and Pfeffer, Jeffrey. Constraints on administrator discretion: The limited influence of mayors on city budgets, *Urban Affairs Quarterly,* in press.

45. Sales, Stephen M. Supervisory style and productivity: Review and theory, *Personnel Psychology,* 1966, 19:275–86.

46. Schultz, Alfred. *The phenomenology of the social world.* Evanston, Ill.: Northwestern University Press, 1967.

47. Selznick, P. *Leadership in administration.* Evanston, Ill.: Row, Peterson, 1957.

48. Spaeth, J. L., and Greeley, A. M. *Recent alumni and higher education.* New York: McGraw-Hill, 1970.

49. Thompson, James D. *Organizations in action.* New York: McGraw-Hill, 1967.

50. Vroom, Victor H. Some personality determinants of the effects of participation, *Journal of Abnormal and Social Psychology,* 1959, 59:322–27.

51. Vroom, Victor H., and Yetton, Phillip W. *Leadership and decision making.* Pittsburgh: University of Pittsburgh Press, 1973.

52. Warner, W. L., and Abbeglin, J. C. *Big business leaders in America.* New York: Harper and Brothers, 1955.

53. Weick, Karl E. *The social psychology of organizing.* Reading, Mass.: Addison-Wesley, 1969.

54. Weinstein, Alan G., and Srinivasan, V. Predicting managerial success of master of business administration (MBA) graduates, *Journal of Applied Psychology,* 1974, 59:207–12.

55. Wolfle, Dael. *The uses of talent.* Princeton: Princeton University Press, 1971.

56. Zald, Mayer N. Who shall rule? A political analysis of succession in a large welfare organization. *Pacific Sociological Review,* 1965, 8:52–60.

Beyond the Magic Leader:
Leadership and Organizational Change

David Nadler

Michael Tushman

INTRODUCTION

The increasingly competitive business environment has demanded that many large organizations undergo significant and profound change. These major organizational transformations are often necessary for those determined to retain their status as major players on the world industrial and commercial stage. The management of large scale organizational changes has become an important and critical task.

There is a growing body of observations and knowledge about large scale planned organizational change. (Goodman, 1982; Kimberly & Quinn, 1984; Nadler, 1981.) An interesting commonality is that virtually all of those who have written about large scale change have in some way discussed the issue of leadership. It seems evident that profound organizational change cannot happen without the presence of a certain type of executive leadership. The leader is a critical player in the drama of organizational change.

This paper proposes an approach to the issue of leadership and organizational change. It attempts to build an initial framework for thinking about the effective leader of change, building from two sources: intensive consulting work with leaders attempting major changes (see Nadler and Tushman, 1987) and macro level analysis of leadership and organizational

changes in several different industries. (Tushman & Romanelli, 1985; Tushman, in press) In the first section, some basic material and terminology about organizational change will be presented and the general importance of leadership discussed. Next, a commonly held view of the nature of effective leadership in change, which is labeled the *magic leader,* is described. In subsequent sections the notion of the magic leader is expanded, and a role for leadership beyond the magic leader is proposed. A final section identifies some implications for organizational change management.

ORGANIZATIONAL CHANGE AND RE-ORIENTATION

Organizations go through change all the time. However, the nature, scope, and intensity of organizational changes vary considerably. In other words, *a change is not always a change.* One way of thinking about the differences among changes is to think about the varying types of planned organizational changes along the following dimensions:

- *Strategic and incremental changes.* Some changes in organizations, while significant, only affect selected components of the organization. The fundamental aim of such change is to enhance the effectiveness of the organization, but within the general framework of the strategy, mode of organizing, and values that already are in place. Such changes are called *incremental changes.* Other changes have an impact on the whole system of the organization, and fundamentally redefine what the organization is or change the basic framework, including strategy, structure, people, processes, and (in some cases) core values. These changes are called *strategic organizational changes.*

· *Reactive and anticipatory changes.* Many organization changes are made in direct response to some external event. These changes, which are forced upon the organization, are called *reactive.* At other times organizational change is initiated, not because of the need to respond to a contemporaneous event, but rather because certain individuals believe that change in anticipation of events still to come will provide competitive advantage. These changes are called *anticipatory.*

If these two dimensions are combined, a basic typology of different changes can be described (see Figure 1). Change which is incremental and anticipatory is called *tuning.* These changes are not system wide redefinitions, but rather modifications of specific components, and they are initiated in anticipation of future events. Incremental change which is initiated reactively is called *adaptation.* Strategic change initiated in anticipation of future events is called *re-orientation,* and change which is prompted by immediate demands is called *re-creation* (for a more detailed discussion of this framework, see Nadler & Tushman, 1986).

Research on patterns of organizational life and death across several industries has provided some insight into the patterns of strategic organizational change (Tushman & Romanelli, 1985). Some of the key findings are as follows:

· *Strategic organization changes are necessary.* These changes appear to be environmentally driven. Various factors—be they competitive, technological, or regulatory—drive the organization (either reactively or

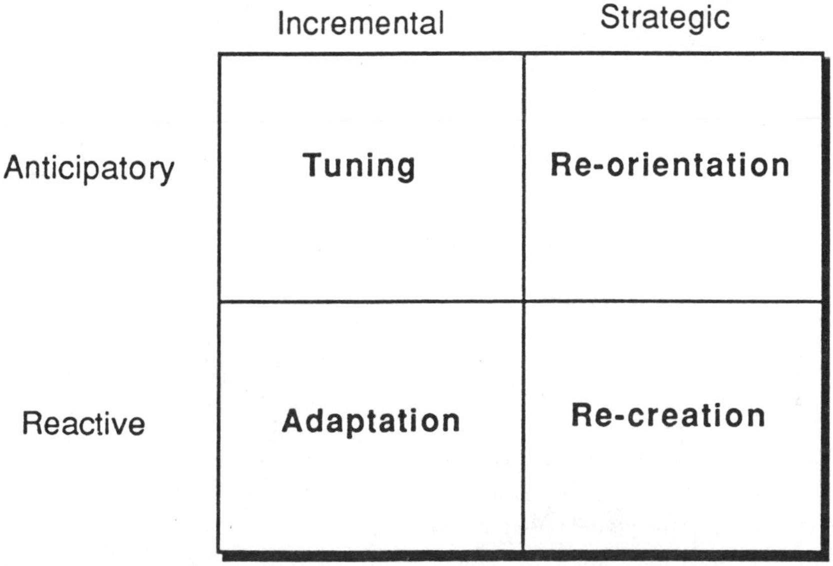

FIGURE 1. *Types of Organizational Changes*

in anticipation) to make the changes. Those organizations that fail to change, generally fail to survive.

- *Re-creations are riskier.* Re-creations are riskier endeavors than re-orientations. The research indicates that fewer than one in ten attempted re-creations succeed. Those that do succeed usually involve changes in the senior leadership of the organization, frequently involving replacement from the outside.

- *Re-orientations are associated more with success.* When re-orientations are initiated in advance of the precipitating external events, success (defined by continued organizational survival, and in most cases continued growth) is more likely. Again, however, many of the successful re-orientations also involve change in the CEO and the executive team. At the same time, a number of re-orientations occur with the same leadership team, and these are among the most successful.

Thus, the role of leadership varies considerably in these different changes. The incremental changes typically can be managed by the existing management structures and processes of the organization, sometimes in conjunction with special "transition structures" (Beckhard & Harris, 1977). In these situations, a variety of leadership styles may be appropriate, depending upon how the organization is normally managed and lead. In the strategic changes, however, the management process and structure itself is the subject of change; therefore, it cannot be relied upon to manage the change. In addition, the organization's definition of effective leadership may also be changing as a consequence of the re-orientation or re-creation. In these situations, leadership becomes a very critical element of change management.

Within this context the focus of this paper will be on the role of leadership in strategic organizational change, and in particular, *the role of leadership in re-orientations.* The reason for this is that re-creations often fail, and they are frequently characterized by the replacement of leadership. Thus, the key challenge for current organizational leadership is to learn how to effectively initiate, lead, and manage re-orientations.

Why is leadership so key to re-orientations? It appears that there are certain aspects of re-orientation that are dependent upon the leader. The first is *strategic anticipation.* Re-orientation requires the organization to accurately anticipate that the conditions for strategic change will arise in the future, and to determine the most effective responses to that change. Unless the leadership somehow becomes involved in this anticipation, no change will be initiated. Second, re-orientation requires a *created sense of urgency.* Since, by definition, the need for change is not apparent to all, some creation of energy is needed to stimulate behavior. Usually, only the leadership can create such a sense of urgency throughout the organization. Third, re-orientation requires effective *creation and management of pain.* Urgency frequently results from pain, either immediate or anticipated. Pain, however, can motivate both functional and dysfunctional behavior. Again, only the leadership has the capacity both to create pain and shape the responses to it. Finally, re-orientations succeed when people perceive the required change to have *centrality,* to be truly critical to the core business and strategic issues of the organization. Centrality, if not apparent, can only be defined by the leadership. (For a more detailed discussion of principles for managing re-orientations, see Nadler, 1987.)

Therefore, it is understandable why no successful re-orientations occur without a major role being played by the organization's leadership—either the existing leadership or new leadership brought in from the outside. The question, then, is what constitutes effective leadership in these situations?

535

THE "MAGIC LEADER"

While the subject of leadership has received much attention over the years, the more specific issue of leadership during periods of change has only recently attracted serious attention (Burns, 1978; Bennis & Nanus, 1985; Tichy & Ulrich, 1984; Tichy & Devanna, 1986). What emerges from various discussions of leadership and organizational change is a picture of the special kind of leadership that appears to be critical during times of strategic organizational change. While various words have been used to portray this type of leadership, we prefer the term "magic leader." It refers to a special quality that enables the leader to mobilize and sustain activity within an organization through specific personal actions combined with perceived personal characteristics. In many cases this is evidenced by the development of a very personal bond between the leader and people in the organization.

At the core of the concept of the magic leader is the model of the charismatic leader. This is not the popular version of the charismatic leader—the great speech maker, the television personality. Rather, this model has emerged from recent work aimed at identifying the nature and determinants of a particular type of leadership that successfully brings about changes in an individual's values, goals, needs, or aspirations. Research on charismatic leadership (Berlew, 1974; House 1977; Bass, 1985) has identified this type of leadership as observable, definable, and having clear behavioral characteristics.

Building from the general concept of charismatic leadership, what specifically characterizes the magic leader of organizational change? We have attempted to develop a first cut description of the leader in terms of the patterns of behavior that he/she seems to exhibit. The resulting approach is outlined in Figure 2, which lists three major types of behavior that characterize these leaders and some illustrative kinds of actions.

The first component of magic leadership is *envisioning*. This involves the creation of a picture of the future, or of a desired future state with which people can identify and which can generate excitement. By creating vision, the leader provides a vehicle for people to develop commitment, a common goal around which people can rally, and a way for people to feel successful. Envisioning is accomplished through a range of different actions. Clearly, the simplest form is through articulation of a compelling vision in clear and dramatic terms. The vision needs to be challenging, meaningful, and worthy of pursuit, but it also needs to

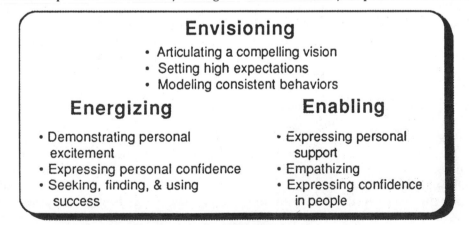

FIGURE 2.   *The Magic Leader*

be credible. People must believe that it is possible to succeed in the pursuit of the vision. However, the vision is communicated in other ways, such as through expectations that the leader expresses and through the leader personally demonstrating behaviors and activities that symbolize and further that vision.

The second component is *energizing*. Here the role of the leader is the direct generation of energy—motivation to act—among members of the organization. How is this done? Different leaders engage in energizing in different ways, but some of the most common include demonstration of their own personal excitement and energy, combined with leveraging that excitement through direct personal contact with large numbers of people in the organization. They express confidence in their own ability to succeed. They find, and use, successes to celebrate progress towards the vision.

The third component is *enabling*. The leader psychologically helps people act or perform in the face of challenging goals. Assuming that individuals are directed through a vision and motivated by the creation of energy, they then may need emotional assistance in accomplishing their tasks. This enabling is achieved in several ways. Magic leaders demonstrate empathy—the ability to listen, understand, and share the feelings of those in the organization. They express support for individuals. Perhaps most importantly, the magic leader tends to express his/her confidence in people's ability to perform effectively and to meet challenges.

Assuming that leaders act in these ways, what functions are they performing that help bring about change? First, they provide a psychological focal point for the energies, hopes, and aspirations of people in the organization. Second, they may serve as the embodiment of some type of organizational "ego ideal." They represent what the organization hopes to become. Through their personal effectiveness and attractiveness they build a very personal and intimate bond between themselves and the organization. Thus, they can become a source of sustained energy, a hero with which people can identify.

LIMITATIONS OF THE MAGIC LEADER

Even if one were able to do all of the things involved in being a magic leader, it might still not be enough. In fact, our observations suggest that there are a number of inherent limitations to the effectiveness of the magic leader, many stemming from the risks associated with leadership which revolves around a single individual. Some of the key potential problems are as follows (see also, Figure 3):

- *Unrealistic expectations.* In creating a vision and getting people energized, the leader may create expectations that are unrealistic or unattainable. These can backfire if the leader cannot live up to the expectations that are created.
- *Dependency and counterdependency.* A strong, visible, and energetic leader may spur different psychological responses. Some individuals may become overly dependent upon the leader, and in some cases whole organizations become dependent. Everyone else stops initiating actions and always waits for the leader to provide direction. They may become passive or reactive. On the other extreme, others may be uncomfortable with strong personal presence and may spend a lot of time and energy demonstrating how the leader is wrong—how the emperor has no clothes.
- *Reluctance to disagree with the leader.* The magic leader's approval or disapproval becomes an important commodity. In the presence of a strong leader, people may become hesitant to disagree or come into conflict with the leader. This may, in turn, lead to stifling conformity.

- *Need for continuing "magic."* The leader may become trapped by the expectation that the "magic" will continue unabated. This may cause the leader to act in ways that are not functional, or (if the magic is not produced) cause a crisis of leadership credibility.
- *Potential feelings of betrayal.* When and if things do not work out as the leader had envisioned, then the potential exists for individuals to feel betrayed by their leader. They may become frustrated and angry, with some of that anger directed at the individual who created the expectations that have now been betrayed.
- *Disenfranchisement of next levels of management.* A consequence of the strong magic leader is that the next levels of management can easily become disenfranchised. They lose their ability to lead because no direction, vision, exhortation, reward, or punishment is meaningful unless it comes directly from the magic leader. The magic leader thus may end up underleveraging his/her management.
- *Limitations of range of the individual leader.* When the leadership process is built around an individual, management's ability to deal with various issues is limited by the time, energy, expertise, and interest of that individual. This is particularly problematic during periods of change when different types of issues demand different types of competencies (e.g. markets, technologies, products, finance) which a single individual may not possess. Different types of strategic changes make different managerial demands and call for different personal characteristics. Finally, there may be limits to the number of strategic changes that one individual can lead over the life of an organization.

In light of these risks, it appears that the magic leader is a necessary component—but not a self-sufficient component—of the organi-

FIGURE 3. *Risks of the Magic Leader*

- Unrealistic expectations
- Dependency and counterdependency
- Reluctance to disagree with the leader
- Need for continuing "magic"
- Potential feelings of betrayal
- Disenfranchisement of next levels of management
- Limitations of range of the individual leader

zational leadership required for effective organizational re-orientation. There is a need to move beyond the magic leader.

INSTRUMENTAL LEADERSHIP

The description of the magic leader as just outlined is not novel. As mentioned earlier, several observers of leadership have described this phenomena. The three components of envisioning, energizing, and enabling are simply one way of describing what these leaders do and how they do it.

Given the risks of magic leadership, there also are more and more examples of individuals who demonstrated the behaviors listed above but failed to successfully initiate or sustain change. Effective leaders of change need to be more than just magic. The effective re-orientations also seem to be characterized by the presence of another type of leadership, which focuses not on the excitement of individuals and changing their goals, needs or aspirations, but on making sure that individuals throughout the organization do indeed behave in the ways needed for the change to occur. The role of leadership is to clarify required behaviors, build in measurement, and administer rewards and punishments so that individuals perceive that behavior consistent with the change is instrumental for them in achieving their own goals. Thus, we will call this type of leadership *instrumental leadership,* since it focuses on the management of structure to create individual instrumentalities. The basis of this approach is in expectancy theories of motivation, which propose that individuals will perform those behaviors that they perceive as instrumental for acquiring valued outcomes (Vroom, 1964; Campbell, Dunnette, Lawler & Weick, 1970). Leadership, in this context, involves the managing of environments to create conditions that will motivate the required behavior (House, 1971; Oldham, 1976).

In practice, instrumental leadership of change involves three elements of behavior (see Figure 4). The first is *structuring.* The leader invests time in creating structures that make it clear what types of behavior are required. This may involve setting goals, establishing standards, defining roles, and similar activities. In re-orientations it involves detailed planning about what people will be needed to do and how they will be required to act during different phases of the change. The second element of instrumental leadership is *controlling.* This involves the creation of systems and processes to measure, monitor, and assess both behavior and results and to administer corrective action (See Lawler & Rhode, 1976). The third element is *rewarding,* which includes the administration of both rewards and punish-

ments contingent upon the degree to which behavior is consistent with the requirements of the change.

Instrumental leadership focuses on the challenge of compliance. The magic leader excites individuals, shapes their aspirations, and directs their energy. In practice, however, this may not be enough to sustain patterns of desired behavior. The followers may be committed to the vision, but over time other forces may influence their behavior, particularly when they are not in direct personal contact with the leader. This is particularly relevant during periods of change when the formal organization and the informal social system may lag behind the leader communicating outdated messages or rewarding traditional behavior. Instrumental leadership is needed to ensure compliance over time consistent with the commitment generated by magic leadership.

The Role of Mundane Behaviors.
Typical descriptions of both magic and instrumental leaders tend to focus on significant events, critical incidents, and "grand gestures." Our vision of the change manager is frequently exemplified by the key speech or public event that is a potential watershed event. While these are important arenas for leadership, the leading of change (including magic and instrumen-

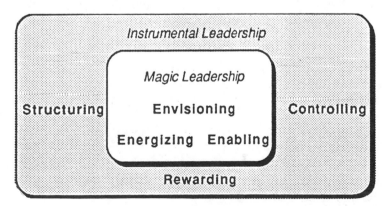

FIGURE 4. Instrumental Leadership

tal leadership) frequently occurs through an accumulation of less dramatic, day-to-day patterns of activity, which have been called mundane behaviors (Peters, 1978). Through relatively unobtrusive acts, the leader can help to shape the patterns of events that people see. Examples of mundane behavior that can have a great impact include:

· Allocation of time and calendar management
· Shaping of physical settings
· Control over agendas of events or meetings
· Use of events such as lunches, meetings, etc.
· Summarization—post hoc interpretation of what occurred
· Use of humor, stories, and myths
· Small symbolic actions, including rewards and punishments

In each of these ways, the leader can use daily activities to emphasize important issues, identify desirable behavior, and help create patterns and meaning out of the various transactions that make up organizational life.

The Complementarity of Leadership Approaches.

It appears that effective organizational re-orientation requires both magic and instrumental leadership. Magic leadership is needed to generate energy, create commitment, and direct individuals towards new objectives, values or aspirations. Instrumental leadership is required to ensure that people really do act in a manner consistent with their new goals. Either one alone seems insufficient for the achievement of change.

The complementarity of leadership approaches (House, in press) and the necessity for both creates a dilemma. Success in implementing these approaches seems to be associated with the personal style, characteristics, needs, and skills of the individual who is the leader. Thus, an individual who is adept at one ap-

proach may have difficulty executing the other. For example, magic leaders may have problems with the tasks involved in achieving control. Many magic leaders have narcissistic tendencies, and in fact a certain degree of narcissism may be necessary to be an effective magic leader. The problem is that these individuals are frequently motivated by a strong desire to be loved or to receive affection from those around them. They therefore have problems delivering unpleasant messages, dealing with performance problems, or creating situations that could attract negative feelings. Only the truly exceptional individual can handle range of both approaches. While such individuals exist, an alternative may be to involve others in leadership roles, thus complementing the strengths and weaknesses of one individual leader.

The limitations of the individual leader (of either type) pose a significant challenge. Magic leadership has a "broad reach." It can influence many people, but is limited by the frequency and intensity of contact with the individual leader. Instrumental leadership is also limited by the degree to which the individual leader can structure, observe, measure, and reward behavior. These limitations present significant problems for achieving re-orientation. One implication is that structural extensions of leadership should be created in the process of managing re-orientations (these are discussed in Nadler and Tushman, 1987). A second implication is that human extensions of leadership need to be created to broaden the scope and impact of leader actions. This leads to a third aspect of leadership and change—the extension of leadership beyond the individual leader, or the creation of institutionalized leadership.

INSTITUTIONALIZING THE LEADERSHIP OF CHANGE

Given the limitations of the individual magic leader, the challenge is to broaden the range of individuals who can perform the critical leadership functions during periods of significant organizational change. There are three potential leverage points for the extension of leadership—the senior team, the broader senior management, and the development of leadership throughout the organization (see Figure 5).

Leveraging the Senior Team.

The group of individuals who report directly to the individual leader—the executive or senior team—is the first logical place to look for opportunities to extend and institutionalize leadership. Development of an effective, visible, and dynamic senior team can be a major step in getting around the problems and limitations of the individual leader. Several actions appear to be important in enhancing the effectiveness of the senior team.

- *Visible empowerment of the team.* A first step is the visible empowerment of the team, or "anointing" the team as extensions of the individual leader. There are two different aspects to this empowerment: objective and symbolic. Objective empowerment involves providing team members with the autonomy and resources to serve effectively. Symbolic empowerment involves communicating messages (through information, symbols, and mundane behaviors) that show the organization that these individuals are indeed extensions of the leader, and ultimately key components of the leadership. Symbolic empowerment can be done through the use of titles, the designation of organizational structures, and the visible presence of individuals in ceremonial roles.

- *Individual development of team members.* Empowerment will fail if the individuals on the team are not capable of capitalizing on their anointed status. A major problem in these people situations is that the members of the senior team frequently are the product of the very systems, structures, and values that the re-orientation seeks to change. Participating in the change, and more importantly, leading it, may require a significant "switching of cognitive gears." It demands that the senior team members think very differently about the business and about managing. This need for personal

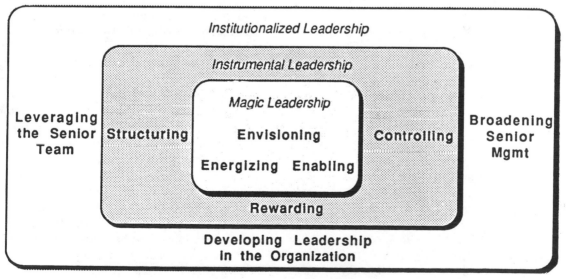

FIGURE 5. *Institutionalized Leadership*

change at the most senior level has implications for the selection of senior team members (see below). It also may mean that part of the individual leader's role is to help coach, guide, and support individuals in developing their own leadership capabilities. Each individual need not (and should not) be a "clone" of the individual leader; but each should be able to initiate credible leadership actions in a manner consistent with their own personal styles. Ultimately, it also puts a demand on the leader to deal with those who won't or can't make the personal changes required for participation in the leadership of the re-orientation.

- *Composition of the senior team.* The need for the senior team to lead change may mean that the composition of that team may have to be altered. Different skills, capacities, styles, and value orientations may be needed. In fact, most successful re-orientations seem to involve some significant changes in the make-up of the senior team. This may require outplacement of people, as mentioned above, and it may require importing new people, either from outside the organization, or from outside the coalition that has traditionally lead the organization.

- *The inducement of strategic anticipation.* A critical issue in organization re-orientations is *strategic anticipation.* By definition, a reorientation is a strategic organizational change that is initiated in anticipation of significant external events. Re-orientation occurs because the organization's leadership perceives competitive advantage from initiating the changes earlier rather than later. The question is, who is responsible for thinking about and anticipating external events, and ultimately deciding that re-orientation is necessary? In some cases, the individual leader does this, but the task is enormous. This is where the senior team can be helpful, because as a group it can scan a larger number of events and potentially be more creative in analyzing of the environment and the process of anticipation.

Companies that are successful anticipators create conditions in which anticipation is more likely to occur. They invest in activities that foster anticipation, such as environmental scanning, experiments or probes inside the organization (frequently on the periphery), and frequent contacts with the outside. The senior team has a major role in initiating, sponsoring, and leveraging these activities.

- *The senior team as a learning system.* For a senior team to benefit from it's involvement in leading change, it must become an effective system for learning about the business, the nature of change, and the task of managing the change. The challenge is to both bond the team together, while avoiding insularity. One of the down sides of such team structures is that they become isolated from the rest of the organization, they develop patterns of dysfunctional conformity, avoid conflict, and over time develop patterns of learned incompetence. All of this diminishes the team's capacity for effective strategic anticipation, and it decreases the team's ability to provide effective leadership of the reorientation process.

There are several ways to avoid negative consequences. One approach is to work hard to keep the team an open system, receptive to outside ideas and information. This can be accomplished by creating a constant stream of events that expose people to new ideas. These can include speakers or visitors brought in to meet with the team, visits by the team to other organizations, frequent contact with customers, and planned "deep contact" in the organization (informal and nondisruptive regular data collection through personal contact—breakfasts, focus groups etc.).

A second approach involves the shaping and management of the internal group process of the team itself. This involves working on effective group leadership, building effective team member skills, creating meeting management discipline, acquiring group problem solving and information processing skills, and ultimately creating norms that promote effective learning, innovation, and problem solving.

As a final note, it is important to remember that frequently there are significant obstacles to developing effective senior teams to lead changes. The issues of skills and selection have been mentioned, but more important is the question of power and succession. A team is most successful when there is a perception of common fate. *Individuals have to believe that the success of the team will, in the long run, be more salient to them than their individual short run success.* In many situations, this can be accomplished through appropriate structures, objectives, and incentives. But this fails when there are pending (or anticipated) decisions to be made concerning senior management succession. In these situations, the quality of collaboration tends to deteriorate significantly, and effective team leadership of change becomes problematic. The individual leader must manage the timing and process of succession in relation to the requirements for team leadership, so that conflicting (and mutually exclusive) incentives are not created by the situation.

Broadening Senior Management.

A second step in moving beyond individual leadership of change is the further extension of the leadership beyond the executive or senior team to include a broader set of individuals who make up the senior management of the organization. This would include individuals one or two levels down from the executive team. This set of individuals, generally ranging in size from 30 to 120 people, is in fact the senior operating management of most sizeable organizations, and is looked upon as senior management by the majority of employees. In many cases (and particularly during times of change) they do not feel like senior management, and thus they are not positioned to lead the change. They feel like participants (at best) and victims (at worst). This group can be particularly problematic since they may be more embedded in the current system of organizing and managing than some of the senior team. They may be less prepared to change, they frequently have molded themselves to fit the current organizational style, and they may feel disenfranchised by the very act of developing a strong executive team, particularly if that team has been assembled by bringing in people from outside of the organization.

The task is to make this group feel like senior management, to get them "signed up" for the change, and to motivate and enable them to work as an extension of the senior team. Many of the implications are similar to those mentioned above in relation to the top team; however there are special problems of size, and lack of proximity to the individual magic leader. Part of the answer is to get the senior team to take responsibility for developing their own teams as leaders of change. Other specific actions may include:

- *Rites of passage.* Creating symbolic events that help these individuals to feel more a part of senior management.
- *Senior groups.* Creating structures (councils, boards, committees, conferences) to maintain contact with this group and reinforce their sense of participation as members of senior management.
- *Participation in planning change.* Involving these people in the early diagnosing of the need to change and the planning of change strategies associated with the re-orientation. This is particularly useful in getting

them to feel more like owners, rather than victims of the change.

- *Intensive communication.* Maintaining a constant stream of open communication to and from this group. It is the lack of information and perspective that psychologically disenfranchises these individuals.

Developing Leadership in the Organization.

A third arena for enhancing the leadership of re-orientations is through the organizational structures, systems, and process for the development of leadership. These frequently lag behind the re-orientation, when they should be in tune with the focus on strategic anticipation. The management development system of many organizations frequently works effectively to create managers who will fit well with the organizational environment that the leadership seeks to abandon. There needs to be strategic and anticipatory thinking about the leadership development process, including the following:

- *Definition of managerial competence.* A first step is determining the skills, capabilities, and capacities needed to manage and lead effectively in the re-orientation and post re-orientation period. Factors that have contributed to managerial success in the past may be the seeds of failure in the future.
- *Sourcing managerial talent.* Re-orientations may require that the organization start identifying significantly different sources for acquiring leaders or potential leaders. Senior managers should be involved in recruiting and hiring. Because of the lead time involved, managerial sourcing has to be approached as a long term (five to ten years) task.
- *Socialization.* As individuals move into the organization and into positions of leader-

ship, deliberate actions must be taken to teach them how the organization's social system works. During periods of reorientation, the socialization process ought to lead rather than lag behind the change.

- *Management education.* Re-orientation may require managers and leaders to use new skills, competencies, or knowledge. This creates a demand for effective management education. On the other hand, recent research indicates that the impact of internal management education on the development of effective leaders may be minimal when compared with job experiences. Thus the use of educational events to expose people to external settings or ideas (through out of company education) and to socialize individuals may be more useful than attempts to teach people to be effective leaders and managers.
- *Career management.* Research and experience indicate that the most potent factor in the development of effective leaders is the nature of their job experiences. The challenge is how to ensure that individuals get the appropriate experiences. Preparing people to lead reorientations may mean a major rethinking of the types of experiences they need (e.g. situation and manager problems rather than function or discipline). It may require the building of processes to ensure that people get appropriate experiences, the sharing of the burden of career management between both the organization and the employee, and finally, the deliberate strategy of balancing current contribution with investment for the future when placing people in job assignments.
- *Seeding talent.* Developing leadership for change may also require deliberate leveraging of the available talent. This implies very thoughtful placement of individual leaders in different situations and parts of the orga-

nization, the use of transfers, and the whole notion of strategic placement.

SUMMARY

This paper has attempted to outline a way of thinking about leadership of strategic organizational change, and in particular, the task of building effective leadership for re-orientations. The starting point was that there are different types of organizational change that make different demands and pose different challenges. In strategic organizational change (and in this case, reorientations) the role of leadership is absolutely critical to success. This paper has attempted to both define what is required and to expand the view of what is involved in the leadership of organizational change.

At the broadest level, the argument has been for dealing with three basic issues: *excitement* of the organization and individuals to change through the concept of the "magic leader", *control* of behavior through structuring, controlling and rewarding, and finally *institutionalization* of leadership by moving beyond the individual leader and focusing on the senior team, the broader senior management, and the question of leadership development through the organization.

Leadership is an area that has stimulated years of exploration and still eludes full understanding. The relationship between leadership and organizational change pose even greater challenges. The task is critical, however, if our knowledge of how to build more effective organizations is to continue to grow.

REFERENCES

Bass, B. M. *Performance beyond expectations.* Academic Press, 1985.

Beckhard, R., & Harris, R. *Organizational transitions.* Reading, Mass.: Addison-Wesley, 1977.

Bennis, W., & Nanus, B. *Leaders: The strategies for taking charge.* New York: Harper and Row, 1985.

Berlew, D. E. Leadership and organizational excitement, in D.A. Kolb, I.M. Rubin, & J.M. McIntyre (Eds.) *Organizational Psychology.* Englewood Cliffs: Prentice Hall, 1974.

Burns, J. M. *Leadership.* New York: Harper & Row, 1978.

Campbell, J. P., Dunnette, M.D., Lawler, E.E., & Weick, K. *Managerial behavior, performances and effectiveness.* New York: McGraw-Hill, 1970.

Goodman, P. A. & Associates (Eds.) *Change in organizations.: New perspectives on theory, research, and practice.* San Francisco: Jossey-Bass, 1982.

House, R. J. Path-goal theory of leader effectiveness. *Administrative Science Quarterly,* 1971, 16, 321–338.

House, R. J. A 1976 theory of charismatic leadership. In J.G. Hunt and L.L. Larson (Eds.) *Leadership: The cutting edge.* Carbondale, Ill.: Southern Illinois University Press, 1977.

House, R. J. Exchange and charismatic theories of leadership. In G. Reber (Ed.) *Encyclopedia of leadership,* in press.

Kimberly, J. R., & Quinn, R. E. *New futures: The challenge of managing corporate transitions.* Homewood, Ill.: Dow Jones-Irwin, 1984.

Lawler, E. E., & Rhode, J. G. *Information and control in organizations.* Pacific Palisades, Calif.: Goodyear, 1976.

Nadler, D. A. Managing organizational change: An integrative perspective. *The Journal of Applied Behavioral Science.* 17, 1981, 191–211.

Nadler, D. A., & Tushman, M. L. Organizational framebending: Principles for managing reorientation. New York: Delta Consulting Group, 1987.

Nadler, D. A., & Tushman, M. L. Managing strategic organizational change. New York: Delta Consulting Group, 1986.

Oldham, G. R. The motivational strategies used by supervisors: Relationships to effectiveness indicators. *Organizational Behavior and Human Performance.* 1976, 15, 66–86.

Peters, T. J. Symbols, patterns and settings: An optimistic case for getting things done. *Organizational Dynamics.* Autumn, 1978.

Tichy, N. M., & Devanna, M. A. *The transformational leader.* New York: John Wiley & Sons, 1986.

Tichy, N. M., & Ulrich, D. The leadership challenge—A call for the transformational leader. *Sloan Management Review,* Fall, 1984.

Tushman, M.L. Patterns of organizational re-orientation. Paper presented at University of Pittsburgh Conference on large scale organizational change, 1986.

Tushman, M.L. & Romanelli, E. Organizational evolution: A metamorphosis model of convergence and re-orientation. in B.M. Straw & I.I. Cummings (Eds.), *Research in Organizational Behavior.* Greenwich, Ct.: JAI Press, 1985, 17.

Vroom, V. H. *Work and motivation.* New York: Wiley, 1964.

When Leaders Are at Their Best:
Five Practices and Ten Commitments

James Kouzes

Barry Posner

I think good people deserve good leadership.

> —Debi Coleman, Vice-President
> and Chief Financial Officer,
> Apple Computer

After twenty-five years in the packaged goods industry, Tom Melohn quit. He quit to become "head sweeper"—that's what it says on his resumé—of North American Tool and Die. Translate "head sweeper" to mean co-owner, president, and chief executive officer of that San Leandro, California, manufacturing company.

When Melohn and his partner, Garner Beckett, took over NATD, the company was a poor performer in an industry being attacked by offshore competitors. In a period of eight years under Melohn's leadership, NATD increased its sales by a factor of 5, increased its pretax profits by 750 percent, reduced annual turnover from 27 percent to 4 percent, and decreased the reject rate from 5 percent to a tenth of a percent. By year eight, NATD had opened its second plant—Melohn calls it "Plant 20" to give people a sense that the company is growing—and received its ninth "vendor of the year" award.

To what does Melohn attribute this extraordinary turnaround? Certainly not to his skills as a machinist. He was a self-described "peddler"—his last position before NATD was senior vice-president of marketing—and claims he cannot even hammer a nail or screw the license plates onto his car. Nor was it his business education. He holds a master's degree in history from Princeton University, and he claims he has never read a book on business. Nor was it his industry experience. Remember, he was a peddler in packaged goods.

And it wasn't geographical advantage in

distribution, proprietary products, or new equipment. NATD is in a region filled with lots of small job shops, it makes parts to the specifications of its customers, and its equipment is old.

So what is the magic?

"We set three objectives for NATD," says Melohn. "First, we planned to grow the company profitably. Second, to share the wealth among employees. And third, and equally critical, it was important to have fun—not just the two owners, but all our employees.

"And that is the key. To have fun. Yes, the numbers are important; they are our report card. Yet the real reason for our success is deceptively simple. It's our employees—our major asset. To see them grow, personally, professionally, financially—to share with them the excitement of building our company. The psychic income alone is enormous."

The strategy for increasing company profits came from the customers. Melohn and his partner went out and interviewed about fifty buyers and twenty-five engineers. They asked them what they needed, what they wanted from a job shop. The answers were always the same: quality, service, price.

So quality became the NATD hallmark. But at NATD, quality doesn't start in quality control. "It's too late there," says Melohn. "They're just the traffic cop. . . . Nope, at NATD quality must be in each employee's head and heart or we're dead." You'll find Melohn on the shop floor preaching the gospel of quality every day at NATD.

At NATD, the owners also share the wealth. They have a company employee stock ownership plan. The employee stock is free, and the owners have waived their rights to participate. They also recognize employees with cash awards for contributing to the goal of "no rejects."

"Another action area that reinforces our belief in the importance of our employees is called caring. Simply stated," says Melohn, "at NATD we care about our people. We care a great deal. Not just as employees, but as human beings, as friends. And we try to help them in any way we can." From sending flowers, to buying doughnuts, to loaning company trucks, to monthly "Super Person" awards, Melohn shows how much he cares.

"The only way to achieve these goals, we decided, was to create an atmosphere of complete trust between us, the owners, and all our employees." But Melohn adds "one admonition: you've got to really mean it when you say you want such an atmosphere. You truly have to believe it. Then you've got to work at improving relations every day in every situation. Otherwise, your employees will sense the hypocrisy, and all will be for naught."

Apple Computer, Inc., is one of North American Tool and Die's customers. At the time of our interviews, the person in charge of the operation to which NATD sells was Debi Coleman. Coleman was the vice-president of worldwide manufacturing for Apple, the only female vice-president of manufacturing in a Fortune 500 company. (In 1987 Coleman was appointed chief financial officer for Apple.)

Coleman began her business career at Texas Instruments. After earning her M.B.A. degree at Stanford, she joined Hewlett-Packard. But Apple Computer offered boundless opportunity, and she joined them, starting as a finance manager for the Macintosh project. In the brief period of five years, she held five other jobs, as Macintosh project controller, Macintosh division controller, product group controller, Macintosh division operations manager, and finally vice-president of worldwide manufacturing.

Manufacturing is not the usual choice for a Stanford M.B.A., but Coleman always wanted to work in the factory. "I don't think you should ever manage something that you don't care passionately about," says Coleman. "The move I made from finance to manufacturing was just not intuitively obvious to people, except if you knew how passionately I cared about manufacturing."

Some of the accomplishments of which Coleman is the proudest occurred while she was Macintosh division operations manager. One of her tasks was to improve the performance of the Fremont manufacturing plant—one of the most innovative personal computer factories in the world.

Under her leadership as factory manager, the throughput yield in the factory went from a first-pass cumulative yield of about 30 percent to one of 70 percent in nine months. Incoming acceptance on materials went from 80 percent to 96–99 percent. They got over thirty inventory turns a year.

A lot of solid manufacturing processes contributed to these results. The Fremont facility was conceived as an integrated factory—everything under one roof, with one management team. They also operated with just-in-time inventory management, bar code serialization to monitor work in progress, unique vendor partnerships, and a host of other impressive innovations.

While all those manufacturing innovations were important, they weren't the only things that made the Mac factory a highly productive and reliable facility. First, says Coleman, "I really can't claim credit for all these things." She attributes them to the people who work there.

So what was her contribution? "One of them was a total willingness to listen to everybody about what was going on." Another was "spending time on the floor . . . five hours a day." And then there were the numerous little things Debi did. She refurbished the bathrooms off the production floor, had the factory floor cleaned around the clock, sealed and waxed the floor, painted the factory walls white, set up an Apple values committee, and for the first two months held catered supper meetings with production folks every Tuesday and Thursday.

Details, details, details. Coleman works very hard at the details. Why work so hard? "I think good people deserve good leadership. The people I manage deserve the best leader in the world. If you could see them, you would understand why somebody would want to work sixty hours a week to make those people more successful."

Tom Melohn and Debi Coleman each seized the opportunity to lead. They chose a pioneering path and led their organizations to new summits of excellence. Melohn and Coleman are exceptional, to be sure, but their stories are not.

We have found such achievements to be commonplace. We have discovered that there are thousands of success stories in business. Getting extraordinary things done in organizations is not restricted to a select few stars or a select few companies. It is something the vast majority of managers are capable of doing in the future.

What can we learn from Tom Melohn, Debi Coleman, and the hundreds of others who have told us their stories? What does it take to get other people, by the force of their own free wills, despite potential risk and hard work, to want to climb to the summit?

Through our studies, we have discovered that the ordinary executives who convinced others to join them on pioneering journeys followed the path of a three-phase strategy. We refer to it as the VIP—vision-involvement-persistence—model of leadership.

When people described their personal best leadership experiences, they told of times when they imagined exciting, highly attractive futures for their organizations. They had *visions* and dreams of what could be. They had absolute and total personal belief, and they were confident in their abilities to make extraordinary things happen.

These leaders recognized that grand dreams do not become significant realities through the actions of a single leader. They knew that scores of people were needed to create, produce, sell, and sponsor the vision. The *involvement* of many others is key to making it all the way to the top.

Our sample of leaders acted on their wise understanding that new tomorrows are not realized without hard work and *persistence.* The personal best projects were distinguished by the fact that all of them required relentless effort, steadfastness, competence, planning, attention.to detail, and encouragement.

FIVE LEADERSHIP PRACTICES COMMON TO SUCCESSFUL LEADERS

As we looked deeper into this dynamic process, through the case analyses and survey questionnaires, we uncovered five fundamental practices that enabled these leaders to get extraordinary things done. When they were at their personal best, our leaders:

1. Challenged the process.
2. Inspired a shared vision.
3. Enabled others to act.
4. Modeled the way.
5. Encouraged the heart.

These practices are not the private property of the leaders we studied. They are available to anyone who wants to accept the leadership challenge.

Challenging the Process.

Leadership is an active, not a passive process. While many leaders attributed their success to "luck" or "being in the right place at the right time," none of them sat idly by or waited for fate to smile upon them. Although the distinctive competencies of a person may fit the needs of the moment, those who lead others to greatness seek challenge. All the cases we collected about leadership personal bests involved some kind of challenge. The challenge may have been an innovative new product, a reorganization, or a turnaround, but the majority of the cases involved a change from the status quo. They involved *challenging the process.*

Leaders are pioneers—people who are willing to step out into the unknown. They are people who are willing to take risks, to innovate and experiment in order to find new and better ways of doing things. But leaders need not always be the creators or originators of new products or work processes. In fact, it is just as likely that they are not. Product innovations tend to come from customers, vendors, and line employees. Process innovations tend to come from the people doing the work.

The leader's primary contribution is in the recognition of good ideas, the support of those ideas, and the willingness to challenge the system in order to get new products, processes, and services adopted. In this sense, it might be more accurate to call them early adopters of innovation.

Innovation, according to Robert Metcalfe, chairperson of 3COM, "requires gambling and risk taking. We tell our folks to make at least ten mistakes a day. If they're not making ten mistakes a day, they're not trying hard enough." And Olle Bovin, a manager at Hewlett-Packard in Europe, claims, "You have to be brave enough to fail as a leader." If this seems like foolish advice, recall the times you have tried to play a new game or a new sport. Did you get it absolutely perfect the first time you played it? Probably not. Experimentation, innovation, and change all involve risk and failure.

It would be ridiculous to state that those who fail over and over again eventually succeed as leaders. Success in business is not a process of simply buying enough lottery tickets. The key that unlocks the door to opportunity is learning. Warren Bennis and Burt Nanus, authors of *Leaders,* tell us that the ninety successful leaders they studied regard almost "every false step as a learning opportunity, and not the end of the world." Leaders are learners. They learn from their mistakes as well as their successes.

Inspiring a Shared Vision.

Robert Swiggett, chairperson of Kollmorgen Corporation, offers a straightforward view about the job of a leader. It is, he says, "to create a vision." Every organization, every social movement begins with a dream. The dream or vision is the force that invents the future.

Leaders spend considerable effort gazing across the horizon of time, imagining what it will be like when they have arrived at their final destinations. Some call it vision; others describe it as a purpose, mission, goal, even personal agenda. Regardless of what we call it, there is a desire to make something happen, to change the way things are, to create something that no one else has ever created before.

In some ways, leaders live their lives backwards. They see pictures in their minds' eyes of what the results will look like even before they have started their projects, much as an architect draws a blueprint or an engineer builds a model. Their clear image of the future pulls them forward. But visions seen only by leaders are insufficient to create an organized movement or a significant change in a company. A person with no followers is *not* a leader, and people will not become followers until they accept a vision as their own. You cannot command commitment, you can only inspire it.

Leaders *inspire a shared vision.* They breathe life into what are the hopes and dreams of others and enable them to see the exciting possibilities that the future holds. Leaders get others to buy into their dreams by showing how all will be served by a common purpose.

To enlist people in a vision, a leader must "know your followers and speak their language," according to Beverly Ann Scott, organization development manager at McKesson. People must believe that you understand their needs and have their interests at heart. Only through an intimate knowledge of their dreams, their hopes, their aspirations, their visions, their values is the leader able to enlist their support.

There is an old Texas saying that "you can't light a fire with a wet match." Leaders cannot ignite the flame of passion in their followers if they themselves do not express enthusiasm for the compelling vision of their group. Leaders communicate their passion through vivid language and an expressive style.

Person after person in our study reported that they were incredibly enthusiastic about their personal best projects. Their own enthusiasm was catching; it spread from leader to followers. The leader's own belief in and enthusiasm for the vision are the spark that ignites the flame of inspiration.

Enabling Others to Act.

Leaders do not achieve success by themselves. When we asked Bill Flanagan, vice-president of manufacturing at Amdahl Corporation, to tell us his personal best, he replied that he couldn't, "because it wasn't my personal best. It was our personal best. It wasn't me. It was us."

After reviewing over 500 personal best cases, we have developed a simple one-word test to detect whether someone is on the road to becoming a leader. That word is *we.*

Exemplary leaders enlist the support and assistance of all those who must make the project work. They involve, in some way, those who must live with the results, and they make it possible for others to do good work. They encourage collaboration, build teams, and empower others. *They enable others to act.* In 91 percent of the cases we analyzed, leaders proudly discussed how teamwork and collaboration were essential. Additionally, our data on others' perceptions of leaders indicate that this is the most significant of all the five practices.

When Versatec needed a table for its conference room, instead of buying one, Renn Zaphiropoulos, president and chief executive officer, invited the managers over to his house to build one. In his garage one Saturday, they built a twenty-one-foot-long teakwood conference table, hauled it to the company on a flatbed truck, and carried it up two flights of stairs to the conference room. This off-line camaraderie illustrates the family feeling that typically develops among highly committed, productive teams.

This sense of teamwork goes far beyond the leader and his or her immediate subordinates. It includes peers, superiors, customers, suppliers—all those who must support the vision. Rosabeth Moss Kanter, a Harvard professor, confirms this in her research on successful innovations inside large corporations. In her book *The Change Masters,* she reports, "The few projects in my study that disintegrated did so because the manager failed to build a coalition of supporters and collaborators." The effect of enabling others to act is to make them feel strong, capable, and committed. Those in the organization who must produce the results feel a sense of ownership. They feel empowered, and when people feel empowered, they are more likely to use their energies to produce extraordinary results.

Modeling the Way.

At a recent faculty convocation at Santa Clara University, the president, Reverend William J. Rewak, S.J., spoke eloquently about the changes anticipated for the campus. After he showed slides of the planned new buildings and gardens, he said: "Vision needs management, electricity, and concrete." Grand dreams, he reminded us, cannot become significant realities with élan alone. Leaders also must have detailed plans. They must steer projects along the course, measure performance, raise funds, and take corrective action. Many conventional management practices are certainly useful. Yet there is an even more demanding leadership task if a person is to direct the course of action. The leader must *model the way.*

Irwin Federman, president and chief executive officer of Monolithic Memories, puts it this way: "Your job gives you authority. Your behavior earns you respect." While managers appraise their subordinates, subordinates also appraise their managers. The test they use is a simple one: Does my leader practice what he or she preaches? Ninety-five percent of our leaders reported that they modeled the way through planning and leading by example.

In order to lead by example, leaders must first be clear about their business beliefs. Managers may speak eloquently about vision and values, but if their behavior is not consistent with their stated beliefs, people ultimately will lose respect for them. It may be best to take the advice of Frank J. Ruck, Jr., former president of Employee Transfer Company and current president of Thermal Designs, Inc., who says of his leadership style: "I began by becoming a role model that exemplifies the organizational and management values I believe are important."

Being a role model means paying attention to what you believe is important. It means showing others through your behavior that you live your values. Tom Melohn believes he should "share whatever wealth was created" at NATD. So each year, employees are given shares of NATD stock. And that stock is newly issued.

Tom Peters, coauthor of *In Search of Excellence* and *Passion for Excellence,* summarizes this practice superbly when he says, "The only magic is brute consistence, persistence, and attention to detail." Leaders act in ways that are consistent with their beliefs, they are persistent in pursuit of their visions, and they are always vigilant about the little things that make a big difference.

Encouraging the Heart.

Each spring at Versatec, about 2,000 non-managerial personnel come together to receive annual bonuses. Recently, Zaphiropoulos arrived at the celebration dressed in a satin costume and riding atop an elephant, accompanying the Stanford Marching Band. Zaphiropoulos likes to say, "If you are going to give someone a check, don't just mail it. Have a celebration."

The climb to the top is arduous and long. People become exhausted, frustrated, and disenchanted. They often are tempted to give up. Leaders must *encourage the heart* of their followers to carry on. With elephants and music and a share of the gain, Zaphiropoulos gives heart to his people so that they will continue the journey.

Of course, it is not necessary to be that dramatic to offer encouragement. Simple things can create similar reactions. Phil Turner, plant manager of the Wire and Cable Division of Raychem Corporation, occasionally will put on a clown costume and give out balloons. He enjoys celebrating milestones and the employees get a good laugh from Turner's playful acts. Sue Cook, former manager of employee development at Apple Computer and now a consultant with the Tom Peters Group, is a master of celebration. She gives out stickers, T-shirts, buttons, and every other conceivable award when people achieve a milestone. Mervyn's top management send note cards that have "I heard something good about you" printed at the top. They are sent not just to other officers but to clerks, buyers, trainers, and other line employees.

People do not start their work each day with a desire to lose. It is part of the leader's job to show them that they can win. In the cases we collected, there were numerous examples of individual recognition and group celebration. The marching bands, the bells, the T-shirts, the note cards, the personal thank-yous are the visible signs of encouragement to keep on winning. If people smell a charlatan making noisy pretenses, they will turn away. But genuine acts of caring draw people forward.

There is one other aspect of encouragement that came through in the cases we examined: the encouragement that leaders give themselves. When we asked George Gananian, owner of Star Graphics, why he worked so hard, he said, "I love to turn the key in the door and put on the coffee pot." Love of their products, their people, their customers, their work—this may just be the best-kept secret of exemplary leadership.

THE TEN COMMITMENTS OF LEADERSHIP

Our research has shown us that leadership is an observable, learnable set of practices. Leadership is not something mystical and ethereal that cannot be understood by ordinary people. It is a myth that only a lucky few can ever decipher the leadership code. We have discovered hundreds of people who have led others to get extraordinary things done in organizations. There are thousands, perhaps millions, more. The belief that leadership cannot be learned is a far more powerful deterrent to development than is the nature of the leadership process itself.

We found the following behavioral commitments in the personal best leadership cases:

Challenging the Process
 1. Search for Opportunities
 2. Experiment and Take Risks

Inspiring a Shared Vision
  3. Envision the Future
  4. Enlist Others

Enabling Others to Act
  5. Foster Collaboration
  6. Strengthen Others

Modeling the Way
  7. Set the Example
  8. Plan Small Wins

Encouraging the Heart
  9. Recognize Individual Contribution
  10. Celebrate Accomplishments

The Top Management Team: Key to Strategic Success

Donald C. Hambrick

For the past fifteen years, strategy researchers and consultants have been preoccupied by a quest for techniques and tools that top managers can reliably use to improve their firms' performance. Many such attempts have fallen flat when tried in real competitive arenas. Others have emerged as useful rules of thumb or as rough guidelines, but carrying so many exceptions as to be only narrowly useful. Also, once in the hands of all competitors in an industry, many of these concepts simply result in a more sophisticated stalemate. Finally, some of the prescriptions—such as those dealing with pay-offs from market share, product quality, innovation, and employee productivity—are a bit like the advice to the investor: "Buy low and sell high." They're unassailable but provide very little concrete guidance.

These disappointing results have caused some theorists to shift their focus away from trying to find new strategic nostrums and toward trying to better understand the process by which successful strategies emerge and get implemented. At the heart of this concern for stra-

tegic processes is the question, "What types of managers, in what combinations, have the best chances of identifying, picking, and implementing successful strategies?" Introduced as the "upper echelons model," this view contends that performance of an organization is ultimately a reflection of its top managers.[1] In the face of the ambiguity and massive bombardment of information that typifies the top management task, no two strategists will necessarily identify the same array of options; if they were to pick the same major options, they almost certainly would not implement them identically. Biases, blinders, skills, aptitudes, interpersonal dynamics and other human factors in the executive ranks greatly affect what happens to companies. The upshot is that general managers who want to improve their organizations' performance will work on improving their management teams.

Obviously, greatness within a team will not in itself assure strategic success. We have many examples of "high-caliber" management teams who have operated in ways that have nullified their raw talents.[2] However, team qualities are the essential foundation for a successful strategic process within the firm. The amounts of open-mindedness, perseverance, communication skills, vision, and other key characteristics that exist within the team clearly set the limits for how well the team—and, in turn, the firm—can operate.

From Glenn R. Carroll and David Vogel, eds., *Organizational Approaches to Strategy* (Cambridge, Mass.: Ballinger Publishing Co., 1988). Copyright © 1988 by Ballinger Publishing Company.

Bert Cannella, Jim Fredrickson, Mike Tushman, and Bob Yavitz made valuable suggestions on earlier versions of this article. The article is based upon research conducted under the sponsorship of Columbia University's Strategy Research Center.

This chapter proposes a framework for systematically assessing and reshaping top management teams. While the logic of the approach could be used at any managerial level, the major focus here is on how the general manager of a business unit should approach this critical task. Following the description of the framework in the next section, the case for a division president in a multibusiness firm who used the framework will be presented.

The analytic framework is diagrammed in Figure 1. It specifies the elements of this important process and identifies the range of issues the manager must consider. The starting point is a careful consideration of the context in which the management team will operate. This context includes external factors (societal, industry, and corporate) as well as internal factors (chosen strategy, competitive weapons, workforce profile, and so on). The profile of the ideal team for managing in this context can then be constructed. There are many dimensions on which managerial qualities can be assessed, but the focus here is on six broad arenas: values, aptitudes, skills, knowledge, cognitive style, and demeanor. The next step is to fairly and carefully assess the mix of qualities within the existing team. Finally, the manager must develop a concrete action plan for closing the gap between what is needed and what exists. There is a substantial array of levers for reshaping a top team—training and development, incentives, coaching and counsel, use of outside or contract talent, team replacements, and team additions.

The framework should not be taken primarily as a way for deciding who needs to be replaced. It may lead to such decisions, but at least in the firms where it has been applied so far, it has tended to lead to the enhancement and unleashing of individuals' talents while making the overall team far more fit for the competitive environment.

Three basic premises underlie this chapter and the framework presented in it. First,

there is no such thing as a universally ideal management team. The appropriate mix of qualities depends on the context in which the managers must operate and how the individuals fit with each other. This means that even the seemingly most desirable qualities can exist in counterproductive amounts. Second, the general manager can and must think proactively about his or her team. The view that the existing team's talents have to be taken completely as a given is an immense disservice to the business as well as to the members of the team. Third, managers must think about their teams in their own highly personalized ways. The ideal team is very much a function of how the general manager operates and what he or she values within the group. For this reason, canned inventories of managerial qualities are dangerous. For the same reason, it may eventually prove difficult for theorists to construct broadly applicable hypotheses about ideal team mixes, since the ideal is so dependent upon the general manager's own preferred mode of operating.

The view that so much hinges upon the general manager appears to imply that the upper echelon should be defined strictly as the top person. In support of such a position, recent research has found convincing evidence that the characteristics of general managers are related to the strategies they pursue[3] as well as to how well their organizations will perform.[4] Such findings are intuitively reassuring to most of us, since we—Americans in particular—tend to hold romantic views about strong leaders.[5] As a society, we seem to need and continually create singular managerial heroes and villains.

However, except in the most extreme cases, management is a shared effort. There are too many options and issues for one person to comprehend, so delegation and collaboration occur. The limited empirical evidence as to whether the top person or the entire top team is a better predictor of organizational outcomes clearly supports the conclusion that the full

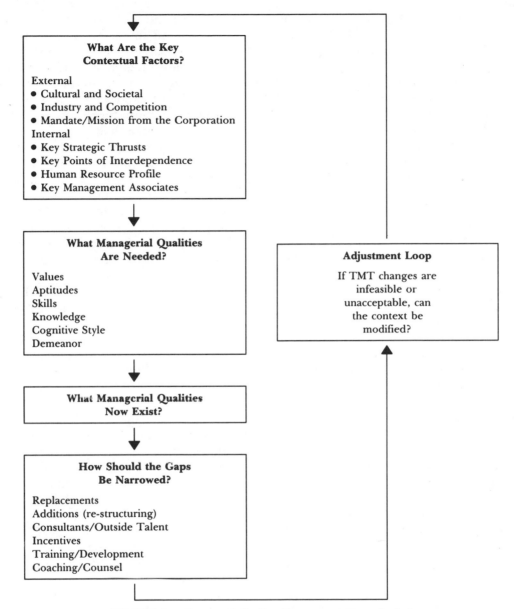

What Are the Key Contextual Factors?

External
- Cultural and Societal
- Industry and Competition
- Mandate/Mission from the Corporation

Internal
- Key Strategic Thrusts
- Key Points of Interdependence
- Human Resource Profile
- Key Management Associates

What Managerial Qualities Are Needed?

Values
Aptitudes
Skills
Knowledge
Cognitive Style
Demeanor

What Managerial Qualities Now Exist?

How Should the Gaps Be Narrowed?

Replacements
Additions (re-structuring)
Consultants/Outside Talent
Incentives
Training/Development
Coaching/Counsel

Adjustment Loop

If TMT changes are infeasible or unacceptable, can the context be modified?

FIGURE 1. Framework for Top Management Team Analysis

team has greater effect. Hage and Dewar found that the values of the entire top teams of health and social service agencies were better predictors of subsequent organizational innovation than were the values of the executive directors alone.[6] Similarly, Tushman, Virany, and Roma- nelli found in a sample of minicomputer firms that major organization changes, or "reorienta- tions," were more likely to be successful when accompanied by changes in the entire top team than when accompanied by a change only in the CEO.[7]

One could also turn to anecdotal accounts of the importance of team dynamics. For example, Exxon's inability to achieve success outside the oil industry has been blamed on the extreme homogeneity and long tenures in the oil industry of Exxon's top management team.[8] Similarly, it was primarily due to the interplay among key partners, rather than due to any one person, that the venerable investment bank, Lehman Brothers, experienced a mutiny and was absorbed by Shearson/American Express[9] It seems clear that the composition of the top team is a crucial element in corporate behavior and performance.

FRAMEWORK FOR TEAM ANALYSIS

Context

The starting point for assessing a managerial team is in reaching a complete understanding of the context in which the team will be operating. Team designers often omit this stage or give it short shrift, preferring to move directly to more action-oriented questions, such as "Who should fill each slot?" However, unless the setting for managerial action is well comprehended, the mix of appropriate team qualities cannot be identified.

A good contextual analysis need not be laborious. Key factors are often readily apparent; moreover, in many firms, a major portion of the context is revealed as part of a good strategic planning process, with its emphasis on environmental opportunities and threats and internal strengths and weaknesses.

The context consists of factors both external and internal to the business. Following are descriptions of several of the key contextual elements that the team architect must grasp.

• *Cultural and Societal Factors*—What are the norms and needs within the broad society in which the business operates? What do *today's* (and tomorrow's) employees, customers, regulatory bodies, press, and other stakeholders require from the business and its managers? For instance, it is now widely observed that today's employees and customers are more highly educated and sophisticated than their predecessors 25, or even 15, years ago; yet, many firms still have not grasped the importance of having senior managers who can deal effectively in this new climate. Societal factors are also extremely important to understand in staffing foreign subsidiaries or even in staffing regional operations in the United States. For instance, many companies have found that very different styles and perspectives are needed for effectively managing West Coast, deep South, Midwest, and Midatlantic operations.

• *Business and Industry Environment*—What are the key success factors in this industry? Where are the big opportunities and threats? How turbulent is the industry? Answers to these questions change over the life cycle of an industry.[10] However, unpatterned pressures can arise as well. For example, the onslaught of low-price foreign competition has made cost controls an essential ingredient for success in the automotive industry. The recent insider-trading scandals that rocked Wall Street have profound implications for managerial selection in the large investment banks.

• *Mandate/Mission from the Corporation*—What is the role of this business in the firm's portfolio? Is it to generate cash flow? growth? technology? What constraints will be imposed? Obviously, a mandate for growth along with big infusions of cash requires very different managerial qualities and temperaments than a mandate for squeezing cash out of the business.[11]

• *Strategic Thrusts*—What product/markets segments have we chosen to emphasize?

What will be our primary basis for competing? low unit costs? product innovation? customization and service? Each of these approaches to the marketplace, as well as others that could be envisioned, requires its own mix of managerial strengths. For instance, Miles and Snow found that firms which compete successfully by continual product innovation (prospectors) have relatively heavier representation of marketing and product development specialists within their top teams than do firms which compete successfully with a stable product line (defenders).[12]

Obviously, if an enduring strategy has yet to be settled, the context then calls for team members who can contribute to development of a sound strategy. However, when a strategy has been decided, and the general manager has confidence in its correctness, it is then crucial that the team possess the special competences required for the plan's execution.[13]

- *Key Points of Interdependence*—Where do information flows, negotiations, and inter-unit decisions have to be particularly smooth and fast? between manufacturing and marketing? R&D and marketing? Derived both from the environment and the chosen strategy of the business, key collaborative nodes create the need for communication and negotiation skills, often even a certain "chemistry," between the parties involved. For example, a company attempting an aggressive product innovation strategy in the medical instrumentation industry found that the heads of marketing and R&D, while both very strong in their own areas, were not compatible or sufficiently compromising with each other. The strategy foundered severely and both individuals had to be replaced.

External interdependencies must also be considered. The business may depend on a tight, symbiotic relationship with outside parties who need to be understood in considering an optimal team. For instance, a business engaged in defense contracting has to achieve a close familiarity with governmental procedures and personalities. The firm engaged in a high-technology strategy may need strong ties to, and an affinity for, university researchers.

- *Human Resource Profile*—What are the capabilities, values, and beliefs of the employees? Are they enthusiastic? cynical? frightened? out of date? The work of the business can only be done through its people, and the managers—particularly their communications and leadership abilities—must be suited to garnering the effective efforts from the workforce. This is a particularly important consideration in turn-around or depressed situations.

- *Key Management Associates*—What are the capabilities and repertoire, of the other key members of the management team? No executive position or person can be considered in isolation. There must be a thorough assessment of the people who are already part of the team, so that the desirable degrees of complementarity and depth can be achieved. Such considerations especially apply when a single position on the team needs to be filled.

Identifying the Ideal Team Profile

Having analyzed the context in which the management team must operate, the team architect turns next to establishing an ideal profile for the team. This can be done in broad overall terms or it can be attempted with substantial precision on a position-by-position basis. The latter approach is far better, since the presence of certain qualities in a specific position are usually far more important than their mere presence somewhere on the overall team. Put another way, there may be certain characteristics which everyone on the team should ideally possess and yet others which are desirable only in certain specific positions.

There are many potential dimensions for assessing managerial attributes. For instance, Levinson identifies 20 dimensions for evaluating leaders, including such factors as tolerance for ambiguity, sense of humor, and perseverance.[14] Similarly, Stringer describes an inventory of 36 managerial attributes which Pepsi-Cola International uses for evaluating managers.[15] The list includes such items as industry knowledge, writing skills, and drive.

These approaches are suggestive but far too limiting. They pretend to completeness and uniform appropriateness, although, in a given situation, neither may be the case.

The preferable approach is to propose very broad arenas of managerial wherewithal but then leave to the general manager the identification of specific dimensions for profiling the team. This choice of specific qualities should be based on the contextual analysis already conducted, as well as on the general manager's own highly personalized model of the key ingredients for managerial or team success. We turn now to a discussion of the broad areas in which the general manager will want to develop his or her own customized set of profiling dimensions.

- *Values*—The first broad area for considering executive makeup is values. Namely, what fundamental beliefs are important to have represented on the team? Values of humanism, aesthetics, hard work, wealth, novelty, and ethics are among those that might be considered in characterizing the ideal team. Values affect an executive's contributions to a team in three ways.[16] First, values cause executives to prefer certain behaviors and outcomes over others. Second, they affect the way in which the person searches and filters data used in decision making. Third, values affect the person's receptivity to any incentives and

norms the general manager may try to establish.

- *Aptitudes*—Positions on the team also need to be mapped out according to the aptitudes, or personal capacities, needed among its members. Examples of aptitudes are creativity, intellect, tolerance for ambiguity, and interpersonal awareness. Essentially, aptitudes are those qualities that are not amenable to short-term change. As such, they typically cannot be manipulated by training or incentives, at least in the short term.

- *Skills*—The team will also require a certain mix of skills. These are more concrete and usually more observable than aptitudes. Examples of skills that might be needed are communications, negotiation, economic analysis, planning, and delegating. Skills are somewhat dependent upon a person's aptitudes, but they are more prone to development and refinement.

- *Knowledge*—The context also imposes certain knowledge requirements on the ideal team. In-depth familiarity with certain industry, technical, or functional-area issues, legal or regulatory factors, and marketplace trends are illustrative of the knowledge bases that may be needed. Obviously, the more technically or legally complex the business, the greater the knowledge requirements. Compared to the other broad arenas, knowledge is perhaps most amenable to immediate and significant change within a person.

- *Cognitive Style*—It is widely accepted among psychologists that people differ appreciably in how they process information and make decisions. While the differences may not be as simple as ascribing "left-brain" and "right-brain" qualities, a major distinction is between orderly/analytic and nonlinear/intuitive thinkers.[17] The mix of the two modes within a team will greatly affect the team's strategic decisions—both their formulation and implementation. In turn, the appropriate mix of the two styles depends on the context in which the team must operate.

For example, the CEO of a large firm consisting primarily of mature, medium-technology, industrial products concluded that his team of highly analytic, engineering-educated managers (including himself) were at a loss in comprehending and anticipating a new environment unfolding around them. Their industries were being rocked by radical technological breakthroughs, emergence of many new small competitors, and globalization. The team was well suited to digesting quantitative, tabular, incremental data, but it had little facility for grasping or acting upon the qualitative, incomplete, and rapid-fire explosion of information around them. The CEO complained, "We're typical engineers. We wait for data to become clear, firm, and graphable. By the time that happens, today's competition has passed us by."

- *Demeanor*—The intangible aura, style, or demeanor of members of a management team is a final area of consideration. Such qualities as enthusiasm, warmth, poise, or stateliness can be of central importance in constituting a management team. These characteristics would be especially relevant when constituencies are skeptical of the firm's prospects and motives, i.e., where the management team needs to provide some outward and immediate measure of legitimacy and strength.

These six arenas, comprising the range of qualities the general manager should consider for his or her team, serve as triggers for identifying specifically relevant dimensions for team success. The specific dimensions should be based on the earlier contextual analysis as well as on the general manager's highly per-

sonal view of the managerial ingredients needed for success of the business. As noted above, the general manager should attempt to specify the amounts of each quality that are needed for specific positions within the team, thus accounting for inherent differences in the tasks of individual positions.

Assessing the Existing Team

A manager of an on-going business rarely has a blank slate for a team. People are already in most, if not all, of the positions. The next step in the team analysis, then, is to carefully and fairly assess the qualities of the incumbents on the dimensions specified in the process discussed above.

Managers typically pride themselves in being good judges of people and in having an accurate and complete sense of the talents of their team members. Yet, many managers—even very good ones—carry only partial, fragmented views of their subordinates' repertoires. Appraising members of the team is something that must be vigorously worked at. It will not occur without pointed effort.

The manager must engage in continual observation, testing and probing, not in a threatening or adversarial manner, but in a way that somehow allows the boundaries of each person's repertoire to become apparent. Talking to each person's peers and subordinates is an important way of gathering insights. Also, getting out from behind the desk—or what Peters and Waterman would call "managing by wandering around"[18]—to watch each person carry out his or her job is an important part of the data-gathering process. Depending on the general manager's style and beliefs, he or she may wish to use standard psychological or assessment techniques with the assistance of trained consultants.[19] However, the reliability of such techniques is mixed, and their administration to senior colleagues is usually not well received.

There is simply no substitute for careful, persistent observation of people engaged in a range of real managerial challenges.

Narrowing the Gaps

After the ideal team profile has been constructed and the incumbents have been gauged against the ideal, a plan for closing, or at least narrowing, the gaps between ideal and actuality must be designed. Required is a blend of ingenuity, open-mindedness, tough-mindedness, and humaneness on the part of the general manager. If the gaps are large, changes must be made or the business has a dim future. Fortunately, the array of possible changes is often immense, some involving less turmoil and discomfort than others.

Several broad categories of options can be considered. Since usually several types of gaps exist, these approaches will typically be used in combination rather than in isolation.

The first three options involve bringing new people on to the team:

- hiring or promoting replacements,
- hiring or promoting additions to the team, which essentially amounts to a re-structuring (either creating a new post or elevating an existing post to the top team level), and
- using consultants or outside talent as adjuncts to the team.

This last option, rarely considered, is particularly useful when a major knowledge deficiency exists within the current team. The use of limited-term adjuncts to managerial teams is a trend of growing importance, and one which provides the general manager maximum flexibility and quickness in securing needed skills.[20] However, "contract players" usually can only be used in staff support areas, since any supervisory or line powers can create serious morale problems among other members of the team.

The remaining three options involve efforts to secure more or different types of contributions from existing members of the team:

- incentives,
- training and development, and
- coaching and counsel.

Basically, these methods should be used if the general manager believes that the targeted team members have the inherent values and aptitudes that are needed in their posts, but that on other key dimensions—particularly skills, knowledge, or demeanor—they are delivering less than is needed. These methods hold great promise for stimulating or re-directing even the most senior executives.[21]

The choice of whether and how to use the six gap-closing alternatives depends on the general manager's assessment of the benefits and costs of each. The general manager should apply his or her own criteria, but at least four tests of each option should be considered.

- What is the *dollar cost?* Namely, can we financially afford to try to reshape the team in this way?
- What is the *organizational cost?* That is, how would this action affect morale, intensity of effort, and team interactions?
- *How quickly* would this action have its desired effect? Often certain avenues are closed because they would simply take too long to achieve their end.
- Finally, what is the likelihood or *assurance* that the action would have its desired effect? Some actions, including the hiring of new people, simply have low or unknown probabilities of solving the problem.

The general manager needs to face up to these sometime remote possibilities and be sure not to undertake costly actions just on the "off-chance" they will work.

Looping-Back to the Context

After applying these tests to the most promising options for closing gaps on the team, the general manager may conclude that the needed changes are flatly infeasible. This could be because of strong norms or personal preferences about removing people, the costs involved, or the amount of time involved. In short, it is possible that the gaps simply cannot be closed, at least not in the timeframe needed for competitive success.

If this impasse occurs, the manager must loop back in his or her analysis and re-think the context in which the team will operate. In short, if the team can't be changed, then the context must be changed. It may be that the manager will have to readjust the intended strategy—the markets emphasized or the competitive weapons used—in order to accommodate the talents now on the team. The manager may also need to modify his or her way of operating with the team—perhaps delegating less than was hoped, requesting more frequent reports from subordinates, serving as mediator, and so on.

In sum, the effective manager understands the critical role of the management team in achieving strategic success. He or she is creative and far-reaching in identifying options, but tough-minded about bringing the team into alignment with the competitive context in which the business must operate. At the same time, however, the successful team architect understands the constraints on the task and possesses the flexibility and fluidity to be able to creatively re-think his or her original game plan. In this way, the exceptional strategist conceives of the top team as a key element of both strategy formulation and implementation.

CASE OF THE SCRIBE DIVISION

Following is a disguised case about a general manager who applied the framework for team analysis as part of his overall effort to turn around the performance of an ailing business. As will be seen, he followed the general logic stream of the framework while tailoring it to his own circumstances and style. Therefore, his approach should not be taken as the only or best way to systematically assess a team, but simply as an illustration of the perspective set forth in this chapter and as an indication of the array of issues and options it helps identify.

A New Strategy

Walter Newberry was brought in from a competing firm to be general manager of the Scribe writing instrument division of a large multibusiness firm. The division, with sales of $300 million, had languished for the previous five years, losing market share and making only modest profits. Its strategy during this period had mirrored some major trends in the industry: offshore (Far East) production, minimal promotion expenditures, price-based competition, and heavy emphasis on the price-sensitive government and commercial markets. Unfortunately, Scribe's moderate market share simply did not allow it the low unit costs to compete well in its chosen segments.

After three months of intense analysis and deliberations with his managers and consultants, Mr. Newberry developed a strategy which he thought would yield a solid future for Scribe. The summary of his strategy, as presented to and approved by corporate top management, was as follows:

> Scribe must do things differently if it is going to compete with the giants. Above all, Scribe must avoid head-on price competition at the low end of the product spectrum. Instead, the emphasis should be on aggressive development of new products and product variations (new product features, new styling, new packaging, etc.) that will sell at a mid-level price (between BIC and Gillette on the one hand and Cross and Parker

on the other hand). An integral part of this strategy depends on being able to segment the market and develop innovations to match. Scribe must become a marketing company, adept at market research, translation of market research into product development, and media advertising. This strategy of innovation requires change in the distribution of our product. We will decrease our emphasis on small stationery and drugstores, as well as the commercial and government markets. A major push will be through national drug, department store, and gift/bookstore chains.

The Team Context—

Newberry knew that the success of his new strategy depended on his management team. He had had a chance to work with these people—particularly the five functional heads who reported directly to him—during the process of formulating the new strategy. He had watched these people closely during this time, trying to observe their range of capabilities and potential. He had formed a number of impressions, but as so often happens, he felt he was lacking a coherent, overarching sense of the team. He felt the same way about his sense of what would constitute an ideal team. He had some scattered, piecemeal thoughts, but he did not feel he had a complete or well-developed picture of the talents he would need. He decided to approach this critical task systematically, using a tailored version of the process discussed in this chapter.

His starting point was to carefully assess the context in which the team would have to operate. His assessment of the external context led him to several conclusions. First, he knew that all external parties—customers, press, distributors, and so on—had higher standards for business communication and openness than had ever existed before. Second, when he looked at the writing instrument industry, he saw increasing price competition from imports and the consequent likelihood that other major

firms would try, like Scribe, to escape by moving into higher styled, more differentiated segments. The industry was going to be more competitive than ever. Third, his mandate from the parent firm was very clear: "We want Scribe to be a balanced generator of profits and growth. We will make modest infusions of cash for up to three years in order to allow the business to achieve this balanced strength."

The key features of the internal context stemmed primarily from the new strategy. The key strategic drivers were going to be product innovation, styling, and creative marketing. In manufacturing, cost control would be important, but quality would be essential. Key points of interdependence—where negotiations and cooperation would need to be fluid—were between marketing and R&D, as well as between manufacturing and R&D. In assessing the human resource profile, Newberry concluded that the limited remaining U.S. production workforce was technically capable but probably lacking in concern for quality. It was among the marketing and sales employees that Newberry was most concerned. Few marketing people, *per se,* even existed, and the unpolished sales force consisted largely of "ordertakers" whose primary selling angle had always been price and delivery. Overall, Newberry also saw a general malaise and cynicism among employees.

The Ideal Team Profile

It was against this backdrop that Newberry set out to identify the attributes he would need on his team. He began only with the six broad categories—values, knowledge, etc.—and then identified specific dimensions of importance under each. The resulting list of 18 dimensions is shown in Table 1.

It is important to emphasize that Newberry's list of profiling areas is uniquely his. As noted earlier, there can be no standard, universal approach to this important task. The choice of areas of concern is derived from the contex-

TABLE 1. *What Managerial Qualities are Needed?*

	General Manager	Director of Marketing	Director of R&D	Director of Manu-facturing	Controller	Director of Human Resources
Values						
High Standards for Business Performance	5	4	4	4	4	4
Commitment to Aesthetics	5	5	5	5	3	3
Work is Fun; Good Humor	5	4	4	4	4	4
High Ethical Standards	5	5	5	5	5	5
Aptitudes						
Creativity	4	5	5	4	3	3
Intellect	4	4	4	4	4	4
Social/Cultural Awareness	5	5	4	3	2	4
Skills						
Interpersonal and Communications	5	5	4	4	3	4
Business/Economic Analysis	4	5	3	5	5	3
Negotiation/Compromise	5	5	4	5	2	3
Knowledge						
Writing Instrument Technology and Markets	4	5	5	5	3	2
Gift and Premium Buyer Behavior	5	5	4	3	3	3
State-of-art Management Concepts	4	5	3	4	4	3
Cognitive Style						
Orderly/Analytic	3	3	4	4	5	3
Nonlinear/Intuitive	5	5	5	3	3	4
Demeanor/Style						
"Stylish/Classy"	5	5	3	4	3	4
Open/Flexible	5	5	5	4	4	4
Sense of Enthusiasm/ Dynamism	5	5	5	4	4	4

tual analysis as well as from the general manager's own values and style. In Newberry's list, for instance, knowledge about Gift and Premium Buyer Behavior and aptitude for Social and Cultural Awareness follow directly from the imperatives of the new strategy. Newberry's inclusion of the value, High Standards for Business Performance, was largely due to his strong feeling that his colleagues in his former company had been content to be survivors and lacked the will to excel. He thus had a "hang-up" about high standards, seeing this dimension as crucial to team success.

After generating his array of relevant

team qualities, Newberry turned to an assessment of how important each quality would be for each position on the team. He decided to approach this step quantitatively, although a numerical approach is neither necessary nor, perhaps in some eyes, even desirable. Newberry's quantitative ratings are presented here not because they are a preferred way, but because they allow a relatively concise portrayal of a complex process. (To Newberry's credit, he had many pages of personal notes which accompanied his numerical tallies.)

Newberry rated each of the six positions on his team, including the general management position, by asking this question of himself: "On a scale of one (very low) to five (very high), what is the minimum amount of each quality that should be held by the ideal incumbent?" Obviously, realism must be borne in mind—all fives are not possible. While it is desirable that the points on such a scale have absolute meaning, in actuality a concrete meaning for, say, a 5, is not essential; what is important is that the same relative frame of reference be used for this step (rating ideals) as for the next step (rating what now exists).

As can be seen, Newberry wanted homogeneity on some dimensions (such as most of the values) and heterogeneity, or complementarity, on other dimensions (such as cognitive style). Not surprisingly, he set very high standards for the marketing and R&D positions, since he considered them of paramount importance for execution of the new strategy.

Evaluating the Current Team

Drawing upon his several months of observation of his team, he then rated each member of the current team on all 18 dimensions (see Table 2). The director of manufacturing had retired just before Newberry arrived and had not yet been replaced, therefore no incumbent ratings were conducted for that position. Otherwise, all ratings were attempted. Asterisks in

Table 2 denote gaps between the ideal and what actually existed.

A number of patterns emerged, but several in particular warrant noting. First, the director of marketing seemed to have serious, pervasive shortcomings for his position. Newberry had found him very bright and hardworking, but gruff, stubborn, and interpersonally and socially ill at ease; he also didn't have the creativity or intuition Newberry thought were needed in the job. The director of human resources was rated below the ideal on 14 of the dimensions, with serious shortfalls in attitudinal areas—good humor and enthusiasm/dynamism. The controller had several shortfalls, perhaps most notably in business/economic analysis and state-of-the-art management concepts.

Taking a different view, by looking across the columns, it can be seen that team-wide deficiencies existed in two major areas: knowledge of gift and premium buyer behavior and openness/flexibility.

It is worth noting that Newberry rated himself below the ideal on several dimensions. Whether he was sufficiently self-critical we cannot assess, however he appeared willing to admit that he himself had room for improvement.

Closing the Gaps

With his assessment done, Newberry began to consider actions. First, he concluded that he would have to modify his new strategy. He had planned to make the complete switch to the higher-priced, higher-styled strategy over a two-year period. Now fully appreciating the limitations of his team—particularly its lack of knowledge of the gift and premium market, but other notable shortfalls as well—he decided to carry out the transition over a four-year period. Thus, his team analysis led to a strategy modification. If he had done a careful team analysis earlier, he might have factored the re-

TABLE 2. *What Managerial Qualities Now Exist?*

	General Manager	Director of Marketing	Director of R&D	Director of Manufacturing	Controller	Director of Human Resources
Values						
High Standards for Business Performance	5	4	3*		4	3*
Commitment to Aesthetics	5	3**	4*		3	2*
Work is Fun; Good Humor	5	4	5		3*	2**
High Ethical Standards	5	5	5		5	5
Aptitudes						
Creativity	4	3**	5		3	2*
Intellect	4	5	4		5	3*
Social/Cultural Awareness	4	3**	4		3	3*
Skills						
Interpersonal and Communications	4*	3**	4		3	3*
Business/Economic Analysis	4	5	3		3**	2*
Negotiation/Compromise	4*	4*	4		2	2*
Knowledge						
Writing Instrument Technology and Markets	2**	5	5		3	3
Gift and Premium Buyer Behavior	4*	3**	2**		1**	1**
State-of-art Management Concepts	3*	4*	3		2**	3
Cognitive Style						
Orderly/Analytic	3	4	4		5	3
Nonlinear/Intuitive	5	2**	4*		3	3*
Demeanor/Style						
"Stylish/Classy"	5	3**	4		3	3*
Open/Flexible	3**	3**	5		3*	3*
Sense of Enthusiasm/Dynamism	5	5	5		3*	2**

*is 1-point shortfall
**is 2-point (or more) shortfall

sults into the initial strategy formulation as part of a customary strengths and weaknesses analysis. The important point, however, is that Newberry recognized how crucial the team's abilities would be to successful execution of the new strategy and had the good sense to know that those abilities simply did not exist and probably could not be acquired or developed on the tight timetable he had envisioned.

This change of strategy then led to a

change in structure. It was clear to Newberry that he would essentially have to run the old and the new businesses in parallel for the foreseeable future. He decided to create a structural subunit for the old business—which he called Government and Commercial—and appoint a director for it. He did not have to look far for the ideal candidate. The current Director of Marketing, although ill-suited for the new high-styled business, was ideally suited for broadened responsibilities in Scribe's traditional domain. His intellect, analytic and business skills, and in-depth knowledge of the writing instrument industry all fit well with the strategic challenges facing the Government and Commercial Market: intense negotiations with off-shore producers, marketing with an emphasis on volume and price, and establishment of efficient logistical systems. Whether Newberry came up with the idea of this new position before or after he had the Director of Marketing in mind for it is not clear. What is very apparent is that the systematic team analysis led to a clarity of options and issues.

In turn, there was the need for a director of marketing for the new line. Newberry turned outside and hired a person whose profile matched very closely with what was needed, including having significant experience in the gift and premium market. One of the first things Newberry asked this new person to do was to design a series of one-day workshops for the entire top management team dealing with the gift and premium market. The new person was to identify the top outside experts in the field to conduct these sessions. He was also charged with setting up a series of visits for Newberry, himself, and the R&D director to major gift and premium buyers. Thus, Newberry used his team analysis to identify the qualities needed in a new hire, but just as important was his use of the analysis to develop a plan for leveraging the new person's repertoire in a way to enhance the whole team.

Newberry decided to have a heart-to-heart, after-hours talk with the human resources director. Fully expecting that he would have to replace this person, Newberry encountered new insights about him. He had known already that the man was going through a divorce, but he had not known how traumatic it had been or that it had caused serious problems for the man's teenage children. Newberry essentially concluded that his assessment of the person had been, or may have been, off the mark. The man's apparent lethargy, distraction, and uninspired behavior were not inherent; they were temporary. The two questions in Newberry's mind were: "Can all this be overcome in time for this guy to be a productive team member? Can I play a role in the process?" The personal meetings continued; Newberry worked hard at listening and encouraging; he worked to make the man feel an integral part of the team, whereas he had been a secondary figure under Newberry's predecessor. Circumstances and good managing allowed this person to become an effective, fully contributing member of the team over the ensuing months. Here, an interesting lesson emerges. Namely, our assessments of people can sometimes be wrong; however, an explicit process of assessment can help guide us to where the problems may lie and where we may want to especially reaffirm our data.

The situation with the controller was somewhat similar. In a one-on-one, after-hours meeting, it became apparent to Newberry that the controller's lack of enthusiasm and good humor came from the fact that he was certain he would be fired. He was out-of-date with his profession, and he knew it. He was sure Newberry would replace him with a younger person, better versed in modern control and information systems. Newberry did come close to firing him, but he kept coming back to the man's strengths, including a great deal of evidence that he was fundamentally a smart, analytic person. Newberry then laid a developmental plan. He asked the controller to head a special project to analyze the economics of the new product strategy. Other insiders would serve on the task force and it would also be supported by outside consultants from the parent firm's auditors. Newberry's implicit agenda was twofold (beyond getting the study done): he wanted the controller to learn a great deal at the hands of the outside consultants, and he wanted the controller to develop confidence in his ability to learn. Newberry made these somewhat uncustomary goals clear to the senior outside consultant when he approached the firm. The result was that the controller made substantial progress— learning a great deal, developing an enthusiasm for learning more, and becoming an integral, effective part of the team.

Newberry's experiences with the controller and the human resources director warrant attention. In both cases, Newberry set out to establish a more intimate and accurate information exchange than he thought could be accomplished in everyday business activity. This did not come naturally for Newberry. In fact, he was struggling to overcome the aloofness and autocratic style that superiors and peers had criticized him for throughout his managerial career. He had taken these criticisms to heart in rating himself (Table 2). In his dealings with these two members of his team, we observe a purposeful, albeit strained, experiment with tremendously positive results for the business and for the people involved. In sum, if the team analysis is well done, it can lead to self-insight and self-development for the general manager himself or herself.

All of these actions, as well as establishment of new aggressive incentives based on overall performance of the business, were carried out within Newberry's first six months in the Scribe division. Two years after Newberry took over, Scribe was recognized within the parent firm as a dramatic turnaround success. Sales were up 35 percent, with about half the gains coming from the traditional line and half from the new line (which achieved an impressive ten percent of its served market within a year of introduction). Profits had doubled, and the division's return on assets was above (well above) the parent firm's average for the first time in many years.

SUMMARY

The strategic success of a business depends not on just one person but on the entire top management team. If the aptitudes, values, skills, and knowledge base of the top few people do not fit with what is required by the competitive environment, or if they do not mesh with each other, the business will encounter serious trouble. Conversely, the business with a top team whose qualities are well suited to emerging trends in the environment, as well as forming a complementary whole, will have the best chance of competitive success.

This chapter has presented a comprehensive framework for conducting this important managerial task. While leaving room for ample tailoring to the general manager's own style and preferences, the framework provides a generalized procedure:

- understand the context in which the team will operate,
- develop a profile of the ideal team for that context,
- fairly and carefully assess the current team, and
- develop a plan for closing the gaps between what is needed and what exists.

Ideally, a well developed, on-going executive development system will reliably address many of these issues. However, at times, an in-depth, *ad hoc* analysis may be important.

The case of Walt Newberry at Scribe illustrates how the framework can help greatly sharpen the issues and options confronting a team architect. His successes were no doubt aided by good fortune and other factors, but his integrated approach to team design was instrumental in the advances he was able to make. Managers who, like Newberry, face increasingly competitive environments must understand the real key to strategic success is the group of people who formulate and implement the strategy. The task of selecting, developing, and molding that group into a fit team is at the heart of the general manager's job.

REFERENCES

1. D.C. Hambrick and P.A. Mason, "Upper Echelons: The Organization as a Reflection of Its Top Managers," *Academy of Management Review*, 9 (1984):193–206.

2. G.T. Allison, *The Essence of Decision: Explaining the Cuban Missile Crisis* (Boston, MA: Little Brown, 1971); I.L. Janis and L. Mann, *Decision Making: A Psychological Analysis of Conflict, Choice, and Commitment* (New York, NY: Free Press, 1977); B.W. Tuchman, *The March of Folly: From Troy to Vietnam* (New York, NY: Ballantine, 1984).

3. D. Miller, M.F. Kets DeVries, and J.M. Toulouse, "Top Executive Locus of Control and Its Relationship to Strategy-Making, Structure, and Environment," *Academy of Management Journal*, 25 (1982):237–253; D. Miller and J.M. Toulouse, "Chief Executive Personality and Corporate Strategy and Structure in Small Firms," *Management Science*, 32 (1986):1389–1409.

4. A.K. Gupta and V. Govindarajan, "Business Unit Strategy, Managerial Characteristics, and Business Unit Effectiveness at Strategy Implementation," *Academy of Management Journal*, 27 (1984):25–41.

5. J.R. Meindl, S.B. Ehrlich, and J.M. Dukerich, "The Romance of Leadership," *Administrative Science Quarterly*, 30 (March 1985):78–102.

6. J. Hage and R. Dewer, "Elite Values Versus Organizational Structure in Predicting Innovation," *Administrative Science Quarterly*, 18/3 (September 1973):279–290.

7. M.L. Tushman, B. Virany, and E. Romanelli, "Executive Succession, Strategic Reorientations, and Organizational Evolution," *Technology and Society*, 7 (1985):297–313.

8. M. Shao, "Exxon's Mining Unit Finds It Tough Going," *Wall Street Journal*, August 31, 1982, p. 1.

9. K. Auletta, "The Fall of Lehman Brothers: The Men, The Money, The Merger," *New York Times Magazine*, February 24, 1985, p. 36.

10. W.L. Moore and M.L. Tushman, "Managing Innovation Over the Life Cycle," in M.L. Tushman and W.L. Moore, eds., *Readings in the Management of Innovation* (Boston, MA: Pitman, 1982), pp. 131–150; M.W. Porter, *Competitive Strategy* (New York, NY: Free Press, 1980).

11. M. Gerstein and H. Reisman, "Strategic Selection: Matching Executives to Business Conditions," *Sloan Management Review*, 24/2 (Winter 1983):33–49; Gupta and Govindarajan, op. cit.

12. R. E. Miles and C.C. Snow, *Organization Strategy, Structure, and Process* (New York, NY: McGraw-Hill, 1978).

13. A.K. Gupta, "Matching Managers to Strategies: Point and Counterpoint," *Human Resources Management*, 25 (1986): 215–234.

14. H. Levinson, "Criteria for Choosing Chief Executives," *Harvard Business Review*, 58/4 (1980):113–120.

15. R.A. Stringer, Jr., *Strategy Traps* (Lexington, MA: Lexington Books, 1986).

16. G.W. England, "Personal Value Systems of American Managers," *Academy of Management Journal*, 10 (1967):53–68; D.C. Hambrick and G.L. Brandon, "Executive Values," in D.C. Hambrick, ed., *The Executive Effect: Concepts and Methods for Studying Top Managers* (Greenwich, CT: JAI Press, 1987).

17. H. Mintzberg, "Planning on the Left Side and Managing on the Right," *Harvard Business Review*, 54/4 (1976):49–58; W. Taggart and D. Robey, "Minds and Managers: On the Dual Nature of Human Information Processing and Management," *Academy of Management Review*, 6 (1981):187–195.

18. T.E. Peters and R.H. Waterman, Jr., *In Search of*

Excellence (New York, NY: Harper and Row, 1982).

19. Gerstein and Reisman, op. cit.

20. S. Lee and S. Flack, "HiHo, Silver," *Forbes,* March 9, 1987, pp. 90–98.

21. J.F. Bolt, "Tailor Executive Development to Strategy," *Harvard Business Review,* 63/6 (1985):168–176; D.C. Hambrick and C.C. Snow, "Strategic Reward Systems," in C.C. Snow, ed., *Strategy, Organization Design and Human Resource Management* (Greenwich, CT: JAI Press, 1987).

Neurotic Style and Organization Pathology

Manfred F. R. Kets de Vries

Danny Miller

Summary *Many parallels can be drawn between organizational and individual pathologies. We believe that the fantasies of top executives and the neurotic styles to which they give rise are important determinants of the nature of organizational dysfunctions. This is particularly true in centralized organizations where the top executives have a major impact upon organizational climate, structure, strategy and even the selection of the environment; and, where organizational recruitment and promotion processes ensure uniformity, or at least conformity, among the top ranks of executives. Using an empirically derived taxonomy, we have isolated five common pathological organizational types and related each of these to the fantasies and neurotic styles of their top executives. Each type is shown to reflect a large number of elements of structure and strategy that are consistent with and probably caused by the neurotic style of the cadre of top executives. The types are called* paranoid, compulsive, histrionic, depressive *and* schizoid. *Implications for management research and organizational change are discussed.*

It may be appropriate to begin this paper with a personal note. One of the authors is a practising psychoanalyst, management professor and organizational consultant. He kept noticing a certain amount of similarity between findings from his psychoanalytic practice and his consulting. Organizational problems and orientations seemed very much to mirror the clinical findings about the personalities of the top echelon of executives. There seemed to be an intimate connection between the two, with, for example, organizations run by those with a paranoid disposition having many manifestations of such paranoia in strategy, structure and organizational climate.

The other author has done extensive research trying to identify recurrent organizational Gestalts or common and predictively useful configurations: those which highlight the integral interdependencies among elements of organizational strategy, structure and environment. His sporadic forays into the psychiatric and psychoanalytic literature seemed to point to the power of using the most common clinical configurations as organizing constructs for erecting a typology of problematic organizational adaptive styles. Our previous work in deriving empirical organizational taxonomies elicited five failure or borderline success types that were intimately related to five very common neurotic styles found among individuals. This was quite surprising since executive personalities were not used to generate the original taxonomy.

Human functioning is generally characterized by a mixture of neurotic styles. The same person may possess elements of many different styles, each of which gets triggered in different circumstances. Among many individuals, however, we can discern the predominance of one specific style that comes to consistently characterize many aspects of behaviour. Any extreme manifestations of one particular style can eventually lead to serious impairment of functioning, and psychopathology. Our experience with top executives and organizations revealed that parallels could be drawn between individual pathology—the excessive use of one neurotic style—and organizational pathology, the latter resulting in poorly functioning organizations. This theme is explored more broadly by Kets de Vries and Miller (1982a).

Admittedly, interdisciplinary research is frought with hazards. It is all too easy to take a conceptual framework from one field and to apply it blindly to another very different field. For example the organismic analogy in organizational theory has been exceedingly popular and perhaps of considerable value, but it has resulted in obscuring key differences between organisms and organizations (Keeley, 1980). We therefore need a plausible rationale for making the link between intrapsychic phenomena as manifested by neurotic style, and organizational adaptive characteristics. This we shall attempt to provide. Although the framework we are about to propose is quite speculative, we do not think that it is by any means facile.

SCOPE

It is important to delimit our scope at the outset to prevent any misunderstandings about the generality of our framework. We shall be focusing upon relatively dysfunctional top executives—that is, those who have *significant* neurotic tendencies that influence their managerial behavior. Most executives of healthy firms do not let their mild neuroses influence their performance. Moreover, we shall be trying to relate the most common neurotic styles to the problems of some very common *pathological* types of organizations. That is, our framework will be more useful to help us to understand dysfunctional rather than healthy organizations. These are very numerous. In fact, of Miller and Friesen's (1978) sample, almost *half* comprised firms with strong pathological elements. Our model will be most applicable to firms in which decision making power is *centralized* in the hands of a neurotic top executive or a small, homogeneous dominant coalition. Where power is broadly distributed throughout a firm, its strategies will be determined by many managers, each of whom may have quite a different personality. This would make it difficult to draw inferences between human and organizational behavior. Finally, we shall be concerned with the *highest level of management,* and with the top *'corporate' level* rather than 'business' level strategies (Schendel and Hofer, 1979:12–13). Top managers normally have the most impact on their organizations, so it is wise, as a first step, to focus our attention upon them. Their concern is usually with corporate level issues and strategies, but where their neurotic tendencies prevent such a focus, and redirect it towards business level policies, our attention will shift accordingly. We believe that neurotic styles can have an impact at all levels of the organization but wish here to limit our scope to top management. At this stage it is not at all clear how the neurotic styles of different organizational members interact to influence overall strategy and structure.

NEUROTIC STYLES AND ORGANIZATIONS

The personality of the top manager can in very important ways influence strategy and even structure (Miller, Kets de Vries and Toulouse, 1982). It can certainly influence organizational climate (Kernberg, 1979; Jaques, 1951, 1970; Maccoby, 1976; Payne and Pugh, 1976; Zaleznik and Kets de Vries, 1975; Kets de Vries, 1980, 1982). There is much formal, empirical and anecdotal evidence to support this link. Unfortunately, the tendency has been to look at one simple aspect of personality, such as locus of control (Phares, 1976; Lefcourt, 1976), need for achievement (McClelland, 1961), need for power (McClelland, 1975) etc., and to relate it to one or two organizational variables such as the participativeness of decision making (Vroom, 1960; Tosi, 1970), formalization or bureaucratization (Merton, 1968), and so on. Research built on single traits or attitudes can be quite misleading. Complex situations are reduced to one dimension as though that dimension alone could explain much of the phenomenon under study or could exist independently of the broader aspects of personality.

We thought that the psychoanalytic and psychiatric literature (especially as represented by the works of Fenichel (1945), Laplanche and Pontalis (1973), Shapiro (1965), Freedman, Kaplan and Sadock (1975) and Nicholi (1978)) might be more useful than the more standard psychological literature, because it provides a more complete and far more integrated view of intrapsychic functioning and behaviour. Instead of focusing on one narrow trait or attitude of the executive, it might be more useful to look at personality styles—those patterns of behaviour by which the individual relates himself to external reality and to his own internal dispositions. Personality styles can explain a multiplicity of behaviours. The focus is on clusters of behaviour patterns which remain relatively stable over the years, as opposed to simple dimensions of behaviour. These may better enable us to make a link between an executive's intrapsychic world and actual behavior in organizations.

THE EMERGENCE OF NEUROSES AND NEUROTIC FIRMS

Psychoanalytic object relations[1] theoreticians stress that interpersonal interactions as well as instinctual needs are central in the development of personality (Klein, 1948; Fairbairn, 1952; Balint, 1965; Guntrip, 1969; Jacobson, 1964; Sandler and Rosenblatt, 1962; Mahler, Pine and Bergman, 1975; Kernberg, 1976). Child observation studies reveal that behaviour is determined by an individual's representational psychic world, populated by enduring images of oneself and others. These images or mental constructs develop through the process of maturation and become encoded into the brain. They become organizing units, enabling the individual to perceive, interpret and react to sensations in a meaningful way. Typically, instinctual needs get linked to these mental representations and are transformed into wishes of various kinds which become articulated through 'fantasies'. Fantasies can be seen as original rudimentary schemata for viewing the world. They evolve in complexity and can be taken as 'scripts (scenarios) of organized scenes which are capable of dramatisation' (Laplanche and Pontalis, 1973:318). It should be noted here that we are not talking about fantasies in the whimsical sense of daydreaming, but about complex and stable psychological structures (Breuer and Freud, 1893–1895:-22). These are the building blocks making for specific neurotic styles and are thereby enduring determinants of behaviour.

We believe that the intrapsychic fantasies of key organization members are major determinants of their prevailing neurotic style. In some organizations, these in turn give rise to shared fantasies which permeate all levels of functioning, colour organizational climate, and make for a dominant organizational adaptive style (Kets de Vries and Miller, 1982b). This style will greatly influence decisions about strategy and structure. Although many specific examples of the link between a leader's neurotic style and organizational behaviour will follow, we can make our argument more concrete by pointing to one now. Let us take an organization in which power is highly centralized in a leader with paranoid tendencies. The prevailing fantasy among individuals possessing this style will be something like: 'everybody is out to get me'. The reality of the past when such experiences might have occurred seems to be reintroduced into the present, creating deviations from rational decision making. What will the strategy and structure look like, and what kind of organizational climate exists in these firms? First, there is likely to be a good deal of vigilance caused by a distrust of subordinates and competitors alike. This will lead to the development of many control and information systems; of a CIA-like fascination with gathering intelligence from inside and outside the firm. Second, paranoia will result in much centralization of power as the top executive responds to his distrust by wanting to control things himself. Third, the strategy is likely to emphasize 'protection' and reducing dependencies upon particular markets or customers. There is likely to be a good deal of diversification with tight control over the divisions and much analytical activity. There are many other links, but the message is clear—the personality of the leader driven by intrapsychic fantasies centered around distrust can set the tone for strategy, structure and organizational climate.

As we noted earlier, the relation between neurotic style and organizational behaviour will only hold when power is centralized in the organization. That way the leader gets his way and has the most impact. Otherwise, a variety of top executive personalities would cancel each other out, resulting in a neutral (or mixed) orientation. However, there is indeed a tendency in many pathological organizations for one or two top executives to strongly set the tone for the firm—to guide its strategy and create a specific structural climate (Miller and Friesen, 1978). Also, there may be uniformity or at least complementarity in neurotic styles among organizational participants in many decentralized organizations that do not have a very powerful leader. Organizational political, selection and promotion processes have a strong moulding effect, enhancing uniformity. Senior executives tend to ensure compatibility and similarity of personnel in their selection, reward-punishment and promotion procedures. For example, the paranoid top executive will seek out and promote others who share his fears; the obsessive compulsive CEO will recruit those who share his obsessions. The histrionic leader will recruit only dependent, passive and second tier managers so that he himself can make all the key decisions. All of these selection biases maximize the impact of the neurotic styles of the top executives and allow them to endure. This tendency can be reinforced by organizational myths, legends and stories, enabling organization members to identify common symbols, attain a sense of community and create *shared* fantasies (Larcon and Reitter, 1979). According to Mitroff and Kilmann: 'The corporate myth is the 'spirit' of the organization and is infused into all levels of policy and decision making' (1976:190).

This brings us to a second rationale for examining the link between neurotic styles and organizational functioning. The use of a rich set of neurotic styles will allow us to predict *many* aspects of each dysfunctional organization. For example, once we have decided that a paranoid climate prevails at the shared fantasy level in an organization, this will be manifested in *many* ways. There will be indications of paranoia in strategy, structure and organizational climate, and there may even be factors in the environment that feed or result from the paranoia. In other words, there may exist a set of mutually complementary elements that appear to be consistent and integral aspects of the same configurations; configurations which have been identified by several independently derived typologies and taxonomies. These configurations strongly suggest the utility of using neurotic styles as organizing constructs for deriving a taxonomy of organizational dysfunction for centralized firms.

We have identified five very common neurotic styles, well established in the psychoanalytic and psychiatric literature. They are: paranoid, compulsive, histrionic, depressive and schizoid. These are discussed in the latest *Diagnostic and Statistical Manual of Mental Disorders* published by the American Psychiatric Association (1980). Each style has its specific characteristics, its predominant motivating fantasy and its associated dangers. In Table 1 we present an overview of the salient characteristics of each neurotic style.

In the following descriptions of organizational pathology we will see how each of these styles strongly parallels the strategic behaviour, climate, structure, and environment of five of the types (S_3, S_2, F_1, F_2 and F_3, respectively) of Miller and Friesen's (1977, 1978) empirical taxonomy of organizations. The paranoid firms seem also to relate to some of Miles and Snow's (1978) 'analysers', the compulsive firms to Mintzberg's (1979) 'machine bureaucracies', the histrionic firms to some of Collins and Moore's (1970) entrepreneurial types, the depressive firms to Thompson's (1961), and Starbuck, Greve and Hedberg's (1978) bureaucracies, and the schizoid firms to Mintzberg's (1983) political arenas. The descriptions of the

five organizational types are based upon the empirically isolated configurations of Miller (1976) and Miller and Friesen (1977, 1978). It was only recently, however, as a result of our consulting experiences that we realized that the most common unsuccessful types seemed to manifest a broad array of attributes that mirrored a specific neurotic style and its related shared fantasy.

Five essential polarities are used to characterize the five common neurotic styles as well as the five common organizational configurations to which they give rise. These dimensions are based on various studies concerning individual differences in styles of functioning. We have selected the following dimensions: internal-external (Jung, 1920), active-passive (Fries and Woolf, 1953), high control-low control (White, 1972), impulsion-deliberation (Murray, 1938), and broad-narrow (Shapiro, 1965). These polarities will guide us in our description of the various organizational neurotic styles and are defined in the following passages.

Internal-External. This polarity is concerned with the way interests are directed. These can be focused on subjective experiences, internal needs and goals or toward external events.

Active-Passive. At one extreme we can find patterns such as initiative, assertion and exploration of surroundings. At the other extreme there is a reliance on others to initiate action.

High Control-Low Control. At one extreme there exists a preoccupation about dominating action by making and enforcing rules, curbing behavior and controlling others. At the other end of the spectrum we can find a more laissez-faire, relaxed attitude toward control.

Impulsion-Deliberation. We find on the one hand the tendency to respond quickly without reflection or forethought. On the other we observe hesitation, caution and reflection before

TABLE 1. *Summary of the Five Neurotic Styles*

Key Factors	Neurotic Styles				
	Paranoid	Compulsive	Histrionic	Depressive	Schizoid
Characteristics	Suspiciousness and mistrust of others; hypersensitivity and hyperalertness; readiness to counter perceived threats; over-concern with hidden motives and special meanings; intense attention span; cold, rational, unemotional	Perfectionistic; preoccupation with trivial details; insistence that others submit to own way of doing things; relationships seen in terms of dominance and submission; lack of spontaneity; inability to relax; meticulousness, dogmatism, obstinacy	Self dramatization, excessive expression of emotions; incessant drawing of attention to self; a craving for activity and excitement; incapacity for concentration or sharply focused attention	Feelings of guilt, worthlessness, self-reproach, inadequacy. Sense of helplessness and hopelessness—of being at the mercy of events; diminished ability to think clearly, loss of interest and motivation; inability to experience pleasure	Detachment, non-involvement, withdrawnness; sense of estrangement; lack of excitement or enthusiasm; indifference to praise or criticism; lack of interest in present or future; appearance cold, unemotional
Fantasy	I cannot really trust anybody. A menacing superior force exists which is out to get me. I had better be on my guard	I don't want to be at the mercy of events. I have to master and control all the things affecting me	I want to get attention from and impress the people who count in my life	It is hopeless to change the course of events in my life. I am just not good enough	The world of reality does not offer any satisfaction to me. All my interactions with others will eventually fail and cause harm so it is safer to remain distant
Dangers	Distortion of reality due to a preoccupation with confirmation of suspicions. Loss of capacity for spontaneous action because of defensive attitudes	Inward orientation. Indecisiveness and postponement; avoidance due to the fear of making mistakes. Inability to deviate from planned activity. Excessive reliance on rules and regulations. Difficulties in seeing 'the big picture'	Superficiality; suggestibility. The risk of operating in a non-factual world—action based on 'hunches'. Overreaction to minor events	Overly pessimistic outlook. Difficulties in concentration and performance. Inhibition of action, indecisiveness	Emotional isolation results in frustration of dependency needs of others. Bewilderment and aggressiveness may be the consequences

initiating action; there is a predilection to pre-plan and organize.

Broad-Narrow. The distinction to be made along this dimension is between organizations that are open to many factors, and those that are preoccupied with a narrow range of details.

The five organizational types are summarized in Table 2.

THE DYSFUNCTIONAL TYPES DESCRIBED

The Paranoid Organization

Shared Fantasy. I cannot really trust anybody. A superior force exists which is out to get me so I had better be on my guard.

Neurotic Style. This style is characterized by suspiciousness and mistrust of others together with a hypersensitivity of being slighted. Undue concern exists about hidden motives and special meanings, making for an intense attention span and a readiness to counter perceived threats. Pride is taken in being objective, cold, rational and unemotional.

Danger. A distortion of reality may occur due to a preoccupation with confirming suspicions. Defensive attitudes deplete the capacity for spontaneous action.

Managerial suspicions translate into a primary *emphasis upon organizational intelligence* and controls. Management information systems are very sophisticated in their methods of scanning the environment and controlling internal processes. Scanning is done to identify threats and challenges that are being levelled by government, competitors and customers. Controls take the form of budgets, cost centres, profit centres, cost accounting procedures and other methods of monitoring the performance of internal operations. Top management are suspicious and wary about people and events both inside and outside the firm. The elaborate information processing apparatus is a product of their desire for perpetual vigilance and preparedness for emergencies.

The paranoia of the top management group also takes another form. It influences the decision making behaviour of executives. Frequently, key decision makers, instead of withholding information from each other as part of their defensive mobilization, decide that it may be safer to direct their distrust externally. To protect against competitors they share informa-

TABLE 2.   *The Five Types Along the Five Dimensions*

| | Organizational Type | | | | |
Orientation	Paranoid Firm	Compulsive Firm	Histrionic Firm	Depressive Firm	Schizoid Firm
Internal-external	External	Internal	External	Internal	Internal
Active-passive	Active	Active/passive	Very active	Very passive	Passive
High control-low control	High	High	Low	Medium	Low
Impulsive-deliberative	Deliberative	Deliberative	Impulsive	Not applicable	Impulsive
Broad-narrow	Broad	Narrow	Broad	Narrow	Narrow

tion. Also, in order *to ensure an adequate response to threats, a good deal of analysis takes place in decision making.* There are concerted efforts devoted to discovering orgnizational problems and in generating and selecting alternative solutions for dealing with these problems. Decision making also tends to be consultative so that a large number of factors can be taken into consideration—thus many aspects of each problem or threat can be addressed. However, decision making can become overly consultative in that similar information is asked from different people. This 'institutionalization of suspicion' ensures that the most accurate information will gravitate to the top of the firm, but it may also result in a drop in organizational morale and trust.

Another organizational characteristic that conforms to the paranoid style is the tendency to *centralize* power in the hands of top executives and their consultants who design control and information systems. Those who feel threatened generally like to have a good deal of control over their subordinates. They use subordinates to find out what's going on, but want to reserve the ultimate power for decision making for themselves. So the locus of power is high up in the organization.

Much use is made of co-ordination and planning committees, sales meetings, sessions with regional managers, etc. Also, the information elicited at these sessions is taken into account in making decisions, but most of the key decisions are both formulated and decided at the top of the organization, leaving out other tiers of management which are affected by the decisions.

The *strategies* of paranoid firms tend to be more reactive than proactive. Firms seem to be active in a *reactive* way. External challenges 'get through' to managers who do their very best to cope with them. If competitors lower prices, the firm may study this challenge and react to it. If other firms introduce and are successful with a new product, the paranoid firm

will probably imitate, but strategic paranoia carries with it a sizeable element of *conservatism.* Fear can take many guises and it often entails being afraid to overinnovate or overextend resources, or to take bold risks. So a reactive strategy dominates. The level of risk taking will be held to a minimum with 'safe' incremental and piecemeal moves being favoured. The level of product-market innovation will slightly lag that among competitors, but the paranoid firm *will* in general be quite responsive to its environment.

A potential problem with the reactive orientation is that it can get in the way of the development of a concerted, integrated and consistent strategy. The firm's direction is too much a function of external forces and not enough one of consistent goals, strategic plans or unifying themes and traditions. This can cause a *'muddling-through'* or 'meandering' strategy under which no forceful distinctive competences are developed. The firm tries alternately to wear too many different hats.

There is one strategy that may be used quite frequently by paranoid firms—that of product-market *diversification.* Here the attempt is to reduce the risk exposure to, or reliance upon, any one environment. A number of often unrelated businesses are entered into. These are each run by separate divisional managers who are responsible for day-to-day operations. The managers, however, are kept in line by developing more sophisticated management information systems and narrowly focused controls. The case of ITT under Harold Geneen is perhaps the best well-known example of the paranoid organization. It seems to suggest a number of interdependent links under which the desire to reduce risk can lead to diversification, which requires more elaborate control and information processing mechanisms, which in turn reinforce the paranoid potential.

A final aspect of the paranoid configuration relates to its possible aetiology. Corporate paranoia may stem from a period of traumatic challenge. The environment may cause the firm to suddenly experience a crisis. A strong market might dry up, a powerful new competitor may enter the market, or a very damaging piece of legislation might be passed. The damage done by these forces may cause managers to become very distrustful and fearful, to lose their nerve, to recognize the need for better intelligence. If this is true we would expect many paranoid firms to be facing or to have faced a very hostile and *dynamic environment.*

We can summarize the paranoid organization along our five dimensions. First, the focus is clearly *external,* as the threats brought about by the environment to a large extent determine the nature of strategy. It is not internal objectives that give the firm direction so much as the jolts given the firm by the environment. Second, we would have to say that the firm has an *active* orientation—there is a diligent effort devoted to adaptation, and changes in strategy do take place, but changes are incremental and conservatism prevails, so the firm is only moderately active. Third, the firm tends to be very *high* on the *control* scale, constantly monitoring what is happening in the environment. These types of organizations are very preoccupied with information gathering. Fourth, the firm is much more *deliberative* than impulsive. All action tends to be purposeful, and is usually directed toward a defensive end. Scanning, analysis and interpreting the information gathered by information systems are the order of the day. Fear causes careful deliberation rather than impulsive action. Fifth, the orientation is *broad* not narrow. Firms try to adapt and react to all kinds of threats. Since there is no concerted strategic emphasis, efforts are made to compete upon a large variety of fronts. Experts from many different areas are brought into the decision making process, and they all have some influence upon the course of action being decided.

The Compulsive Organization

Shared fantasy.   I don't want to be at the mercy of events. I have to master and control all the things affecting me.

Neurotic style.   Perfectionism, meticulousness, dogmatism and obstinacy are dominant patterns in this style. There is an insistence that others submit to one's own way of doing things. All relationships are seen in terms of dominance and submission. A lack of spontaneity and an inability to relax can be observed.

Danger.   The orientation is excessively internal. There exists an indecisiveness symptomized by postponing and avoiding due to a fear of punishment for making mistakes. There is an inability to deviate from planned activity and an excessive reliance on rules and regulations. The preoccupation with trivial details is at the cost of seeing 'the big picture'.

The compulsive firm is wed to ritual. Every last detail of operation is planned out in advance and carried on in a routinized and pre-programmed fashion. Thoroughness, completeness and conformity with standard and established procedures are emphasized. These are central tendencies manifested by the organization structure, decision making processes, and strategies of the compulsive firm.

The external environment has to be fairly *stable* and cannot pose any great challenge. Otherwise, the programmed compulsive firm would rapidly perish. Usually, the firm is quite dominant—being bigger and stronger than its major competitors. If there is some dynamism in the environment because of, say, product-market changes, the firm is sufficiently well positioned and powerful to ignore it. In fact, more often than not, where the compulsive firm *is* found in a dynamic environment, the source of the dynamism is the firm itself.

The organization of the compulsive firm is a bit like that of the paranoid firm. There is an emphasis upon *formal controls* and information systems to ensure that the organizational machine is operating properly. However, a crucial difference between the paranoid and compulsive organizations is that in the latter, controls are really designed to monitor internal operations, production efficiency, costs, and scheduling and performance of projects. The paranoid firm on the other hand places more emphasis on monitoring *external* environmental conditions.

Operations are *standardized* as much as possible and an elaborate set of *formal policies,* rules and procedures are evolved. These have a very wide range and extend not merely to the programming of production or marketing procedures but to dress codes, frequent sales meetings, and a corporate credo that includes suggested employee attitudes. All is prescribed. All is systematized and formally inscribed.

The organization is exceedingly *hierarchical.* Much status is accorded an individual simply because of his position. This may be because the leader himself has many compulsive characteristics, generally manifested by a strong concern with control. The compulsive person is always worried about the next move and how he is going to make it. This constant preoccupation about domination and submission have been reinforced by periods in the firm's history when it actually lost control and was at the mercy of the other organizations or constituencies. Consequently, the compulsive executives try to *reduce uncertainty* at all costs and to attain a clearly specified objective in a determined manner. Surprises must be avoided. The structural attributes that ensure this are, of course, tight controls, standardization of procedures (and, where possible, of personnel and attitudes), and centralization of power through the emphasis upon hierarchy.

The *strategy making* style of the compulsive firm shows the same preoccupation with detail and established procedures. First, every move is very carefully *planned.* There are generally a large number of action plans, budgets, and capital expenditure plans. Each project is very carefully designed, with many checkpoints, exhaustive performance evaluation procedures and incredibly detailed schedules. There is often a substantial planning department which has representatives from many areas of functional expertise.

Another emphasis in strategy making is the long run reliance upon an *established theme.* The firms have a particular orientation and *distinctive competence* and their plans reflect this. This orientation, rather than what is going on in the environment, serves as the major guide for the firm's strategy. For example, some organizations take pride in being the leading innovator in the market-place. They focus their strategy to be the first out with new products, whether these are called for by customers or not. Other organizations try to be the most efficient low-cost producers and are careful to obtain the best equipment, good cost controls, etc. Still other organizations place great emphasis upon product quality. Thus, unlike the paranoid firms which often lack a theme for their strategies, compulsive firms have clear and very well established themes. They also tend to focus in on a carefully circumscribed target market. There are no conglomerates here. Unfortunately, the theme may lose its relevance or appropriateness in the light of new market conditions, but the emphasis upon traditional methods and the strong inward focus prevents any realization of this fact. Change is difficult. The *fixation* on a specific line of thought makes a new strategic orientation hard to push through. Usually, a change-over is preceded by a protracted period of doubt and ambivalence due to the difficulty of relaxing existing decision rules.

We can summarize the compulsive firm along our five dimensions. First, the orientation is *internal,* not external. The firm tries to buffer itself from its environment to do things in a planned, programmed and ritualized way. This deprives it of the adaptive responsiveness of its paranoid counterparts. Second, the firm is both *active* and *passive.* It is active to the extent that its strategic theme requires innovation or to the extent that controlling the internal operations requires more administrative procedures and controls. It is passive in its reluctance to deviate from established policies and methods. Third, the firm scores *high* on the *control* scale, preoccupied as it is with the need to monitor even minute technical details, living with the notion that any relaxation of programmed activity is dangerous. Fourth, the firm is somewhat more *deliberative* than compulsive, although not to the same degree as the paranoid firm. Since the firm acts according to long established guidelines rather than any recent deliberation upon newly discovered facts, we might say that it is deliberative about means, but not about basic goals or strategic themes. The latter are deeply engrained. Finally, it is clear that a *narrow* rather than a broad focus prevails. Strategies are unified by a dominant element and are highly integrated. The organization is designed with particular purposes in mind and these are carefully circumscribed and explicitly articulated. Dominant firms such as Xerox and IBM have many compulsive aspects (Rodgers, 1969; Miller, 1976).

The Histrionic Firm

Shared fantasy.   I want to get attention from and impress the people who count in my life.

Neurotic style.   This style is characterized by self-dramatization, excessive expression of emotions, an incessant drawing of attention to self and a craving for activity and excitement. There exists an incapacity for concentration or sharply focused attention.

Danger.   Problems will emerge given the degree of superficiality and suggestibility. Operating in a non-factual world and basing actions on 'hunches' carries many risks. In addition, there is the danger of overreacting to minor events.

These firms live up to their names in many respects: they are hyperactive, impulsive, dramatically venturesome, and dangerously uninhibited. Their decision makers live in a world of hunches and impressions rather than facts as they address a broad array of widely disparate projects, products, and markets in a desultory fashion. Their flair for the dramatic causes top echelons to centralize power, reserving their prerogative to independently initiate bold ventures. They restrict the power of the second tier, preferring to have these positions occupied by executives with dependent personalities.

It might be best to begin our discussion of the histrionic firm by examining corporate *strategy.* Everything else seems to follow from the strategy as well as the decision making style used to formulate it. *Boldness, risk taking* and *diversification* are the themes. Instead of reacting to the environment, the top decision maker, often an entrepreneur, attempts to enact his own environment. He enters some markets and industries and leaves others; initiates some new products, while abandoning older ones. Generally, these are major and bold actions. A sizeable proportion of the firm's capital is placed at risk. Often the strategic moves are so major that they require the firm to become highly levered financially. Most of these strategic moves are made in the service of grandiosity. Unbridled growth is the goal. The organization's strategy is an extension of its top manager's desire for attention and visibility. It appears that the top man wants to be at centre stage, putting on a show. He likes to be noticed, to finally show 'the others over there' how great an executive he really is.

But while strategy is dramatic, it is by no means consistent or integrated. The ventures undertaken are almost never complementary, and sometimes are downright *conflicting*. It becomes action for action's sake; to have a dramatic impact, to be noticed. It is not uncommon to see firms entering a new market one year, and then abandoning it for another the next as radically different ventures seize the fancy of the man at the top. A multiplicity of market niches are approached and a great deal of organizational resources are squandered in the process. The level of risk taking can be enormously high.

As might be expected, the decision making style is quite *unreflective*. Decisions are made impulsively by someone who really hasn't the time to look into things very carefully. Hunches and superficial impressions guide actions more than facts do. The greater the number of complex ventures addressed, and the more extensive the range of diversification, the more the demands upon the chief executive's time and the less attention he can pay to handling complex decisions and the operating problems to which they subsequently give rise. To aggravate the situation, the top man rarely consults his subordinates or staff experts in making key decisions. Participative decision-making and consultation are alien to the histrionic organization. Analysis rarely takes place, and major ventures are initiated on the basis of only one point of view.

The *structure* of the histrionic organization is far too primitive for its broad product-market scope. The firm has grown and diversified quickly and haphazardly and structure has failed to adapt to the new conditions. First, too much *power* is concentrated with the entrepreneurial chief executive. He meddles even in routine divisional and departmental operating

matters because he wants to put his personal stamp on (and take credit for) everything. Alternating between a broad range of strategic and operating matters contributes to the lack of continuity in the corporate orientation. A second key characteristic of structure follows from this overcentralization: namely, the *absence of an effective information system*. There is not enough scanning of the environment by the top executive since he has too little time, and prefers to act upon intuition rather than facts. Even where information is gathered by lower level managers, they have too little influence upon decisions for it to matter. Because the firms have grown so rapidly, the controls of yesterday are no longer adequate. Operating problems develop quickly because of impulsive ventures and acquisitions but are very slow to be recognized. Finally, the striving for dominance by the leader obstructs effective internal communication which is mostly in a top-down direction. There is a general dearth of upward and lateral communication.

All of these inadequacies of information processing are of course aggravated by the diversified nature of the organization and the *high levels of differentiation* in the goals, methods and interpersonal orientations of sub-units. Automatic Sprinkler, United Shoe Machinery (USM), Gulf & Western Industries, Litton, and Textron are firms that have gone through periods which call forth the histrionic style (Miller, 1976).

We can summarize the histrionic organization along our five dimensions. First, the orientation is *external* more than internal. There is an effort to control the environment, to dominate it, to expand and to become visible. The focus is upon areas of opportunity in different markets and industries. Many internal problems are ignored. Second, histrionic firms fall at the extremely *active* polarity of the active-passive scale. There is much boldness in decision making, a dramatically venturesome and decisive strategy, and a strong proclivity to embrace risk. Third, histrionic firms are very *low* on the *control* scale. The top executive's lack of interest in systems and his preference for quick impressions thwart the implementation or use of well developed control and information systems. Fourth, an *impulsive* rather than a deliberative orientation prevails. Decisions are made quickly, on the spur of the moment. Little effort is devoted to ensuring complementarity among different decisions, or to carefully analysing their implications. Finally, there is a *broad* instead of a narrow focus, at least when it comes to product-market strategy. The firm is broadly diversified and caters to a great variety of markets. In short, the histrionic organization is very much an extension of the hysterical personality of its chief executive officer.

The Depressive Organization

Shared fantasy.   It is hopeless to try to change the course of events in my life. I am just not powerful enough.

Neurotic style.   This style is characterized by feelings of guilt, worthlessness, self-reproach and inadequacy. There exists a sense of helplessness and hopelessness, a feeling of being at the mercy of events. Other elements of this style are a loss of interest and motivation, and an inability to experience pleasure.

Danger.   The outlook is overly pessimistic, leading to inhibition of action, indecisiveness and difficulties in concentration and performance.

Inactivity, lack of confidence, extreme conservatism, and a bureaucratically motivated insularity characterize the depressive organization. There is an atmosphere of extreme passivity and purposelessness. Whatever does get done is that which has been programmed and routinized and requires no special initiative.

This lends a character of automaticity to the organization.

Most depressive firms are found in *stable environments*—the only setting in which they can survive for any length of time. Typically, the firms are well established and serve a mature market, one which has had the same technology, customer preferences and competitive patterns for many years. 'Negotiated environments' which are characterized by trade agreements, collusion, restrictive trade practices, and substantial tariffs to limit foreign competition are the rule. The primary steel industry and the agricultural or industrial chemical businesses are representative of the markets of depressive firms. The low level of change and the absence of serious competition make the administrative task fairly simple, but so does the homogeneity of the set of customers being served. Generally, depressive firms address only one narrowly defined market, a market which is almost never redefined or broadened.

Predictably enough, the orientation is very *bureaucratic*. Technologies are fairly automated, and the same administrative procedures have been used for decades. The firm almost runs itself. Everything functions automatically according to plan, or rather, according to policy and programme. The organization operates as a machine, its gears and energy are formal procedures, routines and prescribed methods. In fact, the depressive organization shows great similarities to the Weberian bureaucracy.

Although the organization is *hierarchical* in the sense that formal authority is centralized and position-based rather than expertise-based, the issue of intra-organizational power is not very salient. The organization is not guided by any real leader and does not show evidence of making decisions. Control and co-ordination are really exercised by formalized programmes and policies rather than by managerial initiatives. Suggestions for change are resisted; inhibition of action seems to be prevalent. It is almost as if the top executive group share a feeling of impotence and incapacity. It is thought that there is no way to change the course of events in the organization. Managers just don't feel they have what it takes to revitalize their firm.

In such firms there is a *leadership vacuum.* The firm drifts aimlessly without any sense of direction. It floats along on a river of ritual without any explicit goals or targets. The top managers have become caretakers who have given up trying to direct the enterprise. They merely serve as passive functionaries, operating at low levels of performance and maintaining the status quo. Their dominant feeling is one of powerlessness, of sensing that the course of events is unalterable.

The final element of organizational structure is the *internal focus of the information system.* Organizations that function automatically, mechanically and passively and are content with the status quo rarely make major decisions. As a result they do not engage in much information gathering to discover the key threats and weaknesses in markets. They do not open up internal communication channels to supply decision makers with the best information or to foster the collaboration of functional specialists. It is difficult to say whether a stagnant orientation induces inattention to, or a disinclination towards, information processing, or whether the opposite causal direction holds. In either event, the two aspects seem to go hand in hand in the depressive firm as well as in many other organizations.

This brings us to the issues of *strategy* and decision making. If there was ever a type of organization that lacked any semblance of conscious strategy it would be the depressive firm. The sense of *aimlessness,* purposelessness, and apathy among top managers seems to preclude any attempts to give the firm any clear direction, orientation or goals. Strategic issues are never explicitly considered, so meaningful *change does not occur.* The general outlook is one of pessimism. Yesterday's products and markets become today's. This is not so much due to an explicit policy of risk aversion or conservatism, but to a lethargy or blindness to strategic matters. Managers are focused inwardly. They do not receive or process much information about the external environment. Most of their time is spent working out minor details and handling routine operating matters. There is an avoidance of decision making and much procrastination. In fact, any outside observer would say that the firm seems to be in a catatonic state. Instead of there being any effort to adapt, to grow or to become more effective, we see mainly inactivity and passivity.

One of the authors has observed a number of instances of this kind of behaviour in organizations. They involved firms taken over by conglomerates. After the departure of the previous top decision maker—often an entrepreneur or an executive with entrepreneurial inclinations—these firms were subjected to a new style of management. Detailed new control procedures were introduced by the parent company, many of which were irrelevant for the specific type of business. This lack of understanding on the part of the parent eventually stifled initiative and induced apathy among the key executive group who felt that they had very little control over the firm. Organizational stagnation resulted in several cases.

We can now situate the depressive firm along our five dimensions. First, there is clearly an *internal* rather than an external focus. The firm concentrates on trivial details of operation rather than key threats or opportunities in the environment. Second, depressive firms are extraordinarily *passive.* There is among managers a sense of helplessness and hopelessness which gives rise to inactivity and an avoidance of decision making. The firm ends up being as paralysed as its top executives feel. It is unsurpassed in this respect by the other four types. Third, although well developed control systems are in existence, they are all form without much substance. The system has become rather meaningless. Consequently, we can rate the depressive firm as being somewhere in the *middle* of the *control* scale. Fourth, the firm is *neither deliberative* nor *impulsive.* These terms can only take on meaning when they describe strategic decision making—an activity too rare to study in the depressive context. Finally, the strategic focus is *narrow*—typically the firm addresses itself to a homogeneous and well established niche of the market and almost never strays from that niche. We can recapitulate all this by saying that the depressive organization is apathetic, somnolent and mechanical.

The Schizoid Organization

Shared fantasy.   The world of reality does not offer any real satisfaction to me. All my interactions will eventually fail and cause harm. Therefore, it is much safer to remain distant.

Neurotic style.   This style is characterized by little or no interest in other people, an air of non-involvement, withdrawnness, detachment and estrangement. In addition, there is a lack of excitement or criticism. What happens in the present or future does not seem to matter. The appearance is one of coldness and lack of emotion.

Danger.   The emotional isolation results in the frustration of the dependency needs of others and may provoke their bewilderment and aggressivity.

The schizoid organization is characterized by a *leadership vacuum.* Its top executive discourages interaction, owing to a fear of involvement. The schizoid leader experiences the world as an unhappy place, populated by frustrating individuals. Perhaps because of past disappointments, he believes most contacts may end painfully for him. Consequently, he is inclined to daydream to compensate for a lack of fulfillment. In some organizations the second tier of executives will make up what is missing from the leader with their own warmth and extroversion. Frequently, however, the schizoid organization can become a political battlefield. Members of the second tier see in the withdrawn nature of the top executive an opportunity to pursue their own needs.

A key repercussion of this behaviour is that the second tier becomes a *political playground* for 'gamesmen (Maccoby, 1976) who try to win favour from the unresponsive leader. There are some interesting strategic and structural implications of the leadership vacuum and the political infighting caused by the schizoid leader. Perhaps the most important one is that no concerted and integrated product market strategy develops. The leader is insecure, withdrawn and non-committal. He seems to have no interest in the organization and refuses to adopt any consistent position, vacillating between the proposals of one favoured subordinate and another. No clear sense of direction emerges. The effective power for strategy making resides in a *shifting coalition* of careerist second tier managers who try to influence the indecisive leader and to simultaneously advance their pet projects and their little empires. As a result, the firm muddles through and drifts, making incremental changes in one area and then reversing them when a new group of managers become ascendent.

Strategy becomes more a product of individual goals, power and politics than any perceived key threats or opportunities in the external environment. The strategy also *may* be a product of the top man's intrapsychic fantasies, but this is not usually the case as his emotional apathy and inactivity thwart the translation of his ideas into actions. Moreover, a conservatism accompanies the aimlessness of the organization. The initiatives of one group of managers are often neutralized or severely mitigated by those of a politically opposing group. The result is that only small, incremental and *piecemeal changes* occur.

We have already hinted at the structure of the schizoid firm. Its primary characteristic is the dispersal of some power, and almost all decision making initiative, to the tier of managers just below the top executive. The political and gamesman-like nature of these second tier managers stems in large part from the characteristics of the leader, whose indecisiveness and withdrawal alienate well adjusted managers and provide a fertile breeding ground for opportunists who are adept at catering to the insecurities of the top man. These second tier managers very rarely collaborate effectively, and so the structure takes the form of a series of warring, or at least unco-operative and *independent fiefdoms*—of alienated departments and divisions.

This divided nature of the organization thwarts effective cross-functional (and, where relevant, interdivisional) co-ordination and communication. Information is used more as a power resource than as a vehicle for effective adaptation. Very real *barriers* are erected *to prevent the free flow of information*. But this is not the only shortcoming of the information system. Another is the absence of environmental scanning. The focus is internal—upon personal political ambitions and catering to the top manager's desires. Second tier managers find it more useful to ignore objective phenomena in the environment, whose identification might reflect poorly on their own past behaviour, or which might conflict with the wishes of the detached leader.

The schizoid organization can now be characterized along our five dimensions. First, the orientation is *internal* rather than external. Very little attention is paid to the external environment. The emphasis is on internal gamesmanship. Second, the firm is much more *passive* than active. The leader is insecure and appears emotionally detached from his subordinates, taking few decisive actions.

His subordinates often neutralize each other's initiatives so that the net result is drifting or muddling through, rather than an integrated or bold strategy. Consequently, there is a lack of control over organizational actions. Although well developed control systems might be in existence they are poorly used making for a *low* rating on the *control* scale. There is little reflection or analysis—decisions or proposals are based upon the *impulsive* pursuit of personal goals. Although Machiavellianism does require a certain degree of calculation, it does not induce a considered analysis of key objective elements of strategy. Finally, the orientation is a *narrow* political one. Whereas the different subunits of the organization may collectively represent a diversity of viewpoints, factionalism prevents these from being integrated into a multifaceted action plan. So one narrow viewpoint eventually falls out of favour and is replaced by another narrow viewpoint. The schizoid firm is thus an insular, isolated, political and fragmented organization with an inconsistent strategy.

Table 2 provided a summary of how the paranoid, compulsive, histrionic, depressive, and schizoid firms ranked on the five personality dimensions. For purposes of comparing the five types of organizations we have included Table 3 which gives an overview of the strengths and weaknesses of each organizational neurotic style. It is notable that neurotic executives contribute strengths as well as weaknesses to their firms. Therefore some neuroses may be somewhat functional in particular environments. For example, paranoid executives may be helpful in setting up sophisticated scanning and control systems and diversification strategies useful in a competitive and hostile environment. Compulsives whose emphasis is upon quality products may be useful in some engineering or high technology industries. Histrionics may be of use in establishing companies and in reviving somnolent firms. In general, however, these neuroses are harmful in

TABLE 3.   *Strengths and Weaknesses of the Five Organizational Styles*

Potential Strengths	Potential Weaknesses
Paranoid style	
Good knowledge of threats and opportunities inside and outside the firm	Lack of a concerted and consistent strategy—few distinctive competences
Benefits of reduced market risk from diversification	Insecurity and disenchantment among second tier managers and their subordinates because of the atmosphere of distrust
Compulsive style	
Fine internal controls and efficient operation	Traditions embraced so firmly that strategy and structure become anachronistic
Well-integrated and focused product-market strategy	Things so programmed that bureaucratic dysfunctions, inflexibility and inappropriate responses become common
	Managers discontent due to their lack of influence and discretion; stifling of initiative
Histrionic style	
Creating the momentum for passing through the start-up phase	Inconsistent strategies which have a very high element of risk and cause resources to be needlessly squandered
Some good ideas for revitalizing tired firms	Problems in controlling widespread operations and in restoring their profitability
	Rash and dangerous expansion policies
	Inadequate role played by second tier of managers
Depressive style	
Efficiency of internal processes	Anachronistic strategies and organizational stagnation
Focused strategy	Confinement to dying markets
	Weak competitive posture due to poor product lines
	Apathetic and inactive managers
Schizoid style	
Second tier managers share in strategy formulation; a variety of points of view may be brought to bear	Inconsistent or vacillating strategy
	Issues decided by political negotiation more than facts
	Lack of leadership
	Climate of suspicion and distrust which prevents collaboration

588

the long run because of the grave strictures they place upon adaptive capacity.

OPERATIONALIZING THE FRAMEWORK

We believe that it would be possible to test the framework we have proposed. There are a number of possible ways to do this, but we shall suggest just one. Miller and Friesen (1977, 1978) have paved the way for a quantitative characterization of paranoid, compulsive, histrionic, depressive, and schizoid firms. These firms resemble their archetypes S_3, S_2, F_1, F_2 and F_3 respectively. Although these types are not perfect exemplars of each of our five pathologies, they can serve as rough approximations. Miller and Friesen's (1977, 1978) thirty-one variables can be measured in a field study of firms that are performing poorly or face other serious problems. The rated firms can then be classified into one of the five types, or into an 'outliner' category using scores on the variables and the classificatory criteria established by Miller and Friesen (1977). A more exacting but precise method of quantifying the framework would be to use the key attributes of each of the five types as outlined earlier in the paper. These could be used to suggest the set of variables to be gauged and the criteria to be used for classifying firms into each group.

For the firms closely resembling the five types, it would be desirable to administer psychiatric assessment interviews to the top decision makers. This can be done using the procedures and questions outlined in the *Diagnostic and Statistical Manual of Mental Disorders* of the American Psychiatric Association (1980). The chapter on personality disorders would be the most relevant. If it is impossible for a qualified psychologist to carry out the psychiatric assessment, the researcher can use the relevant scales available in the well known Minnesota Multiphasic Personality Inventory (e.g. those gauging paranoia, compulsivity, hysteria, depression, etc.). Having classified the firm and its executives, it is a relatively simple matter to compare the results to determine whether the nature of organizational dysfunction bears any relationship to the severity and nature of the neurotic styles of the top executives. Cross-tabulation and analysis of variance procedures could be used for this purpose.

CONCLUSION

One way of looking at organizations is from a hermeneutic perspective (Palmer, 1969; Ricoeur, 1974). In studying organizations we are really engaged in deciphering structures of signification. Order is sought where chaos once reigned. As researchers of organizations we are curious about why certain decisions are made and specific strategies chosen. Why does the organization end up with a particular kind of structure? Why is a certain individual selected for a specific job? What we are trying to do is to recognize the 'signifiers' which determine the organizational configurations, the cues which will give us insight into formal and informal structure; the occurrences that take place at the shared fantasy level of the organization. We are, in some sense, looking for the meaning behind these 'signifiers'; that which gives rise to them and is 'signified'.

We believe that in dysfunctional organizations many aspects of strategy, structure and organizational climate will be signifiers (i.e. a function) of the neurotic styles and fantasies of the top echelon of managers. More specifically, the 'neurotic' characteristics of executives—the pecularities of their styles—seem to give rise to uniformities of organizational culture. These are long lived and self-perpetuating and can in turn foster common *organizational* neurotic styles as manifested by certain strategies, structures and organizational climates. We believe that these psychodynamic and organizational phenomena together form integral Gestalts or configurations. Given some aspects of each configuration it becomes possible to predict many of its other aspects by making reference to the taxonomy. These Gestalts demonstrate mutual complementarities among their elements. They reveal the genesis of particular organizational weaknesses and the way in which these are tied to strategy, structure, organizational climate and managerial personality.

Should the framework we have outlined be borne out by subsequent empirical research, there will be a number of practical implications for the management of organizations. The first is that organizational problems are often deeply ingrained, having as their aetiology the deep-seated neurotic styles and intrapsychic fantasies of top executives. They are manifested by a broad array of structural, strategic, and 'mythical' (shared fantasy) aspects. These are mutually reinforcing and pervasive, and therefore resistant to change. Organizational change agents will be effective only if they get at the roots of dysfunctions, but this might be very difficult if problems are so deeply ingrained and so broadly manifested. Piecemeal changes will not do much good, whereas revolutionary ones are expensive, hard to implement and politically inexpedient. Since our five common pathologies seem to be so multifaceted and thematically unified, it is unlikely that they can be adequately addressed by management consultants who have a standard bag of tools. The implementation of information systems, the use of strategic business units, committees and matrix structures, or the creation of organizational development and quality of working life programmes will be of little help as long as an organization's executives cling to their dysfunctional fantasies and the shared organizational ideologies that they create. The new programmes will have little effect unless they are complemented by more realistic views

of the business and its environment or, failing that, by more adaptive executives.

Our framework also implies that executives must be on the lookout for the five pathological styles. Since it is hard to recognize these in one's own attitudes, it might be easier to examine the organization to see if its concrete structure, strategy, or climate conforms across-the-board to one of our pathological types. If so, it might be time for an open discussion of shared fantasies—to the extent that they can be articulated—in order to scrutinize them. The stimulus for such dialogue usually has to come from a knowledgeable outsider and needs a considerable investment in time and effort. It might also be useful to examine the degree of similarity of these fantasies among top executives. The more uniform they are, the greater the dangers of being out of touch with reality and falling into the trap of insularity. Perhaps the time will have come to open up the organization to those with different personalities and fantasies to create a climate of healthy diversity.

Recruitment and promotion policies might benefit from the attempt to ensure substantial differences in the personalities of key executives. The tendency among executives to select and promote in their own image should not be underestimated. There are also socialization processes which occur in a very subtle way in organizations and which tend to have a moulding effect on character. Since organizations easily become gathering stations for managers with similar styles, there will always be a danger that the lack of diversity may give way to organizational pathology.

NOTE

1. 'Object' is taken in the special sense of referring to the person to whom instinctual needs are directed.

REFERENCES

American Psychiatric Association. *Diagnostic and Statistical Manual of Mental Disorders,* 3rd edn, Washington, D.C., 1980.

Balint, Michael. *Primary Love and Psychoanalytic Technique,* Liveright Publishing Corporation, London, 1965.

Breuer, Josef and Sigmund Freud. 'Studies on hysteria', in *The Standard Edition of the Complete Psychological Works of Sigmund Freud,* Vol. II, The Hogarth Press and the Institute of Psychoanalysis, London, 1893–1895.

Collins, Orvis and David Moore. *The Organization Makers,* Appleton-Century-Crofts, New York, 1970.

Fairbairn, W. Ronald D. *An Object-Relations Theory of Personality,* Basic Books, New York, 1952.

Fenichel, Otto. *The Psychoanalytic Theory of Neurosis,* W. W. Norton and Co., New York, 1945.

Freedman, Alfred M., Harold I. Kaplan and Benjamin J. Sadock (eds). *Comprehensive Textbook of Psychiatry,* Vols I, II, The Williams and Wilkins Co., Baltimore, 1975.

Fries, M. E. and P. J. Woolf. 'Some hypotheses on the role of congenital activity types in personality development', *Psychoanalytic Study of the Child,* **8**, 1953, pp. 48–62.

Guntrip, Harry. *Schizoid Phenomena, Object Relations and the Self,* International Universities Press, New York, 1969.

Jacobson, Edith. *The Self and the Object World,* International Universities Press, New York, 1964.

Jaques, Elliott. *The Changing Culture of a Factory,* Tavistock, London, 1951.

Jaques, Elliott. *Work, Creativity and Social Justice,* International Universities Press, New York, 1970.

Jung, C. G. *Psychological Types, or the Psychology of Individuation,* Harcourt, Brace, Jovanovich, New York, 1920.

Keeley, M. 'Organizational analogy: a comparison of organismic and social contract models', *Administrative Science Quarterly,* **25**, 1980, pp. 337–362.

Kernberg, Otto. *Object Relations Theory and Clinical Psychoanalysis,* Jason Aronson Inc., New York, 1976.

Kernberg, Otto. 'Regression in organizational leadership', *Psychiatry,* **42**, 1979, pp. 29–39.

Kets de Vries, Manfred F. R. (ed.). *The Irrational Executive: Psychoanalytic Explorations in Management,* International Universities Press, New York, 1982.

Kets de Vries, Manfred F. R. *Organizational Paradoxes: Clinical Approaches to Management,* Tavistock, London, 1980.

Kets de Vries, Manfred and Danny Miller. *The Invisible Hand: Hidden Forces in Organizations,* 1982a.

Kets de Vries, Manfred and Danny Miller. 'Group fantasies and organizational functioning', *Working paper,* McGill University, Faculty of Management, Montreal, 1982b.

Klein, Melanie. *Contributions to Psychoanalysis 1921–1945,* The Hogarth Press, London, 1948.

Laplanche, J. and J. B. Pontalis. *The Language of Psychoanalysis,* The Hogarth Press, London, 1973.

Larcon, Jean-Paul and Roland Reitter. *Structures de Pouvoir et Identite de l'Enterprise,* Nathan, Paris, 1979.

Lefcourt, Herbert M. *Locus of Control,* Wiley, New York, 1976.

McClelland, David. *The Achieving Society,* Irvington Publishers, New York, 1961.

McClelland, David. *Power: The Inner Experience,* Halsted Press, New York, 1975.

Maccoby, Michael. *The Gamesman,* Simon and Schuster, New York, 1976.

Mahler, Margaret S., Fred Pine and Anni Bergman. *The Psychological Birth of the Human Infant,* Basic Books, New York, 1975.

Merton, Robert K. 'Bureaucratic structure and personality', in Merton, R. K. (ed.), *Social Theory and Social Structure,* Free Press, New York, 1968, pp. 249–259.

Miles, Raymond and Charles Snow. *Strategy, Structure and Process,* McGraw-Hill, New York, 1978.

Miller, Danny. 'Strategy making in context: ten empirical archetypes', *Doctoral Dissertation,* McGill University, 1976.

Miller, Danny and Peter Friesen. 'Strategic making in context: ten empirical archetypes', *Journal of Management Studies,* **14**, 1977, pp. 258–280.

Miller, Danny and Peter Friesen. 'Archetypes of strategy formulation', *Management Science,* **24**, 1978, pp. 921–933.

Miller, Danny, Manfred F. R. Kets de Vries and Jean-Marie Toulouse. 'Top executive locus of control and its relationship to strategy-making, structure and environment', *Academy of Management Journal*, **25**, 1982, pp. 237–253.

Mintzberg, Henry. *The Structuring of Organizations*, Prentice-Hall, Englewood Cliffs, 1979.

Mintzberg, Henry. *Power in and Around Organizations*, Prentice-Hall, Englewood Cliffs, 1983.

Mitroff, Ian I. and Ralph H. Kilmann. 'Organization stories: an approach to the design and analysis of organizations through myths and stories', in Kilmann, R. H., L. R. Pondy and D. P. Slevin (eds), *The Management of Organization Design Strategies and Implementation*, Elsevier North Holland, New York, 1976.

Murray, Henry A. *Explorations in Personality*, Oxford University Press, New York, 1938.

Nicholi, Armand M. (ed.). *The Harvard Guide to Modern Psychiatry*, The Belknap Press, Cambridge, 1978.

Palmer, Robert. *Hermeneutics*, Northwestern University Press, Evanston, 1969.

Payne, Roy and Derek S. Pugh. 'Organization structure and climate', in Dunnette, M. D. (ed.), *Handbook of Industrial and Organizational Psychology*, Rand McNally, Chicago, 1976.

Phares, Jerry E. *Locus of Control in Personality*, General Learning Press, Morristown, 1976.

Ricoeur, Paul. *The Conflict of Interpretations: Essays in Hermeneutics*, Inde, D. (ed.), Northwestern University Press, Evanston, 1974.

Rodgers, William. *Think: A Biography of the Watsons and IBM*, Stein & Day, New York, 1969.

Sandler, Joseph and Bernard Rosenblatt. 'The concept of the representational world', *Psychoanalytic Study of the Child*, **17**, 1962, pp. 128–145.

Schendel, Dan and Charles Hofer. *Strategic Management*, Little, Brown, Boston, 1979.

Shapiro, David. *Neurotic Styles*, Basic Books, New York, 1965.

Starbuck, William H., A. Greve and B. Hedberg. 'Responding to crises', *Journal of Business Administration*, **9**, 1978, pp. 111–137.

Thompson, Victor. *Modern Organizations*, Knopf, New York, 1961.

Tosi, Henry. 'A reexamination of personality as a determinant of the effects of participation, *Personnel Psychology*, **23**, 1970, pp. 91–99.

Vroom, Victor H. *Some Personality Determinants of the Effects of Participation*, Prentice-Hall, Englewood Cliffs, 1960.

White, Robert W. *The Enterprise of Living*, Holt, Rinehart and Winston, New York, 1972.

Zaleznik, Abraham and Manfred F. R. Kets de Vries. *Power and the Corporate Mind*, Houghton Mifflin, Boston, 1975.

Name Index

ABOUT THE EDITORS

Michael L. Tushman is Professor in the Management and Organizations Division and is the Director of the Innovation and Entrepreneurship Research Center at the Graduate School of Business, Columbia University. He received his M.S. at Cornell University and his Ph.D. at M.I.T. Tushman is on the editorial boards of *Administrative Science Quarterly*, *Management Science*, and the *Journal of Business Venturing*. He is also the editor of *Readings in the Management of Innovation*, published by Harper & Row in 1988.

Charles O'Reilly is Professor of Management in the Graduate School of Business at the University of California, Berkeley, and a staff member at the university's Institute of Personality Assessment and Research. He also obtained his M.B.A. and Ph.D. from Berkeley. O'Reilly is on the editorial board of *Administrative Science Quarterly* and *Communication Research*. He has published extensively in the areas of organizational communication, employee commitment, and human resource management and has consulted for a variety of public and private firms.

David A. Nadler is President of the Delta Consulting Group. Prior to his work at Delta, he was Associate Professor at the Graduate School of Business, Columbia University. He holds an M.B.A. from the Harvard Business School and an M.A. and a Ph.D. from the University of Michigan. Nadler is the author of five books, including *Feedback and Organization Development*, as well as numerous articles and papers on organizational behavior, strategic change, and leadership.

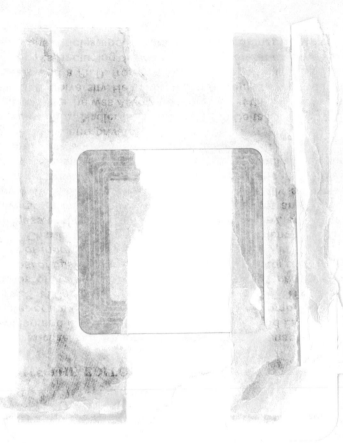

658.42
T96p